C.Thomas — Jan '02

The Letters of

GUSTAVE
FLAUBERT

1830–1880

The Letters of

GUSTAVE FLAUBERT

Volumes I & II

1830–1880

Selected, edited and translated by
FRANCIS STEEGMULLER

With a foreword by Anita Brookner

PICADOR

To Jean Bruneau and
Norbert Guterman

First published 2001 by Picador
an imprint of Pan Macmillan Ltd
Pan Macmillan, 20 New Wharf Rd, London, N1 9RR
Basingstoke and Oxford
Associated companies throughout the world
www.panmacmillan.com

ISBN 0 330 48847 3

The Letters of Gustave Flaubert 1830–1857 first published in Great Britain in 1981 as
a separate volume by Faber & Faber, by arrangement with Harvard University Press.
The Letters of Gustave Flaubert 1857–1880 first published in Great Britain in 1984 as
a separate volume by Faber & Faber, by arrangement with Harvard University Press.

1 3 5 7 9 8 6 4 2

A CIP catalogue record for this book is available from the British Library.

Phototypeset by Intype London Ltd
Printed and bound in Great Britain by
Mackays of Chatham plc, Chatham, Kent

ACKNOWLEDGEMENTS

IN PREPARING THE present volume I have been greatly helped by the cooperation of MM. Gallimard, who have allowed me to use the text of *Flaubert: Correspondance*, Volume I (1973) and Volumes II, III and IV (in preparation), edited by Jean Bruneau (Bibliothèque de la Pléiade). I am also particularly indebted to M. Jean Bruneau himself, for sharing with me some of his preparations for Volume II of that edition and for his patient clarification of many details (I have included his name or initials in a number of my notes). I have also been greatly helped by the cooperation of Professor Alphonse Jacobs and his publisher, Flammarion, who have allowed me to use portions of the texts and notes of his *Gustave Flaubert – George Sand, Correspondance* (Paris, 1981) and whose initials I have also included in a number of my notes. Thanks to Mr Norbert Guterman, for his invaluable help in the search for literal equivalent or proper paraphrase; and to the John Simon Guggenheim Memorial Foundation for its generous grant-in-aid. My warm thanks go also to the following: Mr Jacques Barzun, Mr Leroy C. Breunig, Mr William B. Goodman, Mr Gordon Haight, M. Jean Hugo, Mr Harry Levin, Mr Ved Mehta, Mr Walter Pistole, Mr Gordon N. Ray, Mr Douglas Siler, Ms Camille Smith, Mr Robert Sonkin, M. Jacques Suffel, Mr Frank Tuohy, M and Mme Olivier Ziegel. My thanks go also to the National Endowment for the Humanities for its generous grant-in-aid. I am grateful to Madame Léo d'Erlanger for hospitality in the region of Carthage; to Steele Commager for clarifying many of Flaubert's references to Latin writers; to David Marcus for elucidating certain terms in *Salammbô* and in Flaubert's notes for that novel; to Camille Smith for her editorial help; to Monsieur and Madame Olivier Ziegel for research and information; and, as always, to Shirley Hazzard for – everything.

My warm thanks go also to the following: Lucien Andrieu, Mohammed K. Annabi (Attaché de Recherches, Conservation du site de Carthage, Institut National d'Archéologie et d'Art de Tunisie) and Madame Chedlia Annabi, Max Aprile, Jacques Barzun, Jeanne Bem, Mr and Mrs Steven Bosworth, Erse Breunig, Leroy C. Breunig, Victor Brombert, Anita Brookner, Cavaliere Alfonso Cavotti (Chief Concierge of the Hotel Excelsior, Naples) and his staff, Natalie Datlof, Comtesse Catherine Donin de Rosière, Dr Henry R. Erle, Everett Fahy, William B. Goodman, Lily Gravino, David Hamilton, Edgar Johnson, Carlo Knight, Serge Lancel (Directeur de la Mission Française, Carthage), Monsignor Andrew P. Landi, Harry Levin, Georges Lubin, Kenneth Martin, Stanley Martin, Mark Piel, Jeanine Parisier Plottel, Gordon N. Ray, Jasper Ridley, Edward Said, Dr Alvin A. Schaye, Douglas Siler, Dorle Soria, Alex Szogyi, F. Firat Topçuoğlu (Deputy Turkish Consul-General in New York), and Marietta Tree.

The French texts of Flaubert's letters used for translation have been, whenever possible, those provided by Jean Bruneau in his edition mentioned above. Also used have been the edition published by Louis Conard (1926–1933) with Supplement (1954), and that of the Club de l'Honnête Homme (1971–1975), together with a number of articles in professional publications correcting the dating of certain letters. For the correspondence with Turgenev, I have used chiefly the texts edited by Gérard Gailly (1946).

CONTENTS

APPENDICES

Volume I

Volume II

LIST OF ILLUSTRATIONS

All illustrations courtesy of the Collection de la Bibliothèque munici-
pale de Rouen Photographies Catherine Lancien

INTRODUCTION

By Anita Brookner

IT WAS THROUGH the medium of his letters that Flaubert's life became legendary. Who would guess from simply reading *Madame Bovary*, that apparently uncomplicated, unassuming and limpid account of a woman's fall into the quotidian, that these qualities were achieved by an unremitting exercise of the will, and more, by a transformation of the real self into that of another, diametrically opposed, human being, by the desire to encompass an alternative consciousness, one so at odds with his choleric temperament, as to suggest not merely literary artifice but some sort of necromancy?

Emma Bovary, the wife of a mediocre provincial health officer, herself an unwakened and above all undiscriminating anti-heroine, treated with all the gravity usually allowed to the most Romantic of archetypes, would seem to be an unworthy recipient of Flaubert's manic care, yet his ambition, however he might sympathize with his victim, ranged far above and beyond her. The self he so studiously avoided in the novel is fully expressed in the letters he wrote to Louise Colet, when the work was in progress, describing what he saw as his aim. This was no less than the complete absence of subjectivity, an impassivity so extreme that he perceived it as being analogous to that of God in the universe, so studiedly indifferent to his creation as to cause doubts and misgivings in the faithful. 'Style is achieved only by dint of atrocious labour, fanatical and unremitting stubbornness,' he wrote, something that Colet, his mistress, and an undistinguished poet by profession, could barely understand.

The unremitting labour was not in any doubt. More interesting, and perhaps more important, was the excitement, the euphoria, occasioned by this exercise, a euphoria he sought to convey by even more exalted pronouncements, such as the one familiar to all students of literature: ' . . . what I should like to write is a book about nothing, a book dependent on nothing external, which would be held together by the internal strength of its style, just as the earth, suspended in the void, depends on nothing external for its support; a book which would have almost no subject, or at least in which the subject would be almost invisible, if such a thing is possible.'

Is such a thing possible? *Madame Bovary* is hardly a book about nothing, very much the opposite. Yet the Olympian ambition of the author is there, present in the style which might be that of a provincial onlooker, initially sympathetic, finally indifferent. The chasm that lay between the combustible author and his essentially unaware subject could only be bridged by a treatment that would distance both of them, one from the other. If hardly God in the universe, as he claimed, Flaubert was utterly successful in his stated aim, which was to disappear completely from his creation, only briefly apparent at the end in the vengeful act of awarding the Légion d'Honneur to M. Homais, the most obtuse of self-appointed experts and the recipient of the authorial Flaubert's hatred and sarcasm. Indeed the achievement of the novel is its dreamlike unity and inevitability, its studious absence of blame, its unquestioning acceptance of Fate. Except that Flaubert would not have invoked Fate. Fate was Flaubert himself, the self-obliterating author who merely observed his creation willing herself to her doom.

All this is the more remarkable in that Flaubert was, as he proclaimed on several occasions, a Romantic. Too young to belong to the Romantic generation of 1830 he nevertheless espoused that generation's values, worshipping Victor Hugo, and indulging in many traits familiar to those pioneers of whom Gautier was the spokesman. His own life provides many examples of typical Romantic behaviour, notably his adolescent love for Elise Schlesinger, to whom in some ways he remained faithful throughout his life. Indeed it is in his attitude to women that the seeds of his great novel may be sought. Mme Schlesinger was his youthful ideal, with which he dealt more appropriately, more becomingly, it might be said, than he did with his real-life lover Louise Colet. It was the fact of his never having known a woman like Emma Bovary that made the book such an enthralling prospect, one to which other writers might be blind. The real woman, the one who took sexual activity for granted, as a normal means of exchange, held no mystery for him, and, it might be said, little interest. Admirers of Flaubert are given pause by his treatment of Louise Colet, who complained that her lover treated her like a person of the lowest class and who reacted to his instruction to '. . . live like a bourgeois, think like a demigod', by talking about pregnancy and asking him when she might meet his mother. 'Everything should be done coldly, with poise,' he told her, while continuing to express to her, sometimes in the same letter, his rage, joy, manic excitement and what he quite correctly described as 'ejaculations of the soul'. It was her role to receive these ejaculations: hundreds of letters, very few meetings. He valued her most by keeping her at arm's length, and although quite mundane a lover in many respects he never regarded her as an equal. The extreme cruelty of his final letter to her, a note of dismissal, the cancellation of a contract, stems from the same impassivity that brought about the literary triumph of *Madame Bovary.* 'Madame,' he wrote to her on 6 March 1855, 'I was told that you took the trouble to come here to see me three times last evening. I was not in. And fearing lest persistence expose you to humiliation, I am bound by the rules of politeness to warn you that I shall never be in. Yours, G.F.'

Such were Flaubert's rules of politeness. His harshness towards Louise Colet, all too real, has to be set against his acceptance of the incapacity, also all too real, of Emma Bovary. No living woman would compare with his immaculate creation. Art outweighed life in every respect, though whether it should be allowed to is another matter, one for the moralists, or perhaps for the moralist who resides in us all.

It was not until he made the acquaintance of the fourth woman in his life, George Sand, that he began to meet with some opposition to his ideals and beliefs. We must count Elise Schlesinger, Emma Bovary and Louise Colet as his previous mistresses; in George Sand he encountered someone and something far less compliant. This eminent woman, who was on excellent terms with most of literary Paris, and who had accomplished her own liberation from early constraints, held convictions utterly opposed to those of Flaubert.

She was a democrat, a humanist and a humanitarian, who regarded sympathy for the oppressed as the highest ideal. Well aware of the natural distance between Flaubert and herself, she continued to exercise a benign influence over him. She was a guest at his house at Croisset, and he at Nohant, where he participated in family games. In their letters, the finest exposition of their friendship, they treat each other with affection and respect, aware that no word of criticism should be allowed to escape. George Sand, a prolific and, in some ways, an undistinguished writer, was in every other way a superior woman. She too was a recipient of Flaubert's ejaculations of the soul, to which she had the wit and the experience to respond in a way that would cause no offence. To his deliberate elitism she gently opposed her own warm sympathies. When he claimed, in a letter to her of 7 October 1871, that 'the entire dream of democracy is to raise the proletariat to the level of bourgeois stupidity', she wisely kept the discussion confined within the bounds of literature. Yet on receiving another missive on the impersonality, the atemporality of art, she was finally moved to a brilliant defence of a simple desire to write for simple people, 'those with a thirst to read' (letter of 12 January 1876). She urged him, three days later, to 'portray the honest and the strong, along with the maniacs and the dolts you love to ridicule'. This has become the anti-Flaubert line. It is the voice of common sense, the quality that Flaubert despised above all others.

All writers complain, of the isolation, the imprisonment, the loneliness and, above all, of the sense that they are only good for one thing. Flaubert complains more than most, and after 1870 he was justified in so doing. Those he loved were dead or dying; his health was deteriorating; he was in financial difficulties and was obliged to apply for help to his niece Caroline, to whose bungling husband he had imprudently entrusted his affairs. There is no trace, in the later letters, of the headstrong youth whose epilepsy persuaded his father that he was not best suited for the law, or the entranced traveller who had spent eighteen months in the Middle East, most of them on horseback or in brothels. He was not, however much he favoured the idea, outside history. Prussian troops were quartered in his house during the invasion and occupation in 1870–1871; he returned home one day to find a Prussian helmet on his bed. He became old, like everybody else: thinking like a demigod does not help in this respect. He also became eminent, holding court in his Paris flat on Sunday afternoons. Yet he never repeated the heroic exploit, the wager, that was *Madame Bovary.* His other novels divide uneasily between full-blown Romanticism (*Salammbô*, *La Tentation de Saint Antoine*) and the nerveless realism of *L'Éducation sentimentale*. His last story, *Un Coeur Simple*, even has a touch of pathos, or of bathos, in its conception. But the letters, in Francis Steegmuller's magisterial presentation, remain exemplary to the end, an account of a writer's life that will never be surpassed. In attaining his highest standards Flaubert will for ever remain not only an exceptional artist, but the undoubted hero of his own imaginings.

Volume I

1830–1857

INTRODUCTION

Reflections:
Gustave Flaubert's Correspondence

What seems to me the highest and most difficult
achievement of Art is not to make us laugh or
cry, nor to arouse our lust or rage, but to do
what nature does – that is, to set us dreaming.

Letter to Louise Colet, August 26, 1853

IF THERE IS one article of faith that dominates the Credo of
Gustave Flaubert's correspondence, it is that the function of great
art is not to provide 'answers'. To suppose that art need respond
only to such questions as we are capable of posing is, in Flaubert's
view, a presumption, an egotistic fallacy. If art has a 'function', it is
to extend us into unimagined shocks, experiences, pleasures, reflections. Art is discovery, as much as recognition.

By no means new in Flaubert's time, the view that art should
be 'serviceable' in supplying a text for the management of life – a
view that has played its role, too, in proposing art as an inexhaustible
ground for critical theory and explication – has since then cast its
shadow over much of modern thought and education. It was to be
expected that such an attitude would gain credence with the onset
of the industrial era; and that Flaubert would be, in 1853, aroused to
its dangers. Two decades later, George Eliot was excoriating 'that
dead anatomy of culture which turns the universe into a mere
ceaseless answer to questions'. In our own era, the necessary correc-
tives continue. There is Auden's: 'A work of art is not *about* this or

that kind of life; it *has* life'; and Saul Bellow's charge against intellectuals – against 'the educated people of modern countries' whose 'business is to reduce masterpieces to discourse'.

Flaubert's letter defining 'the highest and most difficult achievement of art' goes on to say:

> The most beautiful works . . . are serene in aspect, unfathomable. The means by which they act on us are various: they are motionless as cliffs, stormy as the ocean, leafy, green and murmurous as forests, forlorn as the desert, blue as the sky. Rabelais, Michelangelo, Shakespeare and Goethe seem to me *pitiless*. They are bottomless, infinite, manifold. Through small apertures we glimpse abysses whose sombre depths turn us faint. And yet over the whole there hovers an extraordinary tenderness. It is like the brilliance of light, the smile of the sun; and it is calm, calm and strong.

When he wrote these words, Flaubert had already been at work on *Madame Bovary* for two years. He had become fully aware of the great possibilities and rich promise of his novel after his first year's labour on it: 'When I think of what it can be, I am dazzled. But then, when I reflect that so much beauty has been entrusted to me – to *me* – I am terrified . . . I have been working like a mule for fifteen long years . . . Oh, if I ever produce a good book I'll have earned it!'

At that time he was thirty, and had published nothing, despite several opportunities to do so. The son of a provincial doctor, he had been raised in a household where scientific, and particularly medical, research was held to be man's noblest activity. In that ambience, the preferred pastimes of his early years – reverie, and the composition of plays to be acted by himself and his friends – were accepted with kindness but with a certain disregard. (Even so, Jean-Paul Sartre may exaggerate in ironically entitling his study of the young Flaubert *L'Idiot de la famille*.)[1] Throughout childhood, youth, and early manhood Flaubert wrote incessantly, producing work

1. Sartre possibly derived his title from 'L'Idiot des Salons', a farcical skit in which Flaubert impersonated a foolish party-goer for the entertainment of his friends. (See *Journal des Goncourt*, March 29, 1862.)

enough to fill several volumes – the earliest plays, essays and stories, then a short novel, a longer novel, half a book on Brittany, and a long, learned fantasy in dramatic form about the fourth-century St Anthony Abbot, his age and beliefs. Almost without exception these works were of progressively greater interest and quality. But at the crucial point in writing *Madame Bovary* he looked back and saw them as mule's work. 'How I congratulate myself on the prescience I had not to publish!' he wrote exultantly to his mistress, Louise Colet.

Earlier, at the age of twenty-five, when he had not yet begun *Saint Antoine*, much less *Madame Bovary*, he had rejected praise from Louise, who, herself a writer, had quickly become aware of what she called his 'sure literary sense'. In 1846 he wrote to her: 'You disparage yourself in comparison with me, you belittle yourself – I surprise you, I astonish you – but who am I, what am I? I am nothing but a literary lizard, warming myself all day in the bright sun of Beauty. That is all.'

The reader of the correspondence will appreciate such self-description: Flaubert is conspicuously a literary lizard from the beginning, warming himself in the bright suns of one great writer after another. But in the early years he had demanded, or expected, direct responses from them: each of the works he himself produced bore the stamp of one or another of these great predecessors, rather than his own. In those days he had even warned his friend Maxime DuCamp against daydreaming: 'Be on your guard against la Rêverie, a vicious monster, siren of the soul, which has already devoured much of my substance.' The near-simultaneity of his perceiving the possibilities of the new work he was engaged in and his realization that the highest good his forefathers in art had done him had been to set him dreaming was no coincidence, but the affirmation of maturing genius. The true Flaubert was born when he recognized that his rewards from great art had come from immersion in it, as in a stream or the sea – not from requiring formulae and solutions from it as from a Sybil. 'Ineptitude,' he had learned, 'consists in wanting to reach conclusions . . . What mind worthy of the name, beginning with Homer, ever reached a conclusion?'

*

It might be rejoined that even after the dazzling vision of his novel's potentialities, the great burden of his letters, whenever *Madame Bovary* is mentioned, is essentially a lament that he was still – especially as he approached the end of the book – working 'like a mule': that, as Henry James oddly put it, in *Notes on Novelists*, 'Flaubert's case was a doom because he felt of his vocation almost nothing but the difficulty'. James's word 'almost' is quite unsuitable here – because on those days when Flaubert did pierce through his difficulties, the glimpse of blue sky brought nothing short of ecstasy. A few years earlier, during his journey to Egypt in 1849–50, when his *cange* lay off Thebes in the sunset, with the Nile 'a lake of molten steel', and the sailors singing and dancing on board, he had expressed, in his journal, a similar conscious rejoicing: 'It was then, while I was observing those things, and enjoying observing them, and just as I was watching three wave-crests curling under the wind at our stern, that I felt a surge of solemn happiness that reached out towards what I was seeing, and I thanked God in my heart for having made me capable of such joy: I felt fortunate at the thought, and yet it seemed to me that I was thinking of nothing: it was a sensuous pleasure that pervaded my entire being.'

Now, it was his own work, *Madame Bovary*, under way and offering its promise, that brought a comparable surge of gratitude:

> . . . it is a delicious thing to write, to be no longer yourself but to move in an entire universe of your own creating. Today, for instance, as man and woman, both lover and mistress, I rode in a forest on an autumn afternoon under the yellow leaves, and I was also the horses, the leaves, the wind, the words my people uttered, even the red sun that made them almost close their love-drowned eyes.
>
> Is this pride or piety? Is it a foolish overflow of exaggerated self-satisfaction, or is it really a vague and noble religious instinct? But when I brood over these marvellous pleasures I have enjoyed, I would be tempted to offer God a prayer of thanks if I knew he could hear me. Praised may he be for not creating me a cotton merchant, a vaudevillian, a wit, etc.! Let us sing to Apollo as in ancient days, and breathe deeply of the fresh cold air of Parnassus; let us strum our guitars and clash

our cymbals, and whirl like dervishes in the eternal hubbub of
Forms and Ideas.

Shortly after the publication of *Madame Bovary*, Flaubert – the same
Flaubert who is credited, or charged, with 'inaugurating the modern
novel' – wrote to the critic Charles Augustin de Sainte-Beuve to
deny that he was a 'realist'. In Sainte-Beuve's review of the novel
(with its celebrated closing words: 'Son and brother of eminent
doctors, M. Gustave Flaubert wields the pen as others wield the
scalpel. Anatomists and physiologists, I find you on every page!'),
the critic, although granting him distinction in the matter of style,
had nevertheless classified Flaubert among the 'more or less exact
observers who in our time pride themselves on conscientiously
reproducing reality, and nothing but reality.' 'Please let me enlighten
you on a purely personal point,' Flaubert wrote. 'I do not belong to
the generation you speak of: at least, in ways of feeling. I insist that
I belong to *yours* – I mean the good generation, that of 1830. It
represents everything I love. I am a rabid old Romantic – or a
fossilized one, whichever you prefer.'

Readers of the correspondence are made aware of Flaubert's
'personal' romanticism almost from the outset. The intricacy of the
pattern of *Madame Bovary* – Flaubert's revelation of the fatality of
living out romantic dreams in the modern world (the dangers, the
dreams and the modern world all being depicted in 'impersonal'
detail) – has long been a cornerstone of literary study. And very
conspicuous is the exotic 'revenge' inherent in the author's subsequently turning from that novel subtitled 'Patterns of Provincial
Life' to the bloody, Carthaginian *Salammbô*. The coexistence of
'personal' romanticism with professional 'realism' is perhaps most
vividly dramatized at the point in the correspondence where, after
laborious days spent chronicling Emma Bovary's frustrations, Flaubert bursts out to Louise Colet in an all but untranslatable apostrophe
reminiscent of Chateaubriand: '*J'aurai connu vos douleurs, pauvres
âmes obscures, humides de mélancolie renfermée, comme vos arrière-
cours de province, dont les murs ont de la mousse.*'

The romantic–realistic dichotomy forms a broad supporting base
for the constant self-contradiction that is one of the joys of the

correspondence and a source of its great vigour. There is perhaps no better characterization of the correspondence itself than Flaubert's phrase already quoted about the 'hubbub of Forms and Ideas'. In the letters, almost every conceivable artistic form is examined. And Flaubert forestalled much present-day academic discourse with his simple: 'Prose was born yesterday: you have to keep that in mind. Verse is the form par excellence of ancient literatures. All possible prosodic [that is, poetic] variations have been discovered; but that is far from being the case with prose.' Scarcely a passage of Flaubert's correspondence is without ideas. That a novelist will deal in contradictory attitudes is not unexpected. Flaubert not only admits this trait: he flaunts it. 'My basic character, whatever anyone may say, is that of the mountebank.' 'With my faculty of arousing myself with my pen, I took my subject seriously; *but only while I was writing.*' 'You are lucky, you poets: you have an outlet in your verse. When something troubles you, you spit out a sonnet, and that relieves you' – followed exactly a month later by the corrective: 'Do not imagine you can exorcize what oppresses you in life by giving vent to it in art. No. The heart's dross does not find its way on to paper: all you pour out there is ink.' How many writers might be quoted in support, contradiction, or extenuation of these outbursts – Auden, in his poem 'The Novelist'; or Yeats exclaiming over his hopeless passion for Maud Gonne: 'How much of the best I have done and still do is but the attempt to explain myself to her?'

Flaubert had his own opinion of 'Systematic thinkers': 'As a rule the philosopher [he was thinking particularly of Victor Cousin] is a kind of mongrel being, a cross between scientist and poet, envious of both. Metaphysics puts a good deal of rancour into the blood – a very curious and most interesting phenomenon. I was considerably engrossed by it for a couple of years, but it was a waste of time I now regret.'

Flaubert might have enjoyed the Chinese sage Chuang Tzu: 'Were we to tell him we had found contradictions in what he said, he would be apt to do a most unphilosophic thing. His students did just that, once: they confronted him to say, "Yesterday *that* happened, now today *this* happens: what position would you take in such a case, Master?" And what did the Master do? – Chuang Tzu laughed.'[2]

As for critics, Flaubert says bluntly that they 'write criticism because they are unable to be artists, just as a man unfit to bear arms becomes a police spy. I'd like to know what poets throughout the ages could have in common with the critics who have analysed their work.' And: 'Criticism occupies the lowest place in the literary hierarchy; as regards form, almost always; and as regards "moral value", incontestably. It comes after rhyming games and acrostics, which at least require a certain inventiveness.'

In contrast to the massive critical and academic attention given to Flaubert's work and to other aspects of his ideas, such reflections as these, and the cautionary truths expressed in them, have been given a wide critical berth.

Attentive readers of *Madame Bovary* have always noticed aspects of the novel – not only the pervasive presence of romanticism – that provide some confirmation of Flaubert's assertion to Sainte-Beuve that he was no 'realist'. There are time sequences that do not coalesce, descriptive details that are alien – all of them, however, achieving an effect of the liveliest realism by virtue of what the French *flaubertiste* Jean-Jacques Mayoux has called Flaubert's 'secret rhythm' – the masterly succession of 'words each exerting the proper weight in itself and in combination with the others'.[3]

In his review, Sainte-Beuve complained that 'there is no goodness in the book. Not a single character represents goodness'; and that this detracts from the novel's 'realism'. Sainte-Beuve's objection has been laughed at as philistine, but it does not lack validity; and there is the further question of the characters' intelligence. In *Madame Bovary* intelligence seems to be reserved solely for the author – and, presumably, for his appreciative reader. A single-questioning or self-appraising intelligence, though intermittently active as in life itself, would disrupt the book's tone. Yet even the dreariest provincial

2. Sebastian de Grazia, 'About Chuang Tzu', *Dalhousie Review*, summer 1974. And see *The Complete Works of Chuang Tzu*, translated by Burton Watson (New York: Columbia University Press, 1968), p. 109.
3. '*Flaubert et le Réel*', *Mercure de France*, 15 Février – 15 Mars 1934.

society (or even the worldliest) cannot be certain of insulating itself from an occasional flash of self-appraisal. The exclusion of both simple humanity (unless we except the aptly named Justin) and intelligent insight from the story, while a source of its power, deprives it of a measure of universality.

The very earliest letters in Flaubert's correspondence, those to his school friend Ernest Chevalier, are youthful and naive (Flaubert's tone to and about Chevalier was later to change, when he had outstripped him); those to the adored Alfred LePoittevin are generally rhapsodic, with interpolations of parroted cynicism; those to his literary 'midwife', Louis Bouilhet, have a tone of frank camaraderie. The two series of letters to Louise Colet, separated by a three-year interval, have their similarities and their contrasts.

In 1846, within the space of six months, Flaubert lost his father, his sister, and – through marriage – his most intimate friend, who was also soon to die. When, in July of that year, he met Louise Colet for the first time, at the studio of the sculptor James Pradier, he was in a state of depression, even of shock. (He was in fact delivering his sister's death-mask to the sculptor.) For the previous two years, following an epileptoid breakdown, he had, furthermore, been celibate. Rather than participate in life, he had resolved to observe it, and, if the artistic power were granted him, to represent it. Two or three nights after meeting Louise, he was in her bed. Or, as he wrote to her half-reproachfully: 'Then you came along, and with the touch of a fingertip stirred everything up again.'

It is to Louise Colet's retentive nature – and her daughter's need for money – that we owe the preservation and publication of approximately two hundred letters written by her celebrated lover during the first half of his life. His first letters to her, while throbbing with physical passion, nevertheless abound in half-reproaches. She had aroused his flesh *malgré lui;* he revelled in the sensuality, and resented it. Hence the peculiar tone of these love letters, for two years continually tipped with an insensitivity amounting to sadism. At this stage Flaubert has an equivocal view of Louise's destiny. He wants her to achieve her possibilities as a writer, and yet to be a 'sex object' to him. He wants to confide his literary dreams to her, but scarcely to share hers. In a moving passage he repudiates her reproach that his reflections on art are what he would say to any casual acquaintance – 'to someone I care nothing for'. Yet he is almost never at ease in the role of a loving man. The complexity of his feelings affects his style and syntax, sometimes to the point of challenging the reader's understanding. He himself speaks of this more than once: 'I feel I am writing badly – you will read this without emotion – I am saying nothing of what I want to say'; 'It's strange how bad my writing is in these letters to you . . . One thing conflicts with another . . . It's as though I wanted to say three words at a time.' Of all the letters, these are the most exigent for the translator – and perhaps for the reader.

After the first rupture (for which Louise eventually had the intelligence to recognize some responsibility), and the interval of Flaubert's 'Voyage en Orient', the liaison was resumed on a different basis. Now it is Louise's 'Memoranda', or 'Mementos' (discovered by M. Jean Bruneau at Avignon in 1974) that record Flaubert's physical response: Flaubert himself refers to it less often. He tells her that he longs to make of her a 'sublime hermaphrodite'; he wants her to be 'a man from the waist up'. And ultimately she becomes little more than a repository, a 'convenient receptacle' for all he has to say about the weird novel he finds himself creating – a book so different from anything he, or any other writer, has done before, that night after night he feels compelled to chronicle its tortuous, tormenting progress. As Louise well realizes, this, from a supposed lover whom one seldom sees, again approaches a form of sadism: 'In his letters, Gustave never speaks to me of anything except art – or himself.' And indeed, in the almost total absence from the archive of Louise Colet's letters to Flaubert, his second series to her, especially, brings to mind the image of a man dancing with a partner from whom he remains detached. Louise's bitter complaints, and her clumsy contrivings to hold Flaubert fast, bring about the unhappy close.

The foregoing pages may suggest why there are readers of Flaubert who from time to time turn from the novels to his correspondence. How often, in the letters, he laments that the art he produces is not the art he most admires. Flaubert's own great heroes among the artists are, in their prodigious spontaneity, his very opposites. His own power in the novels – one need only mention his celebrated and unremitting castigation of the bourgeois ('bourgeois' being defined as 'anyone who thinks basely') – is achieved by the labour revealed in the letters. Whereas: 'how easily the great men achieve their effects by means extraneous to Art. What is more badly put together than much of Rabelais, Cervantes, Molière and Hugo? But such quick punches! Such power in a single word! We must pile up a mass of little pebbles to build our pyramids; theirs, a hundred times greater, are hewn in monoliths.' It is in his correspondence – the writing he does 'after hours' – that Flaubert attains the very spontaneity he covets. In the torrential letters about 'art – or himself', about the 'eternal hubbub of Forms and Ideas', he enters the company of those other great men, the ones who, with such formidable effect, had set him dreaming.

In the present volume – a selection from Flaubert's thousands of letters – dots of omission indicate passages which in the editor's opinion reiterate Flaubert's already expressed views or are less revelatory than other passages of his personality and opinions.

I

The Billiard Table, The Collège

1821–1840

GUSTAVE FLAUBERT WAS born on December 12, 1821, in the residence wing of the Hôtel-Dieu, the municipal hospital of Rouen, where his father, the eminent Dr Achille-Cléophas Flaubert, was director and chief surgeon. For most of his first twenty-five years he lived in this contiguity with blood, suffering, and death – and with scientific research. 'The dissecting room of the hospital gave on to our garden. How many times my sister and I used to climb the trellis, cling to the vines, and peer curiously at the cadavers on their slabs! The sun shone on them, and the same flies that were flitting about us and about the flowers would light on them and come buzzing back to us . . . I still see my father raising his head from his dissecting, and telling us to go away.' As though the continual presence of physical malfunction and destruction were not enough, an uncle saw to it that the boy observed their mental counterpart: 'The first time I saw insane people was here in Rouen, in the asylum, with poor Père Parain. Sitting in cells, chained around the middle, naked to the waist, dishevelled, a dozen women were screaming and tearing their faces with their nails. I was then perhaps six or seven. These are good impressions to have when young: they make a man of you.' During his adolescence, he often visited the morgue.

He was a handsome boy, with the classic Norman fair hair and blue eyes; affectionate with his sister Caroline, but always in the shadow of his brother Achille. Achille, nine years his senior, was an apt and diligent student, trained almost from the cradle to follow his father into medicine, whereas Gustave's favourite childhood occupations were almost exactly those which the young Marcel Proust, another son of a doctor, would later list as his own: 'reading, reverie, poetry, the theatre'.

In Flaubert's case, reading was somewhat delayed. His sister Caroline, three years younger, was – with the advanced aptitude more usual in girls at that age – quick to learn her letters, putting her brother to shame. The little boy's slowness in reading and writing was a grave matter to his exigent family; and Gustave's sufferings over it are reflected in certain tales written in his adolescence. The retardation was brief, and, when overcome, evidently compensated for by a precocity of literary expression to which one of his earliest known letters – written at the age of nine (the first in the present volume) – amply testifies.

On the theme of reverie, or daydreaming, he would have much to say all his life; and his early theatre consisted of presenting and acting in his own dramas and in versions of the classics, before audiences of family and friends, using the home billiard table as a stage.

When he was eleven he became a boarder in the local lycée, the Collège Royal de Rouen, where he remained for several years. Here his friends were enthusiasts for the French Romantic writers. These students were not simply the readers, but, in many of their youthful tastes, the emulators, of literary figures – Chateaubriand, Hugo, Lamartine, Vigny, Musset – who concerned themselves with various forms of social, political, and spiritual agitation. Though typical of contemporary Romanticism throughout Europe, this ferment among French artists was credited by Musset himself, in *La Confession d'un enfant du siècle*, with a national raison d'être: reaction against the increasing flatness of French life following the years of revolution and Napoleonic drama. However, in the 1830s, while Flaubert was still a schoolboy, Balzac was beginning to publish the early volumes of his *Comédie Humaine*; and Flaubert read Balzac as well as the Romantics.

In the summer of 1836, at the seashore in Trouville, when he was almost fifteen, Flaubert conceived a passion – an 'enormous' passion, he later called it – for a woman of twenty-six with a genial husband and a small child. This was Mme Maurice (Elise) Schlesinger, whose warm motherliness was in contrast to the habitually rigid demeanour of Flaubert's own mother. There is no mention of this attachment in the adolescent's letters, but in an 'ideal' form Flaubert continued to cherish it, and it would eventually inspire the main thread of his third published novel, *L'Éducation sentimentale*, which appeared when he was almost fifty – one of the many examples, in Flaubert's literary life, of a very early experience serving as a quarry for much later work.

As a schoolboy he wrote essays and short tales, two of which were printed in a Rouen magazine – his only work published before the appearance of *Madame Bovary*. Two other short pieces were circulated privately by a family friend. He and his schoolmates invented a grotesque character, baptized '*le Garçon*', a raucous amalgam of clichés and boorishness, with a particularly revolting loud laugh, whom they tirelessly impersonated among themselves. Although he already occasionally satirized the contemporary bourgeois, most of the 'narrative compositions' he wrote while at the Collège Royal were gory prose melodramas, laid in the medieval settings often favoured by the Romantics. Gradually these early writings became more autobiographical, infused with ennui and yearning – yearning for love and for the exotic. In later life he painted himself as having been the complete young Romantic:

[At seventeen] I was like the cathedrals of the XVth century, lanceolated, flamboyant . . . Between the world and me there existed a kind of stained-glass window, coloured yellow, with rays of fire and golden arabesques, so that everything was reflected in my soul as on the pavement of a sanctuary, beautified, transfigured, and yet melancholy; and all who walked on it were beautiful. They were dreams – more majestic, more gorgeously costumed, than cardinals in purple robes. Such throbbings from the organ! Such hymns! And what a sweet odour of incense pouring from a thousand censers!

In 1839, his last year at the college, he participated in a student protest against the dismissal of a favourite teacher, and was expelled. The French school system allowed him to prepare for the final examination at home, and he passed it, obtaining his baccalauréat in 1840.

The present correspondence opens with the nine-year-old Flaubert already castigating (and at the same time observing) a bourgeois holiday ritual, commenting on national affairs, and discussing his own writing. In the French original the first few letters are marked by schoolboy errors of spelling and syntax; no attempt has been made to approximate these in the translation.

~

To Ernest Chevalier[1]

[Rouen, before January 1, 1831]

Dear Friend

You are right in saying that New Year's Day[2] is stupid. My friend, they have just dismissed the greatest of them all, the white-haired Lafayette, champion of freedom in the old world and the new.[3] Friend, I'll send you some of my political and constitutional liberal speeches. You are right in saying you'll give me pleasure by coming to Rouen, you will give me a great deal. I wish you a happy 1831, my affectionate greetings to your dear family. The friend you sent me seemed a nice fellow even though I saw him only once. I'll also send you some of my comedies. If you'd like us to work together at writing, I'll write comedies and you can write your dreams, and since there's a lady who comes to see papa and always says stupid things I'll write them too. I'm not writing this letter well because I'm expecting a box of sweets from Nogent.[4] *Adieu*, answer me as soon as possible.

Adieu, good health; your friend for life.

Answer as quickly as possible, please.

1. Ernest Chevalier (1820–1887), a year older than Flaubert and his earliest school friend, was the son of a prosperous farmer-businessman in the nearby country town of Les Andelys. For some years he was a boarder at the lycée in Rouen. His maternal grandparents, M. and Mme Mignot, who lived in Rouen, were friends of the Flaubert family. As he grows older, Chevalier will be, along with Flaubert's older brother Achille, a 'straight man' in the correspondence – the young bourgeois who advances complacently in a normal professional career.

2. Many years later, in a letter to his niece Caroline, the daughter of his long-dead sister, Flaubert would describe ritual New Year's Day visiting in

the Rouen of his childhood: 'In those times, on New Year's Day, Julie [the children's nurse] would take your mother and me by the hand and we'd pay our first call on Mme Lenôtre, who engulfed us in her great bonnet as she kissed us; next, père Langlois; then M. and Mme Bapeaume, Mme Lormier, Mme Énault, old Mme Legros and ending with Mme LePoittevin. So many different houses and faces – I remember them all clearly. My legs still ache when I think of those long boulevards. Our four little buttocks would be icy cold, and we couldn't pry our teeth apart, stuck together with apple taffy. What a din at your grandfather's! The front door wide open from seven in the morning! A salad bowl overflowing with visiting cards; hugs and kisses all day long. And the next day, zero, absolute solitude. That's how it was.' (Julie, old and blind, was still with Flaubert when this letter was written.)

3. The Liberal Lafayette had been dismissed (more precisely, his office as commander-in-chief of the National Guard had been 'abolished') by the Chamber of Deputies, in compliance with the wishes of King Louis-Philippe. There was agitation throughout France following this reactionary move by the recently inaugurated 'July Monarchy'. During the earlier Restoration, Dr Flaubert, suspected of 'progressive ideas', had been investigated but judged not dangerous.

4. Where lived a number of aunts, uncles, and cousins on Dr Flaubert's side of the family.

~

To Ernest Chevalier

[January 15, 1832]

Dear Friend

Your grandfather is a little better, the medicine papa gave him helped and we hope he'll soon be well. I'm making notes on *Don Quixote* and he says they're very good. Somebody I think Amédée has had my eulogy of Corneille printed and I am sending you a copy.[1] The billiard table is deserted, I'm not putting on any plays as you're not here. The Sunday you left seemed to me ten times as long as the others. I forgot to tell you that I'm about to begin a play to be called The miser lover, it will be about a miser who refuses to give his mistress any presents so his friend gets her away from him. All my greetings to your family, I will tell you the end of my play in another letter. Make your parents promise to come here with you for Carnival, work at your geography. I'm going to start also a History of Henry 4, Louis 13 and Louis 14. I must get to work. Answer . . . *Adieu* my best friend till death by God.

Good night. Your old friend.   Rouen this 15 of January
in the year 1832 of Our
Lord Jesus Christ.

Answer

1.   Amédée Mignot, Ernest Chevalier's uncle, finding young Flaubert's compositions precocious and amusing, had several handwritten copies made of two of them: a eulogy of Corneille and a mock treatise on constipation written partly in Latin. He circulated these as a pamphlet, entitled *Trois pages d'un Cahier d'Écolier, ou, Oeuvres choisies de Gustave F****.

∽

To Ernest Chevalier

February 4, 183[2]

Dear Friend

I'm answering you by return of mail. I told you I'd be writing some plays, but no, I'll write some Novels I have in mind, they are the Beautiful Andalusian, the masked ball, Cardenio, Dorothy, the moorish woman, the impertinent eavesdropper, the prudent husband. I have put aside the billiard table and the scenery. In my *proverbes dramatiques*[1] there are several plays that we can do. Your grandfather is still the same. You see I was right in saying that the splendid explanation of that famous condition constipation and my eulogy of Corneille would go down to posterity. That is, down to the posterior . . .

So long. Happy New Year, kiss my arses, come to Rouen.

Your dauntless dirty-minded friend till death.

Answer.

1.   *A proverbe dramatique* is a short play developed from a proverb, such as Alfred de Musset's *On ne badine pas avec l'amour.* Other well-known French writers of *proverbes dramatiques* are Louis Carrogis, known as Carmontelle (1717–1806) and Michel-Theodore Leclercq (1777–1851). (Jean Brunneau, J.B.)

∽

To Ernest Chevalier

Rouen, March 31, 1832

Dauntless One:

You know I told you in one of my letters that we were not having any more theatre, but the last few days we've been busy on the billiard table again. I have about 30 plays and there are many which Caroline and I act together. Be a good boy, come for Easter and stay at least a week. You'll say 'What about my catechism?' but you'd set out on Sunday at six o'clock after vespers, you'd be at Rouen by eleven, and you'd leave us with great regret the next Saturday afternoon. Your grandfather is better. I have written a poem called 'a mother' which is as good as the death of Louis 16. I have also done several plays, among others one called The ignorant antiquary which makes fun of stupid antiquaries and another which is called 'preparations to receive the king', which is very funny.

Listen to this, there's a pupil of old Langlois's[1] named Alexis, called by everybody Jesus. The other day he almost fell into the trench. At the moment he was placing his façade on the hole the boards broke and if someone hadn't caught hold of him he'd have fallen into old Langlois's excrement. *Adieu.*

Answer quickly at the first opportunity.

1. Perhaps a Rouen drawing teacher. (J.B.) One of the recipients of the New Year's Day calls described on p. 16, n. 2.

∾

To Ernest Chevalier

[Rouen, before April 22, 1832]

Victory Victory Victory Victory Victory you'll be coming one of these days, my friend, the theatre, the posters, everything is ready. When you come, Amédée, Edmond, Mme Chevalier, mama, two servants and perhaps some of the medical students will come to see us act. We'll give 4 plays you don't know but you'll learn the lines quickly. The tickets for the first, second, and third performances are done, there will be regular seats, there are also roofs and decorations. The backdrop is ready, perhaps there will be 10 or twelve people. So you must be brave and fear nothing, we'll have a doorkeeper who'll be young Lerond and his sister will be an extra. I don't know whether you have seen Poursognac,[1] we'll give it along with a play by Berquin, one by Scribe and a *proverbe dramatique* by Carmontelle, no use my telling you their titles I don't think you know them. When they told me you weren't coming I was in a frightful rage. If by any chance you didn't come I'd go to Les Andelys to get you on all fours like the dogs of King Louis Fils-Lippe (see the newspaper *La Caricature*) and I think you would do the same for me, for you and I are bound by a love that can be called fraternal. Yes, I, who have deep feelings, yes, I would walk a thousand leagues if necessary to be reunited with my best of friends, for nothing is so sweet as friendship oh sweet friendship how much has been accomplished thanks to this senti-ment, without attachments how could we live. We find this feeling even in the smallest animals, without friends how would the weak live, how could widows and children subsist?

Permit me, my dear friend, these tender reflections but I swear to you I have not been trying to embellish them nor to indulge in rhetoric, but am speaking to you with the frankness of the true friend. There is almost no cholera morbus at the Hôtel-Dieu. Your grandfather is the same. Come to Rouen. *Adieu.*

1.   Molière's *Monsieur de Pourceaugnac*. For a scene from this 'comedy-ballet' see p. 264.

TO ERNEST CHEVALIER

Rouen, Friday August 14, 1835

Dear Ernest

It is with much pleasure that I can now tell you with certainty that in papa's words 'We'll soon be coming to see you.'

Then you will owe us a return visit, and I hope you will adopt the good habit of coming to spend a week with us. About two weeks ago I finished my *Frédégonde*, I've even recopied an act and a half. I have another drama in mind. Gourgaud is assigning me narrative compositions.[1]

Since you saw me I've read *Catherine Howard* and *La Tour de Nesle.* I've also read the works of Beaumarchais: that's the place to find new ideas. Now I am entirely absorbed in the plays of old Shakespeare, I am reading *Othello,* and then I am going to take with me for my trip the *History of Scotland* in three volumes by W. Scott,[2] then I'll read Voltaire. I am working like a demon, getting up at half past three in the morning.

I see with indignation that theatre censorship is going to be reintroduced and the freedom of the press abolished; yes, this law will be passed, for the representatives of the people are nothing but a filthy lot of sold-out wretches, they see only their own interests, their natural bent is toward baseness, their honour is a stupid pride, their soul a lump of mud; but some day, a day that will come before long, the people will unleash the third revolution; kings' heads will roll, there will be rivers of blood. At present they are depriving the man of letters of his conscience, his artist's conscience. Yes, our century is rich in bloody *peripeties. Adieu, au revoir,* and let us continue to devote ourselves to what is greater than peoples, crowns and kings: to the god of Art, who is ever-present, wearing his diadem, his divine frenzy merely in abeyance.

1.   Henri-Honoré Gourgaud-Dugazon, professor of literature at the college. He recognized and encouraged the adolescent Flaubert's narrative gift, and became his friend and confidant. Flaubert preserved these early 'narrative compositions', and they were published posthumously in his *Oeuvres de jeunesse.*
2.   At this time he read both authors in French translation.

~

To Ernest Chevalier

> *[Rouen,] Saturday night [June] 24, 1837. (St John's Day, the longest day of the year, on which it chances that that old jokester the sun, among its other antics, dons its Sunday clothes, turns red as a carrot, draws sweat from grocers – hunting dogs – the National Guard – and dries out the turds in the streets.)*

Now that I am no longer writing, but have become an historian (so-called),[1] now that I read books, display serious tastes, and in the midst of it all preserve sufficient sangfroid and gravity to be able to look at myself in the mirror without laughing, I am all too happy when with the excuse of writing a letter I can let myself go, interrupt my work, and put off making notes, even those on M. Michelet; for the most beautiful woman is scarcely beautiful on the table of a dissecting-room, with her bowels draped over her nose, one leg minus its skin, and half a burnt-out cigar on her foot. Oh no it's a sad thing, criticism, study, plumbing the depths of knowledge to find only vanity, analysing the human heart to find only egoism, and understanding the world only to find in it nothing but misery. Oh how much more I love pure poetry, cries from the soul, sudden transports and then deep sighs, the voices of the soul, the thoughts of the heart. There are days when I would give all the knowledge of chatterers past, present and future, all the stupid erudition of the nitpickers, hairsplitters, philosophers, novelists, chemists, grocers, academicians, for two lines of Lamartine or Victor Hugo. You see me become very antiprose, antireason, antitruth, for what is the beautiful if not the impossible, what is poetry if not barbarism – the heart of man – and where to find that heart when in most cases it is given over to the two enormous preoccupations that fill a man's life: making his fortune and living for himself, in other words compressing his heart to make it fit in somewhere between his shop and his digestion . . .

1.   Adolphe Chéruel, professor of history at the college, later a well-known historian himself, was multiplying Flaubert's assignments, encouraging his historical studies as Gourgaud-Dugazon was encouraging his writing of fiction. The titles of many of Flaubert's youthful tales – ancestors of the *contes* of his maturity – reveal their historical settings: *Mort du duc de Guise, Chronique normande du Xe siècle, La Peste à Florence*, etc.

~

TO ERNEST CHEVALIER

Rouen, Thursday, September 13, 1838
     Your remarks on Victor Hugo are as true as they are unoriginal. Modern criticism now generally accepts that antithesis of body and soul so profoundly expressed in all the works of the great author of *Notre-Dame*. This man has been much attacked because he is great and arouses envy. People were at first astonished, and then they blushed, to see before them a genius as immense as any of those

whom they had been admiring for centuries; for human pride doesn't enjoy paying tribute to laurels that are still green. Is not V. Hugo as great a man as Racine, Calderón, Lope de Vega and many another long admired?

I am still reading Rabelais, and have also taken up Montaigne. I even intend later to make a special philosophical and literary study of these two men. Together they mark the taking-off point, as I see it, of French literature and the French spirit.

Really I deeply value only two men, Rabelais and Byron, the only two who have written in a spirit of malice towards the human race and with the intention of laughing in its face. What a tremendous position a man occupies who places himself in that relation to the world!

. . .

～

To Ernest Chevalier

[Rouen,] Sunday morning, February 24, 1839

What a fine and joyous existence is yours![1] Living from day to day, heedless of tomorrow, no worries about the future, no doubts, no fears, no hopes, no dreams – a life of merry loves and glasses of kirschwasser. A dissolute life, fantastic, artistic, jumping, hopping, bouncing, a life that goes up in its own smoke and drinks itself silly. Masked balls, restaurants, champagne, liqueurs, whores, vast clouds of tobacco – that's your life and you can't get enough of it, that's how you're wasting your days. Well, why not? You go with the wind; caprice is your only guide; when a woman passes, you follow her; you hear music, and it's on with the dance, the cancan, the chahut, squeezings and ticklings. And then the orgies! The 'bacchanalian' orgies! The shrieking! The yelling! The howling! (Here a poem on 'bacchanalian' orgies: I'll skip it.) You'll live this way for three years, and they will be – of course – 'the happiest years of your life', the ones you'll regret when you've settled down into sobriety and sharp dealing, living splendidly, paying your taxes, a convert to the virtue of a lawfully wedded wife and to temperance societies. But what are you going to do? What do you expect to become? What will your future be? Do you ask yourself that, sometimes? No: why should you? And you are right. The future is the worst thing about the present. The question, 'What are you going to do?', when it is cast in your face, is like an abyss in front of you that keeps moving ahead with each step you take. Quite apart from the metaphysical future (which I don't give a damn about because I can't believe that our body, composed as it is of mud and shit and equipped with instincts lower than those of the pig or the crab-louse, contains anything pure and immaterial, when everything around it is so polluted and ignoble) – apart from that future, there is the future of one's life. But don't think that I am undecided as to the choice of a profession: I am quite resolved to embrace none whatever. Because I despise my fellow-creatures too much to want to help them or harm them. Anyhow, I will get myself admitted to the bar, and perhaps even go on for a doctorate as a means of loafing an additional year. But very probably I shall never practise, unless perhaps to defend some famous criminal, or if a case is exceptionally horrible. As for writing . . . I am willing to bet that I will never be printed or acted. Not that I'm afraid of failure: I would simply be too disgusted with the chicaneries of publishing or the theatre. However, if I ever do take an active part in the world it will be as a thinker and de-moralizer. I will simply tell the truth: but that truth will be horrible, cruel, naked. Still, how do I know? For I am one of those people always disgusted from one day to the next, always thinking of the future, always dreaming, or rather daydreaming, surly, pestiferous, never knowing what they want, bored with themselves and boring to everybody else. I went to the brothel for some fun and was merely bored. Magnier[2] gets on my nerves, history I find oppressive. Tobacco? My throat is raw from it. Alcohol? I am pickled in it. The only thing left is eating, and that I do for hours on end. As a result, my body is fatter but my mind emaciated. In the past I used to think, reflect, write, dash down on paper all the verve I felt in my heart. Now I no longer think, no longer reflect – even less, write. Poetry has perhaps left me, too bored to stay. Poor angel, will you never return? And yet I have a confused feeling of something stirring within me, I am in a period of transition, curious to see what the result will be, how I'll come out of it: I am moulting (in the intellectual sense). Will I be hairless, or magnificent? I wonder. We shall see. My thoughts are confused, I am unable to do any work requiring imagination, every-thing I produce is dry, laboured, painful. I began a morality play two months ago – what I have done of it is absurd, absolutely empty of ideas. Perhaps I'll drop it. Too bad: at least I'll have had a glimpse of the sublime, but clouds came up and plunged me back into the inglorious commonplace. My life, in my dreams so beautiful, so poetic, so vast, so filled with love, will be like everyone else's – monotonous, sensible, stupid. I'll attend Law School, be admitted to the bar, and end up as a respectable assistant district attorney in a small provincial town, like Yvetot or Dieppe . . .

1. Chevalier, a year older than Flaubert, had entered the Paris Law School the previous autumn. For the prophetic aspect of this mockery of bourgeois clichés about '*la vie de bohème*' in the Latin Quarter, and its sequel, see Flaubert's letter to his mother from Constantinople on p. 184.
2. Professor of rhetoric at the college.

~

To Ernest Chevalier

[Rouen,] Monday morning. [March 18, 1839]
. . .

As to your horror of '*ces dames*'[1] who are, I might say in passing, very kind-hearted, broad-minded persons – I leave to Alfred[2] the task of changing it logically into a philosophical love consistent with the rest of your moral opinions. Yes, a thousand times yes, I prefer a whore to a grisette, for of all types of human beings the grisette is what I most abominate. Such, I believe, is the name given to that wriggly, properish, coquettish, simpery, perky, stupid something that's always getting on your nerves and wanting to play passion the way she sees it played in vaudeville. No, I much prefer the ignoble that doesn't pretend to be anything else. This preference is a pose like any other, a fact I am well aware of. With all my heart I could love a beautiful, ardent woman with the soul – and the fingers – of a whore. Such is the point I have reached. Such pure and innocent tastes! . . .

You tell me you have an admiration for G. Sand; I share it keenly, and with the same reservations. I have read few things as fine as *Jacques*. Speak to Alfred about it.

At present I am reading scarcely at all. I have resumed a work I put aside a long time ago, a morality play, a ragout – I think I've told you about it already.[3]

· · ·

1. '*Ces dames*' – 'those women' – in Flaubert's letters always means 'prostitutes'; he mocks, simply by using it, a pharisaic bourgeois euphemism. Chevalier had apparently written from Paris expressing 'pure' sentiments on the subject.

    A grisette was a working girl, often a seamstress: more particularly, one living with a student or several students or a succession of students. Mimi, in Puccini's *La Bohème* (its libretto based on Murger's *Scènes de la vie de bohème*, 1847–49), is probably the world's best known grisette. The word originally signified a cheap grey cloth, perhaps the stuff of the girls' workaday smocks, and is now used only historically, in connection with the Latin Quarter of that period.

2. Alfred LePoittevin, of whom much more will be heard.

3. There follows a detailed synopsis of his philosophical drama, *Smarh*, in which Satan guides and misguides a mortal, commenting sardonically on human thoughts and passions. It reflects early readings in Byron, Goethe, Quinet, Spinoza, Michelet.

∾

To Ernest Chevalier
    [Rouen,] Monday afternoon, mathematics class, July 15, 1839
· · ·

I thought I was going to have some ideas just now, and nothing has come – so what? I'm sorry, but it's not my fault if I don't have a philosophical mind, like [Victor] Cousin or Pierre Leroux or Brillat-Savarin – or like Lacenaire,[1] who philosophized also, in his own way. And a strange, deep, bitter philosophy it was. What a lesson he read Morality, what a public whipping he gave that poor desiccated prude – how he pummelled her, dragged her in the mud, in blood. I love to see men like that, like Nero, like the marquis de Sade. When you read history, when you see the same old wheels always rolling along the same old roads in the midst of ruins, turning, turning in the dusty path of the human race, those figures loom up like Egyptian priapi . . . Those monsters explain history for me, they are its complement, its apogee, its moral, its dessert. Believe me, they too are great men, immortals. Nero will live as long as Vespasian, Satan as long as J-C.

Oh, dear Ernest, apropos of the marquis de Sade, if you could find me some of the novels of that honourable writer, I'd pay you their weight in gold. I've read a biographical article about him by J. Janin, which filled me with revulsion – revulsion against Janin, needless to say: he held forth on behalf of morality, philanthropy, deflowered virgins . . .

1.　Pierre-François Lacenaire, thief and assassin, guillotined in Paris in 1836. A volume of his memoirs, reflections, and poems, published after his death, was discussed with horror at the time. His name is known to present generations through his depiction by the actor Marcel Herrand in the film *Les Enfants du Paradis* (1945).

　　Victor Cousin was the most prominent living French philosopher and will re-enter these pages in another role. Flaubert had been reading one of his works at the college.

　　Pierre Leroux was a Saint-Simonian economist; Brillat-Savarin the author of *The Physiology of Taste*; Jules Janin a literary journalist.

II

The Law

1840–1843

AFTER PASSING THE baccalauréat in August 1840, Flaubert was sent by his parents on his first long journey – to Corsica, via the Pyrenees and Provence, with a family friend, Dr Jules Cloquet. Also in the party were the doctor's sister and an Italian abbé friend of the Cloquets. The company was not particularly congenial to Flaubert, but it was in Marseilles during this trip that his erotic initiation was completed[1] by the alluringly named Mme Eulalie Foucault, née Delanglade, who with her mother was co-owner, or co-manager, of the Hôtel Richelieu, rue de la Darse. Unwittingly or otherwise, Dr Cloquet performed a service for his handsome, not virginal, but 'unawakened', romantic young friend when he took him to stay in this hotel for a few days – and nights. Flaubert wrote to Mme Foucault after his return to Rouen, and kept some of her affectionate replies: Jean Bruneau thinks their style suggests that they were copied from printed models. As we shall see, Flaubert never forgot this blessedly aggressive benefactress.

In Provence, Flaubert first saw the Mediterranean and glimpsed the architecture of the ancient world. Both enchanted him and aroused his appetite. Dazzled, he returned to Rouen on November 1, 1840.

1. In their journal, the Goncourt brothers report Flaubert's telling them of having been *dépucelé* by one of his mother's maids. After that initiation came the schoolboy visits to Rouen brothels.

~

To Ernest Chevalier

[Rouen,] November 14, 1840

. . .

My mind is dried up, exhausted. I'm disgusted to be back in this damned country where you see the sun in the sky about as often as a diamond in a pig's arse-hole. I don't give a shit for Normandy and *la belle France*. Ah! To live in Spain, in Italy, even in Provence! Some day I must buy myself a slave in Constantinople, a Georgian girl – a man who doesn't own a slave is a nonentity; is there anything more stupid than equality, especially for those who are crippled by it? – and it cripples me horribly. I hate Europe, France – my own country, my succulent motherland that I'd gladly send to hell now that I've had a glimpse of what lies beyond. I think I must have been transplanted by the winds to this land of mud; surely I was born elsewhere – I've always had what seem like memories or intuitions of perfumed shores and blue seas. I was born to be emperor of Cochin-China, to smoke 100-foot pipes, to have 6 thousand wives and 1400 catamites, scimitars to slice off heads I don't like the look of, Numidian horses, marble pools – and I have nothing but immense, insatiable desires, frightful boredom and incessant yawns. Also a broken pipe and dried-out tobacco.

Shit! *Adieu*; keep well. Too bad if you're shocked by the cynicism of this letter: that would be proof you're stupid, and I like to think you're not.

~

Dr Flaubert had experienced no difficulty in settling his elder son, Achille, in the career he had chosen for him – medicine; Gustave he now directed to the law, overriding the boy's evident and outspoken repugnance.[1] Having obtained his baccalauréat, Flaubert would normally have proceeded to Paris and the Law School at once. Instead, his father allowed him to delay the move for two years – part of the period, apparently, to be spent in preparation. Perhaps Dr Flaubert had already detected symptoms of poor health in Gustave, had prescribed the trip to the south for health reasons, and on his return decided to keep him under observation. This interlude at home seems to have been one of extensive daydreaming. He began a novella, *Novembre*, put it aside several times, and finished it on October 25, 1842. For a time he kept a journal. This was discovered only in 1965, and was published that year in France as *Souvenirs, notes, et pensées intimes*. An English translation of this melancholy, poetic, youthfully cynical diary, *Intimate Notebook, 1840–41*, appeared in 1967.

1. Jean-Paul Sartre's primary thesis in his study of Flaubert, *L'Idiot de la famille*, set forth in the (comparatively) early pages of that three-volume, uncompleted work, may perhaps be summarized as follows: because of Gustave's slight delay in learning his letters, his daydreaming, his general tastes, nervousness, and impracticality (all the foregoing characteristics being in themselves products of the family environment), Dr Flaubert considered him unworthy, unlike his older brother, to be trained in medical science. For the doctor, according to Sartre, medicine was the noblest profession, and he himself one of its noblest practitioners. Gustave was quite aware of this, and aware that his being directed to a career in the law (an inferior, less demanding profession) was a humiliation, exclusion from the dynasty of doctor-scientists; and his eventual breakdown was due primarily to that rejection rather than to mere distaste for legal studies. Sartre then proceeds to expound and analyse the use Flaubert made of the freedom to write, conferred by the breakdown.

~

To Henri-Honoré Gourgaud-Dugazon

Rouen, January 22, 1842

Mon cher Maître,

I begin by saying that I'd like an answer. I count on seeing you in April, and since your letters usually take whole trimesters and semesters to arrive, you might easily leave me without news until then. Come – surprise me, be punctual: that is a scholastic virtue you should make a point of possessing, since you have all the others. I was in Paris at the beginning of this month: I stayed two days, full of business and errands, and hadn't the time to come and embrace you. In the spring I'll come to see you some Sunday morning, and willy-nilly you'll have to make me a present of your entire day. Hours pass quickly when we are together; I have so many things to tell you, and you listen so well!

Now more than ever I need to talk to you, need your wisdom, your friendship. My moral position is critical: you saw that when we were last together. From you I hide nothing, and I speak to you not as to my former teacher, but as though you were only twenty and were here, facing me, beside my fireplace.

I am, as you know, studying law; that is, I have bought my lawbooks and matriculated. I'll start studying soon, and expect to pass my examination in July.[1] I continue to busy myself with Greek and Latin, and shall perhaps be busy with them always. I love the flavour of those beautiful tongues; Tacitus is for me like bronze bas-reliefs, and Homer has the beauty of the Mediterranean; the same pure blue waters, the same sun, the same horizon. But what comes back to me from moment to moment, what makes me drop my pen as I take notes, and obliterates my textbooks as I read, is my old love, the same fixed idea: writing! That is why I am not accomplishing much, even though I get up very early and go out less than ever.

I have arrived at a moment of decision: I must go forward or backward. It is a question of life and death. When I decide, nothing will stop me, even though I were booed and jeered at by everyone. You know my stubbornness and stoicism well enough to believe me. I will pass my bar examination, but I scarcely think I shall ever plead in court about a party-wall or on behalf of some poor paterfamilias cheated by a rich upstart. When people speak to me about the bar, saying 'This young fellow will make a fine trial lawyer', because I'm broad in the shoulders and have a booming voice, I confess it turns my stomach. I don't feel myself made for such a completely materialistic, trivial life. On the contrary, every day I admire the poets more and more. I discover in them a thousand things that formerly I never saw. I grasp analogies and antitheses whose precision astonishes me, etc. This, then, is what I have resolved: I have in mind three novels, three tales, each of them different, each requiring a particular way of writing. This will suffice to prove to myself whether I have talent or not.

Into them I'll put everything I have in the way of style, passion and intelligence, and then we'll see.

In April I expect to have something to show you. It is that sentimental and amatory hodgepodge I spoke to you about.[2] There is no action. I wouldn't know how to give you an analysis of it, since it consists of nothing but psychological analyses and dissections. It is perhaps very fine; but I fear it may be very false, and not a little pretentious and stilted.

Adieu; I leave you, for you've perhaps had enough of this letter in which I've done nothing but speak of myself and my wretched passions. But I have nothing else to talk to you about: I don't go to dances, and don't read the newspapers.

Again *adieu*; all my affection.

P.S. Answer me soon. I should dearly love to correspond with you more often, for after finishing a letter to you I find myself only at the beginning of what I want to say.

1. That is, the Law School's so-called First Examination, based on study of Justinian's *Institutes* and the French *Code Civil*, which formed the pro- gramme of the first year.
2. This is the hundred-page novella, *Novembre*, Flaubert's most accomplished work so far. There are only two characters, an unnamed young man and a shadowy woman, Marie, with whom he placates the 'demon of the flesh'. (Flaubert's nights in Marseilles were a fresh memory.) The very Romantic tone echoes that of Goethe's *Werther* and Chateaubriand's *René*, the latter probably Flaubert's favourite modern fiction at the time. There is a pervasive vagueness; character delineation and realistic detail are almost totally absent. An English translation, by Frank Jellinek, suggests the imitative beauty of Flaubert's early Romantic prose.

    Jean Bruneau thinks that Flaubert's other two projects may have been an oriental tale, *Les Sept Fils du derviche*, which he never finished, and a dictionary of accepted opinions or clichés, of which more will be heard.

    Gourgaud-Dugazon was now teaching at Versailles.

≈

In the early summer of 1842 Dr Flaubert found Gustave well enough to go to Paris for some cramming and to take the first examination for the study of law, apparently scheduled for August.

≈

To Ernest Chevalier

[Paris, July 22, 1842]

A pretty science, the Law! Ah, it's beautiful! From the literary point of view, especially. Professors Oudot and Ducoudray: they have such elegant styles! Professor Duranton: his face – the face of a true artist! and ah! what a splendid physique: pure Greek! To think that for a month I haven't read a line of poetry, listened to a note of music, daydreamed peacefully for three hours, lived a single minute! I am so harassed by it all that the other night I *dreamed* of the law! I felt ashamed at having so dishonoured dreaming. I'm sweating blood and tears, but if I can't find somebody's notes on Oudot it's the end – I'll be rejected for next year. Yesterday I went to watch some other students taking their examinations; I have nothing better to do than that. Soon I too shall have to wear that filthy harness. I care nothing for the law, as long as I retain the right to smoke my pipe and watch the clouds, lying on my back with eyes half-closed. That is all I want. Do you think I have any desire to be important, a great man, a man known in an arrondissement, in a department, in three provinces, a man without flesh on his bones, a man whose digestion doesn't work? Do you think I have ambition, like boot-blacks who aspire to be bootmakers, coachmen who long to be grooms, valets who yearn to be masters – the ambition to be a deputy or minister, to be decorated, to become municipal councillor? All that seems utterly dreary to me and makes my mouth water as little as a 40-sou dinner or a humanitarian speech. But it's everybody's mania. And even if only to retain some distinction (quite apart from following one's own taste) – out of mere good form and not incli-nation – it is well nowadays to keep to oneself and leave that sort of thing to the riffraff, who keep pushing and calling attention to themselves. As for us, we stay at home; from our balcony we watch the public go by; and if at times disgust gets the better of us, then let's just spit down on their heads, and go on talking quietly and watching the sun sink below the horizon.

Good night to you.

∿

To his sister Caroline

[Paris, July 25, 1842]

. . .

I dined yesterday at Monsieur Tardif's, with Monsieur and Madame Daupias.[1] Distinguished in dress and manner (like Murat), I conducted myself very well through dinner. But later the company took it into their heads to speak of Louis-Philippe, and I railed against him because of the museum at Versailles. Think of that pig, when he discovers that a picture by Gros isn't large enough to fill a wall panel, conceiving the idea of tearing off one side of the frame and adding two or three feet of canvas painted by some mediocre artist. I'd enjoy meeting that artist, just to see what he looks like. Naturally Monsieur and Madame Daupias, who are frantic *philipp- istes* – who attend court and therefore, like Madame de Sévigné after dancing with Louis XIV, cry 'What a great king!' – were very shocked by the way I spoke of him. But as you know, the more indignant I make the bourgeois, the happier I am. So I was thoroughly satisfied with my evening. They doubtless took me for a legitimist, because I made just as much fun of the men of the opposition.

... Your friend Gourgaud is coming to have lunch with me today, and I write this while waiting for him. The study of law is souring my temper in the extreme; I'm constantly grumbling, growling, grousing; when I'm alone I mutter even against myself. The night before last I'd have given a hundred francs (which I didn't have) to be able to administer a good thrashing to somebody – anybody ...

1.   Tardif was Dr Flaubert's Paris banker, who remitted Gustave his allowance.

     Daupias, baron d'Alcochete, Portuguese consul-general in Paris, was one of the many types of bourgeois who drove the young Flaubert into a frenzy. In another letter to his sister Caroline he wrote: 'Last night I dined at old Tardif's, who gave me 150 francs. *Le sieur* Daupias was there. You can reassure maman, I behaved well – said almost nothing; or at least I didn't rail against the infamous Louis-Philippe. What a ridiculous imbecile that baron d'Alcochete is, what a pig, what utter, wretched riffraff! He was formerly a pearl dealer, went bankrupt, and is now a diplomat and baron with many ribbons on the lapel of his tail-coat. How I'd have loved to spit in his face, beat him up, make him die by torture befitting the lowest criminal.'

∾

But Flaubert discovered that to be permitted to take the first law examination a student had to 'qualify', on the evidence of preparation done and notes made; and Professor Oudot found Flaubert's notes on the *code civil* (Oudot's specialty) inadequate. Or perhaps he discovered that they had not – as Flaubert hints in his letters – been made by Flaubert himself, but bought or borrowed. The examination was postponed until December, and Flaubert was at home again for the late summer and part of the autumn.

In the late autumn of 1842, after finishing *Novembre*, he returned to Paris, took a flat in the Latin Quarter, registered once more at the Law School, and attended lectures.

~

To his sister Caroline

[Paris, after December 10, 1842]

My nerves are so on edge that I have to let myself go a little in a letter to you. Next Friday I'll definitely make the appointment for my examination. I want to get it over with as soon as possible because things can't go on like this any longer. I'd end up in a state of idiocy or fury. Tonight, for example, I'm enjoying both those agreeable sensations simultaneously. I am so desperately impatient to put the examination behind me that I could weep. I think I'd even be glad if I failed, such a burden do I find this life I've been leading for six weeks. Some days are worse than others. Yesterday, for example, the weather was mild as May: all morning I had a terrible longing to take a cart and drive out into the country. I kept thinking that if I were in Déville I'd be under the shed with Neo[1] watching the rain and quietly smoking my pipe. When preparing for an examination one mustn't pay attention to all the good, delightful things that come into one's mind: I reproach myself for wasting time whenever I open my window to look at the stars (there's a beautiful moon just now) and take my mind off things a little. To think that since leaving you I haven't read a line of French, not six lines of poetry, not a single decent sentence. The *Institutes* are written in Latin and the *code civil* in something even less resembling French. The gentlemen who compiled it didn't offer much of a sacrifice to the Graces. They made it as dry, as hard, as stinking, as flatly bourgeois as the wooden benches of the Law School, where we go to harden our buttocks while hearing it explained. Those who care little about comfort – intellectual comfort, in this case – may find themselves not too badly off there; but for aristocrats like me, who are accustomed to enthroning their imaginations in seats that are more ornate, richer, and above all more softly luxurious, it's damned disagreeable and humiliating. *'There is nothing so grossly and largely offending wronging, as the lawes.'* [2]

1. His dog.
2. Montaigne, *Essais*, book 3, chap. 13, *'De l'expérience'*: *'Il n'est rien si lourde-ment et largement faultier que les loix.'* (The English is John Florio's; 1603.)

～

Flaubert finally passed his first examination on December 28, 1842, and after spending the New Year holidays at home he returned to his Paris lodgings. His letters throughout 1843 are disturbed; he loathed his law studies and dreaded the future they represented. He sought relief in various forms. He began a second novel, which he called *L'Education Sentimentale* – the title he would use again almost thirty years later for his great novel portraying an entire generation of Frenchmen. Once a week or so he left the Latin Quarter to visit friends in other parts of the city: the Schlesingers (Maurice Schlesinger, Elise's husband, was a music publisher); the Colliers, an English family he had also met in Trouville; the sculptor James Pradier and his wife; and Mme Pradier's family, the Darcets, whom the Flauberts had known in Rouen. Otherwise he was lonely: Ernest Chevalier (and Alfred LePoittevin, whom the reader will soon meet) had finished Law School and left Paris; Flaubert patronized some of the brothels whose addresses, with the names of certain girls, Alfred sent him. On one occasion he found himself in financial trouble because of bad company, and had to appeal to his father, apparently through Caroline or his mother.[1] It was a wretchedly unhappy time. In August he failed his second examination[2] and had again to reregister.

Symptoms described in a letter to Caroline on May 12, 1843, are a portent of what was to happen the following January: 'How I wish I were with you! But I'm grinding away like crazy, and from now until August shall be in a perpetual fury of work. Sometimes I'm taken with fits of twitching, and fling myself about with my books as though I had the *danse de Saint-Guy*,[3] patron of tailors, or as though I were stricken with epilepsy, the falling sickness.'

1. Dr Flaubert wrote to him in July:

'You are doubly silly – first to let yourself be gulled like a real provincial, a ninny letting himself be swindled by confidence men or loose women, whose usual victims must be morons or imbecile dodderers, and thank God you are neither stupid nor old; your second mistake is not to have confidence in me ... I thought I was sufficiently your friend to merit being told anything that might happen to you, good or bad ...

'*Adieu*, dear Gustave. Spare my purse a little and above all keep well and working.'

2. A passage in the definitive *Éducation sentimentale* (1870) perhaps evokes this occasion. Frédéric Moreau, the novel's hero, is taking a law examination:

'Standing behind the chair, he fidgeted and kept pulling on his moustache.

' "I'm still waiting for your answer," said the examiner. And because Frédéric's gesture apparently irritated him: "You won't find it in your beard." '

3. St Vitus's dance.

∼

TO HIS SISTER CAROLINE

Sunday, 5 p.m [Paris, December 3, 1843]

Bonjour, vieux rat. I gather your precious health is satisfactory, and that you are beginning to acquire a 'robust constitution'. Continue to take care of yourself, so that soon, in a month, when I come to Rouen,[1] I'll find you more vigorous and flourishing than ever. If you continue well, what a time we'll have at Trouville next summer! You know my vacation begins in June. May God make it as good as I hope to make it long.

. . .

You are expecting details about Victor Hugo. What can I tell you? He is a man who looks like many another, with a rather ugly face and a rather common appearance. He has magnificent teeth, a superb forehead, no eyelashes or eyebrows. He talks little, gives the impression of being on his guard and not wanting to give himself away; he is very polite and a little stiff. I greatly like the sound of his voice. I enjoyed watching him from close by; I looked at him with astonishment, as I would at a casket of gold and royal diamonds, thinking of everything that has come out of him – that man who was sitting on a little chair beside me; I kept looking at his right hand, which has written so many splendid things. There was the man who ever since I was born has done more than any other to make my heart throb; the man whom I have loved best, perhaps, of all those whom I do not know! Some of the conversation was about executions, revenge, thieves, etc. The great man and I did most of the talking, and I no longer remember whether what I said was good or stupid, but I said rather a lot. As you see, I go quite often to the Pradiers'. It's a house I very much like; one doesn't feel at all constrained there; it's my kind of place . . .

1.　For the New Year holidays.

III

Breakdown, Travel, Mourning

1844–1846

LATE IN DECEMBER 1843, Flaubert left Paris to spend the New Year holidays – 'twelve days at the most', he wrote to his sister – in Rouen. The exact date of the dramatic and decisive event which now soon occurred is not certain. In January he apparently returned to Paris and his studies as planned, and then for some reason went back again to Normandy. It seems to have been during that second stay that the prospect of resuming the frustrations of the Law School finally became more than his nerves could bear. One late January night, returning in a carriage with his brother Achille from a visit to Deauville to inspect the site being considered for the construction of a summer cottage, he fell to the floorboards, stricken with epilepsy. At home, cared for by his father, he suffered more attacks.

A few months earlier, he had confided to Alfred LePoittevin (who had been writing him cynical letters about the law, not designed to improve his morale) his intention of telling his father that although he would finish Law School he was determined never to practise; and Alfred had replied: 'If I were capable of pitying anyone, I would pity you, buried as you are under law books. I long to know how things will end, and how Father will take your resolution to make your diploma the end of your active life.' The onset of epilepsy spared Flaubert the need to announce his resolution. That aspect of his future had solved itself.

∼

To Ernest Chevalier

[Rouen, February 1, 1844]

Dear Ernest

Without suspecting it, you came close to going into mourning for the worthy who is writing you these lines. Yes, old man; yes, young man; I barely escaped paying my respects to Pluto, Rhadamanthus and Minos. I am still in bed, with a seton in my neck – a collar even stiffer than the kind worn by an officer of the National Guard – taking countless pills and infusions, and above all plagued by that spectre, a thousand times worse than all the illnesses in the world, called a diet. Know then, dear friend, that I had a cerebral congestion, a kind of attack of apoplexy in miniature, accompanied by nervous symptoms which I continue to display because it's good form to do so. I very nearly popped off in the midst of my family (with whom I had come to spend two or three days to recover from the horrible scenes I had witnessed at Hamard's [in Paris]).[1] They bled me in three places at once and I finally opened my eyes. My father wants to keep me here a long time and observe me carefully; my morale is good, however, because I don't know what worry is. I'm in a rotten state; at the slightest excitement, all my nerves quiver like violin strings, my knees, my shoulders, and my belly tremble like leaves. Well, *c'est la vie, sic est vita,* such is life. I shall probably not be returning to Paris, except for two or three days towards April, to give up my flat and attend to a few small matters. I'll be sent to the seashore early this year and will be made to take a lot of exercise and above all keep very quiet. No doubt I'm boring you frightfully with this tale of my woes, but what can I do? If I'm already suffering from old men's illnesses, I must be allowed to drivel on the way they do . . .

1. Emile Hamard, a school friend, of whom Flaubert had a poor opinion; the future husband of Caroline Flaubert. The 'horrible scenes' were apparently scenes of frantic grief: Hamard's mother had just died, leaving him an orphan and alone; his only brother had died the year before. But Hamard's grief seems scarcely sufficient reason for Flaubert's return to Rouen. The true reason is not known. Perhaps there had been further health warnings.

To Ernest Chevalier

[Rouen,] June 7 [1844]

As to your faithful servant, he is better, without being precisely well. Not a day goes by that I don't see, every once in a while, what looks like a tangle of filaments, or a burst of fireworks, passing before my eyes.[1] That lasts varying lengths of time. Still, my last big attack was lighter than the others. I still have my seton, a pleasure I don't wish on you, and I am still deprived of my pipe – a horrible torture, one not inflicted on the early Christians. And they say the emperors were cruel!!! You see how history is written, dear sir! *Sic scribitur historia!* I am still not allowed to go about by myself . . .

My father has bought a house outside Rouen, at Croisset. We are going there to live next week. Everything is upside down because of the move; we'll be rather uncomfortable there this summer, surrounded by workmen, but next summer I think it will be superb. I go boating with Achille . . .

1. Later, in a letter to Louise Colet, Flaubert wrote more fully about the sensations he experienced during a seizure:
    'Each attack was like a haemorrhage of the nervous system. Seminal losses from the pictorial faculty of the brain, a hundred thousand images cavorting at once in a kind of fireworks. It was a snatching of the soul from the body, excruciating. (I am convinced I died several times.) But what constitutes the personality, the rational essence, was present throughout; had it not been, the suffering would have been nothing, for I would have been purely passive, whereas I was always conscious even when I could no longer speak. Thus my soul was turned back entirely on itself, like a hedgehog wounding itself with its own quills.'

~

To Emmanuel Vasse de Saint-Ouen[1]

[Rouen, January 1845]

. . . I rarely leave my room. I see nobody except Alfred Le Poittevin. I live alone, like a bear. All summer I spent boating and reading Shakespeare, and since we returned from the country I have been reading and working a certain amount, studying Greek and reviewing my history. My illness has brought one benefit, in that I am allowed to spend my time as I like, a great thing in life. For me I can imagine nothing in the world preferable to a nice, well-heated room, with the books one loves and the leisure one wants.[2] As for my health, it is in general better, but in these devilish nervous illnesses recovery is so slow as to be almost imperceptible. I'll be on a diet for a long time to come. But I am patient, and meanwhile time passes. I have suffered a good deal, *pauvre vieux*, since that last night we spent together reading Petronius. I had a seton in my neck which hurt horribly. I almost lost my right hand because of a burn, which has left a great red scar,[3] and to cap it all have had three teeth pulled . . .

1. A school friend, now studying Cretan history.
2. In August he would write to Ernest Chevalier: 'I have never spent better years than the two just ended, because they have been the freest, the least constrained, of my life. I have sacrificed much for this freedom! And I would sacrifice more.'
3. In the course of a treatment, Dr Flaubert had spilled boiling water on the hand, which remained permanently scarred and half-stiffened – 'like the hand of a mummy', Flaubert said.

   Raised to revere the medical profession, Flaubert was learning – literally at first-hand – the fallibility of doctors, to which he would allude more than once in his correspondence and to which he would give formidable illustration in *Madame Bovary.* Sartre points out that the figure of the great Larivière at the conclusion of that novel, commonly accepted as a reverential portrait of Flaubert's father, appears on examination to be quiet mockery. There is no doubt that the man Flaubert revered his father always; Flaubert the artist, however, registered the irreverent truth.

～

A year after his first attack, Flaubert finished *L'Éducation senti-mentale.*[1]

On March 3, 1845, his sister Caroline married Emile Hamard, and a month later the couple set out (from Nogent-sur-Seine, where they were visiting cousins) on the conventional wedding trip to Italy. They were accompanied by Dr and Mme Flaubert and by Gustave, now considered well enough to travel. Caroline herself was frail and had never been further from Rouen than Paris; her father wanted to satisfy himself that she could stand the rigours of the road. His plan was that they would all stay together as far as Genoa – whence, if all went well, the young couple would continue alone to Florence, Rome, and Naples and the others return to France via Switzerland.

But by the time they reached Genoa, Caroline was exhausted and ill. Dr Flaubert briefly thought that the Hamards could perhaps still continue to Naples if he and the others went with them; but Caroline did not improve, Mme Flaubert wept, Dr Flaubert himself developed an eye infection, and in the end they all turned back together. During the trip Flaubert suffered two attacks.

His chief correspondent during the journey was Alfred LePoittevin. With the exception of one schoolboy note written when he was sixteen and already joking about a brothel, these are the earliest of his letters to LePoittevin to have been preserved, and from them can be gauged the importance of this apparently charming and pitiable young man in Flaubert's early life.

Alfred LePoittevin was the voluptuary, Romantic-minded son of a rich Rouen cotton manufacturer. His parents were close friends of Dr and Mme Flaubert (each father was the godfather of the other's son); he was devoted to literature and philosophy; and he had a four-year seniority which qualified him to be cast by Flaubert in the role of substitute for the close older brother that Achille might have been but was not. Alfred's father, like Dr Flaubert, ordered his son to study law and, like Flaubert, Alfred obeyed; but he was without ambition or Flaubert's creative gift, and when his disgust for his enforced profession took the upper hand he did not go on to better things, but wasted himself in whoring, alcohol, a cynical marriage, and, eventually, languor and resignation to early death from tuberculosis.

Before Alfred's departure for Paris and Law School, he and the adolescent Flaubert had been inseparable; Alfred had shared Flaubert's passion for his literary heroes, had perhaps introduced him to some of them; two of Flaubert's works of that time, *Agonies* and *Mémoires d'un fou*, are dedicated to Alfred. Flaubert went to Paris just as Alfred returned to Rouen to practise; only after Flaubert's breakdown were they reunited, and during his convalescence the intimacy was resumed, Alfred already alcoholic, practising law *à contrecoeur*, writing occasional poetry and prose. Now, in 1845, separated from Alfred yet again while travelling, Flaubert let his heart overflow, writing often in the particular tone and vocabulary, a compound of cynicism and rhapsody, which Alfred inspired and which had infused much of Flaubert's early, Romantic fiction.

1. This early novel, three times the length of the graceful *Novembre*, and with a good-sized cast of characters, is Flaubert's most ambitious fiction in a contemporary setting before *Madame Bovary*. It is an awkward attempt at objective narration, which repeatedly, and in the end definitively, relapses into Romantic effusion. There are reflections on art, and longings for exotic scenes, which resemble passages in the correspondence. In its story of two young school friends, Henry and Jules, who follow different paths, this primitive *Éducation sentimentale* contains one of the themes of Flaubert's novel of 1870 to which he would give the same title. Like *Novembre* and the rest, it remained among his unpublished juvenilia until after his death. There is an English translation by Douglas Garman.

~

To Alfred LePoittevin

Nogent-sur-Seine, April 2, [18]45

It is truly wrong for you and me to part, to disrupt our work and our intimacy. Each time we have done so we have found ourselves the worse for it. Once again, at this last separation, I felt a pang; it was less of a shock to me than other times, but still very depressing. For three months we were happy together, alone, each of us alone in himself and with the other. There is nothing in the world to equal those strange conversations we have beside that sooty fireplace where you come and sit – isn't it so, dear poet? Plumb the depths of your life and you will admit, as I do, that we have no better memories; that is, no memories of things more personal, more profound, and all the more tender for being exalted.

I enjoyed seeing Paris again; I looked at the boulevards, the rue de Rivoli, the pavements, as though I were back among them after being away a hundred years; and I don't know why, but I felt happy in the midst of all that noise and all that human flood. (But I have no one with me, alas! The moment you and I part, we set foot in some strange land where people do not speak our language nor we theirs.) No sooner was I off the train than I put on my city shoes, boarded a bus, and began my visits. The stairs of the Mint left me breathless, because there are a hundred of them and also because I remembered the evenings, gone never to return, when I used to climb them on my way to dinner. I greeted Mme and Mlle Darcet,[1] who were in mourning; I sat down, talked for half an hour, and then decamped.

Everywhere I went I walked in my own past, pushing through it as though striding knee-deep against the current of a flowing, murmuring river. I went to the Champs-Elysées, to see the two women[2] with whom I used to spend entire afternoons (which I probably wouldn't do now, I've become such a lout). The invalid was still half-lying in an armchair. She greeted me with the same smile and the same voice. The furniture was still the same, and the rug no more worn. In exquisite affinity, one of those rare harmonies that can be perceived only by the artist, a street-organ began to play under the windows, just as it used to when I would be reading them *Hernani* or *René*. Then I made my way to the home of a great man.[3] Alas! He was away. 'Monsieur Maurice left just this afternoon for London.' You may imagine that I was put out, that I'd have liked to see someone for whom I feel such unconquerable affection. Maurice's clerk found me taller; what do you say to that?

Having got Mme Pradier's address from Panofka, I hurried to the rue Laffitte and asked the concierge of No. 42 for the apartment of that lost lady. Ah! What an interesting study it was! How well I handled myself – at once bourgeois and vulgar gallant! I approved her conduct, declared myself the champion of adultery, perhaps even surprised her by my indulgence. She was certainly extremely flattered by my visit, and invited me to lunch on my return. The whole scene begs to be written, detailed, painted, carved. I would do it for a man like you if it weren't that I hurt my finger the other day, and it forces me to write slowly and hampers me at every word.

I pitied the baseness of all the people who have attacked that poor woman because she spread her legs to admit a prick other than the one officially designated for the purpose. They have taken away her children, taken away everything. She lives on six thousand francs a year in a furnished flat, no maid – wretchedness. When I saw her the time before last she was in her glory – two salons, purple silk chairs, gilded ceilings. When I came in she had been weeping, having learned that morning that the police had been following her for two weeks. The father of the young man with whom she had her affair is afraid that she'll 'get him in her clutches' and is doing everything he can to break up this illicit union. Do you see the beauty of it? The father, terrified of the golddigger? And the son, nervous and uneasy? And the girl, pitilessly persecuted?

We leave tomorrow from Nogent, and go down immediately to Arles and Marseilles. We'll visit the Midi at leisure on our way back from Genoa, after leaving Caroline. So write to me in five or six days at the latest, and address your letter to Marseilles. I'll get to see Mme Foucaud, née Eulalie de Langlade; that will be singularly bitter and funny, especially if I find her grown ugly, as I expect. A bourgeois would say 'If you go, you'll be greatly disillusioned.' But I have rarely experienced disillusion, having had few illusions. What a stupid platitude, always to glorify the lie and say that poetry lives on illusions! As if disillusion weren't a hundred times more poetic in itself! Both words are immensely inept, really.

Today my boredom was terrible. How beautiful are the provinces and the chic of the comfortably off who inhabit them! Their talk is of *The Wandering Jew*[4] and the polka, of taxes and road improvements. The *neighbour* is a wonderful institution. To be given his full social importance he should always be written in capitals: NEIGHBOUR.

Since leaving you, my physical and moral health have been quite good. Only the sore on my tongue is growing larger. What a joke, haha.[5]

Goodbye, dear, very dear, friend. Are you working on your novel? Write it carefully: shit us some good shit. Write to me soon, and make it a long one.

Adieu, je t'embrasse.

I saw nothing on the boulevard, and did nothing obscene.

1. Jean-Pierre-Joseph Darcet, chemist and official of the Paris Mint, whom the Flauberts had known in Rouen, had recently died. The Darcets lived on an upper floor of the Mint itself (the Hôtel de la Monnaie on the Quai des Grands Augustins). Their other daughter, Louise (sometimes called Ludovica), whom Flaubert speaks of in later paragraphs, had recently been repudiated by her husband, the sculptor James Pradier, because of adultery.
2. Gertrude and Henriette Collier, daughters of a British naval officer then living in Paris. Flaubert had met them during the summer of 1842 at Trouville and had seen something of them in Paris during his years at the Law School.
3. Maurice Schlesinger.
4. The novel by Eugène Sue, the best-seller of the moment.
5. Apparently a venereal infection or a symptom resulting from a 'cure'.

~

To Alfred LePoittevin

Marseilles, Tuesday night, [April] 15 [1845] Ten o'clock

Ah! Ah! Ah! Picture to yourself a man catching his breath after a steep climb, a horse resting after a long gallop – picture anything you like, as long as it conveys the idea of liberty, emancipation, relief – and you will picture me writing to you. The longer I go, the more I feel myself incapable of living the life of everybody, of sharing family pleasures, warming to others' enthusiasms, blushing at what shocks them. I try the best I can to keep the sanctum of my heart concealed: useless effort! Alas! The beams pierce through and disclose the God within. Deep down I am serene, but on the surface everything agitates me. It is easier to command one's heart than one's face. By everything you hold sacred, if you hold anything sacred – by everything true and grand – oh my dear sweet Alfred, I conjure you in the name of heaven, in my own name, never travel with anyone! Anyone! I wanted to see Aigues-Mortes and I did not see Aigues-Mortes, nor the Sainte-Baume with the cave where Magdalen wept, nor the battlefield of Marius, etc. I saw nothing of any of those, because I was not alone, I wasn't free. This is the second time I've seen the Mediterranean like a grocer on holiday. Will the third time be better? It goes without saying that I'm 'delighted with my trip', and always in jovial mood – factors favourable to my eventual 'establishment' in life, should I ever wish to be established.

. . . Just now, walking along the shore, I recited to myself passages from your novel: I thought of you again at the Arena in Nîmes and under the arches of the Pont du Gard: that is, in those places I felt a peculiar craving for your presence – because when we are far from one another there is in each of us something one might say lost, indefinite, incomplete.

. . . [At Nîmes] I saw the Arena again, which I first saw five years ago. What have I done since then (words that could be equally well followed by an exclamation point or a question mark). I saw my[1] wild fig tree, growing between the courses of the Velarium, but it was dry, leafless, not rustling; I climbed to the highest tiers, thinking of all who shouted and applauded there – and then it was time to leave. Just as I begin to identify with nature or with history

I'm suddenly snatched away – it's enough to give me bloody guts. On the way to the Pont du Gard I saw two or three wagons of gypsies. At Arles I went with Hamard to the Café de la Rotonde and treated a policeman to a glass of kirsch. Do you sense the sublimity of the scene? I stared at all the young girls – some of them were exquisite, two especially. On Sunday I went to Mass to have a more leisurely look. I saw one, especially, pale and thin, with a warm moistness about her. I walked in the theatre, in the Arena, I spoke with a whore from the brothel opposite the theatre – the old theatre where they played the *Rudens* and the *Bacchides*, where Ballio and Labrax[2] ejaculated their insults and belched their obscenities. I didn't 'go upstairs'. I didn't want to spoil the poetry of it. (In Avignon, too, I talked with whores in the street.) I'll tell you about it all later.

At Marseilles I couldn't find that admirable big-breasted female[3] who gave me such blissful interludes there. She and her mother no longer have the Hôtel Richelieu. I passed it, saw the steps and the door. The shutters were closed: the hotel is abandoned – I could barely recognize it. Isn't that symbolic? The shutters of my heart, too, have been closed a long time, now,[4] its steps deserted; it was a tumultuous hostelry once, but now it is empty and echoing like a great tomb without a corpse! With a little more effort and a little more will I could perhaps have found out where she lives. But the information I was given was so sketchy that I let it go. I lacked eagerness: I always lack eagerness except where art is concerned. Not to mention that I have a strong aversion to revisiting my past; and yet my pitiless curiosity drives me to probe everything, to dig down to the last layers of mud . . . [Five years ago] I returned to the hotel after dinner (it was my last night) and fired four rounds with her. Today I'm writing to you – a superior occupation.

I read nothing, write nothing, and think just about as much. My health remains the same. My stomach is in good shape and I have developed a surprising appetite.

Write to me in Genoa . . .

Take good care with your novel. I don't approve of the idea of a second part. While you're at it, exhaust the subject. Condense it into a single part. Unless there's a better opinion, that's the one I think good.

Adieu, dear and great man, *dimidium animae meae*[5] . . .

1. 'My' because the same fig tree appears in Flaubert's notes on his earlier trip, which Alfred had apparently read or listened to.
2. Comedies by Plautus, and two of his characters.
3. Eulalie Foucault.
4. Since his first attack, Flaubert had been living chastely (see p. 55).
5. 'Half of my soul'.

~

To Alfred LePoittevin

Genoa, May 1 [1845], St Philip's Day

(I should have gone to the French consulate today and left my card.[1] That would have been a way to put myself into the government's good graces and perhaps be given the Cross of the Legion of Honour. Let's get ourselves noticed, why don't we: let's push, climb, kiss the right arses, give thought to 'establishing' ourselves, take wives, 'arrive', etc.)

It is nine o'clock: they have just fired the evening gun. My window is open, the stars are shining, the air is warm; and you, old friend? Where are you? Are you thinking of me? Since my last letter reached you I've been going through agonies, suffering as I haven't suffered for years. You'll need all the intellectual intensity you're capable of to understand it. My father was thinking of continuing as far as Naples, so I thought I'd be going too. But thank God we're not going. We're returning, through Switzerland. In three weeks, a month at the latest, we'll be back in Rouen (good old Rouen, which could be invaded by foreign troops, pillaged and sacked, without my shedding a tear. I've groaned with boredom on every one of its paving stones, yawned with depression on its every street-corner). Do you understand what my fear was? You grasp what I mean? This trip, though very comfortable, has been too crass from the poetic point of view for me to want to prolong it. In Naples I would have experienced such exquisite sensations that the thought of having them spoiled in a million ways was terrible. When I go, I want to get to know that old antiquity to its very marrow. I want to be free, on my own, alone or with you, not with others. I want to be able to sleep under the stars, set out without knowing when I'll return. Then I'll let my thoughts flow without hindrance or reticence before they cool off, giving them all the time they need to boil away at their ease; I'll take on the colour of whatever I see, identify myself with it utterly and passionately. Travel should be a serious occupation. Taken otherwise, unless one stays drunk all day, it is one of the most galling things in life and also one of the silliest. If you knew how continually I am frustrated (never intentionally, of course), everything I'm snatched away from, all the possibilities I'm forced to miss, you would be almost indignant – even you, who never let yourself become indignant about anything, like La Rochefoucauld's *honnête homme.*[2] Of course I conjure you to say nothing of all this to anyone. Despite my best efforts, it may have become all too apparent. Say the opposite: that I'm happy and have been having a charming trip.

I have seen a truly beautiful road, the Corniche, and am now in a beautiful city, a truly beautiful city, Genoa. You walk on marble; everything is marble – stairs, balconies, palaces. The palaces touch one another; walking in the street you look up and see the great patrician ceilings, all painted and gilded. I go into many of the churches, listen to the singing and the organ, watch the monks, look at the chasubles, the altars, the statues. There was a time when I would have indulged in many more reflections than I do now, though I don't know what they would have been: perhaps I would have reflected more and looked less. Now I open my eyes to everything, naively and simply, which is perhaps better.

. . . On the way from Fréjus to Antibes we went over the Esterel, and on the right I saw the immortal Auberge des Adrets. I gazed at it religiously, remembering that it was from there that the great Robert Macaire[3] took his flight towards the future, that out of that house came the greatest symbol of the epoch – the motto, one might say, of our age. Types like that aren't created every day: since Don Juan, I don't know of one who looms so large. Apropos of Don Juan, this is the place to come and think about him: one enjoys imagining him as one strolls in these Italian churches, among the statues, in the rosy light coming through the red curtains, glimpsing the shadowy necks of the kneeling women. They all wear great white veils and long gold or silver earrings. It must be good to fuck there, in the evening, hidden behind the confessionals, at the hour when they're lighting the lamps. But all that isn't for us. We are made to feel it, to talk about it, but not to do it. How is your novel? Coming along? Are you happy about it? I am eager to see it as a whole.

Think only of Art, of that and that alone, because that's all there is. Work! God ordains it. To me that seems clear.

... I expected a letter from you here – I need one ... You promised to write to me often ...

Adieu, dear Alfred. You know I love you and think of you.

1. May 1 was officially celebrated as the name day of Louis-Philippe.
2. La Rochefoucauld: '*Le vrai honnête homme est celui qui ne se pique de rien*'.
3. The bandit-hero of the popular melodrama, *L'Auberge des Adrets*, by Benjamin, Saint-Amant, and Paulyanthe. It was first produced in Paris in 1823, thus antedating by seven years Victor Hugo's *Hernani*, generally considered – on a different literary level – the 'first' Romantic play. In Jean Bruneau's words, Robert Macaire is '*le type romantique du révolté contre la société, sur le mode héroï-comique*'. As such he was immensely appealing to the young Flaubert, who perhaps saw the play in Rouen. He imitated it in some of his earliest writings. The three authors of *L'Auberge des Adrets*, and the play itself, are burlesqued in the film *Les Enfants du Paradis*.

~

To Alfred LePoittevin

Milan, May 13 [1845]

Once again I have left my dear old Mediterranean!! I bade it farewell with a strange sinking of the heart. The morning we were to leave Genoa I went out of the hotel at six o'clock as though to take a stroll. I hired a boat and had myself rowed as far as the entrace of the harbour, to look one last time at the blue waters I so love. The sea was running high. I let myself be rocked with the boat, thinking of you and missing you. And then, when I began to feel I might be seasick, I returned to shore and we set out. I was so depressed for the next three days that more than once I thought I would die. I mean that literally. No matter how great an effort I made, I could not utter a word. I begin to disbelieve that people die of grief, because I am alive.

I saw the battlefields of Marengo, Novi, and Vercelli, but I was in such a pitiable state of mind that it all left me unmoved. I kept thinking of those ceilings in the Genoa palaces, and the proud fucking one would do under them. I carry the love of antiquity in my entrails. I am moved to the deepest depths of my being when I think of the Roman keels that once cut the changeless, eternally undulant waves of this ever-young sea. The ocean is perhaps more beautiful. But here the absence of tides which divide time into regular periods seems to make you forget that the past is far distant and that centuries separate you from Cleopatra. Ah! When will you and I stretch out on our bellies on the sands of Alexandria, or sleep in the shade of the plane trees of the Hellespont?

You are wasting away with boredom, you say? Bursting with anger, dying of depression, stifling? Have patience, O lion of the desert! I myself suffered a long period of suffocation: the walls of my room in the rue de l'Est still echo with the frightful curses, the foot-stampings, the cries of distress I gave vent to when I was alone there. How I roared in that room! And how I yawned! Train your lungs to use only a little air: they will expand all the more joyfully when you're on the high peaks and have to breathe hurricanes. Think, work, write, roll up your sleeves and cut your marble, like the good workman who refuses to be diverted from his task and keeps at it with sweat and good humour. It is in the second part of an artist's life that travel is beneficial: in his earlier years the would-be traveller should cleanse his mind of everything subjective, original, individual. So think what a long wandering in the Orient will mean to you a few years from now! Give your muse free rein, ignore human concerns, and each day you'll feel your mind expanding in a way that will astonish you. The only way not to be unhappy is to shut yourself up in Art and count all the rest as nothing. One's pride, if it is well founded, makes up for everything else. As for me, I've really been fairly well since resigning myself to perpetual illness. You're aware, aren't you, that there are many things lacking in my existence? That I had it in me to be as lavish as the richest men in the world, every bit as tender as the greatest lovers, every bit as sensual as the most unbridled libertines? However, I do not regret the absence of riches, or love, or the flesh, and everyone is astonished to see me behaving so sensibly. I have said an irrevocable farewell to the practical life. My nervous illness was the transition between two states. From now until a day that is far distant I ask for no more than five or six quiet hours in my room, a good fire in winter, and a pair of candles to light me at night.

You distress me, my dear sweet friend (there should be another word, because for me you are not what is commonly meant by 'friend', even in the best sense); you distress me when you speak of your death. Think of what would become of me. A wandering soul, like a bird flying over the flooded earth, I would have not the tiniest stone, not a square inch of ground, where I could rest my weariness. Why are you going to spend a month in Paris? You'll be even more bored than in Rouen. You'll return even more exhausted. Besides, are you sure that steam baths are really so good for your head, O Moechus?[1]

I long to see what you have written since I left. In four or five weeks we'll read it over together, alone, by ourselves and sufficient unto ourselves, far from the world and from the bourgeois, holed up like bears, growling under our layers of fur. I still think about my oriental tale, which I shall write next winter. For the past few days I have had an idea for a rather good play about an episode of the Corsican war which I read in a history of Genoa. I have seen a picture by Breughel, *The Temptation of Saint Anthony*, which made me think of arranging the subject for the theatre. But that would need someone very different from me. I would certainly give the entire collection of the *Moniteur*, if I had it, and a hundred thousand francs besides, for that picture, which most people undoubtedly think bad.

. . . As you recommend, and as I promised, I will go and lunch with Mme Pradier, but it is doubtful that I'll do more than that, unless she invites me *very* openly. Sex games have nothing more to teach me. My desire is too universal, too permanent, too intense, for me to have desires. I don't use women as means to an end: I do what the poet in your novel does – I use them only as objects of contemplation.

1. Adulterer, fornicator.

~

To ALFRED LePOITTEVIN

Geneva, May 26 [1845], Monday, 9 p.m.

Two days ago I saw Byron's name written on one of the pillars of the dungeon where the prisoner of Chillon was confined. The sight afforded me exquisite joy. I thought more about Byron than about the prisoner, and no ideas came to me about tyranny and slavery. All the time I thought of the pale man who came there one day, walked up and down, wrote his name on the stone, and left.'

One would have to be very daring or very stupid to write one's name in such a place after that. The stone is scratched and stained in a hundred places. In the midst of all the obscure names there I saw those of Victor Hugo and George Sand. It gave me bad feelings towards them: I thought they had more taste. Also, written in pencil, I read: 'Mme Viardot, née Pauline Garcia',[1] and that made me laugh. Mme Viardot née Pauline Garcia dreaming of the misfortunes poetized by the master and wanting the public to know about it I found truly grotesque. It 'excited my hilarity', as we say in parliamentary style.

Byron's name is scratched on one side, and it is already black, as though ink had been rubbed into it to make it show. It does in fact stand out on the grey column, and one sees it the minute one enters. Below the name, the stone is a little eaten away, as though the tremendous hand which rested there had worn it with its weight. I was sunk in contemplation before those five letters.

This evening, just now, I lit my cigar and walked to a little island attached to the shore of the lake opposite our hotel, called the Ile Jean-Jacques because of Pradier's statue which stands there. This island is a favourite promenade, where they have music in the evening. When I arrived at the foot of the statue, the brasses were playing softly. One could scarcely see; people were sitting on benches, facing the lake, at the foot of tall trees whose tops were almost still, just slightly swaying. Old Rousseau, motionless on his pedestal, listened to it all. I shivered; the sound of the trombones and flutes went to my very entrails. After the andante came something merry, full of fanfares. I thought of the theatre, the orchestra, boxes full of powdered women, all the thrills of fame, and of this paragraph of the *Confessions*.[2] . . . The music continued a long time. From symphony to symphony I put off returning to the hotel; finally I left. At the two ends of Lake Geneva there are two geniuses who cast shadows loftier than those of the mountains: Byron and Rousseau, two 'sly ones who would have made very good lawyers.'[3]

You tell me that you are falling more and more in love with nature. My own passion for it is becoming uncontrollable. At times

I look on animals and even trees with a tenderness that amounts to a feeling of affinity: I derive almost voluptuous sensations from the mere act of seeing – when I see clearly. A few days ago I met three poor idiot women who asked me for alms. They were horrible, disgusting in their ugliness and cretinism; they could not speak, they could scarcely walk. When they saw me they began to make signs to tell me that they loved me; they smiled at me, lifted their hands to their faces and sent me kisses. At Pont-l'Evêque my father owns a pasture where the caretaker has an imbecile daughter; the first time she saw me she too displayed a strange attachment to me. I attract mad people and animals. Is it because they sense that I understand them, because they feel that I enter into their world?

· · ·

We crossed the Simplon last Thursday. It is the most beautiful thing I have seen in nature so far. You know that beautiful things cannot stand description. I missed you badly; I'd have liked you to be with me, or else I'd have liked to be in the soul of those tall pines that hung, all snowy, over the rim of the precipices. I kept measuring myself against that immensity.

· · ·

It's a singular thing, the way I have drawn away from women. I am satiated with them, as those must be who have been loved too much. Or perhaps it is I who have loved too much. Masturbation is the cause of that: moral masturbation, I mean. Everything has gone out of me; everything has returned and entered into me. I have become impotent as a result of those magnificent effluvia that have seethed in me too furiously ever to flow. It is now two years since I last had coitus; and, in a few days, a year since I performed any lascivious act. I no longer experience in the presence of any skirt even the desire that springs from curiosity, that impels you to strip the veil from the unknown and look for something new. I must have fallen very low, since the sight of a brothel inspires me with no urge to enter it. I approve your project about the trip with a whore. That would indeed be tremendously ironic, and worthy of a great man like you.[4]

· · ·

1. The singer, sister of Malibran. It is not clear whether at this time Flaubert knew who she was. He became acquainted with her later, through Turgenev.

2. Here Flaubert (mis)quotes from memory the opening words of a paragraph in which Rousseau looks back on a moment of youthful fiasco from the height of his triumph with his opera, *Le Devin du village.*
3. Alfred LePoittevin's father had said of Flaubert: 'He's a sly one; he'd make a good lawyer.'
4. Alfred's plan which Flaubert 'approved' was this (written in reply to Flaubert's May 1 letter from Genoa):

    'Le Havre and Honfleur, for many reasons, still play strangely on my emotions. I dreamed of love there when I was very young, of that love which I would refuse today, wherever it might come from, in whatever form. Today I enjoy it as buffoonery, the most exquisite kind of all, but I like to think back on the past, when I *believed*! . . . Of those women, some are married, others still available. It's a strange thing: my sensuality is of the wild, impetuous kind, yet I cannot give a kiss that is not ironic. I don't know what you will think of a project I intend to carry out when I can: it is to spend three days in Le Havre or Honfleur with a whore I'll choose ad hoc. We'll eat, drink, take walks, and sleep together. I'll greatly enjoy taking her to places where, being still young, I *believed* . . . I'll pay her off when we get back. I am like that Greek who could never laugh again after going down into Trophonius's cave.'

~

To Alfred LePoittevin
Croisset, Tuesday night, half past 10 [June 17, 1845]
Back in my cave!

Back in my solitude! By dint of being in a bad way, I'm in a good way. I shan't be wanting any change in my circumstances for a long time. What do I need, after all? Liberty and leisure, isn't it so? I have deliberately weaned myself from so many things that I feel rich in the midst of the most absolute destitution. I still have some way to go. My sentimental education[1] isn't finished, but I may graduate soon. Have you sometimes thought, dear sweet friend, how many tears the horrible word 'happiness' is responsible for? If that word didn't exist we would sleep more serenely and live in greater peace. I am still prey, sometimes, to strange yearnings for love, although I am disgusted by it down to my very entrails. They would perhaps pass unnoticed if I could pay less attention to them; but I'm forever on the watch, spying on the workings of my heart.

I have had no return of the depression of five years ago. Do you remember the state I was in one whole winter, when I used to come to you on Thursday afternoons after leaving Chéruel's class, in my big blue overcoat? My feet would be soaked from the snow, and I'd warm them at your fire.

My youth has really been a bitter one, and I would not care to relive it. But now my life seems to be arranged in a regular way. Its horizons are less wide, alas! – less varied, especially; but perhaps it is the more intense for being restricted. My books are here on the table before me, everything is calm, the rain is dropping softly on the leaves, and the moon is passing behind the great tulip tree, a black silhouette against the deep blue sky.

I have thought about Pradier's advice. It is good: but how to follow it? And where would I stop? If I were to take it seriously, and really throw myself into physical pleasure, I'd be humiliated. But that is what I would have to do, and what I will not do. Normal, regular, rich, hearty copulation would take me too much out of myself, disturb my peace. I would be re-entering active life in the physical sense, and that is what has been detrimental to me each time I've tried it. Besides, if it were destined to be, it would be.

. . . *Adieu, carissimo* – answer me soon, as you promised . . .

1. Flaubert's words are '*mon éducation sentimentale*'. 'Sentimental Education', the literal English translation of the term as the title of Flaubert's novel, is misleading: the book treats of the illusion of romantic love.

∿

To Alfred LePoittevin

[Croisset, July 1845]

. . .

I am still dissecting Voltaire's plays. It is tedious, but may be useful to me later. One does come on some astonishingly stupid lines. I keep doing a little Greek. I have finished Herodotus's *Egypt*. Three months from now I hope to be reading him easily; and in a year, with patience, Sophocles. Also, I'm reading Quintus Curtius. What a lad, that Alexander! The sculptural beauty of his life! He gives the impression of a magnificent actor, continually improvising the play he is starring in. The life of that man was pure art. I saw in one of Voltaire's notes that he preferred the Marcus Aureliuses and the Trajans to Alexander. What do you say to that: good, isn't it? I'll show you several passages from Quintus Curtius that I think you'll find worthy of your esteem, including the entry into Persepolis and the enumeration of Darius's troops. Today I finished Shakespeare's *Timon of Athens*. The more I think about Shakespeare the more overwhelmed I am. Remind me to tell you about the scene where Timon uses the dishes from his table to show his contempt for his parasites.

We'll be neighbours this winter,[1] old man. We'll be able to see each other every day – we'll plan some projects. We'll talk beside my fire while the rain falls or the snow blankets the roofs. No, I don't look on myself as one to be pitied when I think that I have you, that we still have time to ourselves, whole free hours. Bare though a rock may be, it isn't bleak when seaweed comes and clings to it, refreshing the granite with the drops of water sparkling in its tufts. If you were to disappear, what would be left to me? What would I have in my inner life – my real life?

Answer me quickly. You should write to me more often and more fully. When do you return? Soon? Last night in bed I read the first volume of Stendhal's *Le Rouge et le Noir*. A distinguished mind, it seems to me – a mind of great delicacy. The style is French. But is it *style*, true style, as it used to be, unknown today?[2]

. . . *Adieu*, dear Alfred. Try, if you possibly can, and for love of me, to watch the drinking . . .

1. When the Flauberts would move back to the Hôtel-Dieu from the riverside house at Croisset (then well outside the city), which had so far been used only for summer residence. These winter plans were to be sadly disrupted.
2. One recalls Stendhal's words to Balzac: 'While composing the *Chartreuse*, to acquire the tone, I used to read two or three pages of the *code civil* every morning', and Flaubert's remarks concerning the *code* (see p. 35).

∼

To Alfred LePoittevin

[Croisset,] Tuesday night, September 16 [1845]

. . .

I am very eager to read your story . . . Work, work, write – write all you can while the muse bears you along. She is the best battle-steed, the best coach to carry you through life in noble style. The burden of existence does not weigh on our shoulders when we are composing. It is true that the fatigue and the feeling of desertion that follow are all the more terrible. Let it be so, however. Two glasses of vinegar and one of wine are better than one of reddish water. As for me, I no longer feel the glowing enthusiasm of youth, nor those dreadful old waves of bitterness. The two have merged, and the result is a single, universal tone, made up of everything, ground together and compounded. I notice that I seldom laugh any more, and no longer suffer from depressions. I am ripe. You speak of my serenity, dear friend, and are envious of it.[1] It is true that it might seem surprising. Ill, agitated, prey a thousand times a day to moments of terrible anxiety, without women, without wine, without any of the tinsel the world offers, I continue my slow work like a good workman who rolls up his sleeves and sweats away at his anvil, indifferent to rain or wind, hail or thunder. Formerly I was not like that. The change came about naturally. My will, too, played a certain role. It will take me further, I hope. My only fear is lest it give way, for there are days when my torpor is frightening. I think I have finally come to understand one thing, one great thing. That is, that for people like you and me happiness is in the *idea*, nowhere else. Seek out what is truly your nature, and be in harmony with it. '*Sibi constet*,' says Horace. That is everything. I swear to you that I think neither about fame nor – very much – about art. I try to pass the time in the least boring way possible, and I have found it. Do as I do. *Break with the outside world*, live like a bear – a polar bear – let everything else go to hell – everything, yourself included, except your intelligence. There is now such a great gap between me and the rest of the world that I am sometimes surprised to hear people say the most natural and simple things. It's strange how the most banal utterance sometimes makes me marvel. There are gestures, sounds of people's voices, that I cannot get over, silly remarks that almost give me vertigo. Have you sometimes listened closely to people speaking a foreign language you didn't understand? That is my case. Precisely because I want to understand everything, anything at all sets me wondering. Still, it seems to me that this astonishment is not stupidity. The bourgeois, for example, is for me something unfathomable.

. . .

Everyone is quite well here. *Adieu*; answer quickly.

1. Alfred had recently written him: 'I say nothing about my morale: it continues as low as ever, just as listless and exhausted. It seems one doesn't
   shake off boredom and one's disgust with things. If the supreme good is
   action, then I'm a bloody long way from it. I admire your serenity. Does it
   come from your being less distracted than I, less harried by external things?
   Or is it simply that you are stronger? You are lucky to be able to save
   yourself by a means that I too might have had at my command, but which
   so far I haven't felt any urgent need to clutch hold of.'

$\sim$

'Everyone is quite well here' . . .

Within a few months the Flaubert family was shattered by two
deaths. On January 15, 1846, Dr Flaubert died, at sixty-one, following
an operation by his son Achille for 'a deep abscess in the thigh'.
Caroline, who had come to Rouen for the delivery of her first child,
gave birth to a daughter on January 21; after a few days she developed
an infection; she lingered, and died on March 22.

After Caroline's death, Flaubert and his mother moved out of
the Hôtel-Dieu and took the baby girl – to be baptized Caroline –
with them to Croisset; Hamard came to live in a small house
adjoining.

'The good, intelligent man we have lost; the tender, noble soul
that is gone,' Flaubert wrote to Ernest Chevalier. Flaubert unquestionably loved and admired his exigent father; and yet following the
doctor's disappearance the epileptic attacks immediately began to
decrease in frequency.

Maxime DuCamp, who now enters the correspondence and will
continue to occupy a prominent place in it, was introduced to
Flaubert in Paris during the years of law study: Flaubert considered
DuCamp's friendship the only good that came to him during that
time. A year younger than Flaubert, and like him the son of a
prominent doctor, DuCamp had lost both parents and lived in Paris
with his grandmother. He had some independent means, and was
trying his hand at various kinds of writing. In contrast to Flaubert,
he was worldly and efficient, with a wide-ranging curiosity and a
force of ambition that would eventually take him into the French
Academy. At this moment of new crisis in Flaubert's life DuCamp

was planning a trip to the 'Orient' – what is now called the Middle East.

~

To Maxime DuCamp

[Rouen, March 15, 1846]

Hamard has just left my room, where he was standing sobbing beside the fire. My mother is a weeping statue.

Caroline speaks to us, caresses us, says gentle and affectionate things to all of us. Her memory is going, her ideas are confused; she didn't know whether it was I or Achille who had gone to Paris.[1] What grace there is about the sick, what strange movements they make! The baby sucks and cries. Achille says nothing, not knowing what to say. What a house! What a hell!

My own eyes are dry as marble. It is strange how sorrows in fiction flood me with facile emotion, while actual sorrows remain hard and bitter in my heart, crystallizing there as they come.

It seems that calamity is upon us, and that it will not leave until it has glutted itself on us.

Once again I'm to see the house draped in black; once again I'm to hear the hobnailed boots of the undertaker's men – ignoble sound! – descending the stairs.

I prefer to have no hope, but rather to direct my thoughts to the grief that is coming. Dr Marjolin arrives tonight. What can he do?

I had a premonition last night that when I next saw you I would not be gay.

---

1. Flaubert had just seen DuCamp in Paris, where he had gone to enlist the aid of highly placed medical friends of the family concerning his brother Achille's succession to his father's post in the Rouen hospital. Certain doctors on the staff had tried to block the appointment, charging under-qualification and favouritism. Flaubert would always be proud of the successful role he played in this episode of 'practical life'.

~

To Maxime DuCamp

[Croisset,] Wednesday morning [March 25, 1846]

Mon cher vieux, I didn't want you to come here. I was afraid of your affection. It was enough for me to see Hamard, without seeing you. Perhaps you would have been even less calm than we were. In a little while I'll send you a call: I count on you. It was yesterday at eleven o'clock that we buried her, poor girl. They dressed her in her wedding-gown, with bouquets of roses, immortelles and violets. I watched beside her all night. She lay on her bed, in that room where you heard her play her piano. She seemed much taller and much more beautiful than when she was alive, with the long white veil coming down to her feet.[1] In the morning, when everything was done, I gave her a long last farewell kiss in her coffin. I bent over her, and as I lowered my head into the coffin I felt the lead buckle under my hands. It was I who attended to the casts. I saw the great paws of those louts touching her and covering her with plaster. I shall have her hand and her face. I shall ask Pradier to make me her bust and will put it in my room. I have her big coloured shawl, a lock of her hair, her table and writing-desk. That is all – all that remains of those we love!

Hamard insisted on coming with us. There, in the cemetery (I used to walk just outside the walls with my class, and it was there that Hamard saw me for the first time), he knelt at the edge of the grave, threw kisses to her, and wept. The grave was too narrow, the coffin wouldn't fit. They shook it, pulled it, turned it this way and that; they took a spade and crowbars, and finally a gravedigger trod on it – just above Caroline's head – to force it down. I was standing at the side, holding my hat in my hand; I threw it down with a cry.

I'll tell you the rest when we're together, for I'd write it all too badly. I was as tearless as a tombstone, but seething with anger. I wanted to tell you all this, thinking it would give you pleasure. You are sufficiently intelligent, and love me enough, to understand that word 'pleasure', which would make the bourgeois laugh.

We have been back in Croisset since Sunday. (What a journey, alone with my mother, and the baby crying!) The last time I left Croisset was with you: you remember. Of the four who lived here then, two remain. The trees are still leafless, the wind is blowing, the river is high; the rooms are cold and bare.

My mother is better than one would think she could be. She busies herself with her daughter's child, sleeps in her room, rocks her, does everything she can. She is trying to turn herself into a mother again. Will she succeed? The reaction has not yet set in, and I dread its coming.

We face some bad trouble because of the child.[2] It is no longer possible to settle things privately; we must go to court. Even if there is no hitch, it will take three months. Also – and this is the most pressing – we must find a place to live in Rouen.[3]

I am crushed, numb. I greatly need to resume a quiet existence: the grief and the worry have been suffocating. When can I return to my austere life of tranquil art and long meditation? I laugh with pity at the vanity of the human will, when I think that for the past six years I have wanted to learn Greek, and that circumstances have been such that I haven't yet got as far as the verbs.

Adieu, dear Maxime. *Je t'embrasse tendrement.*

It goes without saying that this letter is for you alone, and nothing in it should go any further.

1. Recalling this scene in a later letter to Louise Colet, Flaubert adds the following: 'I was reading Montaigne; my eyes kept turning from my book to the corpse; her husband and the priest were snoring; and I kept telling myself, as I saw all this, that forms disappear, that the idea alone remains; and I kept feeling thrills at turns of phrase in the Montaigne, and reflected that he too would be forgotten. It was freezing, the window was open because of the odour, and from time to time I got up to look at the stars, calm, radiant, eternal.'
2. Hamard was showing signs of mental derangement.
3. For the following winter.

∼

To Maxime DuCamp

[Croisset,] Tuesday, 2 p.m. [April 7, 1846]

I have taken a large sheet of paper with the intention of writing you a long letter; perhaps I shall send you only three lines; we'll see how it goes. The sky is grey, the Seine yellow, the grass green; the trees are just beginning to bud; it is spring, the season of joy and love. 'But there is no more spring in my heart than there is on the highroad, where the wind wearies the eyes and the dust rises in whirling clouds.' Do you remember where that comes from? From my old *Novembre*. I was nineteen when I wrote it, almost six years ago. It is strange, how I was born with little faith in happiness. While still very young I had a complete presentiment of life. It was like a nauseating smell of cooking escaping through a ventilator: you don't have to eat it to know it would make you vomit. This is not a complaint, however; my recent bereavements have saddened me but not surprised me. Without feeling them any the less acutely, I have analysed them as an artist. This task has revived my grief in a melancholy way. Had my expectations been greater, I'd have cursed life. That is just what I have not done. You would perhaps consider me heartless were I to tell you that I do not consider my present state the most pitiable of all. When I had nothing to complain of, I felt much sorrier for myself. This, after all, may be only a question of practice. The soul expands with suffering, thus enormously increasing its capacity; what formerly filled it to the point of bursting now barely covers the bottom. At least I have one great consolation, one firm basis of support: I don't see what further trouble can befall me . . .

～

To Alfred LePoittevin

[Croisset,] Sunday night, 10.30. [May 31, 1846]

Not having asked me for advice, it would be proper for me to give none.[1] So we won't speak about that. There are many things which I foresee. Unfortunately, I am farsighted; I think you are deluded, enormously so – as indeed one is when one takes any Step. Are you sure, O great man, that you'll not end up becoming a bourgeois? In all my artistic hopes, I was at one with you. It is that aspect that distresses me.

Too late! Let be what will be. I will always be here for you. Remains to be seen whether you will be there for me. Don't protest or explain! Time and things are stronger than ourselves. An entire volume would be needed to develop even the least significant word on this page. No one wishes for your happiness more than I, and no one is more doubtful of it. Because in your very seeking it you are doing something abnormal. If you love her, so much the better; if you don't love her, try to love her.

Will we still share those arcana of ideas and feelings, inaccessible to the rest of the world? Who can say? No one.

Come and see me, or I'll come to see you whenever you wish. Only write to me at least a day in advance, because at present I come occasionally to Rouen to help with the move.

I have said nothing to Hamard, as he is away and won't be back until Tuesday morning. If you can, try to come on Tuesday: that would be quite convenient for me.

Adieu, Carissimo.

1. Flaubert had just learned of Alfred's engagement. His syntax itself betrays his agitation.

    Alfred's fiancée was Louise de Maupassant, daughter of a family long acquainted with the LePoittevins and the Flauberts. Both the LePoittevins and the Maupassants were of the prosperous Norman bourgeoisie, with pretensions to noble quarterings. Alfred's marriage would take place on July 6. The following November 9, Alfred's sister, Laure LePoittevin, would marry Louise de Maupassant's brother Gustave; they would become the parents of Guy de Maupassant.

❧

To ERNEST CHEVALIER

[Croisset,] June 4, [1846] Thursday night.

. . .

I'll give you some news of what is happening here. Achille has succeeded my father as resident director of the Rouen hospital: so there he is, settled in the finest medical position in Normandy. The rest of us are living at Croisset, which I never leave and where I work as much as I can, which is not very much, but a step towards something more. This winter we shall spend four months in Rouen: we have taken an apartment at the corner of the rue de Buffon. Here at Croisset we are almost settled, thank God – it has been another sad task. I have quite a nice room, with a little balcony where I can smoke my morning pipe.

Do you want me to tell you something that will make you utter an 'Oh' followed by several exclamation points? It is the marriage – of whom? Of a young man of your acquaintance – not me, rest assured; but of a certain LePoittevin, to Mademoiselle de Maupassant[1] . . . At this point you will give yourself over to astonishment and reverie . . . The 'holy nuptials' will be celebrated in a fortnight, I believe. The contract was to have been signed last Tuesday. After the wedding they will make a trip to Italy and next winter they will live in Paris. So there is one more lost to me, and doubly so – first because he is marrying, and second because he will live elsewhere. How everything vanishes! How everything vanishes! The leaves are unfurling again on the trees, but where is the month of May that will give us back the lovely flowers we have lost, and the fragrance of our early manhood? I don't know whether you feel the same, but I have the sensation of being inordinately aged, older than an obelisk. I have lived enormously, and when I'm sixty shall probably feel very young: that's what is so bitterly absurd about it all.

My poor mother remains inconsolable. You have no conception of such grief. If there is a God, you must admit he isn't always in the kindest of moods. Mme Mignot wrote to me this morning to tell me she'll soon be coming to spend a few days here; I am immensely grateful to her. My courage isn't always equal to the task of carrying, alone, the burden of this great despair that nothing can lighten. *Adieu*, old friend; I embrace you with all my heart.

1.   Deletions in the autograph here. Ernest Chevalier, going over Flaubert's letters in the eminence of his later life (he became a senator), destroyed some and censored others.

IV

Louise Colet I

1846–1848

FLAUBERT'S VISITS TO the salon of the sculptor James Pradier during his dreary terms at the Law School had received the all-important blessing of Alfred LePoittevin. 'I strongly urge you to cultivate that house,' Alfred wrote him on November 26, 1843. 'There is much to be gained there – useful friends at the very least, a mistress perhaps.' We have seen that in 1845 Flaubert found the Pradiers separated, and wrote to Alfred of Pradier's advice that he take a mistress. Then came the double bereavement in Rouen, and Alfred's marriage.

One afternoon in late July 1846, Flaubert paid Pradier a professional visit. The sculptor had already undertaken to carve a bust of Dr Flaubert; now Flaubert brought with him the death mask of his sister Caroline and a cast of her hand, for the same purpose.

That day in Pradier's studio a beautiful woman was posing for the sculptor. Flaubert was introduced to her: Madame Louise Colet.

Flaubert had certainly heard or read about the poet Louise Colet, although at that time he may not have known her entire story.

She was eleven years his senior, born Louise Révoil in 1810 at Aix-en-Provence, where when quite young she reigned as a local muse. At twenty-four she arrived in Paris as the bride of Hippolyte Colet, an assistant professor at the Conservatory of Music. After winning a French Academy poetry prize and being awarded a government pension, she met the celebrated Victor Cousin – whose works Flaubert had studied at the Collège Royal. Philosopher and professor of philosophy, Cousin was now Minister of Education. Within a short time after Cousin's encounter with Louise, Hippolyte Colet had received promotion, Louise had been awarded a second Academy prize, and her pension had been increased. She also became pregnant (after five years of childless marriage); and when the gossip columnist Alphonse Karr suggested in print that for this, too, her 'protector' might be responsible, she called on the slanderer and attempted to stab him with a kitchen knife. Karr gleefully publicized the assault, and thereafter there was always an aroma of ridicule about Louise, although – thanks in part to her beauty[1] and to her continued liaison with Cousin – her work continued to be published and she moved in literary society.

Louise Colet was uncritical towards her own work and remained a very minor poet; but she was sometimes perceptive regarding the work of others, and could write journalism that suited the taste of the time. She was a feminist, and in the face of difficulties, caused both by her own tiresome personality and by the pressures of contemporary society on women, could display considerable courage; but one of her greatest aptitudes was for intrigue, and in pursuit of her ends she exploited whomever and whatever she could. Victor Cousin believed that he was indeed the father of Louise's daughter, Henriette – a belief in which Louise, and apparently Hippolyte as well, encouraged him. The truth of the matter seems not to be known, but Cousin's belief resulted in material advantages to the household. At the time she met Flaubert in Pradier's studio, Louise's fortunes were at a lower ebb than usual: Hippolyte was sick; despite Cousin's help the Colets were in debt, and they were anything but harmonious; with Cousin, too, Louise had been quarrelling.

As Flaubert himself was later to say, the meeting at Pradier's was 'predestined'. It seems likely that on seeing the handsome young man, Louise, never bashful, quickly showed herself available. Long ill, long celibate, Flaubert had recently lost father, sister, and, through marriage, his most intimate friend. It is evident from the letters that he was stimulated by the dual presence of the sculptor, known to be lascivious, and his beautiful model; in that atmosphere he felt himself, as he was to put it later, 'sliding down the slope'. The day he knew Louise would next be posing, he deliberately stayed away, but returned the day after, foreseeing the immediate outcome. They spent the next few nights and days together. Then he returned to Croisset.

In the pages immediately following, Flaubert's first several letters to Louise are translated almost in their entirety. All were written from Croisset within a month of their meeting in Pradier's studio; all derive from their first few days together and from a second, brief tryst in Paris about three weeks later. Primarily they are love letters, passionately – and repeatedly – conveying the erotic sensations Louise inspires. They are the only such effusions Flaubert is known to have written, and they contrast strongly with the flowing, open-hearted letters to male friends that precede and follow them. Flaubert himself was impressed by the difficulty he experienced in expressing his feelings to Louise: 'It's strange how bad my writing is in these letters to you . . . One thing conflicts with another . . . It's as though I wanted to say three words at a time.' Almost immediately he proceeded to intersperse the erotic messages with reminiscences, artistic and literary ideas, and reflections on men and women that he regarded as expressions of candour – all of which provide a foretaste of the rich intellectual content of later letters, but which naturally displeased Louise, who would have preferred pages more exclusively amatory.

There is a reason for this. Reading these first letters to Louise, one recalls Flaubert's words to Alfred LePoittevin about plunging into physical pleasure: 'That is what I will not do.' With Louise he had, in fact, taken that plunge, and the equivocal tone in the letters from the outset betrays his resentment at having been seduced from a principle. The cruelty displayed, for example, in speculating to Louise about her own death, in explaining his gift of flowers, in asking her to forward his letter to a former mistress, is doubtless largely unconscious – Flaubert himself seldom admits to more than 'tactlessness'; but it would be obtuse to accuse Flaubert of mere insensitivity: the reader will be put in mind of his earlier expression of admiration for the works of the marquis de Sade. Concerning her behaviour with her young and quite peculiar lover, Louise, on her side, was later to write (in her 'Memoranda'; all but a few of her letters to Flaubert have been lost): 'I was exasperated, went to extremes, and was not very intelligent about charming him.'

1. See Appendix I, 'A Self-Portrait of Louise Colet'.

~

To Louise Colet

[Croisset,] Tuesday midnight. [August 4–5, 1846]

Twelve hours ago we were still together, and at this very moment yesterday I was holding you in my arms! Do you remember? How long ago it seems! Now the night is soft and warm; I can hear the great tulip tree under my window rustling in the wind, and when I lift my head I see the moon reflected in the river. Your little slippers are in front of me as I write; I keep looking at them. Here, locked away by myself, I have just put away everything you gave me. Your two letters are in the little embroidered bag, and I am going to reread them as soon as I have sealed mine. I am not writing to you on my ordinary writing-paper – that is edged with black and I want nothing sad to pass from me to you. I want to cause you nothing but joy, and to surround you with a calm, endless bliss – to repay you a little for the overflowing generosity of the love you have given me. I am afraid of being cold, arid, selfish – and yet, God can see what is going on within me at this moment. What memories! And what desire! Ah! Our two marvellous carriage rides; how beautiful they were, particularly the second, with the lightning flashes above us. I keep remembering the colour of the trees lit by the streetlights, and the swaying motion of the springs. We were alone, happy: I kept staring at you, and even in the darkness your whole face seemed illumined by your eyes. I feel I am writing badly – you will read this without emotion – I am saying nothing of what I want to say. My sentences run together like sighs, to understand them you will have to supply what should go between. You will do that, won't you? Every letter, every turn of my handwriting will set you dreaming? The way the sight of your little brown slippers makes me dream of the movements of your feet when they were in them, when the slippers were warm from them. The handkerchief, too, is there; I see your blood. I wish it were completely red with it.

My mother was waiting for me at the station. She wept at seeing me return. You wept to see me leave. In other words, such is our sad fate that we cannot move a league without causing tears on two sides at once! Grotesque and sombre thought! Here the grass is still green, the trees are as full, the river as placid, as when I left; my books are open at the same pages; nothing is changed. External nature shames us, her serenity is a rebuke to our pride. No matter – let us think of nothing, neither of the future nor of ourselves, for to think is to suffer. Let the tempest in our hearts blow us where it will at full sail, and as for reefs – we'll simply have to take our chance with them.

. . . On the train I read almost an entire volume.[1] More than one passage moved me, but of that I will talk with you more fully later. As you can well see, I am unable to concentrate. Tonight I am far from being a critic. I wanted only to send you another kiss before sleeping, to tell you I love you. No sooner had I left you – and increasingly as I was borne further and further away – than my thoughts flew back towards you, more swiftly even than the smoke I saw billowing back from the train. (My metaphor implies the idea of fire: forgive the allusion.) Here: a kiss, quickly – you know the kind – the kind Ariosto[2] speaks of – and another, and another! Still another, and finally one more just under your chin on the spot I love, where your skin is so soft, and another on your breast, where I lay my heart. *Adieu, adieu.* All my love.

1. A volume by Louise Colet?
2. Jean Bruneau suggests that Flaubert may mean Aretino, author of erotic sonnets.

~

To Louise Colet

[Croisset, August 6 or 7, 1846]

I am shattered, numb, as though after a long orgy; I miss you terribly. There is an immense void in my heart. Formerly I was calm, proud of my serenity. I worked keenly and steadily from morning to night. Now I cannot read, or think, or write. Your love has made me sad. I can see you are suffering; I foresee I will make you suffer. Both for your sake and for my own I wish we had never met, and yet the thought of you is never absent from my mind. In it I find an exquisite sweetness. Ah! How much better it would have been to stop short after our first ride together! I had forebodings that things would turn out as they have! The next day, when I didn't come to

Phidias', it was because I already felt myself sliding down the slope.
I wanted to stop: what pushed me? So much the worse! So much
the better! God did not give me a merry constitution; no one senses
more keenly than I the wretchedness of life. I believe in nothing –
not even in myself, which is rare. I devote myself to Art because it
gives me pleasure to do so, but I have no faith whatever in beauty,
any more than in anything else. So the part of your letter in which
you speak of patriotism, poor darling, would have made me laugh
if I had been in a gayer mood. You will think that I am hard, I wish
I were. All those who cross my path would benefit from my being
so, and so would I, with my heart that's been cropped close – like
meadow grass in autumn by all the passing sheep. You would not
believe me when I told you I was old. Alas, yes, for every sensation
that enters my soul turns sour, like wine poured into jars too often
used. If you knew all the inner forces that have consumed me, all
the mad desires that have passed through my head, everything I have
tried and experienced in the way of sensations and passions, you
would see that I am not so young! It is you who are a child, you who
are fresh and new, you whose candour makes me blush. The grandeur
of your love fills me with humility; you deserved someone better
than I. May lightning strike me, may all possible curses fall upon
me if ever I forget that! You ask me whether I despise you because
you gave yourself to me too quickly. Have you really been able to
suspect that? *Never, never*: whatever you do, whatever may happen,
I am devoted to you for life, to you, to your daughter, to anything
and anyone you wish. That is a vow. Remember it. Use it. I make
it because I can keep it.

Yes, I desire you and I think of you. I love you more than I
loved you in Paris. I can no longer do anything; I keep seeing you
in the studio, standing near your bust, your long curls stirring on
your white shoulders, your blue dress, your arm, your face – everything. Ah! Now *strength* is beginning to circulate in my blood. You
seem to be here; I am on fire, my nerves tremble . . . you know
how . . . you know the heat of my kisses.

Ever since we said we loved each other, you have wondered why
I have never added the words 'for ever'. Why? Because I always sense
the future, the antithesis of everything is always before my eyes. I
have never seen a child without thinking that it would grow old,

nor a cradle without thinking of a grave. The sight of a naked woman makes me imagine her skeleton. As a result, joyful spectacles sadden me and sad ones affect me but little. I do too much inward weeping to shed outward tears – something read in a book moves me more than a real misfortune. When I had a family, I often wished I had none, so that I might be freer, free to live in China or among savages. Now that my family is gone, I long for it, and cling to the walls that still retain the imprint of its shadow. Others would be proud of the love you lavish on me, their vanity would drink its fill of it, and their male egotism would be flattered to its inmost depths. But after the moments of frenzy have passed, my heart swoons with sadness, for I say to myself: 'She loves me and I love her too, but I do not love her enough. If she had never known me, she would have been spared all the tears she is shedding.' Forgive me, forgive me in the name of all the rapture you have given me. But I have a presentiment of immense unhappiness for you. I fear lest my letters be discovered, that everything become known. *I am sick and my sickness is you.*

You think that you will love me for ever, child. For ever! What presumption on human lips! You have loved before, have you not? So have I. Remember that you have said 'for ever' before. But I am bullying you, hurting you. You know that my caresses are fierce. No matter: I should rather inject some disquiet into your happiness now than deliberately exaggerate its extent, as men always do, to make you suffer the more when it ends – who knows? You will thank me later, perhaps, for having had the courage not to be more tender. Ah! If I lived in Paris, if every day of my life could be passed at your side – yes, then I'd let myself be swept away by this current, without crying for help! I should find in you, for my heart, my body and my mind, a daily gratification that would never weary me. But apart, destined to see each other only rarely, how frightful! What a prospect! What can we do? Still – I cannot imagine how I was able to leave you. But that is how I am; there you see my wretched character. If you were not to love me, I should die; but you do love me, and I am writing to you to stop. I am disgusted by my own stupidity. But in whatever direction I look I see only unhappiness! I wish I might have come into your life like a cool brook to refresh its thirst, not as a devastating torrent. At the thought of me your flesh would have thrilled, your heart smiled. Never curse me! Ah, I shall love you well before loving you no longer. I shall always bless you – your image will stay with me, all imbued with poetry and tenderness, as last night was bathed in the milky vapour of its silvery mist.

Sometime this month I'll come to see you and will stay an entire day. In two weeks or less I shall be with you. When Phidias writes[1] I will come at once, I promise . . .

You want me to send you something I have written. No, you would find everything too good. Have you not given me enough, without literary praise? Do you want to make me completely fatuous? Nothing I have here is legible; you couldn't decipher it, with all its crossings-out and inserts – I have never had anything properly re-copied. Aren't you afraid of spoiling your style by associating with me? You'd like me to publish something immediately; you'd like to stimulate me; you'd end by getting me to take myself seriously (may the Lord preserve me from that!). Formerly the pen ran quickly over my paper; now as it runs it tears. I cannot write a sentence, I keep changing my pen, because I can express nothing of what I want to say. Come to Rouen with Phidias, pretend you met him here by chance, and visit me here. That will satisfy you more than any possible description. Then you'll think of my rug and of the great white bearskin I stretch out on during the day, as I think of your alabaster lamp and how I watched its dying light flickering on the ceiling. Did you understand, that night, that I was waiting for it to go out? I didn't dare; I am timid, despite my cynicism – or perhaps because of it. I told myself I'll wait till the candle dies. Oh! Such forgetfulness of everything! Such exclusion of the rest of the world! The smooth skin of your naked body! And the hypocritical pleasure I took in my resentment as your other guests stayed, and stayed! I shall always remember your look when you were at my knees on the floor, and your ecstatic smile when you opened the door and we parted. I went down through the shadows on tiptoe like a thief. Wasn't I one? And are they all as happy, when they flee with their loot?

I owe you a frank explanation of myself, in response to a page of your letter which makes me see that you harbour illusions about me. It would be cowardly of me (and cowardice is a vice that disgusts me, in whatever aspect it shows itself) to allow these to persist.

My basic character, whatever anyone may say, is that of the mountebank. In my childhood and my youth I was wildly in love with the stage. I should perhaps have been a great actor if I had happened to be born poorer. Even now, what I love above all else, is *form*, provided it be beautiful, and nothing beyond it. Women whose hearts are too ardent and whose minds too exclusive do not understand this religion of beauty, beauty considered apart from emotion. They always demand a cause, an end. I admire tinsel as much as gold: indeed, the poetry of tinsel is even greater, because it is sadder. The only things that exist for me in the world are splendid poetry, harmonious, well-turned, singing sentences, beautiful sunsets, moonlight, pictures, ancient sculpture, and strongly marked faces. Beyond that, nothing. I would rather have been Talma than Mirabeau, because he lived in a sphere of purer beauty. I am as sorry for caged birds as for enslaved human beings. In all of politics, there is only one thing that I understand: the riot. I am as fatalistic as a Turk, and believe that whether we do everything we can for the progress of humanity, or nothing at all, makes no whit of difference. As for that 'progress'. I have but an obtuse comprehension of muddy ideas. I am completely out of patience with everything pertaining to that kind of language. I despise modern tyranny because it seems to me stupid, weak, and without the courage of its convictions. But I have a deep cult of ancient tyranny, which I regard as mankind's finest manifestation. I am above all a man of fantasy, caprice, lack of method. I thought long and *very seriously* (don't laugh, it is a memory of my best hours) of becoming a Mohammedan in Smyrna. The day will come when I will go and settle somewhere far from here, and nothing more will be heard of me. As for what ordinarily touches men most closely, and for me is secondary – I mean physical love – I have always kept it separate from this other. I heard you jeer at J.J.[2] on this account the other day: his case is mine exactly. You are the only woman whom I have both loved and possessed. Until now I used women to satisfy desires aroused in me by other women. You made me untrue to my system, to my heart, perhaps to my nature, which, incomplete in itself, always seeks the incomplete.

I loved one woman from the time I was fourteen until I was twenty, without telling her, without touching her;[3] and after that I went three years without feeling sexual desire. At one time I thought

I should continue so until I died, and I thanked God. I wish I had neither body nor heart, or rather, I wish I might be dead, for the figure I cut on this earth is infinitely ridiculous. That is what makes me mistrustful and fearful of myself.

You are the only woman to whom I have dared to try to give pleasure, the only one, perhaps, to whom I have given it. Thank you, thank you for that! But will you understand me to the end? Will you be able to bear the burden of my spleen, my manias, my whims, my prostrations and my wild reversals? You tell me, for example, to write to you every day, and if I don't you will reproach me. But the very idea that you want a letter every morning will prevent me from writing it. Let me love you in my own way, in the way my nature demands, with what you call my originality. Force me to do nothing, and I will do everything. Understand me, do not reproach me. If I thought you frivolous and stupid like other women, I would placate you with words, promises, vows. That would cost me nothing. But I prefer to express less, not more, than the true feelings of my heart.

The Numidians, Herodotus says, have a strange custom. They burn the scalps of their infant children with coals, to make them less sensitive to the action of the sun, which is so fierce in their country. And of all people on earth they are the healthiest. Imagine that I was brought up in the Numidian way. Wouldn't it be too easy to say to me: 'You don't feel anything! The sun itself doesn't warm you!' Have no fear: my heart is none the worse for being calloused. Don't misunderstand me, however: when I probe myself I don't think myself better than my neighbour. Only, I have some perspicacity, and a certain delicacy in my manners.

Evening is falling. I have spent my afternoon writing to you. When I was eighteen, back from a trip to the Midi, I wrote similar letters for six months to a woman I didn't love.[4] I did it to force myself to love her, to play a role with conviction. Now it is the exact opposite; the antithesis is complete.

One last word: in Paris, there is a man who is at my service, devoted to me unto death;[5] active, bold, intelligent, a great and heroic nature compliant to my every wish. In case of need, count on him as you would on me. Tomorrow I expect your poems, and in a few days your two volumes. Farewell, think of me; yes, kiss your arm for me. Every evening now I read some of your poems. I keep looking for traces of yourself in them; sometimes I find them.

Adieu, adieu; I lay my head on your breasts and look up at you, as to a madonna.

11 p.m.

Adieu, I seal my letter. This is the hour when, alone amidst everything that sleeps, I open the drawer that holds my treasures. I look at your slippers, your handkerchief, your hair, your portrait, I re-read your letters and breathe their musky perfume. If you could know what I am feeling at this moment! My heart expands in the night, suffused with a dew of love!

A thousand kisses, a thousand, everywhere – *everywhere.*

1. About the bust of Dr Flaubert. Because of his mother, Flaubert needed a pretext to go to Paris. 'Phidias', of course, was Pradier.
2. The critic Jules Janin.
3. Elise Schlesinger.
4. Eulalie Foucault.
5. Maxime DuCamp.

∾

To Louise Colet

[Croisset,] Saturday-Sunday, midnight. [August 8–9, 1846]

The sky is clear, the moon is shining. I hear sailors singing as they raise anchor, preparing to leave with the oncoming tide. No clouds, no wind. The river is white under the moon, black in the shadows. Moths are playing around my candles, and the scent of the night comes to me through my open windows. And you, are you asleep? Or at your window? Are you thinking of the one who thinks of you? Are you dreaming? What is the colour of your dream? A week ago we were taking our beautiful drive in the Bois de Boulogne. What an abyss since that day! For others, those charming hours doubtless went by like those that preceded them and those that followed; but for us it was a radiant moment whose glow will always brighten our hearts. It was beautiful in its joy and tenderness, was it not, poor soul? If I were rich I would buy that carriage and put it in my stable and never use it again. Yes, I will come back, and soon, for I think of you always; I keep dreaming of your face, of your shoulders, your white neck, your smile, of your voice that is like a love-cry, at once impassioned, violent, and sweet. I told you, I think, that it was above all your voice that I loved.

This morning I waited a whole hour on the quay for the postman: he was late today. How many heartbeats that red-collared fool must be the cause of, all unknowing! Thank you for your good letter. But do not love me so much, do not love me so much. You hurt me! Let me love you. Don't you know that to love excessively brings bad luck to both? It's like over-fondled children: they die young. Life is not made for that. Happiness is a monstrosity; they who seek it are punished.

Yesterday and the day before, my mother was in a frightful state; she had funereal hallucinations. I stayed by her side. You don't know what it is, the burden of such despair that has to be borne alone. Remember those last words, if ever you think yourself the unhappiest of women. There is one who is more unhappy than it is possible to be: one step further lies death or madness.

Before I knew you, I was calm; I had become so. I was entering a vigorous period of moral health. My youth is over. My nervous illness, which lasted two years, was its conclusion, its close, its logical result. To have had what I had, something very serious must have happened earlier inside my brain pan. Then everything became itself again. I had experienced a clear vision of things – and of myself, which is rarer. I was living soundly, according to my particular system, devised for my particular case. I had arrived at an understanding of everything within myself, I had sorted it all, classified it all, with the result that I was more at peace than at any previous period of my existence, whereas everyone imagined the opposite – that now I was to be pitied. Then you came along, and with the touch of a fingertip stirred everything up again. The old dregs were set boiling once more; the lake of my heart began to churn. But the tempest is for the ocean; ponds, when they are disturbed, produce nothing but unhealthy smells. I must love you to tell you this. Forget me if you can, tear your soul from your body with your two hands and trample on it, to obliterate the traces I left there.

Come, don't be angry. No, I embrace you, I kiss you. I feel crazy. Were you here, I'd bite you; I long to – I, whom women jeer at for my coldness – I, charitably supposed to be incapable of sex, so little have I indulged in it. Yes, I feel within me now the cravings of wild beasts, the instincts of a love that is carnivorous, capable of tearing flesh to pieces. Is this love? Perhaps it is the opposite. Perhaps in my case it's the heart that is impotent.

My deplorable mania for analysis exhausts me. I doubt everything, even my doubt. You thought me young, and I am old. I have often spoken with old people about the pleasures of this earth, and I have always been astonished by the brightness that comes into their lacklustre eyes; just as they could never get over their amazement at my way of life, and kept saying 'At your age! At your age! You! You!' Take away my nervous exaltation, my fantasy of mind, the emotion of the moment, and I have little left. That's what I am underneath. *I was not made to enjoy life.* You must not take these words in a down-to-earth sense, but rather grasp their metaphysical intensity. I keep telling myself that I'll bring you misfortune, that were it not for me your life would have continued undisturbed, that the day will come when we shall part (and I protest in advance). Then the nausea of life rises to my lips, and I feel immeasurable self-disgust and a wholly Christian tenderness for you.

At other times – yesterday, for example, when I had sealed my letter – the thought of you sings, smiles, shines, and dances like a joyous fire that gives out a thousand colours and penetrating warmth. I keep remembering the graceful, charming, provocative movement of your mouth when you speak – that rosy moist mouth that calls forth kisses and sucks them irresistibly in. What a good idea I had, to take your slippers. If you knew how I keep looking at them! The bloodstains are fading: is that their fault? We shall do the same: one year, two years, six, what does it matter? Everything measurable passes, everything that can be counted has an end. Only three things are infinite: the sky in its stars, the sea in its drops of water, and the heart in its tears. Only in that capacity is the heart large; everything else about it is small. Am I lying? Think, try to be calm. One or two shreds of happiness fill it to overflowing, whereas it has room for all the miseries of mankind.

You speak of work. Yes, you must work; love art. Of all lies, art is the least untrue. Try to love it with a love that is exclusive, ardent, devoted. It will not fail you. Only the Idea is eternal and necessary.

There are no more artists as they once existed, artists whose loves and minds were the blind instruments of the appetite for the beautiful, God's organs by means of which he demonstrated to himself his own existence. For them the world did not exist; no one has ever known anything of their sufferings; each night they lay down in sadness, and they looked at human life with wonder, as we contemplate ant-hills.

You judge me from a woman's point of view: am I supposed to complain of your judgement? You love me so much that you delude yourself about me; you find in me talent, intelligence, style. In me! In me! You'll make me vain, and I was proud of not being so! See: you have already lost something as a result of meeting me. Your critical sense is forsaking you, and you imagine this person who loves you is a great man. Would that I were, to make you proud of me! (It is I who am proud of *you*. I keep telling myself: 'But she loves me! Is it possible? *She!*') Yes, I wish that I could write beautiful things, great things, and that you would weep with admiration of them. I think of you at a performance of a play by me, in a box, listening, hearing the applause. But I fear the contrary – that you will weary of constantly raising me to your level. When I was a child I dreamed of fame like everyone else, no more nor less; in me good sense sprouted late, but it is firmly planted. So it is very doubtful that the public will ever have occasion to read a single line written by me; if this happens, it will not be before ten years, at least.

I don't know what led me to read you something; forgive that weakness. I could not resist the temptation to make you think highly of me. But I was sure of success, wasn't I? What puerility on my part! It was a sweet idea you had, that we should write a book together; it moved me; but I do not want to publish anything. This is a stand I have taken, a vow I made to myself at a solemn period in my life. I work with absolute disinterestedness and without ulterior motive or concern. I am not a nightingale, but a shrill warbler, hiding deep in the woods lest I be heard by anyone except myself. If I make an appearance, one day, it will be in full armour; but I shall never have the assurance. Already my imagination is fading, my zest is not what it was. I am bored by my own sentences; and if I keep those that I have written it is because I like to surround myself with memories, just as I never sell my old clothes. I go and look at them sometimes in the attic where I keep them, and dream of the time when they were new and of everything I did when I was wearing them.

By the way – so we'll christen the blue dress together. I'll try to arrive some evening about six. We'll have all night and the next day. We'll set the night ablaze! I'll be your desire, you'll be mine, and we'll gorge ourselves on each other to see whether we can be satiated. Never! No, never! Your heart is an inexhaustible spring, you let me drink deep, it floods me, penetrates me, I drown. Oh! The beauty of your face, all pale and quivering under my kisses! But how cold I was! I did nothing but look at you; I was surprised, charmed. If I had you here now . . . Come, I'll take another look at your slippers. They are something I'll never give up; I think I love them as much as I do you. Whoever made them, little suspected how my hands would tremble when I touch them. I breathe their perfume; they smell of verbena – and of you in a way that makes my heart swell.

Adieu, my life, *adieu*, my love, a thousand kisses everywhere. Phidias has only to write, and I will come. Next winter there will no longer be any way for us to see each other, but [if Phidias writes between now and the beginning of the winter][1] I'll come to Paris for at least three weeks. *Adieu*, I kiss you in the place where I *will* kiss you, where I wanted to; I put my mouth there, *je me roule sur toi, mille baisers. Oh! donne-m'en, donne-m'en!*

1. Clarification suggested by J.B.

~

To Louise Colet

　　　　　[Croisset,] Sunday morning. 10 o'clock. [August 9, 1846]
My child, your infatuation is carrying you away. Calm, calm. You are putting yourself into a state – into a rage against yourself, against life. I told you I was more reasonable than you. Do you think that I too am not to be pitied? Be more sparing with your cries; they are torturing me. What do you want me to do? Can I leave everything here and live in Paris? Impossible. If I were entirely free I would, for with you in Paris I wouldn't have the strength to go into exile – a project of my youth, which I shall carry out some day. For I want to live in a place where no one loves me or knows

me, where the sound of my name causes only indifference, where my death or my absence costs no one a tear. I have been too much loved, you see; you love me too much. I am satiated with affection, and I keep wanting it, alas! You tell me that what I needed was a banal kind of love. I needed either no love at all, or yours, for I cannot imagine one more complete, more full, more beautiful. It is now ten o'clock; I have just received your letter and sent you mine, the one I wrote last night. Scarcely awake, I am writing to you again without knowing what I am going to say. You must see that I am thinking of you. Don't be angry with me when you receive no letter from me. It is not my fault. Those are the very days when I am perhaps thinking of you most of all. You are afraid I am ill, dear Louise. People like me can be ill with impunity; they do not die. I have had every kind of illness and accident, horses have been killed under me, carriages have overturned, and I have never been scratched. I am fated to live a long life and to see everything perish around me and in me. In my soul I have already attended a thousand funerals; my friends leave me one after the other, they marry, move away, change; when we meet we barely recognize each other, find scarcely anything to say. What irresistible impulse drove me towards you? For an instant I saw the abyss, realized its depth, and then vertigo swept me over. But how *not* love you, you who are so sweet, so good, so noble, so loving, so beautiful? I keep remembering your voice, when you spoke to me the night of the fireworks. They blazed for us, that night, a dazzling inauguration of our love.

Your apartment resembles one I had in Paris for almost two years at 19 rue de l'Est.[1] When you pass that way, look up at the second floor. From there too there was a view over Paris. On summer nights I used to look up at the stars, and in winter at the luminous mist of the great city floating above the houses. Just as from your windows, I saw gardens, roofs, the surrounding hills. When I walked into your house it seemed to me I was reliving my past, that I had returned to one of those beautiful, sad twilights of 1843, when I would sit at my window for a little air, utterly bored, deathly depressed. If only I had known you then! Why could that not have been? I was free, alone, without family or mistress, for I have never had a mistress. You will think that I am lying. I have never been more scrupulously truthful, and this is the reason why: the grotesque aspects of love

have always kept me from indulging in it. At times I have wanted
to give pleasure to women, but the idea of the strange spectacle I
must be presenting at that moment made me laugh so much that
all my desire melted under the fire of irony, which sang a hymn of
bitter derision within me. It is only with you that I have not yet
laughed at myself. But when I see you so intense, absolute in your
passion, I am tempted to cry out to you: 'No! No! You are making
a mistake! Take care! Not this man!'

Heaven made you beautiful, devoted, intelligent; I should like
to be other than I am, to be worthy of you. I wish my heart were
newer and fresher. Ah! Do not revive me too much: I'd blaze up like
straw. You will think I am selfish, that I fear you. I admit it: I am
terrified of your love, because I feel it is devouring us both, especially
you. You are like Ugolino in his prison; you devour your own flesh
to appease your hunger.

Some day, if I write my memoirs – the only thing I shall write
well, if ever I settle down to it – you will have a place in them, and
what a place! For you are making a wide breach in my existence. I
had surrounded myself with a wall of stoicism; one look from you
blew it to pieces, like a cannon ball. Yes, I often think I hear your
dress rustling behind me on my rug; I tremble, and turn around –
and it's my curtain rustling in the wind, as though you were entering
the room. I keep seeing your lovely white forehead; you know, don't
you, that your forehead is sublime? Too beautiful even to be kissed;
pure, noble, eloquent of what is within. Do you go to Phidias', to
that studio where I saw you the first time, among the marbles and
the casts?

He should be coming soon. I await a letter from him which will
give me a pretext to go to Paris for a day. Then early in September
I will find another, to go to Mantes or Vernon. After that, we shall
see. But what is the good of getting accustomed to seeing each other,
loving each other? Why treat ourselves to the luxury of affection, if
afterwards we must be miserable? What is the good? But what else
can we do?

Adieu, my darling; I have just gone down into the garden and
gathered this little rose I send you. I kiss it; put it quickly to your
mouth, and then – you know where . . . *Adieu!* A thousand kisses. I
am yours from night to day, from day to night.

1. Not the present rue de l'Est, but an old street, since demolished, near the Law School and the Luxembourg Gardens.

~

To Louise Colet

[Croisset,] Tuesday afternoon. [August 11, 1846]

You would breathe love into a dead man. How can I not love you? You have powers of attraction to make stones rise up at your voice. Your letters stir me to my entrails. So have no fear that I'll forget you! You must know that one doesn't turn away from natures like yours – natures that are deep and emotional, and stir the emotions of others. I hate myself, I could beat myself, for having hurt you. Forget everything I said in my letter of Sunday. I was addressing myself to your virile intellect; I had thought you could disregard the prompting of your heart and understand me in intellectual terms. You saw too many things where there were not that many to see; you exaggerated everything I said. You perhaps thought that I was acting the part of a third-rate Antony.[1] You call me a Voltairean and a materialist. God knows whether I am or not! You speak also of my 'exclusive tastes in literature, which should have made you guess what I am like when it comes to love'. I try in vain to find the meaning of that. I remain completely baffled. On the contrary: whatever I admire, I do so sincerely and if I am worth anything it is thanks to this pantheistic faculty, and to my very 'intransigence' that offended you. Come, let's talk no more about it. I was wrong, I was foolish. I did with you what in the past I have done with those I loved best: I bared my soul, and the acrid dust that rose from its most secret recesses stuck in their throats. How many times, without wanting to, I brought tears to the eyes of my father, who was so intelligent, so perceptive! But he understood nothing of my idiom – like you, like the others. I have the infirmity of being born with a special language, to which I alone have the key. I am not in the least unhappy, not at all blasé: everybody finds me gay by nature, and I absolutely never complain. I don't really think I'm an object of pity, for I envy nothing and want nothing. Come, I'll torment you no longer; I'll touch you gently, as one does a child one fears to injure: I'll turn all my stings inward, on myself. If he's not too angry, the porcupine doesn't always pierce you. You say I analyse myself too much: *I* find that I don't know myself well enough – every day I discover something new. I travel within myself as in a country unknown, even though I have traversed it many times. You are not grateful for my frankness. (Women want you to deceive them: they force you to, and if you resist they blame you.) You tell me that I didn't show myself in that light at first. But think back. Remember all the things I said at our first dinner. You even exclaimed: 'So you excuse everything! For you there is no good or evil!' No, I never lied to you; I loved you instinctively, and I did not set out deliberately to please you. Everything happened because it was fated to happen. Mock my fatalism if you will, and tell me I'm behind the times in being a Turk. Fatalism is the Providence of evil: it is the Providence whose evidence one sees, and I believe in it.

The tearstains I find on your letters – all from tears caused by me: I'd like to redeem them with so many cups of my blood. I am angry with myself: it increases my self-disgust. If I didn't think you liked me, I would abhor myself. But that's always the way: you bring suffering to those you love, or they to you. How can you reproach me for saying 'I wish I had never known you'? I can imagine nothing more affectionate. Do you want me to tell you something comparable? It is something I said the day before my sister died – it came out spontaneously and revolted everyone. We were talking about my mother, and I said: 'If only she could die!' And as everyone protested, I said: 'Yes: if she wanted to throw herself out of the window I'd open it for her.' It seems that isn't the sort of thing one says in polite society; it sounded strange or cruel. But what the devil does one say when one's heart is full to bursting? Ask yourself whether there are many men who would have written you that letter that hurt you so. Few, I think, would have had the courage and the disinterested self-abnegation. You must tear up that letter, my love, and never think of it again; or, reread it from time to time, when you feel strong.

About letters: when you write to me on a Sunday, post it early: you know the offices close at two. Yesterday I didn't get one. I was afraid of I don't know what. But today both came, and the little flower with them. Thank you for the idea of the mitten: if only you could send yourself with it! If I could hide you in the drawer of the cabinet beside me – how carefully I'd lock you in!

Come, laugh! Today I'm gay, I don't know why: the sweetness of your letters of this morning has entered my blood. But don't give me any more commonplaces like these: that it is money that has kept me from being happy, that if I had worked I'd be better off. As though one had only to be an apothecary's boy, a baker or a wine merchant not to be discontented here below! All that has been said to me too often by countless Philistines for me to want to hear it from your lips. That sort of thing doesn't become them: they aren't made for it. But I am grateful that you approve my literary silence. If I am fated to say something new, it will emerge by itself, when the time comes. Oh! How I should love to write great things, to please you! How I should love to thrill you with my style. Though I do not long for fame (and in this respect I am more naive than the fox in the fable) I should love to have some for you, to toss it to you like a bouquet: it would be yet another caress, a soft bed where your mind would bask in the sun of my glory. You find me handsome: I wish I were handsome in the way of Greek youths – I wish my hair were curly, black, falling on ivory shoulders; I wish I were strong, pure. But when I look at myself in the glass and think that you love me, I find myself revoltingly common. My hands are hard; I am knock-kneed, narrow-chested. If only I had a voice, and could sing – oh! how I would modulate those long inhalations that must now evaporate as sighs. If you had known me ten years ago, I was fresh, fragrant;[2] I breathed life and love; but now I see even my maturity beginning to fade. Why weren't you the first woman I knew? Why wasn't it in your arms that I first felt the intoxication of the body and the blissful spasms that hold us in ecstasy?

I regret all my past: I feel I should have held it in reserve, waiting, even without knowing why: then I could have given it to you when the time came. But I never suspected anyone could love me. (Even now that seems unnatural. Love for me! How strange!) And like a prodigal seeking to ruin himself in a single day, I gave away all my riches, great and small. I loved unspeakable things – and furiously. I idolized vile women, I sacrificed at all the altars and drank from every cask. Ah! My moral treasures! I tossed gold pieces out of the window to passers-by, or sent them skimming over the water. The following comparison, which is actually only a simple analogy, will give you my picture. When I was in Paris I squandered six or seven thousand a year, yet went without dinner three times a week. It is the same with my feelings: on what would gorge a regiment, I starve to death. Indigence is in my nature, but don't think of me as being in desperate straits. I used to be, but no longer. There was a time when I was unhappy. The reproaches you send me today might have been justified then.

I will write to Phidias; I don't quite know how to say that he should make it sound urgent that I come immediately. Is he perhaps in the country? Where? When does he get back? I'll arrive one evening, and spend the night and the next day until seven: that's a promise. From Thursday on, address your letter to me like this: M. DuCamp, c/o M. G. Fl., because the letters I receive from you are supposedly from him, and when he is here it would seem odd if I were to get them just the same. I might be questioned, etc. However, if you feel the slightest distaste for this, don't do it: I don't give a damn. I am discreet for your sake. I'm sure that if I so much as uttered your name, I'd blush and all would become obvious.

. . . You wanted me to send you something concerning us. Here is a page written about this time 2 years ago (it is a fragment of a letter to a friend):[3]

. . . From her eyes flowed a lustrous fluid that seemed to enlarge them; they were motionless, fixed. Her naked shoulders (for she wore no fichu, and her dress seemed loose about her), her naked shoulders were pale silvery-gilt, smooth and firm like yellowed marble. Blue veins coursed through her burning flesh. Her pulsing breast rose and fell, and my own chest was filled with the breath she was retaining. That lasted a century. The entire earth had vanished. I saw only the pupils of her eyes, which dilated more and more: I heard only her breathing – the only sound in the silence into which we were plunged.

And I took a step forward; I kissed her on her eyes, which tasted moist and sweet. She looked at me in astonishment. 'Will you love me?' she said. 'Will you really love me?' I let her speak without replying. I held her in my arms, and felt her heart beating against me.

She broke away. 'Tonight I'll come back. Now let me go, let me go. Until tonight!' She ran out.

At dinner she kept her feet on mine, and now and again touched my elbow, turning her face the other way.

Does that ring true?

. . . I haven't the heart for work. I do nothing; I walk up and down in my study, lie on my green leather sofa and think of you. Afternoons, especially, I find fatiguingly long. I am tired of thinking; I'd like to be completely simple, and love you like a child, or else be a Goethe or a Byron.

As soon as I have a letter from Phidias, I'll leave my friend (even though he's coming here particularly to see me), and come running. You can see that I no longer have heart, will, anything. I am a limp, fond thing, entirely at your command. In daydream I live in the folds of your dress, in the fine curls of your hair. I have some of those here: how good they smell! If you knew how I think of your sweet voice – of your shoulders and their fragrance that I love.

. . . I wanted to work today, and not write to you until tonight. I couldn't: I had to surrender.

So: *adieu, adieu:* a great long kiss on your mouth.

Midnight, I have just reread your letters, looked at everything again. I send you a last kiss for the night. I have just written to Phidias. I think I have made him understand that I want to come to Paris right away. I'll mail it in Rouen tomorrow, along with this. I hope to get there in time so you'll have this tomorrow evening.

Adieu. A thousand kisses without end. Till soon, my lovely – till soon.

1.   The hero of the melodrama of the same name by the elder Dumas.
2.   Flaubert wrote to Louise about his earlier appearance in another letter: 'It was ten years ago that you should have known me. My face had a distinction it has lost, my nose was less bulbous and my forehead unlined. There are still moments when, if I look at myself, I seem all right, but much of the time I think of myself as being the very picture of a bourgeois. Do you know that when I was a child, princesses stopped their carriages to take me in their arms and kiss me? One day when the duchesse de Berry was in Rouen, driving along the quays, she noticed me in the crowd: my father was holding me up so that I could see the procession. Her caleche was moving very slowly. She stopped it and obviously enjoyed seeing me and

kissing me. My poor father came home very happy about that triumph – it was certainly the only one I'll ever have.' And Mrs Tennant (Gertrude Collier: see p. 46, n. 2) wrote of the young Flaubert as she knew him as a lycéen at Trouville: 'At that time Gustave Flaubert looked like a young Greek. He was in mid-adolescence, tall and slender, lithe and graceful as an athlete.'

3. Actually a passage from *L'Education sentimentale* (first version). It naturally aroused Louise's jealousy (see p. 97).

~

To Louise Colet

[Croisset,] Wednesday night. [August 12, 1846]

Today you will have gone all day without a letter from me. Once again you must have doubted me, poor love. Forgive me. The fault lies not in my will but in my memory; I thought I had until one o'clock for the last mail from Rouen, whereas actually it was only until eleven. But if you're still holding a little grudge against me I hope to make it disappear on Monday – I have great hopes for Monday! Phidias will please write to me. I count on having his note not later than Sunday.

How I love the plan you propose for the celebration! It brought tears of affection to my eyes. Yes, you do love me; to doubt it would be a crime. And as for me, if I do not love you, what can my feeling for you be called? Each letter you send me penetrates more deeply into my heart. Particularly the one of this morning; it was of an exquisite charm. It was gay, kind, beautiful, like yourself. Yes, let us love each other, let us love each other since no one has ever loved us.

I shall arrive in Paris at four or quarter past. Thus, before half past four I shall be at your house. Already I see myself climbing your stairs: I hear the sound of the bell. . . . 'Is Madame at home?' 'Come in.' Ah! I'm relishing them in advance, those twenty-four hours. But why must every joy bring me pain? I already think of our separation, of your sadness. You will be sensible, won't you? For I feel I'll be more depressed than the first time.

I am not one of those in whom possession kills love; rather, it kindles it. With regard to everything good that has happened to me I am like those Arabs who, one day each year, still turn in the direction of Granada and lament the beautiful place no longer theirs.

A little earlier today I happened to be walking in the rue du

Collège; I saw people on the steps of the chapel; it was Prize Day; I heard the cries of the pupils, the sound of applause and a band. I went in. There it all was again, just as in my time. The same hangings in the same places. It made me remember the smell of the wet oak leaves they used to put on our heads;[1] I thought of the delirium of joy that always gripped me that day, for two months of complete freedom lay open before me. My father was there, and my sister, and friends now dead, gone, or changed. I felt a great pang as I left. The ceremony was less colourful; there were few people as compared to the crowd that filled the church ten years ago. There was less noise, there was no singing of the 'Marseillaise', which I used to bellow madly as I banged the benches. The fashionable crowd no longer attends. I remember that formerly it was full of women got up in great style; actresses would come, kept women with titles.[2] They sat upstairs, in the galleries. How proud we were when they looked at us! Some day I will write about all this, the modern young man, his soul unfurling at sixteen with an immense love that makes him lust for wealth, fame, all the splendours of life – all the overflowing, sad poetry of the heart of an adolescent – this is a new vein which no one has yet explored. Oh Louise! What I am going to say is hard, yet it is born of the deepest, most intense sympathy and pity. If ever you are loved by some poor boy who finds you beautiful, a boy such as I was, timid, gentle, trembling, who fears you and yet seeks you out, who avoids you and yet pursues you, be kind to him, do not reject him; let him only kiss your hand and he will die of ecstasy. Drop your handkerchief, he will take it and sleep with it, press it to him and weep. The spectacle I just saw has reopened the tomb in which my mummified youth has lain sleeping; I've had a whiff of its faded breath. My soul has been haunted by something like those forgotten melodies that come back to us at twilight, during those slow hours in which memory, like a ghost among ruins, stalks our thoughts. But women will never experience any of this, and certainly they will never express it. They love, they love perhaps more than we, more strongly, but not so boldly. And then, is it enough to be possessed by a feeling, to express it? Has a drinking song ever been written by a drunken man? It is wrong to think that feeling is everything. In the arts, it is nothing without form. All this is to say that women who have loved a great deal do not know love, because they have been too immersed in it; they do not have a *disinterested* appetite for the Beautiful. For them, love must always be linked with something, with a goal, a practical concern. They write to ease their hearts – not because they are attracted by Art, which is a self-sufficient principle, no more needful of support than a star. I know very well that this is not what you think, but it is what I think. Some day I will explain these ideas to you clearly, and shall hope to convince you – you, a born poet. Yesterday I read your story *Le Marquis d'Entrecasteaux*. It is written in a good, sober, vivid style; one feels it; it shows true talent. I especially like the opening, the walk, and the scene with Madame d'Entrecasteaux alone in her room, before her husband comes in. As for myself, I keep studying a little Greek. I am reading Chardin's travels to keep up my oriental studies, and to help me with an oriental story I've been planning for a year and a half. But for some time past my imagination has been losing strength. How could it soar, poor little bee? It caught its feet in a pot of jam, and is sinking there up to its neck. *Adieu*, my beloved; resume your usual life, go out, invite your friends, do not refuse to see the people who were there with me on Sunday. I would like to see them again myself. I don't know why. When I love, my feeling is like a flood that spreads over everything around me.

. . . No: let's not go back to the rue de l'Est together. The very thought of the Latin Quarter nauseates me. *Adieu*, a thousand kisses. And – yes – a thousand of Ariosto's[3] kind – and the way we know how to give them.

1. Wreaths for the prize-winners, as in Andrew Marvell's 'How vainly men themselves amaze/To win the palm, the oak, or bays.'
2. Fashionable courtesans sometimes adopted *titres de noblesse*, calling themselves 'comtesse', 'marquise', etc. But Flaubert probably exaggerates the frequency with which such glamorous creatures attended graduation ceremonies at his provincial lycée.
3. See p. 71, n. 2.

$\sim$

TO LOUISE COLET

[Croisset,] Thursday night, 11 o'clock. [August 13, 1846]
Your letter of this morning is sad, full of sorrow and resignation.

You offer to forget me if that is what I want. You are sublime! I knew you were good, wonderfully good, but I did not know you were so noble. I repeat: I feel *humble* at the contrast I see between us. Do you know that you write to me cruel things? And the worst is that it was I who provoked them. You are returning blow for blow – a reprisal. What I want of you, I do not know. But what I want of myself is to love you, to love you a thousand times more. Oh! If you could read my heart you would see the place I have given you there! I can see that you are suffering more than you admit. Your letter sounds strained – you had been weeping before writing it, hadn't you? It sounds crushed, in it I sense the lassitude that grief brings, I hear the faint echo of a voice that has been sobbing. Admit it, tell me right away that you were having a bad day, that it was because my letter had not come. Be frank, not proud; do not do as I have done all too often. Do not restrain your tears, they then fall back into the heart, you know, and leave deep wounds.

Something occurs to me which I must say. I am sure you think me selfish. The thought grieves you, and you are convinced it is true. Is it because I seem so? About selfishness, you know, everyone deludes himself. I am selfish like everyone else – less so than many, perhaps, and perhaps more than others. Who knows? Besides, 'selfish' is a word that everyone applies to his neighbour without really knowing what he means by it. Who is not selfish, to a greater or lesser degree? From the idiot who wouldn't give a sou to redeem the human race, to the man who dives beneath the ice to rescue a stranger, do we not all seek, according to our various instincts, to satisfy our natures? St Vincent de Paul obeyed an appetite for charity, Caligula an appetite for cruelty. Everyone takes his enjoyment in his own way and for himself alone. Some direct all activity towards themselves, making themselves the cause, the centre, the end of everything; others invite the whole world to the banquet of their souls. That is the difference between prodigals and misers: the first take their pleasure in giving, the second in keeping. As for ordinary selfishness (what we usually mean by the word), although it is extremely repugnant to my spirit, I confess that if I could buy it I should give everything to have it. To be stupid, selfish, and have good health are three requirements for happiness, though if stupidity is lacking, all is lost. But there is also another kind of happiness, yes, there is another, for I have seen it, you have made me feel it; you have shown me, in the air, its shining light; before my eyes I have seen the glistening hem of its garment. I hold out my hands to grasp it . . . and then you yourself begin to shake your head and suspect it's but a phantom. (What a stupid mania I have for speaking in metaphors that say nothing!) What I mean is, I am beginning to feel that you too have sadness in your heart, that deep sadness which comes of nothing, and which, rooted in the very substance of being, increases as that substance itself is aroused. I warned you: my misery is contagious. I am infected! Woe to the one who touches me!

Oh, what you wrote me this morning is lamentable and painful: I pictured your poor face, sad at the thought of me, sad because of me. Yesterday I was so happy, confident, serene, joyful as the summer sun between two showers. Your mitten is here. It smells sweet, making me feel that I am still breathing the perfume of your shoulder and the sweet warmth of your bare arm. Come! Here are thoughts of voluptuousness, thoughts of caresses, overwhelming me again; my heart leaps up at the thought of you. I covet all your being, I invoke my memory of you to quench this need that is crying in my very depths. Why are you not here! But – Monday, yes? I await the letter from Phidias. If he writes to me, everything will be as we agreed.

Do you know what I am thinking of? Of your little boudoir, where you work, where . . . (no word here; the three dots say more than all the eloquence in the world). I keep seeing your pale, intense face as you lay on the floor, your head in my lap . . . and the lamp! Oh! Never break it; keep it, light it every night, or rather at certain solemn moments of your inner life, when you are beginning or finishing some great work. An idea! I have some water from the Mississippi. It was brought to my father by a sea captain, who gave it to him as a great treat. I want you, when you have written something you think fine, to wash your hands in it; or else I will pour it on your breast, baptizing you in the name of my love. I am wandering, I think; I don't know what I was speaking of before I thought of that bottle. The lamp, wasn't it? Yes, I love it, I love your house, your furniture; everything, except that frightful caricature in oil hanging in your bedroom. I think also of that worthy Catherine who served us dinner, of Phidias' jokes, of everything, a thousand foolish details that amuse me. But do you know the two pictures of you that predominate? In the studio, standing, posing, the light falling on you from the side, when I was looking at you and you at me. And then the night at the hotel – I see you lying on my bed, your hair streaming over my pillow, your eyes raised, your face pale, your hands joined, flooding me with wild words. When you are dressed, you are fresh as a bouquet. In my arms you're a warm sweetness that melts and intoxicates. And I? Tell me how I seem to you, what sort of picture of me comes to your mind? . . . What a wretched lover I am! Will you believe me when I tell you that what happened to me with you never happened before? (I had been exhausted for three days, taut as a cello string.) If I were a man of great self-esteem I'd have been bitterly chagrined. I was, for you. I feared you might suppose things that you would consider odious; other women would perhaps have found me insulting; they would have thought me cold, or repelled, or depleted. I was grateful to you for your spontaneous intelligence, which kept you from being surprised, whereas I myself was surprised by it as by something inconceivable and monstrous. I must indeed have loved you, and deeply, since my initial reaction with you was the opposite of what it had always been with other women.

You would like to transform me into a pagan, O my muse! You who have Roman blood in your veins. But try as I might, any effort in that direction would be useless, for deep in my soul is the Northern fog that I breathed at my birth. I carry within me the melancholy of the barbarians, with their instinct for migration and their innate disgust for life – which made them leave their own country as though by so doing they could take leave of themselves. They loved the sun, all those barbarians who went to Italy to die; they had a frenzied longing for light, for blue sky, for a warm, vibrant existence. They dreamed of joyful days, full of love, love that would be to the heart what the juice of ripe grapes is to the hand that squeezes them. I've always had a tender sympathy for them, as one has for ancestors. In their tumultuous history, didn't I find the whole mute, obscure story of myself? Alaric's cries of joy on entering Rome found their parallel, fourteen centuries later, in the secret ravings of a poor child's heart. Alas! No, I am no man of antiquity: men of antiquity didn't have sick nerves like mine! Nor you: you are neither Greek nor Latin; you are beyond that – you have passed through Romanticism. Though today we may be reluctant to admit it, Christianity contributed to the growth of these aspirations, at the same time poisoning them by associating them with painful inner conflict. The human heart can be enlarged only by being lacerated.

You tell me ironically, in connection with the article in the *Constitutionnel,* that I have little regard for patriotism, generosity, and courage. Oh no! I love the conquered, but also I love conquerors. That is perhaps difficult to understand, but it's true. As to the idea of a fatherland – that is, a certain portion of the earth's surface drawn on a map and separated from others by a red or blue line – no! My fatherland is for me the country I love, that is, the one I dream of, the one in which I feel at home. I am as Chinese as I am French, and rejoice not at all in our victories over the Arabs, because I'm saddened by their defeats.[1] I love that fierce, enduring, hardy people, the last example of primitive society. I like to think of them as they pause for rest at noon, lying in the shade under the bellies of their camels, smoking their chibouks and jeering at our fine civilization; and I enjoy thinking how their jeering enrages us. Where am I? Whither do I roam? – as a tragic poet of the school of Delille would put it.[2] In the Orient, God help me! Farewell, my sultana! To think that I haven't even a silver-gilt perfume-burner to light when you come to sleep in my couch! What a shame! But I'll offer you all the perfumes of my heart. Farewell; one long, very long, kiss, and others besides.

1.   In Algeria, where Abd-el-Kader had 'rebelled' after the French 'conquest'.
2.   Jacques Delille (1738–1813), a poet of 'sensibility'.

~

To Louise Colet
    [Croisset,] Friday night, 1 o'clock. [August 14–15, 1846]
    How beautiful they are, the poems you send me! Their rhythm is as gentle as the caresses of your voice when you murmur my name among your other endearments. Forgive me if I think them the best you've done. It wasn't pride I felt when I saw they had been written for me; no: it was love, tenderness. Yours are the seductions of a siren, fatal even to the most callous. Yes, my beautiful one, you've enwrapped me in your charm, infused me with your very self. Oh!

if I have perhaps seemed cold to you, if my sarcasms are harsh and hurt you, I want to cover you with love when I next see you, with caresses, with ecstasy. I want to gorge you with all the joys of the flesh, until you faint and die. I want you to be astonished by me, to confess to yourself that you had never even dreamed of such transports. I am the one who has been happy, now I want you to be the same. When you are old, I want you to recall those few hours. I want your dry bones to quiver with joy when you think of them. Not yet having received Phidias' letter (I await it with impatience and annoyance) I cannot be with you on Sunday evening. And even if I could, we wouldn't have the night together. Besides, you'll be entertaining friends. I'd have to dress, and consequently should need luggage. I want to come without anything, without bundles or bags, to be freer, unencumbered.

I understand perfectly your wish to see me again in the same place, with the same people; I too should like that. Don't we always cling to our past, recent though it may be? In our appetite for life we feast again on past feelings and dream of those yet to come. Confined strictly to the present, the soul is stifled; the world is too small for it. I often think of your alabaster lamp and the chain it hangs from. Look at it when you read this, and thank it for lending me its light.

DuCamp (he is the friend I mentioned in one of my earlier letters) arrived today – he is to spend a month. (Continue to address your letters to him, as you did your last.)[1] He brought me your portrait. The frame is of carved black wood and sets off the engraving very well. It is facing me as I write, leaning gently against a cushion on my chintz sofa, in the corner between two windows – just where you would be sitting if you came here. This sofa is the one I slept on so many nights in the rue de l'Est. During the day I would lie on it when I was tired, and refresh my heart with some great poetic dream, or the memory of an old love. I shall leave the picture there like that; no one will touch it. (The other one is in my drawer, with your bag, on top of your slippers.) My mother has seen it; she likes your face, thinks you pretty. You have an 'animated, open, pleasant expression,' she says. I pretended to her that proofs of the engraving happened to be delivered one afternoon when I visited you, and that you presented some of them to the people who happened to be there.

You ask me whether the few lines I sent you were written for you; you would like to know for whom; you are jealous. For no one – like everything I have written. I have always forbidden myself ever to put anything of myself into my works, and yet I have put in a great deal. I have always tried not to make Art subservient to the gratification of any particular person. I have written very tender pages without love, and burning pages with no fire in my blood. I imagined, I recollected and I combined. What you read is a memory of nothing at all. You predict that some day I'll write beautiful things. Who knows? (*That is my favourite motto.*) I doubt it; my imagination is withering. I am becoming too fastidious. All I ask is to be able to continue to admire the masters with that innermost rapture for which I would gladly sacrifice everything, everything. But as for becoming a master myself, never: I am sure of it. I have immense deficiencies: I have no inborn gift, to begin with, and I lack perseverance in my work. Style is achieved only by dint of atrocious labour, fanatical and unremitting stubbornness. Buffon's saying is a great blasphemy;[2] genius is not 'a long patience'. But there is some truth in it, more than is generally believed, especially nowadays.

This morning I read poems in your volume with a friend who came to see me.[3] He's a poor fellow who gives lessons here for a living and who is a poet, a true poet, who writes superb and charming things and will remain unknown because he lacks two requirements: bread and time. Yes, we read you, we admired you.

Do you think I don't find it sweet to be able to say to myself: 'Nevertheless she's mine, mine!' On Sunday two weeks will have passed since you knelt on the floor and gazed at me with sweetly eager eyes; I was looking at your forehead, thinking of all that lay behind it, staring at your face, with infinite wonder at the lightness and thickness of your hair.

I wouldn't like you to see me now: I am frighteningly ugly. I have an enormous boil on my right cheek, which has half closed one of my eyes and swollen the entire upper part of my face. I must look ridiculous. If you saw me thus, love might draw back, for it is alarmed at the grotesque. But don't worry, I'll be all right when we meet; just as I was, the way you love me.

Tell me whether you use the verbena. Do you put it on your handkerchiefs? Put some on your shift. But no – don't use perfume; the best perfume is yourself, your own natural fragrance. Perhaps I shall have a letter tomorrow.

Adieu, I bite your lip: is the little red spot still there?

Adieu, a thousand kisses. Perhaps on Monday I'll taste the sweetness of yours again.

Yours, body and soul.

1. Louise had been sending her letters to DuCamp in Paris, who forwarded them to Croisset in envelopes addressed in his own hand. But see p. 87.
2. '*Le génie n'est qu'une plus grande aptitude à la patience.*' Attributed to the naturalist Georges Louis Leclerc de Buffon (1707–1788) by Hérault de Séchelles, in the latter's *Voyage à Montbard*.
3. This is the first mention in the present correspondence of Louis Bouilhet (1822–1869), whose 'liaison' (as he himself called it) with Flaubert – intimacy in life and work – began about now. The two men, who grew to look strikingly alike, had been rivals in accomplishment at the Rouen lycée – which Bouilhet, whose family was poor, had attended with scholarship aid; and Bouilhet had later been among Dr Flaubert's medical students. He had subsequently been dismissed from the Hôtel-Dieu – as Flaubert had been from the lycée – because of participation in a student protest, and was now devoting himself to poetry, earning his living in a Rouen tutoring school. Increasing esteem and affection for Bouilhet gave Flaubert some consolation for the 'defection' of Alfred LePoittevin.

~

To Louise Colet

[Croisset, August 17, 1846]

An evil spell is on us! It is always so. Isn't it enough to want something in order not to obtain it? That is the law of life. Impossible for me to be in Paris tonight. My head is all wrapped in wet poultices, because of the frightful boils I have all over my body. I'm lying down, unable to move, and write to you from that position. But I am applying remedies more desperate than you can imagine. We'll laugh about them together. I dare not believe I'll arrive in Paris tomorrow, Tuesday: I might, but don't count on it. So it will be for Wednesday, at the same time.

It was impossible for me yesterday, Sunday, to send you a line. I was counting on my brother's servant – my brother comes here for dinner once a week – but yesterday he didn't turn up. I share the disappointment and anxiety you'll be feeling at half past four today when I don't arrive. But forgive me. I am suffering more than you. Come, my lovely, a little patience: in a few hours you'll see me.

... *Adieu*. I am furious, but kiss you on the mouth – *adieu* – all yours, yours.

~

To Louise Colet

[Croisset,] Tuesday morning. [August 18, 1846]

Here I am on my feet, thanks to my stubbornness. By following my own instinct I rid myself in 2 days of what would have lasted a week. And that against everybody's opinion. Only scars are left.

I'll arrive at your house tomorrow between half past four and five. I'm counting on it. *It is sure* – unless the devil himself takes a hand in it this time. He's taken a hand in so many of my affairs that he might well meddle in this one. So: until tomorrow. Shall we go and take Phidias out for dinner? What's your feeling? Think it over carefully beforehand. Ah – in thirty hours I'll be setting out! Pass swiftly, Today! Pass swiftly, Long Night!

It is raining now: the sky is grey. But I have the sun in my soul.

Adieu – I'd love to fill these 4 little pages, but the postman will soon be arriving, so I'll quickly close this and seal it.

A thousand loves.

The real ones tomorrow. Tomorrow I'll be touching you. Sometimes I think it's a dream I have read about somewhere, and that you don't really exist.

~

To Louise Colet

[Croisset,] Thursday, 1 o'clock in the morning. [August 20–21, 1846]

Alone, now! All alone! It's a dream. Oh, how far away they are, those hours that are barely the past! There are whole centuries between a little while ago and now. A little while ago I was with you, we were together. Our poor ride in the Bois! How dreary the weather was last night when I left you. It was raining. There were tears in the air. The weather itself was sad.

I keep thinking of our last 'reunion' at the hotel, with your silk dress open, and the lace coiling over your breast. Your entire face was smiling, wonder-struck with love and ecstasy. How your sweet eyes shone! Twenty-four hours ago: remember! Oh, the impossibility of recapturing any part of a thing that is gone! *Adieu*, I am going to bed now, and before sleeping I'll read there the letter you wrote to me while waiting for me. *Adieu, adieu*, a thousand love-kisses. Were you here, I'd give you more of the kind I gave you. I am still longing for you, my thirst unquenched! *Adieu, adieu*.

~

To Louise Colet

> *[Croisset,] Friday night, midnight. [August 21–22, 1846]*

Last night I wrote you a note, and send it with this letter.

. . . Forty-eight hours ago . . . you filled my heart with such gladness that some of it remains, even though you're no longer with me. The memory of you is radiant, sweet, poignant. I keep seeing the joyful expression on your lovely face when I was looking into it from very close. Do you know, I'll end by not being able to live without you – a thought that sometimes makes my head spin. When I see you in my mind's eye you draw me irresistibly and it makes me dizzy. What will happen? No matter: let us love each other. It's so sweet, so good. I haven't a single word to say to you, I am so full of you. Except the eternal words: I love you.

. . . Our wonderful dinner together the night before last (the night before last: already so far away)! Afterwards, when I gave you my arm, I was so at peace, oblivious of everything! And then alone in my room, when I felt your body against mine . . . Ah, don't accuse me again of having eyes only for the wretchedness of life . . . weren't we happy? And when we were riding in the carriage, talking, hand in hand, I dreamed of what our existence might have been if conditions were different – if I lived permanently in Paris, if you were alone, if I were free. We were like a young couple on their honeymoon – rich, handsome . . . Imagine what a life like that would be – sweet, full, working together, loving each other . . .

Today I have done nothing. Neither written nor read a line. I unpacked my *Temptation of Saint Anthony* and hung it on my wall;[1] that is all. I am very fond of this picture. I had wanted it for a long time. For me the tragic grotesque holds immense charm, it corresponds to the intimate needs of my nature, which is buffoonishly bitter. It doesn't make me laugh, but sets me dreaming. I recognize it wherever it exists.

. . . *Adieu.* I kiss you everywhere. Think of me: I think of you. Or rather no; think less about me; work, be sensible, be happy in your thoughts. Return to your muse, who consoled you on your worst days. I am for days of happiness.

Adieu. I kiss you on the lips.

1. An engraving by Jacques Callot of the subject Flaubert had seen painted by Breughel in Genoa. The engraving now hangs in the Flaubert pavilion at Croisset.

~

To Louise Colet

[Croisset, Sunday, August 23, 1846]

Do you know you are cruel? You reproach me with not loving you, and point, as evidence, to my always leaving. That is wrong of you. How can I stay? What would you do in my place? You always speak to me of your sorrows: I know they are genuine, I have seen proof; and feel it in myself, which makes it the more convincing. But I see evidence of another sorrow, a sorrow constantly at my side; this one never complains, it even smiles, and, alongside it, yours, however exaggerated it may be, will never be more than what a fleabite is to a burn, a spasm to a death-agony. I am caught in a vice. The two women I love most are driving me with double rein: the bit is in my heart, and they are pulling on it with their love and grief. Forgive me if this angers you yet again. I no longer know what to say to you: I hesitate, now. When I speak to you I'm afraid of making you cry, and when I touch you, of wounding you. You remember my violent caresses, how strong my hands were: you were almost trembling. I made you cry out two or three times. But be more reasonable, poor child I love: stop grieving over chimeras.

You reproach me for my habit of analysing. But you attribute to my words a wicked subtlety they do not have. You dislike the cast

of my mind: the rockets it sends up displease you: you'd like me to
be more consistent, more uniform, in my affections and my language.
That it should be you, you! who are now doing as others do, as
everybody does – blaming me for the only good thing about me,
my leaps and starts, my naive outbursts. Yes, you too want to prune
the tree. Its branches may be unruly, but they are thick and leafy,
and they reach out in all directions to breathe the air and the sun.
You want to tame that tree, to make it into a charming espalier that
would be trained against a wall: true, it would then bear lovely fruit,
which a child could pick without a ladder. What do you want me
to do? I love in my way: whether more than you, or less, God knows.
But I love you, and when you say that I have perhaps done for
vulgar women what I have done for you . . . I have done it for *no
one* – no one: I swear it. You are absolutely the first and only woman
whom I have ever been willing to travel to see – whom I have loved
enough to do that for – because you are the first to love me as you
love me. No: no one before you has ever wept the same tears, or
looked at me in that sad and tender way. Yes: the memory of
Wednesday night is my most beautiful memory of love. Were I to
become old tomorrow, it is that memory that would make me regret
what I had lost.

   . . . *Adieu.* This is your name-day.[1] As a bouquet I send you my
best kisses.

1.   St Louis's Day is August 25.

～

To Louise Colet

                    [Croisset,] Monday night. [August 24, 1846]
   I shan't be able to write you tomorrow, dearly beloved, nor
perhaps the day after; but Friday at the latest (I'll try to make it
Thursday) you'll have a long letter from me. We[1] set out tomorrow
morning (I'll see that it's not until after the postman comes), for a
little trip to a region nine leagues from here. We won't be back until
Wednesday night. We are going to visit some old Gothic abbeys –
Jumièges, where Agnès Sorel is buried, Saint-Wandrille, etc. I shall
be thinking of you throughout this trip, and missing you. If you

knew how long my days are now, and how cold my nights, bereft as they are of all the joys of love!

. . .

In the sublime cynicism of your love you are taking pleasure in the hypothesis of a child who may be born. You desire a child – admit it. You are wishing for one, as yet another bond that would unite us; as a contract, sealed by fate that would weld together our two destinies. Oh! It is only because you are you, dear and too tender friend, that I am not angry with you for a wish that poses such an appalling threat to my happiness. I, who have sworn to myself that I will never again link any being to my own: I, to give birth to another! If it happens I'll not complain. Since the heart is so idiotically illogical, who knows whether as a man I may not experience a spasm of divine joy? Yes, I'm sure I would love that child of ours. If you died I'd bring it up, and all my affection would probably be transferred to it. But the very idea sends a shiver up my spine. And if to prevent its coming into the world I had to leave the world, the Seine is right here, and I'd jump in this very moment with a 36-pound cannon ball attached to my feet.

Don't be afraid that I would be reproachful or harsh with you. After all, you have your share of suffering. And so mine will keep silent and out of sight. I confess that in two weeks I shall perhaps be relieved of an enormous weight. My lack of precaution will hang over my soul like the sword of Damocles. In all our future ecstasies I will always keep this possible danger in mind. No matter! That is not the best part of our love. It's only the sauce, as Rabelais would say: the meat is your soul. You wept, the first time on Wednesday; you thought I wasn't happy, isn't it so? I was, though, more so than I have ever been, as happy as I could be. I shall be happier still, for I love you more and more; I want to keep telling you so and proving it to you.

1. Flaubert and Maxime DuCamp. DuCamp had not yet met Louise. Soon, however, after Louise's husband returned to Paris following a summer's absence, DuCamp would be doubly used as the lovers' post office; and later, when relations soured, he would become the repository of their mutual complaints. DuCamp soon became exasperated with Louise, a fact she quickly sensed despite what seems to have been prolonged courtesy on his part. For Flaubert to tell her, at this early date, that he could not write to

her because he was off on a walk with DuCamp was the first step towards
making DuCamp a target of Louise's eventual invective in her letters to
Flaubert. DuCamp was 'a bad influence', he 'came between' them, he
'turned Flaubert against' her.

~

To Louise Colet

[Croisset,] Wednesday, 10 p.m. [August 26, 1846]

What would I learn from those wonderful newspapers you so
want me to take each morning, with my bread and butter and cup
of coffee? Why should I care what they say? I have very little curiosity
about the news, politics bores me to death, and the literary articles
stink. To me it's all stupid-making and irritating . . . Yes, newspapers
disgust me profoundly – I mean the ephemeral, things of the
moment, what is important today and won't be tomorrow. This is
not insensitivity. It is simply that I sympathize as much, perhaps
even more, with the past misfortunes of those who are dead and no
longer thought of – all the cries they uttered, now unheard. I feel
no more pity for the lot of the modern working classes than for that
of the ancient slaves who turned the millstones. I am no more
modern than I am ancient, no more French than Chinese; and the
idea of *la patrie*, the fatherland – that is, the obligation to live on a
bit of earth coloured red or blue on a map, and to detest the other
bits coloured green or black – has always seemed to me narrow,
restricted, and ferociously stupid. I am the brother in God of everything that lives, from the giraffe and the crocodile to man, and the
fellow-citizen of everyone inhabiting the great furnished mansion
called the universe . . . Poetry is a free plant. It grows where no one
has ever seeded it. The poet is simply the patient botanist who scales
mountains to gather it.

And now that I have unburdened my heart – for we have
returned to this subject several times without your wishing to understand it – let's talk about ourselves, and kiss each other, sweetly and
lingeringly, on the lips.

Yesterday and today we had a splendid walk. I saw ruins, ruins
which I loved in my youth, which I already knew, and had often
visited with those who are no more. I thought of them, and of those
other dead whom I never knew, and whose empty graves I was

walking on. I have a particular love for the vegetation that grows in ruins. That invasion of man's work by nature as soon as his hand is no longer there to defend it rejoices me immensely and profoundly. Life comes to superimpose itself on Death: it makes plants grow in petrified skulls; and on the stone where one of us has carved his dream the Life Principle reasserts itself with every new blossoming of the yellow wallflowers. I find it a sweet thought that one day I'll help tulips grow. Who knows? The tree at whose feet I'll be laid may bear splendid fruit. I'll perhaps make superb manure, a superior kind of guano.

. . . It gave you pleasure, poor angel, the name-day bouquet I sent you! It wasn't my idea to put those eloquent flowers in my letter: I was unaware of their symbolic meaning. It was DuCamp who taught it to me and advised me to make use of it. I thought that bit of childishness would amuse your heart. It greatly amused mine!

. . . I often think of our dear Bois de Boulogne. You remember our first ride, on July 30th? How Henriette was sleeping on the cushions?[1] And the gentle motion of the springs; and our hands – and our glances, even more closely entwined. My heart was warm and soft. I saw your eyes shining in the dark. Your pupils stared into mine, and I drank their long emanations with a kind of ecstasy. When will all that happen again? Who knows? Who knows? Oh, never accuse me of forgetting – never! That would be unspeakably cruel. Keep loving me, for my love is constant. *Adieu*, a thousand kisses on your lovely throat, on those breasts you offer to my lips, smiling so sweetly as you say, 'So you like me? You love me?' Do I like you! Do I love you! A deaf man who saw me writing to you would know the answer: he would only have to *look* at my body. Once more *adieu*, a thousand loves. Don't be afraid, my dear: I have your letter telling me that your blood should come on the 10th.[2]

1. Louise Colet's six-year-old daughter.
2. See p. 111, n.2.

~

Such are Flaubert's first 'love' letters to Louise Colet. Barely a month had passed since their first meeting at Pradier's, and already Flaubert had offended by waiting almost three weeks before making the short trip to Paris to see her again. Forced to realize that for him 'affair' seemed to mean chiefly 'correspondence', she responded by sharpening her tone.

During the eighteen months of this, the first of their two liaisons, Flaubert would write Louise about one hundred letters, but he managed to see her only six times. Baffled and irritated by the contrast between Flaubert's eloquent and undoubted passion and his prolonged absences, Louise had to struggle also with his many other inconsistencies; and she continued to object to the amount of extraneous matter – so she found it – with which he filled the pages he sent her.

The letters which follow reflect, perhaps explain – and to some extent excuse – Louise's growing acerbity. In them, Flaubert will continue – to our advantage, if not to hers – to reveal his attitudes on art and literature, on sex and politics; and, above all, to reveal himself.

~

To Louise Colet

[Croisset,] Sunday, 2 p.m. [August 30, 1846]

Anger! Good God! Vituperation, invective! Lurid language! What does it mean? That you like disputes, recriminations, all the bitter daily wrangling that ends by making life a real hell? I don't understand. You complain of my hard words, but it seems to me that I never sent you any to equal these. Perhaps you'll say I have written to you even more harshly: everyone has his illusions. But in your letter of this morning I see something more, a deliberate intent to be nasty, or to seem so. Who knows? Perhaps it's a trial, a ploy. Your neverending reproach is that I'm always posing, theatrical, vain, that I parade my sorrows like a swashbuckler displaying his scars. According to you I keep hurting you to my heart's content, pretending to weep in order to draw tears from you. What an atrocious idea! How can you love me if you see me as such a wretch? If so, you must despise me – perhaps you really do despise me? You are no doubt already having regrets, you see that you made a mistake, and I'm the one who's to blame for your lost illusion. But remember that my very first words were a cry of warning to you; and when our enthusiasm swept us both away I never stopped telling you to save yourself while there was still time. Was that vanity? Was that arrogance? I might have done the opposite – lied, told you how wonderful I was, acted the sublime. You would have believed me. Then you would have thought me good, precisely because I was being a hypocrite.

What shall I tell you? What shall I do? I'm at a loss. It takes courage to write to you, knowing that whatever I say wounds you. The caresses that cats give their females draw blood, and an exchange of jabs is part of their pleasure. Why do they keep doing it? Nature impels them: I must be the same as they. Every word of mine is a wound I give you: every loving impulse is taken as an insult. Ah, my poor dear Louise, nothing prepared me for anything like this, not even my most far-reaching anticipations of possible misfortunes.

How could you think I would love you the less if you had a child by me? On the contrary, I would love you more. A thousand times more. Wouldn't you be much more closely bound to me, by our common suffering, by my gratitude, even pity? That last word still shocks you, perhaps. But don't take it in its banal, narrow sense: think of its most personal, emotional, disinterested implications. You think that because of this continual fear of a new life that might result from a moment of inattention, you and I will no longer know rapture and divine forgetfulness? To tell the truth, I see this very rapture as a disturbing concomitant of love, because it is always followed by remorse. Why confuse your anxiety over an impending disaster with the happiness you give me? Usually I may not be blessed with common sense, as you keep telling me, but in this case it doesn't seem to me that I'm the one who lacks it. If I cared only for my own enjoyment, if all I asked of love were merely physical pleasure, then my behaviour would be different: surely that is obvious to anyone. Come, darling, I am not yet as coarse as you say. There is something I love even more than your lovely body, and that is your self. Do you know what you lack, or rather what you sin against? Discernment. You find hidden meanings where they don't exist, in places where no one dreamed of concealing them. You exaggerate everything, you magnify, you carry things much too far. Where the devil did you ever get the idea that I wrote you anything like this: 'I never loved the women I possessed, and those I loved never granted me anything'?[1] I simply told you that for six years I loved a woman who never in her life knew it. That would have seemed stupid to her. It seems so to me, now. After that, until I met you, I never loved, because I didn't want to love, that's all. Don't think I belong to that vulgar race of men who feel disgust after pleasure, love existing for them only as lust. No: in me, what rises doesn't subside so quickly. If moss grows on the castles of my heart as soon as they are built, at any rate it takes time for them to fall into ruin, if they ever do so completely.

Jeer at me as much as you like – at my life, at that boundless vanity you have just discovered (you are the Christopher Columbus of that discovery), at my pantheist beliefs. In all that, there is not the slightest wish to impress you or to seem original. I don't make a show of extravagance. If I'm extravagant, so much the worse – or the better.

. . . One has to be obsessed with eccentricity to find it in me, who lead the most bourgeois, the most obscure life in the world. I shall die in my corner without anyone being able, I hope, to blame me for a wicked deed or a bad line, the reason being that I do not make others my concern and will do nothing to make myself theirs. It is difficult for me to detect 'extravagance' in so commonplace a life.

But beneath that existence lies another, a secret *other*, all radiant and illuminated for me alone. One that I display to no one, because it would arouse laughter. Is that so unreasonable?

Have no fear that I show your letters to anyone at all. No: you can be sure of that. DuCamp knows only that I write to a woman in Paris who will perhaps need his help next winter with our letters. He sees me writing to you every day. But he doesn't yet know your name. He behaves similarly in matters of his own, and neither of us asks questions of the other. He merely lent me, the other day, the seal that has his motto.

I'm sorry Phidias isn't coming. He is a splendid man and a great artist, yes, a great artist, a real Greek, the most ancient of all the moderns. A man who doesn't let himself worry about anything – not politics, nor socialism, nor Fourier, nor the Jesuits, nor the University. Instead, he rolls up his sleeves like a good workman and is there to do his job from morning till night, desiring to do it well and loving his art. That is everything, love of art. But I'll stop: this must be irritating you again; you don't like to hear me say that I worry more about a line of verse than about any man, and that I'm more grateful to the poets than to saints and heroes. In old Rome, no one would have been shocked had a man approached Horace and said: 'Oh, my good Flaccus, how is your ode to Melpomene coming along? Tell me about your passion for the little Persian boy whom Pollion has let you have: will you be writing about him in Asclepiadics or iambics? Everything you say is much more interesting to me than the Parthian war or the Pontifical College or the Valerian Law they want to bring up again.' In other words, there was something of greater consequence than the men who were dying for their country or praying for it or working to make it more prosperous: namely, the men who were celebrating it in verse. Because only they survive. New worlds have been discovered where they can be read. Printing was invented to spread their fame. Ah! Yes, the love of Glycera or Lycoris will outlive future civilizations. Like a star, Art watches undisturbed as the world spins round. Shining in its blue immensity, the Beautiful keeps its place in the firmament. But all this is annoying you. So what shall I tell you? That I kiss you . . .

1. But see p. 75.

~

TO LOUISE COLET

> *[Croisset,] Sunday night. [September 13, 1846]*
> I am very worried about your health, poor darling, about your vomiting and that cursed blood that doesn't come. I beg you to make sure of your condition as quickly as possible. Ask your doctor. If he has any intelligence he will understand immediately. Or consult another one, some competent doctor who doesn't know you. Tell him it happens with you sometimes, and ask him what one can do to make certain. Before making that journey, you should know how things stand, no?[1] And if you don't try what I advise (a remedy to bring on the Redcoats),[2] how will you know why they are staying away? Quite often something in the mind is enough to keep them back, almost any kind of emotion. You would be mad to travel down there to prevent a danger that may not exist. I think this advice very sensible. I beg you, beseech you, to follow it. And burn this letter,

it is more prudent. We must think of everything. Don't do anything rash, don't tempt misfortune: you know how that monster lies in wait for his victims. If you like, I'll procure and send you an opinion, one that I guarantee in advance will be good. Think about all this and answer me promptly.

I am depressed, troubled, a mass of nerves. I feel the way I did two years ago, horribly on edge. Everything wounds me, tears me to pieces. Your last two letters made my heart beat almost to bursting. They move me so, when I unfold them and your perfume rises from the paper and the fragrance of your caressing words penetrates me to the heart. Spare me; you make me giddy with your love! We must convince ourselves, however, that we cannot live together. We must resign ourselves to a flatter, more pallid existence. I wish that you would accustom yourself to this; I want the thought of me to comfort you, not consume you; to console you, not drive you to despair. What can we do, darling? It must be so. We cannot continue with these convulsions of the soul. The despondency that follows is a kind of death. Work, think of other things. You have so much intelligence: use a little of it to become more serene. I am at the end of my strength. I had plenty of courage for myself: but for two! My role is to sustain everyone, and I am exhausted. Don't distress me with your outbursts, which make me curse myself without seeing any remedy.

. . . I must scold you about something that shocks and scandalizes me, namely how little you care about Art now.[3] You care about fame – so be it: I approve; but Art, the only true and good thing in life! Can you compare any earthly love to it? Can you prefer the adoration of some relative beauty to the cult of the True? Let me say this: there is only one good thing about me, only one thing in myself that I think estimable – I can *admire*. You adulterate the Beautiful with a mass of extraneous things – the useful, the agreeable, and who knows what else. Tell the Philosopher[4] to explain to you the idea of Pure Beauty as he expounded it in his course in 1819, and as I conceive it. We'll speak about it next time.

I am now reading an Indian play, *Sakountala*,[5] and studying some Greek. It isn't going very well, my poor Greek: your face keeps coming between the book and my eyes.

Adieu, chérie; be good, love me *well* and I will love you *much*:

for that's what you want, my voracious darling. A thousand kisses and a thousand tender thoughts.

1. Louise was apparently planning, rather precipitately, to visit a *faiseur d'anges* – an abortionist – in some distant town.
2. '*Les Anglais sont débarqués*' – 'The Redcoats have landed' – is an expression of relief well known to French lovers. Louise's Redcoats landed a day or two later. Flaubert had confided his anxiety to Maxime DuCamp, who wrote to him on September 20: 'My sincere congratulations to you, and to her too, whatever she may say.' Several subsequent delays of the same kind are chronicled in the course of the correspondence.
3. For a remark made by Louise a few days earlier, when the lovers had met in Mantes (between Paris and Rouen) – the remark that triggered the present upbraiding – see p. 133.
4. Victor Cousin.
5. A 'mytho-pastoral drama' in seven acts by the Sanskrit poet Kalidasa – 'abounding', says the *Encyclopaedia Britannica*, 'in stanzas of exquisite tenderness and fine descriptive passages'.

～

To Louise Colet
[Croisset,] Monday, 10 p.m. [September 14, 1846]
. . .

If I were in Paris . . . how I would love you! I would sicken, die, stupefy myself, from loving you; I would become nothing but a kind of sensitive plant which only your kisses would bring to life. No middle course! Life! And life is precisely that: love, love, sexual ecstasy. Or, something which resembles that but is its negation: namely, the Idea, the contemplation of the Immutable – in a word, Religion, in the broadest sense. I feel that you are too lacking in that, my love. I mean, it seems to me that you do not greatly adore Genius, that you do not tremble to your very entrails at the contemplation of the beautiful. It is not enough to have wings: they must bear you aloft. One of these days I will write you a long literary letter. Today I finished *Sakountala*. India dazzles me. It is superb. My studies of Brahminism this winter have nearly driven me crazy. There have been moments when I thought I'd lost my wits . . .

～

To Louise Colet

[Croisset,] Friday, 10 p.m. [September 18, 1846]
. . .

You tell me, my angel, that I have not initiated you into my inner life, into my most secret thoughts. Do you know what is most intimate, most hidden, in my heart, and what is most authentically myself? Two or three modest ideas about art, lovingly brooded over; that is all. The greatest events of my life have been a few thoughts, a few books, certain sunsets on the beach at Trouville, and talks five or six hours long with a friend now married and lost to me.[1] I have always seen life differently from others, and the result has been that I've always isolated myself (but not sufficiently, alas!) in a state of harsh unsociability, with no exit. I suffered so many humiliations, I so shocked people and made them indignant, that I long ago came to realize that in order to live in peace one must live alone and seal one's windows lest the air of the world seep in. In spite of myself I still retain something of this habit. That is why I deliberately avoided the company of women for several years. I wanted no hindrance to my innate moral precept. I wanted no yoke, no influence. In the end I no longer desired women's company at all. Stirrings of the flesh, throbbings of the heart, were absent from my life, and I was not even conscious of my sex. As I told you, I had an overwhelming passion when I was little more than a child. When it ended I decided to divide my life in two parts: to put on one side my soul, which I reserved for Art, and on the other my body, which was to live as best it could. Then you came along and upset all that. So here I am, returning to a human existence!

You have awakened all that was slumbering, or perhaps decaying, within me! I had been loved before, and intensely, though I'm one of those who are quickly forgotten and more apt to kindle emotion than to keep it alive. The love I arouse is always that felt for something a little strange. Love, after all, is only a superior kind of curiosity, an appetite for the unknown that makes you bare your breast and plunge headlong into the storm.

As I said, I have been loved before, but *never the way you love me*; nor has there ever been between a woman and myself the bond that exists between us two. I have never felt for any woman so deep a devotion, so irresistible an attraction; never has there been such complete communion. Why do you keep saying that I love the tinselly, the showy, the flashy? 'Poet of form!' That is the favourite term of abuse hurled by utilitarians at true artists. For my part, until someone comes along and separates for me the form and the substance of a given sentence, I shall continue to maintain that that distinction is meaningless. Every beautiful thought has a beautiful form, and vice versa.[2] In the world of Art, beauty is a by-product of form, just as in our world temptation is a by-product of love. Just as you cannot remove from a physical body the qualities that constitute it – colour, extension, solidity – without reducing it to a hollow abstraction, without destroying it, so you cannot remove the form from the Idea, because the Idea exists only by virtue of its form. Imagine an idea that has no form – such a thing is as impossible as a form that expresses no idea. Such are the stupidities on which criticism feeds. Good stylists are reproached for neglecting the Idea, the moral goal; as though the goal of the doctor were not to heal, the goal of the painter to paint, the goal of the nightingale to sing, as though the goal of Art were not, first and foremost, Beauty!

Sculptors who create real women, with breasts that can contain milk and thighs that suggest fecundity, are accused of sensualism. Whereas, were they to carve wads of drapery and figures flat as signboards, they would be called idealists, spiritualists. 'Yes, he does neglect form, it's true,' people would say, 'but he is a thinker!' Whereupon the bourgeois, with cries of joy, would outdo themselves to admire what bores them. It's easy, with the help of conventional jargon, and two or three ideas acceptable as common coin, to pass as a socialist humanitarian writer, a renovator, a harbinger of the evangelical future dreamed of by the poor and the mad. Such is the modern mania: one blushes to be a writer. If you merely write verse or a novel, merely carve marble, shame! That was acceptable previously, before the poet had a 'social mission'. Now every piece of writing must have its moral significance, must teach its lesson, elementary or advanced; a sonnet must be endowed with philosophical implications, a play must rap the knuckles of royalty, and a watercolour contribute to moral progress. Everywhere there is pettifoggery, the craze for spouting and orating: the muse becomes a mere pedestal for a thousand unholy desires. Poor Olympus! They'd be capable of planting a potato patch on its summit! If it were only the mediocrities who were involved, one would let them do as they liked. But no – vanity has banished pride, and caused a thousand little cupidities to spring up where formerly a single, noble ambition prevailed. Even men of parts, great men, ask themselves: 'Why not seize the moment? Why not impress these people now, hour after hour, instead of being admired by them later?' Whereupon they mount the tribune. They join the staff of a newspaper, and there we see them lending the weight of their immortal names to ephemeral theories.

They intrigue to overthrow some minister who would topple without them – when with a single line of satirical verse they could make his name a synonym for infamy. They concern themselves with taxes, customs-duties, laws, peace and war! How petty all this is! How transient! How false and secondary! All these wretched things excite them – they attack all the crooks, gush over every decent action no matter how commonplace, cry their eyes out over every poor fellow who is murdered, every dog that's run over – as though this were the sole purpose of their lives. To me it seems finer to stand at a distance of several centuries and thrill whole generations, fill them with pure pleasures. Who can measure the ecstasy that Homer has inspired, or count the tears that the excellent Horace has changed into smiles? To speak only of myself, I am grateful to Plutarch because of evenings he gave me at the lycée, evenings filled with warlike ardour, as though the clash of armies were in my very soul.

1. Alfred LePoittevin.
2. Flaubert had read Hegel's *Aesthetics*. (J.B.)

~

To Louise Colet

[Croisset,] Tuesday, 10 a.m. [September 22, 1846]
· · ·

Thank you for your letter of this morning. I was waiting for the postman on the quay, looking unconcerned and smoking my pipe. I love that postman! I've left orders in the kitchen that he's to have a glass of wine to refresh him. He likes this house and is very punctual. Yesterday he brought me nothing, so he got nothing.

You send me everything you can find to gratify my love for you; you pass on to me all the tributes you receive. I read Plato's[1] letter with the keenest possible concentration; I found many things in it, very many. Essentially, he's a man whose heart, despite all he may do to make it appear serene, is cold and empty; his life is dreary, without radiance, I am sure. But he greatly loved you and still does, with a love that is deep and lonely; he will feed on it a long time. I found his letter painful; I looked into the very depths of this colourless existence, filled with tasks undertaken without enthusiasm and carried out with a dogged obstinacy which is the only thing that keeps him going. Your love brought him a little joy. He clung to it with an old man's hunger for life. You were his last passion, and the only thing that reconciled him to himself. He is, I think, jealous of Béranger – the life and fame of this latter can scarcely afford him much pleasure.[2] As a rule the philosopher is a kind of mongrel being, a cross between scientist and poet, envious of both. Metaphysics puts a lot of rancour into the blood – a very curious and very interesting phenomenon. I was considerably engrossed by it for a couple of years, but it was a waste of time I now regret.

You wrote something very true: 'Love is a great comedy, and so is life, when you're not playing one of the roles.' Only I won't concede that it makes you laugh. About a year and a half ago I experienced a living illustration of this, something that happened spontaneously, I mean. I preferred not to witness the very end. At that time I often visited a family in which there was a charming young girl,[3] marvellously beautiful – of a very Christian, almost Gothic, beauty, if I can put it that way. She was a pure spirit, easily susceptible to emotion; one moment she'd be crying, the next laughing, like sunshine after a shower. The feelings of this lovely, innocent creature were entirely at the mercy of my words. I can still see her lying against her pink cushion and looking at me, as I read, with her great blue eyes. One day we were alone, sitting on a sofa; she took my hand, twined her fingers in mine; this I let her do without thinking (most of the time I'm a great innocent), and she gave me a look which still makes me shiver. Just then her mother entered, took in everything, and smiled at what she thought was the acquisition of a son-in-law. I'll not forget that smile – the most sublime thing ever seen. It was a compound of indulgent benevolence and genteel vulgarity. I am sure that the poor girl had been carried away by an irresistible affectionate impulse, one of those moments of mawkish sentimentality when everything within you seems to be melting and dissolving – a voluptuous anguish that would fill you with delight if only it didn't bring you to the verge of sobs and tears. You cannot conceive the terror I felt. I returned home shattered, reproaching myself for being alive. I don't know whether I exaggerated the situation, but even though I did not love her I'd gladly have given my life to redeem that sad, loving look to which I had not responded.

. . . What a horrible invention the bourgeois is, don't you agree? Why is he in the world? And what is he doing there, poor wretch? For my part, I cannot imagine how people unconcerned with art can spend their time: how they live is a mystery to me.

You are perhaps right in what you say about excessive reading killing the imagination, the individual element, the one thing, after all, that has some value. But I'm engaged in a number of tasks I must finish; and besides, these days I am continually afraid to write – afraid of botching my outlines, so I put off doing anything with them.

. . . *Adieu*; it's time for me to leave you. I am yours, dear love, I who love you and kiss your breasts. Look at them, and say: he is dreaming of your roundness, and his desire rests its head on you.

1. Victor Cousin, now fifty-fourth.
2. Pierre-Jean Béranger (1780–1857), the writer of sentimental verse, enjoyed such immense popularity that, in 1828, when for the second time he was fined and imprisoned for satires against the regime, the fine was paid by popular subscription.
3. Henriette Collier.

~

To Louise Colet

    [Croisset,] Sunday morning, 11 a.m. [September 27, 1846]

You're surprised that I judged the Philosopher so accurately, without knowing him? That's because, in spite of appearances, I've had considerable experience. You didn't want to believe that, when I told you at the very beginning. I am ripe. Early ripe, it's true, because I have lived in a hothouse. I never pose as a man of experience – that would be too stupid. But I observe a great deal, and never make conclusions – an infallible way not to be mistaken. In a personal affair I once got the better of some supposedly astute people of importance, which gave me a very poor opinion of their abilities.[1] Practical life is loathsome to me: the mere necessity of sitting down in a dining room at fixed hours fills my soul with a feeling of wretchedness. But when I participate in it (in practical life), when I sit down (at table), I know how to behave like anyone else.

You'd like me to meet Béranger. I should like it, too. He is a grand old man; I find him appealing. But – and now I speak of his works – he is immensely unfortunate in the kind of people who admire him. There are tremendous geniuses who have but one defect, one vice – that of being especially appreciated by the vulgar, by people susceptible to cheap poetry. For thirty years Béranger has been the inspiration for the love life of students and the erotic dreams of travelling salesmen. I know perfectly well he doesn't write for them, but it's those people in particular who appreciate him. Say what you will, popularity, which seems to give genius greater scope, actually vulgarizes it; authentic Beauty is not for the masses, especially in France. *Hamlet* will always give less pleasure than *Mademoiselle de Belle-Isle*.[2] Béranger expresses no passions that *I* feel, no dreams that I dream; his poetry is not mine. I read him historically; he is a man of another age. He was right for his time, but is no longer right for ours. The happy, carefree love that he so joyously celebrates in his garret window is very foreign to us who are young today; we can admire it as we might admire the hymn of some extinct religion, but it cannot move us. I've heard so many fools, so many narrow-minded bourgeois, sing his songs about beggars and the 'God of the good folks' that he must really be a great poet to have kept my esteem despite all the hullabaloo. For my own consumption I prefer geniuses a little less agreeable to the touch, more disdainful of the people, more reserved, more haughty in their manner and their tastes; or else the only man who can take the place of all others, my adored Shakespeare, whom I am now going to start reading from one end to the other, and whom I shall not abandon this time until the volumes fall apart in my hands. When I read Shakespeare I become greater, wiser, purer. When I have reached the crest of one of his works I feel that I am high on a mountain: everything disappears, everything appears. I am no longer a man, I am an *eye*. New horizons loom, perspectives extend to infinity. I forget I have been living like other men in the barely discernible hovels below, that I've been drinking from all those distant rivers that appear smaller than brooks, that I have participated in all the confusion of the anthill. Long ago, in a burst of happy pride (I should dearly love to recapture it), I wrote a sentence that you will understand. Speaking of the joy experienced in reading the great poets, I said: 'I often felt that the rapture they kindled in me made me their equal and raised me to a level with themselves' . . .[3]

1.   The matter of securing Achille Flaubert's succession to his father's post at the Hôtel-Dieu.
2.   A play by Alexandre Dumas.
3.   From *Novembre*.

~

To Louise Colet

[Croisset,] Monday morning. [September 28, 1846]

No! Once again, no! I protest, I swear: others may feel nothing but contempt after possession, but I am not like them, and I glory in not being so. On the contrary, for me possession breeds affection. If I weren't afraid of shocking you yet again, I'd say – indeed I *will* say: '*Je suis comme les cigares, on ne m'allume qu'en tirant.*'[1]

. . . As for Mme Foucaud, she is certainly the one I knew.[2] Is your cousin sufficiently reliable to be entrusted with a letter? Can I be sure he'll deliver it? For I feel like writing to Mme Foucaud. She's an old acquaintance; don't be jealous of her. You shall read the letter if you like, on condition you don't tear it up. Your word will be enough. If I thought of you as a commonplace woman I should not tell you all this. But what you dislike, perhaps, is precisely the fact that I treat you like a man and not like a woman. Try to put some of your intelligence into your relations with me. Later your heart will thank your mind for this. I thought at first that I would find in you less feminine personality, a more universal conception of life. But no! The heart, the heart! That poor heart, that kind heart, that charming heart with its eternal graces, is always there, even in the noblest and greatest women. As a rule men do everything they can to vex the heart, to make it bleed. They steep themselves with subtle sensuality in all those tears that they themselves don't shed, in all those little agonies they see as proofs of their strength. If I had a taste for that sort of pleasure it would be easy for me to enjoy it with you.

But no, I should like to make of you something entirely apart – neither friend nor mistress. Each of those categories is too restricted, too exclusive – one doesn't sufficiently love a friend, and one is too idiotic with a mistress. It is the intermediate term that I seek, the essence of those two sentiments combined. What I want, in short, is that, like a new kind of hermaphrodite, you give me with your body all the joys of the flesh and with your mind all those of the soul. Will you understand that? I fear it isn't clear. It's strange how bad my writing is, in these letters to you; I put no literary vanity into it. One thing conflicts with another. It's as though I wanted to say three words at a time.

. . . In writing this to you, I'm inaugurating my new armchair, in which I am destined to spend long years – if I live. What will I write in it? God knows. Will it be good or bad, tender or erotic, sad or gay? A little of each, probably – adding up to nothing. No matter: may this inauguration bless all my future work! Winter has come, the rain is falling, my fire is burning: now comes the season of long hours shut indoors. Soon now the silent, lamp-lit evenings, watching the wood burn and listening to the wind. *Adieu*, bright moonlight on the green grass, blue nights all spangled with stars. *Adieu*, my darling: I kiss you with all my soul . . .

1. A pun. To light (*allumer*) a cigar, one 'draws' (*tire*); but *tirer* here refers to the expression *tirer un coup* – perform the sexual act. The more he makes love to a woman the more he is attracted. (J.B.)
2. Flaubert had written to Louise a week before: 'By the way, while I think of it, ask your cousin, since he lived in Cayenne, to give you news of two people, M. Brache and Mme Foucaud de Langlade. The latter must have left there some time ago.' Flaubert's spelling of the lady's name varies.

∾

To Louise Colet
                    [Croisset,] Wednesday, 9 p.m. [September 30, 1846]
                              · · ·

So what the devil do you want me to talk to you about if not
Shakespeare, if not what lies closest to my heart? That I have more
imagination than heart, as you remark, I should like very much to
believe; but I doubt it, for I feel I have very little. When I consider
my plans on the one hand and Art on the other, I echo the cry of
Breton sailors: 'Oh God, how vast the sea, and how small my boat!'
Is it possible that you reproach me for the innocent affection I feel
for an armchair? If I spoke to you about my shoes I think you'd be
jealous of them. Come! I love you dearly all the same, and I kiss
you on the lips, my darling. One more kiss between the breasts, and
one on each finger. Take care of your hands, and let your nails grow
longer. You know you promised. *Adieu, adieu,* a thousand warm
caresses.

⌇

To Louise Colet
                         [Croisset,] Saturday, 8 a.m. [October 3, 1846]
                              · · ·

Come now, smile, kiss me. Stop being hurt because I speak to
you about Shakespeare rather than myself. It's simply that he strikes
me as more interesting. And what should one speak of (I ask you once
more) if not what fills one's mind? As for me, I fail to understand how
those people exist who are not from morning to night in an aesthetic
state. I have enjoyed more than many the pleasures of family, as
much as any man of my age the pleasures of the senses, more than
many the pleasures of love. But I know of no delight to compare
with that given me by some of the illustrious dead whose works I
have read or seen. The three finest things God ever made are the
sea, *Hamlet,* and Mozart's *Don Giovanni.* Are you going to be
offended again by all this? You mustn't be, for such a reproach doesn't
represent your true feelings. It may surge up at a moment of nervous
irritation, but cannot persist for ever in the depths of your heart . . .

⌇

To Louise Colet

[Croisset,] Wednesday morning. [October 7, 1846]
· · ·

How rapturous your letter is, how ardent, how heartfelt! Because I tell you I'll soon be coming, you approve everything in me, you shower me with caresses and praise. You no longer reproach me for my whims, my love of rhetoric, the refinements of my selfishness, etc. But should anything arise to prevent my coming, the whole thing would begin over again, would it not? Oh, my child, my child, how young you still are! Love is a springtime plant that perfumes everything with its hope, even the ruins to which it clings. I don't mean by this that you're a ruin, my darling. I mean that though you claim to be older than I in years, you are younger. You think of me a little as Madame de Sévigné thought of Louis XIV: 'Oh, what a great king!' because he danced with her. Because you love me you think me handsome, intelligent, sublime; you predict great things for me. No, no, you're mistaken. Once I had all those ideas about myself. Every moron has dreamed of being a great man, and every donkey who ever peered at himself in the water of the stream he was crossing has enjoyed the sight and been sure he was a handsome horse. I lack many qualities, many of the very best, that are needed if one is to do something good. I have written a few pages here and there that are excellent, but no complete work. I have a book in mind now that would show me whether I am any good.[1] But this book may never be written. Too bad: it would have meant a lot to those who read it.

Among navigators there are some who discover worlds, who add new continents to the earth and new constellations to the heavens: they are the masters, eternally splendid. Others belch terror from their vessels' guns and wax rich and fat from their plunder. Still others leave home to seek gold and silk under foreign skies. And still others merely let down their nets to catch salmon for gourmets and cod for the poor. I am the obscure and patient pearl-fisher, who dives deep and comes up empty-handed and blue in the face. A fatal attraction draws me down into the abysses of thought, down to those innermost recesses that never lose their fascination for the strong. I shall spend my life watching the ocean of art where others are sailing or fighting; and from time to time I'll entertain myself by plunging to the bottom in search of green or yellow shells. No one will want them, so I'll keep them for myself alone, and use them to cover the walls of my hut.

1. Jean Bruneau thinks that this may still be the oriental tale, *Les Sept Fils du derviche*, mentioned on p. 32, n. 2.

~

To Louise Colet

[Croisset,] Thursday, 10 p.m. [October 8, 1846]

. . .

I should love to have you here tonight – kiss your lips, to pass my hands through your lovely curls, lay my head on your breast – even though this last is forbidden since you saw that in my letter to Mme Foucaud I spoke of hers. So you found that letter a little too tender? I shouldn't have thought so. On the contrary, it seemed to me there were moments of insolence in it, and that the general tone was slightly condescending. You say that I seriously loved that woman. It is not so. Only when I was writing to her, with my faculty of arousing myself with my pen, I took my subject seriously; but *only while I was writing*. Many things that leave me cold when I see them or when others talk about them enrapture me, irritate me, or hurt me if I speak of them, and especially if I write. That is one of the effects of my mountebank nature. My father finally forbade me to imitate certain people (he was persuaded that I suffered greatly in doing it – which was true, though I denied it), among others an epileptic beggar I met one day at the seashore. He told me his story: he had begun as a journalist, etc. It was superb. No question that when I acted out that chap I was inside his skin. Impossible to imagine anything more hideous than the spectacle I made at that moment. Do you understand the satisfaction it gave me? I am sure you don't.

To return to that worthy creature, I have given you the entire truth about her. I had other adventures, more or less droll. But even at the time, those bits of foolishness didn't touch my heart very closely, and I had only one true passion. I already told you of it. I was barely 15, and it lasted until I was 18. And when I saw that woman again after several years I had difficulty in recognizing her. I still see her sometimes, but rarely, and I look at her with the same astonishment the émigrés must have felt on coming back to their dilapidated châteaux: 'Is it possible I lived here?' And one tells oneself that these ruins haven't always been ruins, and that this derelict hearth, now exposed to rain and snow, was once a place where people warmed themselves.[1] There would be a magnificent story to write, but I am not the man who will do it, nor will anyone else – it would be too marvellous. The story of a modern man from age 7 to 20. Whoever accomplishes this task will remain as eternal as the human heart itself. When you like, I'll tell you something of this unknown drama that I have observed both in myself and in others. Something similar must take place in women, though I can scarcely believe it. I've never yet met one willing to show me frankly the ashes of her heart: they want to make you believe it's all glowing fire; and they actually believe that themselves . . .

1. Editors have thought that Flaubert wrote thus about Elise Schlesinger to forestall Louise Colet's jealousy of an old love. Elsewhere he speaks of her only with affection and regard, culminating in his portrayal of her as Mme Arnoux in the definitive *Éducation sentimentale*.

∼

TO LOUISE COLET

[Croisset,] Wednesday, 11 p.m. [October 14, 1846]

· · ·

Since my father and sister died, I have had no ambition left. They carried off my vanity in their shrouds, and they keep it. I don't know whether a single line by me will ever be printed. I am not like the fox who said the grapes he couldn't reach were too sour; instead, I am no longer hungry. Success doesn't tempt me. What does tempt me I can provide – my own approval. And even that I shall perhaps dispense with eventually, as I ought to have done with that of others. So I transfer all that to you. Work, meditate, meditate above all; condense your ideas – you know that lovely fragments are no use. Unity, unity, that is everything. The *whole*: that's what's lacking in all writers today, great and small. A thousand fine bits, no complete work. Compress your style: weave a fabric soft as silk and strong as a coat of mail. Forgive this advice, but I'd like to give you everything I desire for myself.

... I am working quite hard at the moment. I have several things I want to finish, things that bore me but with which I continue in the hope of extracting something from them later on. But next spring I'll really start to write again. I keep putting it off. A subject to write about is for me like a woman one is in love with: when she is going to yield, one trembles and is afraid. It's a voluptuous terror. One dares not attain one's desire.

... You mention Albert Aubert and M. Gaschon de Molesnes. Despise all those scamps. Why worry about the chatter of such magpies? It's a waste of time to read criticism. I pride myself on my ability to uphold the thesis that there hasn't been a single piece of good criticism since criticism was invented; that it serves no purpose except to annoy authors and blunt the sensibility of the public; and finally that critics write criticism because they are unable to be artists, just as a man unfit to bear arms becomes a police spy. I'd like to know what poets throughout the ages could have in common with the critics who have analysed their work. Plautus would have laughed at Aristotle had he known his rules; Corneille fought against those strictures. Voltaire, despite himself, felt the pinch of Boileau. We should all have been spared much that's bad in modern drama had it not been for W. Schlegel; and when the translation of Hegel is completed God knows where we'll go. And when to these you add the journalists, who aren't even equipped to hide their leprous jealousy under a show of learning!

There: I've let my hatred for criticism and critics carry me away. Those wretches have left me no room to kiss you; but that's what I do anyway, despite them. So, with their permission, a thousand great kisses on your lovely forehead, and on your eyes, so sweet, and on ...

⌇

To Louise Colet

[Croisset,] Friday, midnight. [October 23, 1846]

No, I do not scorn fame: one doesn't scorn what one cannot attain. More than many another's, my heart has been set pounding by that word. I used to spend long hours dreaming resounding triumphs for myself; the clamour would thrill me as though I really heard it. But, I don't know why, one fine day I awoke relieved of this desire, more completely than if it had been fulfilled. Then I saw myself in smaller dimension, and devoted all my faculties to observation of my nature – to sounding its depth, and especially to discovering its limitations. The poets I admired loomed all the grander, being now at a greater distance, and I truly enjoyed that humility, which might have maddened another man to death. For a gifted person to seek success is wanton self-mutilation, and to seek fame is perhaps self-destruction. For there are two classes of poet. The greatest, the rare true masters, are microcosms of mankind: not concerned with themselves or their own passions, discarding their own personality, they are, instead, absorbed in that of others; they reproduce the Universe, which is reflected in their works, scintillating, varied, manifold, like an entire sky mirrored in the sea with all its stars and all its azure. Then there are others, whose slightest cry is melodic, whose every tear wrings the heart, and who have only to speak of themselves to remain eternal. They might well have been unable to go further had they undertaken any different sort of work; they may lack breadth, but they have ardour and verve; had they been born with different temperaments, they might not have had genius. Byron belongs to this class, Shakespeare to the other. Indeed, who can tell me what Shakespeare loved, hated, or felt? He is a terrifying colossus: one can scarcely believe he was a man. Now, as for fame, one wants it pure, real, permanent, like that of those demigods: one stretches and strains, attempting to reach their level; one prunes the capricious naiveties and instinctive fantasies of one's talent, making them fit into a conventional type, into a ready-made mould. Or else one has the presumption to believe that it is enough to say, like Byron and Montaigne, what one thinks and feels, in order to create fine things. This latter course is perhaps the wisest for original people, because we would often have many more qualities if we didn't strive after them, and anyone capable of writing correctly would produce a superb book by setting down his memoirs, if he did so with complete sincerity. Thus – to revert to myself – I saw that I was neither of sufficient stature to produce genuine works of art, nor eccentric enough to be able to fill volumes with my *self* alone. And not having the ability needed to attain success, nor the genius to conquer fame, I am condemned to write solely for myself, for my own private diversion, as one smokes or rides on horseback. It is almost certain I shall never have a line printed; and my nephews (I say nephews in the proper sense, not wanting family posterity any more than I count on having any of the other variety) will probably make three-cornered hats for their grandchildren with my fantastic novels, and shades for their kitchen candles from my oriental tales, dramas, mystery plays, and the other twaddle I write out seriously, line by line, on good white paper. There, my dear Louise, once and for all, you have the essence of what I think concerning this subject and myself.

Today I've done nothing but think of you. This morning when I went to bed I thought of the thrill I experienced in bed at Mantes when I felt your thigh on my belly and your waist within my arms; and the impression of that thought stayed with me all day. But you don't want me to talk about all that. (What *am* I to talk to you about?) So let's talk of other things. You are right. It would have been better for you not to love me. Happiness is a usurer: for the loan of fifteen minutes of love it makes you pay with a whole cargo of misery . . .

∽

To Louise Colet

[Rouen,] Friday, 4 p.m. [December 11, 1846]

To deny the existence of lukewarm affections because they *are* lukewarm is to deny that the sun sometimes shines when it isn't high noon. There is as much truth in halftones as in violent colours. In my youth I had a true friend who was devoted to me, who would have given his life and his fortune for me, but wouldn't have got up half an hour earlier than usual to please me, or accelerated any of his actions. When you observe life with a little attention, you see cedars as being a little less tall and bushes somewhat higher. All the same, I don't like the habit some people have of disparaging great enthusiasms or minimizing sublime impulses that surpass nature. Thus Vigny's book, *Servitude et grandeur militaires*, shocked me a little at first glance because I saw in it a systematic depreciation of blind devotion (the cult of the Emperor, for example), of man's fanaticism for man, in favour of the abstract, dry idea of duty, a concept I've never been able to grasp and which does not seem to me inherent in human entrails. What is noble in the Empire is adoration of the Emperor, a love that is exclusive, absurd, sublime, truly human. That is why I have little understanding of what *la Patrie*, the fatherland, is for us today. I can readily grasp what it was for the Greek, who had only his city, for the Roman who had only Rome, for the savage tracked down in his forest, for the Arab pursued to his very tent. But for us ... Don't we, at bottom, feel just as Chinese or English as French? Aren't all our dreams of foreign places? As children we long to live in a land of parrots and candied dates, we're nurtured on Byron and Virgil, on rainy days we yearn for the Orient, or we want to go and make our fortunes in India, or grow sugarcane in America. *La Patrie* is the earth, the universe, the stars, the air. It is thought itself: that is, the Infinite within our breasts. But quarrels between one nation and another, between canton and arrondissement, between man and man, interest me little, and engage me only when represented in great pictures with crimson backgrounds.

~

To Louise Colet

[Rouen, end of December, 1846 (?)]

It is impossible for me to continue any longer a correspondence that is becoming epileptic. Change it, I beg. What have I done to you that you should unfold before me, with all the pride of grief, the spectacle of a despair for which I know no remedy? If I had betrayed you, publicly displayed you as my mistress, sold your letters, etc., you could scarcely write me things more atrocious or more distressing.

What have I done, good God? What have I done? You know quite well I cannot come to Paris. You seem to want to force me to answer you brutally; I am too well bred to do so, but it seems to me I have restated this often enough for you to bear it in mind.

I had formed quite a different idea of love. I thought it was something independent of everything, even of the person who inspired it. Absence, insult, infamy – all that does not affect it. When two persons love, they can go ten years without seeing each other and without suffering from it.[1]

You claim that I treat you like 'a woman of the lowest class', I don't know what 'a woman of the lowest class' is, nor of the highest class, nor of the next-highest. Women are relatively inferior or superior by reason of their beauty and the attraction they exert on us, that's all. You accuse me of being an aristocrat, but I have very democratic ideas on this subject. It's possible, as you say, that it is in the nature of moderate affections to be enduring. But in saying that, you condemn your own, for it is anything but moderate. As for myself, I am weary of grand passions, exalted feelings, frenzied loves, and howling despairs. I love good sense above all, perhaps because I have none.

I fail to understand why you are repeatedly offended, and sulk. You are at fault in this, for you are kind, most charming and lovable, and one cannot help holding it against you that you wantonly spoil it all.

Calm yourself, work, and when we meet again welcome me with a good laugh and tell me you've been silly.

1.   'What a sentence!' Louise wrote in the margin here.

≈

To Louise Colet
                    [Rouen,] Monday, 3 o'clock. [January 11, 1847]
                          · · ·

There are certain bourgeois satisfactions that are disgusting, and some ordinary joys whose vulgarity I find repugnant. That is why I have always taken against Béranger, with his lovers in their garrets and his idealization of the mediocre. I have never understood why, as he puts it, 'at twenty you're happy in a garret'. Would one be unhappy in a palace? Isn't it the poet's function to transport us elsewhere? I don't like to come upon grisette-love, a porter's lodge, and my threadbare overcoat in the realm where I go to forget all that. Let people who are happy among such things remain among them, but to represent them as being beautiful, no, no. I still prefer to dream of swansdown divans and hummingbird-feather hammocks, even if I suffer in doing so.

What an extraordinary idea of yours, that someone should continue *Candide*! Is it possible? Who will do it, who *could* do it? There are some works so overpoweringly great (and *Candide* is one of them), that their weight would crush anyone who tried to take them on. Giant's armour: the dwarf who put it on his back would be flattened before taking a single step. You do not admire enough, you do not respect enough. You have a genuine love of art, but not the religion of art. If you experienced a deep and pure delight in the contemplation of masterpieces, you would not sometimes make these peculiar strictures about them. Still, as you are, one cannot help loving you and feeling drawn to you despite oneself.

Adieu. Thine.

～

To Louise Colet

[Paris, ultima, April 30, 1847]

I have never before been so conscious of how little talent I possess for expressing ideas in words. You ask me for a frank, clear explanation. But haven't I given you just that a hundred times, and, if I dare say so, in every letter for many months? What can I say now that I haven't said before?

You want to know whether I love you, so that everything can be cleared up once and for all. Isn't that what you wrote to me yesterday? It is too big a question to be answered by a 'Yes' or a 'No'. Still, I will try to do that, so you'll no longer accuse me of always being evasive. I hope that today you'll at least be fair: you don't spoil me in that respect.

For me, love is not and should not be in the foreground of life; it should remain in the back room. Other things in the soul take precedence over it – things which seem to me nearer the light, closer to the sun. So, if you look upon love as the main dish of existence, the answer is No. As a seasoning. Yes.

If you mean by 'loving' to be exclusively preoccupied with the loved one, to live only through him, to see, of everything there is to see in the world, only him, to be full of the idea of him, to have your heart overflow with him, the way a little girl's apron is so full of flowers that they continually overflow even though she holds the corners in her mouth and squeezes it tightly with both hands – to feel, in a word, that your life is tied to his life and that this has become an integral organ of your soul – then, No.

If you mean by 'loving' the desire to take, from this double contact, the foam that floats on the surface, without stirring the dregs that may be at the bottom; a union combining affection and pleasure; meetings filled with delight and partings free of despair (if the truth be known, even when one kisses, in their coffins, those one has loved the best, one doesn't 'despair'); the ability to live without one another – since it is quite possible to live severed from everything one covets, orphaned of all one's loves, bereft of all one's dreams – yet when together experiencing moments of rapture that make you smile as though you were being tickled in some strange way; in short, the feeling that this happened because it was fated, and will end because everything must end (it being solemnly agreed, in advance, that neither will blame the other), and the determination, in the midst of this joy, to go on living as before, or perhaps a little better than before, with this additional resting-place for your heart when it is tired (not that it makes you feel any happier at facing the world each morning); – if you grant that it is possible to be in love and yet realize how immensely pitiful are the rewards of love as compared with the rewards of art, and feel an amused and bitter scorn for everything that drags you down to earth; – if you admit that it is possible to be in love and yet feel that a line of Theocritus is more intoxicating than your most precious memories, and feel too that you could easily make great sacrifices (I mean of the things generally considered most precious: life, money) whereas small compromises are difficult – then: Yes.

Ah, when I saw you, poor pretty darling, setting sail on this ocean (remember my first letters), didn't I warn you: 'No! Stay where you are! Stay on shore, meagre though your existence there may be!'

Now, put out of your mind your suppositions concerning the outside influences you think are acting on me – my mother, Phidias, Maxime. None of it is true – the part about Maxime no more than the rest. I don't know that anyone up until now has ever made me do anything either good or bad, or even been responsible for a single one of my opinions. Not that I'm inflexible: in these cases I simply act naturally, without being aware of what I do.

As for your differences with Maxime, you must remember that in this whole affair he came to you to serve your interests, not his own. He may have been hurt (since he bruises easily – something in which he and I differ, you see, despite the 'pact' that binds us, as you put it) by a number of vehement things you wrote to him, or he may be tired of being put to use so often on my account. The role of confidant may be honourable, but it isn't always amusing. Besides, you slander him: he was completely devoted to you. If the need arose, he would be so again.

One thing. You keep coming back to the intellectual differences between us, to Nero, etc. (Nero!) Let's talk no more about this: it would be more sensible. Quite apart from the fact that I find it difficult to produce explanations of this kind, they upset me horribly. Yes – incredibly. Because they touch too closely on what lies at the very deepest part of my self.

. . . If this letter wounds you, if it's the 'blow' you have been expecting, it still seems to me not so harsh as all that. You kept begging me so persistently to strike you! Blame only yourself. You asked me, on your knees, to insult you – but no, I send you my affection . . .

～

The heading on that letter of April 30, 1847, including the word *ultima*, is in Louise Colet's hand. *Ultima* because she believed, or pretended to believe, that it was the last letter Flaubert would write to her. He was to leave the next day with Maxime DuCamp for a three-months' walking tour in Brittany, and the affair seemed to be over. In March, Louise had made scenes at Flaubert's Paris hotel, at Maxime DuCamp's house, and at the railway station – all of which, Flaubert wrote to her, made him look ridiculous. Since then they had exchanged several '*ultimas*', of which this one was, in fact, Flaubert's last only in the sense of being written on the eve of his departure. From Brittany he wrote to Louise a number of times, sending her a flower from Chateaubriand's grave, begging her for letters, and assuring her for the thousandth time that he 'had never meant to hurt her'.

Flaubert and DuCamp were in Brittany until late July. In Brest and several other towns they met, by prearrangement, Mme Flaubert, who had come down from Normandy with her granddaughter Caroline and the baby's nurse; and over certain carriageable stretches of the route the hikers travelled with her, then diverging and rejoining her from time to time. 'The poor woman now has only me,' Flaubert wrote to Ernest Chevalier from Saint-Malo on July 13, 'and it would have been cruel to leave her behind . . . [Maxime and I] have had some good moments in the shadow of old chateaux, and smoked our long pipes in many a crumbling moat overgrown with weeds and perfumed with the scent of broom. And the sea! The sea! The fresh air, the fields, the freedom – I mean real freedom, the kind that consists in saying what you like, thinking aloud together, and walking at random, as oblivious of the passing of time as of the drifting smoke of your pipe.'[1]

The two travellers had agreed to write a joint account of their trip, DuCamp to do the even-numbered chapters and Flaubert the uneven; and this they accomplished on their return. They called their narrative *Par les champs et par les grèves – Over Field and Shore* – and had two fair handwritten copies made of the manuscript. Flaubert much later allowed a magazine to print a few of his pages, on Celtic archaeology; posthumously, all his chapters were printed. DuCamp's chapters were published only recently, in the *Club de l'honnête homme* edition of Flaubert's works. Although Flaubert once said, of his part of *Par les champs*, that it was the first thing he had ever written carefully, the general tone is casual and 'occasional'. A few of his passages stand out, particularly one describing the friends reading *René* aloud as they sat by the lake near Chateaubriand's Château de Combourg.

After Flaubert returned to Croisset he resumed his correspondence with Louise; but the affair was foundering. About this time, or perhaps even before leaving for Brittany, he began to enjoy the company of another, less exigent Louise on his trips to Paris – Louise Pradier, the sculptor's discarded wife, who also permitted DuCamp and a number of others certain liberties. (Pradier was kept in ignorance of this particular instance of Flaubert's obedience to his own earlier advice to take a mistress.) Louise Colet quickly suspected the new affair, and added it to her list of complaints.

1.   Flaubert could not resist adding, to tease the now very respectable Chevalier, formerly one of the tumultuous band at the lycée: 'If you are still in Corsica next summer [he had been appointed assistant public attorney in Ajaccio], you will probably have the honour of a visit from the young Maxime DuCamp, who plans to go to Sardinia as well. I'd love to come with him

and drop into your courtroom some morning, to make a shambles of the place – belch behind the door, upset the inkwells, and shit in front of His Majesty's bust: in short, burst in on you like the *Garçon*.'

~

To Louise Colet

[Croisset, November 7, 1847]

. . .

You reproach me for speaking of art with you, 'as though I were speaking with someone I care nothing for'. So you speak about art with people for whom you care nothing? You regard this subject as quite secondary, a kind of entertainment, something between politics and the day's news? Not I! Not I! The other day I saw a friend who lives outside France.[1] We were brought up together; he reminisced about our childhood, my father, my sister, the college, etc. Do you think that I spoke to him about the things closest to me, or even those that I have the highest regard for – my loves and my enthusiasms? I was very careful not to, I assure you, for he would have trampled them underfoot. The spirit observes the proprieties too, you know. He bored me to death, and at the end of two hours I was longing for him to go – which doesn't mean that I'm not devoted to him, and don't love him, if you call it loving. What is there worth discussing except Art? But who is there to talk of Art with? The first person who happens along? You are luckier than I, then, for I never find anyone. You want me to be frank? Well then, I will be. One day, our day together in Mantes, under the trees, you told me that you 'wouldn't exchange your happiness for the fame of Corneille'. Do you remember that? Is my memory correct? If you knew how those words shocked me, how they chilled the very marrow of my bones! Fame! Fame! What is fame? It is nothing. A mere noise, the external accompaniment of the joy Art gives us. 'The fame of Corneille' indeed! But – to *be* Corneille! To feel *one's self* Corneille! But then I have always seen you lump art together with other things – patriotism, love, what you will – a lot of things which other to my mind are alien to it and, far from augmenting its stature, in my opinion diminish it. This is one of the chasms that exist between you and me. It was you who exposed it, and revealed it to me.

· · ·

1. Ernest Chevalier.

~

To Louise Colet

[Croisset, March 1848]

I thank you[1] for the concern you felt for me during the recent events,[2] and on this occasion as on preceding ones I beg your pardon for the worry and distress I caused you. Your letter reached me only after a delay of seven days. That was the fault of the mails, which as you may imagine functioned very badly all last week.

You ask my opinion concerning what has just taken place. Well, it is all very funny. The expressions on the faces of the discomfited are a joy to see.[3] I take the greatest delight in observing all the crushed ambitions. I don't know whether the new form of government and the resulting social order will be favourable to Art. That is a question. It cannot be more bourgeois or more worthless than the old. As for being more stupid, is it possible? I am glad that it improves the prospects for your play. A good play is well worth a king.[4] I'll come to applaud at the first performance, as I already told you. I'll be there, you'll see me, I'll do my best, and gladly.

What is the good of coming back endlessly to DuCamp and the grievances real or not that you hold against him?[5] You must realize that this has long been painful to me. Your persistence, in bad taste from the start, has become cruel.

Also, why all your preambles to telling me the 'news'?[6] You could have given it to me outright from the beginning, without circumlocutions. I spare you the reflections it inspires in me and the feelings it arouses. There would be too much to say. I pity you, I pity you greatly. I suffered for you, and – more to the point – 'I have seen it all'. You understand, don't you? It is to the artist that I speak.

Whatever may happen, count on me always. Even though we may no longer see each other or write, there will always be a bond between us that will not be effaced, a past whose consequences will endure. My 'monstrous personality', as you so amiably call it, does not obliterate in me every last decent feeling – *human* feeling, if you prefer. One day you will perhaps realize this, and regret having expended so much vexation and bitterness on my account.
Adieu, je vous embrasse.

1. Flaubert uses the formal *vous* instead of the familiar *tu* of previous letters.
2. The Revolution of 1848: more particularly, the abdication of Louis-Philippe on 24 February and the proclamation of the Second French Republic by Lamartine. Flaubert had gone to Paris to witness some of the events, and briefly joined Maxime DuCamp in a company of the National Guard (which supported the 'reform' of the government).
3. The monarchists.
4. Louise Colet's five-act play in verse, *Madeleine*. There had been earlier references to it in the correspondence: Louise had hoped that it might be performed at the Comédie Française, with Rachel in the leading role. Its 'better prospects' under the new Republic were perhaps due to its subject, '*une famille en 1793*'. It was never produced.
5. DuCamp had lost all esteem – if he had ever had any – for Louise Colet. In December 1847 he had written to Flaubert: 'The Muse has written me a very calm letter. She says she is resigned [to the end of the liaison with Flaubert] and is going to get to work. Bad news for literature.'
6. Louise, who was frequenting liberal exiles from various countries, was pregnant by a Polish refugee named Franc. Their son died in infancy.

～

In the spring of 1848 there occurred what might be called the second act – the first having been Alfred LePoittevin's marriage – of what Flaubert was always to consider the greatest loss of his life. Alfred, now the father of a son and living with his wife in the country, had been slowly wasting away from tuberculosis.

～

To Maxime DuCamp

[Croisset,] Friday night. [April 7, 1848]

Alfred died on Monday at midnight. I buried him yesterday, and am now back. I watched beside him two nights (the second time, all night), I wrapped him in his shroud, I gave him the farewell kiss, and saw him sealed in his coffin. I was there two days – very full days. While I sat beside him I read Creuzer's *Religions of Antiquity*. The window was open, the night splendid. I could hear a cock crowing, and a night-moth circled around the tapers. I shall never forget all that, or the look on Alfred's face, or, the first night at midnight, the far-off sound of a hunting-horn that came to me through the forest.

On Wednesday I walked all afternoon, with a dog that followed me without being summoned. (It was a bitch that had become attached to Alfred and always accompanied him when he walked alone. The night before his death she howled frightfully and couldn't be quieted.) From time to time I sat on the moss; I smoked, I stared up at the sky. I lay down behind a heap of cut broom and slept.

The last night I read *Les Feuilles d'automne*.[1] I kept coming upon poems that were his favourites or which had special meaning for me in the circumstances. Now and then I got up, lifted the veil covering his face, and looked at him. I was wrapped in a cloak that belonged to my father and which he had worn only once, the day of Caroline's wedding.

At daybreak, about four o'clock, the attendant and I began our task. I lifted him, turned him, covered him. The feeling of the coldness and rigidity of his limbs stayed in my fingertips all the next day. He was horribly decomposed; the sheets were stained through. We wrapped him in two shrouds. When it was done he looked like an Egyptian mummy in its bandages, and I was filled with an indescribable sense of joy and relief on his account. There was a whitish mist, the trees were beginning to be visible through it. The two tapers shone in the dawning whiteness; two or three birds sang, and I recited to myself this sequence from his *Bélial*.[2] '*Il ira, joyeux oiseau, saluer dans les pins le soleil levant*' – or rather I heard his voice saying it to me, and for the rest of the day was deliciously obsessed by it.

He was laid in the coffin in the entry, where the doors had been removed and where the morning air poured in, freshened by the rain that had started to fall. He was carried to the cemetery on men's shoulders. It was almost an hour's walk. From behind, I saw the coffin swaying like a rolling boat. The service was atrociously long. In the cemetery the earth was muddy. I stood by the grave and watched each shovelful as it fell: there seemed to be a hundred thousand of them. When the hole was filled I walked away, smoking, which Boivin didn't think proper.

I returned to Rouen on the box of a carriage with Bouilhet. The rain beat down, the horses went at a gallop, I shouted to urge them on, we were back in 43 minutes – 5 leagues. The air did me much good. I slept all night and most of today, and had a strange dream, which I wrote down lest I lose it.[3]

That, dear Max, has been my life since Tuesday evening. I have had marvellous intimations and intuitions, and flashes of untranslatable ideas. A host of things have been coming back to me, with choirs of music and clouds of perfume.

As long as he was capable of doing anything, he read Spinoza in bed each night until one in the morning.

On one of his last days, when the windows were open and the sun was coming into the room, he said: 'Close it! It is too beautiful – too beautiful!'

There were times, dear Max, when I thought intensely of you, recalling and comparing sad memories.[4]

. . . *Adieu*, dear Max. All my affection. I embrace you, and long to see you, for I need to speak with you of incomprehensible things.

1. By Victor Hugo; a Bible of the young Romantics.
2. See p. 138.
3. The dream is lost.
4. Flaubert knew that the lively, efficient DuCamp had detested the languid, decadent, subtle Alfred and had been jealous of Flaubert's love for him. In 1844, during Flaubert's first year of convalescence, DuCamp had sent him, from Rome, a long letter of encouragement, warning him, however, that association with Alfred was doing him no good. 'You, who have a most brilliant intelligence, have been aping someone corrupt, that "Greek of the Late Empire", as he calls himself. And now, I give you my word, Gustave, he is laughing at you, and doesn't believe a word of anything he has told you. Show him this letter and see if he dares deny what I say.'

~

Flaubert later wrote to a correspondent.[1] 'Ten years ago I lost the man I loved most in the world, Alfred LePoittevin. During his last illness, he spent his nights reading Spinoza. I have never known anyone (and I know many people) of so transcendental a mind as this friend I speak of. We sometimes spent six hours on end talking about metaphysics. We flew *high* sometimes, I assure you. Since his death I no longer *talk* with anyone at all. I chatter, or remain silent. What a necropolis is the human heart!'

Doubtless fearing that scabrous passages might become known, the LePoittevin family demanded that Flaubert return to them Alfred's manuscripts, apparently including his letters, that were in his possession. 'The first great aesthetico-sentimental fury of my life,' he wrote to Louise Colet in 1853, 'was six years ago, over an expurgated edition of Molière, compiled by a priest . . . The second was when [Alfred LePoittevin's family] refused to give me, or rather demanded that I return, certain of his manuscripts.' Some of Alfred's poems and letters (the latter much censored), and his 'philosophical tale', *Une Promenade de Bélial,* resembling in subject Flaubert's earlier *Smarh,* were first printed only in 1909 and 1910, by the Flaubert scholar René Descharmes, to whom they were confided by Alfred's son, Louis LePoittevin. Several passages have been restored by Jean Bruneau in Pléaide, I, and by Sartre in *L'Idiot de la famille.*

1.   To Mlle Leroyer de Chantepie, November 4, 1857.

~

To Ernest Chevalier

Croisset, Monday, July 4 [1848]

I seem fated, poor Ernest, each time I write to you to give sad news.[1] You have read in the newspapers of the atrocities that have been taking place in Paris.[2] DuCamp was struck by a bullet in the calf of his right leg and will be laid up for at least a month: I am told his wound is slight but am not entirely reassured.

While that was taking place the rest of us were coping with a different kind of shock.

Hamard returned from Paris a month ago announcing his intention of becoming an actor and making his debut at the Comédie Française in two weeks. (In the last four months he has squandered thirty thousand francs, not to mention his silver and diamonds, which he gave to the Republic, etc. etc.) In short, completely mad. He came here to claim his daughter. But my mother was advised to keep her away from him because of his condition, and we left hurriedly for Forges, the first place that occurred to us. There, since my mother trembled at the sound of every carriage that arrived in town, she begged shelter from M. and Mme Beaufils, who welcomed her in a way I'll never forget – perfectly. Meanwhile his family wanted to have him committed and his uncle petitioned that he be declared incompetent. But unfortunately the outbreak in Paris kept the police from doing anything. When he learned that action was being taken against him he temporarily regained his sanity. He petitioned that my mother be obliged to return his child; but the judge decided that she should keep her until the hearing on the issue of incompetence. We reached an amicable settlement, and now he has consented that my mother should keep the child until January, and they are going to stay proceedings about his incompetence. Six months from now he will, I hope, be completely insane and will almost certainly be declared incompetent. I spare you countless details, horrible for my mother . . .

And you, what has become of you? Have you a little peace? As for me, as you may imagine, I am living in hell; all conceivable blows are falling on my head. At each new misfortune I think the limit has been reached, but they keep coming and coming! And I haven't told you everything . . .

1. Flaubert had recently written to Chevalier about Alfred LePoittevin's death.
2. The workers' revolution of June 24–26 (the 'June days') against the recently installed republic. It was bloodily suppressed by the National Guard, now pro-government. The 'atrocities' referred to by Flaubert were probably those committed by both sides (J.B.), including the murder of General Bréa and the Archbishop of Paris by the insurgents. Flaubert considered himself nonpolitical, and he was of course vehemently antibourgeois from the aesthetic point of view; but at moments of danger from the Left he feared for his bourgeois foundations. The events of 1848 form part of the story of *L'Éducation sentimentale* (1870).

~

To Louise Colet

[Croisset, August 25, 1848]

Thank you for the gift.[1]
Thank you for your very beautiful poem.
Thank you for the remembrance.

Yours, G.
Friday night.

1. A lock of Chateaubriand's hair. Chateaubriand had died on July 4. Louise had probably been given the memento by her neighbour and friend, Mme Récamier, Chateaubriand's companion.

V

Voyage en Orient

1849–1851

Now with Alfred LePoittevin dead, the connection with Louise Colet at an end, and the weeks in Brittany as evidence that Maxime DuCamp was a congenial travelling companion, Flaubert's thoughts turned to the 'Orient' – to Egypt and the Middle East – where he had always longed to go, and where DuCamp had recently been and was eager to go again. For some years the two friends had spoken of making such a journey together. 'You asked me the other day how I spend my time with DuCamp,' Flaubert wrote in September 1846 to Louise, who was jealous that Maxime should be spending a month at Croisset. 'For three days we've been tracing on the map a great tour of Asia which would take six years and cost us – the way we have conceived it – 3 million 600 thousand and some francs.' Money was one of the hindrances to even a more modest tour: financially, Flaubert was largely dependent on his mother – and for company, as we have seen, she was dependent on him. It took time and careful plotting to get Mme Flaubert to contemplate the venture itself and the separation. She consented only after Flaubert and DuCamp persuaded Dr Achille Flaubert and Dr Jules Cloquet to advise her that travel in warm countries would benefit Gustave's health. The route was to be Egypt, Palestine, perhaps Persia, then Greece, Italy and home.

In his memoirs Maxime DuCamp describes the preparations for the trip. 'I wanted us to enjoy every possible advantage while travelling, and had asked the government to assign us missions that would recommend us to French diplomatic and commercial agents in the

Orient. Need I say that these missions were to be, and were, entirely unpaid? My request was granted. Flaubert – one can scarcely refrain from smiling – was charged by the Ministry of Agriculture and Commerce with the task of collecting, in the various ports and caravan centres, any information that he thought might interest Chambers of Commerce.' DuCamp's mission (of his own choosing) was to photograph monuments and inscriptions. He secured letters of introduction to officials of the Egyptian government; and he had a special map of Egypt prepared, a copy of which was to be left with Mme Flaubert so she could follow their progress. A servant, a Corsican named Sassetti, was hired for the journey.

Meanwhile, shortly before Alfred's death, Flaubert had begun a work which he thought, for the first time, might be worthy of publication – the appearance 'in full armour' that was the only kind of literary debut he was willing to envisage. Inspired by the painting of the Temptation of St Anthony about which he had written to Alfred LePoittevin from Genoa in 1845, and Callot's engraving of the same subject that he had bought and hung on his wall, it would 'bring to life', as Jean Bruneau has put it, 'the religious world of the Fourth Century AD, with all its beliefs, heresies and legends.'[1] He resolved to complete it before setting out.

He would show the Anchorite tempted not merely by sins of the world and the flesh, but by forbidden intellectual and spiritual concepts: by the pagan schools of philosophy, by the dogmas of all the heretical Christian sects, and the doctrines of non-Christian religions. To familiarize himself with these he made use of his old classical and Indian studies, and embarked on wide new reading. Jean Seznec[2] has shown that for a single episode in *La Tentation de Saint Antoine* – the procession of the fallen gods, about one-seventh part of the whole – Flaubert read, re-read or consulted at least sixty ancient texts, histories, and scholarly commentaries. The work would be in dramatic form, each seductive belief and way of thought hurled at the saint by its spokesman. The cast of characters became enormous, the work so long that when he finally finished it, in September 1849, and read it aloud to Maxime DuCamp and Louis Bouilhet, they listened to him – so DuCamp says in his memoirs – for thirty-two hours.

The hours that Bouilhet and I spent listening to Flaubert chant his lines – we sitting there silent, occasionally exchanging a glance – remain very painful in my memory. We kept straining our ears, always hoping that the action would begin, and always disappointed, for the situation remains the same from beginning to end. St Anthony, bewildered, a little simple, really quite a blockhead if I dare say so, sees the various forms of temptation pass before him and responds with nothing but exclamations: '*Ah! Ah! Oh! Oh! Mon dieu! Mon dieu!*' . . . Flaubert grew heated as he read, and we tried to grow warm with him, but remained frozen . . . After the last reading – it was almost midnight – Flaubert pounded the table: 'Now: tell me frankly what you think.'

Bouilhet was a shy man, but no one was firmer than he once he decided to express his opinion; and he said: 'We think you should throw it into the fire and never speak of it again.'

Flaubert leapt up and uttered a cry of horror . . . He repeated certain lines to us, saying 'But that is beautiful!'

'Yes, it is beautiful . . . There are excellent passages, some exquisite evocations of antiquity, but it is all lost in the bombast of the language. You wanted to make music and you have made only noise.'

Mme Flaubert long held our frankness against us. She thought we were jealous of her son, and she let us know it.

DuCamp's account, written after the deaths of both Bouilhet and Flaubert, is perhaps overcoloured; but he and Bouilhet unquestionably did advise Flaubert to put *Saint Antoine* away. Flaubert, crushed, bowed to their opinion. He was sick at heart as he made himself ready to travel. After an emotional parting from his mother, he set off with DuCamp in late October, via Marseilles and Alexandria, for Cairo.[3] There they would hire a sailing boat, a *cange*, and its crew, and explore both banks of the Nile.

1. In *Dizionario critico della letteratura francese* (*Unione tipografico-editrice torinese*, 1973), article 'Flaubert'.

2. In *Les Sources de l'épisode des dieux dans La Tentation de Saint Antoine (Première version, 1849)*. (Paris, 1940.)

This first version of the *Tentation*, earliest of three composed at different periods of Flaubert's life (see pp. 306, n. 2 and 310, n. 2), is much the longest. There is no English translation.

3. Two 'Mementos' of Louise Colet (see note to Appendix I):

'*Memento of October 28, 1849. 9.30 o'clock. Alone.* Today Ferrat told me that Gustave will be passing through Paris on his way to embark on that long trip to the Orient. He is leaving without writing to me, without seeing me, without telling me what he has done with my letters and my keepsakes. Oh! How sombre these amours broken off for ever, leaving no trace! No trace in the *man's* heart: in mine, the wounds never close, and bleed eternally. Is it possible that two beings should have loved one another, loved sincerely, merged each in the other – and that one of the two should break away like this, forget all – *all, mon Dieu!* – about those marvellous hours! He lacks even the poetic, natural curiosity which after a few years makes us yearn for another view of sites and monuments that have impressed us.'

'*Memento of Tuesday, December 4, 1849.* Saturday morning (the 1st of the month), I saw in a newspaper that Maxime and Gustave had set sail for Egypt. Heartache, the wound reopens! Not a word of farewell! And now the sea lies between us ... In the evening, a visit from Ferrat ... How I am suffering, *mon Dieu!* I couldn't keep from crying in front of Ferrat. I spoke of Gustave in the midst of my tears. I am too wretched. I wish I were dead ...'

~

TO HIS MOTHER

[Alexandria, November 17, 1849]

. . .

When we were two hours out from the coast of Egypt I went into the bow with the chief quartermaster and saw the seraglio of Abbas Pasha like a black dome on the blue of the Mediterranean. The sun was beating down on it. I had my first sight of the Orient through, or rather in, a glowing light that was like melted silver on the sea. Soon the shore became distinguishable, and the first thing we saw on land was a pair of camels led by their driver; then, on the dock, some Arabs peacefully fishing. Landing took place amid the most deafening uproar imaginable: negroes, negresses, camels, turbans, cudgelings to right and left, and ear-splitting guttural cries. I gulped down a whole bellyful of colours, like a donkey filling himself with hay. Cudgelings play a great role here; everyone who wears clean clothes beats everyone who wears dirty ones, or rather none at all, and when I say clothes I mean a pair of short breeches. You see many gentlemen sauntering along the streets with nothing but a shirt and a long pipe. Except in the very lowest classes, all the women are veiled, and on their noses they wear ornaments that hang down and sway from side to side . . . On the other hand, if you don't see their faces, you see their entire bosoms. As you change countries, you find that modesty changes its place, like a bored traveller who keeps shifting from the outside to the inside of the stage-coach. One curious thing here is the respect, or rather the terror, that everyone displays in the presence of 'Franks', as they call Europeans. We have had bands of ten or twelve Arabs, advancing across the whole width of a street, break apart to let us pass. In fact, Alexandria is almost a European city, there are so many Europeans here. At table in our hotel alone there are thirty, and the place is full of Englishmen, Italians, etc. Yesterday we saw a magnificent procession celebrating the circumcision of the son of a rich merchant. This morning we saw Cleopatra's Needles (two great obelisks on the shorefront), Pompey's column, the catacombs, and Cleopatra's baths. Tomorrow we leave for Rosetta, whence we shall return in three or four days. We go slowly and don't get overtired, living sensibly and clad in flannel from head to foot, even though the temperature indoors is sometimes thirty degrees.[1] The heat is not at all unbearable, thanks to the sea breeze.

Soliman Pasha,[2] the most powerful man in Egypt, the victor at Nezib, the terror of Constantinople, happens just now to be in Alexandria instead of Cairo. We paid him a visit yesterday, and presented Lauvergne's letter. He received us very courteously. He is to give us orders for all the provincial governors of Egypt and offered us his carriage for the journey to Cairo. It was he who arranged about our horses for tomorrow. He is charming, cordial, etc. He apparently likes the way we look. In addition, we have M. Galis, chief of the army engineers, Princeteau Bey, etc. Just to give you an idea of how we are to travel, we have been given soldiers to hold back the crowd when we want to photograph: I trust you are impressed. As you see, poor old darling, conditions couldn't be better. As for ophthalmia: of the people one sees, only the very lowest orders (as the expression goes) suffer from it. M. Willemin, a young doctor who has been in Egypt five years, told us this morning that he has not seen a single case among the well-to-do or Europeans. That should reassure you. Don't worry, I'll come back in good shape. I have put on so much weight since I left that two pairs of my trousers are with M. Chavannes, a French tailor, being let out to accommodate my paunch.

So – goodbye, old lady. I was interrupted during the writing of this letter by the arrival of M. Pastré, the banker who is to send us our money as we need it and will ship home any packages, in case we buy a mummy or two. Now we are going to our friend Soliman Pasha to pick up a letter from him about tomorrow's expedition: it is addressed to the Governor of Rosetta, seeing to it that he puts us up in his house – i.e. in the fort, apparently the only place to stay. We had intended to push on as far as Damietta. But as we have been told that would be too tiring on horseback because of the sand, we've given up the idea. We'll go to Cairo by boat. As you see, we're not stubborn; it's our principle to follow the advice of experts and behave like a pair of little saints. Goodbye, a thousand kisses, kiss the baby for me, send me long letters . . .

1. Réaumur. 86° Fahrenheit.
2. François Sève, a former colonel in the French army, taken into the Egyptian service in 1815 (after Waterloo) by Mohammed Ali. The latter, viceroy of Egypt, revolted against his sovereign, the Turkish sultan; and his forces, under Soliman Pasha, defeated the Turks in the battle of Nezib (or Nisib) in 1839. A number of other officials mentioned by Flaubert were also Frenchmen, given the title 'bey' or 'pasha' in the Egyptian service.

～

TO HIS MOTHER

Alexandria, Thursday, [November] 22 [1849]

My darling – I am writing to you in white tie and tails, pumps, etc., like a man who has been paying a call on a prime minister: in fact we have just left Artin Bey, Minister of Foreign Affairs, to whom we were introduced by the (French) consul and who received us splendidly. He is going to give us a *firman* with his seal on it for our entire journey. It is unbelievable how well we are treated here – it's as though we were princes, and I'm not joking. Sassetti keeps saying: 'Whatever happens, I'll be able to say that once in my life I had ten slaves to serve me and one to chase away the flies,' and that is quite true.

.   .   .

~

Friday morning. [November 23]

We set out at daybreak last Sunday, saddled and booted, harnessed and armed, with four men running behind us, our dragoman on his mule carrying our coats and supplies, and our three horses, which were ridden with simple halters. They looked like nags but were on the contrary excellent beasts; with two pricks of the spur they were off at a gallop, and a whistle brought them up short. To make them go right or left you had only to touch their neck. The desert begins at the very gates of Alexandria: first sandy hillocks covered here and there with palms, and then dunes that stretch on endlessly. From time to time you see on the horizon what looks like great stretches of water with trees reflected in them, and at their furthest limit, where they seem to touch the sky, a grey vapour that appears to be moving in a rush, like a train: that is the mirage, known to all, Arabs and Europeans – people familiar with the desert as well as those seeing it for the first time. Now and then you come upon the carcass of some animal on the sand – a dead camel three-quarters eaten by jackals, its guts exposed and blackened by the sun; a mummified buffalo, a horse's head, etc. Arabs trot by on their donkeys, their wives bundled in immense black or white veils: you exchange greetings – '*Taieb*' – and continue on your way. About eleven o'clock we lunched near Abukir, in a fort manned by soldiers who gave us excellent coffee and refused *baksheesh* (a wonder!). The beach at Abukir is still littered, here and there, with the wreckage of ships.[1] We saw a number of sharks that had been washed up, and along the water's edge our horses trod on seashells. We shot cormorants and water-magpies, and our Arabs ran like hares to pick up those we wounded: I brought down a few birds myself – yes, *me*! – something new, what? The weather was magnificent, sea and sky bluest blue, an immensity of space.

At a place called Edku (you will find it on your map) we took a ferry and there our runners bought dates from a camel-driver whose two beasts were laden with them. A mile or two further on, we were riding tranquilly along side by side, a hundred feet in front of our runners, when suddenly we heard loud cries from behind. We turned, and saw our men in a tumult, jostling and shoving one another and making signs for us to turn back. Sassetti dashed off at a gallop, velvet jacket flying; and digging our spurs into our horses we followed after to the scene of the conflict. It was occasioned, we discovered, by the owner of the dates, who had been following his camels at a distance and who, coming upon our men and seeing that they were eating dates, had thought they had stolen them and had fallen on them with his cudgel.

But when he saw us three ruffians descending upon him with rifles slung over our saddles, roles were reversed, and from the beater he became the beaten. Courage returned to our men, and they fell upon him with their sticks in such a way that his backside was soon resounding with blow after blow. To escape, he ran into the sea, lifting up his robe to keep it dry, but his assailants followed. The higher he lifted his robe, the greater the area he exposed to their cudgels, which rattled on him like drumsticks. You can't imagine anything funnier than that man's black behind amid the white foam churned up by the combat. The rest of us stood on the shore, laughing like fools; my sides still ache when I think of it . . . Two days later, coming back from Rosetta, we met the same camels as they were returning from Alexandria. Perceiving us from afar, the owner hastily left his beasts and made a long detour in the desert to avoid us – a precaution which diverted us considerably. You would scarcely believe the important role played by the cudgel in this part of the world; buffets are distributed with a sublime prodigality, always accompanied by loud cries; it's the most genuine kind of local colour you can think of.

At six in the evening, after a sunset that made the sky look like melted vermilion and the sand of the desert like ink, we arrived at Rosetta and found all the gates closed. At the name of Soliman Pasha they opened, creaking faintly like doors of a barn. The streets were dark, and so narrow that there was barely room for a single horseman. We rode through the bazaars, where each shop was lit by a glass of oil hanging from a cord, and arrived at the barracks. The [local] pasha received us on his sofa, surrounded by negroes who brought us pipes and coffee. After many courtesies and compliments, we were

given supper and shown to our beds, which were equipped with
excellent mosquito-netting . . . The next morning while we were
washing, the pasha came into our room, followed by the regimental
doctor, an Italian who spoke French perfectly and did us the honours
of the city. Thanks to him we spent a very agreeable day. When he
learned my name and that I was the son of a doctor, he said he had
heard of Father and had often seen his name cited. It was no small
satisfaction to me, dear Mother, to think that Father's memory was
still beneficial to me, serving as a kind of protection at this distance.
That reminds me that in the depths of Brittany, too, at Guérande,
the local doctor told me he had quoted Father in his thesis. Yes,
poor darling, I think constantly of those who are gone; as my body
continues on its journey, my thoughts keep turning back to bury
themselves in days past.

. . . All morning was taken up with things to do in Rosetta. By
the way, when you write to Rouen will you please make enquiries
about M. Julienne, who invented those fuel-saving devices for steam
pumps? What is his address? Would he like to enter into correspondence with M. Foucault, manager of rice production at Rosetta, to
whom I spoke of this invention and who would be glad to hear
more? . . . I promised to do this, and would like to keep my word[2] . . .

1. From the naval battle of August 1, 1798, when Vice-Admiral Horatio Nelson
    destroyed the French fleet?
2. This is one of Flaubert's very rare references to anything that might be
    thought of as relating to his 'mission'. Nevertheless, in this same letter he
    urges his mother, when addressing her envelopes to him, to write 'my
    name, title, and "Cairo, Egypt",' the 'title' being: '*Chargé d'une mission en
    Orient*' – doubtless because the official designation was proving so useful.

∽

To Louis Bouilhet
                Cairo, Saturday night, 10 o'clock. December 1, 1849
Let me begin by kissing both your dear cheeks and blowing onto
this paper all my 'inspiration', so as to bring your 'spirit' close to
me. I imagine that you must be thinking quite a bit about us. For
we think quite a bit about you, and miss you a hundred times a day.
Yesterday, for example, my dear sir, we were in a whorehouse. But
let's not jump ahead. At the present moment the moon is shining

on the minarets – all is silence but for the occasional barking of dogs. My curtains are pulled back, and outside my window is the mass of the trees in the garden, black against the pale glimmer of the night. I am writing on a table with a green cloth, lit by two candles, and taking my ink from an ointment jar: near me, about ten millimetres away, are my ministerial instructions, which seem to be waiting impatiently for the day I'll use them as lavatory paper. Behind the partition I hear the young Maxime, preparing solutions for his negatives. Upstairs sleep the mutes, namely Sassetti and the dragoman – the latter, if truth be known, one of the most arrant pimps, ruffians and old bardashes[1] that could ever be imagined. As for my gracious self, I am wearing a large white cotton Nubian shirt, trimmed with little pompoms and of a cut whose description would take up too much space here. My head is completely shaved except for one lock at the occiput (by which Mohammed lifts you up on Judgement Day) and adorned with a tarboosh which is of a screaming red and made me half die of heat the first days I wore it. We look quite the pair of orientals – Max is especially marvellous when he smokes his *narghile* and fingers his beads. Considerations of safety limit our sartorial splurges: in Egypt the European is accorded greater respect than the native, so we won't dress up completely until we reach Syria.

And you, what are you up to in our wretched birthplace, which I occasionally surprise myself daydreaming about with affection? I keep thinking of our Sundays at Croisset, when I would hear the sound of the iron gate and look up and see first your walking-stick, then your notebook, and finally you. When shall we be back chatting endlessly before the fire in my green armchairs? What of *Melaenis?*[22] And the plays? Send me volumes. Until further notice write to me to Cairo, and don't forget to put on the address: '*Chargé de mission en Orient*'.

. . . I am sure that as an intelligent man you don't expect me to send you an account of my trip . . . In a word, this is how I sum up my feelings so far: very little impressed by nature here – i.e. landscape, sky, desert (except the mirages); enormously excited by the cities and the people. Hugo would say: 'I was closer to God than to mankind.' It probably comes of my having given more imagination and thought, before coming here, to things like horizon, greenery, sand, trees, sun, etc., than to houses, streets, costumes and faces. The result is that nature has been a rediscovery and the rest a discovery. There is one new element which I hadn't expected to see and which is tremendous here, and that is the grotesque. All the old comic business of the cudgelled slave, of the coarse trafficker in women, of the thieving merchant – it's all very fresh here, very genuine and charming. In the streets, in the houses, on any and all occasions, there is a merry proliferation of beatings right and left. There are guttural intonations that sound like the cries of wild beasts, and laughter, and flowing white robes, and ivory teeth flashing between thick lips, and flat negro noses, and dusty feet, and necklaces, and bracelets! Poor you! The pasha at Rosetta gave us a dinner at which there were ten negroes to serve us – they wore silk jackets and some had silver bracelets; and a little negro boy waved away the flies with a kind of feather-duster made of rushes. We ate with our fingers, the food was brought one dish at a time on a silver tray – about thirty different dishes made their appearance in this way. We were on divans in a wooden pavilion, windows open on the water. One of the finest things is the camel – I never tire of watching this strange beast that lurches like a turkey and sways its neck like a swan. Their cry is something that I wear myself out trying to imitate – I hope to bring it back with me – but it's hard to reproduce – a rattle with a kind of tremulous gargling as an accompaniment.

. . . The morning we arrived in Egypt . . . we had scarcely set foot on shore when Max, the old lecher, got excited over a negress who was drawing water at a fountain. He is just as excited by little negro boys. By whom is he not excited? Or, rather, by *what*? . . . Tomorrow we're to have a party on the river, with several whores dancing to the sound of *darabukehs* and castanets, their hair spangled with gold piastres. I'll try to make my next letter less disjointed – I've been interrupted twenty times in this one – and send you something worthwhile. The day before yesterday we were in the house of a woman who had arranged to have two others there for us. The place was dilapidated and open to all the winds and lit by a nightlight – we could see a palm tree through the unglazed window, and the two Turkish women wore silk robes embroidered with gold. This is a great place for contrasts: splendid things gleam in the dust. I performed on a mat that a family of cats had to be shooed from

– a strange coitus, looking at each other without being able to exchange a word, and the exchange of looks is all the deeper for the curiosity and the surprise. My brain was too stimulated for me to enjoy it much otherwise. These shaved cunts make a strange effect – the flesh is hard as bronze, and my girl had a splendid arse.

Goodbye . . . Write to me, write to my mother now and then . . .

December 4, Post scriptum. For you alone.

To amuse the crowd, Mohammed Ali's jester took a woman in a Cairo bazaar one day, set her on the counter of a shop, and coupled with her publicly while the shopkeeper calmly smoked his pipe.

On the road from Cairo to Shubra some time ago a young fellow had himself publicly buggered by a large monkey – as in the story above, to create a good opinion of himself and make people laugh.

A marabout died a while ago – an idiot – who had long passed as a saint marked by God; all the Moslem women came to see him and masturbated him – in the end he died of exhaustion – from morning to night it was a perpetual jacking-off. Oh Bouilhet, why weren't you that marabout?

Quid dicis of the following fact: some time ago a *santon* (ascetic priest) used to walk through the streets of Cairo completely naked except for a cap on his head and another on his prick. To piss he would doff the prick-cap, and sterile women who wanted children would run up, put themselves under the parabola of his urine and rub themselves with it.

Goodbye – this morning I had a letter from my mother – she is very sad, poor thing. Go and talk to her about me . . .

1. Bardash: a catamite. (OED) The dragoman was named Joseph.
2. Before Flaubert's departure, Bouilhet had begun his *Melaenis*, a very long narrative poem about a dancer in ancient Rome. Flaubert's question about its progress was to bring, in Bouilhet's letters, long passages of the poem, on which Flaubert would comment at length in his replies. Most of these comments have been omitted from the present volume.

～

To his mother

Cairo, January 5, 1850.

Your fine long letter of the 16th reached me as a New Year's present last Wednesday, dear old darling. I was paying an official call on our consul, when he was handed a large packet. He opened it immediately, and I seized the envelope that I recognized among a hundred others. (I was itching to open it, but manners, alas! forbade.) Fortunately, he showed us into his wife's salon, and as there was a letter for her too, from her mother, we gave each other mutual permission to read almost before saying how do you do . . .

. . .

I'm bursting to tell you my name. Do you know what the Arabs call me? Since they have great difficulty in pronouncing French names, they invent their own for us Franks. Can you guess? Abu-Chanab, which means 'Father of the Moustache'. That word, *abu*, father, is applied to anyone connected with the chief detail under discussion – thus for merchants selling various commodities they say Father of the Shoes, Father of the Glue, Father of the Mustard, etc. Max's name is a very long one which I don't remember, and which means 'the man who is excessively thin'. Imagine my joy when I learned the honour being paid to that particular part of myself.

. . . Often when we have been out since early morning and feel hungry and don't want to take time to return to the hotel for lunch, we sit down in a Turkish restaurant. Here all the carving is done with one's hands, and everyone belches to his heart's content. Dining room and kitchen are all one, and behind you at the great fireplace little pots bubble and steam under the eye of the chef in his white turban and rolled-up sleeves. I am careful to write down the names of all the dishes and their ingredients. Also, I have made a list of all the perfumes made in Cairo – it may be very useful to me somewhere. We have hired two dragomans. In the evening an Arab storyteller comes and reads us stories, and there is an effendi whom we pay to make translations for us.

. . .

A few days ago I spent a fine afternoon. Max stayed at home to do I forget what, and I took Hasan (the second dragoman we have temporarily hired) and paid a visit to the bishop of the Copts for the sake of a conversation with him. I entered a square courtyard surrounded by columns, with a little garden in the middle – that is, a few big trees and a bed of dark greenery, around which ran a trellised wooden divan. My dragoman, with his capacious trousers and wide-sleeved jacket, walked ahead; I behind. On one of the corners of the divan was sitting a scowling old personage with a long white beard, wearing an ample pelisse; books in a baroque kind of handwriting were strewn all about him. At a certain distance were standing three black-robed theologians, younger and also with long beards. The dragoman said: 'This is a French gentleman (*cawadja fransaoui*) who is travelling all over the world in search of knowledge, and who has come to you to speak of your religion.' Such is the kind of language they go in for here. Can you imagine how I talk to them? A while ago, when I was looking at seeds in a shop, a woman to whom I had given something said: 'Blessings on you, my sweet lord: God grant that you return safe and sound to your native land.' There is much use of such blessings and ritual formulas. When Max asked a groom if he wasn't tired, the answer was: 'It's enough for me to see the pleasure in your eyes.'

But to return to the bishop. He received me with many courtesies. Coffee was brought, and I soon began to ask questions concerning the Trinity, the Virgin, the Gospels, the Eucharist – all my old erudition of *Saint Antoine* came back in a flood. It was superb, the sky blue above us, the trees, the books spread out, the old fellow ruminating in his beard before answering me, myself sitting cross-legged beside him, gesticulating with my pencil and taking notes, while Hasan stood motionless, translating aloud, and the three other theologians, sitting on stools, nodded their heads and interjected an occasional few words. I enjoyed it deeply. That was indeed the old Orient, land of religions and flowing robes. When the bishop gave out, one of the theologians replaced him; and when I finally saw that they were all somewhat flushed, I left. I am going back, for there is much to learn in that place. The Coptic religion is the most ancient of existing Christian sects, and little or nothing is known about it in Europe (so far as I know). I'm going to talk with the Armenians, too, and the Greeks, and the Sunnites, and especially with Moslem scholars.

We're still waiting for the return of the caravan from Mecca. It is too good an event to miss, and we shall not leave for Upper Egypt until the pilgrims have arrived. There are some bizarre things to see, we have been told: priests' horses walking over prostrate bodies of the faithful, all kinds of dervishes, singers, etc.

. . .

Max's days are entirely absorbed and consumed by photography. He is doing well, but grows desperate whenever he spoils a picture or finds that a plate has been badly washed. Really, if he doesn't take things easier he'll crack up. But he has been getting some superb results, and in consequence his spirits have been better the last few days. The day before yesterday a kicking mule almost smashed the entire equipment.

. . .

When I think of my future (that happens rarely, for I generally think of nothing at all despite the elevated thoughts one should have in the presence of ruins!), when I ask myself: 'What shall I do when I return? What path shall I follow?' and the like, I am full of doubts and indecisions. At every stage in my life I have put off facing my situation in just this same way; and I shall die at eighty before having formed any opinion concerning myself or, perhaps, without writing anything that would have shown me what I could do. Is *Saint Antoine* good or bad? That is what I often ask myself, for example: who was mistaken – I or the others? However, I worry very little about any of this. I live like a plant, suffusing myself with sun and light, with colours and fresh air. I keep eating, so to speak; afterwards the digesting will have to be done, then the shitting; and the shit had better be good! That's the important thing.

. . . You ask me whether the Orient is up to what I imagined. Yes, it is; and more than that, it extends far beyond the narrow idea I had of it. I have found, clearly delineated, everything that was hazy in my mind. Facts have taken the place of suppositions – with such perfection that it is often as though I were suddenly coming upon old forgotten dreams.

~

To Louis Bouilhet

Cairo, January 15, 1850

At noon today came your fine long letter that I was so hoping for. It moved me to the very guts and made a crybaby of me. How constantly I think of you, you precious bastard! How many times a day I evoke you and miss you! . . . When we next see each other many days will have passed – I mean many things will have happened. Shall we still be the same, with nothing changed in the communion of our beings? I have too much pride in both of us not to think so. Carry on with your disgusting and sublime way of life, and then we'll see about beating those drums that we've long been keeping so taut. I'm looking everywhere for something special to bring you. So far I have found nothing except that in Memphis I cut two or three branches of palm for you to make into canes for yourself. I'm greatly giving myself over to the study of perfumes and to the composition of ointments. Yesterday I ate half a pastille so heating that for three hours I thought my tongue was on fire. I haunt the Turkish baths. I devoured the lines from *Melaenis*. Come, let's be calm: no one incapable of restraint was ever a writer – at this moment I'm bursting – I'd like to let off steam and use you as a punching bag – everything's mixed up and jostling everything else in my sick brain – let's try for some order[1] . . .

De Saltatoribus

We have not yet seen any dancing girls; they are all in exile in Upper Egypt. Good brothels no longer exist in Cairo, either. The party we were to have had on the Nile the last time I wrote to you fell through – no loss there. But we have seen male dancers. Oh! Oh! Oh!

That was us, calling you. I was indignant and very sad that you weren't here. Three or four musicians playing curious instruments (we'll bring some home) took up their positions at the end of the hotel dining room while one gentleman was still eating his lunch and the rest of us were sitting on the divan smoking our pipes. As dancers, imagine two rascals, quite ugly, but charming in their corruption, in their obscene leerings and the effeminacy of their movements, dressed as women, their eyes painted with antimony. For costume, they have wide trousers and an embroidered jacket. The latter comes down to the epigastrium, whereas the trousers, held up by an enormous cashmere girdle folded double several times, begin only about at the pubis, so that the entire stomach, the loins, and the beginning of the buttocks are naked, seen through a black gauze held tight against the skin by the upper and lower garments. This ripples on the hips like a dark, transparent wave with every movement they make. The music is always the same, and goes on for two hours without stopping. The flute is shrill, the drumbeats throb in your breast, the singer dominates all. The dancers advance and retreat, shaking the pelvis with a short convulsive movement. A quivering of the muscles is the only way to describe it; when the pelvis moves, the rest of the body is motionless; when the breast shakes, nothing else moves. In this manner they advance towards you, their arms extended, rattling brass castanets, and their faces, under the rouge and the sweat, remain more expressionless than a statue's. By that I mean they never smile. The effect is produced by the gravity of the face in contrast to the lascivious movements of the body. Sometimes they lie down flat on their backs, like a woman ready to be fucked, then rise up with a movement of the loins similar to that of a tree swinging back into place after the wind has stopped. In their bowings and salutations their great red trousers suddenly inflate like oval balloons, then seem to melt away, expelling the air that swells them. From time to time, during the dance, the impresario, or pimp, who brought them plays around them, kissing them on the belly, the arse, and the small of the back, and making obscene remarks in an effort to put additional spice into a thing that is already quite self-evident. It is too beautiful to be exciting. I doubt whether we shall find the women as good as the men; the ugliness of the latter adds greatly to the thing as art. I had a headache for the rest of the day, and I had to go and piss two or three times during the performance – a nervous reaction I attribute particularly to the music – I'll have this marvellous Hasan el-Belbeissi come again. He'll dance the Bee dance for me, in particular. Done by such a bardash as he, it can scarcely be a thing for babes.

Speaking of bardashes, this is what I know about them. Here it is quite accepted. One admits one's sodomy, and it is spoken of at table in the hotel. Sometimes you do a bit of denying, and then everybody teases you and you end up confessing. Travelling as we are for educational purposes, and charged with a mission by the government, we have considered it our duty to indulge in this form of ejaculation. So far the occasion has not presented itself. We continue to seek it, however. It's at the baths that such things take place. You reserve the bath for yourself (five francs including masseurs, pipe, coffee, sheet and towel) and you skewer your lad in one of the rooms. Be informed, furthermore, that all the bath-boys are bardashes. The final masseurs, the ones who come to rub you when all the rest is done, are usually quite nice young boys. We had our eye on one in an establishment very near our hotel. I reserved the bath exclusively for myself. I went, and the rascal was away that day! I was alone in the hot room, watching the daylight fade through the great circles of glass in the dome. Hot water was flowing everywhere; stretched out indolently I thought of a quantity of things as my pores tranquilly dilated. It is very voluptuous and sweetly melancholy to take a bath like that quite alone, lost in those dim rooms where the slightest noise reverberates like cannon shot, while the naked *kellaks* call out to one another as they massage you, turning you over like embalmers preparing you for the tomb. That day (the day before yesterday, Monday) my *kellak* was rubbing me gently, and when he came to the noble parts he lifted up my *boules d'amour* to clean them, then continuing to rub my chest with his left hand he began to pull with his right on my prick, and as he drew it up and down he leaned over my shoulder and said 'baksheesh, baksheesh'. He was a man in his fifties, ignoble, disgusting – imagine the effect, and the word 'baksheesh, baksheesh'. I pushed him away a little, saying 'làh, làh' ('no, no') – he thought I was angry and took on a craven look – then I gave him a few pats on the shoulder, saying 'làh, làh' again but more gently – he smiled a smile that meant, 'You're not fooling me – you like it as much as anybody, but today you've decided against it for some reason.' As for me, I laughed aloud like a dirty old man, and the shadowy vault of the bath echoed with the sound.

. . . A week ago I saw a monkey in the street jump on a donkey and try to jack him off – the donkey brayed and kicked, the monkey's owner shouted, the monkey itself squealed; apart from two or three children who laughed – and me, who found it very funny – no one paid any attention. When I described this to M. Belin, the secretary of the consulate, he told me of having seen an ostrich trying to violate a donkey. Max had himself jacked off the other day in a deserted section among some ruins and says he never enjoyed himself more.

Enough lubricities.

By means of *baksheesh* as always (*baksheesh* and the big stick are the essence of the Arab: you hear nothing else spoken of and see nothing else) we have been initiated into the fraternity of the *psylli*, or snake-charmers. We've had snakes put around our necks, around our hands, incantations have been recited over our heads, and our initiators have breathed into our mouths, all but inserting their tongues. It was great fun – the men who engage in such sinful enterprises practise their vile arts, as M. de Voltaire puts it, with singular competency.

. . . We speak with priests of all religions. The people here sometimes assume really beautiful poses and attitudes. We have translations of songs, stories and traditions made for us – everything that is most folkloric and oriental. We employ scholars – literally. We look quite dashing and are quite insolent and permit ourselves great freedom of language – our hotelkeeper thinks we sometimes go a little far.

One of these days we're going to consult the sorcerers – all part of our quest for the old ways of life here.

Dear fellow, how I'd love to hug you – I'll be glad to see your face again . . . Go and see my mother often – help her – write to her when she's away – the poor woman needs it. You'll be performing an act of the highest evangelism, and – psychologically – you'll witness the shy, gradual expansion of a fine and upright nature. Ah, you old bardash – if it weren't for her and for you, I'd scarcely give a thought to home . . .

1. Here follows an account, similar in most details to those written by many travellers, of visits to the pyramids and the sphinx. 'The Second Pyramid,' Flaubert writes, 'has its apex all covered with the droppings of the eagles and vultures that are constantly flying around the top of these monuments. It reminded me of words from *Saint Antoine*: "The gods, with heads of ibises, have their shoulders whitened with the droppings of birds." Maxime kept repeating: "I saw the Sphinx fleeing towards Libya; it was galloping like a jackal." '

    DuCamp, on the other hand, writes in his memoirs: 'When we reached the Sphinx . . . Flaubert reined in his horse and cried, "I have seen the Sphinx fleeing towards Libya; it was galloping like a jackal," and he added: "That's from *Saint Antoine*." '

    In any case, both were highly excited by the great monuments at Giza, and Flaubert wrote to Bouilhet: 'We don't have emotions as *po-hé-tiques* as that every day, thank God; it would kill us.'

~

Between Minia and Assiut. February 23, 1850
. . .

Now I come to something that you seem to enjoy reverting to
and that I utterly fail to understand. You are never at a loss for
things to torment yourself about. What is the sense of this: that I
must have a job – 'a small job', you say. First of all, *what* job? I defy
you to find me one, to specify in what field, or what it would be
like. Frankly, and without deluding yourself, is there a single one
that I am capable of filling? You add: 'One that wouldn't take up
much of your time and wouldn't prevent you from doing other
things.' There's the delusion! That's what Bouilhet told himself when
he took up medicine, what I told myself when I began law, which
nearly brought about my death from suppressed rage. When one
does something, one must do it wholly and well. Those bastard existences where you sell suet all day and write poetry at night are made
for mediocre minds – like those horses equally good for saddle and carriage – the worst kind, that can neither jump a ditch nor pull a plough.

In short, it seems to me that one takes a job for money, for
honours, or as an escape from idleness. Now you'll grant me, darling,
(1) that I keep busy enough not to have to go out looking for
something to do; and (2) if it's a question of honours, my vanity is
such that I'm incapable of feeling myself honoured by anything: a
position, however high it might be (and that isn't the kind you speak
of), will never give me the satisfaction that I derive from my self-
respect when I have accomplished something well in my own way;
and finally, if it's for money, any jobs or job that I could have would
bring in too little to make much difference to my income. Weigh
all those considerations: *don't knock your head against a hollow idea.*
Is there any position in which I'd be closer to you, more yours?[1]
And isn't not to be bored one of the principal goals of life?

1. Flaubert's reminder to his mother that his having no job would keep him
   close to her was possibly effective: there seem to have been no further
   suggestions that he seek '*une petite place*'.

~

To Louis Bouilhet

March 13, 1850. On board our cange, 12 leagues beyond Assuan[1]

In six or seven hours we are going to pass the Tropic of that well-known personage Cancer. It is 30 degrees in the shade at this moment, we are barefoot and wearing nothing but shirts, and I am writing to you on my divan, to the sound of the *darabukehs* of our sailors, who are singing and clapping their hands. The sun is beating down mercilessly on the awning over our deck. The Nile is flat as a river of steel. On its banks there are clusters of tall palms. The sky is blue as blue. *O pauvre vieux! pauvre vieux de mon coeur!*

What are you up to, there in Rouen? It's a long time since I had any of your letters, or rather I have so far had only one, dated the end of December, which I answered immediately. Perhaps another has arrived in Cairo and is being sent on to me. My mother writes that she sees you very seldom. Why is that? Even if it bores you too much, go once in a while anyway, for my sake, and try to tell me everything you can about what is going on in my house in every conceivable respect. Have you been in Paris again and seen Gautier and Pradier? What has happened to the trip to England for your Chinese story? *Melaenis* must be finished? Send me the end, you bloody bastard. I often growl out some of your lines, if you want to know. I must without further delay withdraw as vociferously as possible the objection I made to your word *vagabond* as applied to the Nile:

'*Que le Nil vagabond roule sur ses rivages.*'

There is no designation more just, more precise and at the same time more all-embracing. It is a crazy, magnificent river, more like an ocean than anything else. Sandy beaches extend as far as the eye can see on both its banks, furrowed by the wind like sea shores; it is so enormous that one doesn't know where the current is, and sometimes you feel enclosed in a great lake. Ah! But if you expect a proper letter you are mistaken. I warn you seriously that my intelligence has greatly diminished. This worries me: *I am not joking* – I feel very empty, very flat, very sterile. What am I to do once back in the old lodgings? Publish or not publish? The *Saint Antoine* business dealt me a heavy blow, I don't mind telling you. I've tried in vain to do something with my oriental tale, and for a day or two I played with the story of Mykerinos in Herodotus (the king who slept with his daughter). But it all came to nothing. By way of work, every day I read the *Odyssey* in Greek. Since we've been on the Nile I have done four books; we are coming home by way of Greece, so it may be of service to me. The first days on board I began to write a little; but I was not long, thank God, in realizing the ineptitude of such behaviour; just now it's best for me to be all eyes. We live, therefore, in the grossest idleness, stretched out all day on our divans watching everything that goes by: camels, herds of oxen from Sennar, boats floating down to Cairo laden with negresses and with elephants' tusks. We are now, my dear sir, in a land where women go naked – one might say with the poet 'naked as the hand',[2] for by way of costume they wear only rings. I have lain with Nubian girls whose necklaces of gold piastre hung down to their thighs and whose black stomachs were encircled by coloured beads – they feel cold when you rub your own stomach against them. And their dancing! *Sacré nom de Dieu!!!* But let us proceed in proper order.

From Cairo to Benisuef, nothing very interesting.

. . . At a place called Begel el-Teir we had an amusing sight. On the top of a hill overlooking the Nile there is a Coptic monastery, whose monks have the custom, as soon as they see a boatload of tourists, of running down, throwing themselves in the water, and swimming out to ask for alms. Everyone who passes is assailed by them. You see these fellows, totally naked, rushing down their perpendicular cliffs and swimming towards you as fast as they can, shouting: '*Baksheesh, baksheesh, cawadja christiani!*' And since there are many caves in the cliff at this particular spot, echo repeats '*Cawadja, cawadja!*' loud as a cannon. Vultures and eagles were flying overhead, the boat was flashing through the water, its two great sails very full. At that moment one of our sailors, the clown of the crew, began to dance a naked, lascivious dance that consisted of an attempt to bugger himself. To drive off the Christians he showed them his prick and his arse pretending to piss and shit on their heads (they were clinging to the sides of the *cange*). The other sailors shouted insults at them, repeating the names of Allah and Mohammed. Some hit them with sticks, others with ropes; Joseph rapped their knuckles with his kitchen tongs. It was a *tutti* of cudgelings, pricks, bare arses, yells and laughter. As soon as they were given money they put it in their mouths and returned home the way they had come. If they weren't greeted with a good beating, the boats would be assailed by such hordes of them that there would be danger of capsizing.

In another place it's not men who call on you, but birds. At Sheik Sa'id there is a tomb-chapel built in honour of a Moslem saint where birds go of their own accord and drop food that is given to them – this food is then offered to poor travellers – You and I, 'who have read Voltaire', don't believe this. But everyone is so backward here! You so seldom hear anyone singing Béranger's songs! ('What, sir, the benefits of civilization are not being introduced into this country? Where are your railway networks? What is the state of elementary education? Etc.')[3] – so that as you sail past this chapel all the birds flock around the boat and land on the rigging – you throw them bits of bread, they wheel about, pick it up from the water, and fly off.

At Kena I did something suitable, which I trust will win your approval: we had landed to buy supplies and were walking peacefully and dreamily in the bazaars, inhaling the odour of sandalwood that floated about us, when suddenly, at a turn in the street, we found ourselves in the whores' quarter. Picture to yourself, my friend, five or six curving streets lined with hovels about four feet high, built of dried grey mud. In the doorways, women standing or sitting on straw mats. The negresses had dresses of sky blue; others were in yellow, in white, in red – loose garments fluttering in the hot wind. Odours of spices. On their bare breasts long necklaces of gold piastres, so that when they move they rattle like carts. They call after you in drawling voices: '*Cawadja, cawadja*', their white teeth gleaming between their red or black lips, their metallic eyes rolling like wheels. I walked through those streets and walked through them again, giving *baksheesh* to all the women, letting them call me and catch hold of me; they took me around the waist and tried to pull me into their houses – think of all that, with the sun blazing down on it. Well, I abstained. (Young DuCamp did not follow my example.) I abstained deliberately, in order to preserve the sweet sadness of the scene and engrave it deeply in my memory. In this way I went away dazzled, and have remained so. There is nothing more beautiful than these women calling you. If I had gone with any of them, a second picture would have been superimposed on the first and dimmed its splendour.

I haven't always made such sacrifices on the altar of art. At Esna
in one day I fired five times and sucked three. I say it straight out
and without circumlocution, and let me add that I enjoyed it.
Kuchuk Hanem is a famous courtesan. When we reached her house
she was waiting for us; her confidante had come to the *cange* that
morning escorted by a sheep all spotted with yellow henna and with
a black velvet muzzle on its nose, following her like a dog – it was
quite a sight. Kuchuk had just left her bath. She was wearing a large
tarboosh topped with a gold plaque containing a green stone, and
with a loose tassel falling to her shoulders; her front hair was platted
in thin braids that were drawn back and tied together; the lower
part of her body was hidden in immense pink trousers; her torso
was entirely naked under purple gauze. She was standing at the top
of her staircase, with the sun behind her, sharply silhouetted against
the blue background of the sky surrounding her. She is a regal-
looking creature, large-breasted, fleshy, with slit nostrils, enormous
eyes, and magnificent knees; when she danced there were formidable
folds of flesh on her stomach. She began by perfuming our hands
with rosewater. Her bosom gave off a smell of sweetened turpentine,
and on it she wore a three-strand golden necklace. Musicians were
sent for and she danced. Her dancing isn't at all up to that of the
famous Hasan I mentioned earlier. Still, it was very agreeable and of
quite a bold style. In general, beautiful women dance badly. (I except
a Nubian we saw at Assuan – but that was no longer Arab dancing;
more ferocious, more frenetic, tigerish, negroid.)

That night we visited her again. There were four women dancers
and singers, *almehs*. (The word *almeh* means 'learned woman', 'blue-
stocking', but has come to signify 'whore' – which goes to show,
Monsieur, that in all countries literary ladies . . . !!!) The party lasted
from six to half past ten, with intermissions for fucking. Two rebec
players sitting on the floor made continual shrill music. When
Kuchuk undressed to dance, a fold of their turbans was lowered over
their eyes, to prevent their seeing anything. This modesty gave a
shocking effect. I spare you any description of the dance, I'd write
it too poorly. To be understood it has to be illustrated with gestures
– and even that would be inadequate.

When it came time to leave, I didn't. Kuchuk wasn't too eager
to have us spend the night with her, out of fear of thieves who might

well have come, knowing there were foreigners in the house. Maxime stayed alone on the divan and I went downstairs with Kuchuk to her room. We lay down on her bed, made of palm branches. A wick was burning in an antique-style lamp hanging on the wall. In an adjoining room guards were talking in low voices with the serving woman, an Abyssinian Negress whose arms were scarred by plague-sores. Kuchuk's little dog slept on my silk jacket.

I sucked her furiously, her body was covered with sweat, she was tired after dancing, she was cold. I covered her with my fur pelisse, and she fell asleep, her fingers in mine. As for me, I scarcely shut my eyes. My night was one long, infinitely intense reverie. That was why I stayed. Watching that beautiful creature asleep (she snored, her head against my arm; I had slipped my forefinger under her necklace), I thought of my nights in Paris brothels – a whole series of old memories came back – and I thought of her, of her dance, of her voice as she sang songs that were for me without meaning and even without distinguishable words. That continued all night.[4] At three o'clock I got up to piss in the street – the stars were shining. The sky was clear and immensely distant. She awoke, went to get a pot of charcoal and for an hour crouched beside it warming herself, then she came back to bed and fell asleep again. As for the *coups*, they were good – the third especially was ferocious, and the last tender – we told each other many sweet things – towards the end there was something sad and loving in the way we embraced.

At 7 in the morning we left. I went shooting with one of the sailors in a cotton field, under palm trees and *gazis*.[5] The countryside was lovely. Arabs, donkeys and buffalo were making their way to the fields. The wind was blowing through the fine branches of the *gazis*, whistling as it does through rushes. The mountains were pink, the sun was rising. My sailor walked ahead of me, bending to pass under bushes, and with a silent gesture pointing out to me the turtledoves he saw on the branches. I killed one, the only one I sighted. I walked pushing my feet ahead of me, and thinking of similar mornings – of one among others, at the marquis de Pomereu's at Le Héron, after a ball. I hadn't gone to bed, and in the morning went out in a boat on the pond, all alone, in my lycée uniform. The swans watched me pass, and leaves from the bushes were falling on the water. It was just before the beginning of term. I was fifteen.

In my absorption of all those things, *mon pauvre vieux*, you never ceased to be present. The thought of you was like a constant vesicant, inflaming my mind and making its juices flow by adding to the stimulation. I was sorry (the word is weak) that you were not there – I enjoyed it all for myself and for you – I was excited for both of us, and you came in for a good share, you may be sure.

. . . Just now we have stopped for lack of wind; the flies are stinging my face. Young DuCamp has gone off to take a picture. He is doing quite well – I think we'll have a nice album. As regards vice, he is calming down; it seems to us that I am inheriting his qualities, for I am growing lewd. Such is my profound conviction. When the brain sinks the prick rises. That isn't to say that I haven't collected a few metaphors. I have had a few stirrings. But how to make use of them, and where? . . .

1. Flaubert writes in a postscript: 'Max insists that for the sake of elegance I add: 23°39′ North Latitude. We are now exactly under the Tropic, but I don't see it.'
2. Alfred de Musset, *Namouna, Conte Oriental:* '*Hassan était donc nu, – mais nu comme la main.*' (J.B.)
3. For the significance of these 'quotations', see p. 678, n. 5.
4. In his travel notes Flaubert added a detail that was later to raise objections in a certain quarter: 'I was facing the wall, and without changing my position I amused myself killing the bedbugs that were crawling on it.' (See p. 249.)
5. A kind of low-growing palm.

$\sim$

To Louis Bouilhet

Between Girga and Assiut, June 2, 1850

. . .

I have given much thought to many things since we parted, *pauvre vieux*. Sitting on the divan of my *cange*, watching the water flow by, I ruminate about my past life, sometimes quite intensely. Many forgotten things come back to me, like snatches of songs sung by one's nurse in childhood. Am I about to enter a new period? Or is it the beginning of complete decadence? And from the past I go dreaming into the future, where I see nothing, nothing. I have no plans, no idea, no project, and, what is worse, no ambition. Something – the eternal 'what's the use?' – sets its bronze barrier across every avenue that I open up in the realm of hypothesis. Travelling doesn't make one gay. I don't know whether the sight of ruins inspires great thoughts, but I should like to know the source of the profound disgust that fills me these days when I think of making myself known and talked about. I don't feel within me the *physical strength* to publish, to run to the printer, to choose paper, to correct proofs, etc. And what is that, beside the rest? Better to work for yourself alone. Do as you like and follow your own ideas, admire yourself and please yourself: isn't that the main thing? And then the public is so stupid. Besides, who reads? And what do they read? And what do they admire?

Ah, blessed peaceful times, blessed times of powdered wigs! You lived with complete assurance, poised on your high heels, twirling your cane! But beneath *us* the earth is trembling. Where can we place our fulcrum, even assuming that we possess the lever? The thing we all lack is not style, nor the dexterity of finger and bow known as talent. We have a large orchestra, a rich palette, a variety of resources. We know many more tricks and dodges, probably, than were ever known before. No, what we lack is the intrinsic principle, the soul of the thing, the very idea of the subject. We take notes, we make journeys: emptiness! emptiness! We become scholars, archaeologists, historians, doctors, cobblers, people of taste. What is the good of all that? Where is the heart, the verve, the sap? Where to start out from? Where to go? We're good at sucking, we play a lot of tongue games, we pet for hours: but – the real thing! To ejaculate, beget the child!

. . . Yes, when I return I shall resume – and for a good long time, I hope – my old quiet life at my round table, between my fireplace and my garden. I shall continue to live like a bear, not giving a damn about my country, about critics, or anyone at all. Those ideas revolt young DuCamp, whose head is full of quite different ones; that is, he has very active plans for his return and intends to throw himself into demoniacal activity. At the end of next winter, in eight or nine months from now, we'll talk about all this.

I am going to make you a very frank confession: I pay no more attention to my mission than to the King of Prussia. To 'discharge my duties' properly I should have had to give up my journey – it would have been absurd. I do stupid things now and then, but not of that enormity, I trust. Can you see me in every town, informing myself about crops, about production, about consumption? 'How much oil do you shit here? How many potatoes do you stuff into yourselves?' And in every port: 'How many ships? What tonnage? How many arrivals? How many departures?' And ditto, ditto. *Merde!* Ah, no! Frankly – was it possible? And after committing a sufficient number of such turpitudes (my title itself is quite enough of one), if I had taken certain steps and if my friends had spoken for me and if the Ministry had been well disposed, I should have won the Legion of Honour! *Tableau!* Great satisfaction for my uncle Parain!!! No, no, a thousand times. I want none of it: I honour myself so much that nothing can honour me. (Pompous words!)

. . .

I have seen Thebes:[1] it is very beautiful. We arrived one night at nine, in brilliant moonlight that flooded the columns. Dogs were barking, the great white ruins looked like ghosts, and the moon on the horizon, completely round and seeming to touch the earth, appeared to be motionless, resting there deliberately. Karnak gave us the impression of a life of giants. I spent a night at the feet of the colossus of Memnon, devoured by mosquitoes. The old scoundrel has a good face and is covered with graffiti. Graffiti and bird-droppings are the only two things in the ruins of Egypt that give any indication of life. The most worn stone doesn't grow a blade of grass; it falls into powder, like a mummy, and that is all . . . Often you see a tall, straight obelisk, with a long white stain down its entire length, like a drapery – wider at the top and tapering towards the base. That is from the vultures, who have been coming there to shit for centuries. It is a very handsome effect and has a curious symbolism. It is as though Nature said to the monuments of Egypt: 'You will have none of me? You will not nourish the seed of the lichen? *Eh bien, merde*, I'll shit on you.'

In the rock tombs at Thebes (among the most curious and fascinating things you can imagine) we discovered some pharaonic bawdy which proves, Monsieur, that in all ages of the world man has gone to perdition, has '*aimé la fillette*', as our immortal songwriter puts it.[3] It is a picture showing men and women at table, eating and drinking, couples with an arm around each other's waist and playing tongue games. There are some charming, lewd profiles, marvellous facial expressions of bourgeois on a spree. Nearby are two young girls in transparent dresses, the most whorish shapes imaginable, playing the guitar with a lascivious air. It's a bordello scene from a dirty Palais Royal picture of 1816. It gave us a good laugh and something to think about. Such thoughts make one dizzy, Monsieur! It's all so modern that one is tempted to believe that condoms were known at the time of Sesostris.

At Esna I saw Kuchuk Hanem again; it was sad. I found her changed. She had been sick. I fired only one shot. The day was heavy and overcast; her Abyssinian servant was sprinkling water on the floor to cool the room. I stared at her for a long while, so as to be able to keep a picture of her in my mind. When I left, we told her we would return the next day, but we did not. I intensely relished the bitterness of all that; that's the main thing, and I felt it in my very bowels. At Kena I had a beautiful whore who liked me very much and told me in sign language that I had lovely eyes. Her name is Hosna et-Taouilah, which means 'the beautiful tall one'; and there was another, fat and lubricious, on top of whom I enjoyed myself immensely and who smelled of rancid butter.

I saw the Red Sea at Koseir. It was a journey that took four days going and five for the return, on camelback and in a heat that in the middle of the day rose to over 45 degrees Réaumur. That was a bit scorching: occasionally I longed for some beer, especially since our water smelled of sulphur and soap in addition to the taste of goat given it by the skins. We rose at three in the morning and went to bed at nine at night, living on hard-boiled eggs, dry preserves, and watermelons. It was real desert life. All along the route we came upon the carcasses of camels that had died of exhaustion. There are places where you find great sheets of sand which seem to have been turned into a kind of pavement, areas smooth and glazed like the threshing-floor of a barn: those are the places where camels stop to piss. With time the urine varnishes the sand and levels it like a floor. We had taken some cold meat with us, but in the middle of the second day had to abandon it. The odour of a leg of mutton we left on a stone immediately attracted a vulture, which began to fly round and round it.

We met great caravans of pilgrims going to Mecca (Koseir is the port where they take ship for Jidda, whence it is only three days to Mecca). Old Turks with their wives carried in baskets; a whole veiled harem called out to us like magpies as we passed; a dervish wearing a leopard-skin.

The camels in a caravan go sometimes one behind the other, sometimes all advancing on one broad front. When you see, foreshortened on the horizon, all those swaying heads coming towards you, it is like a horde of ostriches advancing slowly and gradually drawing together. At Koseir we saw pilgrims from the depths of Africa, poor negroes who have been on the march for a year, even two years. There are some curious sights. We also saw people from Bukhara, Tartars in pointed caps, who were preparing a meal in the shade of a shipwrecked boat made of red Indian wood. As for pearl-fishers, we saw only their canoes. Two men go in each canoe, one to row and one to dive, and they go out onto the open sea. When the diver returns to the surface he is bleeding from ears, nostrils, and eyes.

The day after my arrival I bathed in the Red Sea. It was one of the most voluptuous pleasures of my life. I lolled in its waters as though I were lying on a thousand liquid breasts that caressed my entire body.

That night Maxime, out of courtesy, and to honour his host, gave himself an attack of indigestion. We were lodged in a separate pavilion where we slept on divans and had a view of the sea. We were served by a young negro eunuch who had a very stylish way of carrying the tray of coffee cups on his left arm. The morning we were to leave . . . I sat by myself, looking at the sea. Never will I forget that morning. I was stirred by it as though by an adventure; because of all the shells, shellfish, madrepores, corals, etc. the bottom of the sea is more brilliant than a spring meadow covered with primroses. As for the colour of the surface of the water, all possible tints passed through it, iridescent and melting together, from chocolate to amethyst, from pink to lapis lazuli and the palest green, and were I a painter I'd have been very embarrassed, thinking to what degree the reproduction of those real colours (admitting that they were possible) would seem false.

We left Koseir that afternoon at four, very sadly. My eyes were wet when I embraced our host and climbed back on to my camel. It is always sad to leave a place to which one knows one will never return. Such are the *mélancolies du voyage*: perhaps they are one of the most enriching things about travelling.

As to any change we may have undergone during our separation, I do not think, *cher vieux*, that if there is one it will be to my advantage. You will have gained by solitude and concentration; I shall have lost by diffusion and daydreaming. I am becoming very empty and very barren. I feel it. It is overtaking me like a rising tide. Perhaps this is due to being physically active. I cannot do two things at once. Perhaps I have left my intelligence behind, with my drawstring trousers, my leather divan, and your company, dear sir. Where will all this lead us? What shall we have accomplished in ten years? As for myself, it seems to me that if I fail in the next thing I undertake, I might as well drown myself. Once so dauntless, now I am becoming excessively timid – and in the arts timidity is the worst possible thing and the greatest sign of weakness.

. . .

Well, I hope you will agree that this letter is a veritable document and that I'm a good fellow. Send me an answer to Beirut, where we'll be towards the end of July, then at Jerusalem. Work hard, try not to be too bored, don't do too much fornicating; conserve your strength: an ounce of sperm lost is worse than ten pounds of blood. By the way, you ask me if I consummated that business at the baths. Yes – and on a pockmarked young rascal wearing a white turban. It made me laugh, that's all. But I'll be at it again. To be done well, an experiment must be repeated.

Farewell, old man of the pen!

. . . [P.S.] 5 June. Tomorrow is the sixth, birthday of the great Corneille! What a session at the Rouen Academy! What speeches! . . . The Academicians in full dress: white tie! Pomp! Sound traditions! A brief report on agriculture!

1. The travellers explored Thebes on the return downstream to Cairo. Earlier, when the *cange* stopped briefly at Thebes on the way upstream, Flaubert had recorded in his travel notes a moment of particular élan:

'Monday, 4 March . . . We have passed Luxor. I was cleaning my glass when we sighted Luxor on the left: I climbed on to the roof of the cabin. The seven columns, the obelisk, the French House, Arabs sitting beside the water near an English *cange*. The caretaker of the French House calls out that he has a letter for us . . . We stop. Among the people at the landing, a negro, swathed like a mummy – all cartilage, desiccated, with a small, dirty *takieh* [cap] on the top of his head; women are bathing their feet in the river, a donkey has come down to drink.

'Sunset over Medinet Habu. The mountains are dark indigo (on the Medinet Habu side); blue over dark grey, with contrasting horizontal stripes of purplish red in the clefts of the valleys. The palms are black as ink, the sky is red, the Nile has the look of a lake of molten steel.

'When we arrived off Thebes our sailors were drumming on their *darabukehs*, the mate was playing his flute. Khalil was dancing with his castanets: they broke off to land.

'It was then, while I was observing those things, and enjoying observing them, and just as I was watching three wave-crests curling under the wind at our stern, that I felt a surge of solemn happiness that reached out towards what I was seeing, and I thanked God in my heart for having made me capable of such joy: I felt fortunate at the thought, and yet it seemed to me that I was thinking of nothing: it was a sensuous pleasure that pervaded my entire being.'

2. Béranger.

⌇

To Louis Bouilhet

Cairo, June 27 [1850]

Here we are back in Cairo. That is all the news I have to tell you, dear good friend, for after my last letter nothing of interest happened on our trip. In a few days we leave for Alexandria, and at the end of next month, if all goes well, we'll be not far from Jerusalem.

Leaving our little boat put me into a frightful melancholy.[1] Back in the hotel here in Cairo my head was buzzing, as though after a long journey by stage-coach. The city seemed empty and silent, though actually it was busy and full of people. The first night of my arrival here (last Tuesday), I kept hearing the soft sound of oars in the water – that cadenced accompaniment to our long dreamy days for the past three months. The city palm trees looked to me like brooms used for sweeping public lavatories. I relived the entire trip, and in my heart I felt a bitter sweetness that was like the taste of a belch after good wine – when you say to yourself: 'Well, that was it.'

. . . A bizarre psychological phenomenon! Back in Cairo (and since reading your good letter), I have been feeling myself bursting with intellectual intensity. The pot suddenly began to boil! I felt a burning need to write! I was wound up tight.

. . .

Your idea for a Chinese tale seems to me excellent in general. Can you send me the outline? Once you have decided on your main ideas for local colour, do no more reading and begin to write. *Let's not get lost in archaeology* – a widespread and fatal tendency, I think, of the coming generation . . . Poor wretches that we are, we have, I think, considerable taste because we are profoundly historical: we admit everything, and adopt the point of view of whatever we are judging. But have we as much inner strength as we have under-standing of others? Is fierce originality compatible with so much breadth of mind? Such are my doubts concerning the artistic spirit of the times, that is, concerning the few artists there are. At least, if we do nothing good we shall perhaps have paved the way for a generation that will have our fathers' boldness (I'm looking for another word) along with our own eclecticism. That would surprise me – the world is going to become bloody stupid and from now on will be a very boring place. We're lucky to be living now.

You won't believe that Max and I talk constantly about the future of society. For me it is almost certain that at some more or less distant time it will be regulated like a college. Schoolmasters will make the laws. Everyone will be in uniform. Mankind will no longer commit barbarisms as it writes its insipid theme, but – what wretched style! What lack of form, of rhythm, of spirit! . . .

No matter. God will always be there, after all. Let us hope that He will always hold the upper hand and that the old sun will not perish. Last night I re-read Paulus's apostrophe to Venus [in *Mela-enis*], and this morning I upheld (as I did at eighteen) the doctrine of Art for Art's Sake against a Utilitarian – a good man, however. I resist the torrent. Will it carry us along with it? No – rather than that, let us beat ourselves to death with a leg of our own writing table! 'Let us be strong! Let us be beautiful! Let us wipe off on the grass the dust that soils our gold buskins!'[2] Or not wipe them – I haven't the slightest idea what makes me quote this. So long as there is gold underneath, who cares about the dust on top? . . . Literature! That old whore! We must try to dose her with mercury and pills and clean her out from top to bottom, she has been so ultra-screwed by filthy pricks!

. . .

1. A fuller account of the Egyptian portion of the journey is contained in *Flaubert in Egypt*. (See Works of Related Interest.)
2. A slightly inaccurate quotation from his own *Saint Antoine*.

~

To Louis Bouilhet

Jerusalem, August 20, 1850

I can certainly say, like Sassetti: 'You won't believe me, Monsieur, but when I caught sight of Jerusalem I must confess it gave me a funny feeling.' I checked my horse, which I had spurred on ahead of the others, and stared at the holy city, quite astonished at the sight. It looked very near; the walls were in much better state than I expected. Then I thought of Christ, and saw him climbing the Mount of Olives. He was wearing a blue robe, his temples were beaded with sweat. And I thought of his entry into Jerusalem, the shouting, the green palm branches, etc. – Flandrin's fresco that we saw together in Saint-Germain-des-Prés, the day before I left.

. . .

The Holy Sepulchre is the agglomeration of all possible execrations. Within this tiny space, four churches: Armenian, Greek, Latin, and Coptic. All heartily insulting and cursing one another, each quarrelling with its neighbours over candlesticks, rugs, pictures – and what pictures! It's the Turkish Pasha who keeps the keys to the Holy Sepulchre. When you want to visit it, you must get them from him. I find that quite striking. On the other hand, it's the most humane solution. If the Holy Sepulchre were given over to the Christians, they would unfailingly massacre each other. Such cases have been known.

'*Tanta religio!* etc.,' as gentle Lucretius said.[1]

. . . After my first visit to the Holy Sepulchre I returned to the hotel bone-tired and disgusted. I took up a St Matthew and read the Sermon on the Mount, my heart expanding as though nothing had ever touched it before. That relieved the cold, sour feeling I had experienced. Everything possible has been done to make the holy places ridiculous. It's all whorish to the last degree: hypocrisy, cupidity, falsification, impudence, yes: but as for holiness, go fuck yourself. I resent not having been moved: I wanted nothing better than to be so – you know me. Still, I do have one relic that I'll keep. Here is the story. The second time I was in the Holy Sepulchre I was in the Sepulchre itself, a small chapel all lit by lamps and full of flowers stuck in china vases of the kind you see decorating dressmakers' mantelpieces. There are so many lamps crammed one next to the other that it's like the ceiling of a lamp shop. The walls are marble. Facing you is a grimacing Christ in bas-relief, life-size and horrible, his ribs painted red. I was staring at the holy stone; the priest opened a cupboard, took out a rose, laid it on the stone of the Sepulchre, and proceeded to say a prayer, blessing the flower. I was flooded with a wry kind of sentimentality. I thought of the pious souls who would have been enchanted by such a present in such a place, and how wasted it was on me. My lack of proper response caused me no tears, I had no regrets, but there came over me that strange feeling which two men like you and me experience when we are alone beside our fire, straining with all the might of our souls to explore the ancient abyss represented by the word 'love', and imagining what it might be – if it were possible. No, at that moment I was neither Voltairean nor Mephistophelian nor Sadist. On the contrary, I was being quite simple. I was examining the question in all sincerity, and remained quite calm even in my imaginings.

· · ·

At Beirut we made the acquaintance of a splendid fellow, Camille Rogier, the Postmaster of the place. He is a painter from Paris, one of Gautier's cronies, who lives here in native style. Very intelligent: we enjoyed meeting him. He has a pretty house, a pretty cook (male), and an enormous prick, compared with which yours is a mere tack. When he was at Constantinople, its reputation was such that Turks came to his house in the mornings especially to see it. (Gospel.) He treated us to a morning of nymphets. I fucked three women, four shots in all, three before lunch and one after dessert. At the end, I even proposed doing it with their bawd, but, because I had refused when she offered herself earlier, she made it her turn to say no. Still, I'd have enjoyed pulling that one off, to crown the day's work and give me a good opinion of myself. Young DuCamp only fired once – his prick was sore from the remains of a chancre he picked up from a Walachian girl in Alexandria. I revolted the Turkish women by my cynicism in washing my prick in full view of the company. Which didn't prevent them from quite affably accepting the postilion position. (In a country where all travel is on horseback, there's nothing surprising about that.) Which in turn goes to show, dear Sir, that women are women everywhere: say what you will, upbringing and religion make no difference: they only cover up a little: they conceal, conceal, that's all. The damsels weren't bashful about downing alcohol. I remember one of them, with a spray of jasmine in her frizzy black hair; she seemed to me to smell very sweet as I ejaculated inside her. She was slightly snub-nosed, and there was a bit of matter beside the inner pupil of her right eye. This was in the morning: she probably hadn't had time to wash. These were Society ladies, as we would call them at home; through the kind agency of the procuress they do these tricks for fun and a little money . . .

Nota bene, under the seal of the greatest secrecy: Μαξίμ ουάντεδ τοῦ σόδομάϊζ ε βάρδασ ιν ϑη γρόττο οφ Ιερεμία.—— Θάτς ε λαϊ!²

P.S. No! No! It's true. What think you of our young friend? *Adieu, je t'embrasse. À toi.*

1. Lucretius, *De natura rerum*, Book I, 1.101: ' *Tantum religio potuit suadere malorum!*' ('Such are the crimes to which religion leads.')
2. In the original, the 'Greek' is an accusation by Flaubert, consisting of the following French words written in Greek characters: '*Maxime a voulu sodomiser un bardache dans la grotte de Jérémie,*' followed by Maxime's denial, also in 'Greek': '*C'est faux!*' In the present 'translation', English words in Greek characters have been substituted. Flaubert's P.S. is written in normal French.

∽

TO LOUIS BOUILHET

Damascus, September 4, 1850

'You too, Brutus!' – which doesn't mean that I'm a Caesar!

You too, poor fellow, whom I so admired for your unshakeable faith! . . . In the midst of my lassitudes, my discouragements and my nausea you were always the seltzer water that helped me digest life. I used to soak myself in you as in a tonic bath. When I was alone and full of self-pity I used to say to myself: 'Look at him!' and then I would return to my work with new strength. You were my great moral example, my continual edification. Is the saint now to fall from his niche? Don't stray from your pedestal!

Are we idiots, perhaps? Maybe so, but it is not up to us to say it, still less to believe it. However, we should by now have finished with our migraines and our failures of nerve. One thing is our ruin, one stupid thing shackles us: 'taste' – good taste. We have too much of it – or rather, we worry about it more than we should. Fear of bad taste engulfs us like a fog (a dirty December fog that suddenly appears, freezes your guts, stinks, and stings your eyes), to such a point that we stand still, not daring to advance. Don't you realize how captious we are becoming, that we have our own poetics, our own ready-made ideas, our own rules? . . . What we lack is daring. Oh for the time of my youth, when I dashed off a five-act play in three days! With our scruples we resemble those poor believers who daren't live for fear of hell and who wake their confessor early in the morning to unburden their consciences of having had a miscarriage in a dream. Let's worry less about results. The thing is to keep fucking, keep fucking: who cares what child the muse will give birth to? Isn't the purest pleasure in her embraces?

To do badly, to do well – what's the difference? As for myself, I have renounced thinking of posterity – a wise move. My stand is taken. Unless some excessively literary wind begins to blow in a few years, I am resolved not to 'make the presses groan' with any elucubration of my brain. You and my mother and others (for it is a wonderful thing, how no one will let people live as they like) used to scold me for my manner of life. Just wait a bit till I come back, and see whether I don't resume it. I'll burrow into my hole, and though the world crumble I'll not budge out of it. I have just sent back without even looking at them several silk scarves that were brought me to choose from. I had only to raise my eyes and decide, but the thought of the effort so overpowered me in advance that I sent the merchants away without buying anything. Had I been the sultan, I'd have thrown them out of the window: I was full of rancour towards anyone trying to force me into any activity whatever. But let's get back to our bottles, as old Michel says.[1]

If you think that your worry is going to worry me a long time, you're mistaken. I have shared the burden of greater worries; I fear nothing in that line. If the bedroom in the Hôtel-Dieu now sheltering the young Juliette Flaubert[2] could recount all the disgust that two young men gave vent to there throughout twelve years, I think the establishment would collapse on the heads of its present bourgeois occupants. Poor Alfred! Astonishing how much I think of him, and all the unshed tears for him my heart still holds! How we talked! We looked each other in the eye. We *soared*.

Be careful: one comes to enjoy worrying about things – it's a kind of addiction. What's the matter with you? How I should like to be there, to kiss you on the forehead and kick you in the tail! What you are feeling now is the result of the long labour you put into *Melaenis*. Do you think a poet's brain is like a cotton-spinning machine, which perpetually turns out stuff without fatigue or inter-mittence? Come now, little man! Head up! Give yourself a good talking-to in the mirror. Is it the state of society at the moment that's upsetting you? It's natural for the bourgeois to worry about it behind his counter; and I too have moments of adolescent fears. *Novembre* keeps recurring to me. Am I approaching a Renaissance, or would this be decrepitude in the guise of a second bloom? Still, I have recovered (though not without pain) from the terrible blow dealt me by *Saint Antoine*. I can't boast that I'm not still staggering a little from it, but I'm no longer sick about it, as I was for the first four months of this trip. I was seeing everything through the veil of despondency cast over me by that disappointment, and I kept repeating the same inept words you now send me: 'What's the use?'

However, I am making progress (?). (Perhaps you'd rather I wrote about travel – fresh air, wide horizons, blue skies?) Every day I feel myself becoming more sensitive, more easily moved. The slightest thing brings a tear. My heart plays the very whore, gushingly receptive to anything and everything. Insignificant details stir my guts. I keep falling into endless reveries and distractions. I continuously feel as though I'm a little drunk, and along with that I'm more and more inept and incapable of understanding anything that's explained to me. My memory fails me more and more often. Then, great literary frenzies. I promise myself some sprees when I get back. There you have it.

You do well to think about the *Dictionary of Accepted Opinions*.

Such a book, covering the field *completely*, and opening with a good preface in which we would indicate just how the work was intended to reconcile the public to tradition, to order and conventional morality, and written in such a way that the reader couldn't tell whether or not we were pulling his leg – that would perhaps be a strange book, and it might well have some success, for it would be very topical.

If the presidential election of 1852 doesn't result in a great debacle, if the bourgeois emerge triumphant, we may remain bogged down in our stupid state for another century.[4] In that case the public, weary of politics, may seek diversion in literature, may want to escape from action into fantasy. Might our day then come? If on the contrary we are precipitated into the future, who can tell what kind of Poetry will spring up? There will certainly be poetry, so let's not lament or curse; let's just accept everything, learn to be tolerant . . .

In Jerusalem I read a socialist book (*Essai de philosophie positive*, by Auguste Comte).[5] It was lent me by a raging Catholic, who insisted that I read it to see how dangerous Positivism is. I skimmed a few pages: it is deadly stupid. As I expected, in fact. It contains vast mines of the comic, whole Californias of the grotesque. And perhaps something else, as well. That is possible. One of the first subjects I intend to study on my return is 'those deplorable utopias which are agitating our society and threatening to reduce it to ruins'. Why not accommodate ourselves to the goal proposed to us? It's as good as any other: looking at things impartially, there have been few more fertile. *Ineptitude consists in wanting to reach conclusions.* We tell ourselves: 'But our point of departure is uncertain – which of the two will win out?' I see a past in ruins and a future in bud; the one is too old, the other too young: all is confusion. But that amounts to misunderstanding the nature of all transitions – wanting twilight to be either noon or midnight. What do we care what tomorrow will look like? We see only the face labelled Today. It grimaces horribly – and is thereby all the more expressive of Romanticism.

When has the Bourgeois ever loomed larger than now? What is Molière's Bourgeois in comparison? M. Jourdain doesn't come ankle-high to the first merchant you'll meet in the street. And the envious mug of the proletariat? And the young man on the make? And the

Judge? And everything that's fermenting in the brains of the brainless, everything simmering in the hearts of rogues?

Yes, stupidity consists in wanting to reach conclusions. We are a thread, and we want to know the whole cloth. It recalls the eternal discussions about the decadence of art. Now we spend our time telling ourselves: 'We're completely finished, we're at the last gasp,' etc. What mind worthy of the name, beginning with Homer, ever reached a conclusion? Let's accept the picture. That's how things are. So be it . . .

Now I must go to bed. It is eleven o'clock. I can hear the water plashing into the basin in the courtyard. It reminds me of the sound of the fountain at Marseilles, in the Hôtel Richelieu, while I was fucking that worthy Mme Foucaud, née de Langlade. Ten years ago . . .!

1. Montaigne.
2. The daughter of Flaubert's brother, Dr Achille Flaubert.
3. Flaubert long cherished this project. Over the years he compiled such a dictionary, and he had planned to make it the second part of his last, unfinished novel, *Bouvard et Pécuchet*. It is commonly printed in editions of that work. In English it exists also as a separate volume, *The Dictionary of Accepted Ideas*, translated by Jacques Barzun. (See Works of Related Interest and p. 241 et seq.)
4. The struggle in France between Right and Left, reflected in this letter and others, had persisted after the Revolution of 1848 and the election of Louis-Napoléon Bonaparte as President in December of that year; and it culminated in the latter's coup d'état of December 1 and 2, 1851. In 1852 there would be no 'presidential election': instead, Louis-Napoléon would be given supreme power, with the title of Emperor.
5. Perhaps one of the six volumes of Comte's *Cours de philosophie positive* (1839–42).

~

TO HIS MOTHER

Constantinople, November 14, 1850

. . .

P.S . . . As to the idea that's worrying you, that I'll be bored on my return, rest easy. I have passed the age of boredom, and I left part of myself with it. Besides, I shall have too much work to do. Something new is germinating in me: a second manner, perhaps? But at some point I'll have to give birth. I am impatient to discover what I am capable of. Shall I be able to retrieve, for another piece of work, everything I invested – and lost – in *Saint Antoine???*

~

To Louis Bouilhet
Constantinople, November 14, 1850

. . .

About Constantinople, where I arrived yesterday morning, I'll tell you nothing today, except to say that I have been struck by Fourier's idea that some time in the future it will be the capital of the world. It is really fantastic as a human anthill. That feeling of being crushed and overwhelmed you had on your first visit to Paris: here one is penetrated by it, elbowing as one does so many unknown men, from the Persian and the Indian to the American and the Englishman, so many separate individualities which in their frightening total humble one's own. And then, the city is immense. One gets lost in the streets, which seem to have no beginning or end. The cemeteries are forests in the midst of the city. From the top of the tower at Galata, looking out over all the houses and all the mosques (beside and between the Bosphorous and the Golden Horn, both full of ships), the houses too seem like ships – a motionless fleet, with the minarets as masts. (A rather tortuous sentence – skip it.) We walked through (no more than that) the street of the male brothels. I saw bardashes buying sugared almonds, doubtless with bugger-money – the anus thus about to provision the stomach instead of the usual other way round. I heard the sound of a scratchy violin coming from ground-floor rooms: they were dancing a Greek dance. These young boys are usually Greeks. They wear their hair long.

Tomorrow I'll have your name, *Loue Bouilhette* (Turkish pronunciation), written on a sheet of blue paper in gold letters – a present intended as a decoration for your room. When you are alone and look at it, it will remind you that I have had you much with me during my journey.

. . .

I want you to know, dear Sir, that in Beirut I picked up (I first noticed them at Rhodes, land of the dragon)[1] VII chancres, which eventually merged into two, then one. In that condition I rode my horse from Marmaris to Smyrna. Every night and morning I dressed my wretched prick. Finally it cured itself. In two or three days the scar will be closed. I'm being desperately careful about it. I suspect a Maronite woman of making me this gift, or perhaps it was a little Turkish lady. The Turk or the Christian? Which? *Problème!* Food for thought! That's an aspect of the 'Eastern Question' the *Revue des Deux Mondes* doesn't dream of. We discovered this morning that Sassetti has the clap (from Smyrna), and last night Maxime discovered, even though it's six weeks since he did any fornicating, a double abrasion that looks to me very much like a two-headed chancre. If it is, that makes the third time he's caught the pox since we set out. There's nothing like travel for the health.

Where are you, with the muse? I expected to find a letter from you here, with some lines of verse . . . What are you reading? What are you doing? How I long to see you!

As for me, literarily speaking, I've lost my bearings. At times I feel annihilated (the word is weak); at other times my 'aural' style (i.e. in the state of an aura, an imponderable fluid) passes and circulates within me with intoxicating heat. Then it dies down. I meditate very little, daydream occasionally. My observation is preponderantly of the moral kind. I should never have suspected this facet of travel. The psychological, human, comic side abounds. One meets splendid specimens – variegated, iridescent existences very lustrous to the eye, like tattered embroidered garments heavy with filth and gold braid. And underneath it all, the same old low-life, immutable, invincible. That's the basis. How much of it one sees! From time to time, in the towns, I open a newspaper. Things seem to be going at a dizzy rate. We are dancing not on a volcano, but on the rotten seat of a latrine. Before very long, society is going to drown in nineteen centuries of shit, and there'll be a lot of shouting. I am thinking seriously of 'studying the question'. If you'll forgive my presumption, I'd like to squeeze the whole thing in my hands, like a lemon, to acidulate my drink. After my return I want to immerse myself in the Socialists' theories, and do, in theatrical form, something very brutal, very farcical, and – of course – impartial. I have the words on the tip of my tongue and the tone at my fingertips. Many subjects for which I have more defined plans are less eager to be born than that one.[2]

As for subjects, I have three; perhaps they are all the same, a thought that galls me considerably. *One: Une Nuit de Don Juan*,[3] which I thought of in quarantine at Rhodes. *Two: Anubis*,[4] the story of the woman who wants to be laid by the God. This is the loftiest of the three, but full of atrocious difficulties. *Three:* my Flemish novel about the young girl who dies a virgin and mystic after living with her father and mother in a small provincial town, at the end of a garden full of cabbages and fruit trees, beside a stream the size of the Robec.[5] What torments me is the kinship of idea of these three projects. In the first, insatiable love in the two forms: earthly love and mystical love. In the second, the same story, only there is fornication in it, and the earthly love is less exalted because more precise. In the third they are combined in the same person, and the one leads to the other; only, my heroine dies of religious masturbation after indulging in digital masturbation. Alas! It seems to me that when one is as good as this at dissecting children yet to be born, one doesn't harden up enough to create them. My clear-cut metaphysics fills me with terrors. But I must get rid of them. I need to know my measure. In order to live in peace, I want to have an opinion of myself, a definite opinion that will regulate me in the use of my powers. I have to know the quality and extent of my land before beginning to plough. I am experiencing a need, with relation to my personal literary situation, which everyone of our age feels to some extent with relation to the life of society: I feel the need of 'becoming established'.

At Smyrna, during a rain that kept us indoors, I took Eugène Sue's *Arthur* from the reading room. It's enough to make you vomit; there's no word to describe it. You have to read this book to realize the pitifulness of money, success and the public. Literature has become consumptive. It spits and slobbers, covers its blisters with salves and sticking-plasters, and has grown bald from excessive hairbrushing. It would take Christs of art to cure this leper. To return to the Antique in literature has been done already. The Middle Ages, the same. Remains the present. But the ground is shaky: where to lay the foundation? And yet there is no other way of constructing something vital and therefore durable. All this worries me so much that I have come to dislike being spoken to about it. I am irritated by it sometimes, like a released convict listening to a discussion of the penal system. Especially with Maxime, who strikes hard and isn't an encouraging fellow – and I badly need to be encouraged. On the other hand, my vanity is not yet resigned to being awarded encouragement prizes only!

I am about to re-read the whole of the *Iliad*. In a fortnight we are to make a little trip to the Troad, and in January we shall be in Greece. I fret at my ignorance: if only I knew Greek! And I have lost so much time over it!

'La sérénité m'abandonne!'

The man who retains the same self-esteem while travelling that he had when he looked at himself every day in the mirror of his room at home is either a very great man or a very sturdy fool. I don't know why, but I'm becoming very humble.

Passing Abydos, I thought much about Byron. That is his Orient, the Turkish Orient, the Orient of the curved sword, the Albanian costume, and the barred window looking on the blue sea. I prefer the baked Orient of the Bedouin and the desert, the vermilion depths of Africa, the crocodile, the camel, the giraffe.

I regret not getting to Persia (money! money!). I keep dreaming of Asiatic journeys, of going overland to China, of impossibilities – the Indies, or California, which always excites me on the human side. At other times I get so choked up with emotion that I could weep, thinking of my study at Croisset, of our Sundays. Ah, how I'll miss these days of travel, how I'll keep reliving them, how I'll repeat the eternal monologue: 'Fool! You didn't enjoy it enough!'

. . . Why has Balzac's death 'affected me strongly'? One is always saddened by the death of a man one admires. I had hoped to know him later, hoped he would like me. Yes, he was a stout fellow, one who had an extraordinary understanding of his age. He, who had studied women so well, died just after he married – and when the society he knew was approaching its end. With Louis-Philippe, something disappeared that we shall not see again. Now we must dance to a different tune.

Why have I a melancholy desire to return to Egypt, to go back up the Nile and see Kuchuk Hanem? All the same, it was a rare night I spent there, and I tasted it to the full. How I missed you!

. . . Good night. I must attend to that dressing.

1. A species of large lizard found on the island is known as 'the dragon of Rhodes'.

2. It would be born, twenty years later, in novelistic rather than dramatic form, in the definitive *Éducation sentimentale*.

3. Flaubert's outline for *Une Nuit de Don Juan* exists. It consists chiefly of two dialogues: between the Don and Leporello, about the Don's way of life; and between the Don and a dead nun with whom he spends the night in her convent, about earthly and mystical love.

4. No outline for *Anubis* is known. From Flaubert's brief description, however, it must have been what Jean Bruneau suggests – a foreshadowing of *Salammbô*.

5. For the role of the projected 'Flemish novel' in the genesis of *Madame Bovary*, see p. 199. In *Par les champs et par les grèves*, Flaubert notes his conception of a similar subject when in Blois with DuCamp in 1847. ('Flemish' here probably means, roughly, 'realistic' – as in Flemish painting, with its 'humbler' subjects drawn from daily life.)

The Robec was a small stream flowing through an old quarter of Rouen. It is mentioned in the first chapter of *Madame Bovary*.

~

To his mother

December 15, 1850. Constantinople

When is the wedding to be, you ask me, apropos of the news of Ernest Chevalier's marriage. When? Never, I hope. As far as man can answer for what he will do, I reply in the negative. Contact with the world – and I've been rubbing shoulders with it now for fourteen months – makes me feel more and more like returning to my shell. Uncle Parain, who claims that travel changes a man, is wrong as far as I am concerned. As I set out, so shall I return, except that there are fewer hairs on my head and considerably more landscapes within it. That is the only difference. As to the principles that guide me, I shall retain the ones I have always had until further notice. Besides, if I had to say how I feel deep down, and if it doesn't sound too presumptuous, I would say: 'Too late, now. I'm too old to change.' When one has lived, as I have, a completely inner life, full of turbulent analyses and repressed enthusiasms, when one has so frequently excited and calmed oneself by turns, and employed all one's youth in learning to manage one's soul, as a horseman manages his horse, making it gallop across fields at the touch of the spur, walk with short steps, jump ditches, trot, and amble, all simply for his own enjoyment and to learn more about such things – well, what I mean is, if one doesn't break one's neck at the outset, the chances are one won't break it later. I, too, am 'established', in that I have found my seat, my centre of gravity. And I don't imagine that any jolt from within could ever unseat me and throw me to the ground. For me, marriage would be an apostasy: the very thought terrifies me. Alfred's death has not erased the memory of how shocked I was by his marriage – as pious folk react to the news of a great scandal caused by their bishop. If a man, whether of low or high degree, wishes to meddle with God's works, he must begin, if only as a healthy precaution, by putting himself in a position where he cannot be made a fool of. You can depict wine, love, women and glory on the condition that you're not a drunkard, a lover, a husband, or a private in the ranks. If you participate actively in life, you don't see it clearly: you suffer from it too much or enjoy it too much. The artist, to my way of thinking, is a monstrosity, something outside nature. All the misfortunes Providence inflicts on him come from his stubbornness in denying that axiom. He suffers from that denial and makes others suffer. Ask women who have loved poets, or men who have loved actresses. So (and this is my conclusion) I am resigned to living as I have lived: alone, with my throng of great men as my only cronies – a bear, with my bear-rug as company. I care nothing for the world, for the future, for what people will say, for any kind of establishment, or even for literary renown, which in the past I used to lie awake so many nights dreaming about. That is what I am like; such is my character.

The devil take me if I know why I've written you these two pages of tirade, poor dear. No, no: when I think of your sweet face, so sad and loving, and of the joy I have in living with you, who are so full of serenity and such grave charm, I know very well that I shall never love another woman as I do you. You will have no rival, never fear! The senses or a momentary fancy will not take the place of what lies locked in the fastness of a triple sanctuary . . .

Good old Ernest! There he is, married, established – and a magistrate to boot. What a perfect bourgeois and gentleman! How much more than ever he'll be the defender of order, family, property! But then he has followed the normal course. He too was an artist; he carried a hunting knife and dreamed of plots for plays. Then he was a student in the Latin Quarter; he had what he called his 'mistress', a neighbourhood grisette whom I scandalized with my talk when I went to see him in their sordid ménage. He danced the cancan at the Chaumière, drank punch at the Café Voltaire. Then he got his doctorate. Immediately there began the comedy of being serious, following what had been the serious business of living a comedy. He became very solemn; concealed his few wild oats; bought a watch (definitive step!), and 'gave up imagination' (his own words). How painful that separation must have been! My heart bleeds to think of it. Now I'm sure that down where he is[1] he's thundering against Socialist doctrines, talking about the 'edifice', the 'basis', the 'helm of State', the 'hydra-headed monster'. As a magistrate, he is reactionary; married, he'll be a cuckold; and so, spending his life between his female and his children on the one hand, and the turpitudes of his profession on the other, there he is, the perfect example of the man who has managed to attain everything life has to offer. Ouf! Let's talk about something else.

1. Ernest Chevalier was now assistant public attorney in Grenoble.

~

To Louis Bouilhet

Athens, in the Lazaretto at the Piraeus. December 19, 1850. Thursday
I have been here since yesterday – we are being kept in quarantine until Sunday. I'm reading Herodotus and Thirlwall.[1] The rain falls in torrents, but at least it's warmer here than in Constantinople, where these last few days the snow was covering the houses. I was truly happy yesterday when I caught sight of the Acropolis, shining white in the sun under a sky heavy with clouds.

. . .

We spent five weeks in Constantinople; one would have to stay there six months . . . I saw the mosques, the seraglio, Santa Sophia. In the seraglio, a dwarf, the sultan's dwarf, was playing with white eunuchs outside the throne room; the dwarf was hideous, expensively dressed in European style – gaiters, overcoat, watch-chain. As for eunuchs, I had no particular feeling about the black ones, the only ones I had seen until then. But the white! I wasn't prepared for them. They look like nasty old women. The sight of them makes you nervous, and torments the imagination. You find yourself devoured by curiosity, and at the same time the bourgeois in you makes you loathe them. The anti-normality of their appearance is a shock to one's virility. Explain that to me. No question, though, that they are one of the most curious products of the human hand. What wouldn't I have given, in the Orient, to become the friend of a eunuch! But they are unapproachable. Apropos of the dwarf, dear Sir, it goes without saying that he brought to mind your nice Caracoïdes.[2]

.   .   .

One day we went to a filthy whorehouse in the Galata quarter to fuck some negresses. They were so disgusting my heart failed me. I was about to walk out when the madam of the place signalled to my dragoman and I was ushered into a separate room, very clean. There, hidden behind curtains, in bed, was a very young girl, 16 or 17, white, a brunette, silk corsage tight at the waist, delicate hands and feet, face sweet and sulky. She was Madame's own daughter, reserved for special circumstances. She made objections; they forced her to stay with me. But when we were in bed together and my forefinger was already in her vagina, and my hand had slowly explored two lovely alabaster columns sheathed in satin (it was like a naughty Empire engraving), I heard her ask me in Italian to let her examine my tool, to make sure I wasn't sick. Well! Since on the lower part of my glans I still have an induration, and was afraid she would see it, I acted the Monsieur and jumped down from the bed, saying loudly that she was insulting me, that such behaviour was revolting to a gentleman; and I left, very annoyed not to have fired such a pretty shot and thoroughly humiliated to think of myself as having a nonpresentable prick.

The law permitting private persons to correspond 'by electricity' has inspired me with strange thoughts.[3] For me it is the clearest possible sign of imminent debacle. It shows how, thanks to 'progress', all government is becoming impossible. It is wildly grotesque to see the law torturing itself almost to death in an attempt to keep up with the New that is breaking out everywhere ... Don't you often think about balloons? The man of the future may have tremendous fun. He'll travel among the stars, with air-pills in his pocket. We – you and I and the rest of us – have come on the scene too early and too late. We'll have performed the most difficult and least glamorous of all tasks: transition.

To accomplish something lasting, one must have a solid foundation. The thought of the future torments us, and the past is holding us back. That is why the present is slipping from our grasp.

1.	Connop Thirlwall, British author of a celebrated *History of Greece*, one volume of which had been translated into French. (J.B.)
2.	A dwarf in Bouilhet's poem *Melaenis*.
3.	The electric telegraph, then gradually replacing the aerial telegraph, and hitherto reserved for government use, was 'put at the disposition of the public' by the law of November 29, 1850. (J.B.)

~

To Louis Bouilhet

Patras, February 10, 1851

. . .

What has become of you? What are you up to? I refer to the material aspect of your life. *Quid de Venere?*[1] It's a long time since I last heard about your 'youthful exploits'. As for me, my frightful chancres have finally closed. The induration is still hard, but seems to be disappearing. Something else that is disappearing, and faster, is my hair. Expect to see me with a skullcap. Bald, like an office clerk or a worse-for-wear notary – the stupidest kind of premature senility. I am depressed about it. Maxime makes fun of me; he may be right. It is a feminine feeling, unworthy of a man and a republican, I know. But I see this as the first symptom of a humiliating decline, and feel it keenly. I am getting fat and paunchy and repulsively common-looking, about to enter the category of those the whore finds it unappetizing to handle. Perhaps I'll soon be lamenting my youth – and my wasted time, like the grandmother in Béranger. Where are you, luxuriant locks of my eighteen summers, falling to my shoulders with such hopes and such pride![2]

Yes, I am growing old. I feel that I am no longer capable of coming up with anything good. I have a terror of everything to do with style. What am I going to write when I return? That is what I keep asking myself. These last days, in the saddle, I have thought a good deal about my *Nuit de Don Juan*. But it seems to me very commonplace, old stuff; it would be just another treatment of the nun theme. To carry it off would require an excessively strong style, without a single weak line. Add to all this the fact that it's raining, that we're in a filthy little inn where we have to wait several more days for the steamer, that my trip is over and that I'm depressed. I want to go back to Egypt. I keep thinking of India. What a foolish creature is man, and especially me!

Even after the Orient, Greece is beautiful. I was immensely moved by the Parthenon. It's as good as the Gothic, whatever anyone may say to the contrary; and above all, I think, it is harder to understand.

. . .

Nature did everything for the Greeks – language, landscape, anatomy, the sun; even the forms of the mountains, which are as though sculptured, with lines more architectural than anywhere else.

I saw the cave of Trophonius, visited by that Apollonius of Tyana of whom I once sang.[3]

The choice of Delphi as the abode of the Pythoness was a stroke of genius. The landscape is one to inspire religious terrors – a narrow valley between two nearly perpendicular mountains, its floor a forest of dark olive trees, the mountains red and green; precipices on all sides, the sea at the far end, and snow-capped peaks on the horizon.

We lost our way in the snows of Mt Cithaeron and narrowly escaped spending the night there.

As we gazed at Parnassus, we thought of the exasperation the sight would have caused a Romantic poet of 1832, and the diatribe he would have hurled against it.

. . .

The Parthenon is the colour of brick, with, in places, tones of bitumen and almost of ink.[4] The sun shines on it almost constantly, whatever the weather. It gleams gloriously. Birds come and perch on the dismantled cornice – falcons, crows. The wind blows between the columns; goats browse amid pieces of white marble, fragments that shift under your feet. Here and there, in holes, piles of human bones: reminders of the war. Small Turkish ruins amid the great Greek ruin; and then, in the distance and always, the sea!

Among the pieces of sculpture found on the Acropolis I noticed especially a bas-relief representing a woman fastening her shoe. There remains only a fragment of the torso, just the two breasts, from the base of the neck to above the navel. One of the breasts is draped, the other uncovered. What breasts! Good God! What a breast! It is apple-round, full, abundant, widely spaced from the other: you can feel the weight of it in your hand. Its fecund maternity and its love-sweetness make you swoon. The rain and sun have turned the white marble to yellow, a tawny colour, almost like flesh. It is so calm, so noble! It seems about to swell; one feels that the lungs beneath it are about to expand and breathe. How well it wore its sheer pleated drapery! How one would have rolled on it, weeping! How one would have fallen on one's knees before it, hands joined! Standing in front of it, I felt the beauty of the expression *Stupet aeris.*[5] A little more and I'd have prayed . . .

1. 'What about your love-life?' The first paragraph of this letter, and numerous passages in most of the letters to Louis Bouilhet, consist of Flaubert's comments on drafts of poems Bouilhet has sent him.
2. Two weeks later, in Naples, Flaubert would write to his mother: 'I bought some razors, and now I no longer have my beard – my poor beard, bathed in the Nile, blown by desert winds, long perfumed by tobacco smoke! Underneath it I discovered a face enormously fatter than before. I am disgusting. I have a double chin and jowls.' It seems that already, in his thirtieth year, Flaubert had begun to look as he does in the well-known later photographs.
3. In *Saint Antoine.*
4. 'What colour is the Parthenon?' is a perennial question, the tones are so variegated and so changeable with the light. Perhaps everyone sees the building differently. Alberto Moravia greeted the present translator in Athens with the words: 'Have you been to the Parthenon yet? It's like lobster meat.'
5. Properly *Stupet Albius aere* ('Albius is in ecstasy before bronze statues.') (Horace, *Satires,* Book I, Satire IV, 1.28).

~

To his mother

Rome, April 8, 1851

This letter is the last, I think. It is the sixtieth . . .

.   .   .

A thought came to me yesterday apropos of Michelangelo's *Last Judgement.* It is this: that there is nothing viler on earth than a bad artist, a poor wretch who all his life sails just offshore from beauty without ever landing and planting his flag. To go in for art as a way of making money, to flatter the public, to spin facetious or dismal yarns for reputation or cash – that is the most ignoble of prostitutions; whereas the true artist seems to me master among men. I would rather have painted the Sistine Chapel than won many a battle, even Marengo. The former will last longer, and was perhaps more difficult. And I consoled myself for my own inadequacy by the thought that at least I am sincere. Everybody can't be Pope. The lowliest barefoot itinerant Franciscan, with limited intellect and no understanding of the prayers he recites, is perhaps as worthy of respect as a cardinal, if he prays with conviction and does his work with ardour. It is true that at moments of discouragement the poor man can't take comfort in the sight of his own purple, or in the hope of some day setting his behind on the Holy See.

1. The sixtieth to his mother alone. Approximately one hundred letters written during the journey survive. Mme Flaubert was soon to join her son in Rome, whence they would return to France together via Tuscany, Venice, and Milan.

~

To Louis Bouilhet

Rome, April 9 [1851]

. . .

The *Don Juan* goes ahead *piano*; from time to time a few ideas for it are 'committed to writing'.

But let's talk about Rome. You're waiting to hear about it, naturally. Well, I'm sorry to confess it, but my first impression was unfavourable. Like a bourgeois, I 'experienced a disillusion'. Seeking the Rome of Nero, I found only that of Sixtus V. The priest-ridden atmosphere casts a miasma of boredom over the city of the Caesars. The gown of the Jesuits has covered everything with a gloomy, seminarist murk. In vain I whipped myself on to continue the quest: invariably churches – churches and convents; and long streets, neither empty enough nor animated enough, bordered by high, blank walls; and Christianity so ever-encroaching, so omnipresent, as to swamp and overwhelm the antiquities that survive in its midst.

Antiquity does survive in the Campagna – fallow, empty, accursed as the desert, with its great stretches of aqueduct and its herds of large-horned cattle. That is truly beautiful, the antique beauty one has imagined. As for Rome itself, in this respect, I haven't yet recovered from my first impression, and must wait until it has subsided a little. What the wretches have done to the Colosseum! Stuck a cross in the centre of the circus, and built twelve chapels around the arena! But for pictures, statues, the XVIth century, Rome is the most splendid museum in the world. The number of masterpieces in the city is dizzying. It is certainly the artists' city. One could spend one's life here in a completely *ideal* atmosphere – outside the world, above it. I am overwhelmed by Michelangelo's *Last Judgement*. It partakes of Goethe, Dante, Shakespeare, merged into an art that is unique. It is beyond description. Even the word 'sublime' seems to me inadequate: shrill and over-simple.

I have seen a *Virgin* by Murillo that haunts me like a perpetual hallucination, a *Rape of Europa* by Veronese that excites me enormously, and two or three other things one could say a great deal about. I have been in Rome a fortnight. I'll tell you more about it later. But Greece has made me exigent concerning ancient art. The Parthenon spoiled Roman art for me: it seems lumpish and trivial in comparison. Greece is so beautiful!

Ah, poor fellow, how I missed you at Pompeii! I enclose some flowers I picked in a lupanar whose door was marked with a phallus in a state of erection. There were more flowers in that house than in any other. Sperm from the pricks of the ancients had perhaps fertilized the ground. The sun was blazing on the grey walls.

I saw Pozzuoli, Lake Lucrinus, Baiae – each of them an earthly Paradise. The emperors had good taste. I melted with melancholy in those places.

Like a tourist, I climbed to the top of Vesuvius and arrived exhausted. The crater is strange. Sulphur has accumulated around the edges in weird growths, yellow and purplish-red. I have been to Paestum. I was set on going to Capri; and very nearly remained there – in the deep. Despite my prowess as a boatman, I thought my last hour had come, and I confess I was worried and even afeared, much afeared. I was within an inch of annihilation, like Rome at the worst moments of the Punic wars.

Naples is a charming city thanks to its great numbers of pimps and whores. One quarter is garrisoned with girls who stand in their doorways: it's like the antique world, a real Suburra. As you go down the street, they hoist their dresses up to their armpits and show you their behinds to earn a penny or two. They run after you in that state. We were in a carriage, and the coachman, holding his reins and slowing the horse, tried to flick the tip of his whip into the cunt of one of them. It was the rawest bit of prostitution and cynicism I've seen yet. When we reached the end of the street Maxime and I both let our heads fall to our chests and sighed, '*Ce pauvre Bezet!*'[1]

I did a certain amount of fornicating in Naples – quite pretty girls. Maxime caught the clap.

Naples is the place to come to for a bath in the fountain of youth and to fall in love with life all over again. The sun itself is enamoured of the place. Everything is gay and easy. The ears of the horses are decked with bunches of peacock feathers.

The Chiaia is a long shorefront promenade, rows of live oaks arching overhead and the sea murmuring alongside. The newlyweds sitting there on moonlit nights warm their behinds on benches made of lava. The immemorial heat of the volcanos reaches their hearts by way of their buttocks: they squeeze each other's hands and choke with emotion. I envy them their sensations.

For almost a week I was tormented by desire for an actress (a French girl! and a vaudeville actress, at that!), and since I had neither enough money to pay her, nor enough nerve to accost her with empty purse, nor enough patience to woo her, I gave up. That cost me a pang. By dint of watching her in the theatre, I got over my temptation, and now think of her no longer. So much for passion.

. . .

As for my moral state, it is a strange one. *I feel the need of a success.* That would restore me, give me new strength, purge me a little . . .

1. Bouilhet's nickname – his name as pronounced by Flaubert's infant niece Caroline.

∾

So it was that, as the travelling approached its end, Flaubert's earlier, hesitant 'Unless some excessively literary wind begins to blow in a few years, I am resolved not to "make the presses groan" with any elucubration of my brain' gave way, in that last letter to Louis Bouilhet from Rome, to the outright 'I feel the need of a success'.

The 'excessively literary wind' probably referred less to a national upsurge of splendid writing than to impulses within Flaubert's own spirit; and the reader of the letters has seen such impulses intensifying. The remark on the death of Balzac – 'I had hoped to know him later, hoped he would like me' – is itself eloquent of ambition and self-confidence: for why might Balzac have later 'liked' Gustave Flaubert if not for some future writing? And now Balzac's own place was empty . . .

VI

Louise Colet II: Madame Bovary

1851–1855

In a memento dated June 16, 1851, Louise Colet, recently widowed, records her great emotion on having learned the previous evening that Flaubert was in Paris, arrived there a few days earlier with his mother on the way back to Croisset after his long trip to the East. Promptly the next morning she had a note delivered to his hotel, suggesting that they meet, only to have it brought back with word that he was not there. After sending someone to enquire of Maxime DuCamp (who told her messenger 'He won't see her'), she learned that Flaubert had already left the city; and she sent either the same letter, or a copy, or a different letter, to Croisset. (The draft of a second letter exists, teeming with reproaches, guaranteed to antagonize.) A week passed without an answer; she determined to see him. 'On Thursday I will go to Rouen,' she promised herself in her Memento of the 23rd, 'and I will bring him this letter:

"I am in Rouen, and shall soon be going on quite a long journey. I come to bring you some news that I think will interest you. My visit will be short, and I hope may be well received. I could not accept even a half-day's hospitality. But I shall be happy to offer my respects to your mother, if she has not entirely forgotten having met me,[1] and I shall be happy to talk with you. Life passes so swiftly, its joys and vanities are so fleeting, that we should be kind to one another. That is the feeling I shall count on for an hour. *Votre dévouée.* L.C." '

The morning of Thursday the 26th, as she was preparing to leave for Rouen, an answer from Flaubert arrived. It has not been preserved. Evidently it was anything but cordial; but it did not deter Louise.

She boarded a train to Rouen (so she records in her Memento of the 27th), took a room there at the Hôtel d'Angleterre, wrote Flaubert a note probably similar to the one she had planned, hired a river-boatman, and, taking the note with her, had herself rowed downstream to Croisset. About half past six she found herself before 'a charming two-storey house in the English style beside the Seine, standing in the midst of a green lawn with flower-beds, and separated from the river only by the road and an iron grille.' Passing through a gate, she walked around to a farm-like courtyard, and asked an employee to take her note in to Monsieur Flaubert. The servant returned: ' "Monsieur cannot see you; he will write to you." ' A maid came out of the house: ' "Monsieur is dining with guests. If Madame will give me her address in Rouen, he will write to Madame."

'I replied that I was returning to Paris that same evening, and would like to speak with him here for a moment.

'The maid went in and returned: "Monsieur will meet Madame this evening at eight o'clock if Madame will give her address. It is impossible for Monsieur to see Madame here." '

'Wounded to the heart,' Louise walked away.

She lingered on the quay, however, and as she stared wistfully at the 'elegant white house . . . where my own image had dwelled so long, where he had written me such tender, beautiful letters,' the front gate opened and Flaubert appeared.

' "What do you want with me, Madame?" he said rudely, perhaps making an effort to be rude.

' "I would like to speak with you."

' "That is really impossible, here."

' "You send me away? You think a visit from me would dishonour your mother?"

' "Not at all, but it is impossible." '

After a few moments:

' "Madame, I will meet you in Rouen at eight o'clock, if you wish . . . Yes or no?"

' "Yes."

' "At eight o'clock I will be at the Hôtel d'Angleterre." '

'Mortified', Louise was rowed back to Rouen.

At the hotel, Flaubert was at first harsh and sarcastic, reproaching her for her intrusion. 'He told me that what he found offensive about me was his knowing that I was capable of just such rash acts as this – coming and asking for him at Croisset.' She spoke of her 'difficult situation' (by which she meant chiefly her poverty, her reluctant financial dependence on Victor Cousin for the expenses of her daughter's upbringing), and of her continuing love for him, Flaubert.

'Marry the Philosopher,' was his only reply.

' "Shall I never, never, be in your arms again?" '

' "Marry the Philosopher," he said, laughing, "and then you and I will see each other." '

She was revolted by the cynicism: ' "*Oh! Profanation de l'amour!*" '

But she made herself as seductive as she could – 'I tried to assume his tone, and joked a bit'; she knew she was still pretty; and after some kissing Flaubert promised to meet her later, in Paris. They walked in the Rouen streets, 'the night was splendid, the stars were shining, the air smelled sweet'. Several times they were about to separate, but each time Louise said, 'Just to the next street-light'; finally, after more kissing, they parted, saying '*Au revoir.*'

'I returned to the hotel. As I walked, the thought of Croisset, closed against me, against *me*, rose up in my heart like an affront, like a poignant pain. As long as he had been with me, I had thought only of loving him, of awakening in him the memory of the past.'

She took the midnight train back to Paris.

She went to England, sent him a letter, enclosing a flower from Windsor Park.

A month after their meeting, he wrote to her.

1. 'Met' in the sense of encountering by chance, probably at some time several years before when Flaubert was escorting his mother in Paris. As will be seen, despite Louise's best efforts she and Mme Flaubert never formally 'met'.

~

To Louise Colet

Croisset, July 26, [1851]

I write you because 'my heart prompts me to speak to you kindly',[1] *pauvre amie*. If I could make you happy, I would do so with joy: it would be only fair. The thought that I have made you suffer so much weighs on me heavily: you know that, don't you? But for this and for the rest neither you nor I are, or ever were, to blame: everything was inherent in the circumstances.

You must have found me very cold the other day in Rouen. But I was as little cold as I possibly could be. I made every effort to be kind. Tender, no: that would have been dishonourable, hypocritical, an insult to your sincerity.

Read. Do not brood. Immerse yourself in long study: only the habit of persistent work can make one continually content; it produces an opium that numbs the soul. I have lived through periods of atrocious ennui, spinning in a void, bored to distraction. One preserves oneself by dint of steadiness and pride. Try it.

I wish you were in such a state that we could see each other calmly. I love your company when it is not tempestuous. The storms one so enjoys in youth are tiring in maturity. It is like riding: there was a time when I loved to gallop: now I let my horse walk, and the reins lie loose. I am growing very old; every jolt upsets me, and feeling is as repugnant to me as action.

You tell me nothing about what would interest me most: your plans. I sense that you have not yet reached any decision. The opinion I gave you was good: as Phidias used to say, you must always have mutton and beef on the table.[2]

I will see you soon in Paris, if you are there. (Weren't you to stay in England a month?) I expect to be in Paris at the end of next week. I shall go to England towards the end of August: my mother wants me to take her there.[3] I dislike the interruption, but . . . If you are still there I will come to see you. We'll try to be happy together.

In Paris, I will leave at your house the two manuscripts you left with me. Also, I want to return, but personally, into your own hands, a bronze medal I was weak enough to accept long ago. I must not keep it: it belongs to your daughter.

Farewell. God bless you, poor child.[4]

1. '*Mon coeur me porte à vous dire quelque bonne parole.*' Perhaps Flaubert is quoting words Louise herself had once used. (J.B.)
2. That is, in Louise's case, more than one project, or the possibility of choice.
3. To see the Great Exhibition at the Crystal Palace.
4. In English in the original.

~

A few days earlier, on July 21, Maxime DuCamp had written to Flaubert from Paris: 'What are you up to? . . . Is it still Don Juan? Or is it the story of Mme Delamare, a splendid subject?'

What seems to have happened is that Flaubert had learned from his mother, after his return, or from Louis Bouilhet, of the death, during his absence, of a Norman country doctor whom the Flauberts had known, named Eugène Delamare, and that this brought to mind certain country gossip. Delamare had been an impecunious and mediocre medical student under Dr Flaubert at the Hôtel-Dieu. He never passed all his examinations, and became not an MD but an *officier de santé* – a licensed 'health officer', practising in a small town near Rouen. His second wife, Delphine, who had died before him, had been the subject of scandalous local talk: the details, unknown today, were apparently such as to make both DuCamp and Bouilhet urge Flaubert to make use of them.

With extraordinary rapidity, thus encouraged by his friends, Flaubert abandoned two of the three subjects he had considered, the exotic *Une Nuit de Don Juan* and the even more exotic *Anubis*, in favour of one from modern life; and he saw that for him, elements of the Delamare story held more promise than that earlier contemporary project, the 'Flemish' novel about the virgin mystic.[1]

He made outlines.

In preparation for his trip to London with his mother, he went to Paris. He and Louise Colet were reunited.[2]

Then, just after leaving her and before going to London, he took the first steps in his narrative.

1. Flaubert seems to have first thought of the name 'Emma Bovary' for the heroine of the earlier, 'Flemish' project, and then used it in the new novel. DuCamp says in his memoirs that the name first came to Flaubert in Egypt. (One of their Cairo hotel-keepers was a former French actor named Bouvaret.)

After the publication of *Madame Bovary*, Flaubert wrote to his faithful correspondent Mlle Leroyer de Chantepie: 'The first idea I had was to make my heroine a virgin, living in the depths of the provinces, growing old in her sadness and so reaching the ultimate stages of mysticism and imagined passion. Of this plan I retained the setting (landscapes and characters quite sombre) – the colour, in short. However, to make the story more comprehensible and entertaining (in the good sense of that word), I invented a more human heroine, a woman of a kind more often seen. Besides, I foresaw such difficulties in the execution of the earlier plan that I didn't dare go ahead with it.'

2.   Louise Colet's Memento of Monday, September 15, 1851:
'. . . He came for me on Saturday at four o'clock. We went to Fleury and Meudon via the Bois and the other woods, dined chez Michel, and thence to Saint-Cloud on foot . . . No constraint, very expansive. On his part, sweetness, kindness, but no deep feeling. Returned in a carriage from Saint-Cloud. The same violent emotions, even in the carriage, but always controlling himself; renunciation of everything he likes. The evening at my house; but there is always that bitter sadness at possessing him so little and having so little influence on his character. We said goodbye without speaking of my material situation – not that I would have accepted anything from him. Distressing of him, for his indifference to my poverty makes me realize how shallow his love is. And yet he is kind-hearted, generous (that is, an easy spender). Still, for all that, he is untroubled by the humiliations torturing the woman he presses so passionately in his arms. I have exactly ten francs in the house to keep me going until the October quarter.' (The reference is probably to the next quarterly instalment of her pension.)

~

To Louise Colet

Croisset, Saturday night [September 20, 1851]

Ma chère amie, I leave for London next Thursday.

. . . Last night I began my novel. Now I foresee difficulties of style, and they terrify me. It is no small thing to be simple. I am afraid of becoming another Paul de Kock[1] or producing a kind of chateaubriandized Balzac.

I have had a sore throat since my return. My vanity likes to think that this is not due to fatigue, and I think my vanity is right. And you? How are you?

I am very busy at the moment on a temporary task I will tell you about later.

Adieu, chère Louise; I kiss your white neck. A long kiss[2] . . .

1. The author of best-selling humorous novels about the French bourgeoisie.
2. From Louise Colet's Memento of September 22, 1851:
    'At last a note from Gustave. What a personality! The wretchedness of my poor life can expect nothing from such an affection as his. What I need is continuous hard work and unshakeable moral courage. All in all, it is better to have him back: even the palest gleam of light is better than total darkness.'

～

Soon after his return from the East, Maxime DuCamp had bought, with a few friends, the title of a defunct magazine, the *Revue de Paris*, and had revived it, planning to publish fiction, poetry, and articles on literature and the social scene. The first issue, which included a story by DuCamp himself, 'Tagahor, a Hindu Tale', appeared on October 1, 1851, and was generally well received. DuCamp was looking for new talent and, despite some opposition from his fellow editors (Théophile Gautier was one of them), who found its 2400 lines excessive, he decided to publish in an early issue Louis Bouilhet's *Melaenis*, the poem about the dancer in old Rome. It would be Bouilhet's debut.

DuCamp invited Flaubert, too, to contribute to the *Revue*, and reminded him that it was time to think of publication. Just launched on the hazardous adventure of a long novel about the bourgeoisie (which at that time he thought would take him 'a year, at least'), Flaubert hesitated: all he had to offer the magazine were his chapters from *Par les champs et par les grèves* – and *Saint Antoine*, which DuCamp, along with Bouilhet, had declared unpublishable. DuCamp, a year his junior, had already published stories, articles, and a travel book; and now Bouilhet, who had had none of Flaubert's freedom, most of whose time had been spent in necessary drudgery, was about to achieve public notice. Perhaps *parts* of *Saint Antoine* could be printed?

Several documents – two Mementos by Louise Colet, and an exchange of letters between Flaubert and DuCamp – paint a somewhat confused picture; with DuCamp, if Louise is to be believed, not always telling the same story.

Memento of Saturday, October 4, 1851 . . . In the evening, visit from DuCamp. What he tells me about Gustave. He is fed up with him, and thinks there is nothing worthwhile in his heart or his intelligence, that he has no literary future, no centre. Perhaps he is right. That tremendous personality of his will have its punishment; and yet I still think he has talent. Perhaps the memories of my love mislead me, but his imagination seems magnetic to me, like his eyes. We must judge him by his first published work. I have just read DuCamp's story in the *Revue de Paris*: it is quite boring. It does show, however, a genuine gift for style and a grasp of Hindu archaeology. But even the slightest wisp of sensibility would be more appreciated by the reader.

Saturday, October 18, 1851 . . . Gustave came at half past eight. He arrived [from England] only last evening, he told me. I found him changed, deteriorated in looks. He had a cold, and said he was more disgusted with life than ever, that Gautier and DuCamp were advising him to publish fragments of his *Saint Antoine*, and that the idea was worrying him. Is it he, or DuCamp, who is not being sincere? The latter told me that *Saint Antoine* was worthless, and that he would be distressed if Gustave wanted to publish it in the *Revue*. Gustave told me that his friend was enchanted by the outline of the novel he is going to work on, whereas DuCamp told me in so many words that it would be a 'tremendous fiasco'. So who is being honest? I am not in a position to tell Gustave the truth; he does not love me enough . . . Despite what DuCamp says about him, I do not find that his imagination has become dulled; he has a highly developed, very sure literary sense . . .

It is clear from DuCamp's letter to Flaubert printed as Appendix III at the end of this book that DuCamp was against publishing anything from *Saint Antoine* in the *Revue*. But perhaps he had not yet told Flaubert this. Théophile Gautier may have felt differently; as we shall see, he would later publish several sections from it in another magazine.

Meanwhile, Flaubert expressed agonies of indecision.

~

To Maxime DuCamp

[Croisset,] Tuesday, October 21 [1851]

. . .

I am very impatient for you to come here for a long, detailed talk, so that I can reach some decision. Last Sunday, with Bouilhet, we read over parts of *Saint Antoine:* Apollonius of Tyana, some of the gods, and the second half of the second part – that is, the Courtesan, Thamar, Nebuchadnezzar, the Sphinx, the Chimera, and all the animals. It would be very difficult to publish excerpts: you'll see. There are some very good things, but – but – but! They are not satisfying in themselves, and 'curious', I think, would be the verdict of the most indulgent readers, indeed the most intelligent. It is true that I would have on my side a lot of worthies who wouldn't understand a word and would admire it for fear their neighbours might understand it better. Bouilhet's objection to publication is that I have put into this all my defects and only a few of my good qualities. According to him, it diminishes me as a man. Next Sunday we shall read all the speeches of the gods; perhaps that would be the best single section. I have no more feelings of my own about this matter of choice than about the main question of publication. I don't know what to think. My position is exactly in the middle. So far, no one has ever reproached me for lacking individual traits, nor for being insensitive to the demands of my own little person. Well, in this question, perhaps the most important in the life of an artist, I completely lack all that. I cancel out. My very self is dissolved, with no effort on my part, alas: indeed I do everything I can to have some sort of opinion, but find myself utterly without one. The arguments for and against seem to me equally valid. If I were to toss a coin for it, I wouldn't regret the result, whichever it might be.

If I do publish, it will be for the stupidest of reasons – because I am told to, because I choose to emulate or obey others, not from any initiative of my own. I feel neither the need nor the desire to publish. And don't you think that we should do only as our hearts prompt us? The idiot who goes to a duel because his friends urge him to and tell him that he must, even though he himself has no desire to go and thinks it stupid, etc., is, at bottom, much more miserable than the self-confessed coward who swallows the insult without even noticing it and stays calmly at home. Yes, I repeat: what I dislike is that the idea comes not from me but from someone else, from others – proof, perhaps, that I am wrong.

And then, let's look further: if I publish, I'll publish; and it won't be by halves. When one does a thing one must do it well. I'll go to Paris for the winter. I'll be a man like other men. I'll lead a life given over to love affairs and scheming. I'll have to do many things that will revolt me and that I find lamentable in advance. Now: am I made for all that? As you well know, I am a man given to great élans and deep discouragements. If you knew all the invisible nets that keep me physically inactive, all the mists that float in my brain! Often, when I am faced with doing no matter what, I am overwhelmed by weariness and am ready to die of boredom; and I grasp even the most straightforward idea only by dint of great effort. My youth (you knew only its latter phase) steeped me in an opiate of boredom, sufficient for the remainder of my days. I hate life. There: I have said it; I'll not take it back. Yes, life; and everything that reminds me that life must be borne.[1] It bores me to eat, to dress, to stand on my feet, etc. I have dragged this hatred everywhere, wherever I have been: at school, in Rouen, in Paris, on the Nile. You, with your clear-cut, forthright nature, always rebelled against these vague Normandisms. In my clumsy way I used to excuse them, and that brought harsh words from you, Maxime, which were often bitter to swallow. I always put them out of my mind, but they were painful at the time.

Do you think it has been out of mere perversity, without long deliberation, that I have lived to the age of thirty in this way you scold me for? Why have I not had mistresses? Why have I preached chastity? Why have I stayed in this provincial backwater? Do you think I don't have erections like other men, and that I wouldn't enjoy cutting a fine figure in Paris? Indeed, I'd enjoy that considerably. But take a good look at me and tell me whether it's possible. I am no more cut out for that sort of thing than to be a fine waltzer. Few men have had fewer women than I (that is the punishment for my cult of 'plastic beauty', so admired by Theo), and if I remain unpublished, that will be the punishment for all my youthful dreams of glory. Must one not follow one's own path? If I find it repugnant to move about, maybe I am right not to. Sometimes I even think it wrong of me to want to write a rational book, instead of letting myself indulge in all the lyricism, all the bombast, all the fantastic philosophical extravagance that might enter my head. Who can tell? Some day I may give birth to a work that will be my own, at least.

Suppose I do publish. Will I be able to stand up against the consequences? They have been the ruin of stronger men than I. Who can tell whether in four years I might not become an ignoble fool? Am I really to have a goal other than Art itself? It alone has been sufficient for me until now; and if I need something more, that is proof that I am deteriorating. And if I *enjoy* the additional something, that is proof that I have deteriorated already.

Only the fear lest I be giving voice to the demon of pride keeps me from saying immediately, 'No! A thousand times no!' Like a snail afraid of touching something unclean on the sand or of being crushed underfoot, I retreat into my shell. I don't say I am incapable of activity of any kind. I plunged into the fray on two occasions, to help Achille and to help you,[2] and both times I was successful. It has to be of short duration and something that I enjoy. I have the physical strength for it, but not the patience, and patience is everything. Were I a strong man at a fair, I could lift the weights perfectly well, but not walk about brandishing them in my fists. Brashness, dissembling, the necessary tact, knowing how to get on in the world – all that's a closed book to me, and I'd make many blunders. The two deletions you made in your story, *Tagahor* – 'urine' and 'women who love other women' – shocked me as being humiliating concessions. That offended me, and I am not sure I forgive you even now. You see what I am like.

The Muse reproaches me for being tied to my mother's apron strings.[3] Just now I followed those apron strings to London; before that, they met me in Rome; and they might well come with me to Paris. Ah, if you could rid me of my brother-in-law and my sister-in-law,[4] how little the apron strings would bother me! Yesterday I had a long talk about all this business with my mother. Like me, she came to no conclusion. Her final word was: 'If you have written something you think good, publish it.' How far that gets me!

So there you are, old fellow. I assign you all the foregoing as a theme for meditation. Only, do meditate – and consider my whole self. Despite what I wrote in the *Éducation* – that even in the most intimate confidences there is something that remains unsaid – I have told you everything, insofar as a man can be honest with himself. It seems to me that I am that. I am showing you my very entrails. I am putting my trust in you – in you, my dear, old friend; in your instinct, which I sense is sure, and in your intelligence, which is keen when not outweighed by extraneous considerations. I will do whatever you wish, whatever you tell me. I entrust my *self* to you: I am weary of it. I had no idea, when I began my letter, that I was going to write all this. It came of itself; let it go off to you. It may make things easier when we have our discussion two weeks from now. *Adieu: je t'embrasse* with all manner of feelings.

1. A passage often cited, usually by those who dislike Flaubert the writer because of his famous self-styled 'impersonality' – his abstaining from expressing his own feelings concerning his characters (an abstinence which was, however, far from total). Taking Flaubert's words *au pied de la lettre*, not seeking any deeper meaning, such critics point to this outburst as constituting a fatal handicap, a disqualification, for a novelist.
2. For the help to Achille, see p. 61, n. 1. DuCamp had apparently been aided by Flaubert in a financial crisis. (J.B.)
3. As Louise Colet was called by Flaubert, DuCamp, and Bouilhet among themselves.
4. Hamard, who was still making trouble, and Achille's wife, Anathalie-Julie, never a favourite.

≈

If the 'discussion' mentioned by Flaubert took place, Louis Bouilhet was probably one of the participants. In any case, on October 29–30, 1851, Maxime DuCamp – without waiting for the two weeks to elapse – sent Flaubert the long reply printed as Appendix III at the end of this book.

Meanwhile, in letters usually written – like his earlier messages to her – late at night, after the day's work was done, Flaubert was beginning to cast Louise Colet in the role for which she has come to be chiefly known – his epistolary confidante concerning the progress of *Madame Bovary*. The passages translated from this second series of Flaubert's letters to Louise have been chosen primarily to chronicle that progress, and to reveal some of the ideas that occupied

Flaubert while he was writing his novel. The uneven course of the renewed liaison is charted, but it takes second place to the drama of the novel itself. Louise constantly sent Flaubert drafts of the poems she was writing in competition for the cash prizes awarded by the French Academy; and in his letters he returned detailed suggestions, often in collaboration with Bouilhet. These have almost invariably been omitted here.

~

To Louise Colet

[Croisset,] Thursday night, 1 a.m. [October 23, 1851]

Poor child! So will you always refuse to understand things as they are said? Really, that remark you find so harsh requires no apology or commentary. And if it tastes bitter to anyone, it can only be to me. Yes: I do wish that you did not love me, and that you had never known me; and in so wishing I think I express a regret that concerns your happiness.[1] Just as I wish I were not loved by my mother, did not love her or anyone in the world, so I wish there were nothing in my heart that reached out to others, and nothing in the hearts of others that reached out to me. The more one lives, the more one suffers. To make existence bearable, haven't there been inventions ever since the world began – imaginary worlds, opium, tobacco, strong drink, ether? Blessed be he who invented chloroform. The doctors object that one can die of it. But that is the very point! You lack sufficient hatred of life and of everything connected with it. You would understand me better if you were inside my skin: what you now consider unwarranted harshness you would see to be heart-felt compassion, something tender and generous, it seems to me. You believe I am wicked, or at least selfish, that I think only of myself, love only myself. Surely that is no more true of me than of anyone else: less, perhaps, if one may sing one's own praises. In any case, you will grant me the merit of always speaking the truth. Perhaps I feel more than I say, for I have relegated all my emphasis to my written style; there it stays, and doesn't budge. Each of us can only do what he is capable of. A man steeped for years, as I was, in all the excesses of solitude, nervous to the point of losing consciousness, agitated by repressed passions, racked by doubts from within and without: that is not the man for you to love. I love you as best I can; badly, not enough, I know it, I know it, oh God! Who is to blame? Chance! Fatality – that old ironic fatality, which joins things together for the greatest harmony of the whole and the greatest disharmony between the parts. Individuals meet only to collide; and each, bearing his torn entrails in his hands, accuses the other – who is gathering up his own. Still, there are some good days, some delicious moments. I love your company, I love your body, yes, your body, poor Louise, when you lean on my left arm and bend back your head and I kiss your neck. Stop weeping; think not about past or future, but about today. 'What is your duty? Whatever each day requires,' Goethe said. Submit to that requirement and you will have a tranquil heart.

Look at life from a loftier viewpoint, stand high on a tower (even though the foundation may crack, have faith in its solidity); then around you you will see only the blue ether. Sometimes the blue will change to mist: what matter, if everything disappears, drowned in placid vapour?

One must esteem a woman, to write her such things as these.

I am finding it very hard to get my novel started. I suffer from stylistic abscesses; and sentences keep itching without coming to a head. I am fretting, scratching. What a heavy oar the pen is, and what a strong current ideas are to row in! This makes me so desperate that I enjoy it considerably. In this state I spent a good day today, with the window open, the sun on the river, and the greatest serenity in the world. I wrote one page and sketched three more. A fortnight from now I hope to be in gear, but the colours I am working with are so new to me that I keep staring at them in astonishment.[2]

My cold is ending; I feel well. The middle of next month I shall come to Paris for two or three days. Work, think of me, and if you see me in your mind, avoid dark colours; let my image evoke happy memories. After all, we have to laugh. *Vive la joie! Adieu.* One more kiss . . .

1. From Louise Colet's Memento of October 18, 1851:
    ' . . . We talked amicably for an hour and a half. His personality is very hard. He said, "I would like you to find me disagreeable, so that you would stop loving me, for I see how it makes you suffer." I replied that those words demonstrated a total absence of love, and tears came to my

eyes. Then he wanted to embrace me and to kiss my eyes – the eyes, he said, that were shedding tears because of him.'

2. It is easy to picture Flaubert's astonishment at finding himself using the colours of the everyday Norman lives and places he was describing with deliberate objectivity in *Madame Bovary,* 'so new' as contrasted with the Eastern and Mediterranean pictures he had been painting in recent letters, with the fantasmagoria of *Saint Antoine* – and, especially, with the emotional, confessional tones of his earlier work.

    We ourselves are tempted to feel a certain astonishment at the mastery rapidly displayed by Flaubert in working with these 'new' colours – which characterize the novel, as we know it, from its very opening; even though preliminary drafts, many extant and published in a variorum edition, testify to his difficulty in getting started. However, the correspondence has already revealed the constant coexistence, in Flaubert, of these 'new' colours along with the old; and especially the most prominent of the 'new' colours – detachment. One has only to reread the account of the night spent with Kuchuk Hanem: the bedbugs on the wall exemplify elements in the picture as striking as the exoticism.

~

Following the exchange of letters with DuCamp, and perhaps as an aftermath of the 'discussion', the question of Flaubert's publishing parts of *Saint Antoine* – or anything else[1] – in the *Revue de Paris* at present was dropped, and he devoted himself entirely to his novel. Louis Bouilhet, coming to Croisset almost every Saturday or Sunday, hearing the week's work read aloud, became his dearest friend, his mentor.

Flaubert called Bouilhet something more – his 'midwife'. As such, Bouilhet neither conceived nor bore the child (his own poetry reveals no great creative power), but his assistance was devoted and invaluable; he was a gifted, highly sensitive reader and editor. The varying existing drafts of sections of *Madame Bovary,* especially its earlier parts, are suggestive of Bouilhet's role – tantalizing hints of unrecorded conversations between author and editor.

1. In his memoirs, Maxime DuCamp (who several years before had published an account of his earlier trip to the 'Orient') says that he had made Flaubert an alternative suggestion: 'I had urged him to write up the Greek portion of our journey; it could make a short, interesting book, excellent for a debut in letters. He rejected my advice, saying that travel, like the humanities, should serve only to "enliven one's style", and that incidents

gleaned abroad might be used in a novel, but not in a straight account. Travel writings were to him the same as news items, he said, a low form of literature, and he had higher aspirations.'

~

To Louise Colet

[Croisset,] Monday night. [November 3, 1851]
. . .

It is splendid to be a great writer, to put men into the frying pan of your words and make them pop like chestnuts. There must be a delirious pride in the feeling that you are bringing the full weight of your ideas to bear on mankind. But for that you must have something to say. Now, I will confess to you it seems to me I have nothing that everyone else doesn't have, or that hasn't been said equally well, or that can't be said better. In the life you preach to me, I would lose the little I do have;[1] I would take on the passions of the crowd, in order to please it, and would descend to its level. Rather sit by the fire and make Art for oneself, the way one plays ninepins. When all is said and done, Art is perhaps no more serious than a game of ninepins. Perhaps everything is an immense bluff. I am afraid of that. And when we turn the page we may be very surprised to find that the answer to the riddle is so simple.

In the midst of all this I am advancing painfully with my book. I spoil a considerable quantity of paper. So many deletions! Sentences are very slow in coming. What a devilish style I have adopted! A curse on simple subjects! If you knew how I was torturing myself you'd be sorry for me. I'm certainly saddled with this book for a year, at least. Once under way, I'll enjoy it, but it is hard. I have also resumed a little Greek and Shakespeare.

I was forgetting to tell you that the governess arrived ten days ago. Her 'physique', incidentally, does not impress me. I have never felt less venereal . . .

1. Despite his self-doubts as he tries to get his novel under way, Flaubert is resisting Louise's renewed urging that he come and lead the literary life in Paris.

~

Caroline's new governess, her second, was an Englishwoman, Isabel Hutton, called by the Flauberts 'Miss Isabel'. (Her predecessor, 'Miss Jane', also English, had left to be married, and will be met later as Mrs Farmer.) The mention of Miss Isabel's 'physique', in that last letter of Flaubert's, suggests that Louise had already made some remark about her possible charms. Despite Flaubert's denial of them, it would seem that the thought of the young woman's presence in the house at Croisset inspired the jealousy now recorded by Louise and the murderous gesture she – who had already shown herself physically violent with Alphonse Karr – now contemplated.

Memento of Friday night, November 21, 1851. Horrible night, Sunday-Monday – the thought of killing him rather than see him take up with another woman. Until four in the morning, in bed, revolving the most sinister projects. Arranged to be alone to receive him – sent my daughter to spend the night with her teacher. Put on my velvet gown; the dagger. Finally he rings – nine o'clock. I collect myself: what's the use? DuCamp is right, he is a being apart, perhaps a non-being. I had guessed right instinctively: the solemn decision he had come to discuss was whether or not he should publish something and whether or not he should come to Paris.

The decision is put off for a year. Meanwhile, he will work. He was kind and sweet with me, but as for solicitude, devotion – no hope of that.

He came again Tuesday night. On Wednesday we walked in the Bois. About four o'clock. (Pale sun setting behind Mont Valérien.) He was depressed, out of sorts. He showed me the dregs of his heart – that sediment that life precipitates in all of us. We must keep it down and let it harden, I told him, to prevent its nauseating us – whereas he keeps stirring up its stench. I said profound, tender things that moved him ... Everyone has his own anguish, believe me (I said); and some have the additional affliction of being poor, etc. etc. If you haven't determined to die, then have the strength to live and not suffer too much nor cause suffering to those who love you. He was affected: '*Oh, bonne Louise!*' he said. '*Si tu savais quelles bénédictions je te donne devant Dieu!*' We embraced.

When he left he seemed revived. Yesterday we spent a last evening together; he was more passionate than ever, told me he had never loved me more, that he would come back in three weeks. His ideas about the bliss of being a priest – (career) – the stationary brain. I am eager to read a complete work by him. He said he would send me his manuscripts[1] . . . All in all, the feeling that even as he is, he is preferable to the others,[2] he will stimulate me to work.

Still without funds! I need 500 francs. Where to turn. He is going to write to England for that album.[3] Think of his not having the idea of helping me in this way, delicately, without my knowing about it. Strange! If I had a million, I would give it to him! . . .

1. Flaubert sent Louise three of his manuscripts, on all of which she commented in her Memoranda.
    Novembre: ' . . . weak, mediocre, except for the dramatic part, the woman's story; I wrote him 12 pages about it today.'
    L'Éducation sentimentale (version of 1843–1844): 'Admirable pages about art. He is a great artist.'
    Saint Antoine (earliest version): 'I admire his *Saint Antoine* tremendously, and was greatly surprised by it. He is a genius.'
2. There had been several 'others' during the past two years.
3. Louise had given Flaubert her autograph album, asking him to 'try to sell it in England'. He had done just that, leaving it there with a friend in the hope a buyer might turn up. Louise would always resent his not taking the hint and quietly buying it himself.

∾

To Louise Colet

[Croisset,] Friday night. [January 16, 1852]
· · ·

There are in me, literarily speaking, two distinct persons: one who is infatuated with bombast, lyricism, eagle flights, sonorities of phrase and lofty ideas; and another who digs and burrows into the truth as deeply as he can, who likes to treat a humble fact as respectfully as a big one, who would like to make you feel almost *physically* the things he reproduces. The former likes to laugh, and enjoys the animal side of man.

· · ·

[In *Saint Antoine,*] having taken a subject which left me completely free as to lyricism, emotions, excesses of all kinds, I felt in my element, and had only to let myself go. Never will I rediscover such recklessness of style as I indulged in during those eighteen long months. How passionately I carved the beads of my necklace! I forgot only one thing – the string . . .

What seems beautiful to me, what I should like to write, is a book about nothing, a book dependent on nothing external, which would be held together by the internal strength of its style, just as the earth, suspended in the void, depends on nothing external for its support; a book which would have almost no subject, or at least in which the subject would be almost invisible, if such a thing is possible. The finest works are those that contain the least matter; the closer expression comes to thought, the closer language comes to coinciding and merging with it, the finer the result. I believe the future of Art lies in this direction. I see it, as it has developed from its beginnings, growing progressively more ethereal, from Egyptian pylons to Gothic lancets, from the 20,000-line Hindu poems to the effusions of Byron. Form, in becoming more skilful, becomes attenuated; it leaves behind all liturgy, rule, measure; the epic is discarded in favour of the novel, verse in favour of prose; there is no longer any orthodoxy, and form is as free as the will of its creator. This progressive shedding of the burden of tradition can be observed everywhere: governments have gone through similar evolution, from oriental despotisms to the socialisms of the future.

It is for this reason that there are no noble subjects or ignoble subjects; from the standpoint of pure Art one might almost establish the axiom that there is no such thing as subject – style in itself being an absolute manner of seeing things.

I should need an entire book to develop what I want to say. I'll write about all that in my old age, when I'll have nothing better to scribble. Meanwhile, I'm working hard on my novel. Will the great days of *Saint Antoine* return? May the result be different, Lord God! I go slowly: in four days I have done five pages, but so far I find it good fun. It brings me some peace of mind. The weather is ghastly, the river like an ocean; not a cat passes under my windows. I keep a big fire going . . .

∽

To Louise Colet
[Croisset, February 8, 1852]

So you are decidedly an enthusiast for *Saint Antoine*. At last! I'll at least have had *one*! That's something. Though I don't accept all you say about it, I think my friends were unwilling to see everything that is there. It was lightly judged; I don't say unjustly, but lightly. As for the correction you suggest, we'll talk about it; it is *splendid*. It is repugnant to me to re-enter a sphere of ideas I have moved away from, and that is what I would have to do in order to make corrections in the tone of the rest. To do my saint over would give me a great deal of trouble: long absorption would be needed to enable me to invent something. I don't say I won't try, but it will not be right away.

Now I am in an entirely different world, that of close observation of the most trivial details. My attention is fixed on the mouldy mosses of the soul. It is a long way from the mythological and theological extravagances of *Saint Antoine*. And just as the subject is different, so I am writing in an entirely different way. I do not want my book to contain a *single* subjective reaction, nor a single reflection by the author. I think it will be less lofty than *Saint Antoine* as to *ideas* (which I don't think very important), but it will perhaps be stronger and more extraordinary, without seeming so.

But let's not talk any more about *Saint Antoine*. It disturbs me to do so – my mind becomes filled with the subject and I waste time thinking about it. If it is good, so much the better; if bad, too bad. In the former case, what difference does it make *when* it is published? In the latter, since it is destined to perish, why speak of it?

.   .   .

Yes, for me you are a diversion, but one of the best, the most complete kind. You relieve me emotionally, for the thought of you fills me with tenderness, and my heart reposes on this thought, just as when I lie on you. You loved me very much, *pauvre chère femme*, and now you admire me very much, and you love me still. Thank you for all that. You have given me more than I have given you, for what is noblest in the soul is the enthusiasm it radiates.

Adieu, chère et bonne Louise . . .

~

To Louise Colet

[Croisset,] Wednesday night, 1 a.m. [March 3, 1852]
. . .

I have just been re-reading a number of children's books for my novel.[1] I am half crazy tonight, after all the things I looked at today – from old keepsakes to tales of shipwrecks and buccaneers. I came upon old engravings that I coloured when I was seven or eight and hadn't seen since. There are rocks painted in blue, and trees in green. Some of them, a wintry scene showing people stranded on ice floes, for instance, made me re-experience the terrors I felt when I was a child. I wish I had something to distract me; I'm almost afraid to go to bed. There is a story about Dutch sailors in the icy sea, with bears attacking them in their hut (this picture used to keep me awake), and one about Chinese pirates sacking a temple full of golden idols. Tonight my travels and my childhood memories are all colouring off from each other; they keep following one after the other and spiralling upward in a prodigious flamboyant dance . . .

For two days now I have been trying to enter into the dreams of young girls, and for this have been navigating in the milky oceans of books about castles, and troubadours in white-plumed velvet hats. Remind me to speak to you about this. You can give me exact details I need. So: *adieu* until soon. If I am not with you by ten o'clock on Monday, it will be for Tuesday. A thousand kisses.

1. *Madame Bovary,* Part I, Chapter 6.

~

Louise Colet has left a record of the time Flaubert spent with her – and, one evening, with two of her friends – the following week:

Memento of Sunday night, March 14, 1852. How boring everyone has seemed whom I saw today, after the splendid, marvellous day spent with him yesterday! His arrival at half past two, our reading my poems and those of Mme Valmore, his telling me the outline of his novel *Bovaris* [sic], our embraces, his passion, his tender words; our dinner at the Restaurant Durant, Place

de la Madeleine – like our first days, long ago! Our return in
a carriage – Place de la Concorde, Champs-Elysées as far as the
Rond-Point, our reading the *Dialogue de Sylla*,[1] our two hours
of bliss. This morning I found his handkerchief in my bed! He
left me his Egyptian ring! What a splendid week! Monday,
Tuesday, Wednesday – short visits; then Thursday, full fête!
Bouilhet's arrival; dinner, the evening, Babinet, the Captain.
Gustave took Bouilhet away and they spent the night at the
Café Anglais discussing art and feelings, at six o'clock they
went to watch the sunrise from the Place de la Concorde; then
Bouilhet left. The next day Gustave talked happily with me
about that evening – he thanked me, kissed me, he loves me; I
think he can no longer do without me, as I cannot do without
him. We are at a level where we should understand one another,
and we are alone enough to feel that we are necessary to each
other . . . For me there is nothing but Gustave and work. I
would like to shut the doors of my house and wall myself up
in work, like him, but with my daughter this is very difficult.
Then the complication of being poor. He never thinks of saying
a word to me about that, of using the pretext of the album to
oblige me – that seems to me ever more strange. He has all
the essential intellectual virtues; he should also have those
of the heart. Such as he is, he is superior to anyone I have ever
known. I love him; he lifts my spirits. I am going to resume
hard work.

Tonight I am sunk in lassitude and depression. The flight
of time is heart-rending. Never, never, can one stop the hours;
the happy ones speed by, reminding us of our nothingness.
Yesterday I was in his arms, today he is far away! And now,
two months of absence. To work! To work!

1. Montesquieu's *Dialogue de Sylla et d'Eucrate.*

~

Flaubert wrote to her a few days after his return to Croisset.

~

To Louise Colet

[Croisset,] Saturday night, 1 a.m. [March 20, 1852]

I did nothing for two days – very bored, very idle, very drowsy. Then I gave my clock a mighty winding, and now my life has resumed the tic-tac of its pendulum. I have gone back to my eternal Greek, and will master it in a few months, because that is what I have sworn to do; and to my novel – which will be finished God knows when. There is nothing at once so frightening and so consoling as having a long task ahead. There are so many obstacles to overcome, the hours one devotes to it are so satisfying. For the moment, I am up to my neck in a young girl's dreams . . . The entire value of my book, if it has any, will consist of my having known how to walk straight ahead on a hair, balanced above the two abysses of lyricism and vulgarity (which I want to fuse in a narrative analysis). When I think of what it can be, I am dazzled. But then, when I reflect that so much beauty has been entrusted to me – to *me* – I am so terrified that I am seized with cramps and long to rush off and hide, no matter where. I have been working like a mule for fifteen long years. All my life I have lived in this maniacal stubbornness, keeping all my other passions locked up in cages and visiting them only now and then, for diversion. Oh, if I ever produce a good book I'll have earned it! Would to God that Buffon's blasphemous words were true.[1] I should certainly be among the foremost.

·   ·   ·

1. See p. 98, n. 2.

⁓

To Louise Colet

[Croisset,] Saturday night, half-past midnight. [March 27, 1852]

·   ·   ·

Tonight I finished scribbling the first draft of my young girl's dreams. I'll spend another fortnight sailing on these blue lakes, after which I'll go to a ball and then spend a rainy winter, which I'll end with a pregnancy, and about a third of my book will be done.

·   ·   ·

⁓

To Louise Colet

[Croisset,] Saturday night [April 24, 1852]
. . .

If I haven't written sooner in reply to your sad, discouraged letter, it's because I have been in a great fit of work. The day before yesterday I went to bed at five in the morning and yesterday at three. Since last Monday I have put everything else aside, and have done nothing all week but sweat over my *Bovary,* disgruntled at making such slow progress. I have now reached my ball, which I will begin Monday. I hope that may go better. Since you last saw me I have written 25 pages in all (25 pages in six weeks). They were rough going. Tomorrow I shall read them to Bouilhet. I have gone over them so much myself, copied them, changed them, shuffled them, that for the time being I see them very confusedly. But I think they will stand up. You speak of your discouragements: if you could see mine! Sometimes I don't understand why my arms don't drop from my body with fatigue, why my brain doesn't melt away. I am leading an austere life, stripped of all external pleasure, and am sustained only by a kind of permanent frenzy, which sometimes makes me weep tears of impotence but never abates. I love my work with a love that is frantic and perverted, as an ascetic loves the hair shirt that scratches his belly.

Sometimes, when I am empty, when words don't come, when I find I haven't written a single sentence after scribbling whole pages, I collapse on my couch and lie there dazed, bogged in a swamp of despair, hating myself and blaming myself for this demented pride that makes me pant after a chimera. A quarter of an hour later, everything has changed; my heart is pounding with joy. Last Wednesday I had to get up and fetch my handkerchief; tears were streaming down my face. I had been moved by my own writing: the emotion I had conceived, the phrase that rendered it, and the satisfaction of having found the phrase – all were causing me the most exquisite pleasure. At least I think that all those elements were present in this emotion, which after all was predominantly a matter of nerves. There exist even higher emotions of this same kind: those which are devoid of the sensory element. These are superior, in moral beauty, to virtue – so independent are they of any personal factor, of any human implication. Occasionally (at great moments of illumination) I have had glimpses, in the glow of an enthusiasm that made me thrill from head to foot, of such a state of mind, superior to life itself, a state in which fame counts for nothing and even happiness is superfluous. If everything around us, instead of permanently conspiring to drown us in a slough of mud, contributed rather to keep our spirits healthy, who can tell whether we might not be able to do for aesthetics what stoicism did for morals? Greek art was not an art; it was the very constitution of an entire people, of an entire race, of the country itself. In Greece the profile of the mountains was different from elsewhere, and they were made of marble, for sculptors, etc.

The time for beauty is over. Mankind may return to it, but it has no use for it at present. The more Art develops, the more scientific it will be, just as science will become artistic. Separated in their early stages, the two will become one again when both reach their culmination. It is beyond the power of human thought today to foresee in what a dazzling intellectual light the works of the future will flower. Meanwhile we are in a shadowy corridor, groping in the dark. We are without a lever; the ground is slipping under our feet; we all lack a basis – literati and scribblers that we are. What's the good of it all? Is our chatter the answer to any need? Between the crowd and ourselves, no bond exists. Alas for the crowd; alas for us, especially. But since there is a reason for everything, and since the fancy of one individual seems to me just as valid as the appetite of a million men, and can occupy an equal place in the world, we must (regardless of material things and of mankind, which disavows us) live for our vocation, climb up our ivory tower, and there, like a bayadère with her perfumes, dwell alone with our dreams. At times I have feelings of great despair and emptiness – doubts that taunt me in the midst of my simplest satisfactions. And yet I would not exchange all this for anything, because my conscience tells me that I am fulfilling my duty, obeying a decree of fate – that I am doing what is Good, that I am in the Right.

. . .

. . . I envision a style: a style that would be beautiful, that someone will invent some day, ten years or ten centuries from now, one that would be rhythmic as verse, precise as the language of the sciences, undulant, deep-voiced as a cello, tipped with flame: a style that would pierce your idea like a dagger, and on which your thought would sail easily ahead over a smooth surface, like a skiff before a good tail wind. Prose was born yesterday: you have to keep that in mind. Verse is the form par excellence of ancient literatures. All possible prosodic variations have been discovered; but that is far from being the case with prose.

~

To Louise Colet
                              [Croisset,] Saturday night [May 29, 1852]
. . .

Since my humour is particularly bad today (and frankly my heart is heavy with it), I'll drain it to the last drop. You talk about your 'days of pride', when 'people seek you out, flatter you', etc. Come! Those are days of weakness, days you should blush for. I'll tell you which are your days of pride. When you're at home at night in your oldest dressing gown, with Henriette getting on your nerves, the fire smoking and money worries and other troubles looming large, and you get ready for bed with heavy heart and weary mind; when you walk restlessly up and down your room, or sit staring at the fire, telling yourself you have nothing to back you up, that there isn't a soul you can count on, that you have been abandoned by all; and then – somewhere underneath your dejection as a woman you feel the stirring of the muse, deep within you something begins to sing, to sing something joyous and solemn, like a battle-hymn, a challenge flung in the face of life, a surge of confidence in your own strength, the flaring-up of works to come. The days when *that* happens to you are your days of pride. Don't talk to me about other kinds of pride. Leave those to weaklings – to the great Enault,[1] flattered to be published in the *Revue de Paris*, to DuCamp, enchanted to be received chez Mme Delessert,[2] to all who honour themselves so little that they can be 'honoured' by others. To have talent, you must be convinced that you possess it; and to keep your conscience pure you must set it above everybody else's. The way to live serenely, in clean, fresh air, is to install yourself atop some pyramid, no matter which, provided it be lofty and have a solid foundation. Ah! It isn't always 'amusing' up there, and you are utterly alone; but there is consolation to be taken in spitting from so high a place.

. . .

1. Louis Énault (1824–1900), lawyer, journalist, author of novels and travel books.
2. Valentine, née de Laborde, the elegant wife of Gabriel Delessert, ex-Prefect of Police and son of a wealthy banker, presided over a fashionable Paris salon. She had become DuCamp's mistress the year before. One of her earlier lovers had been Prosper Mérimée. DuCamp wrote Flaubert the most precise details of this amatory victory.

   Relations between Flaubert and DuCamp were beginning to sour. In letters now lost, DuCamp was again reproaching Flaubert for his way of life and urging him to live in Paris.

≈

To Louise Colet

[Croisset,] Sunday, 11 p.m. [June 13, 1852]

. . .

I like clear, sharp sentences, sentences which stand erect, erect while running – almost an impossibility. The ideal of prose has reached an unheard-of degree of difficulty: there must be no more archaisms, clichés; contemporary ideas must be expressed using the appropriate crude terms; everything must be as clear as Voltaire, as abrim with substance as Montaigne, as vigorous as La Bruyère, and always streaming with colour.

. . .

≈

To Maxime DuCamp

[Croisset, June 26, 1852]

Mon cher ami

It seems to me that where I am concerned you suffer from a tic, or an incurable lack of comprehension that vitiates your judgement. It does not bother me – have no fear of that. I have long since made up my mind on the matters you mention.

I shall merely tell you that all the words you use – 'hurry', 'this is the moment', 'it is high time', 'your place will be taken', 'become established', 'inadmissible' – are for me a vocabulary devoid of sense. It is as though you were talking to an Algonquin. I don't understand.

'Get somewhere' – where? To the position of MM. Murger, Feuillet, Monselet, Arsène Houssaye, Taxile Delord, Hippolyte Lucas, and six dozen others? Thank you.[1]

'To be known' is not my chief concern: that can give complete gratification only to very mediocre vanities. Besides, is there ever any certainty about this? Even the greatest fame leaves one longing for more, and seldom does anyone but a fool die sure of his reputation. Fame, therefore, can no more serve you as a gauge of your own worth than obscurity.

I am aiming at something better – to please myself. Success seems to me a result, not the goal. Now it is this goal that I am trying to attain; and it seems to me that for a long time I have not strayed an inch from the path, whether to make love to the ladies or to take a nap on the grass. If I must chase will-o'-the-wisps I may as well chase the most exalted.

Perish the United States, rather than a principle! May I die like a dog rather than hurry by a single second a sentence that isn't ripe!

I have conceived a manner of writing and a nobility of language that I want to attain. When I think that I have harvested my fruit I shan't refuse to sell it, nor shall I forbid hand-clapping if it is good. In the meantime I do not wish to fleece the public. That's all there is to it.

If by that time it is too late and nobody wants it, too bad. I assure you I wish I had much greater facility, much less toil, and larger profits. But I see no remedy for this.

It may well be that from a commercial point of view there are 'favourable moments', a ready market for one kind of article or another, a passing public taste which raises the price of rubber or cotton. Let those who wish to manufacture those things hasten to set up their factories: I well understand that they should. But if your work of art is good, if it is authentic, its echo will be heard, it will find its place – in six months, six years, or after you're gone. What difference does it make?

You tell me that it is only in Paris that one breathes 'the breath of life'. In my opinion your Parisian 'breath of life' often has the odour of rotten teeth. In that Parnassus to which you invite me one is visited more often by a miasma than by divine madness, and you will agree that the laurels gathered there are apt to be somewhat spattered with shit.

I am sorry to see a man like you go one better than the marquise d'Escarbagnas,[2] who thought that 'outside Paris there was no salvation for gentlefolk'. That judgement seems to me itself provincial, that is, narrow. Humanity exists everywhere, my dear Sir, but in Paris nonsense is more prevalent than elsewhere, I agree.

And there is unquestionably one thing that you do acquire in Paris – and that is impertinence; but at the cost of losing a bit of your lion's mane.

Anyone raised in Paris who nevertheless becomes a man of real consequence was born a demigod. He grew up straitjacketed and with heavy burdens on his head; whereas one must be born destitute of natural originality if solitude, concentration, and persistent work fail in the end to create in you something comparable.

As for deploring so bitterly my 'ineffectual' way of life, it is as though you were to reproach a shoemaker for making shoes or a blacksmith for striking his iron or a painter for living in his studio. Since I work every day from one in the afternoon until one in the morning, except from six o'clock to eight, I scarcely see how I can make use of the remaining time. If I led a genuinely provincial or rural existence, devoting myself to dominoes or raising melons, I could understand the reproach. But, if I am becoming stultified, you will have to lay the blame on Lucian, Shakespeare, and writing a novel.

I told you I shall move to Paris when my book is done, and that I shall publish it if I am satisfied with it. My resolution has not changed in the slightest. That is all I can say, and nothing more.

And believe me, my friend, you would do well not to fret about me. As for the waxing and waning of literary quarrels, I don't give a damn. As to whether or not Augier has a success I don't give a double damn. And as to whether Vacquerie and Ponsard so inflate themselves as to occupy the place that should be mine, I don't give a triple damn, and I have no intention of troubling them to give it back to me.[3]

Whereupon *je t'embrasse.*

1. The present obscurity of these names speaks for itself.
2. The comtesse d'Escarbagnas, in Molière's one-act comedy of that name.

3. Flaubert wrote to Louise Colet that same night:

'Apropos of Ponsard's *Ulysse* [a play], Monsieur DuCamp has written to me very bluntly. Once again he deplores – "bitterly" is his word – my not being in Paris, where my place is between Ponsard and Vacquerie. It is only in Paris that one really lives, etc. I lead an "ineffectual" life. I have sent him a severe, concise reply on this subject. I think he won't return to it, or show my letter to anyone.'

~

To Maxime DuCamp

[Croisset, early July, 1852]

Mon cher bonhomme

It pains me to see you so sensitive. Far from intending to make my letter wounding, I tried to make it the opposite. To the extent that I could, I kept within the limits of the subject, as they say in rhetoric.

But why begin the same old story all over again? Are you forever going to preach diet to a man who insists he is in good health? I find your distress on my account comical, that's all. Do I reproach you for living in Paris, for having published, etc.? Even when you wanted, once, to move into Hamard's house, did I applaud that project? Have I ever advised you to lead a life like mine? Have I ever tried to put leading-strings on your talent, saying 'Baby mustn't eat that', 'Come here, baby', or 'You mustn't dress like that, darling'? To each what suits him. All plants don't require the same cultivation. And besides, if destiny is not with us, you will strive in vain in Paris and I here; if we haven't the vocation, nothing will come of our efforts; and if, on the contrary, we have it, why worry ourselves about other things?

Everything you can tell me, I assure you, I have already told myself, whether it be blame or praise, bad or good. Everything added by you will be merely a repetition of many a monologue I know by heart.

One thing more, however. I deny the existence of the literary renascence which you proclaim. So far, I see no new writer, no original book, no idea that isn't outworn. (Everyone is trailing at the backside of the masters, as in the past.) The same old humanitarian or aesthetic saws are repeated over and over again. I don't deny the good intentions of the young men of today who want to create a new school, but I challenge them to do it. Glad if I find myself mistaken: I'll profit from the discovery.

As for my 'post' as man of letters, I gladly relinquish it to you. I abandon the sentry-box – walk away from it with my gun under my arm. I disown the honour of such a title and such a mission. I am simply a bourgeois living retired in the country, occupying myself with literature, and asking nothing of others, neither consideration nor honour nor even esteem. So they will get along without my bright lights. All I ask in return is that they not poison me with the reek of their kitchen candles. That is why I keep my distance.

As for 'helping' them, I will never refuse assistance in any cause. I would plunge into the water to save a good line of verse or a good sentence, no matter by whom. But I don't think that humanity needs me for that, or vice versa.

And correct this idea of yours: that as long as I am alone 'I shall never be satisfied with myself'. On the contrary, it's when I become satisfied with myself that I'll emerge from this retreat, where no one is spoiling me with encouragement. If you could see deep into my brain, you would think that sentence you wrote a monstrosity.

If your conscience prompted you to give me advice, you did the proper thing, and I thank you for your intention. But I think that you extend that conscience of yours to include others, and that our friend Louis [de Cormenin] and good old Théo [Théophile Gautier], who, you say, share your wish to fashion a little wig to cover my baldness, don't really give a shit about my way of life, or at least never think about it. They may be convinced that 'poor Flaubert has gone bald', but 'distressed' about it I doubt. Try to be like them, resign yourself to my premature baldness, to my having become an incurable stick-in-the-mud. That mud clings to me like scales: you'll break your nails on it. Save them for lighter work.

You and I are no longer following the same road; we are no longer sailing in the same skiff. May God lead each of us to where each of us wants to go! As for me, I am not seeking port, but the high seas. If I am shipwrecked, I absolve you from mourning[1] . . .

1. The assured, uncompromising tone of these letters from Flaubert to DuCamp strikes us in retrospect as triumphantly right, and even inspired – knowing, as we do, that his confidence in his course was vindicated. It is

a kind of assurance that can be compared to the revelling of the Allied officers at the Duchess of Richmond's ball in Brussels on the eve of Waterloo: their defiance seems to us superb – since we know they won the ensuing battle; had they lost, we might condemn their bravado.

Flaubert wrote to Louise: 'DuCamp's reply was "benevolent" and aggrieved. I have sent him another letter from the same barrel (of vinegar) as my first. I think he'll be reeling for some time from such a blow, and that he will now keep quiet. I am a very peaceable fellow up to a certain point – up to a certain frontier (that of my freedom), which no one is to pass. So, since he chose to trespass on my most personal territory, I knocked him back into his corner.'

∽

In a Memento dated the previous February 12 (1852), Louise had written: 'Oh, what a joy to have Gustave back. I love him more than anyone else: he appreciates me; and then, all those affairs ending with a break are hurtful and humiliating.' But Louise continued to court hurt and humiliation. Several of Flaubert's letters written during the summer of 1852 refer to a flirtation on which she now embarked with Alfred de Musset, who, as a member of the French Academy, might help advance her career. The details, confided to her Memoranda and to Flaubert, included her leap, one moonlit night, from a speeding fiacre in which the drunken Musset had become 'insulting'. Flaubert expressed indignation against Musset, and concern for the bruises Louise suffered on the pavement of the Place de la Concorde, but he pointed out: 'Instead of jumping from the cab, you had only to order the driver to stop, and tell him: "Please throw out M. Alfred de Musset: he is insulting me." ' However, Flaubert's chief reactions to what she told him about Musset were literary ones.

∽

To Louise Colet

[Croisset,] Tuesday [July 6, 1852]

. . .

Convention has it that one doesn't go for a moonlight drive with a man for the purpose of admiring the moon, and milord de Musset is devilishly conventional: his vanity bespeaks bourgeois blood. I do not share your belief that what means most to him are works of art. What means most to him are his own passions. Musset is more poet than artist, and now much more man than poet – and a poor kind of man at that.

Musset has never distinguished between poetry and the feelings it supplements. Music, according to him, was made for serenades, painting for portraits, and poetry for consolations of the heart. When you undertake in that way to put the sun in your breeches, you burn your breeches and piss on the sun. That is what happened to him. Nerves, magnetism: *voilà la poésie!* No: poetry is built upon a more settled foundation. If having sensitive nerves were sufficient qualification for being a poet, I would be better than Shakespeare – or than Homer, who, I take it, was far from nervous. Such confusion is ungodly. I am qualified to speak of such things, for I have been known to hear what people were saying in low voices beyond closed doors thirty paces away; I have watched the viscera quiver beneath my skin; and sometimes, within the space of a single second, I have been aware of a thousand thoughts, images and associations of all kinds illuminating my brain like so many brilliant fireworks. Such displays are excellent subjects for conversation, and people find them quite moving.

Poetry is not a sort of spiritual languor, whereas those nervous susceptibilities are precisely that. Abnormally keen feeling is a weakness. Let me explain.

Had my brain been sounder, I would not have fallen sick from studying law and being bored. I would have turned those circumstances to my advantage, instead of being hurt by them. My unhappiness, instead of remaining confined within my mind, overflowed into the rest of my body and sent it into convulsions. It was a 'deviation'. There are many children who are upset by music: they are immensely gifted, remember songs after hearing them only once, get overexcited when they play the piano, their hearts pound, they grow thin and pale, fall sick, and their poor nerves, like the nerves of a dog, quiver with pain at the sound of the notes. These children are not future Mozarts. Their vocation has been displaced; the idea has been misdirected to the flesh; once there, it remains sterile, while the flesh perishes; the result is neither genius nor health.

The same in art. Passion does not make verses; and the more personal you are, the weaker. I myself always sinned in that respect:

I always put myself into everything I did. Instead of St Anthony, for example, *I* was in that book; my *Tentation* was written for myself, not for the reader. The less you feel a thing, *the more capable you are of expressing it as it is* (as it *always* is, in itself, in its universality, freed from all ephemeral contingencies). But one must be able to *make oneself feel it.* This faculty is, simply, genius: the ability to *see,* to have the model posing there before you.

That is why I abhor rhetorical poetry, pompous poetry. To express things that are beyond words, a look is enough. Exhalations of the soul, lyricism, descriptions – I want all that to be in the *style.* Elsewhere, it is a prostitution of art and of feeling itself.

It is that constraint that has always prevented me from paying court to a woman. I would have been afraid, had I uttered the 'poetical' phrases that sprang to my lips, that she might say to herself 'What a charlatan!'; and the fear of actually being one held me back.

. . .

What beautiful weather, Louise; how the sun is shining! All my shutters are closed; I am writing to you in the shade. We have had two or three lovely nights. Such moonlight! I am well physically and spiritually, and I hope that my *Bovary* will begin to move ahead again, a little. Heat affects me like brandy: it dries out the fibres and excites me . . .

$\sim$

To Louise Colet

[Croisset,] Thursday, 4 p.m. [July 22, 1852]

I am in the midst of copying and correcting (with much scratching out) all my first part of *Bovary.*[1] My eyes are smarting. I should like to be able to read these one hundred and fifty-eight [manuscript] pages at a single glance and grasp them with all their details in a single thought. A week from Sunday I shall re-read the whole thing to Bouilhet; and the next day, or the day after, you will see me. What a bitch of a thing prose is! It is never finished; there is always something to be done over. However, I think it can be given the consistency of verse. A good prose sentence should be like a good line of poetry – *unchangeable,* just as rhythmic, just as sonorous. Such, at least, is my ambition (one thing I am sure of: no one has ever conceived a more perfect type of prose than I; but as to the execution, how many weaknesses, how many weaknesses, oh God!). Nor does it seem to me impossible to give psychological analysis the swiftness, clarity, and impetus of a purely dramatic narrative. This has never been attempted, and it would be beautiful. Have I succeeded a little in this? I have no idea. As of this moment I have no clear opinion about my work.

. . . In a fortnight, dear Louise, I hope to be beside you (and on top of you). I need that. The end of this part of my novel has left me a little tired. I am becoming aware of it, now that the oven is beginning to cool . . .

1. Ending with Emma Bovary's pregnancy and the move to Yonville. The shortest of the novel's three parts.

~

To Louise Colet

[Croisset,] Monday night, 1 a.m. [July 26, 1852]
. . .

Yes, it is a strange thing, the relation between one's writing and one's personality. Is there anyone who loves antiquity more than I, anyone more haunted by it, anyone who has made a greater effort to understand it? And yet in my books I am as far as possible from being a man of the antique world. From my appearance one would think I should be a writer of epic, of drama, of brutally factual narrative; whereas actually I feel at home only in analysis – in anatomy, if I may call it such. Fundamentally I am the man of the mists; and it is only by patience and study that I have rid myself of all the whitish fat that clogged my muscles. The books I am most eager to write are precisely those for which I am least endowed. *Bovary,* in this respect, will have been an unprecedented tour de force (a fact of which I alone shall ever be aware): its subject, characters, effects, etc. – all are alien to me. It should make it possible for me to take a great step forward later. Writing this book I am like a man playing the piano with lead balls attached to his knuckles. But once I have mastered my fingering, and find a piece that's to my taste and that I can play with my sleeves rolled up, the result will perhaps be good. In any case, I think I am doing the right thing. What one does is not for oneself, but for others. Art is not interested in the personality of the artist. So much the worse for him if he doesn't like red or green or yellow: all colours are beautiful, and his task is to use them.

Have you read *The Golden Ass*? Try to read it before I come, and we'll talk about it a little. I will bring you Cyrano.[1] There's a fantasist for you, that fellow! And a real one, for a change. I have read the Gautier volume:[2] lamentable! Here and there a fine strophe, but not a single good poem. It is strained, contrived; he has pulled all the old strings. One feels it's a mind that has taken Spanish fly. An inferior kind of erection – the erection of a weakling. Ah, all these great men are old; they are old; they drool. And as for the state they're in, they have done all they could to bring it on themselves.

. . .

1. Flaubert had written to Louise of Cyrano de Bergerac's *Les Estats et Empires du Soleil* (1662): 'I recommend the fighting "Icicle Animal" and the Kingdom of the Trees. I find it marvellously poetic.'
2. *Émaux et Camées.*

~

According to Louise Colet's Memento of August 15, 1852, Flaubert arrived in Paris for one of his periodic visits on August 3. He saw Louise several times; he and Louis Bouilhet spent an afternoon with her, choosing from among her poems those to be included in a volume. On Monday the 9th, he and Louise dined with a friend. Louise records what happened later that night:

> His seizure at the hotel. My terror. He begs me not to call anyone. His convulsions, his *râle.* He foams at the mouth: my arm is bruised by his clenched hands and nails. In about ten minutes he comes to himself. Vomiting. I assure him the attack lasted only a few seconds, and that there was no foaming. Deep sympathy for him on my part, great tenderness. I return home at one o'clock, exhausted by fatigue and sadness. He spends the entire next day with me, more amorous, more passionate, than ever; tired, but looking very well.

It was apparently Louise's first view of the kind of attack to which Flaubert had been subject since the onset of epilepsy during

his New Year vacation from the Law School in 1844. Flaubert sometimes said that during these attacks he was never fully unconscious
(see p. 41, n. 1).

~

To Louise Colet

[Croisset,] Wednesday, midnight. [September 1, 1852]

You speak about women's sufferings: I am in the midst of
them. You will see that I have had to descend deeply into the well
of feelings. If my book is good, it will gently caress many a feminine
wound: more than one woman will smile as she recognizes herself
in it. Oh, I'll be well acquainted with what they go through, poor
unsung souls! And with the secret sadness that oozes from them, like
the moss on the walls of their provincial backyards[1] . . .

1. The original is an apostrophe à la Chateaubriand: '*J'aurai connu vos douleurs,
    pauvres âmes obscures, humides de mélancolie renfermée, comme vos arrière-
    cours de province, dont les murs ont de la mousse.*' Flaubert was 'letting
    himself go' in writing *about* his current work, from which he was rigorously
    excluding any such effusions.

~

To Louise Colet

[Croisset,] Saturday, 5 o'clock. [September 4, 1852]
. . .

Since we last saw each other, I have written eight pages of my
second part – the topographical description of a village. Now I am
going to begin a long inn scene,[1] which worries me considerably.
How I wish it were five or six months from now! I would be over
the worst – the parts where I find myself least productive: that is,
where the idea must be struck most persistently in order to force it
to yield a return.

Your letter of this morning makes me sad. Poor darling, how I
love you! Why are you hurt by a sentence that was, on the contrary,
an expression of the strongest love one human being can offer
another? Oh Woman! Woman, be less so! Be so only in bed! Doesn't
your body set me afire when I am there? Haven't you seen me stare
at you, entranced, while my hands rapturously stroke your skin? The

very thought of your body always excites me: and if I don't dream of you more often, it is because one doesn't dream of what one desires.[2] Breathe deeply of the woodland air this week, and look closely at the leaves for what they are: to understand nature we must be calm, like nature itself.

Let nothing distress us: to complain of everything that grieves or annoys us is to complain of the very nature of life. You and I were created to depict it, and nothing more. Let us be religious. As for myself, everything disagreeable that happens to me, whether large or small, makes me hold the faster to my one great concern. I grasp it tightly, with both hands, and close both eyes. I keep calling for Grace until it comes. God is merciful to the meek, and the sun always shines for the strong-hearted, who survey the world from the top of their mountain.

I am turning towards a kind of aesthetic mysticism (if those two words can go together), and I wish it were more intense. When you are given no encouragement by others, when the outside world disgusts, weakens, corrupts, and stupefies you, so-called 'decent' and 'sensitive' people are forced to seek somewhere within themselves a more suitable place to live. If society continues on its present path, I think we shall once again see mystics, such as existed in all dark ages. Unable to expand, the soul will concentrate on itself. The time is not far off when there will be a resurgence of melancholy fantasies, the expectation of a Messiah, beliefs in the approaching end of the world. But lacking any theological foundation, what will be the basis of this fervour? (It will certainly be ignorant concerning itself.) Some will seek it in the flesh, others in the ancient religions, still others in Art; and Mankind, like the Jews in the desert, will adore all kinds of idols. People like us were born a little too soon. Twenty-five years from now, the point of intersection of all these quests will provide superb subjects for a master. Then prose – prose especially, the younger form – may serve to orchestrate a symphony with an extraordinarily rich human content. We may once again have books like the *Satyricon* and *The Golden Ass*, but bubbling over with intellect as those bubble over with sensuality.

This is the very thing that the socialists of the world, with their incessant materialistic preaching, refuse to see. They have denied suffering; they have blasphemed three-quarters of modern poetry, the blood of Christ that stirs within us. Nothing will extirpate suffering, nothing will eliminate it. Our purpose is not to dry it up, but to create outlets for it. If the sense of man's imperfection, of the meaninglessness of life, were to perish – as would follow from their premise – we would be more stupid than birds, who at least perch on trees. The human soul is at present sleeping, drunk with the words it has heard; but some day it will awake in a frenzy and give itself over to a freed-man's pleasures; for there will no longer be anything to restrain it, neither government, nor religion, nor any formula. Republicans of every stripe seem to me the most primitive pedagogues in the world – they dream of organization, legislation, a society like that of a monastery. I believe, on the contrary, that all rules are on their way out, that barriers are crumbling, that all is being reduced to the same level. This great confusion will perhaps bring freedom in its train. At least Art, which is always in the van, has followed this course. What poetics survives today? Plastic form itself is becoming increasingly impossible as our languages become increasingly limited and precise, and our ideas vague, confused, and elusive. All we can do, then, is to use our brains; we must tighten the frayed strings of our guitars, and above all we must become virtuosos, since in the present age naivety is a chimera. Moreover, the picturesque has almost disappeared. Even so, poetry will not die; but what will be its fate in the future? I cannot conceive. Who can tell? Beauty will perhaps become a feeling useless to mankind, and Art something halfway between algebra and music.

Since I cannot see tomorrow, I wish I might have seen yesterday. Why didn't I at least live under Louis XIV, with a great wig, smooth stockings and the company of M. Descartes! Why didn't I live at the time of Ronsard! Or Nero! How I would have talked with the Greek rhetors! How I would have travelled in great chariots over the Roman roads, and slept at night in the hostelries with the itinerant priests of Cybele! Why, above all, didn't I live at the time of Pericles, to sup with violet-crowned Aspasia and sing verses in white marble halls? Ah! All that is past: it is a dream, never to return. I certainly did live in all those places in some former existence. I am sure that in the Roman Empire I was the leader of a troupe of strolling players, one of those who went to Sicily to buy women to make actresses of them, and who were at once professor, pimp, and performer. They are great characters, those rogues in Plautus's plays, and when I read about them they seem to evoke memories in me. Have you occasionally experienced something like that – the shiver of history?

Adieu, je t'embrasse, tout à toi, partout.

1.   *Madame Bovary,* Part II, Chapters 1 and 2.
2.   Flaubert had apparently told Louise that he seldom dreamed about her.

~

To Louise Colet

[Croisset, Sunday, 11 p.m., September 19, 1852]

What trouble my *Bovary* is giving me! Still, I am beginning to see my way a little. Never in my life have I written anything more difficult than what I am doing now – trivial dialogue. This inn scene will perhaps take me three months, I can't tell. There are moments when I want to weep, I feel so powerless. But I'll die rather than botch it. I have to portray, simultaneously and in the same conversation, five or six characters (who speak), several others (who are spoken about), the setting itself, and the entire town, giving physical descriptions of people and objects; and in the midst of all that I have to show a man and a woman who are beginning (through a similarity in tastes) to be a little taken with each other. If only I had space! But the whole thing has to move quickly without being dry, and it requires a certain development without being spread thin; and many details which would be more striking here, have to keep in reserve for use later. I am going to put everything down quickly, proceeding by a series of sketches of the ensemble. By repeated revision I can perhaps pull it together. The language itself is a great stumbling block. My characters are completely commonplace, but they have to speak in a literary style, and the politeness of the language takes away so much picturesqueness from their way of expressing themselves!

Once again, poor dear Louise, you talk to me about fame, the future, applause. That old dream no longer obsesses me, because it did so too much in the past. I am not showing false modesty here: no, I believe in nothing. I doubt everything, and why shouldn't I? I am quite resigned to working all my life like a nigger with no hope whatever of reward. It is a sore that I keep scratching, that's all. I have more books in my head than I'll have time to write between now and the day of my death, especially considering my pace. I'll never lack occupation (and that's the important thing) . . . And then, even admitting the hypothesis of success, what certainty can we derive from it? Unless one is a moron, one always dies unsure of one's own value and that of one's works. Virgil himself, as he lay dying, wanted the *Aeneid* burned. When you compare yourself to what surrounds you, you find yourself admirable; but when you lift your eyes, towards the masters, towards the absolute, towards your dream, how you despise yourself! These last days I have been reading something good, the life of Carême, the cook.[1] Some association of ideas led me to think of that famous inventor of sauces, and I looked up his name in the *Biographie universelle.* His is a magnificent example of the life of an enthusiastic artist: it would be the envy of more than one poet. Here is what he said when he was urged not to work so hard, to take care of his health: 'Coal gas kills, but what of it? Shorter life and longer fame.' And in one of his books, admitting that he was a glutton: ' . . . but I had such a sense of my vocation that I didn't stop eating.' That 'didn't stop eating' is marvellous, coming from a man for whom eating was his art . . .

1. Marie-Antoine Carême (1784–1833), '*chef de bouche*' of Talleyrand and of the emperors of Russia and Austria.

∾

To Louise Colet

[Croisset,] Saturday night [September 25, 1852]
. . .

What is characteristic of great geniuses is their faculty of generalizing and their power of creation. They create types, each of which epitomizes a class, and by doing so they enrich the consciousness of mankind. Don't we believe that Don Quixote is as real as Caesar? Shakespeare is formidable in this regard. He was not a man, he was a continent; he contained whole crowds of great men, entire landscapes. Writers like him do not worry about *style*: they are powerful in spite of all their faults and because of them. When it comes to us, the little men, our value depends on finished execution. Hugo, in this century, will rout all his contemporaries, even though he is full of bad things: but what lung-power! What inspiration! I will risk a proposition here that I wouldn't dare utter to anyone else: that very great men often write very badly – and bravo for them. To discover the art of form, one should go not to them but to writers of the second class (Horace, La Bruyère). It is essential to memorize the masters, idolize them, try to think like them, and then put them aside once and for all. To learn technique, it is more profitable to go to the erudite, the skilful. *Adieu* – I have been constantly interrupted while writing the above – it must lack common sense . . .

~

To Louise Colet

[Croisset,] Saturday, 1 a.m., [October 9, 1852]

. . .

Things have been going well for two or three days. I am doing a conversation between a young man and a young woman about literature, the sea, the mountains, music – all the poetical subjects.[1] It is something that could be taken seriously, and yet I fully intend it as grotesque. This will be the first time, I think, that a book makes fun of its leading lady and its leading man. The irony does not detract from the pathetic aspect, but rather intensifies it. In my third part, which will be full of farcical things, I want my readers to weep.

. . .

1. *Madame Bovary*, Part II, Chapter 2.

~

To Louise Colet

[Croisset,] Tuesday night. [October 26, 1852]

. . .

On Sunday I read to Bouilhet the twenty-seven pages (just about finished) that are the work of two long months. He didn't dislike them at all, and that means much, as I was afraid they might be execrable. I was no longer able to see them clearly, and then the material lent itself so little to any stylistic effect. Perhaps it is an achievement to have made this part passable. Now I am coming to things that will be more entertaining to do. Forty or fifty pages more and I'll reach the climax of adultery. That's when all of us will have a romp, including my little lady.

. . .

～

To Louise Colet

[Croisset,] Monday night. [November 22, 1852]

I am going to read *Uncle Tom* in English. I admit I'm prejudiced against it. Literary merit alone doesn't bring that kind of success. A writer can go far if he combines a certain talent for dramatization and a facility for speaking everybody's language, with the art of exploiting the passions of the day, the concerns of the moment. Do you know what books sell best year after year? *Faublas* and *L'Amour conjugal,*[1] two inept productions. If Tacitus were to return to earth he would sell less well than M. Thiers. The public respects monuments, but has little love for them. They are given conventional admiration and no more. The bourgeoisie (which today comprises all of mankind, including the 'people') has the same attitude towards the classics as towards religion: it knows that they exist, would be sorry if they didn't, realizes that they serve some vague purpose, but makes no use of them and finds them very boring.

I have had *La Chartreuse de Parme* brought to me from the lending library and shall read it carefully. I know *Le Rouge et le Noir,* which I find badly written and incomprehensible as regards characters and intentions. I am quite aware that people of taste are not of my opinion; but people of taste are a queer caste: they have little saints of their own whom nobody knows. It was our friend Sainte-Beuve who launched this fashion. People swoon with admiration before parlour wits, before talents whose only recommendation is that they are obscure. As for Beyle, after reading *Le Rouge et le Noir* I failed completely to understand Balzac's enthusiasm for such a writer. Speaking of reading, I read Rabelais and *Don Quixote* every Sunday with Bouilhet and never tire of them. What overwhelming books! The more one contemplates them the bigger they grow, like the pyramids, and in the end they almost frighten you. What is prodigious about *Don Quixote* is the absence of art, and that perpetual fusion of illusion and reality which makes the book so comic and so poetic. All others are such dwarfs beside it! How small one feels, oh Lord, how small one feels!

I am working quite well, I mean with plenty of energy, but it is difficult to give adequate expression to something one has never felt: long preparations are necessary, and one must devilishly rack one's brains to achieve one's aim without going too far. The gradual development of my character's emotional life is giving me a lot of trouble; and everything in this novel depends on it: for in my opinion ideas can be as entertaining as actions, but in order to be so they must flow one from the other like a series of cascades, carrying the reader along amid the throbbing of sentences and the seething of metaphors. When we next see each other, I shall have made a great step ahead: I'll be plunged into love, the core of my subject, and the fate of my book will be decided; but I think that just now I'm in a dangerous pass.

.   .   .

1. *Tableau de l'amour conjugal,* by Dr Nicolas Venette (1686) and *Amours du Chevalier Faublas,* by J. B. Louvet de Couvray (one of the three parts of his novel, *Les Aventures du Chevalier Faublas,* 1787–1789).

∽

To Louise Colet

[Croisset,] Thursday, 1 p.m. [December 9, 1852]

.   .   .

The author's comments [*in Uncle Tom's Cabin*] irritated me continually. Does one have to make observations about slavery? Depict it: that's enough. That is what has always seemed powerful to me in *Le Dernier jour d'un condamné.*[1] No observations concerning the death penalty (it is true that the preface spoils the book, if that book could be spoiled). Look at *The Merchant of Venice* and see whether anyone declaims against usury. But the dramatic form has that virtue – of eliminating the author. Balzac was not free of this defect: he is legitimist, Catholic, aristocrat. An author in his book must be like God in the universe, present everywhere and visible nowhere. Art being a second Nature, the creator of that Nature must behave similarly. In all its atoms, in all its aspects, let there be sensed a hidden, infinite impassivity. The effect for the spectator must be a kind of amazement. 'How is all that done?' one must ask; and one must feel overwhelmed without knowing why. Greek art followed that principle, and to achieve its effects more quickly it chose characters in exceptional social conditions – kings, gods, demigods. You were not encouraged to identify with the dramatis personae: the *divine* was the dramatist's goal.

Adieu. It is late. Too bad! I was in a mood to chat. A thousand and a thousand kisses. And – my God! – see that *it* happens![2]

1. By Victor Hugo.
2. See the following letter.

~

To Louise Colet

[Croisset,] Saturday, 1 o'clock [December 11, 1852]

I begin by devouring you with kisses, I am so happy. Your letter of this morning lifted a terrible weight from my heart. It was high time. Yesterday I could not work all day. Every time I moved (literally), my brain throbbed in my skull, and I had to go to bed at 11 o'clock. I was feverish and completely despondent. For these past three weeks I have suffered from horrible apprehensions: I never stopped thinking of you, but in a way that was scarcely pleasant. Yes, the thought tortured me; once or twice I actually saw stars before my eyes – on Thursday, among other days. The idea of bringing someone into this world fills me with *horror*. I would curse myself if I were to become a father. A son! Oh, no, no, no! May my flesh perish utterly! May I never transmit to anyone the boredom and the ignominies of existence! My soul rebelled against this hypothesis; and then, and then . . . Well, now there is nothing to fear, thank God. Blessed be the Redcoats.

I also had a superstitious idea: tomorrow I shall be 31. I shall have passed that fatal age of thirty, which *ranks* a man. That is the age at which you assume your future shape, take your place in society, embrace a profession. There are few people who do not become bourgeois at 30. Paternity would have relegated me to the ordinary condition of life. My innocence in relation to the world would have been destroyed, and that would have cast me into the pit of common miseries. Well, today I am overflowing with serenity. I feel calm and radiant. My entire youth has passed unmarred, unsapped by weakness. From my childhood to this very hour it has followed a single straight line. And since I have sacrificed nothing to the passions, have never said 'Youth must end', youth will not end. I am still full of freshness; I am like a springtime. I have a great, flowing river in me, something that keeps churning and never ceases. My style and my muscles are still supple; and if the hair is gone from my brow, I think there is still many a plume in my mane. One more year, poor dear Louise, *ma bonne femme aimée*, and we will spend long days together.

Why did you wish that bond? Oh, no! You do not have to reassume woman's lot, to be loved by me. On the contrary, I love you because you have so little femininity – you lack woman's social hypocrisy, her weakness of intellect. Don't you feel that between us there is an attachment superior to that of the flesh? Independent, even, of love's tenderness? Do not spoil any of this for me. One is always punished if one strays from one's true road. So let us remain in our own private path: that separate path which is for us alone. The less one's feelings have in common with those of the world, the less they partake of the world's fragility. Time will not affect my love, because it is not a love 'such as love should be'. And I am going to say something that will seem strange to you. It does not seem to me that you are my mistress. Never does that banal term enter my mind when I think of you. In me you have a special place, which has never been occupied by anyone. If you were absent, it would remain empty; and yet my flesh loves your flesh, and when I see myself naked it seems to me that every pore of my skin is yearning for you; and what rapture there is in our embraces!

I am not talking literature; I am only now recovering from my long worry, and my heart is expanding. I breathe: it is a beautiful day, the sun sparkles on the river, at this moment a brig is passing in full sail; my window is open and my fire burning. *Adieu*, I love you more than ever, I stifle you with kisses, for my birthday.

Adieu, chère amour, mille tendresses. Encore à toi.

～

To Louise Colet
> *[Croisset,] Thursday night, 1 a.m. [December 16, 1852]*
What is wrong with your health, *pauvre chérie?* What are all these vomitings, stomach pains, etc.? I am sure that you came close to doing something foolish. I should like to hear that you were well again – completely. No matter: I'll not hide from you that the

landing of the Redcoats was a tremendous relief for me. May the god of coitus grant that I never again go through such agony . . . But the joy I subsequently felt has been profitable for me, I think.[1]

.   .   .

Have you noticed that I'm becoming a moralist? Is it a sign of old age? But I am certainly turning towards high comedy. Sometimes I have an itch to lash out at my fellow humans, and some day I will, ten years from now,[2] in a long novel with wide range. Meanwhile an old idea has come back to me – that of my *Dictionary of Accepted Opinions* (do you know what it is?).[3] The preface, especially, greatly excites me, and in the way I conceive it (it would be a book in itself) no law could touch me although I would attack everything.[4] It would be the historical glorification of everything generally approved. I would demonstrate that majorities have always been right, minorities always wrong. I would immolate the great men on the altars of the fools, deliver the martyrs to the executioners – and that in a style pushed to the extreme, with all possible fireworks. For example: I would show that in literature, mediocrity, being within the reach of everyone, is alone legitimate, and that consequently every kind of originality must be denounced as dangerous, ridiculous, etc. I would declare that this apologia for human vulgarity in all its aspects – and it would be raucous and ironic from beginning to end, full of quotations, proofs (which would prove the opposite), frightening texts (easily found) – was aimed at doing away, once and for all, with all eccentricities, whatever they might be. That would lead to the modern democratic idea of equality, using Fourier's remark that 'great men won't be needed'; and it is for this purpose, I would say, that the book is written. It would include, in alphabetical order and covering all possible subjects, 'everything one should say if one is to be considered a decent and likeable member of society'.

For example:

Artists: never interested in money.
Crayfish: the female of the lobster.
France: must be ruled with an iron hand.
Bossuet: 'the eagle of Meaux'.
Fénélon: 'the swan of Cambrai'.
Negresses: hotter than white women.

Erection: must be said only when speaking of monuments, etc.

I think that as a whole it would deliver a strong punch. There would not be a single word invented by me in the book. If properly done, anyone who read it would never dare open his mouth again, for fear of spontaneously uttering one of its pronouncements. Furthermore, certain items could be gone into in quite splendid detail, for example MAN, WOMAN, FRIEND, POLITICS, MORES, JUDGE. And a concisely written list of types could be included, to show not only what one should *say,* but what one should *seem to be.*

· · ·

Poetry has to be disguised, in France: the French hate it, and of all our writers perhaps only Ronsard was quite simply a poet, what a poet was in antiquity and is today in other countries.

Perhaps all plastic forms have been done and redone: that was the work of the earlier masters. What remains to us is the exterior[5] of man – more complex, but far less subject to the conditions of 'form'. And so I think that the novel has only just been born: it awaits its Homer. What a man Balzac would have been, had he known how to write! But that was the only thing he lacked. An artist, after all, would not have done so much, would not have had that amplitude.

· · ·

Just now a frightful wind is blowing; the trees and the river are roaring. This evening I was writing a summer scene, with midges, sun on the grass, etc.[6] (The greater the contrast between what I am writing and my actual surroundings, the better I see my subject.) The high wind has been fascinating me all evening – it is both soothing and distracting. At ten o'clock, when my mother came into my study to say goodnight, my nerves were so taut that I frightened her by giving a great shout of terror. This set my heart pounding, and it took me a quarter of an hour to calm down. Such is my absorption when I am working . . . What a poor machine is ours! And all that because a little man was shaping a sentence!

· · ·

1. Meaning, no doubt, 'good for my work'?
2. Not ten years later, but eleven, Flaubert would keep his word and begin the definitive version of *L'Éducation sentimentale.*

3. See pp. 177–8, and p. 179, n. 3.

4. This is Flaubert's first reference to the heavy press censorship that marked the early Second Empire – a censorship from which he himself was to suffer with *Madame Bovary.*

   Soon, on February 23, 1853, he was to write to Louise from Croisset:

   'We have here, since Monday, an old lady, a friend of my mother's (wife of a former consul in the Orient), with her daughter. Her son, who was one of my school friends, is at this moment in Sainte-Pélagie [a place of detention for political prisoners, especially dissenting writers] for a year (plus 500 francs fine) for distributing copies of *Napoléon le Petit* [by the exiled Victor Hugo]. Watch out! No one has news of him.'

   As we shall see, Flaubert and Louise were themselves in touch with Hugo. Flaubert's imprisoned school friend was Emmanuel Vasse, the student of Cretan history (see p. 41). He had borrowed books for Flaubert from the Bibliothèque Royale in Paris (today the Bibliothèque Nationale) when Flaubert was reading for his oriental tale and *Saint Antoine.*

5. Flaubert wrote 'exterior' here. Some scholars have believed he intended the opposite.

6. *Madame Bovary,* Part II, Chapter 3.

~

TO LOUISE COLET

[Croisset,] Monday, 5 o'clock. [December 27, 1852]

At this moment I am as though in the grip of a ghastly terror, and if I am writing to you it is perhaps to avoid being alone with myself, the way one lights one's lamp at night when one is afraid. I don't know whether you are going to understand me, but it is very strange. Have you read a book by Balzac called *Louis Lambert*? I finished it five minutes ago: I am thunderstruck by it. It is the story of a man who goes mad from thinking about intangible things. I cannot shake it off: it has grappled itself on to me in a thousand places. This Lambert is, in all but a few particulars, my poor Alfred. I have found some of *our* sentences (from years ago) almost word for word: the conversations between the two school friends are our conversations, or analogous. There is a story about a manuscript stolen by the two of them, and remarks made by the schoolmaster – *all of which happened to me,* etc. etc. Do you remember my speaking to you about a metaphysical novel (in outline) in which a man thinks himself into hallucinations that culminate in the ghost of his friend appearing to him and drawing the (ideal, absolute) conclusion from his (worldly, tangible) premises? Well, this idea is suggested in *Louis Lambert*: the entire novel is the preface to it. At the end, the hero wants to castrate himself, in a kind of mystical madness. During my wretchedness in Paris, when I was nineteen, I had that same wish. I will show you where I stopped in front of a shop in the rue Vivienne one night, intensely, imperiously gripped by this idea, and later I spent two entire years without touching a woman. (Last year, when I told you about my idea of entering a monastery,[1] it was my old leaven rising in me again.) There comes a moment when one needs to make oneself suffer, needs to loathe one's flesh, to fling mud in its face, so hideous does it seem. Without my love of form, I would perhaps have been a great mystic. Add to that my nervous attacks, which merely mark moments when, without my being able to do anything about it, ideas and images begin to fade. At such moments the psychic element is leaping above and beyond me, and self-awareness is disappearing, along with all sensation of life. I am sure I know what dying is. I have often distinctly felt my soul was escaping, as one feels blood flowing from the incision when one is being bled. This devilish book made me dream of Alfred all night.

.   .   .

Another case of similarity: my mother showed me a scene in Balzac's *Un Médecin de campagne* (she discovered it yesterday) *exactly the same* as one in my *Bovary:* a visit to a wet nurse. (I had never read that book, any more than I had *Louis Lambert*.) There are *the same details*, the same effects, the same meaning. One would think I had copied it, if it weren't that my page is infinitely better written, no boasting intended. If DuCamp knew all this, he would say I am comparing myself to Balzac, as [he said] I did to Goethe.[2] In the past, I was annoyed by people who thought I looked like this person or that; now it is worse, it is my soul. I find it everywhere: everything reminds me of it. Why, I wonder?

Louis Lambert begins, like *Bovary*, with a first day at school, and there is one sentence the *same* as one of mine . . .

I think that *Bovary* will move along, but I am bothered by my tendency to metaphor, decidedly excessive. I am devoured by comparisons as one is by lice, and I spend my time doing nothing but squashing them: my sentences swarm with them.

Adieu . . .

1. Compare Louise Colet's Memento on p. 212: 'the bliss of being a priest'.
2. Probably in connection with *Saint Antoine.*

∽

Flaubert's next letter to Louise, dated December 29, 1852, was devoted almost entirely to suggestions concerning a long poem she was writing, entitled *La Paysanne.* It is a letter of minimal interest to anyone else, but it was of a kind to delight Louise, and it was probably what inspired part of her Memento of Saturday, January 1, 1853: 'This past year has been the sweetest and best in my life. Gustave has truly loved me, and through him I have tasted art and love more fully than ever before . . . What a good letter he wrote to me yesterday morning; I wept with joy on reading it.'

A few months later, in her Memento of April 7, Louise was writing differently: 'In his letters, Gustave never speaks to me of anything except art – or himself.'

But this is somewhat misleading. For the 'art' to which many of Flaubert's letters refer during these months was the 'art' which he felt would improve the poems she sent him for comment – comment which she demanded, resented, resisted, and often repudiated. Her next poem after *La Paysanne* was *L'Acropole d'Athènes,* that having been announced by the Académie Française as the subject for its 1853 prize contest. (The contest was to be postponed for a year, and Louise would win it.) These letters about Louise's work are omitted from the present volume.

∽

To Louise Colet

[Croisset,] Wednesday, 1 a.m. [January 12, 1853]

I am hideously worried, mortally depressed. My accursed *Bovary* is torturing me and driving me mad. Last Sunday Bouilhet raised some objections to one of my characters and to the plan. I can do nothing about it: though there is some truth in what he says, I feel the opposite is true also. Ah, I am very tired and very discouraged! You call me Master. What a wretched Master!

No – perhaps the whole thing hasn't had enough spadework, for distinctions between thought and style are a sophism. Everything depends on the conception. So much the worse! I am going to push on, and as fast as I can, in order to have a complete picture. There are moments when all this makes me want to croak. Ah! I'll be well acquainted with them, the agonies of Art![1]

1.   Such, at least, would seem to be the least inadequate translation of Flaubert's famous phrase '*les affres de l'Art*'.

~

To Louise Colet
                [Croisset,] Saturday night, 3 o'clock. [January 15, 1853]
                    · · ·

Last week I spent *five days writing one page*, and I dropped everything else for it – my Greek, my English; I gave myself up to it entirely. What worries me in my book is the element of *entertainment*. That side is weak; there is not enough action. I maintain, however, that *ideas* are action. It is more difficult to hold the reader's interest with them, I know, but if the style is right it can be done. I now have fifty pages in a row without a single event. It is an uninterrupted portrayal of a bourgeois existence and of a love that remains inactive[1] – a love all the more difficult to depict because it is both timid and deep, but alas! lacking in inner turbulence, because my gentleman is of a sober temperament. I had something similar in the first part: the husband loves his wife somewhat after the same fashion as her lover. Here are two mediocrities in the same milieu, and I must differentiate between them. If I bring it off, it will be a great achievement, I think, for it will be like painting in monotone without contrasts – not easy. But I fear all these subtleties will be wearisome, and that the reader will long for more movement. Still, one must be loyal to one's concept. If I tried to insert action, I would be following a rule, and would spoil everything. One must sing with one's own voice, and mine will never be dramatic or attractive. Besides, I am convinced that everything is a question of style, or rather of form, of presentation.

A bit of news: our young friend DuCamp has been promoted to *officier* in the Légion d'Honneur! How pleased he must be! When he compares himself with me and surveys the distance he has travelled since leaving me, he must certainly think that I am very far behind him indeed, and that he has done very well for himself (externally). You'll see: he'll end by getting himself a good post and turning his back on literature.[2] He makes no distinctions: women, decorations, art, fashion – for him all these things are on the same level, and whatever advances his career is important. These are fine times we are living in (curious symbolisms, as old Michelet would say) – we decorate photographers and exile poets;[3] how many good pictures do you suppose a painter would have to produce to be made an *officier?* Of all the writers in the Légion d'Honneur only one has the rank of *commandeur,* and that is Monsieur Scribe! How immensely ironic it all is! And how honours swarm where there is no honour!

1. Part II, Chapter 3, et seq. Léon and Emma.
2. Maxime DuCamp never held a post (on one occasion he was an unsuccessful candidate for the Senate); he always remained what we would call today a 'freelance writer'. From the point of view of a writer of genius, such as Flaubert, he did 'turn his back on literature', in the sense that his later work consisted chiefly of factual books on social questions – Parisian life, the Commune, and so on.
3. The reference is to Victor Hugo, in exile on Jersey, and to DuCamp, whose book of Egyptian photographs had been published in splendid format. The photographs are excellent, and the collection is prized today as an example of early photography and as a record of Egyptian monuments as they were at the time. But the contrast made by Flaubert can scarcely be faulted.

～

To Louise Colet
[Croisset,] Sunday night, 1.30 a.m. [February 27, 1853]
· · ·

We must be on our guard against that feverish state called inspiration, which is often a matter of nerves rather than muscle. At this very moment, for example, I am keyed up to a high pitch – my brow is burning, sentences keep rushing into my head; for the past two hours I have been wanting to write to you and haven't been able to wrench myself away from work for an instant. Instead of one idea I have six, and where the most simple exposition is called for I am tempted to elaborate. I am sure I could keep going until tomorrow noon without fatigue. But I know these masked balls of the imagination! You come away from them exhausted and depressed, having seen only falsity and spouted nonsense. Everything should be done coldly, with poise.

. . .

~

To Louise Colet
                    [Croisset,] Easter Sunday, 4 o'clock. [March 27, 1853]
                              . . .

The impression my travel notes make on you has inspired me with some strange reflections, dear Muse, concerning a man's heart and a woman's. Decidedly, they are not the same, whatever people may say.

We, on our side, are frank, if not delicate. We are wrong, however, for our frankness is a harshness. If I had omitted my impressions of women, nothing would have wounded you! Women, on the other hand, keep everything hidden. Their confidences are never the whole story. The most they do is let you guess; and when they tell you things, everything is so covered over with sauce that the meat of the matter disappears. But if we admit to two or three mediocre lays, in which our heart wasn't even involved, just listen to their moans! Strange! Strange! I rack my brain trying to understand it all, and yet I have thought about it much of my life.

. . .

As for Kuchuk Hanem,[1] ah! Set your mind at rest, and at the same time correct your ideas about the Orient. You may be sure that she felt nothing at all: emotionally, I guarantee; and even physically, I strongly suspect. She found us very good *cawadjas* (seigneurs), because we left a goodly number of piastres behind, that's all. Bouilhet's piece is very fine, but it is poetry and nothing else. The oriental woman is no more than a machine: she makes no distinction between one man and another. Smoking, going to the baths, painting her eyelids and drinking coffee – such is the circle of occupations within which her existence is confined. As for physical pleasure, it must be very slight, since the famous button, the seat thereof, is sliced off at an early age. What makes this woman, in a sense, so poetic, is that she relapses into the state of nature.

. . . You tell me that Kuchuk's bedbugs degrade her in your eyes; for me they were the most enchanting touch of all. Their nauseating odour mingled with the scent of her skin, which was dripping with sandalwood oil. I want a bitter undertaste in everything – always a jeer in the midst of our triumphs, desolation in the very midst of enthusiasm.

. . . To go back to Kuchuk. You and I are thinking of her, but she is certainly not thinking of us. We are weaving an aesthetic around her, whereas this particular very interesting tourist who was vouchsafed the honours of her couch has vanished from her memory completely, like many others. Ah! Travel makes one modest: one sees what a tiny place one occupies in the world.

· · ·

As for me, the more I realize the difficulties of writing, the more daring I become; this is what keeps me from pedantry, into which I would otherwise doubtless fall. I have plans for writing that will keep me busy till the end of my life, and though I sometimes have bitter moments that make me almost scream with rage (so acutely do I feel my own impotence and weakness), I have others when I can scarcely contain myself for joy. Something deep and ultra-voluptuous gushes out of me, like an ejaculation of the soul. I feel transported, drunk with my own thought, as though a hot gust of perfume were being wafted to me through some inner conduit. I shall never go very far: I know my limitations. But the goal I have set for myself will be achieved by others: thanks to me, someone more talented, more instinctive, will be set on the right path. It is perhaps absurd to want to give prose the rhythm of verse (keeping it distinctly prose, however), and to write of ordinary life as one writes history or epic (but without falsifying the subject). I often wonder about this. But on the other hand it is perhaps a great experiment, and very original. I know where I fail. (Ah, if only I were fifteen!) No matter: I shall always be given some credit for my stubbornness. And then, who can tell? Some day I may find a good motif, a melody completely suited to my voice, neither too high nor too low. In any case, I shall have lived nobly and often delightfully.

There is a saying by La Bruyère that serves me as a guide: 'A good author likes to think that he writes reasonably.'[2] That is what I ask – to write reasonably; and it's asking a good deal. Still, one thing is depressing, and that is to see how easily the great men achieve their effects by means extraneous to Art. What is more badly put together than much of Rabelais, Cervantes, Molière and Hugo? But such quick punches! Such power in a single word! We have to pile up a mass of little pebbles to build our pyramids; theirs, a hundred times greater, are hewn in monoliths. But to seek to imitate the methods of those geniuses would be fatal. They are great for the very reason that they have no methods.

. . .

1. Flaubert had allowed Louise to see his travel notes, which he had transcribed and expanded from the jottings in the notebooks he had carried with him. Bouilhet's poem, 'Kuchiuk-Hanem: Souvenir', dedicated to Flaubert, was based on Flaubert's letter of March 13, 1850. Bouilhet depicted the almeh as brooding, 'sad as a widow', after her visitors' departure.
2. La Bruyère's words: '*Un esprit médiocre croit écrire divinement, un bon esprit croit écrire raisonnablement.*'

~

To Louise Colet

[Croisset,] Thursday, half past four [March 31, 1853]

I am just back from Rouen, where I went to have a tooth pulled. It was not pulled: my dentist urged me to wait. However, I think that very soon I shall indeed have to part with one of my dominoes. I am ageing: there go the teeth, and soon I shall be quite hairless. Well, provided one keeps one's brain: that's the main thing. How annihilation stalks us! No sooner are we born than putrefaction sets in, and life is nothing but a long battle it wages against us, ever more triumphantly until the end – death – when its reign becomes absolute. There were only two or three years in my life (approximately from seventeen to nineteen) when I was *entire*. I was splendid – I can say it now: sufficiently so to attract the attention of an entire theatre audience – it was in Rouen, the first night of *Ruy Blas*. But since then I have deteriorated shockingly. There are mornings when I am afraid of myself, I am so wrinkled and worn. Ah! It was then that you should have come into my life, poor Muse. But such a love would have driven me mad; or worse – it would have made me vain to the point of idiocy. If I still have a warm heart, it is because for many years I conserved my fire: what I have not spent, I can put to use. There is enough heat in me to feed all my books. No, I regret none of my youth. I was hideously depressed; I contemplated suicide; I was prey to every possible kind of melancholy. My nervous sickness was beneficial, in that it converted all those feelings into physical symptoms, leaving me with a cooler head; and furthermore it made me acquainted with peculiar psychological phenomena that no one has any idea of, or rather that no one has ever experienced. Some day I will have my revenge, in a book (that metaphysical novel with ghosts I spoke to you about).[1] But that subject frightens me, speaking from the medical point of view. I must wait until I'm sufficiently distant from such impressions to be capable of using them factitiously, as symbols, ideal projections, without danger to myself or the book.

Here is my opinion about your idea of a Review:[2]

All the Reviews in the world began with the intention of being virtuous: none has been. The *Revue de Paris* itself (when a project) had the ideas you express, and was very determined to follow them.[3] One swears to be chaste; one is, for a day, two days; and then . . . then . . . Nature! Secondary considerations! Friends! Enemies! Don't you have to boost some, bury others? Admitting that for a time you do stick to the programme the public gets bored, subscriptions don't come in. Then people give you advice outside the lines you set for yourself, you follow it as an experiment, and it becomes a habit. In fact, there is nothing more pernicious than being able to say everything and having a convenient outlet.[4] You become very indulgent with yourself; and your friends are the same with you, in order that you may be so with them. And there you are, fallen into the trap out of pure naivety. A model Review would be a splendid thing, and would require nothing less than the full time of a man of genius. The directorship of a Review should be a post for a patriarch; he should be dictator, with great *moral* authority acquired through his own writings. The authority cannot possibly be shared, for then immediate muddle is unavoidable. You talk a lot and spend all your talent skimming pennies on the river, whereas with greater economy you could in time buy fine farms and excellent châteaux.

What you say, DuCamp used to say: and see what he and his friends have done! Let's not think ourselves stronger than they; for they failed, as we would fail, from being carried away, and because of the slippery slope of the thing itself. After all, a magazine is a shop. And being a shop . . . sooner or later the question of pleasing the customers comes to dominate all others. I well know that it is impossible to publish anywhere these days, and that all existing reviews are squalid whores acting like coquettes. Rotten to the marrow of their bones with the pox, they grimace with distaste at the thought of opening their thighs to healthy creations which badly need to get in. So, do as you've been doing: publish your work in book form – it's more intrepid; and be on your own. Who needs to hitch himself up as one of a team dragging an omnibus when he can still be a *cheval de tilbury*? As for me, I should be very glad if your ideas could be realized. But as to actually participating in anything at all in this world, no! no! a thousand times no! I no more want to be associated with a review, or to be a member of a society, a club, or an academy, than to be a city councillor or an officer in the national guard.

.   .   .

We marvel at the men of the age of Louis XIV, and yet they were not men of enormous genius. Reading them we experience none of that awe which makes us feel that Homer, Rabelais, and above all Shakespeare were more than human; certainly not. But what conscientious workmen! How they strained to find the exact expression for their thoughts! Such labour! Such tireless revision! How they sought one another's advice! How well they knew Latin! How attentively they read! That is why we have their thought in its entirety, why their form is so full, charged with substance to bursting point. Well, *there are no degrees: all good things are of equal value.* LaFontaine will live as long as Dante, and Boileau as long as Bossuet or even Hugo.

.   .   .

1. The novel mentioned on p. 243 as being 'in outline'. Never written, it was to have been called *La Spirale*.
2. Louise Colet had thought of starting a magazine to be called *La Revue Française*. Nothing came of it. (J.B.)
3. The first issue of the *Revue de Paris* had contained a manifesto, called 'Liminaire' – 'Introduction' – signed by Théophile Gautier, which was to be one of the ironic elements in the story of the publication of *Madame Bovary*. It reads, in part:
    'We have but one literary principle: absolute liberty . . . We shall refuse manuscripts, but we will not deface them . . . Those who write for the

Revue will feel no need even to exercise that preliminary self-censorship which forestalls correction . . . Let the poet spread the wings of his strophe to their fullest: we will not clip them . . .

    'What we desire above all is to have every author, obscure or famous, in his own idiosyncratic form, in his most characteristic originality, in his own frank and free nature, without timidity or reticence, with his own bitter or sweet savour . . . as though he were writing, for himself and in solitude, a work which was never to see the light . . . We desire the anarchy and the autonomy of art.'

4. '*Un déversoir commode*': could there be a better description of the role in which Flaubert cast Louise?

∼

To Louise Colet
    [Croisset,] Wednesday, half after midnight. [April 13, 1853]
    . . .

Finally I am beginning to see a little light in my accursed dialogue with the curé.[1] But frankly, there are moments when I almost feel like vomiting *physically,* the whole thing is so low. I want to express the following situation: my little lady, in an access of religiosity, goes to church; at the door she finds the curé, who, in a dialogue (on no definite subject) shows himself to be so stupid, trivial, inept, sordid, that she goes away disgusted and undevout. And my curé is a very good man, indeed an excellent fellow, but he thinks only of the physical side (the sufferings of the poor, no bread, no firewood), and has no inkling of my lady's moral lapses or her vague mystical aspirations; he is very chaste, faithfully performs all his duties. This must have six or seven pages at the most, and must contain no comment, no analysis (it will all be in direct dialogue). Furthermore, since I consider it very cheap to write dialogue substituting dashes for 'he said' and 'he answered', you can imagine it isn't easy to avoid repetitions of the same turns of phrase. So: you are thus initiated into the torture I have been undergoing for a fortnight. By the end of next week, however, I hope it will all be off my hands. Then, after ten more pages (two long passages), I'll have finished the first section of my Part Two. My lovers are ready for adultery: soon they will be committing it. (I too, I hope.) . . .

1. *Madame Bovary,* Part II, Chapter 6.

~

To Louise Colet

[Croisset,] Tuesday night, 1 a.m. [April 26, 1853]

. . .

At the present moment I believe that a thinker (and what is an artist if not a triple thinker?) should have neither religion, country, nor even any social conviction.[1] Absolute doubt now seems to me so completely substantiated that it would be almost silly to seek to formulate it. Bouilhet told me the other day that he felt the need to proclaim himself publicly, in writing, setting down all his reasons, an apostate Christian and an apostate Frenchman. And then to leave Europe and if possible never hear of it again. Yes, it would be a relief to vomit out all the immense contempt that fills the heart to overflowing. What good cause is there these days to arouse one's interest, let alone one's enthusiasm? . . .

I am reading Montaigne in bed, now. I know of no more soothing book, none more conducive to peace of mind. It is so healthy, so down to earth! If you have a copy, read the chapter on Democritus and Heraclitus. And reflect on the last paragraph.[2] One has to become a stoic when one lives in such sad times as ours . . .

1. Seventy years later, Marcel Proust was to make a similar assertion, with particular reference to the work of Flaubert, when he wrote that the artist can serve the glory of his country 'only by being an artist, or, in other words, on condition that when he is studying the laws of Art, making his experiments and his discoveries, as delicate as those of Science, he think of nothing – not even his country – except the truth that is before him . . . It was not out of the kindness of his virtuous heart – and he was very kind – that Choderlos de Laclos wrote *Les Liaisons Dangereuses,* nor because of his liking for the *petite bourgeoisie* – or the *grande,* either – that Flaubert selected for subjects those of *Madame Bovary* and *L'Éducation sentimentale.'* (*The Past Recaptured,* translation by Frederick A. Blossom.)

    In this connection, Oscar Wilde, who in a letter to W. E. Henley (December 1888) had announced 'Flaubert is my master', wrote in a subsequent letter to Henley: 'Flaubert did not write French prose, but the prose of a great artist who happened to be French.' (*The Letters of Oscar Wilde,* ed. Rupert Hart-Davis. London: Rupert Hart-Davis, 1962.)

2. 'Of the same stampe was the answer of Statilius, to whom Brutus spake to

win him to take part, and adhere to the conspiracie against Caesar. He allowed the enterprize to be very just, but disallowed of the men that should perform the same, as unworthy that any man should put himself in any adventure for them. Conformable to the discipline of Hegesias, who said, "That a wise man ought never to do anything, but for himself; forasmuch as he alone is worthy to have any action performed for him"; and to that of Theodorus, who thought it an injustice, that a wise man should in any case hazard himself for the good and benefit of his country, or to endanger his wisdom for fooles.

'Our own condition is as ridiculous as risible.'

(John Florio translation.)

~

To Louise Colet

[Croisset,] Wednesday midnight. [June 1, 1853]

I have just written to the great man (the letter will go off tomorrow at the latest).[1] It wasn't easy, because of the moderate tone I wanted to employ. He has been guilty of too many abominations for me to express my admiration without reserve (his encouragement of mediocrities, the Academy, his political ambition, etc.). On the other hand, he has afforded me so many fine hours of enthusiasm, given me so many splendid erections (if one may put it that way), that it was hard for me to strike a balance between constraint and adulation. However, I think I was both polite and sincere (a rarity).

. . .

I am not inveighing against our good friend de Lisle,[2] but I do say that to me he seems a little *ordinary* in his passions. The true poet, for me, is a priest. As soon as he dons the cassock he must leave his family . . .

There is another thing that seemed to me slightly bourgeois in this same individual: his saying 'I have never been able to go with a whore.'

Well, let me declare that *I* have, and often! Speaking of disgust, all these disgusted people disgust me profoundly. Did he think he wasn't wallowing in prostitution when he wiped from his body the leavings of the husband? The little lady doubtless had a third, and, in the arms of all three, was thinking of a fourth. Oh the irony of love-making! Still, since she carried no card,[3] our nice de Lisle could 'go with' her.

Let me say that that theory makes me gag. There are certain things that tell me immediately with what manner of man I have to deal: (1) admiration for Béranger; (2) dislike of perfumes; (3) liking for thick cloth; (4) a fringe beard; (5) aversion to brothels. How many nice young men I have known who had a pious horror of 'houses' and yet picked up the most beautiful cases of clap you can imagine from their so-called mistresses. The Latin Quarter is full of this doctrine and such occurrences. It is perhaps a perverse taste, but I like prostitution – and for its own sake, independently of what lies underneath. My heart has never failed to pound at the sight of one of those provocatively dressed women walking in the rain under the gas lamps, just as the sight of monks in their robes and knotted girdles touches some ascetic, hidden corner of my soul. Prostitution is a meeting-point of so many elements – lechery, frustration, total lack of any human relation, physical frenzy, the clink of gold – that a glance into its depths makes one giddy and teaches one all manner of things. It fills you with such sadness! And makes you dream so of love! Ah, elegy-makers, it is not on ruins that you should lean, but on the breasts of these light women.

Yes, that man has missed something who has never awakened in an anonymous bed beside a face he will never see again, and who has never left a brothel at sunrise feeling like throwing himself into the river out of pure disgust for life. And just their shameless way of dressing – the temptation of the chimera – the aura of the unknown, of the *maudit* – the old poetry of corruption and venality! During my first years in Paris, I used to sit in front of Tortoni's on hot summer evenings and watch the streetwalkers stroll by in the last rays of the sun. At such moments I ate my heart out with biblical poetry. I thought of Isaiah, of 'fornication in high places', and I walked back along the rue de la Harpe saying to myself: 'And her mouth is smoother than oil.'[4] I swear I was never more chaste. My only complaint about prostitution is that it is a myth. The kept woman has invaded the field of debauchery, just as the journalist has invaded poetry; everything is becoming mongrelized. There are no more courtesans, just as there are no more saints; there are only '*soupeuses*' and '*lorettes*' – even more sordid than *grisettes* . . .

1. Victor Hugo. (See the following letter.) Flaubert was helping the exiled

Hugo correspond surreptitiously with friends in France, including colleagues in the French Academy who might vote for Louise in the 1854 poetry contest.

2. Louise had introduced Flaubert to Charles-Marie-René Leconte de Lisle (1818–94), whose first volume of 'Parnassian' poetry, *Poèmes antiques*, had been published the previous year. Flaubert liked him, but found him and his poetry somewhat pallid. Both Flaubert and Louise vary in the spelling of his name.

3. That is, the married woman in question (she is not identified) was not licensed as a prostitute.

4. Flaubert is possibly thinking of Jeremiah 3:6 or 13:27, and of Proverbs 5:3.

~

To Victor Hugo

Croisset, June 2, 1853

I think, Monsieur, that I should warn you about the following:

Your communication dated April 27 arrived here badly damaged. The outer envelope was torn in several places and a few words in your handwriting were exposed. The inner envelope (addressed to Mme C.) had been torn along the edges, and portions of its contents were visible – two other letters and a printed sheet.

Was it the Customs that opened the envelope, hoping to find a bit of lace? It would be naive, I think, to suppose that; the indiscretion must be laid at the door of the saviours of society. If you have something of importance to transmit to me, Monsieur, I think that the following procedure would be the most secure: you could address your letters from Jersey to a family of honest merchants I know in London; they would open the outer envelope and re-enclose the inner (addressed to me) in one which would thus bear their English handwriting and a London postmark. Communications *from* Mme C. would be forwarded by me via the same route.

Your later envelope, dated May (via Le Havre) arrived here intact.

However, please allow me, Monsieur, to thank you for all your thanks and to accept none of them. The man who in my restricted life has occupied the greatest place, and the best, may indeed expect some service of me, since you call it service!

The diffidence one feels in declaring any true passion inhibits me, despite your exile, from telling you what underlies my attachment to you. It is my gratitude for all the enthusiasm you have aroused in me. But I do not wish to become entangled in sentences which would serve but poorly to specify its extent.

I have already seen you 'in person'. We have met several times – you unaware of me, I gazing eagerly at you. It was in the winter of 1844, in the studio of poor Pradier, of happy memory. There were five or six of us; we drank tea and played 'the game of the goose'; I even remember your large gold ring, with its engraved lion rampant, which we used as a stake.

Since then you have played for higher stakes, and in more fearsome games; but in whatever you do, the lion rampant plays its part. *He*[1] bears on his brow the mark of its claws, and when he passes into history, the centuries will know him by that red scar.

As for you – who knows? Future makers of aesthetic will perhaps thank Providence for this atrocity, this consecration. For is it not by martyrdom that virtue is brought to perfection? Is it not by outrage that grandeur is rendered yet more grand? And in you there is no lack either of inherent grandeur or of that conferred by circumstances.

I send you, Monsieur, together with all my admiration for your genius, the assurance of my entire devotion to your person.

Gust. Flaubert.

(*Mme Farmer, Upper Holloway Manor Road, No. 5, London*)[2]

1. Napoleon III, excoriated by Hugo in *Napoléon le Petit*.
2. Mrs Richard Farmer was Caroline's former governess, 'Miss Jane'. The envelopes to her would be addressed in the hand of the present governess, 'Miss Isabel' (soon, however, to be discharged: see p. 262).

~

TO LOUISE COLET

[Croisset,] Saturday night, 1 o'clock. [June 25, 1853]

Only now have I finished my first section of Part Two,[1] the very section I had planned to have ready before our last meeting in Mantes. You see how slow I have been. I'll spend a few more days reading it over and recopying it, and a week from tomorrow will spill it all out to the Hon. Bouilhet. If it passes the test, that will be one great worry the less – and a good thing, too, believe me, for the substructure was very flimsy. Apart from that, I think the book will have a big defect, namely faulty proportions in regard to length. I already have two hundred and sixty pages which are merely preliminary to the action, containing more or less disguised descriptions of character . . . of landscapes, of places. My conclusion, which will be my little lady's death, her burial and her husband's subsequent grief, will be at least sixty pages. That leaves, for the body of the action itself, one hundred and twenty to one hundred and sixty pages at the most. Isn't that a great flaw? What reassures me (though only moderately) is that the book is a biography rather than a story with a complicated plot. The drama plays only a small part in it, and if this dramatic element is skilfully blended with the rest, so that a uniform, overall tonality is achieved, then perhaps the lack of harmonious development of the various phases will pass unnoticed. Besides, I think that this is rather characteristic of life itself. The sexual act may last only a minute, though it has been anticipated for months! Our passions are like volcanoes: they are always rumbling, but eruption is only intermittent.

Unfortunately the French spirit is mad for entertainment. It demands so much that is showy. It takes so little pleasure in what for me is the essence of poetry, namely exposition, whether our treatment of it is descriptive or moral, whether we stress picturesque aspects or psychological analysis . . . I would like to produce books which would entail only the writing of sentences (if I may put it that way), just as in order to live it is enough to breathe. What I dislike are the tricks inherent in the making of an outline, the arranging of effects, all the underlying calculations – which are, however, Art, for they and they alone account for the stylistic effect.

. . .

If the book I am writing with such difficulty turns out well, I'll have established, by the very fact of having written it, these two truths, which for me are axiomatic, namely: (1) that poetry is purely subjective, that in literature there are no such things as beautiful subjects, and that therefore Yvetot is the equal of Constantinople; and (2) that consequently one can write about any one thing equally well as about any other. The artist must raise everything to a higher level: he is like a pump; he has inside him a great pipe that reaches down into the entrails of things, the deepest layers. He sucks up what was lying there below, dim and unnoticed, and brings it out in great jets to the sunlight.

1. *Madame Bovary,* Part II. Chapters 1–7. From the Bovarys' arrival in Yonville to the first appearance of Rodolphe.

~

To Louise Colet

[Croisset,] Tuesday, 1 a.m. [June 28, 1853]

. . .

I find Musset's remarks about *Hamlet* utterly bourgeois, and this is why. He criticizes this 'inconsistency': that Hamlet is sceptical even after seeing his father's soul with his own eyes. But in the first place it was not the soul that he saw. He saw a ghost, a shade, a *thing*, a material living thing, which was in no way popularly or poetically related, at that period, to the abstract idea of the soul. It is we, metaphysicians and moderns, who use that language. And Hamlet does not *doubt* at all, in the philosophical sense; rather, he *wonders*.

I think that Musset's observation is not original with him; that he took it from Mallefille's preface to his *Don Juan.*[1] In my opinion it is superficial. A peasant of our own day may perfectly well still see a ghost, and next morning, in the crude light of day, think coolly about life and death, but not about the flesh and the soul. Hamlet thinks in terms not of scholastic concepts, but of human attitudes. On the contrary, his perpetual state of fluctuation, his constant uncertainty, his irresolution, and his inability to resolve his thoughts – these are what make the play sublime. But our clever friends want characters to be all of a piece, consistent – as they are in books only. The truth is that Shakespeare's conception of Hamlet reaches into the remotest corners of the human soul. Ulysses is perhaps the greatest type in all ancient literature, and Hamlet in all modern.

If I weren't so weary, I would develop my ideas at greater length. It is so easy to chatter about the Beautiful. But it takes more genius to say, in proper style: 'close the door', or 'he wanted to sleep', than to give all the literature courses in the world.

Criticism occupies the lowest place in the literary hierarchy: as regards form, almost always; and as regards 'moral value', incontestably. It comes after rhyming games and acrostics, which at least require a certain inventiveness.

Allons, adieu. Mille bons baisers. À toi, coeur sur coeur.

1. Félicien Mallefille (1813–1868), playwright and novelist. As delegate of the provisional government in 1848, he is credited with saving the museum of Versailles from incendiarists.

~

To Louise Colet

Croisset, Saturday midnight, [July 2, 1853]

. . .

Tomorrow I shall read to Bouilhet 114 [sic] pages of *Bovary*, pages 139 to 251. That is what I have done since last September – in ten months! This afternoon I finally stopped making corrections, not being able to see straight any longer: continuous concentration on a piece of writing results in your being dazed; what seems a mistake now, five minutes later no longer seems so; it's a never-ending series of corrections and of recorrections of corrections. Eventually one begins to function badly, and it's more sensible to stop. The entire week has been rather tedious, and today I feel a great relief in the thought that I've got something finished, or almost; but I have had to remove a lot of cement that was oozing out from between the stones, and the stones had to be reset so that the joints wouldn't show. Prose must stand upright, from one end to the other, like a wall whose ornamentation continues down to its very base: seen in perspective, it must make a long continuous line. Oh! If I wrote the way I know one has to write, I'd write so well! Still, it seems to me that among these 114 pages there are a good many strong ones, and that the whole thing, though not dramatic, moves at a lively pace.[1] Also, I have been musing on what's to follow. I have a fornication coming up that worries me considerably, and which I mustn't shirk, although I want to make it chaste – that is, literary, without gross details or lascivious images: the carnality must be in the emotion.

. . .

I never talk to you about domestic matters, in fact they are usually quite boring: however, some can be interesting as examples of the grotesque. (1) My mother has just discovered that the gardener is swindling us. Only we, in all the village, have no vegetables, because the village lives somewhat at our expense. Our flowers are sold in Rouen: bunches of them are taken there by steamer. Can't you picture the gardener 'making his gravy' by cheating the boss, and the boss not being happy about it? (2) The governess has been so arrogant, so capricious and rude, and was so mistreating the little girl, that we told her she was no longer needed, and she is leaving. (3) We have discovered by chance that last winter my brother gave a soirée for 'important people' without telling us, so as not to have to invite us. (He and his wife come here every Sunday.) Nice, isn't it? You can gauge from that the degree of warmth and cordiality that surrounds us, my mother and me. But these worthies (not so worthy), who are banality itself, can barely understand – and consequently do not like – anyone out of the ordinary. However that may be, you see how little consideration I enjoy on my native heath and in my family! You'll find the same thing in any life: it's the norm.

1.   A few days later, Flaubert wrote to Louise:
     'I don't know whether Bouilhet has written you. If so, he must have told you he was pleased with what I had done; and so was I, frankly. As a difficulty overcome, it seems to me excellent, but that is all. The subject in itself (so far, at least) precludes the great outbursts of style that ravish me in other writers and which I think I am suited to. The good thing about *Bovary* is that it will have been a splendid exercise. I shall have produced written reality, which is rare. But I will take my revenge: just let me find a subject suited to my voice, and I'll go far.' The first rumble of *Salammbô*.

∾

To Victor Hugo

Croisset, July 15 [1853]

How am I to thank you, Monsieur, for your magnificent gift?[1] What am I to say – unless perhaps I echo the dying Talleyrand when visited by Louis-Philippe: 'This is the greatest honour ever conferred upon my house!'? But there the parallel ends, for any number of reasons.

I will not hide from you that you have profoundly '*Chatouillé de mon coeur l'orgueilleuse faiblesse*' as good old Racine would have said.[2] A true poet! And how many monsters he would find now to depict, different from his dragon-bull and a hundred times worse!

Exile at least spares you the sight of them. Ah, if you knew into what filth we are plunged! Private infamies proceed from political turpitude, and it is impossible to take a step without treading on something unclean. The atmosphere is heavy with nauseous vapours. Air! Air! For that, I open my window and turn towards you. I hear the great wings of your Muse as she passes, and I breathe, as one might breathe the fragrance of the forests, the exhalations that rise from the depths of your style.

And in addition, Monsieur, you have been a charming obsession in my life, a long love that has never weakened. I have read you during awesome nights spent beside the dead, and on soft beaches by the sea in the full sunshine of summer. I carried you with me to Palestine, and it was you who comforted me, ten years ago, when I was dying of ennui in the Latin Quarter. Your poetry became a part of me, like my nurse's milk. Many of your lines will remain in my memory for ever, unforgettable as a momentous exploit.

Here I stop. But if anything is sincere, it is what I have just said. From now on, I shall importune you no longer with my person, and you may make use of the correspondent without fear of his correspondence.

But since you extend your hand to me across the ocean, I take and grasp it. I grasp it proudly, the hand that wrote *Notre-Dame* and *Napoléon le Petit*, the hand that has hewn colossi and fashioned bitter cups for traitors, that has culled the most glorious delights from the loftiest reaches of the intellect, and that now, like the hand of the biblical Hercules,[3] alone stays raised amid the twofold ruins of Art and of Liberty!

I am, Monsieur, yours, with once again a thousand thanks.

Ex imo.

1. Hugo's note accompanying the gift (a photograph of himself) had said, in part: 'Allow me to send . . . you my portrait: it is the work of my son, done in collaboration with the sun.' See the following letter for Flaubert's comment on his present reply to the great man, which reads like an embarrassing parody of Hugo's own grandiose epistolary style.
2. Agamemnon, in Racine's *Iphigénie: 'Ces noms de roi des rois, et chef de la Grèce,/Chatouillaient de mon coeur l'orgueilleuse faiblesse.'*
3. 'The biblical Hercules' is, of course, Samson.

∿

To Louise Colet

[Croisset,] Friday night, 1 o'clock. [July 15, 1853]

. . .

What artists we would be if we had never read, seen, or loved anything that was not beautiful; if from the outset some guardian angel of the purity of our pens had kept us from all contamination; if we had never associated with fools[1] or read newspapers! The Greeks were like that. As regards plastic form, they lived in conditions that will never return. But to want to wear their shoes is madness. What we in the North need are not chlamyses but fur coats. Classic form is insufficient for our needs, and our voices are not created to sing those simple tunes. Let us, if we can, be as dedicated to art as they were, but differently. The human consciousness has broadened since Homer. Sancho Panza's belly has burst the seams of Venus's girdle. Rather than persist in emulating old styles, we must exert ourselves to invent new ones. I think de Lisle is unaware of this. He has no instinct for modern life; he lacks heart. By this I do not mean personal or even humanitarian feelings, no – but *heart*, almost in the medical sense of the word. His ink is pale; his muse suffers from lack of fresh air. Thoroughbred horses and thoroughbred styles have plenty of blood in their veins, and it can be seen pulsing everywhere in them, under the skin and the words. Life! Life! To have erections! That is everything, the only thing that counts! That is why I so love lyricism. It seems to me the most natural form of poetry – poetry in all its nakedness and freedom. All the power of a work of art lies in this mystery, and it is this primordial quality, this *motus animi continuus* (vibration, continual movement of the mind – Cicero's definition of eloquence), which results in conciseness, relief, form, energy, rhythm, diversity. It doesn't require much brain to be a critic: you can judge the excellence of a book by the strength of the punches it has given you and the time it takes you to recover from them. And then, how dauntless are the great masters! They pursue an idea to its furthermost limits. In Molière's *Monsieur de Pourceaugnac* there is a question of giving a man an enema. Not just *one* enema is brought in: a whole troupe of actors carrying syringes pour down the aisles of the theatre! Michelangelo's figures have cables rather than muscles; in Rubens's bacchanalian scenes men piss on the ground; and think of everything in Shakespeare, etc., etc., and the most recent member of the family, old Hugo. What a beautiful thing *Notre Dame* is! I lately re-read three chapters in it, including the sack of the church by the beggars. That's the sort of thing that's *strong*! I think the greatest characteristic of genius is, above all, *power*. Hence, what I detest most of all in the arts, what sets me on edge, is the *ingenious*, the clever. This is not at all the same as bad taste, which is a good quality gone astray. In order to have what is called bad taste, you must have a sense for poetry; whereas cleverness, on the contrary, is incompatible with genuine poetry. Who was cleverer than Voltaire, and who less a poet? In our beloved France, the public will accept poetry only if it is disguised. If it is given to them straight, they protest: they must be treated like the horses of Abbas-Pasha, which are fed a tonic of meatballs masked in flour. That's what Art is: knowing how to disguise! But never fear: if you offer this sort of flour to lions, to real carnivores, they will smell the meat twenty paces away and spring at it.

I have written a monumental letter to the Grand Crocodile. I won't pretend it didn't give me trouble (but I think it quite high-styled, excessively, perhaps); in fact it gave me so much that now I know it by heart. If I still remember it when we meet, I will repeat it to you. The parcel leaves tomorrow.

I have been in excellent form this week. I have written eight pages, all of which I think can stand pretty much as they are. Tonight I have just sketched my entire big scene of the Agricultural Show.[2] It will be enormous — thirty pages at least. Against the background of this rustico-municipal celebration, with all its details (all my secondary characters will be shown talking and in action), there must be continuous dialogue between a gentleman and the lady he is 'warming up'. Moreover, somewhere in the middle I have a solemn speech by a councillor from the Prefecture, and at the end (this I have already done) a newspaper article written by my pharmacist, who gives an account of the celebration in fine philosophical, poetical, progressive style. You see it is no small chore. I am sure of my local colour and of many of my effects; but it's a devilish job to keep it from getting too long. And yet this kind of thing must be full and ample. Once this is behind me, I shall soon reach my fornication in the autumn woods, with the lovers' horses cropping the leaves beside them; and then I think I'll have clear sailing — I'll have passed Charybdis, at least, even though Scylla may remain to be negotiated.

. . .

1. In a recent letter to Louise, Flaubert had written: 'Another law of mathematics to be discovered is: How many imbeciles do you have to know before wanting to cut your throat?'
2. *Madame Bovary,* Part II, Chapter 8.

∽

To Louise Colet
[Croisset,] Friday night, one o'clock. [July 22, 1853]

. . .

Today I had a great success. You know that yesterday 'we' had the 'pleasure' of having Monsieur Saint-Arnaud.[1] Well, in this morning's *Journal de Rouen* I came on a sentence in the Mayor's speech – a sentence which, the day before, I had written *word for word* in my *Bovary* (in the Prefect's speech at the Agricultural Show). Not only the same idea, the same words, but the same assonances of style. I don't mind telling you that this is the sort of thing I enjoy. When literature attains the precision of an exact science, that's something!

. . .

1. Maréchal de Saint-Arnaud, Minister for War. Replying to a speech by the Mayor of Rouen, he assured the citizens that the Emperor intended to help the farmers of the region, whose crops had been largely destroyed by a recent heavy hailstorm.
   About the storm, Flaubert had written to Louise:
   'It wasn't without a certain pleasure that I surveyed my ruined espaliers, all my flowers torn to pieces, the dishevelled vegetable garden. As I contemplated all these factitious little man-made arrangements which five minutes of nature had sufficed to destroy, I admired the way the true order had reimposed itself on the false. These things so tormented by us – trees pruned and shaped, flowers growing where they don't want to, vegetables brought from other countries – they all found a kind of revenge in this atmospheric rebuke . . . It is too generally believed that the sun has no other function here below than to help the cabbages along. Now and then we must restore God to his pedestal.'

∽

To Louise Colet

[Trouville,][1] Sunday 14, 4 o'clock. [August 14, 1853]
· · ·

I spent an hour yesterday watching the ladies bathe. What a sight! What a hideous sight! The two sexes used to bathe together here. But now they are kept separate by means of signposts, wire netting, and a uniformed inspector (what an atrociously lugubrious object, this grotesque figure!) And so, yesterday, from the place where I was standing in the sun, with my spectacles on my nose, I could contemplate the bathing beauties at my leisure. The human race must indeed have become completely moronic to have lost all sense of elegance to this degree. Nothing is more pitiful than these bags in which women encase their bodies, and these oilcloth caps! What faces! And how they walk! Such feet! Red, scrawny, covered with corns and bunions, deformed by shoes, long as shuttles or wide as washerwomen's paddles. And in the midst of it all, scrofulous brats screaming and crying. Further off, grandmas knitting and respectable old gentlemen with gold-rimmed spectacles reading newspapers, looking up from time to time between the lines to survey the vastness of the horizon with an air of approval. The whole thing made me long all afternoon to escape from Europe and go to live in the Sandwich Islands[2] or the forests of Brazil. There, at least, the beaches are not polluted by such ugly feet, by such foul-looking specimens of humanity.

The day before yesterday, in the woods near Touques, in a charming spot beside a spring, I found old cigar butts and scraps of pâté. People had been picnicking. I described such a scene in *Novembre*, eleven years ago: there it was entirely imagined, and the other day it was experienced. Everything one invents is true, you may be sure. Poetry is as precise as geometry. Induction is as good as deduction; and besides, after reaching a certain point one no longer errs about matters of the soul. My poor Bovary, without a doubt, is suffering and weeping at this very hour in twenty villages of France.

The other day I saw something that moved me – something not having to do with myself. We were a league from here, at the Château de Lassay (built in six weeks for Mme Dubarry, who used to come to this coast for sea-bathing). All that remains is a staircase – a great Louis XV staircase, a few empty windows, a wall, and wind, wind.

It is on a plateau, visible from the sea. Beside it stands a peasant's hovel. We went in to get some milk for Liline, who was thirsty. In the tiny garden there were fine hollyhocks as high as the roof, string beans, and a cauldron full of dirty water. Nearby a pig was grunting . . . and further off, beyond the wall, free-running colts were grazing and neighing, their long manes blowing in the sea wind. Inside, on the walls of the cottage hung a picture of the Emperor and another of Badinguet.[3] I would probably have made some joke, when I saw, sitting half-paralysed in a corner by the fireplace, a gaunt old man with a two-weeks' growth of beard. Above his armchair, attached to the wall, were two gold epaulettes! The poor old fellow was so feeble that he had trouble taking his pinch of snuff. No one paid any attention to him. He sat there regurgitating, groaning, eating from a bowl of white beans. The glint of the sun on the metal bands around the pails was making him blink. The cat was lapping milk from an earthenware dish on the floor. And that was all. I thought that in the perpetual half-sleep of old age (which precedes the other sleep, and is like a transition from life to oblivion), the old fellow was probably having visions of the snows of Russia or the sands of Egypt. What other visions were floating before those dulled eyes? And the jacket he was wearing – so patched, so clean! The woman who served us (his daughter, I think) was a dame of fifty, in short skirts and a cotton cap, with wrists like the balustrades of the Place Louis XV.[4] She bustled about the room in her blue stockings and heavy petticoat; and Badinguet, splendid amid it all, was there on his rearing yellow horse, tricorne in hand, saluting a cohort of disabled veterans, all their wooden legs neatly in line. The last time I visited the Château de Lassay was with Alfred. I still remember the conversation we had, the poetry we recited, the plans we made.

How little Nature cares about us! And how impassive the look of the trees, the grass, the waves! (The bell on the steamer for Le Havre is ringing so fiercely that I must break off here.) What a din industry makes in the world! What a clackety thing the machine is! Speaking of industry, have you sometimes thought of the quantity of stupid professions it begets, and the vast amount of stupidity that must inevitably accrue from them over the years? Such a statistic could be frightening! What can be expected of a population like that of Manchester, which spends its life making pins? And the manufacture of a pin involves five or six different specialities! As work is broken down into compartments, men-machines take their places beside the machines themselves. Think of spending one's life selling tickets in a railway station, or pasting on labels in a printing shop, etc., etc. Yes, mankind is becoming increasingly brutish. Leconte is right: he formulated that in a way I shall never forget.[5] The 'dreamers' of the Middle Ages were a different breed from the 'men of action' of modern times.

Mankind hates us: we serve none of its purposes; and we hate it, because it injures us. So let us love one another 'in Art', as mystics love one another 'in God'. Let everything else pale before this love. May all life's kitchen candles (every one of which reeks) disappear in the light of that great sun. In periods when every common bond is broken, and when Society is but one vast banditry (governmental term), more or less well organized, when the values of the flesh and those of the mind are far apart, howling at each other from a distance, like wolves, we must, like the rest of the world, fashion ourselves an egoism (but one that is nobler), and live inside our den. Each day I feel a greater distance between myself and my fellow men; and I am glad of it, for my ability to recognize what is sympathetic to me increases thanks to this very distance.

. . .

1. Flaubert was spending a few weeks in Trouville with his mother and Caroline, 'Liline'. In this letter and in others from Trouville he evokes his adolescent days there and the birth of his passion for Elise Schlesinger, causing Louise to write to him jealously about his obsession with 'Trouville ghosts'.

2. The Hawaiian Islands. The 'unpolluted beaches' alluded to by Flaubert are therefore such present-day funfairs as Waikiki.

3. Napoleon and Napoleon III. Flaubert tended to sentimentalize about the first Empire. In 1853 he still considered his own Emperor a shoddy figure, and was glad to use the popular, comic-sounding nickname, which had originated in a satirical cartoon by Gavarni.

4. One of the earlier names of the Place de la Concorde, but still in common use.

5. 'Since Homer and Aeschylus, who represent poetry as it was at its most vital, in its greatest fullness and harmony, decadence and barbarism have buried the human spirit.' (Leconte de Lisle, preface to *Poèmes antiques*, 1852.) (J.B.)

∾

To Louise Colet
[Trouville,] Sunday, 11 o'clock [August 21, 1853]
. . .

Yes, I maintain (and in my opinion this ought to be a practical dogma in the artist's life) that you should divide your existence into two parts: live like a bourgeois, and think like a demigod. Physical and intellectual satisfactions have nothing in common. If they happen to be combined, seize hold of them and never let go. But do not *seek* the combination, for that would be artificial. Incidentally, that idea of 'happiness' is the cause, almost single-handed, of all human misfortunes . . .

If you seek happiness and beauty at the same time, you will find neither the one nor the other, for the latter is attained only by sacrifice. Art, like the God of the Jews, feasts on holocausts.

. . .

∾

To Louis Bouilhet
[Trouville,] Wednesday, 1 o'clock. [August 24, 1853]
. . .

How eager I am to finish *Bovary, Anubis,* and my three prefaces,[1] so that I can enter on a new period and revel in pure beauty. My idleness of these past few weeks has given me a burning desire to transform, by art, everything that originates in myself, everything I have ever felt. I have not the slightest urge to write my memoirs. I find my own personality repugnant, and everything around me hideous or stupid, I am so fed up with it all. In my desperation I take refuge in fantasy. I see the fishing boats here as feluccas; I strip the sailors as they pass by, and turn them into savages striding naked on vermilion strands. I think of India, of your China,[2] of my oriental story (ideas for bits of it keep coming to me); I feel the need for gigantic epics. It is you, *cher bougre,* who fill me with this tail wind, from afar.

But life is so short! I want to cut my throat when I think that I shall never write the way I want, or set down a quarter of what I dream. All this energy we feel ourselves choking on: we are fated to die with it still in us, unexpended. It is like those sudden cravings for a lay. In imagination we lift up every passing petticoat; but after the fifth discharge no sperm is left. Blood comes to the glans, but our lust is confined to our hearts.

It is six years since I was last here. Where will I be six years from now?[3] And what will I have accomplished?

. . .

1. For *Anubis*, see pp. 182 and 184, n. 4. Of the 'three prefaces', mentioned as projects in other letters to Louise, one, an introduction to the works of Pierre Ronsard, was never written; another, a foreword to a volume of poems by Louis Bouilhet, would be written only after Bouilhet's death; and the third, a preface to the *Dictionary of Accepted Opinions* (see pp. 177–8, 179, n. 3., and 241), would be absorbed in *Bouvard et Pécuchet*.
2. Bouilhet was studying Chinese.
3. He would be at Croisset, writing his second published novel, *Salammbô* – satisfying his 'need for gigantic epics'.

~

To Louise Colet
     [Trouville,] Friday night, 11 o'clock. [August 26, 1853]

. . .

What seems to me the highest and most difficult achievement of Art is not to make us laugh or cry, nor to arouse our lust or rage, but to do what nature does – that is, to set us dreaming. The most beautiful works have this quality. They are serene in aspect, inscrutable. The means by which they act on us are various: they are as motionless as cliffs, stormy as the ocean, leafy, green and murmurous as forests, forlorn as the desert, blue as the sky. Homer, Rabelais, Michelangelo, Shakespeare and Goethe seem to me *pitiless*. They are unfathomable, infinite, manifold. Through small apertures we glimpse abysses whose sombre depths turn us faint. And yet over the whole there hovers an extraordinary tenderness. It is like the brilliance of light, the smile of the sun; and it is calm, calm and strong.

. . .

~

To Louise Colet
     [Croisset,] Wednesday, midnight. [October 12, 1853]
My head is on fire, as it used to be after a long day on horseback. Today it's my pen that I've been riding – and hard. I have been

writing since half past noon without stopping, except for an occasional five minutes to smoke my pipe, and just now an hour for dinner. My agricultural show[1] was giving me such trouble that I decided to put aside Greek and Latin until it was finished, and beginning today I am devoting myself to it exclusively. It is taking too long! Sometimes I think it will be the death of me, and I want to come and see you.

Bouilhet says it will be the best scene in the book. What I am sure of is that it will be new, and that I am aiming at something good. If the effects of a symphony have ever been conveyed in a book, it will be in these pages. I want the reader to hear everything together, like one great roar – the bellowing of bulls, the sighing of lovers, the bombast of official oratory. The sun shines down on it all, and there are gusts of wind that threaten to blow off the women's big bonnets. The most arduous passages in *Saint Antoine* were child's play in comparison. I achieve dramatic effect simply by the interweaving of dialogue and by contrasts of character. I am in the midst of it now. In less than a week I'll have tied the knot on which all the rest depends. I keep feeling that my brain is too small to encompass this complex situation in a single glance. I write ten pages at a time, dashing from one sentence to another. However, one of these days I must write to the Crocodile. He has lost Mrs Farmer's address, and would have to send letters directly to us from Jersey, which is to be avoided if at all possible.

. . .

What a strange creature you are, dear Louise, sending me more 'diatribes', as my pharmacist would say. You ask me a favour, I say yes, I promise again, and you still scold! Well, since you hide nothing from me (a habit I approve of), I won't hide from you that this idea strikes me as one of your obsessions. You want to link two very different kinds of affection, and I don't see the sense of it, much less the use. I fail completely to understand how your hospitality to me in Paris puts my mother under the slightest obligation. For three years I went continually to the Schlesingers', where she never once set foot. Similarly, Bouilhet has been spending the night at our house and having Sunday lunch and dinner here for eight years, without our having had a single glimpse of his mother, who comes to Rouen almost every month. I assure you that doesn't shock my mother in the slightest. However, it shall be as you wish. I promise, I swear, that I will explain your reasons to her and ask her to arrange a meeting. As for what happens then, with the best will in the world I can do nothing. Perhaps you will get along very well, perhaps you will dislike each other intensely. The good lady tends to be stand-offish. She has stopped seeing not only all her old acquaintances, but her friends as well. She has only one that I know of, and that one doesn't live in Croisset.

. . .

1. *Madame Bovary,* Part II, Chapter 8.

~

To Louise Colet
> *[Croisset,] Tuesday night, midnight. [October 25, 1853]*

. . .

You are lucky, you poets: you have an outlet in your verse. When something troubles you, you spit out a sonnet, and that relieves you. But we poor devils, writers of prose, who are forbidden (myself in particular) any expression of personal feelings – think of all the bitterness that remains in our souls, all the moral mucus we gag on!

There is something faulty in my character and in my vocation. I was born a lyricist and I write no poetry. I want to shower good on those I love, and I make them weep. Look at Bouilhet: there's a man for you! Such a complete nature! If I were capable of being jealous of anyone, it would be of him. With the stultifying life he has had and the misfortunes that have befallen him, I would certainly be an imbecile by now, or deported, or hanged by my own hand. The buffetings he has suffered have only improved him. That is what happens to forests of tall trees: they keep growing ever higher in the wind, and they force their roots through silex and granite; whereas espaliers, with all their fertilizer and their straw matting, die against the wall that supports them, in full sun. Be fond of him – that is all I can say to you about him – and never doubt him for an instant.

Do you know what I talked about with my mother all last evening? About you. I told her many things she didn't know, or which she had at most half guessed. She appreciates you, and I am sure that this winter she will be glad to see you. So that question is settled.

Bovary is marching ahead again. Bouilhet was pleased on Sunday. But he was in such high spirits, and so preoccupied with Eros (not that I was the object of his passion), that perhaps he judged too favourably. I am waiting for his second reading, to be sure I am on the right track. I can't be far off it, however. This agricultural show will take me another full six weeks (a good month after my return from Paris). But the difficulties that remain are mostly in the execution. Then I will have to go over the whole thing, as the style is a little choppy. Some passages will have to be rewritten, others eliminated. So it will have taken me from July to the end of November to write *one scene*! If at least I enjoyed doing it! But I will never like this book, no matter how successfully I may bring it off. Now that I have a clear view of it as a whole, it disgusts me. But at least it will have been good training. I'll have learned how to do dialogue and portraits. I will write other books! The pleasure of criticism surely has a charm of its own, and if a fault you find in your work leads you to conceive a greater beauty, isn't this conception alone a delight in itself, almost a promise?

Adieu, à bientôt. Mille baisers.

∼

A few months after the appearance of Louis Bouilhet's first published poem, *Melaenis*, in the *Revue de Paris*. Louise Colet had given a reception in his honour, in the course of which an attractive Parisienne, Mme Edma Roger des Genettes, read a portion of the poem to the assembled guests. Poet and *diseuse* were soon on the best of terms, and they continued to see each other from time to time. Now, in the autumn of 1853, Bouilhet was taking the risk of giving up his tutoring, borrowing money, and moving to Paris, hoping to profit from the favourable impression created in literary circles there by *Melaenis*. He was finishing a second long work, a 'scientific' poem to be called *Les Fossiles*, and was planning a play. It was perhaps the prospect of being reunited more regularly with Edma that caused him, on that Sunday, October 23, 1853, to be 'preoccupied with Eros'.

With Bouilhet in Paris, recommended to her anew by Flaubert, Louise Colet did her best to use him as go-between, as she had earlier tried to use DuCamp. But as usual she followed, with Flaubert, a course little calculated to further her interests: few things could have irritated him more than her insistence on meeting his mother – to which she added the bizarre grievance that he had never brought about a meeting between her daughter Henriette (now thirteen) and his niece Caroline (ten). Writing his novel, Flaubert was portraying his heroine ever more fully; and his depiction of one trait increasingly displayed by Emma Bovary – vehemence – was doubtless nourished somewhat by Louise's shrill demands.

Even at this late date, neither of the lovers ceased attempting to reform the other. One of the causes for conflict at this time was an intolerable literary crime committed by Louise – her newest, very feminist poem, *La Servante*, over two thousand lines long, didactic, sentimental, flat, infelicitous, in which she insisted on retaining, despite Flaubert's strongest pleas, the vengeful portrait of a drunken, decayed poet-seducer, blatantly modelled on Alfred de Musset. Other lines depict actresses as being little more than prostitutes, 'protected' by rich, coarse businessmen. Flaubert continued to use literary objection as a vehicle for broader reproof.

~

To Louise Colet
> *[Croisset,] Friday night, 1 o'clock. [November 25, 1853]*
> . . .

Must I speak to you about art?[1] Won't you accuse me of passing quickly over affairs of the heart? But in fact everything is bound up together, and what distorts your life is also distorting your style. For you continually alloy your concepts with your passions, and this weakens the first and prevents you from enjoying the second. Oh, if I could make you what I dream of! What a woman, what a human being, you would be! And first and foremost, how happy you would be!

. . . You are a poet shackled to a woman, just as Hugo is a poet shackled to an orator . . . Do not imagine you can exorcize what oppresses you in life by giving vent to it in art. No. The heart's dross does not find its way on to paper: all you pour out there is ink, and no sooner do you voice your sorrows than they return to the soul through the ear, louder, reaching deeper than ever. Nothing has been gained . . . Only in the Absolute are we well off. Let us hold fast to that; let us keep climbing.

And so, let nothing – me, above all – disturb your sleep. Rest assured that you are, and always will be, the woman for whom I have had the greatest, the most complete affection. But I am all frayed at the edges, and you must have consideration for my tics, for my upbringing, and for my nerves. Next year, even if *Bovary* isn't finished, I will come. I will take lodgings. I will stay at least four consecutive months each year, and the rest of the time will come to Paris more often than I ever did. Meanwhile, I will see you every two months, as I promised.

As for your work, you will write beautiful things, very beautiful, and you will succeed materially, provided you confine yourself to your subjects, make outlines, and offer the public what it can conceivably accept. I am not telling you to be in tow to public taste. But in our beloved France one's form must be disguised. Whereas you flaunt your form. For *La Servante* you would have been tried, jailed, and perhaps physically assaulted by actresses.[2]

This letter is not long, but I beg you, for the love I bear you, to weigh its every line. It is pregnant with truths. Do not be upset. The sweet things I might have written to you instead of this would have carried less affection.

1.   The reference is to Louise's insistence on discussing *La Servante*.
2.   Nevertheless, in *La Servante* Louise persisted in portraying actresses, as a class, in the guise of near-prostitutes – courtesans with crude, coarse 'protectors'. In another letter about *La Servante*, Flaubert wrote: 'You have made Art an outlet for passions, a kind of chamber-pot to catch the overflow of I don't know what. It doesn't smell good! It smells of hate!'

~

To Louis Bouilhet
                    [Croisset,] Thursday, 11 o'clock. [December 8, 1853]
                              · · ·

She makes me very sad, our poor Muse. I don't know what to do about her. I assure you that this grieves me in all kinds of ways. How do you think things will end? I suspect her of being thoroughly tired of me. And for her own peace of mind it would be best if she broke with me. She is a girl of twenty as far as feelings are concerned, and I am a sexagenarian. (Surely you yourself must have interesting things to say on this subject.) In her letter of today she tells me she is sick. If she were *really* sick, I would count on you to tell me and would come running. In two weeks my mother will be passing through Paris again. I hesitate to have her call on the Muse. It would be a kind action, I think, and one should try to be as kind as possible. But . . . but . . . *quid*? Not a word to her about this, needless to say . . .

❧

Smarting under Flaubert's repeated warnings that to publish *La Servante* as it stood would be an indignity and a dangerous folly, and exasperated by his total behaviour, Louise made a resolution (in her Memento of December 9, 1853): 'I am giving up writing to him. DeLisle is right. It is beneath my dignity to complain. Silence or short letters. If he is going to change, he will do so of his own accord. Complaining weakens my position. Oh! *mon Dieu*, how I am suffering! Never a great and noble heart.'

❧

To Louise Colet
   [Croisset,] Friday night, 2 o'clock. [December 23, 1853]
  I must love you to write to you tonight, for I am *exhausted*. My skull feels encased in an iron helmet. Since two o'clock yesterday afternoon (except for about twenty-five minutes for dinner), I have been writing *Bovary*. I am in full fornication, in the very midst of it: my lovers are sweating and gasping. This has been one of the rare days of my life passed completely in illusion, from beginning to end. At six o'clock tonight, as I was writing the word 'hysterics', I was so swept away, was bellowing so loudly[1] and feeling so deeply what my little Bovary was going through, that I was afraid of having hysterics myself. I got up from my table and opened the window to calm myself. My head was spinning. Now I have great pains in my knees, in my back and in my head. I feel like a man who has been fucking too much (forgive the expression) – a kind of rapturous lassitude. And since I am in the midst of love it is only proper that I should not fall asleep before sending you a caress, a kiss, and whatever thoughts are left in me.
  Will what I have written be good? I have no idea – I am hurrying a little, to be able to show Bouilhet a complete section when he comes. What is certain is that my book has been going at a lively

rate for the past week. May it continue so, for I am weary of my usual snail's pace. But I fear the awakening, the disillusion that may come when the pages are copied. No matter: for better or worse, it is a delicious thing to write, to be no longer yourself but to move in an entire universe of your own creating. Today, for instance, as man and woman, both lover and mistress, I rode in a forest on an autumn afternoon under the yellow leaves, and I was also the horses, the leaves, the wind, the words my people uttered, even the red sun that made them almost close their love-drowned eyes.[2]

Is this pride or piety? Is it a foolish overflow of exaggerated self-satisfaction, or is it really a vague and noble religious instinct? But when I brood over these marvellous pleasures I have enjoyed, I would be tempted to offer God a prayer of thanks if I knew he could hear me. Praised may he be for not creating me a cotton merchant, a vaudevillian, a wit, etc.! Let us sing to Apollo as in ancient days, and breathe deeply of the fresh cold air of Parnassus; let us strum our guitars and clash our cymbals, and whirl like dervishes in the eternal hubbub of Forms and Ideas.[3]

. . .

1. Flaubert often shouted aloud (*gueulait*) the sentences he was writing. He called his study his *gueuloir*.
2. *Madame Bovary*, Part II, Chapter 9.
3. This note of exaltation and gratitude is reminiscent of the prayer of thanksgiving on the Nile (p. 171, n. 1), and joins it among the exceptions to the oddly phrased remark by Henry James in *Notes on Novelists:* '[Flaubert's] case was a doom because he felt of his vocation almost nothing but the difficulty.'

∼

To Louis Bouilhet

[Croisset, December 26, 1853]

. . .

How is our poor Muse? What do you think about her? What does she say? She writes to me less often. I think that at bottom she is tired of me. Who is to blame? Destiny. For I feel my conscience perfectly at ease in this whole affair, and consider that I have nothing to reproach myself for; and as for her being tired of me, so would anyone else be, in her place. There is nothing lovable about me, and when I say lovable I use the word in its deepest sense. She is indeed the only woman who has loved me. Is that a curse sent her from heaven? If she dared, she would say I do not love her. She is mistaken, however.

~

It is probable that Flaubert's letter of Monday, December 26, crossed one that Bouilhet had written to Paris the previous Saturday. Bouilhet's letter did more than merely answer some of Flaubert's recent questions. If Flaubert, as he had been saying in his last two letters, sincerely, or even partially, believed that Louise was tired of him, Bouilhet gave him cause to change his mind.

> [Paris, Saturday, December 24, 1853]
> ... I have just been having impossible, interminable conversations with her. *You* are 'an egoist, a monster', and many other things besides. Apart from the deadly boredom of such confidences, they cast me in the role of a fool. The Muse's intentions seem to me neither frank nor disinterested. This display of emotion masks a great egotism that I find repellent. For the sake of physical pleasure she has jeopardized the future of her daughter, her darling daughter, her charming daughter, etc.
>
> Do you want me to tell you what I feel? Do you want me to say straight out what she is after, with her visits to your mother, with the comedy in verse,[1] her cries, her tears, her invitations and her dinners?
>
> She wants, and expects, to become your wife![2]
>
> I was thinking so without daring to formulate the idea to myself, but the word was boldly uttered to me, not by her, but as positively coming from her. That is why she refused the Philosopher.[3]
>
> All that seems to me monstrous. There is nothing physically wrong with her: she is frustrated and furious. Now I see her game. She is playing every possible card – your friends, DuCamp in the past, me today, pleasant acquaintances, Babinet, Préault, etc., and finally your family. That is the culmination, the last scene of the comedy (in verse).
>
> She knew from me that your mother was in Paris. She

came to invite me to dinner that day, and I saw no reason to keep your family's presence a secret from her. Whereupon she proposed – wrote to me, half an hour later – that I talk about her to your mother, tell her how she loves you, etc. I declared in no uncertain terms that I would do nothing of the sort, and that I wanted no such commissions.

In short, *cher vieux adoré*, at this moment I am extremely exasperated. To such a point that I don't know whether I shall continue to see the Muse as hitherto. She has been very obliging to me, but it was all done for so obvious a purpose that I am ashamed. I shall send her some suitable present as thanks for her help in finding me a place to live, and gradually, without any fracas, I will let her go. Perhaps I am taking too dark a view of things. Write to me by return. Give me your advice, as sage and as friend.

Tomorrow, Sunday, I am to dine with her. She will want to see your letter. I will refuse; perhaps we shall quarrel. I don't give a damn. From the moment your future is at stake I ignore the niceties: I want no one to meddle with that.

. . .

Our poor Muse is making enemies of all her acquaintances, past and present. No one here takes her seriously. She makes herself wantonly ridiculous. I am distressed by it all, because at bottom I am fond of her, and it is always sad to be disappointed.

Louis Bouilhet (Flaubert's '*cher bougre*') and Louise Colet were probably jealous of each other. Flaubert (Bouilhet's '*cher vieux adoré*') had facetiously assured Louise that he himself was not the object of Bouilhet's 'passion' that recent Sunday, October 28; and Bouilhet, in the present letter, speaks of Louise's wish to marry Flaubert as though it were a crime, rather than the normal ardour of such a woman to possess the man she loved in her way – as he had possessed her in his. A futile 'game', undoubtedly, considering how well she knew him; but scarcely 'monstrous'.

1. A play by Louise, never performed and its text now lost, entitled *Les Lettres d'amour*. One of its characters (ignoble) was modelled on Victor Cousin,

and another (flatteringly admirable) on Flaubert. (J.B.) Flaubert found it a lamentable work and said so in several letters to Louise.

2. The French reads: '*Elle veut, elle croit devenir ton épouse!*' – to which Bouilhet has added the parenthetical remark: '*Le vers y est, ma foi!*' – meaning that he had unwittingly written an alexandrine.

3. Victor Cousin was now Honorary Professor at the Sorbonne, having been deprived of his post in the Ministry of Public Instruction by the Imperial regime. Continuing to believe himself the father of Louise's daughter, he contributed regular sums for the child's support. Recently, according to Louise, he had proposed marriage.

∼

To Louise Colet

[Croisset,] Wednesday, 11 p.m. [December 28, 1853]

·   ·   ·

Do not worry, *pauvre amie*, my health is better than ever. Nothing that comes from myself ever harms me. It is the world outside that hurts me, agitates me, wears me down. I could work for ten years, uninterruptedly, in the austerest solitude, without suffering as much as a headache; whereas a creaking door, the face of a bourgeois, a ridiculous suggestion, give me palpitations, upset me.[1] I am like those Alpine lakes which roughen under valley breezes, gentle winds that blow over low-lying ground; but great gusts from the mountains pass over them without ruffling their surface, and serve only to chase away the mists. And then, is one ever harmed by what one enjoys doing? A vocation patiently and candidly pursued becomes almost a physical function, a way of existence that occupies one's whole being. Excess holds no dangers for those who by nature tend to exaggerate.

·   ·   ·

Have you ever remarked how all *authority* is stupid concerning Art? Our wonderful governments (kings or republics) imagine that they have only to order work to be done, and it will be forthcoming. They set up prizes, encouragements, academies, and they forget only one thing, one little thing without which nothing can live: the *atmosphere*. There are two kinds of literature: one that I would call 'national'[2] (the better of the two); and the other, 'individual' – works produced by gifted writers. For the first to be realized, there must be a fund of opinions shared by the mass of the people, a common

bond such as does not now exist; and for the full development of
the second, there must be *liberty.* Nowadays, however, what can we
say, what can we talk about? This situation will worsen: I dearly
hope I am right. I prefer absolute Nothing to evil; dust, rather than
putrefaction. And eventually there will be a revival, a new dawn. We
shan't be here to see it. But who cares?

.   .   .

1. Flaubert had written to Louise two weeks before, when his mother and
    Caroline were away, that the increased solitude at Croisset was 'charming'
    and 'superb'. 'I hear no human step, no human voice, I don't know what
    the servants are up to, they wait on me like shadows. I dine with my
    dog . . .'
        Sadistic 'tactlessness' of that kind has been more characteristic of
    Flaubert when writing to Louise than the innuendo the present letter seems
    to carry, in its mention of a 'ridiculous suggestion' and the 'stupidity' of
    authority in matters of art. (In addition to her government pension, Louise
    had been awarded three prizes by the French Academy, and the following
    year was to win her fourth.) It was probably Bouilhet's letter of December
    24, about Louise's 'game', that generated the change of tone.
2. Flaubert is here referring to his concept of Greek art as 'the very constitution
    of an entire people', as expressed in his letter of April 24, 1852 (see p. 219).

~

To Louise Colet
                  [Croisset,] Monday night, 1 a.m. [January 2, 1854]
                              .   .   .

Bouilhet was here Friday night, Saturday, and yesterday morning.
He will come again, on Wednesday for the rest of the week. So far,
we have had time only to talk about ourselves; most of it was taken
up with the *Fossiles* and *Bovary.*[1] He was pleased with my fornication
scene. However, before said passage I had one of transition, eight
lines, which took me three days and doesn't contain a superfluous
word – but which I have to do over again because it's too slow. It is
direct dialogue, which I must change to indirect, and there isn't
room to say what needs to be said. It must all be very fast and
incidental, to be as though thrown away, almost unnoticeable in the
book. Following which I still have three or four corrections to make
– infinitely small, but they will take me all next week. How slow!
How slow! No matter: I keep going. In fact I've taken a long step
ahead, and feel a great inner relief, which makes me quite gay and

cheerful, even though tonight I was literally sweating from the effort. It's so hard to undo what has been done, and done well, in order to insert something new in its place without revealing the joint.

. . .

Preoccupation with morality makes a work of imagination so false and boring! I am strongly attracted to criticism. The novel I am writing sharpens my ability in this respect, for it is above all a work of criticism, or rather of anatomy. The reader will be unaware, I hope, of all the psychological workings concealed beneath the form, but he will feel their effect. Another side of me longs to write great, sumptuous things – battles, sieges, descriptions of the fabulous ancient Orient. Thursday night I spent two lovely hours with my head in my hands, thinking of the bright multicoloured walls of Ecbatana.[2] Nothing has been written about all that. How many things still float in the limbo of human thought! It isn't subjects that are lacking, but men.

. . .

1. In other words, they had as yet had no time to look at Louise's *La Servante*, which she had finally consented to let them 'edit'. Whatever suggestions they may have made, the poem as printed remains immensely overlong, scurrilous, and generally deplorable. Louise's defiant publication of so sorry a work unquestionably played a role in the now imminent rupture.

2. Today the city of Hamadan, in Iran. 'The Medes were again obedient [to Deioces] and built the city now called Agbatana, the walls of which are of great size and strength, rising in circles one within the other . . . The number of the circles is seven, the royal palace and the treasuries standing within the last. The circuit of the outer wall is very nearly the same with that of Athens. Of this wall the battlements are white, of the next black, of the third scarlet, of the fourth blue, of the fifth orange; all these are coloured with paint. The two last have their battlements coated respectively with silver and gold.' (Herodotus, *History*, I, c. 98. Translated by George Rawlinson.)
   As we now know, it was *Salammbô's* Carthage that would eventually emerge from Flaubert's 'lovely hours' of meditation.

~

TO LOUISE COLET

[Croisset,] Friday night, 1 a.m. [January 13, 1854]

. . .

In your note that came this morning, you ask me to reply to your letter of last Friday. I have just re-read it; it is here, lying open on my table. What kind of answer can I give you? You must know me as well as I know myself, and you keep bringing up things we've discussed a hundred times without getting anywhere. You even reproach me for the affectionate expressions – you call them 'bizarre' – that I use in my letters to you (though it seems to me I do not overindulge in sentimentalities). I will be even more sparing of them in the future, since they 'make you gag'. Let us go back, start over again. I will be categorical, explicit:

1. About my mother. Yes: your guess is correct. It is because I am persuaded that if she were to see you she would behave coldly towards you, less than politely, as you put it, that I prefer you not to see one another. Besides, I dislike this confusion, this bringing together of two very dissimilar kinds of affection. (You can picture what kind of woman my mother is, in this respect, when I tell you that she will never visit her elder son without invitation.) Besides: what would be her pretext for calling on you? When I told you she would visit you, I had at last overcome a tremendous obstacle, after several days of parleying, because I wanted to please you. You took no account of that, and rushed most inopportunely to reopen an irritating subject, one extremely antipathetic to me, on which I had expended great effort. I would have gone on, but you told me not to. Too bad. Now once again I beg you: leave this alone. When the time is ripe and an occasion presents itself, I will know what to do. Your persistence in this matter strikes me as very odd. Your continually asking to meet my mother, wanting me to bring her to your house, wanting her to see you, seems to me just as peculiar as though she, on her side, were to want me not to see you, not to have anything to do with you, because, because, etc. And I assure you that if she were to open her mouth concerning such matters she would soon shut it again.

Next question: financial. I am not 'sulking' about this at all. I am not playing a game. I never hide my money (when I have some). There are few people as meagrely off as I who have such an air of wealth about them. (I do give the impression of being rich: that is quite true.) This is unfortunate, as it can cause me to be taken for a miser. You seem to consider me niggardly because I don't offer assistance when I am not asked. But when did I ever refuse? (No one knows the trouble I have sometimes gone to to oblige a friend.)

You say I never feel a spontaneous urge to be generous? I say that is not true, that I am quite capable of such impulses. But this is no doubt a strange delusion. Didn't DuCamp, too, once tell me: 'Your purse strings are stiff from disuse'?

To sum up: I told you that I will *always* oblige you, and yet I keep saying I haven't a sou. That seems suspect to you, but I deny none of it, and I repeat it again. Let me explain. It is quite true that I haven't a farthing. (At the moment, 20 francs must carry me through till February.) Don't you think I would buy 100 copies of Leconte's book, etc. if I could? But one must first pay one's debts. Of the 2000 francs I have coming to me this year,[1] I already owe almost 1200. On top of that there are my trips to Paris. Next year, in order to live in Paris I shall have to dig deep into my capital. *That is unavoidable.* I have decided on a certain sum for living expenses in the city. Once that is used up, I'll have to resume my present existence, unless I earn something – a supposition I find absurd.

But, but! – pay close attention to this *but*: if you needed it, I would find money for you anyway, even if I had to pawn the family silver. Do you understand me now?

As for finishing *Bovary,* I have already set myself so many dates, and been mistaken so often, that I refuse not only to speak of it, but to think of it. I no longer have any idea, and can only trust in God. It will be finished in its own good time, even if I die of vexation and impatience – which might very well happen were it not for the fury that sustains me. Meanwhile I will come to see you every two months, as I promised.

Now, poor dear Louise, do you want me to tell you what I really think, or rather what you really feel? I think that your love is wavering. Your dissatisfactions, the sufferings I inflict on you, can have only that cause; for as I am now, so I have always been. But now you see me more clearly, and your judgement is a reasonable one, perhaps. I don't know. However, when you love a person *completely* you love him just as he is, with his faults and his monstrousnesses; you adore even his scabs, and the hump on his back; you love to inhale the breath that poisons you. The same is true of the spiritual aspect. Now, I am 'warped, squalid, selfish', etc. You know, you'll end up by making me insufferably proud, always finding fault with me as you do. I think there cannot be a mortal on this earth less commended than I; but I will not change. I will not reform. I have already erased, corrected, blotted out or suppressed so many things in myself that I am weary of it. Everything has its end, and I think I'm now a big enough boy to consider my education complete. Now I have other things to think about. I was born with all the vices. I have radically suppressed some, and kept the rest on a starvation diet. God alone knows the martyrdoms I have undergone in this psychological training school; but now I give up. That path leads to the grave, and I want to live through three or four more books; so behold me crystallized, immobile. You say I am made of granite. I admit it. But if my heart is inflexible, it is at least firm, and never gives way. Desertions and injustices do not change what is engraved on it. Everything that is there remains; and the thought of you, whatever you or I may do, will not be effaced.

Adieu – a long kiss on your beloved forehead.

1. Flaubert's personal income came from property left him by his father; he had no expenses while living at home. In her letter of 'last Friday', Louise had characterized her many complaints as 'further proof of [my] love'. Flaubert had lent her 800 francs, which she had so far been unable to repay.

~

To Louise Colet
                [Croisset,] Wednesday midnight [January 18, 1854]
                        . . .

This week I re-read the first act of *King Lear*. Shakespeare frightens me the more I think of him. In their entirety, I find his works stupendous, exalting, like the idea of the planetary system. I see only an immensity there, dazzling and bewildering to the eye.

But I well know, *pauvre chère amie*, that we cannot always live with our noses pointed at the stars! No one suffers more than I from the necessities, the penuries, of life. My flesh lies heavy – some 75 thousand kilograms of it – on my soul. But when I urge you to renounce action, I don't mean that you should live like a brahmin. I mean merely that we should immerse ourselves in real life only up to the navel. Let movement be confined to the region of the legs; let us not be passionate about picayune, ephemeral, ugly, or mortal things. If we have to seem to be moved by all that, then we can pretend to be; but let us only pretend. Something filmier than a cloud and more resistant than a cuirass is needed to protect those natures that are rent by a mere nothing and vibrate from top to bottom at the slightest touch. We have to carry the burden (let us not forget it) of *all* other people's sufferings. And how can the vase be expected to stay full when you shake it by both handles? Brothels provide condoms as protection against catching the pox from infected vaginas. Let us always have a vast condom within us to protect the health of our soul amid the filth into which it is plunged. The pleasure is diminished, it is true, and sometimes the sheath splits.

. . .

~

It is tempting to let the epistolary record of the liaison end there, with the vision of Shakespeare, the flattering evocation of twin special souls, and the distasteful metaphor, all combining to epitomize the Flaubert whom Louise had perhaps been 'cursed', as he put it, to love. But 'the union of this ever diverse pair' still had a short time to run.

The possibility of Louise's association with a magazine was still in the air, and with Flaubert she sometimes talked of what might be printed in it. 'There is something quite new and charming that could be done for your magazine,' he wrote to her in January 1854, 'something that could almost be a literary creation and which hasn't occurred to you: an article on fashion. I will explain what I mean, in my next.'

In the manuscript of *Madame Bovary*, Flaubert had already written several passages that touched on women's fashions; and fashion was to play a crucial, even diabolical, role in the last part of the novel. He had introduced the lovely young Emma, still a girl on her father's farm, opening her parasol of 'rosy iridescent silk' on a day of thaw. There was a picturesque description of clothes worn at a country wedding. At a fashionable dinner party in a château, 'Madame Bovary was surprised to notice that several of the ladies had failed to put their gloves in their glasses', which meant that unlike provincially bred Emma, these sophisticates saw no reason to signal that they did not drink wine in public. There was Emma as she danced: 'Her hair, drawn down smoothly on both sides and slightly fluffed out over the ears, shone with a blue lustre; in her chignon a rose quivered on its pliant stem, with artificial dewdrops at the leaftips. Her gown was pale saffron, trimmed with three bunches of pompom roses and green sprays.' In the end, many of Emma's fatal debts were to be for clothes.

Now Flaubert sent Louise his suggestions for a fashion article – incorrigibly inflicting on her, as a preamble, yet more passages to do with himself or with Shakespeare.

~

To Louise Colet

[Croisset,] Sunday night [January 29, 1854]

. . .

Do you know how many pages I have written this week? One, and I cannot even say a good one. A quick, light passage was needed, and I was in a frame of mind better suited to gravity and unhurried exposition. What trouble I am having! What an atrociously delicious thing we are bound to say writing is – since we keep slaving this way, enduring such tortures and not wanting things otherwise. There is a mystery in this I cannot fathom. The writer's vocation is perhaps comparable to love for one's native land (of which I have little, by the way), a certain fated bond between men and things. The Siberian in his snow and the Hottentot in his hut both live content, not dreaming of the sun or of palaces. Something stronger than they keeps them attached to their miserable environment, while we flounder about in our search for Forms. Whether poets, sculptors, painters or musicians, we perceive existence as refracted in words, shapes, colours or harmonies, and we find that the most wonderful thing in the world.

And then I was overwhelmed for two days by a scene in Shakespeare (the first scene in Act Three of *King Lear*).[1] That man will drive me mad. More and more all the others seem like children beside him. In that scene all the characters, wretched beyond endurance and completely crazed by their sufferings, go off their heads and talk wildly. There are three different kinds of madness howling at once, while the Fool cracks jokes and rain pours down amid thunder and lightning. A young gentleman, whom we have seen rich and handsome at the beginning of the play, says this: 'Ah! I knew women, etc. I was ruined by them. Distrust the light sound of their gown and the creaking of their satin shoes, etc.' Ah! *Poésie françoyse!* How clear your waters run in comparison! When I think of how faithful we are to those busts – Racine! Corneille! And other talents just as mortally boring! It makes me groan! I long (another quotation from the Bard) to 'tread them into mortar and daub the walls of a jakes with them'.[2] Yes, it bowled me over. I could think of nothing but that scene on the heath, where wolves are heard howling and old Lear weeps in the rain and tears his beard in the wind. It is when one contemplates such peaks that one feels small: 'Doomed to mediocrity, we are humbled by transcendent minds.'[3]

But now to talk about something other than Shakespeare: about your magazine. Well, I think that everywhere, apropos of everything, Art has its place. Now who, up to the present, has dabbled in writing about fashion? Dressmakers! But just as upholsterers have no understanding of furniture, cooks little understanding of cuisine, and tailors none whatever of costume, so dressmakers have no idea of Art. For the same reason, portraitists paint bad portraits (the good ones are painted by thinkers, by creators, who alone know how to *reproduce*). The narrow specialization in which they spend their lives blinds them to the very significance of their speciality, and they constantly confuse the accessory with the essential, the trimming with the cut. A great tailor might be an artist, as in the XVIth century goldsmiths were artists. But mediocrity is creeping in everywhere: the very stones under our feet are becoming dull, and our highways are boring beyond words. Perish though we may (and perish we shall in any case), we must employ every means to stem the flood of trash invading us. We must take flight into the ideal, since we can no longer dwell in marble halls and wear the purple, recline on hummingbird-feather divans, enjoy swansdown carpets, ebony chairs, tortoise-shell floors, solid gold candelabra, lamps carved in emerald. And so we must raise our voices against gloves made of shoddy, against office chairs, the mackintosh, cheap stoves, against imitation cloth, imitation luxury, imitation pride. Thanks to industrialism, ugliness has assumed gigantic proportions. How many good people who a century ago could have lived perfectly well without Beaux Arts now cannot do without mini-statues, mini-music and mini-

literature! Take a single case: the ominous proliferation of bad drawings by lithography. And the extraordinary notions of the human
anatomy those lithographs convey! On the other hand, cheapness
has made real luxury fabulously expensive. Who is willing these days
to buy a good watch? (It costs 1200 francs.) We are all fakes and
charlatans. Pretence, affectation, humbug everywhere – the crinoline
has falsified the buttocks. Our century is a century of whores, and
so far what is least prostituted is the prostitute.

But since our purpose here is not to sermonize the bourgeois
(who aren't even bourgeois any more, for since the invention of the
public bus the bourgeoisie is dead; they sit there in the bus alongside
the 'lower classes' and not only think like them and look like them
but even dress like them: take the fashion for coarse cloth, the new
styles in overcoats, the jerseys worn for boating, and the blue work
shirts for field sports, etc.) – still, since there is no question of
sermonizing them, this is what I would do: I would accept it all,
and write straight from the democratic point of view: point out that
nowadays everything is for everybody, and that the greatest possible
confusion exists for the good of the greatest number. I would try to
establish *a posteriori* that consequently there is no such thing as
fashion, since there is no authority, no rule. In the past it was known
who set the fashions, and every fashion had some sense to it. (I
would return to this point later: it would be part of a history of
costume – which would be a very good thing to write, by the way,
a totally new subject.) But now there is anarchy, and everyone is free
to follow his own caprice. Perhaps from this a new order will emerge.

And here are two further points that I would develop. This
anarchy is the result, among a thousand other things, of the histori-
zing tendency of our epoch. (The Nineteenth Century seems to be
taking a survey course in history.) Thus in the space of less than
thirty years we have seen vogues for the Roman, the Gothic, the
Pompadour and the Renaissance, and something remains of all that.
So: how take advantage of this for beauty's sake – or, forgive the
pun, for our Beauties' sake? I see it this way: by studying what form,
what colour, is suitable for a given person in a given circumstance.
This involves the ability to sense a certain harmony between colour
and line. The great courtesans and the true dandies are particularly
good at this: they do not dress in obedience to fashion magazines.

That is the art such a magazine must address itself to if it wants to be new and realistic. Study, for example, how Veronese dresses his golden women, what ornaments he places on the necks of his negresses, etc. Isn't there such a thing as a 'seemly' way of dressing? Isn't there a libidinous way, or an elegiac, or a provocative? On what do such effects depend? On an exact harmony, so subtle as to be unnoticeable, between features and facial expression on the one side, and apparel on the other. A further consideration is the relation between costume and function; and some forms of the beautiful are rooted in this utilitarian idea. For example, the majesty of church vestments: the gesture of benediction is stupid without wide sleeves. The Orient is de-Moslemizing itself by adopting the frock-coat. They can't even make their ablutions any more, poor things, what with their buttoned cuffs! Similarly, the introduction of the *sous-pied*[4] will sooner or later cause them to give up the divan (and perhaps even the harem, for such trousers also have *buttoned flies*. For the importance of the fly, see the great Rabelais). As for the *sous-pied*, it is now being given up in France because of the proliferation and speed of commercial business. Note that the stockbrokers were the first to adopt spats and low-cut shoes: the *sous-pied* hindered them from rushing up the steps of the Exchange, etc. And is there anything stupider than the 'fashion bulletin', which reports what costumes were worn *last* week, so that the reader can wear them *next* week, and which sets rules for everybody? Not to mention that to be well dressed, everyone must dress in the way best suited to himself. It is always the same question, the question of poetics. Each individual piece of work contains its own innate poetics, and each of these must be discovered.

So: I would attack and put to rout that idea of a general fashion. I would rampage against stove-pipe hats; and against dressing gowns with designs of palm-leaves, and those '*bonnets grecs*' embroidered with flowers.[5] I would terrify the bourgeois and the bourgeois spirit. The fashion for corsets must go – hideous things, revoltingly lubricious and excessively inconvenient at certain moments. I have sometimes suffered grievously because of corsets!!! Yes, I have suffered greatly from those nothings, which a man 'mustn't talk about' (because that 'isn't done' by the virile type we are all supposed to pattern ourselves on, at the risk of being considered eunuchs). There are certain styles of interior decoration, certain costumes, certain colours in clothes, shapes of chairs, borders on curtains, that make me really sick. In the theatre I never see the coiffures of women '*en toilette*' without being nauseated, because of all the fish glue veneering their hair, etc.; and the sight of actors wearing gloves from Jouvin even when playing *William Tell* is enough to make me hate the opera. What imbeciles! What about expressive movements of the hand – what happens to them, constrained in a glove? Imagine a statue wearing gloves! Styles must always say something; they must express, to the greatest extent possible, the soul of the wearer.

Enough talk about rags, no?

Ah! I have spent many hours of my life at my fireside, furnishing palaces, dreaming of liveries, for the day when I would have a million a year! I have seen myself wearing buskins studded with diamonds. I have heard horses neighing at many an imaginary porte cochère, harnessed to equipages that would make all England die of envy. Such banquets! Such sumptuously decked tables! Such service, such good fare! Fruit, from every country in the world, poured out of baskets made of its own leaves! Oysters were served on beds of seaweed, and all around the dining room ran an espalier of flowering jasmine alive with exotic birds.

Oh! Our ivory towers! Let us climb them in our dreams, since the hobnails on our boots keep us anchored here below!

In my entire life I have *never* seen anything luxurious except in the Orient. There you find people clad in rags and swarming with vermin, yet with gold bracelets on their arms. The Beautiful is more useful to them than the Good. They cover themselves with colour, not with cloth. Their need for smoking is greater than that for food. Admirable predominance of the Idea, whatever else may be said.

So – *adieu*, it is very late; *je t'embrasse, à toi.*

1. What follows is in *Lear*, Act III, not Scene I, but Scenes II and IV. Only if one is to consider the Fool mad, which Flaubert seems not to do, can one conceivably find here 'three different kinds of madness howling at once'; and the paraphrase is inaccurate, for the 'young gentleman' (Edgar) does not say he was ruined by women, nor was he. Flaubert's inexactitudes concerning these scenes which he had apparently been reading only recently, and yet his undoubted enthusiasm for them, are the subject of interesting comment by Sartre (*L'Idiot de la famille*, II, 2034 et seq.). Flaubert was still

reading Shakespeare with the help of a French translation. Three years later, while reading *Macbeth*, he would write to Louis Bouilhet: 'If I persist a little longer, I will be able to understand . . . Shakespeare very well.' Flaubert's Shakespeare was rather like his Greek. As for his impatience with the French classics, see his contrasting remarks to Louise about Corneille (p. 133).

2. *Lear*, Act II, Scene II. The French here in the letter is: '*Je voudrais les broyer dans un pilon, pour peindre ensuite avec les résidus les murailles des latrines.*'

3. '*Nés pour la médiocrité, nous sommes accablés par les esprits sublimes.*' From Montesquieu, *Dialogue de Sylla et d'Eucrate*, which Flaubert and Louise had read together almost a year before (see p. 216).

4. A strap attached to the bottom of the trouser leg and passing under the foot, to keep the trouser trim.

5. What we would now call men's 'paisley' dressing gowns; and, to be worn with them, at home, small round 'Greek' caps, sometimes tasselled.

In another sense, too, it was late – too late for the faltering liaison to last much longer. Even after Bouilhet's warning about Louise's 'game', Flaubert continued for a time to use her as his outlet – for chronicle, ideas, protests, and his brand of affection; talking to her, as it were, from the solitude of Croisset, seeing her occasionally in Paris and presumably making love. But the last surviving letters (about a dozen of them[1] after the letter concerning fashion) do not go beyond April 1854. There follows a gap of almost a year. Then, in March 1855, in circumstances whose immediate details are unknown, Flaubert wrote his real 'ultima'.

1. Omitted from the present volume, these abound in outrages:

'You ask for love, you complain that I don't send you flowers. Flowers, indeed! Go find some nice fresh-faced young boy with perfect manners and all the right ideas. I am like the tiger, who has bristles of hair at the tip of his glans, which lacerate the female.'

'You tell me you are hardly ever troubled by erotic thoughts. I can make you the same confidence: I confess I no longer have any sexual urge, thank God.'

'I have always tried (but I think I failed) to turn you into a sublime hermaphrodite. I want you to be a man down to the navel; below that, you get in my way, you disturb me – your female element ruins everything.'

Yet, along with this heightened abuse, there are some fine Flaubertian strokes:

'I am like Egypt: in order to live, I need regular floods – of style.'

'Sentences must stir in a book like leaves in a forest, each distinct from each despite their resemblance.'

～

To Louise Colet

[Paris, March 6, 1855]

Madame: I was told that you took the trouble to come here to see me three times last evening.

I was not in. And, fearing lest persistence expose you to humiliation, I am bound by the rules of politeness to warn you that *I shall never be in.*

Yours,

Tuesday morning. 　　　　　　　　　　　　　　　　　G.F.

～

On that sheet of Flaubert's blue notepaper Louise has dashed down the words '*lâche, couard et canaillè* – 'poltroon, coward, cur'.

It must have been about this time that Flaubert was describing, in his novel, the way in which a lover he had created, the brutal gentleman-farmer Rodolphe Boulanger, chose to break with his mistress, Emma Bovary. 'Then,' the passage about Rodolphe's letter of rupture to Emma reads, 'looking around for something to seal the letter with, his eye fell on the signet ring [given him by Emma] with the motto "*Amor nel Cor*". "Scarcely appropriate under the circumstances, but what the . . ." Whereupon he smoked three pipes and went to bed.'

The coarse-grained, uncultured Rodolphe is scarcely to be identified with his creator Gustave Flaubert. Yet there is something redolent of 'smoking three pipes and going to bed' in Flaubert's manner of breaking with the mistress – importunate and intolerable though she had become – whom he had loved, known long, and confided in most intimately. This brutality towards Louise is emphasized in a detail of the rupture he invented for Rodolphe and Emma: for Flaubert himself had received, as a gift from Louise, not a signet ring but a cigar holder, inscribed with the words '*Amor nel Cor*'.

In *Madame Bovary,* Emma reads Rodolphe's letter 'through, now and then giving an angry sneer'. Louise Colet was in no sense the 'model' for Emma Bovary; and yet (to anticipate), when the novel was published and Louise read it, she was inevitably made to think of herself in the scenes of lovers' meetings and in Emma's vehemences. She expanded the angry sneer she had written on Flaubert's letter of rupture into a poem, printed in a Parisian magazine, with *Amor nel Cor* as its title. Intended to be bitter but achieving, alas, only mawkishness, the poem is an embarrassing justification of Flaubert's warning against putting one's 'heart's dross' on paper. Certain of its lines refer to a novel, written by the brutish recipient of the woman's gift, as *'un roman de commis voyageur'* – a novel for travelling salesmen.

With her *'lâche, couard et canaille'*, Louise makes her exit from Flaubert's correspondence, except as a memory occasionally evoked in letters to people who had known them both. Flaubert seems never to have seen her again; she once glimpsed him in a crowd. He heard of her as a voice reported speaking ill of him to friends, and as a writer of fiction who used him as a model for characters in novels, much as she had excoriated Alfred de Musset in her poem, 'La Servanté'.[1]

Because of the cessation of letters to Louise, the composition of the last third of *Madame Bovary* is scarcely recorded. But now the great drama of the novel's publication was imminent.

1. Louise Colet continued her career as poet, novelist, and journalist until her death in 1876. She became an ever more outspoken feminist, was never well off, and displayed courage in adverse circumstances. Often these were of her own making: she quarrelled with almost everyone, including her daughter Henriette, and left, on the whole, a reputation entitling her to be more fitly remembered not as 'Penserosa' (the title of one of her early books), but rather, perhaps, as 'Clamorosa'. Henriette, who inherited Flaubert's letters to her mother, sold them to a publisher in the early 1900s. They have been printed in various editions of Flaubert's correspondence ever since, culminating in that of the Bibliothèque de la Pléiade, definitively edited by Jean Bruneau.

VII

Publication, Trial, Triumph

1856–1857

A T THE TIME of the final rupture between the lovers, Louis Bou-ilhet, in Paris, had had his second long poem well received and had almost completed an historical drama in verse. Flaubert had himself taken an apartment in Paris for the winter of 1854–1855, and he did the same the next winter. He and Bouilhet saw each other constantly, had affairs with Parisian actresses, and afforded each other professional help and consolation, Flaubert sustaining and scolding the rather timid Bouilhet in the face of repeated rebuffs by theatrical producers, and Bouilhet continuing his role of 'midwife' as *Madame Bovary* neared its conclusion.

In one of his last letters to Louise Colet, in 1854, Flaubert had written:

> I think I have taken a big step – made the *imperceptible* transition from psychology to drama. Now that I'll be in the midst of action, the passions I depict will be conveyed more effectively. I'll no longer have to use so many half-tones. This will be more amusing, for the reader, at least ... When will the blessed day come when I will write the words 'The End'? Next September it will be three years that I've been at work on this book. That's a long time, three years spent on the same idea, writing in the same style (especially when the style is one which expresses my personality as little as that of the Emperor of China), living continuously with the same characters, in the

same surroundings, clobbering oneself to maintain the same illusion.

Now, a year later, he was still at it. There were times when he found his labour on the last chapters almost intolerable. 'I am working badly, quite without any taste for it, or rather with *dis*taste. I am profoundly sick of this task. It is a real pensum for me now,' he wrote to Bouilhet from Croisset in September 1855. 'My wretched novel won't be finished before February. This is becoming ridiculous. I don't dare mention it any more.' What he was writing, and what he saw about him, intensified his misanthropy: 'I feel waves of hatred for the stupidity of my age. They choke me. Shit keeps coming into my mouth, as from a strangulated hernia . . . I want to make a paste of it and daub it over the nineteenth century, the way they coat Indian pagodas with cow dung.' And he told Bouilhet: 'You know, about six weeks ago my mother made a remark I find sublime, enough to make the Muse hang herself out of jealousy at not having thought of it herself. "Your mania for sentences," my mother said, "has dried up your heart." '

Especially for the later chapters of the book, those dealing with Emma's extravagances and promissory notes, and the resultant forced sale of the contents of the Bovarys' house, he made detailed use of a strange document concerning his old friend Louise Pradier.[1] (He continued to see this other Louise from time to time, and the tone of his occasional letters to her was always quite formal: '*Chère Madame,*' and so on – in order, Jean Bruneau thinks, that she might share them with her mother and sister, who were well known to Flaubert and his family. This formality was in strong contrast to the nature of his other relations with the lady, who seems to have remained good-natured and easygoing in her 'disgrace'.)

The completed manuscript of *Madame Bovary* in Flaubert's hand bears the dates 'September 1851–April 1856'.

Flaubert and Maxime DuCamp never fully recovered the degree of friendship that had preceded their disagreement over Flaubert's chosen way of life, but the bitterness of that episode had abated, and DuCamp was one of the first to be shown the completed novel. Although, as will be seen, he had strong reservations, he seems not to have found it the 'total fiasco' he had prophesied to Louise Colet; in any case, he kept the 'pledge' he had made to Flaubert five years before, and offered to print it in the *Revue de Paris* in six bi-monthly parts and to pay Flaubert two thousand francs. Flaubert accepted, asserting in a letter to his cousin Olympe Bonenfant in Nogent that the sum proved him to be 'an excellent businessman'.[2] DuCamp, for his part, was to boast for the rest of his life of being the first publisher of *Madame Bovary.*

Delivery to the *Revue* was delayed because Bouilhet, on re-reading the manuscript as a whole, advised some cutting, and Flaubert reluctantly removed thirty pages. After the novel had been read by Léon Laurent-Pichat, one of DuCamp's codirectors on the *Revue*, DuCamp sent Flaubert a letter whose tone and content will surprise no serious creative writer who has had to do with publishers and editors of magazines:

July 14, 1856

Cher Vieux: Laurent-Pichat has read your novel, and I enclose his remarks about it. You will realize when you read them how I must agree, for they reproduce almost all the observations I made to you before you left. I gave the book to Laurent with no comment beyond a warm recommendation; it is not by collusion that we harass you along the same lines. The advice he gives you is good – the only advice, let me say, that you should follow. Let us take full charge of the publication of your novel in the *Revue*; we will make the cuts we think indispensable, and later you will publish it in a volume in whatever form you choose: that is your affair. My personal opinion is that if you do not do this, you will be gravely compromising yourself, making your first appearance with a muddled work to which the style alone does not give sufficient interest. Be brave, close your eyes during the operation, and have confidence – if not in our talent, at least in the experience we have acquired in such matters and also in our affection for you. You have buried your novel under a heap of details which are well done but superfluous: it is not seen clearly enough, and must be disencumbered – an easy task. We shall have it done under our supervision by someone who is experienced and clever; not a word will be added to your manuscript, it will merely be pruned; the job will cost you about a hundred francs, which will be deducted from your payment, and you will have published something really good instead of something imperfect and padded. You are doubtless cursing me with all your might at this very moment, but you may be sure that in all this I have only your own interest at heart.

On that letter Flaubert scrawled '*Gigantesque!*'; and retorted to DuCamp that the novel was to be published as it was or not at all. After some dispute it was agreed that only one passage would be omitted – that describing the careening course, through the streets of Rouen, of the erotic cab containing Emma and her lover Leon. That, DuCamp flatly said, was 'impossible'.

The first instalment, originally scheduled for July or August, finally appeared in the issue of October 1, 1856.

1. Among the Flaubert papers in the Municipal Library of Rouen, Mlle Gabrielle Leleu found, and summarized in 1947, a manuscript entitled *Mémoires de Madame Ludovica*, an account of Louise Pradier's debts and adulteries written by an unnamed woman. The American scholar Douglas Siler, who published the document in full in 1973, has identified the author as a friend of Mme Pradier's, a certain Mme Louise Boyé. It is not known how the document came into Flaubert's possession. One of Flaubert's major 'scenarios' – outlines – for *Madame Bovary*, recently discovered by Dr Siler (who is preparing an edition of Pradier's correspondence), is none other than a partial summary of the *Mémoires de Madame Ludovica*.

2. It is difficult to assess the 'real' value of Flaubert's 2000 francs (magazine payment for four and a half years' work) except by comparing it with certain incomes of the time. The reader will recall Flaubert's writing to Alfred LePoittevin in 1845 that Louise Pradier, cast out by her husband, was living 'wretchedly' on 6000 francs a year. Jacques Desmarets, in *La France de 1870* (Hachette, 1971), lists the following annual averages: 'bourgeois', 13,000 to 17,000; artisans and shopkeepers, 1600 to 1800; minor officials, 1000 to 1200; labourers and shop employees, under 1000. According to Theodore Zeldin, in *France 1848–1945*, a doctor might expect to average 3000 francs a year in 1842, a good Parisian carpenter could earn 1300 francs during the early Second Empire, and an *agrégé de l'université* (a particularly qualified teacher in a lycée) began at 2200 francs and could rise to 6600.

❦

To Leon Laurent-Pichat
                    Croisset, Thursday night. [October 2,] 1856
Cher Ami

I have just received *Bovary*,[1] and first of all want to thank you for it (I may be vulgar, but I am not ungrateful); you did me a service by taking it as it is and I will not forget it.

Confess that you thought me and still think me (more than ever, perhaps) wildly ridiculous. If some day I come to agree that you were right, I promise you faithfully that I will make you the most humble apologies. But you must understand that this was a *test* which I wanted to make; let us hope that what I learn from it will not be too much of a jolt.

Do you think that this ignoble reality, so distasteful to you in reproduction, does not turn my stomach as it does yours? If you knew me better you would know that I abhor ordinary existence. Personally, I have always held myself as aloof from it as I could. But aesthetically, I wanted this once – and only this once – to plumb its depths. Therefore I plunged into it heroically, into all its minutiae, accepting everything, telling everything, depicting everything, pretentious as that may sound.

I am expressing myself badly, but well enough for you to understand the general trend of my resistance to your criticisms, judicious as they may be. You were rewriting my book. You were damaging the inner poetics that determined the pattern (as a philosopher would say) of its concept.

In short, in acting out of deference and not out of conviction, I would have considered that I was failing in my duty to myself and to you. Art requires neither complaisance nor politeness: nothing but faith – faith always, and freedom.

1.   i.e. the first instalment in the *Revue de Paris*.

❦

The instalments of *Madame Bovary* made a considerable impression from the beginning. The night of November 6, 1856, Bouilhet's play, *Madame de Montarcy*, was acclaimed at the Théâtre de l'Odéon. The two friends were jubilant about their simultaneous success.

However, as serialization proceeded, the editors of the *Revue de Paris* received an increasing number of protests from subscribers, especially readers in the provinces, outraged by the novel's 'immorality'; and during November they learned that because of certain passages the government 'examiner of books and periodicals' – Napoleon III's censor – had asked the Department of Justice to prosecute the magazine and Flaubert for 'outrage of public morals and religion'. When Flaubert opened his copy of the issue of December 1, he found the newest instalment headed by an editorial note: 'The editors find themselves obliged to omit from this instalment a passage which they consider unsuitable for publication in the *Revue de Paris*. They hereby advise the author of their action and assume full responsibility for it.'

And the *Revue* asked Flaubert to make more cuts.

～

To Leon Laurent-Pichat

[Paris,] Sunday. [December 7, 1856]

Mon Cher Ami

First, thank you for disclaiming personal responsibility; I therefore now address not the poet Laurent-Pichat, but the *Revue*, an abstract personality, whose interests you represent. This is my reply to the *Revue de Paris*:

1. It kept the manuscript of *Madame Bovary* for three months, and thus it had every opportunity, before printing the first line, to know what to make of it. The alternatives were to take it or leave it. The *Revue* took it, and must abide by the consequences.

2. Once the agreement was concluded, I consented to the elimination of a passage which I consider very important, because the *Revue* claimed it presented a risk. I complied gracefully, but I will not conceal from you (and now I am speaking to my friend Pichat) that that day I bitterly regretted having had the idea of publishing.

Let us speak our minds fully or not at all:

3. I consider that I have already done a great deal, and the *Revue* thinks that I should do still more. *I will do nothing*: I will not make a correction, not a cut; I will not suppress a comma; nothing, nothing! But if the *Revue de Paris* thinks that I am compromising

it, if it is afraid, the simple thing to do is to stop publication of *Madame Bovary* at once. I wouldn't give a damn.

Now that I have finished addressing the *Revue*, let me point out one thing to my friend:

By eliminating the passage about the cab you have not made the story a whit less shocking; and you will accomplish no more by the cuts you ask for in the sixth instalment.

You are objecting to details, whereas actually you should object to the whole. The brutal element is basic, not superficial. Negroes cannot be made white, and you cannot change the *blood* of a book. All you can do is to weaken it.

Needless to say, if I break with the *Revue de Paris* I shall nevertheless remain a friend of its editors.

I know how to distinguish between literature and literary business.

～

The *Revue* replied that if Flaubert would not make the new cuts, they would. He threatened suit, but was dissuaded by a lawyer friend in Rouen: the law, it appeared, was on the *Revue's* side. He then asked that the last instalment be cancelled. The *Revue* refused, but consented to his prefacing it with a note:

> Considerations which it is not in my province to judge compelled the *Revue de Paris* to omit a passage from the issue of December 1; its scruples having been again aroused on the occasion of the present issue, it has thought proper to omit several more. Consequently, I hereby decline responsibility for the lines which follow. The reader is asked to consider them as a series of fragments, not as a whole.
>
> Gustave Flaubert

On December 26, Flaubert signed a contract with the publisher Michel Lévy for the publication of *Madame Bovary* in book form, giving Lévy the rights to the novel for five years in return for the sum of 800 francs.

Meanwhile, the government proceeded with its charge.

~

To Edmond Pagnerre[1]

[Paris, December 31, 1856]

My dear Pagnerre

You know better than anyone else that I have published a novel in the *Revue de Paris*, since in your newspaper you wrote very amiably about me in that connection. Now I stand accused of having 'outraged public morals and religion' in that book. I have already been interrogated by the examining magistrate, and it is very probable that I shall be summoned to court on a criminal charge. I shall be sentenced in any case, and this is why:

I am a pretext. The government is out to destroy the *Revue de Paris*, and I have been chosen as its instrument.[2] The situation is this: if the case is dropped, I will have saved the *Revue de Paris*; if it is not dropped, I face ruin.

Our friend Cormenin,[3] in whose presence I am writing this, tells me that you are an intimate friend of M. Abbatucci.[4] Do me the service of writing to him and explaining the situation as it really is.

I think I have written a book that is moral by its effect as a whole. As for details, I am being blamed for a scene of Extreme Unction which is copied almost word for word from the Missal. The ridiculous character in my novel is a Voltairean, a materialist philosopher (like the *Garçon!*).[5] I do not preach adultery or irreligion, since I show, as every good author should,[6] the punishment incurred by immoral behaviour.

If I am sentenced, it will be impossible for me ever to write a line again. I will be watched; and a second offence would bring me five years in prison. Besides, it is not pleasant to be sentenced for immorality. It puts one in the company of the Alexis Duponts or the Hervés.[7]

So be a good fellow and do what you think proper to extract me from this hornet's nest.

Write to the Minister telling him who I am as a man and what kind of book I have written. If they want to nab the *Revue*, there are plenty of opportunities. But they should leave me in peace to write my little stories.

Adieu, thank you in advance, for I am counting on you.

1. A Bonapartist, editor-in-chief of *Le Journal du Loiret*, published at Orléans, Flaubert had known Pagnerre as a boy in Rouen. DuCamp had urged Flaubert to seek help from all the Bonapartist friends he could think of. (J.B.)
2. DuCamp and his fellow editors believed this (the magazine had received one or two warnings), and they had apparently persuaded Flaubert it was so. But Jean Bruneau thinks that although the *Revue de Paris* was unquestionably in disfavour with the government because of the liberalism of some of its articles (it was, in fact, later suppressed), the target at this time was really Flaubert and his 'immoral' book. See Flaubert's own mention of 'Jesuits' on p. 307.
3. Louis de Cormenin, a former co-director of the *Revue de Paris*.
4. Charles Abbatucci, senator and Minister of Justice.
5. For the '*Garçon*', see p. 15. Pagnerre, Flaubert later told his niece Caroline, had been 'one of the creators of the *Garçon*. That is a freemasonry one doesn't forget.'
6. It is difficult to know whether Flaubert is being totally ironic here or suggesting to his old friend that these words be repeated to the important senator and Minister of Justice.
7. Dupont, a singer, and Hervé, an actor, had been arrested for abusing young children of both sexes. Dupont, sixty years old, hanged himself. (J.B.)

Despite the rigorous press censorship of the period, the affair of *Madame Bovary* and the *Revue de Paris* did not go unreported. Throughout January, Parisian literary journals commented on the scandal facing the *Revue*. In its issue of January 3, 1857, the Brussels newspaper, *L'Indépendence Belge*, which was sometimes forbidden the French mails, carried a 'Paris letter' entitled '*Madame Bovary et ses persécuteurs*', with a sequel on January 27. Flaubert, who from his solitude at Croisset had expressed his contempt for the press, now found himself *in* the press. The rhythm of his life radically changed, he 'plunged into the fray' – as he had once reminded Maxime DuCamp he was capable of doing if the affair were 'of short duration and something that I enjoy'. He busied himself preparing his defence, writing letters like the one to Pagnerre, soliciting help from friends and acquaintances who might influence government officials. His brother Achille, through the Prefect in Rouen, saw to it that the Ministry of Justice was informed of the Flauberts' being 'an important family, whom it might be dangerous to attack because of the approaching elections'; a powerful defender was found in the prominent trial lawyer Antoine-Marie-Jules Senard, who had been a friend of the elder Dr Flaubert. Nevertheless, the government persisted in its case. Flaubert continued defiant and outspoken. 'At any moment,' he wrote to his brother in mid-January, 'I expect the summons that will name the day when I am to sit – for the crime of writing in French – on the bench usually occupied by pickpockets and prostitutes.'

~

To his brother Achille

[Paris, c. January 20, 1857]

I am very surprised not to have received my summons; there is a delay; are they hesitating, perhaps? I think so; the people who have spoken on my behalf are furious; and I hear that one of my protectors, who is a *very* highly placed personage, is becoming 'enraged', and threatens to 'smash some windows at the Tuileries'. The outcome will be favourable, I am sure, whether the affair is quashed or whether I go on trial.

The various steps I have taken have been very beneficial, in that *opinion* is now on my side; there isn't a literary man in Paris who hasn't read me and doesn't defend me; they are all sheltering behind me – they feel that my cause is theirs.

The police have blundered. They thought they were attacking a run-of-the-mill novel and some ordinary little scribbler; whereas now (in part thanks to the prosecution) my novel is looked on as a masterpiece; as for the author, he has for defenders a number of what used to be called '*grandes dames*'; the Empress, among others, has twice spoken in my favour; the Emperor said, the first time, 'They should leave him alone'; and despite all that the case was taken up again. Why? There begins the mystery.

While waiting, I am preparing my statement, which is simply my novel itself; but I am cramming the margins next to the incriminated passages with embarrassing quotations drawn *from the classics*, to show by means of that simple parallel that for the past three hundred years there hasn't been a line of French literature that couldn't be indicted as undermining morality and religion. Have no fear: I shall be quite calm. As for not appearing at the trial, that would be a retreat; I shan't say anything, but will sit next to Senard, who will need me there. Besides, I can't afford not to display my criminal countenance to the populace.

I thank you and Pottier for your future visit.[1] Come and dine with me in my Venetian oubliette. I'll provide a bundle of straw and some chains, and have my portrait painted as 'the author in fetters, sitting on dank straw in his dungeon'!!!

It is all so stupid that I have come to enjoy it greatly.

As you see, nothing is certain as yet: we must wait.

By the middle of next week you should receive some pieces by me published in *L'Artiste*. There will be four numbers in all, containing fragments of *La Tentation de Saint Antoine*.[2] If I should forget to send them, remind me: the last fragment will appear next Sunday.

Adieu, cher frère, je t'embrasse.

1. Conservateur of the Rouen Municipal Library.
2. Immediately after finishing *Madame Bovary*, Flaubert had taken up his manuscript of *Saint Antoine*, and during the summer and autumn of 1856 he 'corrected' it – a process which resulted in its being cut by half. When *Madame Bovary*, appearing in the *Revue de Paris*, showed signs of becoming a *succès de scandale*, Théophile Gautier urged Flaubert to lose no time in publishing the new version of *Saint Antoine* in the magazine *L'Artiste*, of which Gautier was one of the editors: 'It's a good idea to keep dropping tons of bricks on those stupid bourgeois, without interruption.' The new *Saint Antoine* appeared in the issues of December 21 and 28, 1856, and January 11 and February 1, 1857.

～

To Alfred Blanche[1]

[Paris, January 23, 1857]

This is to inform you that tomorrow, Saturday, January 24, I shall honour by my presence the swindlers' bench in Room 6 of the Criminal Court, at 10 a.m. Ladies are admitted; decent and tasteful dress required.

I am not counting on anything like justice. I shall be sentenced, and perhaps given the maximum – sweet recognition for my labours, noble encouragement to literature.

I dare not even hope that proceedings will be postponed for a fortnight: Maître Senard cannot appear for me either tomorrow or a week from now.[2]

But one thing consoles me for this nonsense: namely, having met with so many expressions of sympathy for myself and my book in so many quarters. I count yours among the first, dear friend. The commendation of certain enlightened minds outweighs the dishonour of criminal prosecution. And I defy the whole French judiciary, with its gendarmes, and the whole Criminal Investigation Service, including its informers, to write a novel that will please you as much as mine.

Such are the proud thoughts that will keep me company in my dungeon.

If my work has real value – if you find that you have not been mistaken about it – I pity my prosecutors. This book that they are seeking to destroy will survive all the better for its very wounds. They are trying to shut my mouth: their reward will be a spit in the face that they won't forget.

Some day, perhaps, you may have occasion to speak to the Emperor about these things. You could cite my trial as illustrative of the inept turpitudes taking place under his rule.

Which doesn't mean that I am becoming a wild man of the Opposition, and that you will soon be having to seek my release from Cayenne.[3] No, no: don't worry. In my deep immorality I stand alone, with no love for any party or clique, not even allied to any coterie, and – naturally – supported by no one. I am detested by the Jesuits in short gowns as much as by the Jesuits in long gowns; my metaphors irritate the former, my frankness scandalizes the latter.

That is all I had to tell you. That, and that I thank you again for your kind help. It has proven useless, for anonymous stupidity has shown itself more powerful than your devotion.

1. A very high Imperial official – Secrétaire Général du Ministère d'Etat. His family was prominent in medical circles in Rouen and Paris. (J.B.)
2. The trial was postponed until January 30.
3. At that time a penal settlement for political offenders.

~

TO HIS BROTHER ACHILLE

[Paris,] Sunday, 6 p.m. [January 25, 1857]

My trial is definitely fixed for next Thursday; there are chances for, and chances against; nothing else is being talked about in the literary world.

Today I spent a whole hour alone with Lamartine, who paid me the most extravagant compliments. Modesty prevents me from repeating the ultra-flattering things he said; what is certain is that he knows my book by heart, understands all I mean by it, and has a clear perception of me as a writer. He will give me a laudatory letter to be offered in court; I am also going to get certificates as to the morality of my book from a number of the most established literary men; Senard says this is important.[1]

My stock is rising; I have been asked to write for the *Moniteur* at 10 sous a line, which for a novel like *Bovary* would amount to about 10,000 francs. Such is the result of prosecution.

Whether I am sentenced or not, my position is now assured.

It was Lamartine who initiated the courtesies: that surprises me considerably – I would never have expected the bard of Elvire[1] to conceive a passion for Homais.

. . .

Adieu. I haven't an idle moment. I have appointments all day, and at night I write and correct proofs.[2]

1. A name which appears frequently in Alphonse de Lamartine's *Méditations poétiques*. Flaubert considered Lamartine soft, both as poet and as politician. 'What a mediocre man that Lamartine is!' he had written to Louise Colet a few years before. At the trial, Senard was able only to mention some of the flattering things Lamartine had *said* about *Madame Bovary* to its author – for to Flaubert's displeasure Lamartine never sent the promised letter.
2. Of *La Tentation de Saint Antoine*.

~

TO HIS BROTHER ACHILLE

[Paris, January 30, 1857]

Mon cher Achille

This morning you should have received a telegram from me sent by one of my friends, saying that the Court will announce its decision a week from tomorrow. Justice still hesitates! . . .

Maître Senard's speech was splendid. He crushed the attorney from the Ministry of Justice, who writhed in his seat and made no rebuttal. We flattered him with quotations from Bossuet and Massillon, smutty passages from Montesquieu, etc. The courtroom was packed. It was marvellous, and I was in fine form. At one point I allowed myself personally to contradict the attorney, who was immediately shown to be acting in bad faith, and retracted. In any case, you will see the rest of the proceedings word for word: I had a stenographer (at 60 francs an hour) taking it all down. Senard spoke for four hours without interruption. It was a triumph for him and for me.

He began by talking about Father, then about you, and finally about me; then followed a complete analysis of the novel, refutation of the list of charges and of the incriminated passages. Here he was particularly strong: the attorney must have been given a good dressing-down after the session.[1] But the best was the passage about Extreme Unction. The attorney was completely discomfited when Maître Senard took a Missal from under his seat and read from it. The passage in my novel is nothing but a *softened* reproduction of what is in the Missal: we certainly stuffed them with a famous bit of literature.

Throughout his speech, Senard spoke of me as a great man and treated my book as a masterpiece. He had about a third of it read aloud. He made the most of Lamartine's commendation. 'You owe him not only an acquittal, but apologies!' was one of the things he said. And: 'Ah! You are attacking the second son of M. Flaubert! . . . No one, M. l'avocat général, and not even you, can give him lessons in morality!' And when the attorney talked nonsense about one passage, Maître Senard replied: 'I do not question your intelligence, but I am struck by your obsession [with adultery].'

All in all, it was a proud day, and you would have enjoyed it had you been there.

Say nothing; keep quiet; after the verdict, if I lose I will appeal in the *Cour d'appel*; if I lose there, in the *Cour de cassation.*

Adieu, cher frère, je t'embrasse.

1. By his superiors at the Ministry of Justice.

～

The decision was announced on February 7, 1857. The Court was unable to resist a certain amount of 'literary' comment, and expressed its preference, at once stern and wistful, for literary works which deal less with life as it is than with life as it should be; but in the end it stated: 'In the circumstances, be it known that it is not sufficiently proven that Pichat, Gustave Flaubert, and Pillet [the printer of the *Revue de Paris*] are guilty of the offence with which they are charged; the Court acquits them of the indictment brought against them, and decrees a dismissal without costs.'

$\backsim$

To Maurice Schlesinger[1]

[February, 1857]

Mon cher Maurice

Thank you for your letter. I shall answer briefly, for all this has left me so exhausted physically and mentally that I haven't the strength to walk a step or hold a pen. The fight was hard, but I finally won.

I have received very flattering compliments from all my *confrères*, and my book is going to sell unusually well for a writer's first. But the fact is, I am infuriated whenever I think of the trial: it has deflected attention from the novel's artistic success, and I dislike Art to be associated with things alien to it. To such a point that all this row disgusts me profoundly, and I hesitate to publish *Madame Bovary* as a volume. I long to return, and for ever, to the solitude and silence I emerged from; to publish nothing; never to be talked of again. For it seems to me impossible in the present day to say anything, social hypocrisy is so ferocious!!!

. . . The volume I was going to publish after my novel, a book that cost me several years of painstaking research and study, would send me to the penitentiary![2] And all my other plans have similar drawbacks. Do you realize now what a bad joke my situation is?

1. The Schlesingers were now living in Baden.
2. The first instalments of *Saint Antoine* in *L'Artiste* had appeared in time to be quoted by the Public Prosecutor as further evidence of Flaubert's immorality. Serial publication continued to the end, however, without interference. Although Flaubert apparently did have some fear that he might eventually be prosecuted for this work as well, his decision not to publish it as a volume at this time was probably largely motivated by continued dissatisfaction with the work itself. *Saint Antoine* would finally appear as a book only in 1874,

still further shortened, and intensified, to the form in which it is now known.

~

To Edmond Pagnerre

[c. February 11, 1857]

If I haven't replied sooner to your congratulations, it is because I was so utterly exhausted for several days following my political bouts that I could neither take a step nor hold a pen. I am still numb and dazed, and not a little anxious about my future books. What can I write that would be more inoffensive than my poor novel?

I am even hesitant about publishing it as a volume, because I want to restore the passages deleted by the *Revue de Paris* – all of them inoffensive, in my opinion. The cuts were idiotic, and create a lubricious effect utterly foreign to the book.

The Prosecutor still has two months in which to appeal. Could you find out definitely from Abbatucci whether he intends to appeal? Must I wait the two months? How am I regarded? Who has it in for me? I'll end up like Rousseau, believing in a Holbachian conspiracy. Because, although everyone I saw personally was favourably disposed, underneath there was an incomprehensible determination to get me.

Meanwhile, Lévy is after me to publish. I don't know what to do.

People advise me to omit some of the passages picked out by the prosecution. But that is *impossible* for me. I will not commit absurdities to please the authorities – not to mention that I find such a method of handling the matter a real bit of asininity.

Such is the sad plight of your unfortunate friend. You know I expect you to dinner one of these days, on the '*boulevard du crime*'.[1]

1. Flaubert was spending the winter in lodgings on the Boulevard du Temple, nicknamed '*le boulevard du crime*' because of its numerous theatres specializing in melodramas. Possibly he was facetiously implying that he himself was one of the boulevard's 'criminals'.

~

The Ministry of Justice did not appeal the verdict, but it was doubtless out of prudence that book publication was delayed until mid-

April. In this first edition of 6750 copies, *Madame Bovary* was printed in two volumes, with a dedication to Louis Bouilhet and a note of thanks to Maître Senard.[1]

During and after serialization, Flaubert had received letters and comment from readers unknown to him – responses which, whether in their praise or in their moralistic shock at the author's unwavering, intransigent view of society,[2] anticipated the flood of conflicting reviews that would greet the published book. More than once he was asked who had been his 'model' for Emma Bovary. Among those who wrote asking that question was a literary spinster in Angers, Mlle de Chantepie, who sent him some of her fiction and, apparently, a portrait of herself. She and Flaubert never met, but maintained a correspondence for many years.

1. The note reads, in part, 'After the detailed analysis you gave of my novel in your magnificent pleading, I find it has acquired a kind of authority such as I myself never supposed it to possess.'
2. Predictably, comment from sources close to the Church or the regime was particularly hostile. Flaubert wrote to Bouilhet on October 8, 1857:

    'Have I told you, apropos of success, that the curate of Canteleu [the parish that included Croisset] is thundering against me? He snatches my book from his parishioners' hands! I confess I enjoy this immensely. No praise has tickled me more. Now nothing is lacking: attack by the government, abuse by the press, hatred from the priests. *Taieb! Buono!*'

    Some of the dismayed critical reactions to *Madame Bovary* read like confirmations of Flaubert's own vow made when he was not yet eighteen: 'I will simply tell the truth, but that truth will be horrible, cruel, naked.' (See p. 24.)

⁓

To Mademoiselle Leroyer de Chantepie

Paris, March 18, [1857]

Madame:

I hasten to thank you: I have received everything you sent. Thank you for the letter, the books – and especially for the portrait: that was a delicate thought, and I am touched by it.

I am going to read your three volumes slowly and carefully – in the way, that is, I am sure they deserve.

But I am prevented from doing so for the moment, because before returning to the country I am busy with some archaeological work dealing with one of the least-known periods of antiquity – a task which is preparation for another. I am going to write a novel whose action will take place three centuries before Christ. I feel the need of leaving the modern world: my pen has been dipped in it too long, and I am as weary of portraying it as I am disgusted by the sight of it.

With a reader as sympathetic as you, Madame, frankness is a duty. Therefore, in answer to your questions: *Madame Bovary* has nothing 'true' in it. It is a totally invented story; into it I put none of my own feelings and nothing from my own life. The illusion (if there is one) comes, on the contrary, from the *impersonality* of the work. It is a principle of mine that a writer must not be his own theme. The artist in his work must be like God in his creation – invisible and all-powerful: he must be everywhere felt, but never seen.

And then, Art must rise above personal affections and neurotic susceptibilities! It is time to banish anything of that sort from it, and give it the precision of the physical sciences. Nevertheless, the capital difficulty for me remains style, form; the indefinable Beauty *resulting from the conception itself* – and which is, as Plato said, the splendid raiment of the Truth . . .

~

To his cousin Olympe Bonenfant

[Croisset, June 14, 1857]

I see I haven't replied to your last letter, which came more than a month ago, in the midst of the flurry of publication. Everything is going smoothly, and if I hadn't been a fool I would now be well off, since my publisher has already sold 15 thousand copies, which at two francs a volume makes 30 thousand francs, and sales keep increasing. In *sum*, I'll have let slip the *sum* of 40 or 50 thousand francs.[1]

Voilà, It's true that I am being showered with honours. I have been attacked and commended, vilified and extolled. But I wouldn't mind having made a little cash.

. . .

1. On August 31, 1857, Lévy voluntarily gave Flaubert an extra 500 francs.

～

Flaubert's letters to only two of *Madame Bovary's* many reviewers have been preserved: those to Sainte-Beuve and Baudelaire. He may have written to others, but the notice paid to his novel by those two writers meant more to him, for different reasons, than the rest of the critical comment.

The article by Sainte-Beuve (whom Flaubert had met through Théophile Gautier) was especially valuable because of the critic's eminence and respectability: his literary feuilleton had for a number of years appeared every Monday in the semi-official *Moniteur Universel*, which had a national circulation among the upper bourgeoisie. To a young writer, favourable notice by Sainte-Beuve was the opening of the door. His article on *Madame Bovary*, which he had cautiously delayed writing until specifically asked to do so by the newspaper, appeared on May 4, 1857. Although not remarkably penetrating, it nevertheless exalted Flaubert above other novelists of his generation: 'One precious quality distinguishes M. Gustave Flaubert from the other more or less exact observers who in our time pride themselves on conscientiously reproducing reality, and nothing but reality, and who occasionally succeed: he has *style*. He even has a trifle too much.'

Its closing words were picked up by the caricaturist Lemot in a celebrated cartoon: 'Son and brother of eminent doctors, M. Gustave Flaubert wields the pen as others wield the scalpel. Anatomists and physiologists, I find you on every page!'

～

To Charles-Augustin Sainte-Beuve

Tuesday night [May 5, 1857] Croisset, near Rouen
Monsieur et cher maître

I am covered with confusion: I have just read your article in the *Moniteur.* How can I express to you all the feelings it evoked in me, and all the pleasure it gave me? To tell you I found it splendid would border on the ridiculous, seeing that you treat me as a friend – that is to say, with the closest attention and the highest praise.

In four newspaper columns you have repaid me for all my labours. Now I have my recompense. *Merci, Monsieur, merci.*

What an exquisite pleasure it is for me, remembering how I read

Volupté and *Les Consolations* at college, that one of the men one looks up to should condescend to interest himself in my thoughts and take me by the hand.[1]

But please let me enlighten you on a purely personal point. Do not judge me by this book. I do not belong to the generation you speak of: at least, not in ways of feeling. I insist that I belong to *yours* – I mean the good generation, that of 1830. It represents everything I love. I am a rabid old Romantic – or a fossilized one, whichever you prefer.

I regard this book as a work of pure art, the result of an inflexible resolve. Nothing more. It will be a long time before I write anything else of the kind. It was *physically* painful for me to write it. Now I want to live – or rather resume living – amid less nauseating scenes.

Next winter, will you allow me to come some evening and sit with you by your fire, for a good talk about our beloved literature, which so few care about in this day and age? I will ask you, apropos of *Bovary*, some practical advice – the kind that is worth more than all the theories and aesthetics in the world. It will be a pleasure and a lesson.

Looking forward to that honour, let me assure you that I am

Most gratefully yours –

1. Flaubert may well have read Sainte-Beuve's novel and poems while at the college, although, as Jean Bruneau points out, there is no mention in the early letters of his doing so. The first reference to Sainte-Beuve in the correspondence is in a letter to Louis de Cormenin of June 7, 1844: 'I am flattered to see that you agree with me in hating Sainte-Beuve and all his group.' And to Louise Colet, in 1852, Flaubert calls him a '*lymphatique coco*' – Sainte-Beuve having expressed the wish, in one of his *Lundis*, that Louis Bouilhet, as poet, would 'stop picking up the butts of Alfred de Musset's cigars'.

∿

Although a number of Charles Baudelaire's poems had been published in magazines, he was known at this time to comparatively few readers, and to them chiefly as art critic and translator of Poe. Before meeting him, and before reading any quantity of his verse, Flaubert had expressed, in a letter of 1854 to Louise Colet, an imperative for modern writers calling for much the same poetic temper that Baudelaire was soon to display so powerfully. 'We must make a break with the tail end of Lamartinism, and adopt an impersonal poetics; or if we choose to practise a subjective lyricism it should be unfamiliar, reckless, in short so intense as to be an absolutely new *creation*. But as for saying weakly what everybody feels weakly, No.'

When novelist and poet became acquainted through Théophile Gautier, it was not strange that they found each other's 'poetics' admirable, and Baudelaire undertook to review *Madame Bovary*. Meanwhile, on June 25, 1857, *Les Fleurs du mal* was published, and Flaubert wrote to Baudelaire as he had not previously written to anyone his own age.

~

TO CHARLES BAUDELAIRE

Croisset, July 13 [1857]

Mon cher Ami

I began by devouring your volume from beginning to end, like a kitchen maid pouncing on a serial, and now for the past week I have been re-reading it line by line, word by word, and I must tell you that it delights and enchants me. You have found the way to rejuvenate Romanticism. You resemble no one – the greatest of all virtues. The originality of your style springs from the conception; each phrase is crammed to bursting with its idea. I love your sharpness, with the refinements of language which enhance it, like damascene work on a fine blade.

These are the pieces which struck me most: Sonnet XVII, *La Beauté*, for me a work of the highest quality; and then *L'Idéal*, *La Géante* (which I already knew), No. XXV.[1]

Avec ses vêtements ondoyants et nacrés

Une charogne, Le Chat, Le Beau navire, A une dame créole, Le Spleen, which went straight to my heart, its tone is so right. Ah! How well you understand the boredom of existence! Of that you may boast without false pride. I won't go on, lest I seem to be copying your table of contents. But I must tell you that I am utterly enchanted by LXXV, *Tristesses de la lune*:

> *. . . Qui d'une main distraite et légère caresse*
> *Avant de s'endormir le contour de ses seins . . .*

and I deeply admire the *Voyage à Cythère*, etc. etc.

As for criticisms, I make none, because I am not sure that I should agree with them myself after a quarter of an hour. In short, I am afraid of mouthing ineptitudes that I would immediately regret. When I see you this winter in Paris, I shall merely ask you a few humble, tentative questions.

To sum up, what I love above all in your book is that in it Art occupies first place. Furthermore, you write of the flesh without loving it, in a melancholy, detached way that I find sympathetic. You are as unyielding as marble and as penetrating as an English fog.

Once again, a thousand thanks for your gift; I shake your hand warmly.

1. Flaubert read the first edition of *Les Fleurs du mal*. Some of the numberings are different in later editions.

~

Further sympathy was created between Flaubert and Baudelaire by a juridical coincidence, news of which reached Flaubert in the country.

~

To CHARLES BAUDELAIRE

[Croisset,] Friday, August 14 [1857]

I have just learned that you are being prosecuted because of your book. Apparently I am rather late in hearing about this. I am in ignorance of everything, for I live here as though I were a hundred thousand leagues from Paris.

Why? Against what have you committed an 'offence'? Religion? 'Public morals'? Have you been 'brought to justice'? When will that be? Etc.

This is something new, to prosecute a book of verse. Up to now the bench has left poetry severely alone.

I am deeply indignant. Give me details about the affair, if it is not too much trouble, and accept a thousand very cordial greetings.

~

To that letter, and to another from Flaubert suggesting certain lines of defence, Baudelaire replied:

> *Cher ami*
>
> I am sending you this short and hasty note before five o'clock merely to express my contrition at not having replied to your affectionate words of sympathy. But if you knew into what an abyss of puerile business I have been plunged! And the article on *Madame Bovary* again postponed for a few days! What an interruption in one's life a ridiculous misadventure can be!
>
> The comedy was played out on Thursday. It was a lengthy affair.
>
> Result: 300 francs fine for me, 200 for the publishers, suppression of Nos. 20, 39, 80, 81, and 87.[1] I will write to you at greater length tonight.

Baudelaire's review of *Madame Bovary* was delayed not a few days, but almost two months, appearing in *L'Artiste* for October 18, 1857.

1. The verdict was later revised, and those poems are now included in all editions.

~

To Charles Baudelaire

Croisset, Wednesday night [October 21, 1857]

I thank you very much, *mon cher ami*. Your article gave me the greatest possible pleasure. You entered into the arcana of the book as though my brain were yours. It is understood and felt to its very depths.

If you find my book stimulating, what you wrote about it is no less so, and we will speak about it all when we see each other, in six weeks.

Until then, once again a thousand greetings.

~

Baudelaire had written in his review that following the death of Balzac, interest in the novel had disappeared; Flaubert had now revived it. And Baudelaire proceeded to expound what he thought must have been in Flaubert's mind when he conceived *Madame Bovary*:

> On a banal canvas, we shall paint in a style that is vigorous, picturesque, subtle and exact. We shall put the most burning and passionate feelings into the most commonplace adventure. The most solemn utterances will come from the most imbecile mouths.
>
> What is the very home of imbecility, the most stupid society, most productive of absurdities, most abounding in intolerant fools?
>
> The provinces.
>
> Which of its inhabitants are the most insufferable?
>
> The common people, incessantly engaged in petty employments, the very exercise of which distorts their ideas.
>
> What is the tritest, the most prostituted, human situation, the most broken-down barrel organ of all?
>
> Adultery.

'To accomplish the tour de force in its entirety,' Baudelaire continued, 'it remained for the author only to divest himself (to the extent possible) of his sex, and to become a woman. The result is a marvel; for despite all his zeal as an actor he was unable to keep from infusing male blood into the veins of his creation, and Madame Bovary, in the most energetic and ambitious aspects of her character, and also in her strong predilection for reverie, remained a man.'

In another paragraph he praised Flaubert for being the first to utilize hysteria, 'that psychological mystery', as the 'base and bedrock of a literary work'; and he ended by saying: 'It would be easy for me to show that M. Gustave Flaubert has deliberately concealed, in *Madame Bovary*, the lofty lyrical and ironic faculties manifested without reserve in *La Tentation de Saint Antoine*, and that the latter work, the secret chamber of his mind, remains clearly the more interesting for poets and philosophers.'

Some of Baudelaire's remarks sound much like Flaubert himself as we have read him in the correspondence, and the review may well have benefited from conversations between the novelist and the poet. Perhaps Flaubert had said to Baudelaire, as he was to say to others, '*Madame Bovary, c'est moi, d'après moi!*': 'Madame Bovary is myself – drawn from life.'

Flaubert must have particularly enjoyed the references to his beloved *Saint Antoine*. For now he was engaged on the project he had announced to Mlle Leroyer de Chantepie – a project which would display, he hoped, all the extravagance he had lavished on the saint, enhanced by the control he had learned from portraying the sinner. Another of the 'three subjects' he had listed in his letter to Bouilhet from Constantinople was assuming modified form. Much as his 'Flemish' novel had become *Madame Bovary*, so *Anubis*, 'the story of the woman who wants to be laid by the God', was emerging as *Salammbô*, the story of the Carthaginian princess whose golden chainlet of virginity is snapped by a giant mercenary – a man she persuades herself may be a god in disguise.

Volume II
1857–1880

INTRODUCTION

Reflections:
Gustave Flaubert's Correspondence

THE POPULAR AND literary success of Gustave Flaubert's first published novel, *Madame Bovary*, brought him notoriety but did not greatly change his daily life. His greatest departure from existence as the 'hermit of Croisset' was an eighteen-month tour of Egypt and the Near East in 1849–1851 with his friend Maxime DuCamp. In the spring of 1858 he visited Tunisia briefly in preparation for his second novel, the exotic *Salammbô*, but otherwise he seldom strayed far from home. When he reached his early fifties the modest financial independence he had enjoyed was undermined by the assistance he gave his niece's husband during years of business failure, but he scrupulously retained his literary independence. Although his later works were often harshly reproached at publication with their dissimilarity to *Madame Bovary*, and although material rewards from his books were meagre, his reputation as a writer of high seriousness and great style never diminished. Flaubert always generated a respect which at difficult moments earned him a degree of indulgence. 'This morning the newspapers vie with one another in trying to cushion Flaubert's fall,' Edmond de Goncourt wrote in his diary following the disastrous reception of Flaubert's only produced play, *Le Candidat*. A curious and growing public sympathy was extended to this uncompromising artist who held himself aloof.[1]

If melancholia and misanthropy – or rather a supreme irritation with human folly – intensified in Flaubert during his later years,

1.   See Volume I, and *Flaubert in Egypt*, in Works of Related Interest.

events appeared to justify that development. He lived through the Franco-Prussian War of 1870–1871 and the subsequent catastrophe of the Commune. These conflicts wrung him, both for their larger meaning and in the sorrow and turmoil they brought to his secluded existence. Under their influence, too, he became – if not quite a patriot – more overtly a Frenchman. We find Flaubert – of all people – drilling the local company of the National Guard and going to Rouen 'to take lessons in military art'. The occupation by Germans of his mother's house at Croisset polluted it in his eyes: 'If [it] belonged to me, I would certainly have it demolished.'

Flaubert suffered with the victims of famine and privation and endured the humiliations of defeat; embittered by the tragic divisions between his countrymen, he was indignant with both Right and Left. And he marked, with habitual prescience, the onset of a new chaos in which technology, political and social fluctuation, and gigantic wars would overwhelm the claims of civilized order and fatally reduce the possibilities for imagination and reflection in human affairs. Having ever despised 'current opinion' and its insistent purveyors, he watched its contagion spread, under the impetus of events, into the domain of intellect, scholarship, and art; infecting all concepts of quality and excellence, and of truth itself, and blighting his closest associations. Before the war he walked out of one of the Magny dinners – those gatherings of literary men and scholars founded by Sainte-Beuve and a few friends – because the other guests insisted on discussing politics, 'an indecency among intellectuals'; and in 1874 he wrote to George Sand: 'The men of my profession are so *little* of my profession! There is scarcely anyone except Victor Hugo with whom I can talk about what interests me. Two days ago he quoted to me by heart from Boileau and Tacitus. It was like receiving some gift, the thing is so rare.'

The great 'Realist' refused to exalt 'modernism', and retained to the end his vision of the long individuality of art: 'This mania for thinking . . . that you're more true than your predecessors exasperates me . . . There is no "True". There are only ways of perceiving . . . Down with Schools, whatever they may be! Down with words devoid of sense! . . . Material truth (or what is so called) must be only a springboard, to help one soar the higher.' At such moments Flaubert

– who had once declared himself 'a rabid old Romantic' – brings to mind the Leopardi of 'La Ginestra'.

In 1872 his mother's death dissolved Flaubert's strongest emotional tie. Seclusion was intensified by the deaths of most of his close friends and became, at times, isolation: 'Almost all human beings are endowed with the gift of exasperating me, and I breathe freely only in the desert.'

Exhorted – in a fine exchange – by George Sand to acknowledge the beneficence of 'mercy' and 'humanitarianism', Flaubert emphatically declined, labelling them 'sentimental' and calling instead for justice – 'the blood of the wounded Themis' – and the spirit of enquiry. On the modern ideal of material and social 'progress' he was similarly unyielding: 'The entire dream of democracy is to raise the proletariat to the level of bourgeois stupidity.' His views were arrived at not through animus or posturing, but with immense suffering: 'Everything moves me, everything lacerates and ravages me, and I make every effort to soar.' Flaubert had painfully earned his right to the despair that often possessed him.

Together with despair there were close affections, great generosity of spirit towards younger writers, an ebullient sense of absurdity, and a generally fastidious code of private behaviour. It is the astringent Edmond de Goncourt who records, at their final meeting, Flaubert's 'kind face'. The remark is unexpected, but somehow not surprising. It is notable that Flaubert did not often or frivolously speak ill of others in his letters, or indulge in trivial gossip and mockery. Men of stature liked and respected him. He cultivated no little court of inferiors to whom he might hold forth without contradiction; and to those who disagreed with him he was not vengeful. He recognized – and indeed held sacred – the private bonds of tenderness, loyalty, goodwill; of shared experience and common suffering; and of an ultimate humility before the great creations of art.

Two significant instances, during the period covered by the present volume, in which Flaubert violated his own standards derive from 'bourgeois' considerations of the kind he himself most savagely condemned. His harmless infatuation with the world of society and court influence was brief – although his friendship with Princesse Mathilde Bonaparte survived. But his role in allowing his beloved niece to be forced into a loveless marriage with a seemingly prosperous bourgeois, a union that later brought him immeasurable grief, was undertaken for thoroughly unworthy reasons. 'I'd rather see you marry a millionaire philistine than an indigent genius': those are the words not of a petty or grand bourgeois, of Monsieur Homais or Monsieur Dambreuse, but of Gustave Flaubert. The consequences were to cost him a precious friendship and to plunge him into mercenary wrangles of the kind his soul had always abhorred: 'I feel spiritually *soiled* by all these sordid concerns, by all this commercial talk; I feel I'm being turned into a shopkeeper. Imagine a virtuous woman made to prostitute herself in a brothel, or a fastidious person being dragged about in a garbage cart, and you have my situation.'

These curious episodes make uneasy reading – if only because we seek from genius a consistency greater than our own. They may, without too much insistence, be linked to endless manifestations of the greater dichotomy of Gustave Flaubert's spirit. Kindliness and misanthropy; the quandary of a novelist who debated whether his next work would deal with Thermopylae or a pair of nineteenth-century copy-clerks; the genius who sought, in his work, 'to be like a God' – and the man who declared he would 'die of suppressed rage at the folly of my fellow men.'

For the most part these later letters of Flaubert's are less well known than their predecessors; nevertheless, some are individually renowned. One might mention the pair to the critics Sainte-Beuve and Froehner rebutting their objections to *Salammbô* – letters of which Jacques Barzun has said: 'Flaubert had his fingers rapped by authoritative pedants, but he knew his subject and crushed their knuckles with the finality of a sledge hammer.' There are the two analytical letters to Taine; the moving congratulations to his young 'disciple', Guy de Maupassant, on having produced a masterpiece in 'Boule de Suif'; the passages on the German occupation; and almost any of the letters to George Sand. Each reader will make his own selection. Flaubert's genius as a correspondent was immune to the fluctuations of fortune and expresses itself with equal force under every variety of circumstance.

The difference between the younger and the older Flaubert is perhaps most manifest in the contrast between the sensual outpourings to Louise Colet in Volume I and what can be thought of as their *pendant* in the present pages – the celebrated series to George Sand, infused with a riper sentiment. Unlike the Flaubert–Colet correspondence, that between Flaubert and Madame Sand survives almost intact on both sides. A number of their exchanges, particularly illuminating of Flaubert's character, life and work, have been included here.[2]

When the fourth and last volume of the first edition of Flaubert's general correspondence was published by Charpentier early in 1893 (the volumes having been issued separately over a period of several years), a long review of the whole, by Henry James, was printed in *Macmillan's Magazine*. James's immediate concern was, he claimed, for the ethical aspects of this disclosure of Flaubert's private circumstances, feelings, and statements, as contrasted with Flaubert's own attitude to such revelations. ' "May I be skinned alive before I ever turn my private feelings to literary account",' James quoted from a letter dated 1854; whereas 'Flaubert's niece, Madame Commanville' (who edited the series) had given the letters to the world 'without attenuation and without scruple . . . In our merciless age,' James went on, 'ineluctable fate has overtaken the man in the world whom we most imagine gnashing his teeth under it.'

James had no way of knowing how inapposite were his words 'without attenuation and without scruple'. In fact, Mme Commanville had been sparing, to say the least, when it came to inserting the series of dots which, in a quoted text, signify ellipsis. (In 1906 she would edit a fifth volume, composed entirely of letters from her uncle to herself, entitled *Lettres à sa nièce Caroline*: here the indications of omission would be much more frequent – although, as we know today, still not frequent enough to meet the case.)

Mme Commanville's censorship took several forms. Most obviously superfluous, in her view, were the passages, very numerous in the later letters to her, in which her uncle – fond of her as he was

---

2. The entire corpus, as recently edited by Alphonse Jacobs (with acknowledgements to Georges Lubin and Jean Bruneau), invites integral translation into any number of languages. (*Gustave Flaubert – George Sand, Correspondance*, Paris: Flammarion, 1981.)

– complained of ill-treatment by her, or, more frequently, by her unlucky and rapacious husband. The image of a niece always affectionate and considerate had to be preserved. (That she had deep cause, if not justification, for the imperfections of her devotion, the reader of the present volume will discover.)

The next category of her omissions related to unflattering, or possibly libellous, references to persons then still alive.

Third, there was Flaubert's tendency to be obscene, profane, and scatological. In these realms he was fluent and, particularly in youth, linguistically inventive. In France phrases of the kind have always been in somewhat wider use than in English-speaking society; and here Mme Commanville – who, though genteel, was thoroughly Gallic – sometimes surprises us by her permissiveness. She might have been yet more liberal in this respect had it not been for her 'spiritual director', the Reverend Father Didon. 'In publishing your uncle's correspondence,' this Dominican priest wrote to her, 'you have not pledged yourself to say everything, and your private conscience must guide you in using judgement as to what you allow to be printed – since it is through you that these letters will be made public. You are responsible before God and man for the moral result of this publication.'[3]

Flaubert sometimes commented on the letters of other artists and writers. On New Year's Eve, 1876, he wrote to Caroline:

> I have read Balzac's Correspondence. Well, for me it was edifying reading. Poor man! What a life! How he suffered and worked! What an example! It would be indecent ever to pity oneself when one knows the tortures he underwent – and one loves him for it. But what an obsession with money! And so little concern for Art! *Not one single time does he talk about it!* Fame was the goal of his ambition, not Beauty. And such

3. Over the years more and more of Flaubert's letters have come to light. The four-volume first edition, plus the volume of letters to Caroline, included something over two thousand letters. The Pléiade edition of the correspondence (Paris: Gallimard), edited and annotated by Jean Bruneau and at present in the course of publication, will include about five thousand.

limitations! – legitimist, Catholic, dreaming of the Chamber of Deputies and the French Academy! With all that, ignorant as a pot, and provincial to the marrow of his bones: luxury dazzled him. His greatest literary admiration was for Walter Scott. I prefer Voltaire's correspondence. The compass spreads wider there!

There were also the letters of Hector Berlioz, for whose tormented life Flaubert expressed a similar pity. (Flaubert and Berlioz had known each other, and Berlioz had written to Flaubert of his admiration for *Salammbô*, which he had thought of making the subject of an opera.) Once again to Caroline, in April 1879:

Reading Berlioz's *Unpublished Correspondence* has revived me. Read it, I beg you. There's a man for you! and a true artist! What a hatred of mediocrity! What marvellous anger against the vile bourgeois! What scorn for 'Them'! It beats Balzac's letters hollow! I'm no longer surprised that we found each other so congenial. Would I had known him better! I'd have adored him!

Even though he enjoyed those letters written by other artists, and expressed no scruples over their publication, it is conceivable that Flaubert might nonetheless have been aghast at the thought of his own letters in print. Who is an exception if not oneself? And Flaubert was a man of contradictions. We cannot be certain. Like everyone else acquainted with the Goncourt brothers, Flaubert knew that they kept a journal intended for publication; nevertheless, in the Goncourts' presence he often spoke openly about the most intimate aspects of his own life and told some of his most scabrous stories – as he did in letters to them. It would hardly have surprised Flaubert to learn that these remarks were commemorated in the journal. In response to queries from Hippolyte Taine, who was writing his treatise *On Intelligence*, he discussed his thoughts concerning the creation of his fictional characters and even described the hallucinations preceding his own epileptiform attacks. We see today what James could not: that Flaubert's remark, 'May I be skinned alive before I ever turn my private feelings to literary account', refers predominantly to his novels rather than to his letters. Caroline Commanville's prime motive for publishing the letters was financial – that consideration was always prominent with her and her husband; and it is true that in her day it was customary to remove anything 'unseemly' from letters before publication. Nevertheless, we, at this distance, inevitably find her culpable – not because she sent her uncle's letters to the printer, but because she censored them before doing so.

Even in their truncated condition, the early printed volumes of Flaubert's correspondence immediately fascinated readers. The several fuller editions that have been published since Caroline's series have led some critics to hail the correspondence, with varying degrees of enthusiastic exaggeration, as 'the best of Flaubert's novels'. There have also been dissenting voices. James himself, in addition to stating his 'ethical' objection, was so repelled by Flaubert's personality as revealed in the letters that the prose in his long review became opaque: he found Flaubert, if 'impossible as a companion, [yet] deeply refreshing as a reference'; and the letters themselves he pronounced productive of a 'compassion . . . full of mystifications and wonderments.'

Marcel Proust, in his essay 'On Flaubert's "Style"' (the quotation marks around 'Style' are Proust's own), expressed astonishment that whereas most writers whose books are written badly (as, in his judgement at the time, was the case with Flaubert) *improve* their style immensely when writing spontaneously in letters, Flaubert's epistolary style is 'even worse' than that of his novels. Proust – who paid a late tribute, in his own novel, to *Madame Bovary* – disagreed with the critic Albert Thibaudet, who found in Flaubert's correspondence 'the expression of the ideas of a first-rate intellect'.

The art and the private correspondence of a great writer are not in rivalry. Yet there will always be those who enjoy setting the one against the other. In an ironic passage dealing with such literary pretensions in *The Guermantes Way* – and included only in recent editions of Proust's novel – the Comtesse d'Arpajon converses with the Narrator:

'As a matter of fact I find that old correspondences have a

peculiar charm,' the lady who was well up on literature and had such fascinating letters in her château went on . . . 'Have you noticed how often a writer's letters are superior to the rest of his work? What's the name of the author who wrote *Salammbô?*'

I should have liked not to have to reply in order not to prolong the conversation, but I felt it would be disobliging to the Prince d'Agrigente, who had pretended to know perfectly well who *Salammbô* was by and out of politeness to be leaving it to me to say, but who was now in a painful quandary.

'Flaubert,' I ended up by saying, but the vigorous signs of assent that came from the Prince's head smothered the sound of my reply, so that my interlocutress was not exactly sure whether I had said Paul Bert or Fulbert, names which she did not find entirely satisfactory.

'In any case,' she went on, 'how intriguing his correspondence is, and how superior to his books! It explains him, in fact, because one sees from everything he says about the difficulty he has in writing a book that he wasn't a real writer, a gifted man.'[4]

Few readers will now share the reservations of either the American mandarin or the French concerning Flaubert's letters. For many, the correspondence is fundamental. Jean Bruneau, in the preface to his first volume, quotes André Gide: 'For more than five years his correspondence took the place of the Bible at my bedside. It was my reservoir of energy. It made me realize that the force impelling me could be consecrated in a new way.'

---

4. *Remembrance of Things Past*, trans. C. K. Scott Moncrieff and Terence Kilmartin (New York: Random House, 1981), II, 508.

VIII

The Writing of Salammbô

1857–1862

ON ITS PUBLICATION in two volumes in April 1857, *Madame Bovary* was an immediate 'success'. That is, it sold widely and was soon reprinted – partly, no doubt, because of the scandal of the prosecution following its serialization in Maxime DuCamp's *Revue de Paris*. On a more serious plane, thoughtful critics recognized the book's importance; and a penetrating review by Baudelaire contributed to the general acceptance of *Madame Bovary* as a masterpiece that depicted human existence with a degree of realism hitherto unknown in fiction.

Unlike many a writer who has achieved immediate fame with his first published work, Flaubert did not remain a man of that one book, or even of one kind of book. He went on to produce a variety of extraordinary works. *Salammbô*, his Carthaginian story, was his second published book – aloof (as contrasted with *Madame Bovary*) from the study of human character; rather, a richly coloured historical and imaginative reconstruction of a vanished civilization. Guy de Maupassant has evoked the nature of what he calls Flaubert's 'Homeric tale':

Is it a novel? Is it not rather a kind of opera in prose? The tableaux unroll with prodigious magnificence, with astonishing splendour, colour and rhythm. The sentences sing and shout with the fury and resonance of trumpets; they murmur like oboes, surge like cellos; they are as flexible as violins, delicate as flutes.

The characters, heroic in their stature, give the impression of being always on a stage; they speak superbly, with an elegance now mighty, now charming; they seem to move in a decor antique and grandiose.

This book, written by a giant, and plastically the most beautiful of all his works, creates the impression of a magnificent dream.

Did the events related by Gustave Flaubert really occur in this way? Certainly not. Exact though the facts may be, the brilliance of the poetry he showers on them displays them to us in a kind of apotheosis, whose lyric art envelops everything it touches.[1]

The writing and reception of *Salammbô*, the 'magnificent dream' of a nineteenth-century novelist in love with antiquity, would be one of the subjects of his correspondence for the next several years.

Even before *Madame Bovary* was published, Flaubert had known what his next book would be.

Abandoning his thought of preparing at that time a definitive version of his early extravaganza, *The Temptation of Saint Anthony*, most of which remained in manuscript (a few revised sections had been printed in Théophile Gautier's magazine *L'Artiste* during the excitement about *Madame Bovary*), he deliberately chose a subject equally exotic. Distance from his own life and times was essential, for *Madame Bovary*, he told Mlle Leroyer de Chantepie, his literary spinster correspondent in Angers, had filled him with 'a long disgust' for anything to do with the French bourgeoisie. The new book, he wrote to her on March 18, 1857, would be a historical novel whose action took place 'in one of the least known periods of antiquity . . . three centuries before Christ'. More precisely, its subject would be the bloody revolt and annihilation of the unpaid polyglot mercenary army of Carthage, following that city's first defeat by Rome in 241 BC – and the end of the first Punic war. He wanted, he told the Goncourt brothers, to 'write something purple'.

Such would be *Salammbô*. The immense difference between Flaubert's first and second novels is proclaimed in their titles, the names of their heroines: Madame Bovary, the bourgeois wife of a provincial French health officer, and Salammbô, daughter of the Carthaginian general Hamilcar – 'a daughter', Flaubert wrote to a friend, 'invented by your humble servant'. (The historian Polybius, writing in the second century BC, mentions a daughter of Hamilcar but does not name her; Flaubert baptized her from the Babylonian and Syrian pantheons, where the goddess whose name can be transcribed as 'Salambo' – we shall see that Flaubert's spelling is specifically French – corresponds to the Greek Aphrodite, or, more particularly, to the mourning Venus of the legend of Venus and Adonis.)

In reply to a letter from Flaubert now lost, Louis Bouilhet, his old friend and literary counsellor, who was now librarian in the town of Mantes, wrote in warning on July 18, 1857:

Either you misunderstood me, or I expressed badly my feelings about your future book. Like you, I not only think it possible, but hope it will be splendid. However, I see it as being so difficult that it alarms me, and I was surprised from the start to see you throw yourself so blithely into so scabrous a subject. That's all. Now, what is of lesser, indeed not of the slightest, importance, from the artistic point of view, is, in my opinion, the inopportuneness of the book at this critical point of your reputation. I may be mistaken, but I think it would be more astute, whatever you may say, to write another work of close observation, making it your last production of that kind. This is certainly the case as far as money is concerned, and also from the standpoint of reputation. At least, such is my sincere opinion. I hope I may be wrong. I'm not afraid that what you propose doing will be a fiasco, but even assuming the same level of excellence it will never, because of its very subject, make the sensation that *Bovary* did, and I'd like you to fire two cannonballs in rapid succession, both of them red-hot.

Everything I'm saying is silly and useless, but I wanted to explain my lack of enthusiasm. *This has nothing to do with the book itself, which will certainly be very fine.* It has to do with its *timing.*

From now on there must be no turning back, and besides I may be making quite a blooper. One never knows how the public will react. So: get to work, start writing as soon as possible. Don't wear yourself out making new notes; digest your old ones; take up your pen, and if something turns up that has to be researched, then research it.

Some years before, during his travels in Egypt, Flaubert had written to Bouilhet: 'Let's not get lost in archaeology': and with typical inconsistency it was into archaeology that he himself now deeply plunged. He is said to have had a Carthaginian subject in mind since his schoolboy reading of Michelet's *Histoire Romaine*: almost the entire background of his story, and most of its military incidents, are based (as is Michelet's account) on Polybius's narrative in his *History*. Until he was well into his new novel, Flaubert sometimes referred to it as *Carthage*, or *The Mercenaries*. Though he was not deterred by Bouilhet's doubts, his letters of 1857 and early 1858 tell of dread caused by Bouilhet's injunction to *begin* – and of near despair, followed by resolve.

1. From Maupassant's preface to *Lettres de Gustave Flaubert à George Sand* (Paris: Charpentier, 1884).

~

To Ernest Feydeau[1]

[Croisset, July 26 [?], 1857]

. . .

I am sick with fear, filled with terrors of all kinds: I'm about to start to write. No, my friend, I'm not so stupid: I'll not show you any part of *Carthage* until the last line is written, because I already have enough doubts of my own without adding those you would give me. Your remarks would drive me crazy. As for my archaeology, it will be 'probable', that's all. As long as no one can *prove* that I've written absurdities, that's all I ask. As for the botanical side, I have no worries; I've seen with my own eyes all the plants and trees I need.

Besides, that's of little importance: it's a secondary matter. A book can be full of enormities and blunders and be no less splendid for that. Such a doctrine, once admitted, would be deplorable, I know, especially in France, where pedantry and ignorance reign. But in the opposite tendency (which is mine, alas!) I see a great danger. Concentration on costume makes us forget the soul. I would give the demi-ream of notes I've written during the last five months and the ninety-eight volumes I've read, to be, for only three seconds, really moved by the passion of my heroes.

· · ·

1. Flaubert had met Ernest Feydeau (1821–1873, father of the playwright Georges Feydeau), through Théophile Gautier, at the time when Feydeau had begun his archaeological study, *Histoire des usages funèbres et des sépultures des peuples anciens*. In 1858 Feydeau would publish his first novel, *Fanny*, which enjoyed a popular and, in some quarters, even critical success equal to that of *Madame Bovary*, but which is forgotten today along with most of Feydeau's subsequent fiction. Flaubert envied him the financial aspect of his success (the publisher Lévy had paid only 800 francs for five years' rights to *Madame Bovary*, plus a voluntary extra 500 francs when it had sold widely); but he greatly liked Feydeau, and spent much time and effort granting his pleas for help in the composition of his novels. Although they were the same age, Flaubert sometimes addressed Feydeau as 'nephew'.

∼

Flaubert apparently lamented similarly to Bouilhet, who wrote to him on September 19, 1857: 'Consider especially that given the milieu and period you have chosen, the book can never be as living as *Bovary*. That is impossible. I'll go further: it would be wrong if it were. Over distant subjects there should always be a haze: the stump is better than the hard pencil, and real life should appear only at rapid intervals, like flashes of lightning on a very distant horizon. That is the danger, but also the beauty and the originality, of your subject.'[1]

1. As *Salammbô* advanced, Flaubert would ask Bouilhet for help at a number of delicate moments. Most of his letters to Bouilhet are lost; many of Bouilhet's replies survive, in the Bibliothèque Lovenjoul at Chantilly. Salammbô's betrothal to the Numidian chieftain, Narr' Havas, despite her broken ankle-chain; the substitution of the slave boy for the child Hannibal; the forced combat between two groups of Theban friends: Flaubert's treatment of all these scenes, and others, owes something to Bouilhet's suggestions. The episodes were conceived by Flaubert, but Bouilhet assisted in their realization. Benjamin F. Bart has written an interesting exposition of Bouilhet's role in his article 'Louis Bouilhet and the Redaction of Salammbô,' *Symposium*, Fall 1973.

⌒

To Ernest Feydeau

[Croisset,] Thursday night [August 6, 1857]

. . .

For the past six weeks I've been shying away from *Carthage* like a coward. I'm accumulating reams of notes, and reading book after book, for I don't feel ready to begin writing. I don't see my objective clearly. In order for one's book to *sweat* truth, one has to be stuffed to the ears with its subject. Then the colour comes quite naturally, like a result decreed by fate, and like a flowering of the very idea.

. . .

⌒

By early October he took a somewhat more hopeful tone in a letter to Jules Duplan, a businessman who performed various friendly services for him in connection with his books: 'Finally I'm beginning to have an erection. That's the important thing. But how hard it's been to get it up! Will it stay?'

⌒

To Mademoiselle Leroyer de Chantepie

[Croisset, November 4, 1857]

. . .

The more experience I acquire in my art, the more tormenting that art becomes. The trouble is, imagination remains stationary while taste matures. Few men, I think, will have suffered as much as I for literature. Now I am going to spend two months in complete solitude, with no company except that of the yellow leaves as they fall on the flowing river . . . Have you noticed how we love our miseries? You cling to the religious ideas that cause you such suffering, and I to the chimera of style, which consumes me body and soul. But perhaps we are worth something only because of our sufferings, for these are all aspirations. There are so many people whose joys are so ignoble and whose ideals so shallow, that we must bless our troubles if they make us more worthy.

. . .

⌒

To Ernest Feydeau

> *[Croisset, about November 20, 1857]*

Oh, I'm done for, my friend, done for! . . . Let me tell you confidentially that for the past month I've found it impossible to write. I can't find a single word. I'm horribly bored, and keep staring at the fire. *Voilà.*

I'm being punished for wanting, like a fool, to begin to write a book before carrying it long enough in my belly. I assure you I'm not very gay . . .

. . .

∾

To Ernest Feydeau

> *[Croisset,] Tuesday night [November 24 [?], 1857]*

. . .

At last I've finished, for better or worse, my first chapter, and am preparing the second. I have undertaken something bold, my boy, something very bold, and I may well break my neck before reaching the end. Never fear, I'll not shirk it. Sombre, grim, desperate, but no coward. But just think, intelligent nephew, of what I've let myself in for: trying to resuscitate an entire civilization with nothing whatever to go on!

How difficult it is to write something that has substance and at the same time *moves!* This is essential, however. On every page there must be food and drink, action and colour.

. . .

∾

To Ernest Feydeau

> *[Croisset,] Saturday [December 12, 1857]*

. . .

I'm not going ahead, which is better than continuing to make mistakes. I stopped because I felt I was on the wrong track. I'm baffled by the psychology of my characters. So I'm waiting, and sighing.

I'll be in Paris on Tuesday or Wednesday of next week, Christmas Eve at the latest . . . Once there, I swear I'm going to go in for some monstrous debauches, to restore my morale. I'm longing for them.

Perhaps by sticking something up my arse I can give my brain a good fucking. I hesitate between the column in the Place Vendôme and the obelisk [in the Place de la Concorde]. I'm laughing – but I'm not merry. It's true that I've gone through similar periods before, and come out of them all the livelier. But this one is lasting too long, too long!

~

Flaubert became increasingly dissatisfied with what he was doing. Might it help if he were to see for himself the site and surroundings of Carthage? One of the basic difficulties was, as he had said, that there was 'nothing to go on': the city had been all but obliterated by Rome following the end of the third Punic war in 147 BC. On January 23, 1858, he wrote to Mlle Leroyer de Chantepie:

> I absolutely must make a trip to Africa; so, towards the end of March I'll return to the land of dates. I'm thrilled at the prospect. Once again I'll live on horseback and sleep under a tent. What deep breaths of air I'll treat myself to when I board my ship at Marseilles! But this trip will be a short one. I need to go only to El Kef[1] (thirty leagues from Tunis), and explore the environs of Carthage within a radius of twenty leagues, in order to acquaint myself thoroughly with the landscapes I'll be describing. My outline is done, and I'm a third of the way through the second chapter. The book will have fifteen. As you see, I've barely begun. Under the best of circumstances, I'll not be finished for two years.

Leaving Croisset, the village on the Seine near Rouen where he lived with his widowed mother and his motherless niece, Caroline Hamard (now twelve years old), he took ship at Marseilles on April 16, 1858. He went ashore at Stora, Algeria, for a preliminary look at Philippeville and Constantine; at Bône (for Bizerta, the ancient Hippo); and on the twenty-fourth disembarked at Tunis, near the site of Carthage. He was well supplied with notebooks. His earliest known letter from this voyage is to Louis Bouilhet.

1. The antique Sicca.

~

To Louis Bouilhet

Midnight [April 23–24, 1858]
Night of Friday–Saturday, aboard the
Hermus, *abreast Cap Nègre and Cap Serat.*
Latitude 37° 10 – longitude 6° 40 – (look
at the map and you'll see where I am!!!)

Mon Vieux,

It's a beautiful night, the sea flat as a lake of oil; old Tanit[1] is shining, the ship's engine panting, the captain smoking beside me on his sofa, and the deck packed solid with Arabs Mecca-bound. Barefoot, swathed in their white burnouses, their faces covered, they look like shrouded corpses. There are women, too, with their children. The entire lot of them are sleeping, or wretchedly vomiting; we are skirting the Tunisian coast, visible in the mist. Tomorrow morning we'll be at Tunis; I'm not going to bed – I want to miss none of this lovely night. Besides, my impatience to see Carthage would keep me awake.

From Paris to Constantine, in other words from Monday to Sunday, I scarcely exchanged a word with a soul. But at Philippeville we took on some fairly agreeable passengers, and since then I've been having various conversations – some quite philosophical and very indecent. I am initiating a young Russian gentleman into the arcana of pederasty . . . though I suspect that as a Scyth he may know more than I about such matters.

At Marseilles I saw the well-remembered house where eighteen years ago I fucked Mme Foucaud, née de Langlade.[2] All changed! The ground floor, then the salon, is now a bazaar, and upstairs is a barbershop. I went there twice to be shaved. I spare you any Chateaubriandesque comments and reflections on the flight of time, on falling leaves and falling hair. No matter: it's a long time since I have thought – or is it *felt*? – so deeply . . .

I was extremely solitary during my two days in Marseilles. I went to the museum, to the theatre. I visited the brothel streets, I sat and smoked in sailors' cafés, looking out at the sea.

The only important place I have seen so far is Constantine, Jugurtha's city. It is surrounded by an immense ravine, tremendous, vertiginous. I walked along its edge and rode a horse along its floor. It was the evening hour, when lines begin to form outside the little theatres on the Boulevard du Temple.[3] Vultures were wheeling in the sky, etc.

In the realm of the ignoble, I have never seen anything better than the three Maltese and an Italian who were with me in the coach from Constantine – drunk as Polacks, stinking like corpses, roaring like tigers. These gentlemen excelled in obscene jokes and gestures, accompanied by farts, belches, and much chewing of garlic, their pipes glowing in the dark. What a journey! What company! It was Plautus to the twelfth degree, lowlife par excellence.

At Philippeville, in a seaside garden full of roses in full bloom, I saw a fine Roman mosaic of two women, one riding a horse and the other a sea monster. The place was filled with exquisite silence: nothing could be heard but the sound of the sea. The gardener, a Negro, brought an old watering-can and sprinkled the mosaic to bring out the lovely fresh colours. And then I left.[4]

And you, old chap, what are you up to? Are you beginning something? My greetings to Léonie[5] and the old bridge at Mantes with the mill creaking beside it. My next letter will be longer. I expect one from you at the end of the week, and I embrace you tenderly, *mon pauvre vieux.*

1. The Carthaginian moon goddess, a great presence in *Salammbô.*
2. See Volume I. Flaubert considered Mme Foucaud his true sexual initiatress, when he was nineteen. She was the inspiration for his early novel, *Novembre*, published only posthumously.
3. Where Flaubert had his Paris apartment, at no. 42.
4. Flaubert's notebook gives a few more details: 'Arrived at Philippeville 6 a.m. [April 19, 1858]. Visited the garden belonging to Mr Nobeli, overlooking the sea. Fragrant with rosebushes in bloom. A mosaic, found on the site, shows two women, one seated and driving an eagle-beaked sea monster, another seated on and driving a horse, iris between its ears like red flames; a third, a dancer, with anklets; feet and legs remarkable for their form and movement, the right crossing over the left; the background dotted with fish. The Negro gardener who showed it to me goes to fill a watering can and sprinkles the mosaic to make it brighter. I am filled with tender feelings here in this garden. The weather hazy, soldiers on the terrace opposite playing fanfares.'
5. Léonie Leparfait, Bouilhet's companion. Bouilhet adopted her illegitimate

son, Philippe Leparfait, whose father was believed to be Philippe de Chenne-
vières (1820–1899), director of the Beaux-Arts in the 1870s. (J.B.)

~

To Ernest Feydeau

Tunis, Saturday, May 8, 1858

It's very good of you to write to me, but I'm *exhausted*, and
unless you long for my death don't ask for letters. This week I was
at Utica, and I spent four entire days at Carthage, from eight to
fourteen hours on horseback every day. At five this afternoon I leave
in a caravan for Bizerta, riding a mule: I scarcely have time to make
notes. Don't worry about me: there's nothing to be afraid of in
Tunisia. The worst of the inhabitants hang around the city gates; it
isn't a good idea to frequent those regions at night, but I think the
European residents here are egregious cowards. I discharged my
dragoman because he was similarly afflicted, trembling at every bush
– not that that kept him from robbing me at every step. His successor,
beginning today, is a hideous Negro, very black.

I miss you greatly. You'd enjoy it here – we'd enjoy it together.
The sky is splendid. At evening and in the morning the lake of
Tunis is covered with flocks of flamingos: when they fly off they're
like a mass of little pink and black clouds.

I spend my evenings in Moorish cafés listening to Jewish singers
and watching the obscenities of Karagöz.[1]

The other day, on my way to Utica, I slept among dogs and
chickens in a Bedouin douar, between two walls made of cow dung;
all night I heard jackals barking. In the morning I hunted scorpions
with a gentleman addicted to that form of sport. And with a whip
I killed a snake a yard or so long that was coiling itself around the
legs of my horse. Such is the sum of my exploits.

I shall probably leave here for Constantine *by land* – it is feasible
– with two of the Bey's horsemen. At the [Algerian] frontier, four
days from here, the commanding officer at Suk Ahras will give me
some men to take me on to Constantine. This journey is easier
going from Tunis to Constantine than from Constantine to Tunis,
yet few Europeans have done it, so far. In this way I'll have seen *all*
the places I'll be writing about in my book.

.   .   .

1. Karagöz ('Black Eye') is the Turkish name both of the traditional Turkish-Arab-Egyptian shadow-theatre (puppets manipulated behind a transparent lighted screen), and of one of its two principal stock characters – much like 'Punch and Judy'. Its popularity began in the seventeenth century. Even by Flaubert's time it was declining; today it is occasionally revived, usually on television. In his Carthaginian notes, Flaubert describes the performance he saw:

   '[When we arrived] in the long, narrow, very crowded theatre there was as yet nothing taking place behind the transparency. In the narrow space between two of the benches a man was performing a rhythmic walk, lifting his knees very high, or dancing without flexing his knees, shaking his belly Egyptian style (very inferior version). What was good was the three musicians, who from time to time, at regular intervals, took up what he was saying, or rather *reflected* it quite loudly, like a chorus; that was very dramatic, and made me feel I understood. As for Karagöz, his penis is about the size of a wooden beam; it soon ceases to seem indecent. Karagöz has several identities: I think the type is falling into decay. The whole thing is to display the penis as much as possible. The biggest had a bell at the tip, which rang with every movement of the haunches; that aroused much laughter. What a deplorable spectacle for a man of taste! and for a gentleman with principles!'

For two more weeks Flaubert remained close to the site of Carthage, filling his notebooks; then he returned westward, bound for Constantine, this time travelling overland as he had announced in his letter to Feydeau. Riding with armed escorts, sleeping outdoors or in native inns, devoured by fleas but happy in his adventure, he spent a week in the mountains and valleys of the Atlas, continuing to make notes on encounters and on the topography he would later describe, in *Salammbô*, in his narrations of the marches of the Mercenaries. On June 2 he took ship at Stora, reached Marseilles on the fourth, and within a week, after spending a few days in Paris, was back at Croisset.

There he 'slept for three days' and went over the notes he had brought back. Notes on the vestiges of Carthage, on the colours of North African land and sea, and on wayside encounters, with details that he might or might not use. On eating lion, for instance:

[*Bizerta.*] Father Jérémie, jovial . . . *Chéchia* on the back of his head, hair ruffled, witty, very comical, setting a great value on '*bons vivants*' (his words). Formerly curate at Boufarik. He has eaten lion, jackal, panther, hyena; he claims that lion is excellent fare. He is raising a wild boar, 'having only four parishioners', and is much occupied with silkworms.

Or on entertainment, much inferior to what he had enjoyed in Egypt:

[*Tunis*,] *Thursday, [May]* 20. Evening party at the house of M. de Kraft. Jewish musicians, whom I had already seen in a café. M. de Montès, Colonel Caligaris, Dubois, Cavalier. In the patio . . . a high torch standing in the middle, like a church candelabrum. Ra'hel, small, thin, long nose, eyebrows completely joined by copper-red paint. The toad dance. Arse smaller than all the rest. Very free behaviour. Marsen's servant in red vest, combines both tastes. Left at 2 a.m.

Friday. Visit to Ra'hel near the leather souk. Stairs. Shit. One room at the back, one to the left. The whores in the salon! A handsome gold necklace of large rings, very flat. My room! Stones! Two stones to hold the door shut; thin calico curtain at the back. Shouting of Jews outside. The women block the window with a pillow. Big bed with mosquito netting, horrible sheets, red-striped blanket. Filthy mattress. Daylight visible through the walls – fear of bringing the house down while fucking. Continuous frying-pan movement. Cavalier arrived ten minutes after me – laughter! And Marsen had been there just before us.

He added more notes,[1] and ended the whole with an invocation:

Midnight, Saturday–Sunday, June 12–13, [1858] Oh, may I be suffused with all the energies of nature I have inhaled, and may they breathe forth in my book! Powers of artistic emotion, come to my aid! Help me resurrect the past! Beauty must guide my pen, but all must be living and true! Have pity on my purpose, oh God of all souls! Give me Strength – and Hope![2]

---

1. A visitor to the region of ancient Carthage who is familiar with Flaubert's

Tunisian notebooks (now in the Bibliothèque Historique de la Ville de Paris) is impressed by the accuracy of their topography and archaeology. Today, recent excavations of the upper part of the city, particularly of its principal ascending street, confirm other details in the novel, which Flaubert took from ancient authors. Following the death, in 1931, of his niece and heir, Mme Caroline Hamard Commanville Grout, the notes of his reading were sold at auction in several lots and widely dispersed. A portfolio in the Pierpont Morgan Library, New York, includes some of these notes, as well as replies to Flaubert from correspondents in Tunisia and France to whom he wrote for information.

The history of the region, together with the literary nostalgia of the former French protectorate, has produced place names evocative of Flaubert's brief visit. A station on the railway line which serves those suburbs of Tunis now occupying the site of ancient Carthage is named Salammbô. Another, Amilcar, recalls not only the first chapter of Flaubert's novel, but particularly its opening sentence: 'It was at Mégara, suburb of Carthage, in the gardens of Hamilcar'. Amilcar is, in fact, close to the present site of beautiful private gardens between that stop and the next – the picturesque Arab village of Sidi-Bou-Saïd, The ancient Mégara is now La Marsa, an adjacent community.

2.   *'Que toutes les énergies de la nature que j'ai aspirées me pénetrent et qu'elles s'exhalent dans mon livre. A moi, puissance de l'émotion plastique! résurrection du passé, à moi! à moi! Il faut faire, à travers le Beau, vivant et vrai quand même. Pitié pour ma volonté, Dieu des âmes! donne-moi la Force – et l'Espoir!'*

~

TO MADEMOISELLE LEROYER DE CHANTEPIE

Croisset, July 11 [1858]

. . .

Living in a house is one of the sadder aspects of civilization. I think we were made to sleep on our backs, looking up at the stars. In a few years mankind (thanks to new developments in locomotion) will revert to its nomadic state. People will travel the world from one end to the other, as they used to cross prairies and mountains: this will calm their spirits and inflate their lungs . . .

I thought of you from time to time down on the African coast, where I enjoyed myself thinking a lot of historical thoughts and meditating on the book I am going to write. I breathed deeply of the air, and stared long at the sky, the mountains, and the sea. I needed to! I've been stifling since my return from the East six years ago.[1]

I made a thorough exploration of the country around Tunis and the ruins of Carthage, I crossed the Regency from east to west, reentering Algeria via the frontier at El Kef, and crossed the eastern part of the province from Constantine to Philippeville, where I re-embarked. I was alone the whole time, very well, on horseback, and in high good spirits.

And now, everything I had done on my novel has to be done over: I was on the wrong track entirely. So it turns out that a little over a year since I first had the idea for the book, and after working hard on it most of that time, I am still only at the beginning. It will be a weighty thing to execute, I assure you. For me, at least. It's true that my intentions are not middling. I am tired of ugly things and sordid environments. *Bovary* inspired me with a long disgust for bourgeois ways. Now I'm going to live, perhaps for several years, in a splendid subject, far from the modern world I'm fed up with. What I am undertaking to do is insane, and will have no success with the public. No matter! One must write for oneself, first and foremost. Only that way does one stand a chance of producing something good . . .

1.   It was in June 1851 that Flaubert had returned to France after his eighteen-month '*voyage en Orient*' with Maxime DuCamp.

~

To Ernest Feydeau

[Croisset,] Saturday night [August 28, 1858]
· · ·

You send me news of the arts: let me repay you with an item from the country.

The Croisset baker has, as assistant breadmaker, a lad of consider-able corpulence. Maestro and servant bugger. They knead each other in the heat generated by their oven. But (and here begins the nice part) the aforesaid baker has a wife, and the two gentlemen, not satisfied with —ing[1] each other, join forces in beating the poor woman. They go at it so lustily – both for fun and out of cunt-hatred (*système Jérôme*)[2] – that the lady is sometimes bedridden for days. Yesterday, however, for the first time, she turned on them with a knife, and the arms of both of them are in horribly sliced condition. Such are the ways of our good rustics – charming, no?

You ask me what I'm doing. During the past two weeks I have read, without interrupting my work, and *for* my work, six *Mémoires* of the Academy of Inscriptions, two volumes of Ritter,[3] Samuel Bochart's *Chanaan*,[4] and various parts of Diodorus.[5] I can't possibly be finished before two years at the earliest, and once again everybody will have it in for me.

No matter. I think this is going to be a very lofty enterprise, and since our aspirations weigh more heavily in the scale of values than our works, and our desires more heavily than our actions, I may acquire considerable merit – who knows?

1. Dubiously effective censoring of the autograph or editorial copy here, perhaps by Flaubert's niece. The autograph, like those of most of the letters to Feydeau, has disappeared.
2. The reference is to '*L'Histoire de Jérôme*', in Sade's *Justine*.
3. Karl Ritter, German geographer (1779–1859): *Die Erdkunde im Verhältnis zur Natur und zur Geschichte des Menschen* (Geography in Relation to Nature and World History), 20 vols, 1817–1858. Only the volumes on Africa, doubtless those read by Flaubert, had been translated into French.
4. Samuel Bochart, French scholar (1599–1667). The *Chanaan* is part of his *Geographia Sacra*.
5. Diodorus Siculus, Greek historian of the age of Julius Caesar and Augustus.

～

The reader will hereafter be temporarily spared further annotation of Flaubert's vast, continuous reading for *Salammbô*. Indication of its extent will be copiously afforded in Chapter IX.

～

To Ernest Feydeau

Croisset, Sunday [December 19, 1858]

. . .

You ask me what I'm up to. Here's your answer.

I get up at noon and go to bed between three and four in the morning. I take a nap about five in the afternoon. I scarcely see the daylight – a horrible way to live in winter – and am thus totally unable to distinguish the days of the week or day from night. My existence is extravagantly unsociable; I love its uneventfulness, its quiet. It is complete and objective nothingness. And I am not working too badly, at least for me. In eighteen days I have written ten pages, read *The Retreat of the Ten Thousand*[1] in its entirety, and analysed six treatises by Plutarch, the great hymn to Ceres (in the Homeric poems, in Greek), and Erasmus's *Encomium moriae*; plus Tabarin[2] at night, or rather in the morning, in bed, for diversion. So there you are. And in two days I'll begin Chapter III. This will be Chapter IV if I retain the preface; but no – no preface, no explanation. Chapter I took me two months last summer. Nevertheless I shan't hesitate to scrap it even though in itself I'm very fond of it.

I'm in a terrific funk because in Chapter III I'm going to repeat an effect already used in Chapter II.[3] Clever writers would think up tricks to conjure the difficulty away, but I'm going to plunge straight into it, like an ox. Such is my system. But how I'll sweat! And how I'll despair while putting said passage together! Seriously, I think that no one has *ever* undertaken a subject so difficult as regards style. At every line, every word, language fails me, and the insufficiency of vocabulary is such that I'm very often forced to change details. It will kill me, my friend, it will kill me. No matter: it begins to be tremendous fun.

I've finally achieved the erection, Monsieur, by dint of self-flagellation and masturbation. Let's hope there's joy to come . . .

1. Xenophon's *Anabasis*.
2. Tabarin was a seventeenth-century Parisian street comedian. A collection of farces and dialogues attributed to him had recently been reprinted.
3. Max Aprile points out that this refers to Flaubert's numbering of chapters in early drafts, not in the volume as published: 'Flaubert's fear of repetition therefore refers to the Hannon and Giscon episodes, Chapters II and IV.' (Personal communication.)

~

To ERNEST FEYDEAU
[Croisset] Tuesday evening [January 11, 1859]
. . .

No, my friend! I do not admit that women are competent to judge the human heart. Their understanding of it is always personal and relative. They are the hardest, the cruellest, of creatures. 'Woman is the desolation of the righteous,' said Proudhon. I have little admiration for said gentleman, but that aphorism is nothing less than a stroke of genius.

As far as literature is concerned, women are capable only of a certain delicacy and sensitivity. Everything that is truly sublime, truly great, escapes them. Our indulgence towards them is one of the reasons for the moral abasement that is prostrating us. We all display an inconceivable cowardice towards our mothers, our sisters, our daughters, our wives, and our mistresses. Never has the tit been responsible for more kinds of abject behaviour than now. And the Church (Catholic, Apostolic, and Roman) has given proof of the greatest good sense in promulgating the dogma of the Immaculate Conception – it epitomizes the emotional life of the nineteenth century. Poor scrofulous swooning century, with its horror of anything strong, of solid food, its fondness for lolling in the laps of women, like a sick child!

'Woman, what have I to do with thee?'[1] is a remark that I find more splendid than any of the celebrated sayings of history. It is the cry of the pure intellect, the brain's protest against the womb. And it has this to be said for it: it has always aroused the indignation of idiots.

Our 'mother-cult' is one of those things that will inspire future generations to helpless laughter. So too our reverence for 'love': this will be thrown into the same rubbish bin with the 'sensibility' and 'nature' of a hundred years ago.

Only one poet, in my opinion, understood these charming animals – namely, the master of masters, Shakespeare the omniscient. His women are *worse* or *better* than his men. He portrays them as overenthusiastic beings, never as reasonable ones. That is why his feminine characters are at once so ideal and so true.

In short, *never* pay any attention to what they say about a book. For them, temperament is everything – the occasion, the place, the *author*. As for knowing whether a detail (exquisite or even sublime in itself) strikes a false note in relation to the whole – no! A thousand times no!

I note with pleasure that printer's ink is beginning to stink in your nostrils. In my opinion it is one of the filthiest inventions of mankind. I resisted it until I was thirty-five, even though I began scribbling at eleven. A book is something essentially organic, a part of ourselves. We tear out a length of gut from our bellies and serve it up to the bourgeois. Drops of our hearts' blood are visible in every letter we trace. But once our work is printed – goodbye! It belongs to everybody. The crowd tramples on us. It is the height of prostitution, and the vilest kind. But the platitude is that it's all very fine, whereas to rent out one's arse for ten francs is an infamy. So be it! . . .

1. John 2:4.

~

To Mademoiselle Leroyer de Chantepie
Croisset, February 18, 1859

. . .

It's a sad story about your relative, the girl driven insane by religious ideas, but not an uncommon one. A robust constitution is needed if one is to scale the peaks of mysticism without losing one's head. And then the whole thing involves (especially for women) questions of temperament, which complicate the malady. Don't you see that they are all in love with Adonis? The eternal bridegroom is what they yearn for. Whether ascetic or lustful, they dream of love, *le grand amour*; and in order to be cured (at least temporarily) what they need is not an idea, but something tangible – a man, a child, a lover. That may sound cynical to you. But human nature is not my invention. I am convinced that the most raging material appetites express themselves unwittingly in outbursts of idealism, just as the most obscene carnal excesses are engendered by pure desire for the impossible, ethereal aspiration toward supreme bliss. Besides, neither I nor anyone else knows the meaning of those two words: 'soul' and 'body' – nor where one leaves off and the other begins. We are aware of certain *drives*, and that is all. Materialism and spiritualism still weigh too heavily on the study of man to permit an impartial investigation of all these phenomena. The anatomy of the human heart is as yet uncharted. So how can you expect it to be cured? To have embarked on such studies will remain the nineteenth century's sole claim to fame. The historical sense is a very new thing in the world. Ideas will now be studied like facts; beliefs dissected like organisms. There exists an entire school that is quietly working on these things, and it will bring results, I am sure.

Do you read Renan's splendid books? Do you know Lanfrey's, or Maury's?[1]

I have had occasion recently to return to those psychomedical studies that so fascinated me ten years ago, when I was [first] writing my *Saint Anthony*. In connection with my *Salammbô* I have been investigating hysteria and mental derangement. There are treasures to be discovered in those fields. But life is short and Art is long, indeed nearly impossible when one is writing in a language that is worn to the point of being threadbare, so worm-eaten that it frays at every touch. What discouragement, what anguish, the love of Beauty brings! Besides – I have undertaken something that is unachievable. No matter: if I stimulate a few noble imaginations I'll not have wasted my time. My task is about a quarter done. Still two years' work ahead.

1. Pierre Lanfrey (1828–1877), French historian and politician, republican, author of works of an anticlerical and rationalizing tendency.

    Alfred Maury (1817–1892), professor at the Collège de France, who wrote studies of psychology and religion and collaborated with Napoleon III on the latter's biography of Julius Caesar. He was later appointed Director General of the National Archives. (See Flaubert's letter to Maury of August 20, 1866.)

∾

To Ernest Feydeau

[Croisset, early August 1859 (?)]

. . .

I don't think that everything can be said well. Some ideas are impossible (for example, those which are hackneyed, or radically wrong), and since *style is merely a manner of thinking*, if your conception is weak your writing will never be strong. For instance: I have just recorrected my fourth chapter. It is a tour de force (I think) of conciseness and clarity if one examines it sentence by sentence; which doesn't keep said chapter from being utterly boring and seeming very long and very dim, because the concept, the basis, or the plan (I don't know what, exactly) has a hidden defect – which I will ferret out. Style *underlies* words as much as it is embodied in them. It is as much the soul of a work as its flesh.

Tonight I am going to begin my sixth chapter. I have thus reached the end of my first third; and yet there still remains much in it that will have to be changed, I'm sure.

Oh, my friend, don't fall into that easy old cliché that is such a plague to me: 'You're lucky to be able to work without pressure, thanks to having private means.' My fellow writers are constantly throwing in my face the few francs of income that keep me from starving. It's easier to do that than to imitate me. I mean, to live as I do: (1) in the country three-quarters of the year; (2) without a wife (a rather delicate little point, but considerable), without friends, horse, or dog – in short, without any of the attributes of human life; (3) and then, for me everything outside the work itself counts for nothing. Success, time, money, publication, are relegated to the lowest level of my mind, off in some very vague horizons that are of no concern to me whatever. All that seems to me dull as dishwater, and unworthy (I repeat the word, *unworthy*) of exciting one's brain about.

The impatience of literary folk to see themselves in print, acted, known, praised, I find astonishing – like a madness. That seems to me to have no more to do with a writer's work than dominoes or politics. *Voilà.*

Anybody can do as I do – work just as slowly as I, and better. All you have to do is rid yourself of certain tastes, and sacrifice a few pleasures. I am not at all virtuous, but I am consistent. And though I have great needs (which I never mention), I would rather be a wretched monitor in a school than write four lines for money. I could have been rich; I said fuck all that, and I continue to live like a Bedouin, in my desert and my pride. Shit, shit, *shit*: such is my motto. And I embrace you tenderly.

~

To Mademoiselle Amélie Bosquet[1]

Wednesday morning [November (?), 1859]

You mistook the *sense* of my last letter. And I doubtless overdid my reproaches, since you ask me to excuse you. One thing is sure: the pleasure afforded by the amends is greater than the pain caused

Flaubert, portrait drawing by E. Liphart

Louise Colet,
by Winterhalter

Flaubert in his twenties,
by Desandré

Ernest Commanville –
'His forehead is *flat*',
George Sand

Caroline Commanville

27. avril 1880. SAINT POLYCARPE

ÉDUCATION SENTIMENTALE

MADAME BOVARY.

SALAMMBÔ

LA TENTATION DE St·ANTOINE

M. Gustave Flaubert.

MENU

Potage velouté à la Bovary
Saumon, sauce matho
Poulet Homais
Filet. Éducation Sentimentale
Jambon St antoine
Salade au Cœur Simple
Haricots verts, Hamilcar
Glace Salammbô
Fromage (aux mangeurs de choses
immondes.)
Dessert
café. vins St Julien (Legende) champagne etc

The last Saint Polycarp dinner:
'The Saint Polycarp celebration left me speechless! . . . The menu
[was] composed of dishes all named for my books.'

by the offence. Only women know how to wound and how to caress! We men are heavy-handed in comparison.

My liaison with Mme Colet left me with no lasting 'wound', in the usual emotional and deep sense of the word. What remains is rather the memory (and, even now, the sensation) of prolonged irritation. Her book has been the crowning touch. Add to it the comments, questions, jokes, and allusions I have been subjected to since the publication of said work. When I saw that you, too, were joining in the game I lost my patience a little, I admit, because in public I keep my dignity. Don't you see? Don't think I hold it against you. No, I embrace you warmly for the nice things you say to me. Please believe me.

Why *did* you join in the taunts? Why did you act like the others? 'They' have a cut-and-dried opinion of me that nothing will eradicate (it's true that I do nothing to undeceive them), namely: that I'm utterly devoid of feeling, that I'm a buffoon, a womanizer (a kind of Romantic Paul de Kock),[2] something between a bohemian and a pedant. Some even suspect me of being a habitual drunkard, etc. etc.

But I think I am neither a hypocrite nor a poseur. No matter: people always take me for something I'm not. Whose fault is that? Mine, no doubt? I am more elegiac than people think: I pay a price for my five feet eight inches[3] and my ruddy complexion.

I am still as timid as an adolescent, and quite capable of preserving withered bouquets as keepsakes. In my youth I *loved*, inordinately – loved without any return, deeply, silently.[4] Nights spent gazing at the moon, dreams of eloping with a beloved, of travels in Italy, dreams of conquering fame for *her* sake, spasms at the scent of a perfumed shoulder, sudden blanchings when eye met eye – I have experienced all that, and know it well. In the heart of each of us there is royal chamber. I have walled mine up, but it is there.

Everyone has talked ad nauseam about the prostitution of women. But not a word about that of men. I have suffered the tortures of a whore, as has every man who after loving long has wanted to love no longer.

And then one reaches the age when one is *afraid*, afraid of everything – of a liaison, of being shackled, interfered with: one longs for happiness, yet dreads it. Isn't it so?

And yet it would be so easy to live a tolerable life! But we seek emotions that are intense, excessive, unqualified, whereas only the composite, the greyed, is practicable. Our grandfathers, and especially our grandmothers, had more sense than we, no?

It seems to me that our little disagreement has made us even better friends than before. Is this an illusion? No: you have learned that I am more serious than I seem, and I have come to know how very good you are. So let us exchange a long, firm handshake.

Tell me about yourself, when you have nothing better to do. Work as much as you can: that is still the best way. The moral of *Candide*, 'we must cultivate our gardens', must be the rule for people like us, those 'who haven't found the answer'. Does one, in fact, ever find it? And when one does, one seeks something else.

1. A feminist writer in Rouen. Louise Colet, the mistress with whom Flaubert had broken in 1855, and who had thereupon depicted him unfavourably in a novel, *Une Histoire de Soldat* (1856), now in 1859 had renewed the attack in another novel, *Lui*. Mlle Bosquet was indiscreet enough to refer to this in a letter to Flaubert. His sharp reply to which he alludes here is missing from the collection of his letters that she gave to the Municipal Library of Rouen in 1892.

    In August 1859, Flaubert wrote to Ernest Feydeau, whose novel, *Fanny*, Louise Colet had recently reviewed: 'As for the widow Colet, she has plans, I don't know just what. But she has plans. I know her through and through. Her praising *Fanny* was done for a *purpose*. Now that you've written to her she'll invite you to come to see her. Go, but be on your guard. She's a pernicious creature. If you want a good laugh, read her *Histoire de Soldat* . . . You'll recognize your friend in it, painted in odious colours – an attempt to smear. And that's not all. She has made me the subject of an unperformed play and a number of short pieces. All because I withdrew *my* 'piece' from her . . .'

2. Charles-Paul de Kock (1794–1871), the author of best-selling humorous novels about the French bourgeoisie.

3. At this height Flaubert was so conspicuously taller than most Frenchmen of his time that he was sometimes called a 'giant' or a 'gendarme'.

4. Flaubert is probably thinking of Elise Schlesinger (see Volume I and pp. 488–9 and 564 below).

∼

To Madame Roger des Genettes[1]

[1859 or 1860?]

. . .

I pity you on the death of your friend. It's no light matter to lose those we love. I myself have wrapped one after another in their shrouds, sat through many a wake. The body of the man I loved best in the world practically fell apart in my hands.[2] Once you have kissed a corpse on the forehead, something of it always remains on your lips – an infinite bitterness, an aftertaste of annihilation that nothing ever effaces. One must look up at the stars, and say 'There perhaps I will go.' But I am repelled by the way all religions speak about God – they treat him with such certainty, such nonchalance and familiarity. I am especially revolted by priests, who have his name on their lips incessantly. It's like a chronic sneeze with them: 'God's goodness', 'God's anger', 'an offence against God'. That's the way they talk. It means thinking of him as a man, and, what's worse, as a bourgeois. They still persist in bedecking him with attributes, the way savages put feathers on their fetish. Some paint infinity in blue, others in black. It's all at the level of cannibals. We're still at the stage of browsing on grass and going on all fours, despite our balloons. The idea of God that mankind has made for itself doesn't go beyond that of an oriental monarch surrounded by his court. The religious concept is thus several centuries behind the social, and there are plenty of clowns pretending to swoon with admiration before it.

1. Mme Edma Roger des Genettes, so graceful that she was known as 'La Sylphide', had become for a time the mistress of Louis Bouilhet after reading aloud from his poem *Melaenis* in Louise Colet's salon in 1852. Later she became Flaubert's friend and correspondent. His letters to her exist chiefly in the form of copies in her hand, undated and incomplete.
2. A reference to Flaubert's helping enshroud his friend Alfred Le Poittevin in April 1848 (see Volume I, p. 135).

∼

To Madame Roger des Genettes

[1861?]

. . .

A good subject for a novel is one that comes all at once, in a single spurt. It is a matrix idea, from which all the others derive. An author is not at all free to write this or that. He does not choose his subject. That is what the public and the critics do not understand. Therein lies the secret of masterpieces – in the concordance of the subject and the author's temperament.

You are right: Lucretius must be spoken of with respect. I see only Byron as comparable with him, and Byron has neither his seriousness nor his sincerity in sorrow. The melancholy of the antique world seems to me more profound than that of the moderns, all of whom more or less imply that beyond the dark void lies immortality. But for the ancients that 'black hole' was infinity itself; their dreams loom and vanish against a background of immutable ebony. No crying out, no convulsions – nothing but the fixity of a pensive gaze. With the gods gone, and Christ not yet come, there was a unique moment, from Cicero to Marcus Aurelius, when man stood alone. Nowhere else do I find that particular grandeur. But what makes Lucretius intolerable is his physics, which he presents as certainty. It is because he didn't *doubt* enough that he is weak: he wanted to explain, to conclude. If he had had only the *spirit* of Epicurus, without his system, all aspects of his work would have been immortal and *radical.* No matter: our modern poets are meagre thinkers compared with such a man.

∼

To Charles Baudelaire

Croisset, Monday [June 25, 1860]

You are very kind, my dear Baudelaire, to have sent me such a book.[1] Everything about it pleases me – the topic, the style, even the paper. I have read it very attentively. But first of all I must thank you for introducing me to so charming a man as *le sieur* De Quincey! How one loves him!

Here – to get the 'but' over with quickly – is my sole objection: it seems to me that with a subject you have treated so loftily, in a study that marks the beginning of a new science, a work of observation and induction, you have (and repeatedly) insisted too much (?) on 'the Spirit of Evil'. One senses something like a leaven of Catholicism here and there. I would have preferred you not to condemn hashish, opium, overindulgence. How do you know what may ultimately come of all that?[2]

But note that this is merely my personal opinion, which I do not insist on at all. I refuse utterly to admit the right of criticism to substitute its opinion for another's. And what I object to in your book is perhaps what constitutes its originality and the very mark of your talent. Not to resemble one's neighbour: that is everything.

Now that I have confessed the sum of my grievance, I can scarcely begin to tell you how excellent I found your book from beginning to end. The style is very lofty, very assured, very incisive. In '*Le Poëme du haschisch*' I deeply admire pages 27–33, 51–55, 76,[3] and everything that follows. You have found the way to be classical while remaining the transcendent Romantic we love.

As for the part called '*Un mangeur d'opium*', I don't know what you owe to De Quincey, but in any case it is a *marvel*. I know of no figure more sympathetic than he, to me at least.

These particular drugs have always raised great longings in me. I even own some excellent hashish, prepared by Gastinel, the pharmacist. *But I am afraid of it.* For which I blame myself.[4]

Do you know, in Escayrac de Lauture's *Soudan*,[5] an entire particular theogony and cosmogony invented by an opium-smoker? I remember it as being 'quite something', but I prefer Mr De Quincey. Poor man! What became of Miss Ann?[6] Thanks are due you, too, for the little note about moral critics. I for one was touched, or rather flattered in my sensitive spot.

I impatiently await the new *Fleurs du mal.**[7] How hard you work! and how well!

Adieu – here's a handshake that will dislocate your shoulder.

*Here my objection is not valid, for the poet has the perfect right to think what he likes. But a scientist? Perhaps I'm talking nonsense? Nevertheless I think I know what I mean. We'll talk about it another time.

1. Baudelaire's new volume, *Les Paradis artificiels*, whose two principal parts are '*Le Poëme du haschisch*', a prose poem about hashish-taking, its effects

and after-effects; and '*Un mangeur d'opium*', an adaptation and partial translation of Thomas De Quincey's *Confessions of an English Opium-Eater* and *Suspiris de Profundis*. There are interesting discussions of *Les Paradis artificiels* in Enid Starkie's *Baudelaire* (London: Faber and Faber, 1957; New York, New Directions, 1958), and in Alethea Hayter's *Opium and the Romantic Imagination* (London: Faber and Faber, 1968).

2. Flaubert means 'Who knows what beautiful works of art may result from taking opium and hashish?' (J.B.)

3. Pages 27–33 of the first edition of *Les Paradis artificiels* provide a description of hashish, the circumstances under which it is most safely taken, and some of its effects. Pages 51–55 treat of hallucinations that may be caused by hashish. On pages 76 et seq. Baudelaire describes the human type 'whom the eighteenth century called *l'homme sensible* [the sensitive man], whom the Romantic school dubbed *l'homme incompris* [the incomprehensible man], and whom bourgeois families and the bourgeoisie in general commonly stigmatize with the epithet *original*'. For the impression made on Flaubert by the terms in this last passage, see his letter to Laure de Maupassant, p. 372–4.

4. Flaubert is responding self-consciously to a passage in which Baudelaire says: 'The man who has long been addicted to opium or hashish and is enfeebled by his long bondage, and who nevertheless has been able to find the energy necessary to free himself, seems to me like an escaped prisoner. He inspires me with more admiration than the prudent man who has never succumbed, having always been careful to avoid temptation.'

    J. B. Gastinel was professor of pharmacology in Cairo, author of works on hashish and opium.

5. *Le Désert et le Soudan*, by Comte d'Escayrac de Lauture (Paris, 1853).

6. The fifteen-year-old girl who was De Quincey's companion in the night streets of London, who brought him 'port wine and spices' when he fainted, and whom he sought in vain on his return from Oxford. Baudelaire's words, in his paraphrase of De Quincey, are similar to Flaubert's: '*Mais la pauvre Ann, qu'en est-il advenu?*' De Quincey's are: 'Meanwhile, what had become of Ann?'

7. Flaubert had seen, in his copy of *Les Paradis artificiels*, that the publisher advertised the first edition of *Les Fleurs du mal* as being 'sold out' and announced the second as being in press. It was published in 1861. Actually, most of the first edition had been destroyed by court order following Baudelaire's conviction for 'offence against public morality'.

CHARLES BAUDELAIRE TO FLAUBERT

June 26, 1860

My dear Flaubert:

I thank you most heartily for your excellent letter. I was much struck by your observation, and after delving very sincerely into the memory of my daydreams I saw that I have always been obsessed by the impossibility of accounting for certain precipitate human actions or thoughts without the hypothesis of the intervention of an exterior evil force. That is a mighty confession, for which the entire confederated nineteenth century will not make me blush. Note, however, that I do not renounce the pleasure of changing my ideas or of contradicting myself.

One of these days, if I may, on my way to Honfleur I will stop at Rouen, but since I presume you are like me and hate surprises, I will give you ample notice.

You tell me that I work a great deal. Are you making fun of me? Many people, myself included, consider that I do very little. To *work* is to work ceaselessly, to renounce the senses, never daydream – and to be *pure will,* always in motion. Perhaps I shall reach that point.

All yours – your very devoted friend.

I have always dreamed of reading the *Temptation of Saint Anthony* in its entirety, and also another singular book which you have never published even in part (*Novembre*).[1] And how goes *Carthage?*

1. Baudelaire had read the portions of *The Temptation of Saint Anthony* printed in Théophile Gautier's magazine *L'Artiste* for December 1856 and January 1857, and in his review of *Madame Bovary* had called *The Temptation* 'the secret chamber' of Flaubert's mind, 'clearly the more interesting for poets and philosophers'. Baudelaire did not live to see the final version, which was not published until 1874. Flaubert's short, youthful, very Romantic novel *Novembre*, written when he was twenty, he would occasionally read to friends, but its publication would be only posthumous.

∾

TO EDMOND AND JULES DE GONCOURT

Croisset, July 3 [1860]

Since you are worried about *Carthage,* here is what I can tell you about it:

I think my eyes were bigger than my stomach. 'Reality' is almost impossible with such a subject. There remains the dodge of 'going poetic'. But that would mean rehashing old stuff, familiar from Télémaque to *Les Martyrs*. I don't speak of the archaeological research, which mustn't call attention to itself, or of the language to fit the form – a near impossibility. To be authentic I'd have to be obscure, talk gibberish, and stuff the book with notes; whereas if one sticks to 'Ye Olde Frensh' literary tone one becomes banal. '*Problème!*' as *Père* Hugo would say.

Despite all that, I press on, though devoured by worries and doubts. I console myself with the thought that I'm attempting something worthwhile. That's the whole story.

The standard of the Doctrine will be boldly unfurled this time, you may be sure.[1] For this book proves nothing, states nothing. It is neither historical, nor satirical, nor humorous. However, it may be stupid.

I am now beginning Chapter VIII. After which there will remain seven to be done: I shan't be finished for at least another eighteen months.

It was not out of mere politeness that I congratulated you on your last book[2] and on the kind of work you do. I love history, madly. The dead are more to my taste than the living. Whence this lure of the past? Why have you made me fall in love with Louis XV's mistresses? This kind of love, incidentally, is something new in mankind. The historical sense dates from yesterday. And it is perhaps the best thing about the nineteenth century.

What are you going to do now? As for me, I am giving myself over to the Cabala, to the Mishna, to the military art of the ancients, etc. (a mass of reading that is of no service to me but which I undertake through excess of conscience and also, a little, for the fun of it); and I keep being distressed by the assonances I come upon in my prose. My life is as flat as the table I write on. Day follows day, and outwardly, at least, each is like the other.

In my periods of despair I dream of travel – a poor remedy.

The two of you seem to be virtuously bored in the bosom of your family, amid the delights of the country. I understand this condition, having very often endured it myself . . .

1.   The doctrine of 'Art for art's sake' – '*L'Art pour l'art*'.

2. *Les Maîtresses de Louis XV.*

~

Flaubert's correspondence is slimmer concerning the progress of *Salammbô* than was the case with *Madame Bovary* (or will be, with *L'Éducation sentimentale*). During these years there is lacking any intimate correspondence with a woman to whom he could pour out his thoughts and his news as he once had to Louise Colet; most of his letters to Louis Bouilhet are lost, and, besides, the two friends saw each other at Croisset almost every Sunday. When Flaubert was not writing *Salammbô* he was reading for it. After three years of work the Carthaginian novel had inevitably become a kind of intoxication, and as in all intoxications tristesse was one of its elements. 'I'm on a spree with antiquity, the way others gorge themselves on wine'; '*In order not to live*, I plunge into art, like a man in despair; I make myself drunk with ink as others do with wine' were two of the messages he sent to friends as the book advanced. 'The things I'm reading,' he told Ernest Feydeau, 'weren't written to be amusing – Mosander, the Emperor Leo, Vegetius, Justus Lipsius'; and also among his authors were 'Cedrenus, Socrates, Sozomen, Eusebius, and a treatise by M. Obry on the immortality of the soul among the Jews'. 'When people read *Salammbô* they won't think of the author, I hope. Few will suspect how depressed one had to be to undertake the resuscitation of Carthage: it's a Thebaid I was pushed into by my disgust with modern life.'

In letters to friends he groaned about climactic scenes:

> I shall soon be in the middle of my Chapter VIII (The Battle of the Macar) . . . The narration and description of a battle of antiquity is no small task, for one keeps falling into the eternal 'epic battle' that all your high-toned writers have imitated from translations of Homer. There's no end to the asininities I keep skirting with this damned book. There will be a pretty weight off my mind when it's finished. If only I were at the end of my tenth chapter: that's where the fucking's about to begin.
>
> At the moment, I'm overwhelmed with fatigue. I'm carrying two entire armies on my shoulders – thirty thousand men on one side, eleven thousand on the other, not counting

the elephants with their elephantarchs, the camp followers, and the baggage!

Let's be ferocious . . .! Let's pour brandy on to this century of sugar water. Let's drown the bourgeois in a grog eleven thousand degrees strong, and may his mouth burn! May he roar with pain!

My determination doesn't weaken, and as background the thing is becoming quite dainty: my men have already begun to *eat* each other. But imagine my anxiety: I am just now composing a sex scene – *the* sex scene of the book. It must be at once lewd, chaste, mystical, and realistic. A slavering such as was never seen, and yet the reader must see it.

The ferocities he was inventing, or gathering from old sources, stimulated Flaubert's habitual impatience with niceties. Writing to the Goncourts to congratulate them on their novel *Soeur Philomène*, he nevertheless complained, as one familiar with doctors and medical students, of the insipidity of its hospital scenes. 'In the Rouen asylum there was an idiot known as "Mirabeau", who *for a cup of coffee* would copulate with dead women on the dissecting table. I'm sorry you couldn't have introduced this little episode into your book: it would have pleased the ladies. It's true that "Mirabeau" was a coward, and unworthy of such an honour, for one day he funked it badly when faced with a woman who had been guillotined.'

Indeed the composition of his Carthaginian slaughterings seems to have turned his thoughts back more often than usual to the hospital where his father had been surgeon-in-chief (his brother Achille was now co-director), and where he and his sister, as children, had peered through windows into the dissecting room at 'the cadavers on their slabs'.

~

To Ernest Feydeau

[1861 (?)]

. . .

It's a strange thing, the way I'm attracted by medical studies. That's the way the intellectual wind is blowing nowadays. I long to dissect. If I were ten years younger I'd do just that. In Rouen there is an excellent man, the medical director of the insane asylum, who is giving a very curious little course for his close friends on hysteria, nymphomania, etc. I haven't the time to attend, and yet I've long been meditating a novel on insanity, or rather on how one becomes insane. I'm furious at being so slow a writer, at being stuck in all kinds of reading and revising. Life is short and Art is long! And then, what's the use? No matter: 'We must cultivate our gardens.' The day before his death Socrates in his prison asked a musician to teach him an air on the lyre. 'What's the use,' said the man, 'since you're about to die?' 'To know it before I die,' answered Socrates. That is one of the loftiest things, morally speaking, that I know of, and I would rather have said it than taken Sebastopol.

. . .

～

During the labours on *Salammbô* there was printed in Brussels and more or less openly 'smuggled' into France a new book of ultra-Romantic poetry by one of Flaubert's old heroes, a political self-exile who was denied French publication – a book whose sonority, sweep and blazing imagery, although Flaubert claimed it made him despair about his own work, quite clearly had the opposite effect, rousing him from his fatigue and giving him new wind. 'Something magnificent has just been published,' he wrote to Mlle Leroyer de Chantepie, '*La Légende des siècles*, by Hugo. This colossal poet has never been so lofty. To you who love the ideal, and recognize it, I recommend the tales of chivalry in the first volume. Such enthusiasm, such strength, such language! It makes one despair, to write in the wake of such a man. Read this, gorge yourself on it, for it is beautiful and salutary.'

To Ernest Feydeau, on the same theme: 'What a poet! Good God, what a poet! I have just swallowed both volumes at one gulp. I miss you! I miss Bouilhet! I long for intelligent ears, since I feel like shouting three thousand lines such as have never before been written! And when I say shouting – No! *Yelling!* I'm beside myself! Tie me up! Ah, I feel better! Old Hugo has driven me mad!'

And to Jules Duplan: 'What a tremendous, marvellous man! Never has anyone written poetry like *Les Lions!*'

When *Salammbô* was almost complete, Flaubert was willing to read parts of it to friends.

~

To EDMOND AND JULES DE GONCOURT
Paris [shortly before May 6, 1861]

The solemn event will take place on Monday, grippe or no grippe. And I beg your pardon for having made you wait so long. Here is the programme:

1. I'll begin my bellowing at four o'clock sharp. So come about three.

2. At seven, *dîner oriental.* You will be served human flesh, bourgeois' brains, and tigresses' clitorises sautéed in rhinoceros butter.

3. After coffee, resumption of Punic caterwauling until listeners' last gasp.

Does this suit you?

P.S. *Punctuality!* And *mystery*!

~

The Goncourt brothers describe the 'solemn event' in one of the worst-written entries in their immense *Journal* (that of May 6, 1861). The following is an attempt to render into readable English the opinions expressed in the unwieldy French of their first paragraphs:

At four o'clock we arrive chez Flaubert, who has invited us to a grand reading of *Salammbô*, along with a painter whom we find there, Gleyre . . .

From four to six, Flaubert reads in that resounding, bellowing voice of his, which has the lulling effect of a purr, but a *bronze* purr. At seven we dine . . . Then, after dinner and a pipe, the reading is resumed. Certain portions he doesn't read completely, but summarizes, and we go all the way through to the last completed chapter, Salammbô's fornication with Mâtho. By this time it is two in the morning.

I am going to set down here what I sincerely think of this book by a man whom I love — there are few of whom I can say that — a man whose first book I admired.

Salammbô does not come up to what I expected of Flaubert. His personality, so very carefully concealed in *Madame Bovary* as to be in fact absent from that very impersonal book, is here revealed – inflated, melodramatic, declamatory, luxuriating in over-accentuation and in crude, almost garish, colours. Flaubert sees the Orient, and the antique Orient, in the guise of present-day Algerian decor. Some of the effects are childish, others ridiculous. His struggle with Chateaubriand is the great defect, and deprives the book of originality: the reader is constantly put in mind of *Les Martyrs*.

Immensely fatiguing are the eternal descriptions, the minute, button-by-button itemizations of every character and every costume, which destroy any possibility of grand group effects. All the effects are minuscular, concentrated on a single point; faces are obscured by trappings, feelings are lost in landscapes.

Unquestionably, immense effort, infinite patience, and rare talent have gone into this attempt to reconstruct a vanished civilization in all its detail. But this project – in my opinion doomed from the start – Flaubert has not been able to *illuminate*: there are none of those revelations by analogy which enable one to discover something of the soul of a nation no longer in existence.

. . . The feelings of his characters . . . are the banal feelings of mankind in general, not of Carthaginian mankind; and his Mâtho is basically nothing but an operatic tenor in a barbaric poem.

The Goncourts' verdict was prophetic.

With the end of *Salammbô* in sight, Flaubert was again exhausted and prey to depression. Again he confided in Ernest Feydeau.

❦

To Ernest Feydeau

Croisset, July 15, 1861

You say you're not very cheerful: well, I'm not precisely joyful, myself. *Carthage* will make me die of fury yet. I am now full of doubts about the ensemble, about the general plan; I think there are too many military men about. That is historical, I know. But if a novel is as boring as a scientific book, *bon soir*! Goodbye, Art! In short, I pass my time telling myself I'm an idiot, and my heart is full of sadness and bitterness.

But my will is as strong as ever, and I press on. Now I'm beginning the siege of Carthage. I'm lost in battle-engines – ballistas and scorpions[1] – and it all passes my understanding as well as everybody else's. There has been a lot written about such things, but nothing very clear. To give you an idea of the nice little preparatory work that certain passages call for, I have read since yesterday sixty pages (folio, double-column) of Justus Lipsius's *Politicorum*.

· · ·

1. 'Scorpions': the ancient name for a kind of catapult.

~

To ERNEST FEYDEAU

Croisset, September 16, 1861

If I don't write, my friend, blame only my extreme lassitude. There are days when I haven't the strength to lift the pen. I sleep ten hours a night and two during the day. *Carthage* will be the end of me if it goes on, and I'm not yet at the end of *it*. Still, by the beginning of next month I'll have finished my siege; but it will take all of October to reach my Chapter XIV, which will be followed by a single short one. It's taking a long time, and the *writing* is becoming more and more impossible. In short, I'm like a toad squashed by a paving-stone, like a dog with its guts crushed out by a shit-wagon, like a clot of snot under a policeman's boot, etc. The military art of the ancients makes my head swim; I'm stuffed with it; I vomit catapults, have hoisting machines up my arse, and piss scorpions.

As for what everybody is going to say, do you want to know how I really feel? As long as they don't say it to my face, that's all I ask.

· · ·

~

To JULES DUPLAN

Croisset, September 25, 1861

I'm physically tired, my muscles are sore. The poisoning of Bovary made me throw up into my chamber pot; the assault on

Carthage is giving me aches and pains in my arms – such, nonetheless, is one of the more agreeable effects of my profession! – and then the thought of all the ineptitudes I'm going to hear offered about my book depresses me in advance. That prospect I found rather entertaining when I was in the middle of the book, but now it nauseates me.

. . .

∿

To Jules de Goncourt

Croisset, Friday [early October 1861]

. . .

I'm at the end of my tether! The siege of Carthage, which I'm just finishing, has been the end of me. War machines are sawing my back in half, I'm sweating blood, pissing boiling water, shitting catapults and farting slingsmen's stones . . . I've succeeded in introducing, into the same chapter, a shower of shit and a procession of pederasts. I've stopped there. Am I being too sober? . . .

∿

For one of his last scenes he read treatises on the eating of human flesh, by Plutarch and by 'Dr Savigny, the doctor of the raft of the Méduse';[1] and in his 1862 New Year letter to the Goncourts: 'I'm about halfway through my last chapter. The funfair I'm producing will make honest citizens vomit with disgust. I'm piling horror on horror. Twenty thousand of my characters have just died from starvation and cannibalism; the rest will end up trodden by elephants and devoured by lions.'

On April 24, 1862, he wrote from Paris to Mlle Leroyer de Chantepie: 'Last Sunday, at seven in the morning, I finally finished my novel *Salammbô*. Corrections and copying will take another month, and I'll return here in mid-September to watch over publication, which will be in late October. But I'm at the end of my tether. I run a temperature every evening, and can scarcely hold a pen. The end was heavy work, very hard to bring off.'

Only at the beginning of July could he write to the Goncourts: '*Salammbô* is off my hands at last. The fair copy went to Paris on

Monday . . . The work was interminable, but I finally resigned myself to considering it finished. Now the umbilical cord is cut.'

About publication, he had written to Mlle Leroyer de Chantepie in January 1862: 'I don't know whether I'll publish immediately or wait until October, because of the great Hugo's *Les Misérables*, the first two volumes of which will appear next month. This colossal publication will continue until May (two volumes are to appear each month), and after May is a bad season for books. I think it would be a bit imprudent and impudent to risk appearing alongside something so great. There are certain people to whom one has to bow, and say "*Après vous, Monsieur.*" Hugo is one of them.'

But then he read *Les Misérables*.

1. The raft (made famous by Géricault's painting, exhibited in the Salon of 1819) carrying survivors of a shipwreck off the west coast of Africa in 1816.

∼

To Madame Roger des Genettes

[Croisset, July 1862]

[. . .][1] such threadbare stuff as *Les Misérables*. But it is not permitted to say anything against it. One would have the air of a police spy.[2] The author's position is impregnable, unassailable. I, who have spent my life adoring him, am at the present moment *indignant*! I have to explode.

I find neither truth nor greatness in this book. As for the style, it strikes me as deliberately incorrect and low. It's a way of flattering the populace. Hugo is taking pains to be nice to everybody: Saint-Simonians, Philippistes, and even innkeepers – the lot. [. . .] Let truth take care of itself, if it can. Where are there prostitutes like Fantine, convicts like Valjean, and politicians like the stupid cocos of the ABC? Not once do you see them *suffer*, in the depths of their souls. They are puppets, figures made of sugar, beginning with Monseigneur Bienvenu. In his socialist mania Hugo slanders the Church just as he slanders the poor. Where will you find a bishop who asks a *conventionnel*[3] for his blessing? Where will you find a factory that would discharge a girl for having had a baby? Etc. And the digressions! So many! So many! The passage about fertilizers must have enchanted Pelletan.[4] This book is designed for the

Catholic-socialist rabble, for all the philosophical-evangelical vermin. What a charming character is Monsieur Marius, living three days on a cutlet.[5] And Monsieur Enjolras, who has given only two kisses in his life,[6] poor chap! As for what they say, they talk very well, but all alike. Old Gillenormand's drivel, Valjean's last ravings, the humour of Cholomiès and Gantaise – it's all from the same mould. Innumerable quips and jokes, artificial high spirits, and never anything comic. Endless explanations of irrelevancies, and none whatever of things indispensable to the subject. But instead, sermons to show that universal suffrage is a very fine thing, that the masses must be educated: this repeated ad nauseam. Despite its good passages, and they are rare, this book is decidedly infantile. Observation is a secondary quality in literature, but a contemporary of Balzac and Dickens hasn't the right to depict society so falsely. The subject was certainly a very good one. But it called for such unemotional handling, such broad, scientific consideration. It's true that *Père* Hugo despises science. And he demonstrates just that . . .

Posterity will not forgive this man for wanting to be a thinker – a role contrary to his nature. What has he been brought to by his mania for posing as a philosopher! And such philosophy! That of Prud'homme, of Poor Richard, or Béranger.[7] He is no more a thinker than Racine or La Fontaine, of whom his opinion is not very high. That is, like them he summarizes the drift and substance of the banal ideas of his time, and with such persistence that he forgets his own work, and his art. That is my opinion [. . .]. I am keeping it to myself, needless to say. Everyone who touches a pen must be too grateful to Hugo to allow himself to criticize. But – privately – I think the gods are growing old. What lack of regard for beauty! Just quote *one page* of the kind he used to write [. . .].

1. The autograph is mutilated here and at other spots marked [. . .].
2. That is, of siding with the government of Napoleon III against Hugo, who was in self-imposed political exile.
3. A member of the revolutionary National Convention of 1792–1795.
4. In this passage, a portion of the long introduction to Jean Valjean's journey through the Paris sewers, Hugo calls on French agriculturists, in the name of 'progress', to learn to use human excrement as fertilizer. Eugène Pelletan, a left-wing politician, author of a work called *Le Monde marche*, was a leading celebrant of 'progress' – a concept anathema to Flaubert.

5. 'The first day he ate the meat, the second day he ate the fat, the third day he gnawed the bone' (third part, book 5, ch. 1: 'Marius Indigent').

6. And both to a corpse (that of M. Mabeuf) (fourth part. bk. 14, ch. 2; and fifth part. bk. 1, ch. 22).

7. Joseph Prud'homme is the quintessential bourgeois, as invented by the writer and caricaturist Henri Monnier. Poor Richard is Benjamin Franklin's sayer of maxims, and Pierre-Jean Béranger was a popular versifier whom Flaubert despised.

∽

Worse than *Les Misérables*, from Flaubert's point of view, was soon to come from Hugo. In 1864 he would publish his magnificent *William Shakespeare*, full of explicitly socialistic pages, culminating in the famous sentence that one hopes Flaubert never saw: 'Art for art's sake is perhaps splendid, but art for the sake of progress is more splendid still.'

Salammbô was published on November 24, 1862.

One of Flaubert's gift copies went to Laure LePoittevin de Maupassant, sister of the long-dead friend of his youth, Alfred LePoittevin. After fifteen years, Laure's marriage to Gustave de Maupassant had disintegrated; she had obtained an agreement of separation and was now living with her two sons, Guy, twelve, and Hervé, six, in the seaside village of Étretat, near Le Havre, whence she wrote Flaubert her thanks.

∽

LAURE DE MAUPASSANT TO FLAUBERT

Étretat, December 6, 1862

I am very grateful to you, my dear Gustave, for sending me *Salammbô*, and my pleasure in first opening the book was a double one. It was proof that I was remembered by an old friend whose affection and regard I hold ever dear; and then the book, just out, was already famous, and I knew I would spend charming hours in the ancient Carthage you have so painstakingly resurrected. My first thought should have been to thank you, but I was drawn at once to your pages, and felt a compulsion to read and re-read them before taking up my pen.

Here in the depths of my hermitage I lead a very active life: my sons' education, for which at the moment I am solely responsible, takes up much of my time; there are long walks, necessary to their health; and in addition, my mother is here just now. All this keeps me excessively busy, and my free moments become fewer and fewer. Still, I have pared away a bit here and there, and can now say that I know this novel, so much and so loudly spoken of in Paris that our Étretat cliffs ring with the echo. Before expressing the humble opinion of this provincial lady, before burning my bit of incense, let me say that your successes of today, as well as those of yesterday, invariably carry me back into the past, to memories of our poor Alfred, whom you too have never forgotten. Do you not feel, as I do, that he has had his part in all this, that some of it goes back to him, and to his praise – the first you had – of your early efforts? I can say things like this to you, and I am sure you agree with me that there are fond memories which occupy an increasingly greater place in our lives, instead of disappearing with time. My mother and I enjoy reliving all the past these long autumn evenings, and our hours together pass a bit sadly, but not without a certain charm. For the last few days, however, *Salammbô* has left us no time to chat: as soon as dinner is over, we sit around the fire, I take up the book, and begin to read aloud. My son Guy is by no means the least attentive member of the group; his eyes flash at your descriptions, some of them so charming and others so terrible, and I swear he hears the din of your battles and the trumpeting of your elephants. It goes without saying that my first reading was complete and for myself alone; now I am re-reading it for the others as well as for myself, and very probably I shall go through it several times more. Your heroine is in my opinion a strikingly original creation: I think you fashioned her out of moonbeams. Around this woman – almost a goddess, and suffused with a mysterious perfume – the action develops, powerful, grandiose, terrible. We are present at the scenes you describe, we touch them with our fingers; and when at the end we see Mâtho fall, and see his living heart offered to the sun, we close our eyes against the unspeakable horror. It is Ribera, I think, who lent you his brush, and you will do well to keep it, for no one will be able to use it as you do. The few summer people still here are besieging me with requests to lend them *Salammbô*; everyone wants to read it; so far, I have given it to no one – to avoid stirring up jealousy.

Your dear mother has already learned from mine of some of the troubles I have had; but to all you dear friends of other days I want to say a little more. I have suffered greatly – I know you understand that: but I am one of those who can make, and keep, a resolution, and I hope you know and esteem me sufficiently to make it unnecessary for me to say that this resolution is absolutely irrevocable, and that I shall know how to preserve the dignity of my life. I am quite well situated here in my pretty village, in my modest house, and in this new-found tranquillity there is a kind of happiness. My sons are growing up and developing; the elder is almost a man in his intelligence, and I have to work hard to keep up with him – I who have grown so ignorant. I have plunged into being a student again: I enjoy it, and it does me good. I have greatly improved the appearance of my house this year – painted it white, and made a garden that goes down to the Fécamp road. I greatly hope that Madame Flaubert won't fail to pay us a visit next summer; my mother is counting on all of you, and you must not deprive us of the joy your presence here would bring us.

. . .

~

To Laure de Maupassant

Paris [January 1863]

Your good letter touched me deeply, my dear Laure; it stirred old feelings, old feelings that are perennially young. It brought back to me, like a breath of fresh air, all the fragrance of my youth, in which our poor Alfred had so large a place. That memory never leaves me. Not a single day passes, I dare to say almost not an hour, without my thinking of him. I am now acquainted with what are commonly called 'the most intelligent men of the day', and I compare them with him and find them mediocre. Not one of them has ever dazzled me as your brother used to. What excursions into the empyrean he used to take me on, and how I loved him! I think I have never loved anyone, man or woman, as much. When he married, I suffered torments of jealousy: it was a rupture, an uprooting. For me he died twice, and I carry his memory with me constantly, like an amulet, like something private and intimate. How often, in the weariness of my work, or during an interval in some Paris theatre, or alone beside the fire at Croisset on a long winter evening, I am carried back to him – see him and hear him! With delight and sadness mingled I think of our interminable conversations, talks made up of everything from farce to metaphysics – the books we read, our dreams, our high aspirations! If I am worth anything, it is certainly because of those things. I have retained a great respect for that part of the past: we were not commonplace, and I have done my best not to fall short.

I can see all of you at your house in the Grande-Rue,[1] strolling in bright sunshine on the terrace, beside the aviary. I arrive, you greet me with the '*Garçon's*' loud laugh,[2] etc. How I would love to talk about all that with you, dear Laure! It's a long time since we've seen each other. But I have followed your life from a distance, and have sensed and inwardly shared some of your sufferings. I have 'understood' you, in sum. That's an old-fashioned word, a word from our day, from the school of the Romantics. It expresses everything I mean, and I hold to it.[3]

Since you mention *Salammbô*, you will be glad to hear that my Carthaginian girl is making her way in the world. My publisher announces the second edition for Friday.[4] Big and little newspapers are speaking about me; I'm the occasion for large quantities of stupid talk. Some critics vilify me, others exalt me. I have been called a 'drunken helot', charged with 'poisoning the air' around me, compared to Chateaubriand and Marmontel, accused of trying to get myself elected to the Institute; and one lady who had read my book asked a friend of mine whether Tanit wasn't a devil. *Voilà!* Such is literary fame. Gradually the mentions come at longer and longer intervals, then you're forgotten and it's over.

No matter: I wrote the book for a very limited number of readers, and it turns out that the public is snatching it up. Blest be the god of the book trade! I was very glad to know that you liked it, for you know how I value your intelligence, my dear Laure. You and I are not only old friends from childhood, but almost schoolmates. Do you remember our reading the *Feuilles d'automne*[5] together at Fécamp, in the little upstairs room? Please give my excuses to your mother and sister for not sending them the book, but I had a very limited number of copies, and many presents to make. Besides, I knew that Mme LePoittevin was with you at Étretat, and counted

on your reading it aloud. Hug your sons for me – and to you, dear
Laure, a double, long, hand-clasp, and fondest thoughts, from your
old friend,

Gustave Flaubert

1. In Rouen.
2. A grotesque character, with a particularly revolting laugh, invented by the
   adolescent Flaubert and his school friends.
3. Cf. p. 358, n. 3.
4. The second printing of *Salammbô* was announced for January 10, 1863.
5. This volume of Victor Hugo's poems had been a bible for the young,
   Romantic Flaubert and his friends.

Flaubert would always be proud of his 'Carthaginian girl'. 'People
don't sufficiently realize the trouble it takes to produce a well-made
sentence,' he wrote to Mme Roger des Genettes in 1873. 'But what
a joy when everything turns out right! I mean colour, relief, harmony.
You were speaking to me the other day about the Banquet of the
Mercenaries. I can tell you I sweated over that chapter, but [when I
finished reading it to you] you gave a cry of satisfaction that I can
still hear. Ah, that little flat in the Boulevard du Temple was the
scene of some great literary feasts!'

IX

The Battle of Salammbô

1862–1863

As Flaubert wrote to Laure de Maupassant, *Salammbô* was greeted with high praise and with vituperation. Victor Hugo, Hector Berlioz,[1] Jules Michelet, George Sand and Eugène Fromentin were among those who sent him splendid letters about it; and to Théophile Gautier, who praised the book in the newspaper *Le Moniteur Universel*, Flaubert wrote: 'If someone had told me, twenty years ago, that the Théophile Gautier who filled my imagination would write such things about me, I'd have gone mad with pride.'[2] The book's detractors, a less distinguished group, proclaimed themselves disgusted by its bloodiness, its eroticism, its 'obscenity', its pictorial extravagance. Its erudition made them uneasy; some called it exhibitionistic, others cast doubt on its authenticity.

Flaubert's defence of *Madame Bovary* in a court of law in 1857 had been a necessity, forced on him by the public prosecutor. Now, he was to defend his new book twice – on both occasions voluntarily: first in a personal letter to the literary critic Sainte-Beuve (who later printed the letter, with Flaubert's permission); and second in a letter of rebuttal to a scholar, written for publication in a newspaper.

These were the last occasions in Flaubert's career when he allowed himself to reply in writing to adverse published comments on his work. Both letters are noteworthy, and are included here as examples of Flaubertian polemics, as illustrations of Flaubert's code of literary morality, and to suggest the extraordinary extent of his research for *Salammbô*. They bring to mind what he had written to Ernest Feydeau just before beginning his first pages: that in the realm of fiction it is possible to consider archaeological accuracy a 'secondary' matter, whereas the opposite tendency, Flaubert's own, to 'concentrate on costume', tends to make one 'forget the soul'. My extensive annotation of these two letters is intended to illuminate the habits of research applied by Flaubert to all his books published after *Madame Bovary*.[3]

As soon as his publisher, Michel Lévy, had proof sheets of *Salammbô*, Flaubert sent a set to Charles-Augustin Sainte-Beuve.

By far the most influential critic in France, Sainte-Beuve had in 1857 confirmed the respectability of *Madame Bovary* by making it the subject of one of his weekly *Causeries du Lundi*, his 'Monday chats' – reviews of new books or articles on aspects of literature – in *Le Moniteur Universel*. The review of *Madame Bovary*, apparently written with some reluctance at the particular request of the paper's editor, could scarcely be called enthusiastic or perceptive. Nevertheless, by its very appearance it had contributed to the book's success, and Flaubert had written his thanks to Sainte-Beuve. Since then the two men had become – if not quite friends – friendly acquaintances, and they would soon be meeting at the 'Magny Dinners', literary evenings at the Restaurant Magny, which Sainte-Beuve and a few friends inaugurated about that time, and which Flaubert would be invited to attend. Sainte-Beuve's *Lundis* were now appearing in the newspaper *Le Constitutionnel*.

With the proof sheets Flaubert sent the critic a note:

Mon cher Maître

Here is my Carthaginian girl at last. I send her to you in fear and trembling. Now I have nothing further to do except discover printers' errors, mistakes in style, mistakes in grammar, etc. – in short, undergo the usual humiliations.

I am impatient to know what you think. When you finish reading this big bundle, send me a note to tell me the day and time you can see me, and I'll come at once.

Sainte-Beuve wrote in the margin of that letter: 'Grammatical mistakes not very important! The essential is that a book should have life and interest, catch hold of the reader, *bite* him – be absorbingly real, or magic.'

He and Flaubert apparently had a conversation about the novel; and Sainte-Beuve's long critique, one of its chief points being that *Salammbô* did not do what his marginal note said a book should, appeared in *Le Constitutionnel* on three successive Mondays, December 8, 15 and 22. The first instalment contained a prefatory paragraph: 'This long-awaited book, on which M. Flaubert has worked for several years, is now published. We intend to forget our connection with the author, even our friendship with him, and to pay his talent the greatest possible tribute: namely, a verdict based on careful reading; impartial, and unrestricted by conventional rules of politeness.'

After reading those words and the text of the comparatively mild first instalment, Flaubert sent Sainte-Beuve a brief note of thanks; and then, remaining cordial with him despite the severity of the second and third articles, prepared a long letter of justification. It is included here in full translation. The charges made by Sainte-Beuve in his review are for the most part sufficiently indicated by Flaubert's specific ripostes.

1. Berlioz, whose opera *The Trojans at Carthage* had been completed four years before and was still awaiting production, wrote to Flaubert on November 4, 1862:

    My dear Monsieur Flaubert,

    I wanted to run over to see you today; that has proven impossible, but I cannot wait any longer to tell you that your book has filled me with admiration, astonishment, and even terror . . . It frightened me: I've been dreaming about it these last few nights. Such style! Such archaeological knowledge! Such imagination! Oh! Your mysterious Salammbô and her secret love – ungovernable and so full of horror – for the enemy who has violated her is an invention of the highest poetry, and yet true to supreme truth.

    Let me clasp your powerful hand and sign myself your devoted admirer,

    Hector Berlioz

    P.S. *Now* let anyone slander our native tongue!

    A few months later, on July 6, 1863, with his opera finally scheduled for production, Berlioz wrote to Flaubert again:

Learned Poet:

I stopped by today to ask a service of you. At this moment we are busy staging my opera, *The Trojans at Carthage*. The manager of the Théâtre Lyrique [Léon Carvalho] and I would be grateful if you would be willing to give us a little advice concerning the Phoenician and Carthaginian costumes. Certainly there is no one who knows more about this than you. When you return, would you be good enough to let me know when we might see each other? Carvalho will come with me and we shall both listen to you as·to the Delphic Oracle.

All admiration from your devoted
Hector Berlioz

As Jacques Barzun points out in his *Berlioz and the Romantic Century*, 'Flaubert insisted on being the one who should call on the other'; and on July 15 Berlioz wrote to thank him for the 'precious notes' he had sent him.

2. For more on Gautier and *Salammbô*, including a discussion of his possible role in its genesis, see Joanna Richardson, *Théophile Gautier* (listed in Works of Related Interest).

3. Flaubert had of course carefully verified details of topography, medicine, fashion, and so on for *Madame Bovary.* But the setting and timing of that novel – in Flaubert's native Normandy, less than a generation before the years of its composition – had made the task less onerous. He had done extensive research for the first, unpublished *Temptation of Saint Anthony*, and would do more for the final version.

~

To Charles-Augustin Sainte-Beuve

[December 23–24, 1862]

Your third article on *Salammbô* has mollified me (I was never very outraged). My friends were a bit annoyed by the two others; but remembering how frankly you told me what you thought of my big tome, I am grateful to you for the leniency of your criticism. Therefore, once again, and very sincerely, I thank you for the marks of affection you show me; and now, bypassing the usual compliments, I begin my 'Apologia'.

Are you quite sure, first of all, that your general judgement isn't a little over-influenced by your emotional reaction? The world I depict in my book – barbarian, Oriental, Molochian – is displeasing to you *in itself.* You begin by doubting the verisimilitude of my reproduction of it, and then you say: 'After all, it *may* be true'; and, in conclusion, 'So much the worse if it *is* true!' You keep being surprised, and hold it against me that you should be. But that I cannot help! Should I have embellished the picture, sweetened, distorted, frenchified it? But you yourself reproach me for having written a poem, for being classical in the unfavourable sense of that word, and you use *Les Martyrs*[1] as a stick to beat me with.

Now, Chateaubriand's system seems to me diametrically opposed to mine. He started from a completely ideal viewpoint: he was thinking of the martyr as a certain type. Whereas I, by applying to antiquity the technique of the modern novel, wanted to capture a mirage, and I tried to be simple. Laugh as much as you like! Yes, I say *simple*, and not sober. Nothing is more complicated than a Barbarian.

But now for the points you make. I defend myself: I fight you inch by inch.

From the outset, I clash with you head-on about Hanno's *Periplus*,[2] which Montesquieu admired and I do not. Who can be persuaded to believe today that it is an 'original' document? It is obviously translated, shortened, pruned and arranged by a Greek. Never did an Oriental, whoever he might be, write in that style. Witness the inscription of Eshmunazar,[3] so bombastic and redundant. People who have themselves called 'son of God', 'eye of God' (see Hamaker's inscriptions)[4] are not simple in the way you mean. And then you will grant me that the Greeks understood nothing about the barbarian world. If they had understood something about it, they would not have been Greeks. The Orient was repugnant to the Hellenic spirit. What travesties they made of everything that came to them from abroad! The same is true of Polybius. He is for me an incontestable authority as to facts; but for anything he has not seen (or which he omits intentionally, for he too had a preconceived framework and belonged to a 'school') I am perfectly entitled to look elsewhere. Hanno's *Periplus* is thus not a 'Carthaginian monument', let alone the 'only one', as you say it is. One true Carthaginian monument is the inscription at Marseilles,[5] written in real Punic. That one is 'simple', I admit, because it is a list of charges; and even so, it is less 'simple' than the famous *Periplus*, in which a touch of the marvellous comes through the Greek – to mention only those gorilla-skins, mistaken for human skins, that hung in the temple of

Moloch (i.e. Saturn), and whose description I spared you. (You can thank me for that.) So: one point settled. I will even tell you, *entre nous*, that Hanno's *Periplus* is completely odious to me, the result of my having read and re-read it together with Bougainville's four dissertations (in the *Mémoires* of the Academy of Inscriptions), not to mention many a doctoral thesis, the *Periplus* being a thesis subject.[6]

As for my heroine, I do not defend her. According to you, she resembles a 'sentimental Elvire', Velléda, Mme Bovary.[7] No: Velléda is active, intelligent, European; Mme Bovary is the prey of many passions; Salammbô, on the contrary, remains adamantine, immobilized by her obsession. She is a maniac, a kind of St Teresa. No matter! I am not sure how real she is; for neither I, nor you, nor anyone, whether ancient or modern, can understand the Oriental woman, for the reason that association with her is impossible.

You accuse me of lacking logic, and you ask: 'Why did the Carthaginians massacre the Balearics?' The reason is very simple: they hate all the Mercenaries; they happen to have that one group of them, the Balearics, in their power; they are stronger, and they kill them. But, you say: 'The news could reach the camp from one moment to the next.' How? Who would have brought it? The Carthaginians? What would have been their purpose? Or some of the Barbarians? But there were none left in the city. Foreigners? Persons unconcerned? But I was careful to show that there was no communication between Carthage and the army.

As for Hanno[8] . . . (The 'bitches' milk', let me say in passing, is not a 'joke'. It was, and *still is*, a remedy against leprosy. See the *Dictionnaire des sciences médicales*, article 'Leprosy' – a poor article, by the way: I corrected parts of it from my own observations in Damascus and Nubia.) Hanno escapes because the Mercenaries deliberately let him escape. They are not yet 'unleashed' against him. They become indignant later, when they reconsider the matter: they are slow to grasp all the perfidy of which the Elders are capable. (See the beginning of my Chapter IV.) Mâtho 'prowls like a madman' around Carthage. 'Madman' is the right word. As conceived by the ancients, wasn't love a madness, a curse, a sickness sent by the gods? Polybius would be 'astonished', you say, to see his Mâtho so depicted. I do not think so, nor would M. de Voltaire have shared this astonishment. Remember what he has the old woman in *Candide* say about the violence of passions in Africa: 'Like fire, vitriol, etc.'

Concerning the aqueduct: 'Here the reader is up to his neck in improbability.' Yes, *cher maître*, you are right, and even more so than you think; but not in the way you think. I will tell you further along my own view of this episode, introduced not to describe the aqueduct itself (which gave me a lot of trouble), but to enable my two heroes to enter Carthage. Actually, it is taken from an anecdote recounted by Polyaenus[9] (*Strategica*) – the story of Theodorus, the friend of Cleon, at the capture of Sestos by the people of Abydos.

'One needs a dictionary.' This is a reproach that I consider supremely unfair. I could have bored the reader to death with technical terms. Far from doing so, I was careful to translate everything into French. I used not a single special term without immediately furnishing an explanation. I except the names of coins, measurements, and the months, which are indicated by the context. But surely, when you encounter on a page such words as 'kreutzer', 'yard', 'piastre', or 'penny', they are not beyond your understanding? What would you have said had I called Moloch 'Melek', Hannibal 'Han-Baal', Carthage 'Karthadhadtha', and if instead of saying that the slaves in the mill wore muzzles, I had written 'pausicapes'?! As for the names of perfumes and precious stones, it is true that I had to take names that are in Theophrastus, Pliny, and Athenaeus. For plants, I used Latin names – 'commonly accepted names' – instead of Arab or Phoenician. Thus I said 'Lausonia' instead of 'Henneb', and I was even considerate enough to write 'Lausonia' with a 'u', which is wrong, and not to add 'inermis', which would have been more precise. The same for 'Rokh'eul', which I call 'antimony', sparing you 'sulphide', O ungrateful one! But out of respect for the French reader I cannot write 'Hannibal' and 'Hamilcar' without the 'H' (since there is a 'rough breathing' on the *alpha*), and remain faithful to Rollin.[10] Be a bit gentle with me, please!

As for the temple of Tanit, I am confident that I reconstruct it correctly, on the basis of the treatise on the Syrian Goddess,[11] the duc de Luynes' medals, our knowledge of the temple at Jerusalem, a passage from St Jerome quoted by Selden[12] (*de Diis Syriis*), the plan of the temple at Gozo[13] (which is certainly Carthaginian), and the ruins of the temple of Thugga,[14] which I have seen with my own eyes and which, so far as I know, is mentioned by no traveller or antiquarian. 'No matter,' you will say, 'it is a strange-sounding place.' Granted. The description itself, from the literary point of view, I find perfectly comprehensible. And it does not impede the action: Spendius and Mâtho remain in the foreground; the reader never loses sight of them. The descriptions in my book are never isolated or gratuitous: they all serve some purpose relating to my characters, and sooner or later they are seen to play a role in the plot.

Nor do I accept the word 'chinoiserie' as applied to Salammbô's chamber, despite the 'exquisite' you add to take the curse off it (like 'devouring' applied to 'dogs' in the famous Dream),[15] because I have not included a single detail that is not in the Bible or not still to be seen in the Orient. You tell me more than once that the Bible is not a guide to Carthage (a debatable point); but surely the Hebrews were closer to the Carthaginians than were the Chinese! Besides, there are climatic considerations, which are eternal. For furniture and costumes, I refer you to the texts included in the twenty-first dissertation by the Abbé Mignot (*Mémoires* of the Academy of Inscriptions, Volume LX or XLI, I forget which).

As for everything in the book having a flavour of 'opera, pomp, and bombast', why should you think that things were not like that then, considering that that is how they are now? Ceremonies, state visits, obeisances, panegyrics, and all the rest were not invented by Mohammed, I suppose.

The same applies to Hannibal. Why do you maintain that I have made his childhood 'fabulous'? Because he kills an eagle? A miracle indeed, in a land where eagles abound! If the scene had been Gaul, I would have made it an owl, a wolf, or a fox. Being French, you are accustomed, automatically, to think of the eagle as a noble bird, more symbol than living thing. However, eagles do exist.

You ask me where I derived 'such an idea of the Council of Carthage'. But in all situations of the kind, in periods of revolution, from our own Convention to the American Parliament,[16] where until quite recently there were duels with canes and pistols, said canes and pistols (like my daggers) were brought in hidden in coat sleeves. And even my Carthaginians were more seemly than the Americans, since the public was not admitted to the Council. Against me you quote a weighty authority: Aristotle. But Aristotle lived more than eighty years before my period, and carries no weight here. Besides, the Stagirite is grossly mistaken when he states that 'in Carthage there was never an uprising or a tyrant'. Would you like a few dates? Carthalo's conspiracy in 530 BC; the usurpation of the two Magos, 460; Hanno's conspiracy, 337; Bomilcar's conspiracy, 307. But here I go beyond Aristotle's time. On to something else.

You scold me about the 'carbuncles formed by lynxes' urine'. That is from Theophrastus, *On Stones*. So: poor Theophrastus![17]

I was forgetting Spendius. No, *cher maître*, his stratagem is neither 'bizarre' nor 'strange'. It is almost a stereotype. I took it from Aelianus (*History of Animals*) and Polyaenus (*Strategica*). In fact, it was so well known following the siege of Megara by Antipater (or Antigonus) that pigs were deliberately fed alongside elephants in order that the larger animals not be frightened by the smaller. In short, it was a common device, probably often used in Spendius's day. I didn't have to go back as far as Samson, because I avoided, as much as possible, details belonging to legendary periods.

Now I come to Hamilcar's treasure. This description, whatever you say, is not in the foreground: Hamilcar himself is the dominant figure, and I think the description is well warranted. The magistrate's anger gradually increases as he sees the depredations made in his house. Far from being 'continuously beside himself', he doesn't explode until the end, when he is insulted personally. That he 'does not gain in stature from this visit' is quite all right with me, since I am not writing his panegyric; but I do not think that in this scene I 'caricature him, to the detriment of the rest of his characterization'. The man who later kills the Mercenaries in the way I have shown (his son Hannibal went in for the same charming behaviour, in Italy), is very much the same man who orders his merchandise to be adulterated and his slaves to be whipped unsparingly.

You quibble about the 'eleven thousand three hundred and ninety-six men' who form his army, asking me 'How do you know this number? Who told you?' But you have just seen that for yourself, since I mentioned the number of men in the different corps of the Punic army. It is simply the sum total: not a figure recklessly invented to create an effect of precision.

There is nothing 'sly' or 'depraved' in the scene of the serpent, no 'bagatelle'.[18] This chapter is a kind of rhetorical precaution, to attenuate the effect of the chapter about the tent. The latter has not shocked readers; but it would have, had it not been preceded by the snake. I preferred a salacious scene with a snake (if there is salaciousness here) to one with a man. Before leaving her house, Salammbô embraces the genius of her family, the very religion of her country and its most ancient symbol. That is all. Quite possibly it would be 'unseemly in an Iliad or a Pharsalia'; but I make no claim to be writing the Iliad or the Pharsalia.

Nor is it my fault if there are frequent storms in Tunisia at the end of the summer. Chateaubriand no more invented storms than he did sunsets; and both, it seems to me, are everyone's property. Besides, please note that the heart of this story is Moloch – Fire, Thunder. Here the god himself acts, in one of his forms: he subdues Salammbô. Thus the thunder is appropriate: it is the voice of Moloch, speaking from without. Furthermore, you must admit that I spared you the 'classic description of a storm'. Besides, my poor storm occupies only *three lines* – separated, at that. The fire that follows was inspired by an episode in the story of Massinissa,[19] by another in the story of Agathocles,[20] and by a passage in Hirtius[21] – all three in analogous circumstances. As you see, I don't stray from the milieu, from the very country in which my action takes place.

About Salammbô's perfumes: you credit me with more imagination than I possess. Just take a whiff of Judith and Esther in the Bible. They literally soaked themselves, poisoned themselves, with perfumes. Which is what I was careful to say at the beginning, as soon as there was a question of Salammbô's sickness.

Why do you object to 'the disappearance of the *zaïmph* being a factor' in the loss of the battle, since the army of Mercenaries included men who believed in the *zaïmph*? I indicate the principal reasons (three military movements) for this defeat; then I add the other, as a secondary, final reason.

To say that I 'invented tortures' at the funeral of the Barbarians is not true. Hendrich (*Carthago, seu Carth. respublica*, 1664) assembled texts to prove that it was a custom of the Carthaginians to mutilate the corpses of their enemies. And you are surprised that the Barbarians, defeated, desperate, enraged, should retaliate in kind, doing so on this one occasion only? Must I remind you of Mme de

Lamballe, of the Garde Mobile in '48, and what is taking place this very moment in the United States?[22] In fact I have been moderate and very considerate.

And since you and I are exchanging truths, I confess to you frankly, *cher maître*, that your 'element of sadistic imagination' wounded me a little. Every word you write is serious. Such words from you, when they are printed, become almost a stigma. Are you forgetting that I once sat on a bench in Criminal Court, accused of offences against public decency, and that fools and knaves use any weapons that come to hand? So do not be surprised if one of these days you read in the *Figaro*[23] some such words as these: 'M. G. Flaubert is a disciple of Sade. His friend, his sponsor, a master critic, has said so himself, quite clearly, although with that finesse and laughing good humour which, etc.' What would I reply – or do?

I bow before the following. You are right, *cher maître*: I did add finishing touches; I did do violence to history; as you so well say, I had 'made up my mind to depict a siege'. But with a military subject, what is wrong with that? And then I did not completely invent this siege. I merely laid it on a bit thick. That is my only sin.

But concerning the 'passage in Montesquieu' about immolating children, I rebel. This horror does not 'raise a doubt' in my mind. (Remember that human sacrifices were not completely abolished in Greece at the time of the battle of Leuctra, 370 BC.) Despite the condition imposed by Gelon (480), in the war against Agathocles (392) two hundred children were burned, according to Diodorus; and as for later periods, I refer you to Silius Italicus, to Eusebius, and especially to St Augustine, who states that such things sometimes took place in his day.

You regret that among the Greeks I have not included a philosopher, a dialectician who would be portrayed as giving a course in morals, or as performing good actions – a gentleman, in short, who 'feels as we do'. Come, now! Would that have been possible? Aratus,[24] whom you mention, was in fact the very person I thought of when imagining Spendius. He was a man of ruses and sudden assaults, capable of killing sentinels at night, and a man who had attacks of vertigo in broad daylight. True, I sidestepped a contrast, but such a contrast would have been a facile one, forced and false.

So much for your 'analysis'. Now as to your 'judgement'.

You are perhaps right in your reflections concerning the historical novel as applied to antiquity, and quite possibly I have failed.[25] However, judging from my own impressions, it seems to me quite probable that the picture I have painted does resemble Carthage. But that is not the question. I care nothing for archaeology. If the colour is not unified, if details jar, if the ways of life I depict are not what can be derived from what we know of the religion, or the action from what we know of human passions, if the delineations of character are not consistent, if the costumes are inappropriate to the life of the people and the architecture to the climate – if, in a word, harmony is lacking – then my book is wrong. If not, not: it is all of a piece.

But you find the milieu itself detestable. I know you do, or rather I sense that you do. Instead of continuing to regard it from your viewpoint, your viewpoint as a man of letters, as a modern, a Parisian, why not come and look at it from mine? The human soul is not the same everywhere, whatever M. Levallois[26] may say. The briefest glance at the world provides sufficient proof of the opposite. Actually, I think I have been less hard on humanity in *Salammbô* than in *Madame Bovary*. The curiosity and love that impelled me to deal with religions and people that are no more has something moral and sympathetic about it, I think.

As to style, I sacrificed less in this book than in the other to rounding out my phrases and my periods. Metaphors are few, and epithets are factual. If I put 'blue' beside 'stones', it is because 'blue' is the right word, believe me; and you may be equally sure that it is indeed possible to distinguish the colour of stones by starlight. Ask any traveller in the Orient, or go and see for yourself.

And since you reproach me for certain words – '*énorme*', for example, which I will not defend (even though excessive silence does give the effect of clamour) – let me in turn object to some of your expressions. I did not understand the quotation from Désaugiers,[27] or why you included it. Your 'Carthaginian knick-knacks' made me frown, as did your calling the *zaïmph* 'a kind of crazy cloak', your speaking of Salammbô's 'romping with the snake' as being a kind of 'spicy come-on', your calling my Libyan a 'handsome rogue' when he is neither handsome nor a rogue, and your reference to Schahabarim's 'libertine' imagination.

One last question, O *maître* – an unseemly question. Why do you find Schahabarim [the high priest] almost comic, and yet take your friends at Port-Royal[28] so seriously? For me, your M. Singlin is deadly, compared with my elephants. I regard the tattooed Barbarians as less inhuman, less 'special', less ludicrous, less exceptional, than men living a communal life who address each other as 'Monsieur' to the end of their days. And it is precisely because they are remote from me that I admire your talent for making me understand them. For I *believe* your picture of Port-Royal, and I would enjoy living there even less than in Carthage. Port-Royal, too, was an exclusive group, unnatural, forced, all of a piece – and yet true. Why will you not allow two truths to exist, two diametrically opposed examples of excess, two different monstrosities?

I am almost done. Be patient a bit longer! Are you curious to know the *enormous* defect ('*énorme*' is used properly here) that I find in my book? It is this:

1. The pedestal is too big for the statue. Or rather, since 'too little', rather than 'too much', is the great sin, there should have been a hundred pages more, devoted to Salammbô alone.

2. A few transitions are lacking. I had them, but removed them or overpruned them, for fear of being boring.

3. In Chapter VI, everything relating to Gisco is of the same tonality as the second part of Chapter II (Hanno). The situation is the same, and the effect is not enhanced.

4. Everything from the battle of the Macar to the serpent, and all of Chapter XIII, up to the enumeration of the Barbarians, sink out of sight, vanish from the reader's memory. These are areas of middle ground, dull and of ephemeral effect. Unfortunately I could not avoid them, and they give a heaviness to the book despite my best efforts at briskness. Those are the parts that gave me the most trouble; I like them the least, and yet they are the ones I am proudest of.

5. The aqueduct. A confession! My *secret* opinion is that there was no aqueduct at Carthage at that period, despite the ruined aqueduct we see today. Therefore I was careful to anticipate possible objections with a hypocritical sentence intended for archaeologists – a clumsy reminder that aqueducts were a Roman invention, new at the time, and that the aqueduct one sees now was a new construction,

on the foundations of an older one. I was obsessed by the memory of Belisarius cutting the Roman aqueduct at Carthage;[29] and besides, it made such a splendid entrance for Spendius and Mâtho! But no question, my aqueduct *is* an evasion. *Confiteor!*

6. One more, final, fraud: Hanno. For the sake of keeping the picture clear, I falsified the story of his death. He was indeed crucified by the Mercenaries, but in Sardinia. The general crucified at Tunis, opposite Spendius, was named Hannibal. Think of the confusion that would have caused the reader![30]

Such, *cher maître*, are what I consider the worst features of my book. I will not tell you what I think the good ones. But you may be sure that my Carthage is no mere fantasy. Documents on Carthage exist, and not all of them are in Movers.[31] They must be sought for a bit further. For example, Ammianus Marcellinus[32] provided me with the exact form of a gate; a poem by Corippus[33] (the *Johannis*) with many details about African tribes, etc.

And besides: few will be following my example. So where is the danger? The Leconte de Lisles and the Baudelaires are less to be feared than the Nadauds and the Clairvilles[34] in this dear land of France, where superficiality is a *quality* and where the banal, the facile, and the foolish are invariably applauded, adopted, and adored. One does not risk corrupting anyone in aspiring to greatness. Am I forgiven?

I end by thanking you once again, *mon cher maître*. You have clawed me, but you have also given me the handshake of affection; and though you have mocked me a little, you have nevertheless given me three great salutes – three long articles, very detailed, very distinguished, which must have been more painful for you than they are for me. It is for that, especially, that I am grateful. Your closing advice will not be forgotten,[35] and you will see that you have not been dealing with a fool or an ingrate.

1. Chateaubriand's Romantic prose epic, *Les Martyrs, ou le Triomphe de la réligion chrétienne* (1809).
2. *The Periplus* is an account of a voyage around Africa, written in the Punic language by a Carthaginian (Hanno was a common Carthaginian name) and later translated into Greek.
3. Eshmunazar (the name means 'the god Eshmun has helped') was a king

of Sidon, about the early fifth century BC. The inscription is on his sarcophagus, discovered in 1855.

4. Hendrik Arent Hamaker, a Dutch orientalist (1789–1835), published works on Phoenician and Punic inscriptions.

5. The so-called Marseilles Tariff, a third- or second-century BC stone inscription in Punic listing sacrifices and dues, found at Marseilles in 1845 and thought to have come from Carthage.

6. That is, permitted as a subject for theses in French universities.

7. Elvire is Lamartine's idealized heroine in his Romantic *Méditations poétiques* (1820). Velléda is a druidess in *Les Martyrs*.

8. This Hanno is a Carthaginian general and magistrate, a character in the novel.

9. Greek author of a book on military stratagems.

10. Charles Rollin (1661–1741), historian, Rector of the University of Paris, where he reintroduced the study of Greek. 'Rough breathing' and 'smooth breathing' are terms referring to the pronunciation of ancient Greek.

11. Lucian: *De dea syria*.

12. John Selden (1584–1654), English jurist and oriental scholar. The book consulted by Flaubert was his *De dis syris syntagmata II* (London, 1617). Flaubert would later be scolded for his misspelling of the title (see letter to Froehner, January 21, 1863, p. 402, n. 14).

13. The second-largest island in the Maltese group.

14. In Tunisia. Sometimes written Dougga. When Sainte-Beuve published Flaubert's letter, with permission, as a note to his review as reprinted in a volume of *Nouveaux Lundis*, he appended the following footnote: 'M. Flaubert, whom I asked to re-read this passage of his letter, has agreed that he was neither the first nor the only writer, as he had previously thought, to speak of the temple of Thugga.'

15. The dream in Racine's *Athalie*, II, 5.

16. One supposes Flaubert means the Congress. The reference might be to the beating of Charles Summer in the Senate in 1856.

17. Sainte-Beuve had jeered at Flaubert's description of Hamilcar's collection of gems: 'Here we have to do with an auctioneer, amusing himself in this underground treasure house by reeling off for us a list of all the mineralogical marvels imaginable, even including "carbuncles formed by lynxes' urine". This is too much, and shows up the author as a dilettante who is making sport of us.'

   André Gide wrote more understandingly of this aspect of *Salammbô* in his *Journal* (April 9, 1908): 'It seems to me that in the texts he used as sources, Flaubert was seeking less for documentation than for authorization. In his horror of daily reality, he was enchanted by everything in these texts that differed from it. Did he really believe that carbuncles were "formed by lynxes' urine"? Certainly not! But he was delighted that a passage in

Theophrastus authorized him to pretend to believe so; and so on throughout the book.'

This inner, or secret, way of the artist, Flaubert would not, or perhaps could not, explain to someone who, like Sainte-Beuve, did not sense it.

18. 'Bagatelle' in the eighteenth-century sense: the act of coition.

19. King of Numidia (c. 238–149 BC), vassal and ally of Carthage, who was married to Sophinisba, daughter of the Carthaginian Hasdrubal, transferred his allegiance to Rome.

20. Sicilian tyrant (d. 289 BC).

21. Roman historian (d. 43 BC).

22. The Princesse de Lamballe, friend of Queen Marie-Antoinette, met an atrocious end at the hands of a mob during the September massacres of 1792. The Garde Mobile (a portion of the National Guard) mowed down demonstrating workmen during the 'June Days' of 1848; Flaubert refers to the National Guard again in his letter of September 29, 1868, to George Sand, and it plays a large role in *L'Éducation sentimentale*. Bulletins concerning the events of the American Civil War were appearing in the newspapers Flaubert read.

23. 'in the *Figaro*.' Responding to Flaubert's request that in his letter as printed the name of the newspaper be omitted, Sainte-Beuve substituted 'in some little scandal sheet'.

24. Achaean general, ally and then enemy of Philip of Macedon.

25. In his review, Sainte-Beuve had written: 'On this subject chosen by M. Flaubert, little information is provided either by monuments or by books. What he tried to accomplish was thus a complete tour de force, and it is little wonder that, in my opinion, he has failed.'

26. Jules Levallois (1829–1903), Sainte-Beuve's former secretary, had written unfavourably about *Salammbô* in the *Opinion Nationale*.

27. Antoine Désaugiers (1772–1827), composer of light songs. Sainte-Beuve, whose taste in humour was not always the most appropriate, had quoted, quite ineptly, some jolly lines from Désaugiers 'as a relief from the solemnity and monotony' of *Salammbô*.

28. The reference is to Sainte-Beuve's *Port-Royal*, his study of the community of seventeenth-century Jansenists.

29. In AD 534 – approximately eight hundred years after the events recounted in *Salammbô*.

30. That is, they would probably have thought that Flaubert was speaking of the younger, greater, Hannibal.

31. Franz Karl Movers (1806–1856), German orientalist. His *Die Phönizier*, one of Flaubert's sources for Carthaginian names and other particulars, was published in two separate parts: Bonn, 1841, and Berlin, 1856.

32. Roman historian in the age of Julian.

33. Flavius Cresconius Corippus, Roman epic poet of the sixth century AD.

34. Gustave Nadaud (1829–1893), composer of light songs; and Louis-François

Nicolaie, called Clairville (1811–1879), composer and *vaudevilliste*. Flaubert was probably unaware, when writing his 'Apologia', that a few months later a vaudeville by Clairville and a collaborator, entitled *Folammbô, ou les Cocasseries carthaginoises*, would open at the Théâtre du Palais-Royal, then as now the home of the farce.

35. Sainte-Beuve's 'closing advice' to the author of *Salammbô* had been:

'A new book by him is due us, and let us hope that this time we shall not have to wait so long. To men – even to the most genuine talents – few years of fertility are granted: one must know how to make use of them, in order to establish oneself before it is too late – anchor oneself in the hearts and memory of one's contemporaries. Besides, that is the surest route to posterity. So let him give us, without too much delay, and without excessive concern for that style of which he is such a master that he can afford to relax a little, a strong, powerful, well-observed, vital work. Certainly it must have some of the bitter, refined qualities of his first novel; it must be earmarked with his originality and his inimitable nature (no one wishes him to abdicate!); but one hopes it will contain at least one vein that will please all of us, if only as a measure of consolation.'

Perhaps Flaubert was referring to that 'closing advice' when he wrote to his niece, on Sainte-Beuve's death seven years later: 'I wrote *L'Éducation sentimentale* in part for Sainte-Beuve.'

The text of Flaubert's 'Apologia' used for this translation is chiefly that printed by Sainte-Beuve in the fourth volume of his *Nouveaux Lundis* along with his own reply to it (translated below). Notice has been taken of the corrections pointed out by Benjamin F. Bart in '*Lettres Inédites de Flaubert à Sainte-Beuve*,' in *Revue d'histoire littéraire de la France*, 64 (1964), which contains also the texts of Flaubert's two shorter letters. For the identification of certain persons, places, and works mentioned in this letter and the next, and for the proper anglicization of certain terms and names, I am particularly grateful to David Marcus.

∾

CHARLES-AUGUSTIN SAINTE-BEUVE TO FLAUBERT

December 25, 1862

My dear friend,

I was waiting impatiently for the promised letter. I read it last night, and have re-read it this morning. I no longer regret having written those articles, since by doing so I induced you to bring out all your reasons. The African sun has had the singular effect of causing the humours of all of us, even our secret humours, to erupt. *Salammbô*, independently of the lady, is from now on the name of a battle, of several battles. I plan to do the following: when I reprint

my articles, I will keep them as they are, and will place, at the end
of the volume, what you call your 'apologia', with only these few
words of reply from me. I had my say; you responded; attentive
readers will judge. What I appreciate especially, and what everyone
will feel, is the high-mindedness and nobility of character which
enabled you quite naturally to tolerate my contradictions, and
which increase the esteem in which you are held. M. Lebrun (of the
Academy), a just man, said this about you to me the other day:
'After all, he comes out of this a more considerable person than
before. That will be the general, and definitive, impression . . .'[1]

1. Those last dots of deletion were substituted by Sainte-Beuve, in the pub-
    lished text of his letter, for the closing words of the autograph. Those
    words, or their sense, can be deduced from Flaubert's brief note of reply:
    ' "Less good friends than before", *cher maître*? Come: *better!* What a
    charming man you are. This time I don't shake your hand: I embrace you.'

∼

In connection with one particularly infuriating review of *Salammbô*
Flaubert wrote to Jules Duplan on January 13, 1863:

> I had taken all imaginable precautions to keep my mother from
> learning about the article in *Le Figaro*, but two of her women
> friends (it's always friends, in such a case) found nothing better
> to do than recite the article to her by heart. She was very upset
> about it on Sunday night, and whenever I go out she imagines
> I'm on my way to fight a duel. So you see my life at home is
> disturbed by those bastards. Such are the rewards of literature.
> Lévy is rubbing his hands and printing the third edition.

The newspaper notices emphasizing the novel's 'horrors' were
indeed helping the sale, and Flaubert was persuaded by Bouilhet not
to reply to any of them.

However, Flaubert would not agree to ignore one magazine
article, signed 'G. Froehner', which he viewed as belonging to an
order of its own. The author, a twenty-seven-year-old German
(naturalized French, hence the 'G' for 'Guillaume' rather than 'W'
for his baptismal 'Wilhelm'), was not a literary critic but an assistant

curator in the Department of Antiquities at the Louvre, and the provocation of his remarks was undeniably acute. When couched in a certain tone, *all* accusations of error can be equally maddening, whether justified or not. Those made in Froehner's article were of both kinds; and its author, who held a degree from the University of Bonn, excelled in a Teutonic variety of tactlessness which always offends – most of all, perhaps, when it condescends to praise. Flaubert's reply appeared in the newspaper *L'Opinion Nationale* for January 24, 1863, and was reprinted in the magazine *La Revue Contemporaine* (where the attack had appeared) for February 15. As in the case of the letter to Sainte-Beuve, the critic's objections are for the most part made evident by Flaubert's ripostes.

~

To Guillaume Froehner

Paris, January 21, 1863

Monsieur:

I have just read your article on *Salammbô* in the *Revue Contemporaine* of December 31, 1862.[1] Despite my practice of never replying to reviews, I find yours unacceptable. It is very courteous, and contains many things extremely flattering to me; but since it casts doubt on the sincerity of my studies, you will kindly allow me to use this space to challenge a number of your assertions.

Let me first ask you, Monsieur, why you so obstinately link me with the Campana collection,[2] claiming that it was my source, my continual inspiration. The fact is that I completed *Salammbô* last March, six weeks before the opening of that museum. Already an error, you see: we shall be finding others, more serious.

I have, Monsieur, no pretensions to archaeology. My book is presented as a novel, without preface and without notes, and I marvel that a man of your eminence should waste his time and effort on such light literature! However, I know enough to risk saying that you err completely, from the beginning of your article to the end, on every one of your eighteen pages, in every paragraph, and in almost every line.

You reprimand me for not having consulted either Falbe or Dureau de la Malle,[3] from whom I 'might have profited'. A thousand pardons! I have read them – more often than you, perhaps, and amid the ruins of Carthage itself. It is indeed quite possible that you 'know of no satisfactory work dealing with the configuration of the city or with its principal districts'; others, however, better informed, do not at all share your scepticism. We may lack information as to the whereabouts of the suburb Aclas, or the place called Fuscianus, or concerning the exact sites of the principal gates whose names we have, etc.; but we do know, and quite well, the position of the city, the architectonic construction of the walls, the Taenia, the Mole and the Cothon.[4] We know that the houses were faced with tar and the streets paved with blocks; we have an idea of the Ancô,[5] described in my Chapter XV; we have heard about Malqua, about Byrsa, about Megara, about the Mappalia and the Catacombs, and about the temple of Eshmun, situated on the Acropolis, and that of Tanit, a little to the right as one stood with one's back to the sea. All that is to be found (not to mention Appian, Pliny, and Procopius) in that same Dureau de la Malle whom you accuse me of not knowing. So it is really regrettable, Monsieur, that you did not, as you put it, 'go into tedious detail' to prove that I had no idea of the situation and plan of ancient Carthage – 'even less than Dureau de la Malle', you add. What is one to believe? On whom is one to rely? – since you have so far not had the kindness to reveal your own system with respect to Carthaginian topography.

It is true that I can quote no text to prove that there existed a street of the Tanners, or of the Perfumers, or of the Dyers. Still, you must agree that it is a likely hypothesis. But I most certainly did not invent Kinisdo and Cynasyn – 'names', you say, 'whose structure is foreign to the spirit of the Semitic languages'. Not so foreign as all that, however, since they are in Gesenius.[6] Almost all my Punic names ('disfigured', according to you) were taken from Gesenius (*Scripturae lingaeque phoeniciae (monumenta quotquot supersunt)*) [1837], or from Falbe, whom I assure you I did consult.

An orientalist of your erudition, Monsieur, should have been a bit more indulgent concerning the Numidian name Naravasse, which I write Narr'Havas, from Nar-el-haouah, *feu du souffle*.[7] You could have guessed that the two *m*'s in Salammbô were put there on purpose, so that the name would be pronounced Sala*m* and not as in Salan;[8] and you might have had the charity to suppose that Égates, instead of Ægates, was a typographical error – corrected, incidentally, in the second edition of my book, which appeared a fortnight before the article in which you offer me advice. The same goes for Scissites, instead of Syssites, and for the word Kabires, which has always been printed without an *h* (horrors!) even in the most serious works, such as Maury's *Les Religions de la Grèce antique.* As for Schalischim, if I did not write (as I should have) Rosh-eisch-Schalischim, it was to shorten a name that I found too forbidding – it not having occurred to me that I would be quizzed by philologists. But since you choose to descend to these chicaneries about words, I will take you up on two (among others) of your own: (1) *Compendieusement,* which you employ in the opposite sense from its meaning, making it signify 'abundantly', 'prolixly', and (2) *carthachinoiserie,*[9] an excellent jest, but not your own: you took it from the little newspaper in which it appeared early last month. As you see, Monsieur, if you are sometimes unacquainted with my authors, I know yours. But it might have been better had you passed over 'those minutiae', as you so properly call them, 'which do not survive critical examination'.

One more such, however. Why did you underline the *and* in this sentence (a little shortened) from my page 156: 'Buy me some Cappadocians *and* some Asiatics'? Was it because you wanted to impress a few ignoramuses, to make them think that I don't distinguish Cappadocia from Asia Minor? But I know the country, Monsieur: I have seen it, I have ridden through it![10]

You have read me with so little care that almost always you *quote me incorrectly.* Nowhere did I say that the priests formed a particular caste, nor, on page 109, that the Libyan soldiers 'were possessed by the desire to drink iron', but that the Barbarians threatened to make the Carthaginians 'drink iron';[11] nor, on page 108, that the guards of the Legion 'wore, in the middle of the forehead, a silver horn to make them look like rhinoceroses', but that *their great horses* were so adorned; nor on page 29, that the peasants amused themselves one day by crucifying two hundred lions. The same goes for those unfortunate Syssites,[12] which, according to you, I spoke of 'doubtless not knowing that the term signified special guilds'. Your 'doubtless' is charming. But doubtless I did know what those guilds were, and the etymology of the word, since I translate it into French the first time it appears in my book, on page 7: 'Syssites, companies (of merchants) who ate together'. Furthermore, you have falsified a passage from

Plautus: his *Poenulus* does not at all prove that 'the Carthaginians knew all languages' (which would be a curious privilege for an entire nation); the prologue reads simply (line 112): '*Is omnes linguas scit*', which must be translated as '*This man* knows all languages' – the Carthaginian in question, not all Carthaginians.

It is not true to say that 'Hanno was not crucified in the war of the Mercenaries, since he was still commanding armies long afterwards': for you will find in Polybius, Monsieur, Book I, Chapter XVII, that he was indeed captured by the rebels and crucified (in Sardinia, it is true, but at this same time). Thus it is not a question of 'that gentleman' having 'grounds for complaint against M. Flaubert', but rather of Polybius having grounds for complaint against M. Froehner.

As for the sacrificing of children, it is very far from 'impossible' that they were being burned alive at the time of Hamilcar, since they were still being so sacrificed at the time of Julius Caesar and Tiberius, if one is to trust Cicero (*Pro Balbo*) and Strabo (Book III). 'The statue of Moloch,' you say, 'does not resemble the hellish device described in *Salammbô*. This figure, composed of seven compartments, one above the other, for the confinement of victims, belongs to the Gallic religion. M. Flaubert has no pretext for making the analogy: his audacious transposition is unjustified.' No! I have no *pretext*: quite true. But I have a *text*, namely *the text*, the actual description by Diodorus,[13] which you may recall, and which is the source of mine – as you may verify should you care to re-read, or read, Book XX in Diodorus, Chapter IV, to which please add the Chaldean paraphrase by Paul Fage,[14] which you do not mention, and which is quoted by Selden, *De diis syriis*, pp. 164–170, along with Eusebius, *Preparatio evangelica*, Book I.

How can it be that 'history makes no mention of the miraculous mantle',[15] since you yourself state that 'it was exhibited in the temple of Venus, but much later, and only at the time of the Roman emperors'? Now I find in Athenaeus, XII, 58, a very minute description of this mantle of which 'history makes no mention'. It was bought from Dionysius the Elder for 120 talents, brought to Rome by Scipio Aemilianus, returned to Carthage by Caius Gracchus, brought again to Rome under Heliogabalus, and then again returned to Carthage. All of which is found also in Dureau de la Malle, from whom I most decidedly did 'profit'.

Three lines further down, you affirm, with the same – candour, that 'most of the other gods invoked in *Salammbô* are completely invented', and you add: 'Who has ever heard of an Aptouknos?' Who? D'Avezac[16] (in his *Cyrénaique*), in connection with a temple near Cyrene. – 'Of a Schaoûl?' But that is a name I give to a slave (see my page 91). – 'Or of a Matisman?' He is mentioned as a god by Corippus.[17] (See his *Johannis* and *Mémoires de l'Académie des Inscriptions*, Vol. XII, p. 181.) 'Who doesn't know that Micipsa was not a divinity, but a man?' But that is what I say, Monsieur, and very clearly, on that same page 91, when Salammbô calls her slaves: 'Help! Help! . . . Kroûm, Ewa, Micipsa, Schaoûl!'

You accuse me of taking Astareth and Astarté to be two distinct divinities. But early in the book, page 48, when Salammbô invokes Tanit, she invokes her by all her names at once: 'Anaïtis! Astarté! Derceto! Astareth! Tiratha!' And I was even careful to say, a little further on, page 52, that she repeated 'all these names, which had no distinct meaning for her'. Are you perhaps like Salammbô in this? I am tempted to think so, since you make Tanit the goddess of war rather than of love, of the female, humid, fecund element: you do so despite Tertullian, and despite the very name Tiratha, of which you will find the scarcely decent, but very explicit, explanation in Movers,[18] *Phenic.*, Book I, page 574.

Next, you are astonished by my apes consecrated to the moon and horses consecrated to the sun. 'These details' – you are sure – 'are found in no ancient author nor in any authentic monument.' But let me remind you, Monsieur, that baboons were consecrated to the moon in Egypt, as one still sees on the walls of the temples, and that Egyptian cults had penetrated into Libya and the oases. As for the horses, I do not say that they were consecrated to Aesculapius, but to Eshmun – who was assimilated to Aesculapius, Iolas, Apollo, the Sun. Horses consecrated to the sun are mentioned in Pausanius (Book I, Chapter I), and in the Bible (II Kings 23:11). But perhaps you will deny that the Egyptian temples are authentic monuments, and that the Bible and Pausanias are ancient authorities?

Apropos of the Bible, I will take another vast liberty, Monsieur, and draw your attention to Volume II of Cahen's translation,[19] page

186, where you will read this: 'Around their necks they wore, suspended from a gold chain, a small figure made of precious stones, which they called The Truth. Debates opened when the president set before himself the image of The Truth.' That is a text from Diodorus. Here is another, from Aelian:[20] 'The eldest among them was their chief, and the judge of all; around his neck he wore an image carved in sapphire. This image was called The Truth.' So be it, then, that [as you say], 'this "Truth" is a very pretty invention by M. Flaubert'.

But everything surprises you: malobathrum, which is quite properly written (if you have no objection) either 'malobathrum' or 'malabathrum' – the gold powder that is still gathered today, as in the past, on Carthaginian beaches; the elephants' ears painted blue; the men who daub themselves with vermilion (cinnabar) and eat vermin and apes; the Lydian men in women's dress, the carbuncles formed by lynxes' urine;[21] the mandragoras (which are in Hippocrates); the ankle-chainlet[22] (which is in the *Song of Songs* – Cahen, Volume XVI, 37); the sprinkling of pomegranate trees with silphium; bound beards; crucified lions, etc. – everything!

Well, no, Monsieur, I did *not* 'borrow all those details from the negroes of Senegambia'. I refer you, concerning the elephants, to the work by Armandi,[23] page 256, and to the authorities he indicates, such as Florus, Diodorus, Ammianus Marcellinus, and other such Senegambian Negroes.

As for the nomads who eat apes, munch lice and daub themselves with vermilion: since you might be 'asked from what source the author has drawn these precious bits of information', and would be, as you confess, 'very embarrassed as to know what to say', let me humbly give you a few hints that may help you in your research.

'The Maxyans . . . paint their bodies with vermilion.' 'The Gyzantians all paint themselves with vermilion, and eat apes.' 'Their women [the women of the Adyrmachidae] . . . if they are bitten by a louse, take it up, bite it, etc.' You will find all this in the Fourth Book of Herodotus, Chapters CXCI, CXCIV, and CLXVIII.[24] (I feel no 'embarrassment' in telling you this.)

It was Herodotus from whom I learned (in his description of Xerxes' army) that the Lydians wore women's dress. Athenaeus, also, in his chapter on the Etruscans and their resemblance to the Lydians, says that they wore women's dress. Finally, the Lydian Bacchus is always portrayed in feminine costume. Is that enough about the Lydians and their garb?

Beards bound up as a sign of mourning are mentioned in Cahen (Ezekiel 24:17),[25] and are found on Egyptian colossi, such as those at Abu Simbel; carbuncles formed by lynxes' urine, in Theophrastus's treatise *On Stones* and in Pliny, Book VIII, Chapter LVII. And as regards the crucified lions (you increase their number to two hundred, no doubt to impute to me an absurdity not my own), do me the favour of consulting Pliny yet again – same book, Chapter XVIII – where you will learn that Scipio Aemilianus and Polybius, riding together in the countryside near Carthage, saw several strung up in that position. '*Quia ceteri metu poenae similis absterrerentur eadem noxa.*'[26] Are those, Monsieur, some of the passages taken indiscriminately [as you suggest] from the *Univers pittoresque*, and 'which the higher criticism has tellingly used against M. Flaubert'? What is the 'higher criticism' you speak of? Your own?

You make very merry about the pomegranate trees sprinkled with silphium. But this detail is not my invention, Monsieur. It is in Pliny, Book XVII, Chapter XLVII. And I am very sorry to have to spoil your joke about the hellebore that 'should be grown at Charenton';[27] but as you yourself say, 'the most penetrating mind cannot make up for the lack of acquired knowledge'. Of which, by the way, you display a complete lack in affirming that 'among the precious stones in Hamilcar's treasury more than one properly belongs to Christian legend and superstition'. No, Monsieur: they are *all* in Pliny and Theophrastus.

The emerald steles at the temple entrance, which make you laugh (you have a delightful sense of humour), are mentioned by Philostratus (*Life of Apollonius*) and by Theophrastus (treatise *On Stones*), whom Heeren[28] (Volume II) quotes as follows: 'The largest Bactrian emerald is at Tyre, in the temple of Hercules. It is a column of considerable size.' Another passage from Theophrastus (Hill's translation): 'In their temple of Jupiter there was an obelisk composed of four emeralds.'

Despite your 'acquired knowledge', you confuse jade, which is a greenish-brown nephrite and comes from China, with jasper, a variety of quartz found in Europe *and* in Sicily. Had you chanced to open the *Dictionnaire de l'Académie française* at the word *jaspe*, you would have discovered without looking further that there is black, red and white jasper. You would then perhaps have moderated your marvellous mirth and not heaped hilarious reproaches on my master and friend Théophile Gautier for giving a woman (in his *Roman de la Momie*) 'green feet' – when the feet he gives her are white. Thus it is not he, but you, who have made 'a ridiculous error'. If you were a bit less disdainful of travel,[29] you could have seen in the Turin museum the very arm of this mummy, brought from Egypt by M. Passalacqua, and in the gesture described by Th. Gautier – 'a gesture' which, according to you, 'is certainly not Egyptian'.[30]

Even without being an engineer you would have learned the functioning of the *sakiehs* which carry water into the houses, and would have been convinced that I was not mistaken in speaking of black clothing: it is generally worn in those countries, where women of the upper classes never go out except swathed in black. But since you prefer written testimony, let me recommend, in the matter of women's clothing, Isaiah 3:18–24; the Mishna ('de Sabbatho'); Samuel 13:18; St Clement of Alexandria, *Paedagogus*, II, 13; and Abbé Mignot's dissertations in the *Mémoires de l'Académie des Inscriptions*, Vol. XLII. And as for that abundance of ornamentation which so astonishes you, I am certainly correct in attributing it to a people who encrusted the floors of their apartments with precious stones. (See Cahen, Ezekiel 28:14.) But you are unlucky, as regards precious stones.[31]

In closing, let me thank you, Monsieur, for your charming manners – a rare thing nowadays. I have called attention to only the grossest of your inaccuracies, those relating to specific points. As to your vague criticisms, your personal allusions, and your consideration of my book from a literary point of view, I have left them unmentioned. I have kept strictly to your own territory – erudition; and I repeat once more that there I am but middling strong. I know neither Hebrew, nor Arabic, nor German, nor Greek, nor Latin, and I make no boast of knowing French. I have often used translations; on occasion, the originals. In my uncertainties I have consulted the men who in France are considered the most competent, and if I have not been 'better guided' it is because I have not had the honour, the advantage, of knowing you: forgive me! Had I taken advice from you, would I 'have been more successful'? I doubt it. In any case, I would have been deprived of those proofs of benevolence which you display throughout your article, and I would have spared you the kind of remorse which you express at the close. But let me reassure you, Monsieur: though you seem to be terrified of your own strength, and though you seriously think that you have 'torn my book to shreds', have no 'fear': set your mind at rest! For you have not been 'cruel': you have merely been – trivial.[32]

1. More accurately, the article, entitled '*Le Roman archéologique en France*', was 'on' three publications: principally *Salammbô*, but also Théophile Gautier's *Le Roman de la Momie* and Ernest Desjardins' *Promenade dans les galeries du Musée Napoléon III*.

2. Le Musée Campana, also called Le Musée Napoléon III, was an assemblage of antiquities bought by the French state from an Italian collector, the Marchese Campana, and opened to the public in Paris in April 1862. For complex legal reasons it was forced to close, amid some scandal, after only a few months. It was dispersed, and some of its contents are now in the Louvre.

    Froehner had strangely called *Salammbô* 'the natural daughter of *Les Misérables*' – a work of which we have already heard Flaubert's opinion – 'and of the Campana collection'. Flaubert's riposte has been questioned because of what he wrote to Mlle Leroyer de Chantepie on April 24: 'Last Sunday . . . I at last finished my novel *Salammbô*.' But a novel is apt to be 'finished' several times. Flaubert possibly meant something like: 'Six weeks before the Musée Campana opened, everything that would appear in *Salammbô* was down on paper.' Indeed in that same letter of April 24 he mentions that the Musée Campana has opened.

3. Christian Tuxen Falbe, *Recherches sur l'Emplacement de Carthage, avec le plan topographique du Terrain et des Ruines de la Ville* (Paris, 1833); Adolphe-Jules-César-Auguste Dureau de la Malle, *Recherches sur la topographie de Carthage* (Paris, 1835).

4. These and the following are identifiable sections or landmarks of Punic Carthage. The Taenia ('ribbon') was the strip of land, south of the city, dividing the present Lake of Tunis from the sea; the Cothon was the military harbour, and so on.

5. The Ancô, which is not mentioned by name in Chapter XV or elsewhere in the novel, is identified by Flaubert in one of his working notes as the dungeon, hollowed in the rock of the Acropolis, where Mâtho is held in solitary confinement and from which he emerges, on the day of his execution, 'bowed almost double, with the bewildered air of wild beasts when they are suddenly released from captivity'.

6. Heinrich Friedrich Wilhelm Gesenius (1786–1842), German orientalist and biblical scholar.

7. On introducing Narr'Havas, the Numidian prince, in the early pages of *Salammbô*, Flaubert emphasizes his 'blazing, staring eyes'. *Feu du souffle* can be translated 'fire of the breath', or perhaps 'fiery current'. One wonders whether Flaubert was aware that *haouah* is also a form of a word meaning 'passion'. It seems likely that had he known this he would have profited from the word's double intensity.

8. Meaning that the *m* should be pronounced hard, rather than merely giving the syllable a nasal sound, as when *m* or *n*, preceded by a vowel, is written singly.

9. A humorous word coined from the French *chinoiserie*, literally 'Chinese knick-knacks,' but in common use as 'foolish intricacies', 'stuff and nonsense'. This was one of many journalistic lampoonings of *Salammbô*.

10. The point here seems to be a distinction between Cappadocia, the name of the Roman province north of Cilicia, and the narrow antique application of the name 'Asia' to the country around Ephesus. Flaubert had ridden through both regions with Maxime DuCamp in 1850.

11. Probably a metaphor: 'to cut their throats'. But the more literal 'to make them drink [molten] iron' would not be out of place in the *Salammbô* torture repertoire.

12. The Syssites were doubly unfortunate in the printed French spellings of their name. There was the misprint in the first edition, already alluded to; and furthermore, as Froehner had properly shown (a point ignored by Flaubert), the correct French spelling would be 'Syssities' (from the Greek *Syssitia*). In English it is usually written 'Syssitia'. Flaubert's definition of the term is correct. (David Marcus – D.M.)

13. Diodorus Siculus, Greek historian of the first century BC.

14. Froehner, in his riposte, makes fun of Flaubert's Gallicization of the name of the seventeenth-century German scholar 'Paulus Fagius' – which was, he says, in itself a Latinization of the original 'Paul Bucheim'. Froehner also corrects Flaubert's '*De diis syriis*' to '*De dis syriis*'. Selden's title page says '*De dis syris*'.

15. The '*zaïmph*', the sacred veil, or mantle, of the goddess Tanit, stolen, in the novel, from her temple by the giant Mâtho and retrieved by Salammbô in Mâtho's tent at the price (ecstatically paid) of her virginity.

16. Marie-Armand-Pascal d'Avezac-Macaya (1799–1875), French geographer.

17. See letter to Sainte-Beuve, p. 390, n. 33.

18. For Movers see letter to Sainte-Beuve, p. 390, n. 31. The 'explanation', as given in Movers' original German text (p. 583), is left in Latin: *pudendum muliebre*.

19. The Hebraicist Samuel Cahen (1796–1862) published his French translation of the Old Testament in eighteen volumes (1831–1851). They include the Hebrew text and ample notes by Cahen. The passages from Diodorus and Aelian quoted by Flaubert are in Cahen's 'supplementary notes' to Exodus 28:30. ('I have just read Cahen's book from one end to the other,' Flaubert

had written Ernest Feydeau in August 1857. 'I know perfectly well that it's very faithful, very good, very scholarly: no matter! I prefer the old Vulgate, because of the Latin! How it rumbles, beside this poor little puny consumptive French! I'll even show you two or three mistranslations, or embellishments, in the Vulgate, which are much finer than the true meaning.')

20.   The anecdotal *Various History* of Claudius Aelianus (Aelian), Roman rhetorician of the age of Hadrian.

21.   See letter to Sainte-Beuve, p. 389, n. 17.

22.   This is the gold chainlet joining Salammbô's ankles, first described by Flaubert as worn *'pour régler sa marche'*, and which later snaps when she is in Mâtho's arms. Cahen, in his note to a variant of the Song of Songs 2:7, refers to 'the chainlets attached to both legs, to prevent accidents that might befall girls taking overlong strides. This kind of fetter served as a sign of virginity – a sign whose absence could give rise to great scandal at the time of marriage.'

23.   Pierre-Damien Armandi, *Histoire militaire des éléphants* (Paris, 1843); L. Florus (other names and exact identity uncertain), Latin historian of the age of Hadrian and Trajan: *Epitome de T. Livio Bellorum omnium annorum DCC Libri duo*; for Marcellinus, see letter to Sainte-Beuve, p. 390, n. 31.

24.   George Rawlinson's translation of Herodotus, IV, 168 reads: 'Their women . . . when they catch any vermin on their persons, bite it and throw it away.'

25.   Cahen's translation, ' . . . *ne fais pas de deuil; . . . ne te voile pas le menton'* is closer to Flaubert's 'beards' than is the King James: 'cover not thy lips'.

26.   Flaubert's slightly faulty Latin has been corrected here. The meaning is: 'because the others might be deterred from the same mischief by fear of the same penalty'. The *'Univers pittoresque'* (begun in 1844) was a popular series of seventy illustrated volumes describing the countries of the world.

27.   Charenton is a famous mental hospital of seventeenth-century origin in a suburb of Paris, popularly thus called by the name of its location; now officially named L'Hôpital Esquirol. The expression *'bon pour Charenton'* ('fit for the loony bin') is still current. Froehner's jeer at the 'pomegranate trees sprinkled with silphium' reads: 'I know that an infusion of this plant was a well-known herbal drink . . . What would we say of a gardener who sprinkled his orange trees with linden tea? We would probably send him to grow hellebore at Charenton.' (In ancient times hellebore was thought to cure madness.)

28.   Arnold Hermann Ludwig Heeren (1760–1842), German author of numerous works on ancient history. It is not certain to which of them Flaubert refers. As to the huge 'emeralds', both Theophrastus himself and John Hill, in his notes to his translation (London, 1746), say that they are the stuff of legend and cannot possibly be true emeralds. Flaubert had

apparently read Hill carelessly. Froehner, in his riposte, continued to jeer
at Flaubert's 'emeralds'.

29. Froehner had written of some of Flaubert's details that 'they smack of the
     modern traveller, who is perhaps an excellent recounter of traditions picked
     up along the way, but whose testimony has not the slightest value when
     it comes to reconstituting the society of ancient Carthage'. Flaubert, of
     course, was 'the modern traveller'. For example, in connection with Flaub-
     ert's mention (a few lines further on) of *sakiehs*, which he had seen in
     Egypt, Froehner had expressed doubt that they could raise water to the
     upper floors of Carthaginian houses, some of which were six storeys high.

30. Gautier himself says, in the novel, that the gesture of his beautiful Tahoser,
     '*celle de la Vénus de Milo*', is '*peu fréquent chez les momies*'.

31. Flaubert himself seems 'unlucky' in this reference. Ezekiel 28:14 does not
     speak of the floors of apartments. The King James reads: ' . . . thou hast
     walked up and down in the midst of the stones of fire'. Cahen's French
     translation is almost identical.

32. Flaubert's word is *léger*.

~

Froehner defended himself, and counter-attacked, in a second article,
in which he spoke of his own 'urbanity' as contrasted with Flaubert's
bad manners. He granted Flaubert 'a certain talent for light literature'
and urged him not to stray again, in his novel writing, from his
native Normandy. The Flaubert–Froehner engagements in what
Sainte-Beuve had called the 'battle' of *Salammbô* ended with a letter
from Flaubert to the editor of *L'Opinion Nationale*:

~

To Adolphe Guéroult

[Paris,] February 2, 1863

Mon cher Monsieur Guéroult:

Forgive me for bothering you once again. But since M. Froehner
is to publish in *L'Opinion Nationale* what he has just printed in the
Revue Contemporaine, I venture to draw his attention to the following:

I did, in fact, commit a *very* grave error. Instead of Diodorus,
Book XX, Chapter IV, read Chapter XIX. Another error: I forgot a
text concerning the statue of Moloch, in Dr Jacobi's *Mythologie*,
Bernard's translation, page 322, where M. Froehner will once again
find the seven compartments that so arouse his indignation.

Also, although he has not deigned to give me a single word of reply concerning (1) the topography of Carthage; (2) the mantle of Tanit; (3) the Punic names I 'travestied'; (4) the gods I 'invented'; and though he has maintained the same silence regarding (5) the horses consecrated to the Sun; (6) the statuette of The Truth; (7) the bizarre customs of the nomads; (8) the crucified lions; (9) the sprinkling with silphium; along with (10) the lynx carbuncles and (11) the Christian superstitions regarding precious stones; keeping similarly silent about (12) jade, and (13) jasper; making no mention of anything concerning (14) Hanno; (15) women's costumes; (16) the dresses of the Lydian men; (17) the fantastic gesture of the Egyptian mummy; (18) the Campana museum; (19) his quotations (inaccurate) from my book; and (20) my Latin, which he urges you to consider incorrect, etc., I am nonetheless quite ready, concerning all that and all the rest, to admit that he is right, and that antiquity is his private property. Let him therefore enjoy himself in peace, 'destroying my edifice', and proving that I know nothing at all . . . For I will not answer him. I will pay no further attention to this gentleman.

I withdraw a word that seems to have displeased him. No: M. Froehner is not *léger*. He is just the opposite. And if I 'chose him as a victim, from among so many writers who have disparaged my book', it was because he had seemed to me the most serious. I was certainly mistaken.

Finally, since he interests himself in my biography (as though I troubled myself about his), affirming twice (he *knows!*) that I was six years writing *Salammbô*, I will confess to him that I am not entirely sure, by now, that I was ever at Carthage.

It remains, Monsieur, for both of us to thank you: I, for your having spontaneously offered me such generous hospitality in your newspaper; and as for M. Froehner, he must be infinitely grateful to you. You have given him the opportunity to apprise many people of his existence. This foreigner[1] desperately wanted to become known. Now he is: to his – advantage.

A thousand greetings.

1. Readers of Volume I may nevertheless recall Flaubert's claiming that he cared nothing for 'the idea of a fatherland, that is, a certain portion of the earth's surface drawn on a map and separated from others by a red or blue line', and that 'I am as Chinese as I am French'.

~

About *Salammbô*, André Malraux once said that what Flaubert wanted it to be was 'a series of poetic moments'.[1] Surely *Salammbô* is that: a concentrated essence, distilled by Flaubert's imagination from observation and research. Sainte-Beuve, in objecting to Flaubert's method and hating the subject, and Froehner, picking flaws in the research, do not touch the heart of the matter. It is as though one of Delacroix's paintings – say one of his Arab horsemen disembowelling a wild beast – were to be disparaged on the grounds of technique, subject, and some 'incorrect' details. Whereas it is Delacroix's fire that counts. Is there fire – one might say 'the sacred fire' – in *Salammbô*? Readers have always been, and continue to be, divided in their opinions. The burden of these two chapters has been to display, chiefly in Flaubert's own words, his struggle to light such a fire and keep it burning, and the alternations in his own estimates of what he had accomplished. Even so, his prodigious effort will be considered in conjunction with the observation he himself made when he was beginning the novel: 'I would give the demi-ream of notes I've written during the last five months and the ninety-eight volumes I've read, to be, for only three seconds, really moved by the passion of my heroes.'

1. André Malraux, '*Professions délirantes*', in *L'Homme précaire et la littérature* (Paris: Gallimard, 1977). Translated by Jeanine Parisier Plottel in *New York Literary Forum*, 1979.

X

Interlude: Society

1863–1866

IN JANUARY 1863, two months after the publication of *Salammbô*, there opened in Flaubert's life a curious new episode which is perhaps best introduced by a series of short letters, all of them dated in that month and having to do with a great house in Paris, in the rue de Courcelles.

~

TO EUDORE SOULIÉ

[Paris,] Tuesday [January 13, 1863]

My dear Soulié

We should like to know – Saint-Victor, the Goncourts, and myself – what is customary regarding the staff in the rue de Courcelles. What does one give as New Year's presents? And to whom does one give them? You will be going there tomorrow, Wednesday . . . It would be kind of you to find out about this from Giraud or Mme de Fly . . .[1]

---

1. Eudore Soulié (1817–1876), curator of the Musée de Versailles, was a member of the 'inner circle' surrounding Princesse Mathilde Bonaparte; it is not clear why he, presumably *au courant* with the customs of the princess's household in the rue de Courcelles, should have to seek information from the artist Eugène Giraud (1806–1881), the princess's instructor in watercolour painting, and Mme de Fly, the princess's lady-in-waiting.

Paul de Saint-Victor was a critic of literature and art. He and Flaubert were friendly until he refused to write an article about *L'Éducation sentimentale*, which he disliked.

~

CAMILLE DOUCET TO FLAUBERT[1]

January 18, 1863 Ministère d'État Théâtres

Mon cher Confrère et Ami,

Here is a letter I promised to hand you myself, but I am a little unwell and send it to you instead.

You are definitely expected on Wednesday, 9 o'clock.

Confidentially, the Emperor and Empress will be there, and – this I whisper in your ear – have expressed the desire to see you.

I have promised you will be there: don't let me down.

All yours,
Camille Doucet

I am writing to Bouilhet today, sending him 2000 francs.

1. Camille Doucet (1812–1895), in addition to being a bureaucrat charged with certain responsibilities regarding ceremonies and the dispensing of grants-in-aid to needy dramatists like Louis Bouilhet, was himself a dramatist, characterized as follows in Larousse, *Grand Dictionnaire Universel*: 'His temperament was devoid of those vigorous hatreds felt by genius . . . and this smoothed his path to the Academy.' This amiable man succeeded to Alfred de Vigny's chair in the French Academy in 1865.

~

TO THÉOPHILE GAUTIER

[Paris, January 19, 1863]

Mon vieux Théo,

Don't come on Wednesday. I'm invited that evening to Princesse Mathilde's, and we wouldn't have time for a leisurely talk after dinner. Come on Saturday instead. I have alerted DuCamp . . .

Agreed? Till Saturday.

~

TO FÉLICIEN DE SAULCY[1]

[Paris,] Saturday morning [January 24, 1863]

Mon cher Ami

. . . Do you remember showing me, two or three years ago, a gold repoussé plaque that was brought back from Kamiros by Salzmann?[2] This plaque represented the figure of a woman, which served me for one of Salammbô's costumes. I need to see it again. Where is it? Do you have a drawing of it, or a detailed description?

I have had a request from a very high source, on behalf of a great lady of your acquaintance, for Salammbô's costumes[3] (there are four in my book, including the one taken from the plaque). I am having them drawn by Bida, and shall add an explanatory note, as clear as possible. Such are my occupations at the moment . . .

1. Félicien de Saulcy, archaeologist and numismatist, had published the discovery of the Punic 'Marseilles Tariff' (see p. 389, n. 5). Flaubert had met him in Constantinople in 1850.

2. August Salzmann, another archaeologist, would publish his *Nécropole de Kamiros* in 1865. Alexandre Bida was a well-known painter of Oriental subjects and illustrator of the Bible. Maxime DuCamp says in his memoirs that Bida declined the commission to design *Salammbô* costumes.

3. Sainte-Beuve wrote to Matthew Arnold on January 13, 1863: '*Salammbô* is our great event! The Empress is so struck by it that she wants to dress as Salammbô at some court masquerade or other, and has expressed a wish to know the author.'

∽

In 1863 Princesse Mathilde Bonaparte, niece of the great Napoleon, daughter of his brother Jerome, was forty-three years old. In youth she had been spoken of as a bride for her first cousin, Louis Napoleon, now Emperor Napoleon III (there was in reality no blood tie, the Emperor's illegitimacy being well known); but she had married, instead, the wealthy Russian Count Anatole Demidoff. Mistreated by him, she had successfully petitioned Czar Nicholas to order her husband to grant her a legal separation and a large financial settlement; and now she reigned in Paris as what might be called her imperial cousin's unofficial – but subsidized – cultural representative. Her love of society and her taste, of sorts, for the arts, brought her a pension from the civil list, the government favouring her salon in the belief (which proved to be well founded) that it might win the support, or at least moderate the opposition, of members of the 'liberal' professions, seduced by the princess's charm and flattered to mingle with ministers and courtiers.

With memorable exceptions, writers have historically been far from immune to the appeal of official pomp, whether royal, republican or totalitarian; and by 1863 Flaubert was regularly attending the princess's evenings in the rue de Courcelles during those few months of the year he spent in Paris – along with the Goncourts, Sainte-Beuve, Taine, Renan and others. In addition to being able to help them, Princesse Mathilde – '*Notre Dame des Arts*', she was sometimes called by her familiars – was capable of true friendship with the artists and writers among her guests, and Flaubert was not the only one to reciprocate. Despite the constant mention of her in memoirs and letters of the time, and the efforts of biographers, the princess remains rather a figure of 'a lady of position' than a distinct personality.

Her older brother, Prince Jerome Napoleon, the so-called republican member of the imperial family, nicknamed 'Plon-Plon' and married to Princesse Clothilde (Clotilda, daughter of King Victor Emmanuel of Italy), was also interested in the arts. He was said to have tried to stop the government's prosecution of Flaubert as the author of *Madame Bovary* in 1857, and since then the two men had become acquainted. Flaubert came to know, also, one of the prince's many mistresses, the beautiful courtesan Jeanne de Tourbey, and wrote her a number of letters, rather forced in their gallantry and of insufficient interest to include here. His activities in imperial society lasted a few years, ending with the collapse of the regime in 1870. The friendship with Princesse Mathilde was the chief survival.

A passage from a letter he wrote to his niece Caroline in January 1864 is typical of his references – half boastful, half abashed – to this side of his life: 'Saturday I dined chez la Princesse Mathilde, and last night (Saturday–Sunday) I was at the Opera Ball until five in the morning (!) with Prince Napoleon and the Ambassador from Turin, in the big imperial box. *Voilà*. The following should be read as spoken by the sheik: "How different from our dull life in the provinces!" '[1]

1. 'The sheik', a character invented by Flaubert and Maxime DuCamp, was the type of pompous French bourgeois to whom they attributed all possible clichés (see Volume I).

To Jules Duplan

> *Palais de Compiègne*[1] *corridor de la Pompe*
> *Second floor, no. 85 [November 12 (?), 1864]*

My dear Jules,

Do me the following service pronto. Get yourself to the Passage de l'Opéra and order a bouquet of white camellias[2] from Mme Prévost – the finest possible; I insist that it be ultra-chic. (One has to cut a fine figure when one belongs to the lower orders of society.) The box must arrive here on Monday morning, so that I can present the flowers that evening. The florist can post the bill to me here or you can pay it, as you prefer. Don't forget, for Christ's sake – I'm counting on you. Immediate reply, please. *Je t'embrasse.*

1. From the following description of imperial weekends at the Château de Compiègne, given in the Larousse *Histoire de France*, it will be seen that at least as far as the date of his visit is concerned, Flaubert was a particularly honoured guest:

    'During the three weeks of the Compiègne season (from All Saints' Day to the opening of the legislature), five groups of guests were entertained at the chateau, each group staying for four days, not including the evening of arrival and the morning of departure. It was a particular favour to be invited for November 15, the *fête de l'Impératrice* . . . For each series, the Empress herself supervised the assignment of rooms, with the guest's name on a card on each door. She did not always manage to satisfy everyone. The painter Couture has been quoted as replying to the sovereign, when she asked him whether he was comfortably installed: "All the more so, Madame, since my room reminds me of the garret I lived in when I was beginning my career."

    'The guests arrived at four o'clock. The chamberlains took them to their apartments, and they foregathered at 7.15, the ladies in ball gowns, the men in tails and either knee-breeches or narrow trousers, in the grand salon, where the sovereigns soon made their appearance. Dinner was served at 7.30. After dinner, before half past eight, everyone returned to the salon, where there were charades, card games and dancing. The next day there was a shoot, and in the evening a gala theatrical performance, serious or light as the case might be. The second day, rides in the forest and excursion to Pierrefonds [the nearby medieval chateau recently restored by Viollet LeDuc]. The third day, riding to hounds; and the fourth, small-game shooting, in which the ladies joined. The following day, after lunch, the guests left, driven to the railway station in the chateau carriages.'

    Maxime DuCamp has written about Flaubert at Compiègne:

    'He did not dislike grandeur, and wherever he was, he was always himself. Into that society, so subservient and right-thinking, he carried the spirit of literary independence, which he of all men possessed to the highest degree. One night, in a group gathered around the Empress, someone spoke irreverently of Victor Hugo: I don't know whether sincerely or in an attempt to flatter the imperial pair. [Victor Hugo was a political exile at this time.] Gustave Flaubert interrupted in no uncertain terms: "Stop right there! That man is the master of us all. Hats off when his name is mentioned!" The other persisted: "Still, you would agree, Monsieur, that the man who wrote *Les Châtiments*..." Flaubert glared: "*Les Châtiments!* Magnificent poetry! I'll recite it, if you like!" The subject was quickly changed.'

2. White camellias were the favourite flower of the Empress, whose celebrated beauty and grace were not lost on Flaubert. He was ordering the flowers to arrive for her fête on the fifteenth. (Readers may recall his broadside at poor Louise Colet when she reproached him for never sending her flowers.) On a later occasion, after seeing the Empress, Flaubert asked Jules Duplan to give Mme Cornu (see p. 505, n. 1) a message, clearly meant to be passed on, which included the words 'I love Her', the capitalization – '*Je L'aime*' – reverentially identifying the object of his affection.

But by 1869, in a letter to Caroline telling her of seeing the Emperor at a ball given in his honour by Princesse Mathilde, he adds ruefully: 'His spouse seems to have forgotten me.' By that time, having finished *L'Éducation sentimentale*, for which he had immersed himself in the history and politics of the past several decades, he was referring ironically to the Emperor as 'our Saviour'.

~

To his niece Caroline

[Paris,] Wednesday [February 22, 1865]

· · ·

What do you want me to tell you about the Prince's ball?[1] It was a very big affair, and very luxurious as far as the decoration of the apartments was concerned. What surprised me most was the number of salons – twenty-three, each opening into the next, not counting the smaller side-rooms. 'Monseigneur'[2] was astonished by the number of people I knew. I must have spoken with two hundred. In the midst of this 'brilliant society', what did I see? Several mugs from Rouen! Old Lédier, old Corneille, old Barbet, old Rouland, the four of them together. Horrified, I put a distance between myself and that group and went and sat on the 'steps of the throne', beside Princesse Primoli. On Saturday said princess sent me her album, for me to inscribe some mighty thoughts therein. I wrote one thought

– but it wasn't mighty. Half the ladies who attended the ball are now in their beds, having caught cold on leaving: the confusion in the cloakroom and in the calling of carriages was staggering. I gazed with admiration at the Régent[3] (15 millions) on my Sovereign's head; it's quite a pretty thing. I was never very close to her, but her little spouse passed so near me that if I had chosen to bow to him I'd have fallen on his nose.[4] Princesse Clothilde, seeing me with Mme Sandeau[5] on my arm, asked her cousin [Princesse Mathilde] if that was my wife – inspiring many pleasantries by both princesses at my expense. Such are the witty cancans I have to report to you.

. . .

1. by Prince Jerome Napoleon at his Paris residence, the Palais Royal.
2. Louis Bouilhet. So called, according to Flaubert's niece Caroline, because of his 'imposing appearance and slightly unctuous manner'.
3. The 136-carat diamond (reduced from 410 carats by cutting) bought by Thomas Pitt (grandfather of William Pitt the elder, earl of Chatham) when he was Governor of Madras and sold in 1717 to the duc d'Orléans, regent of France. It remained 'the property of the French crown' and is now in the Louvre.
4. Napoleon III was considerably under Flaubert's 'gigantic' height of five feet eight inches.
5. Mme Sandeau's husband, the novelist Jules Sandeau, had been an early lover of the young Baronne Dudevant, who had appropriated part of his name to become George Sand. Sandeau was now librarian at the Palais de Saint-Cloud and a member of the French Academy.

～

To Princesse Mathilde

Caude-Côte, near Dieppe, August 16 [1866]

Madame *et Princesse,*

How kind of you to write to me at once! A sign of your large heart.

I don't doubt the good will of M. Duruy,[1] but I imagine that the idea was somewhat suggested to him by someone else? So the red ribbon[2] is for me more than a favour, almost a memento. I did not need that, to have Princesse Mathilde often in my thoughts.

. . . Awaiting the pleasure and the honour of seeing you, *Princesse,* I kiss your hands and beg you to believe me your very grateful, devoted, and affectionate

Gustave Flaubert

1. Victor Duruy (1811–1894), Minister of Education.
2. The red ribbon of the Légion d'Honneur.

~

To CHARLES-AUGUSTIN SAINTE-BEUVE

Caude-Côte, near Dieppe, August 16, 1866

Cher Maître,

I have received M. Duruy's letter along with your note. Thank you for the one and especially for the other. But I am long accustomed to your way of doing things.[1]

Haven't friends had a little hand in this affair? I mean *un ami* or *une amie*? The latter has been very kind also: it was from her that I first learned of my nomination.[2]

A thousand thanks from your sincerely devoted

G. Flaubert

P.S. This should be the occasion for thinking of something witty or heartfelt to say. But my mind is a blank. So – another handshake.

1. Sainte-Beuve was Flaubert's chief proposer for the Légion d'Honneur.
2. A fortnight later Flaubert wrote again to Princesse Mathilde, who had told him that she herself was sending him the cross that is the emblem of the Légion d'Honneur. (The crosses the princess gave her protégés were diamond-studded.) 'The present from you will be more precious to me than the nomination in itself. For the honour is shared by many, but not this.'

~

It has been said that Flaubert persuaded himself that he had 'fallen in love' with Princesse Mathilde, and that on one occasion he was about to declare himself to her but was overcome by timidity and rushed from the room; and Enid Starkie has noted that in one of his letters to the princess he told her he wished she were a simple bourgeoise so that he could speak to her more easily. The tone of certain of his letters about the court, and some of his language in those to the princess (formulas he used in writing to no one else – '*Je me mets à vos pieds*'; '*Votre très humble, très devoué et très affectionné*') bring to mind Voltaire's letters to Catherine the Great.

No doubt to himself, and defensively to at least one friend, Flaubert insisted that favour at court did not soften his memory of his earlier prosecution by the regime, or – by implication – cause him to swerve from his principles. Mlle Amélie Bousquet, the Rouen novelist who had been tactless about Louise Colet's 'portrayals' of him (and whose continued presumptions would eventually put an end to their friendship) had now teased him about his acceptance of the Légion d'Honneur; he replied in August 1866:

> What gives me pleasure about the red ribbon is the joy it causes those who love me: that is the best part of it, I assure you. Ah! if one had been given it when one was eighteen! As to forgetting my trial and no longer feeling resentment – not at all! I am made of slate when it comes to receiving impressions, and of bronze when it comes to retaining them; with me, nothing is ever effaced; all is cumulative.

In writing certain of those lines, Flaubert was perhaps remembering the lack of confidence his family had shown in him as a youth, with his father a famous surgeon, his elder brother already studying medicine, and he himself, in their eyes, with aptitude for nothing but scribbling. Had some honour, or at least recognition, befallen him at that time, it would have carried far greater weight than now.

XI

The Beginning of L'Éducation sentimentale

1863–1866

SHORTLY AFTER THE publication of *Madame Bovary*, and when she had already begun to make notes for *Salammbô*, Flaubert had written to Mlle Leroyer de Chantepie (March 18, 1857): 'I feel the need to step out of the modern world, which I've dipped my pen into too much; and besides, I find it as wearying to reproduce as disgusting to contemplate.' But readers who have become acquainted with Flaubert through his letters will not be surprised to learn that as early as June 1859, before he had reached even mid-point in the Carthaginian novel, he was writing to Ernest Feydeau: 'The deeper I plunge into antiquity, the more I feel the need to do something modern, and inside my head I'm cooking up a whole crew of characters.'

Who were those modern characters whom he was pondering even while struggling with the Mercenaries of the third century BC?

Most probably they were the provisional cast of what would, in fact, be his next – what he would call his 'Parisian' – novel: *L'Éducation sentimentale*.[1] But at this same time he was considering a different novel – one about a pair of '*bonshommes*' whom he referred to as 'my two copy-clerks', or 'my two troglodytes'. (This novel, eventually to be called *Bouvard and Pécuchet*, would be postponed and would be his last work, unfinished at his death.) An entry in one of his notebooks, dated 'Today, December 12, 1862, my forty-first birthday' – that is, two weeks after the publication of *Salammbô* – contains the first mention of the 'Parisian' novel:

Stopped by at M. de Lesseps to leave a copy of *Salammbô* for
the Bey of Tunis. Also left copies for [Jules] Janin, Ed[ouard]
Delessert, H[ector] Berlioz. At the Palais Royal, signed the
Prince's visitors' book. Bought two Carcel lamps. Received a
letter from B[ouilhet]. And applied myself seriously to the
outline of the first part of my modern Parisian novel.

For some time he hesitated between the two projects. 'I'm slaving
at my Parisian novel, which doesn't advance at all,' he wrote to Jules
Duplan at the end of March, 1863. 'It's stupid, stale stuff, nothing
sharp or new about it. I haven't thought up a single major scene;
I'm not *caught* by this book. I can't manage an erection, and keep
masturbating my poor brain in vain. I'm attracted by the story of
my troglodytes, and have been working at an outline for that, as
well. *It* is good, I'm sure, despite what would be frightful difficulties
in varying the monotony of the effect. But I'll be hounded out of
France and Europe if I write it!' And to the Goncourts: 'I'm working
on the outlines of two novels. So far, I don't know which of them
to harness myself to.'
He kept appealing to Louis Bouilhet to help him make up his
mind. 'If you really don't feel yourself primed for the sentimental
novel, then go full steam ahead with your two clerks,' Bouilhet wrote
to him about this time. And again: 'If your Parisian subject is
definitely not ripe, that's no cause for despair – it will come later;
and in the meantime you have another project, very tart and original,
to get to work on.'[2]
In early April he was busy at the 'sentimental' novel. 'I'm working
uninterruptedly on the outline of my *Éducation sentimentale,*' he
wrote to Jules Duplan. 'Perhaps it's beginning to take shape. But its
general design is bad! It doesn't form a pyramid! I doubt that I'll
ever become enthusiastic about this idea. I'm far from cheerful.' A
week later, also to Duplan:

> 'I'm not in a state of grace,' as pious folk say; 'I can't get it
> up,' as pigs put it. *L'Éducation sentimentale* doesn't move. I lack
> *facts* . . . In short, I'm disgusted with it. Very probably I'm
> going to fall back on *The Two Troglodytes*. It's an old idea that
> I've had for years, and perhaps I should get it off my chest. I'd

rather write a book about passion, but one doesn't choose one's subjects: one submits to them. Tomorrow I expect Monseigneur: we're going to talk about all this, and I'll make up my mind, but I feel very empty and very tired, and quite glum.

Once again he wrote to Duplan: 'Decidedly, I wasn't born to write modern things; I pay too high a price for dealing with them. After *Salammbô* I should have immediately set to work on *Saint Antoine*.[3] I was all set for it, and it would be done now. At the moment, I'm bored to death: my idleness (which isn't idleness: I keep racking my brains like a poor wretch), my non-writing, rather, weighs heavy on me. A cursed state!' To the Goncourts he wrote again lamenting his dilemma: 'Besides, spring is giving me wild longings to take off for China or the Indies, and Normandy with its greenery sets my teeth on edge like a dish of bitter sorrel. To cap it all, I'm having stomach cramps . . .'

It was in this state of indecision that he wrote his first letter to a new friend, a Russian now living in France, whom he had met at one of the Magny dinners.

1. Flaubert had given this title to a novel written in his twenties. He had wisely put it aside, and it would be published only posthumously, as an example of his juvenilia. 'Sentimental Education', the literal and usual translation of '*L'Éducation sentimentale*', is somewhat ambiguous. 'The Story of a Romantic Passion' would be closer to the theme of both books. In spirit, Flaubert's title is related to Goethe's *Die Wahlverwandtschaften* (Elective Affinities). Both versions of *L'Éducation sentimentale* treat of love and its illusions: not, as the English title might suggest, of sentimental schooling.
2. Benjamin F. Bart has written about Bouilhet's role in 'Louis Bouilhet, Flaubert's "Accoucheur" ', in *Symposium*, autumn 1963.
3. Except for the few extracts printed in *L'Artiste* during the first excitement over *Madame Bovary*, *The Temptation of Saint Anthony* was still in manuscript.

~

To Ivan Turgenev

Croisset, near Rouen, March 16 [1863]

Dear Monsieur Turgenev,

How grateful I am for your present! I have just read your two volumes, and cannot resist telling you that I am enchanted by them.

For me, you have long been a Master. But the more I study you, the more I marvel at your talent. I admire your manner, at once intense and restrained: that sympathy which extends even to the humblest beings and endows landscapes with reflection. We see, and we dream.

Just as when I read *Don Quixote* I long to ride a horse along a road white with dust and eat olives and raw onions in the shade of a rock, so your *Scènes de la vie russe*[1] makes me want to be jolted in a telega among snow-covered fields, listening to the howling of the wolves. Your works emanate a perfume at once sweet and pungent, a charming sadness that reaches to the depths of my soul.

What art you possess! What a mixture of tenderness, irony, observation, and colour! And how they are all combined! How you bring off your effects! What sureness of touch!

You are *particular*, and at the same time general. How many things that I have felt and experienced myself I find and recognize in you! In '*Trois Rencontres*', among others; in 'Jacques Passynkof', in the '*Journal d'un homme de trop*', etc. – everywhere.

But what has been insufficiently praised in you is *heart* – that is, ever-present *feeling*, some profound, secret sensibility.

I was very happy to make your acquaintance a fortnight ago and to shake your hand. Now I do so again, more firmly than ever, and beg you to think of me, *cher confrère*, as

> All yours –
> G^ve Flaubert

1. 'Scenes from Russian Life', an early collection of Turgenev's short stories in French translation. Of those mentioned by Flaubert in this letter, '*Journal d'un homme de trop*' is recognizable as the tale known in English translation as 'Diary of a Superfluous Man'; but other titles seldom correspond to their English versions.

~

Still hesitating between the two novels, Flaubert spent the next few months working on an unlikely theatrical piece, *Le Château des coeurs* (The Castle of Hearts), in collaboration with Louis Bouilhet and another Norman friend, a witty politician, Charles d'Osmoy. This was undertaken in the hope of earning some money: *Madame Bovary* and *Salammbô* had both sold well, but the agreements Flaubert had signed with Michel Lévy were much in the latter's favour. Belonging to the French theatrical genre called *féerie* – a spectacle with super-natural characters (fairies, wizards, and so on), requiring special scenic effects – *Le Château des coeurs* is an allegory, a contest between good impulses (fairies) and bad (gnomes) for possession of the human heart. Flaubert would keep tinkering with it, and proposing it to producers, for many years. Never performed, it was the first of his several theatrical misadventures. Later in his life it was printed in instalments in a magazine.

Introductory paragraphs of a letter to Bouilhet about this *féerie*, written during a July vacation in Vichy, are more Flaubertian than the unfortunate piece itself:

> I don't know whether it's hot in the Celestial Empire [Bouilhet was studying Chinese], but here the heat is one great fart-blast. Mercury plus humidity means sweat-through-clothes; under-wear wringing wet; trickle-trickle between arse-cheeks; underarms, phew!; shoes hell on feet; skin scorched; air stifling, gasp-making, murderous. Frantically oppressive; the only breeze the panting of human breasts; every bourgeois metamorphosed into a hot-air furnace . . . In short, the brain melts and animal spirits are disordered. I feel as flabby as a dog's prick after coitus . . . I have read Renan's *Life of Jesus*, a work about which, between you and me, I am none too enthusiastic . . .

Late in 1863 Flaubert's much loved, motherless, seventeen-year-old niece, Caroline Hamard, who lived with him and her grand-mother, and whom he had helped educate, was under family pressure to accept her suitor, Ernest Commanville, a Rouen lumber-merchant, for whom she felt no affection. In writing her the following letter, rather than encouraging her to resist, Flaubert – the self-professed enemy of the bourgeois – incurred a responsibility that was to cost him dear (see Appendix IV).

∽

To his niece Caroline

Paris, Wednesday, 3 o'clock [December 23, 1863]

. . . Now let's talk about the big thing.

So, my poor Caro, you're still in the same uncertainty, and perhaps now, after a third meeting, you've advanced no further? It's such a serious decision to make that I'd be in exactly the same state of mind were I in your pretty skin. Look, think, explore yourself heart and soul; try to discover whether this gentleman can offer you any chance of happiness. Human life feeds on more than poetic ideas and exalted sentiments. But on the other hand if bourgeois existence kills you with boredom, what to do? Your poor grandmother wants you to marry, fearing to leave you alone in the world, and I too, dear Caro, should like to see you united with a decent young man who would make you as happy as possible. The other night, when I saw you crying so bitterly, your distress nearly broke my heart. We love you dearly, my darling, and the day of your marriage will not be a merry one for your two old companions. Little jealous though I am by nature, I shall begin by having no liking for the fellow who becomes your husband. But that's not the question. As times goes on I'll forgive him, and I'll love him and cherish him if he makes you happy.

So you see I can't even pretend to advise you. What speaks well for M. Commanville is the way he has gone about things. Moreover, we are acquainted with his character, his background and connections, things it would be next to impossible to know in a Parisian milieu. Here in Paris you might perhaps find young men who are more brilliant; but charm – *l'agrément* – is almost exclusively the property of bohemians. Now the idea of my poor niece being married to a man without means is so dreadful that I won't consider it for a moment. Yes, my darling, I declare I'd rather see you marry a millionaire philistine than an indigent genius. For the genius wouldn't be merely poor; he would be brutal and tyrannical, and make you suffer to the point of madness or idiocy.

The bugbear of living in Rouen has to be considered, I know; but it's better to live in Rouen with money than to be penniless in Paris; and for that matter why shouldn't you move to Paris later if the business goes well?

I am like you, you see; I don't know what to think; I keep saying white one moment and black the next. It's hard to see straight in questions that concern one too deeply.

It will be hard for you to find a husband who is your superior in mind and upbringing. If I knew one who had those qualifications and met all other requirements I'd set off and secure him for you very quickly. So you are faced with having to take a young man of good character who is nevertheless inferior. But will you be able to love a man whom you'll inevitably look down on? Will you be able to live happily with him? That's the whole question. You'll doubtless be badgered to give a quick answer. Don't do anything in a hurry. And whatever happens, my poor Loulou, you know you can depend on the affection of your old uncle, who sends you a kiss.

Take good care of your grandmother. Kiss her for me.

Write me long letters with many details.

~

Caroline married Ernest Commanville on April 6, 1864. By the time she was off on her melancholy wedding journey, Flaubert had ended his indecision between the two novels: the 'sentimental' one, the '*livre de passion*',[1] had won out. 'I'm hard at work on the outline of my big Parisian novel,' he wrote to Caroline in Venice. 'I'm beginning to see it clearly, but never have I so belaboured my poor brain. Ah! How I'd rather be floating on the Grand Canal or strolling on the Lido!' On May 4, after Caroline's return to France: 'Yesterday I worked all day with Monseigneur on the outline of my book . . . The principal theme has emerged, and the course is now clear. I don't intend to begin writing before September.' Meanwhile he studied the historical background for the scenes he would invent: the novel would be laid in the 1840s, and research for it made him more concerned with politics than in the past.

1. '*Inactive* passion', as Flaubert himself would qualify it (see letter to Mlle Leroyer de Chantepie, October 6, 1864).

~

To Madame Roger des Genettes

[Croisset, summer 1864]

... Before long I'll be able to give a course in socialism; at least I know its spirit and meaning. I have just swallowed Lamennais, Saint-Simon, and Fourier, and am now going over all of Proudhon. If you want to know *nothing* about these people, then read the critiques and résumés written about them; they have always been refuted or praised to the skies, never expounded. One salient feature is common to them all: hatred of liberty, hatred of the French Revolution and of philosophy. All those people belong to the Middle Ages; their minds are buried in the past. And what schoolmasters! What pedants! Seminarians on a spree, bookkeepers in delirium! The reason for their failure in '48 was that they stood outside the mainstream of tradition. Socialism is one face of the past, just as Jesuitism is another. Saint-Simon's great teacher was M. de Maistre, and how much Proudhon and Louis Blanc owe to Lamennais has never been sufficiently told. The Lyons school, the most active, is entirely mystical, like the Lollards. The bourgeois understood nothing of all this. They instinctively sensed what stands at the core of all social utopias: tyranny, antinature, the death of the soul ...

∼

For Part One of his novel, Flaubert visited the scenes of his hero's birth and education.

∼

To Jules Duplan

Sens, Hôtel de l'Ecu de France
Wednesday, 9.30 p.m. [August 17, 1864]
... What weather! *Miséricorde!* I was so soaked at Corbeil that I took a hot bath while my clothes were hung to dry. The aquatic establishment of that wretched locality is staffed by fifteen-year-old girls and a woman who half-opens the door of your bath cabin with unparalleled decorum – never did I see anything so discreet as that arm stretching out along the wall to take my duds ...

After nearly coming to blows with two coal men and the proprietor of a livery stable, I took the omnibus for Melun in the company of two highly alcoholized masons and a farmhand who kept guzzling brandy and garlic; and reached Melun at 9 p.m., dying of hunger and cold. Beware the Hôtel de Commerce! Then, this morning, I had an *exquisite* drive from Melun to Montereau along the river, past rocky slopes covered with vineyards, in bright sunshine. My driver wore four military decorations on his lapel, which brought me salutations from people in passing vehicles. Arrived here at two o'clock. I visited the collège, austere retreat that saw the education of our great dramatic poet, him whom decency forbids me to name and who is giving himself over to a Richard Darlington kind of existence, as you will see from the enclosed piece of bumf.[1] The concierge of the collège is a woman of about forty, big tits, brunette, good-natured. While she was showing me the dormitory, the idea occurred to me of pushing her down on to one of the beds and skewering her in honour of Doucet. But I reflected that that might have serious consequences, and therefore abstained.

Oh! the lovely sacristan in the cathedral! What an Onuphre![2] A fortnight's growth of beard, a hump on each shoulder blade, turd-shaped proboscis, and a mug! a mug! He showed me the coronation robe of Charles X, various heads of saints, clothes belonging to Thomas à Becket, etc., and 'recognized me at once for an art lover'. I also saw a tremendous candle, presented by the Pope to Monseigneur;[3] it weighs twenty pounds and is used only once a year. To make it last, it is *never* lit; a seminarian carries it in procession, ahead of Monseigneur.

Think of me on two consecutive evenings 'going to the café'![4] Yesterday, to the café favoured by Messieurs the military; today, to that preferred by Messieurs the travelling salesmen. They repeat lines from *Lambert*[5] and laugh over items in the *Charivari*.[6] Oh, France!

Adieu, little one. I expect to be back in Paris on Saturday, during the day or in the evening. *Je t'embrasse.*

Ton vieux.

1. In the second chapter of *L'Éducation sentimentale* we learn that Frédéric Moreau, born in Nogent-sur-Seine and eighteen years old when the novel opens in 1840, had been a boarder at the Collège de Sens. In real life the collège had been attended by the 'great dramatic poet' Camille Doucet, whom we have already met as a bureaucrat. Richard Darlington, in the

play of that name by Alexandre Dumas (the elder) and a collaborator, is ambitious for official posts and honours. The enclosed bumf was, of course, a newspaper clipping.
2. A hypocrite in LaBruyère's *Caractères*.
3. Here not Louis Bouilhet, but the Archbishop of Sens.
4. Elsewhere in the correspondence Flaubert speaks with shame of being on some occasion 'reduced' to sitting in a café. He considered it a low and stupid pastime.
5. A play, *Lambert Simnel*, by Scribe and Mèleville.
6. A popular satirical journal.

~

To Charles-Edmond[1]

[August 1864?]

I'm very sorry that you can't make the little trip to Villeneuve with me. I get so fed up on a train that after five minutes I'm howling with boredom. Passengers think it's a neglected dog; not at all, it's M. Flaubert, sighing. Such is my reason for desiring your company, my dear chap. The which said, *passons* (as Hugo might put it).

I will send your letter to Mme Regnier, and I have no doubt that in her longing to 'see herself in print' she'll succumb to your exhortations; but if she asks my opinion in the matter I'll advise her to tell you to go straight to blazes (even admitting that you may be right). Yes, my friend, that I shall do – out of conviction, stubbornness, pride, and were it only to uphold my principles.

Ah! How right I am not to write for periodicals, and what deadly emporiums they are! Their mania for 'correcting' manuscripts submitted to them results in everything they print having the same absence of originality. If five novels are published per year in a newspaper or magazine, since all five are 'corrected' by one man or by a like-minded committee, the result is five books that are all the same. Look for example at the style of the *Revue des Deux Mondes*. Turgenev told me recently that Buloz cut something from his last story. By that alone, Turgenev has lowered himself in my esteem. He should have thrown his manuscript in Buloz's face, with a couple of slaps added and a blob of spit as dessert. Mme Sand also lets herself be advised and cut. I have seen Chilly open up aesthetic horizons to her! Whereupon she rushed to adopt his suggestions! It was the same with Théo[phile Gautier] at the *Moniteur* in Turgan's time, etc. Good God! In my opinion this condescension on the part of such geniuses comes close to corruption. Because the moment you offer something you've written, it means, if you're not a rascal, that you think it good. You have presumably put all your effort into it, all your soul. One individuality isn't to be substituted for another. A book is a complicated organism. Any amputation, any change made by a third party, denatures it. It may be less bad: no matter – it won't be *itself.*

This is not a plea for Mme Regnier, but I assure you, my friend, that you're on a downward path, and that all you newspapermen are contributing to the further debasement of human character – to the degradation, greater every day, of intellectual matters.

I will show you the manuscript of *Bovary,* adorned with the corrections and cuts made by the *Revue de Paris*. It's a curiosity. To calm me, they urged on me the examples of Frémy and Delessert.

It is certain that Chateaubriand would have spoiled a manuscript by Voltaire; nor could Mérimée have 'corrected' Balzac. In short, the *Revue* and I quarrelled to such a point that the result was my trial. Those gentlemen were wrong, and yet how shrewd! Laurent-Pichat, my good friend DuCamp, old Kauffmann the silk merchant from Lyon, Fovard the notary.

At which point, *mon vieux,* I blow you a kiss and say farewell.

1. Charles-Edmond Chojecki (1822–1899), the Polish-born editor of the Parisian newspaper *La Presse*, did not use his family name in his French career as journalist and dramatist. Mme Regnier (1840–1887), wife of Dr Raoul-Emmanuel Regnier of Mantes, had submitted a novel, *Un Duel de salon* – apparently through Flaubert – to *La Presse*; and the editor's insistence on 'corrections' rekindles Flaubert's memories of the battle of *Madame Bovary.* His eloquence renders unnecessary the identification of obscure names. *Un Duel de salon* apparently remained in manuscript. Mme Regnier later published several novels, using the nom de plume 'Daniel Darc'.

~

Launched on his novel at last, Flaubert revealed its theme and character as he had come to see them:

~

To Mademoiselle Leroyer de Chantepie
Croisset, October 6, 1864

No, *chère Demoiselle*, I have not forgotten you. I think of you often, of your mind, which is so distinguished, and of your sufferings, which seem to me utterly without remedy.

Our existences are perhaps not as different as they appear to be on the surface and as you imagine them to be. Between the two of us there exists something amounting to a bit more than mere literary sympathy, I believe. My days are spent in solitude, sombre and arduous. It is thanks to work that I am able to stifle the melancholy I was born with. But often the old dregs resurface, the old dregs that no one knows of, the deep, secret wound.

Here I am, harnessed now and for the past month to a novel about modern life, which will be laid in Paris. I want to write the moral history of the men of my generation – or, more accurately, the history of their *feelings*. It's a book about love, about passion; but passion such as can exist nowadays – that is to say, inactive. The subject as I have conceived it is, I believe, profoundly true, but for that very reason probably not very entertaining. Facts, drama, are a bit lacking; and then the action is spread over a too extended period. In short, I'm having a good deal of trouble and am full of anxieties. I shall remain here in the country for part of the winter, in order to push ahead a little with this long task.

· · ·

∼

To Madame Roger des Genettes
[Croisset, December 1864]

Just now I am in complete solitude. A fog has been gathering, deepening the silence and seeming to shroud me in a great whitish tomb. I hear no sound except the crackling of my fire and the ticking of my clock. I work by lamplight ten hours out of the twenty-four, and time passes. But I waste so much of it! What a dreamer I am, in spite of myself! I'm beginning to be a little less discouraged. When you next see me, I'll have done almost three chapters – three, not more. But I thought I'd die of disgust during the first. One's faith in oneself is worn down with the years, the flame dies, strength declines. I have a fundamental reason for being depressed – the conviction that I'm writing something useless; I mean contrary to the goal of Art, which is exaltation, of one kind or another. But with the scientific requirements of today, and a bourgeois subject, that goal seems to me altogether impossible. Beauty is not compatible with modern life. So this is the last time I'll deal with it: I've had enough.

. . .

~

After Flaubert had shown him the beginning of the book, Bouilhet wrote to him, late in 1864: 'What is particularly serious and strange about your new novel is "*le pavé de Paris*".[1] The first pages are in line with your usual literary habits – descriptions, psychological longings, the birth of love. I am sure in advance that you have found, in general, the right tone, whether your opinion be more or less favourable about any particular passage. And you seem to me quite excited and clairvoyant about what's to come. Weigh the thing, peer into it . . .'

The Goncourts, who dined with Flaubert at Croisset on January 6, 1865, on their way back to Paris from a visit to Le Havre, wrote (with some exaggeration) in their Journal: 'He certainly works fourteen hours a day. That goes beyond work; it's the life of a Trappist.' Over a year after Flaubert's announcement to Mlle Leroyer de Chantepie that he had begun Part One of the novel, he wrote to her, on January 23, 1866, that he had finished it. 'When will the whole book be done? That's what I don't know.' Soon he was writing to Caroline about being 'holed up in porcelain factories', and about reading treatises on faience, and Paris newspapers for the year 1847 – research which readers of the novel will recognize as underlying sections of Part Two. 'Could you tell me what I should read to learn something about the neo-Catholic movement of around 1840?' he asked Sainte-Beuve in March. 'My story extends from 1840 to the Coup d'État [December 1851]. I need to know everything, of course, and must get into the atmosphere of the period before writing about it.' Several times he mentioned long sessions with Bouilhet, who was continuing his role of literary 'midwife', and he sought information from Jules Duplan about laws regulating businesses in 1847, as he wanted to show his entrepreneur Arnoux to be 'only a demi-crook – chiefly rattlebrained'.

His doubts about the novel persisted.

1. 'The streets of Paris', as we might say 'the sidewalks of New York' – that is, the atmosphere, the life, of the city. Bouilhet finds it 'serious and strange' that Flaubert, no Parisian, should undertake a Parisian novel.

∽

To Alfred Maury

Croisset, near Rouen, August 20, 1866

. . .

You are too kind, my dear friend. I do not share your hopes concerning the novel I'm now writing. On the contrary, I fear it may prove to be a mediocre work, because the conception is faulty. I want to depict a psychological state – an authentic one, in my opinion – which has not yet been described.[1] But the ambience in which my characters live and move is so dense and teeming that time after time they barely manage to avoid disappearing into it. Thus I am forced to relegate to a middle ground precisely those things that are the most interesting. I skim over many subjects that one would like to see treated more deeply. My purpose is complex – a bad aesthetic method: in short, I think I have never undertaken anything more difficult. We must trust in God, after all!

1. The state of 'inactive passion' mentioned earlier.

XII

Enter George Sand. The Completion and Reception of L'Éducation sentimentale

1866–1869

OF THE COPIES of *Madame Bovary* which Flaubert or his publisher had sent to prominent literary people, one was inscribed 'To Madame Sand, *Hommage d'un inconnu*'. This may well have been more advertisement than tribute. Although at the age of eighteen Flaubert had written to Ernest Chevalier, 'I have read few things as fine as *Jacques*', his opinion of George Sand's writing had changed in the intervening years. 'I read some G. Sand every day, and regularly remain indignant for a quarter of an hour,' he wrote to Louis Bouilhet in May 1855, when Mme Sand's *Histoire de ma vie* was being serialized in *La Presse*. At that time they had apparently not met.

Shortly after receiving *Madame Bovary*, Mme Sand noted in her diary for April 30, 1857, that 'G. Flaubert' had been at a theatrical opening she had attended; he had perhaps been presented to her there. The following September 29, an article about literary realism, paying particular attention to *Madame Bovary*, was printed in a series she was contributing to the newspaper *Le Courrier de Paris*.[1] Learning of it, Flaubert wrote to Jules Duplan: 'Send me Mme Sand's article. Wouldn't it be "the proper thing" for me to write a little word of thanks to that latter-day Dorothée? The comparison is perhaps irreverent. Still, isn't it widely said of her that she "ejaculates like a man"? For she, too, has her "philosophy".'[2]

If Flaubert read the article in question, he discovered a new defender. Though finding *Madame Bovary* 'desolating', and dismayed by its pessimism, George Sand recognized 'the hand of a master' and 'great talent': the novel was 'a brilliant debut', and not at all immoral. It is not known whether Flaubert wrote to her at this time, but it is certain that he never again wrote scabrously about her.

Two years later, after seeing her occasionally, he wrote to Ernest Feydeau: 'I gather you idolize *la mère* Sand. I find her personally a charming woman. As for her doctrines, as expressed in her writings – beware! A fortnight ago I reread *Lélia*. Read it. I beg you, read that book again!'[3] Even when their friendship came to full flower Flaubert would have trouble reconciling the George Sand who was so 'charming' – as well as good, wise, and adorable – with the George Sand of the inadmissible 'doctrines'.

La Presse published Mme Sand's laudatory review of *Salammbô* in January 1863, and she replied to Flaubert's letter of thanks (now lost):

1. '*Le Réalisme*', posthumously reprinted in *Questions d'Art et de Littérature* (1878).
2. Dorothée, Mme d'Esterval, in Sade's *La Nouvelle Justine*, is endowed with a physical trait which makes her (like other women in Sade's pages) 'more man than woman'. In this respect she resembles the Comtesse Gamiami, the chief character in a later pornographic novel, *Gamiami ou deux nuits d'excès* (1833–1835), by 'Alcide de M . . .' (widely thought to be Alfred de Musset, writing spitefully about George Sand after their rupture). The 'philosophy' refers to the peculiar moral doctrines professed by characters in Sade's *La Philosophie dans le boudoir*.
3. One of George Sand's lifelong 'doctrines', preached with particular explicitness in her early novel *Lélia*, was 'reciprocity' – woman's right to experience, rather than merely provide, physical and spiritual ecstasy in love. 'Where liberty and reciprocity do not exist,' she would write in one of her letters to Flaubert, 'there is outrage against holy nature.'

~

GEORGE SAND TO FLAUBERT

Nohant, January 28, [18]63

Mon cher frère,

You must not be grateful to me for having done a duty. Whenever the critics do theirs I will keep silent, for I prefer producing to judging. But everything I had read about *Salammbô*, before reading *Salammbô* itself, was unjust or inadequate. Silence would have seemed to me cowardice – or laziness, which closely resembles it. I don't at all mind adding your adversaries to my own. A few more, a few less . . .

I must ask you to forgive my rather puerile criticism regarding the Defile of the Axe. If I let it stand it was because a reservation added to the sincerity of my admiration.

We are but slightly acquainted. Come and see me when you have time. It's not far, and I am always here. But I am an old woman;[1] don't delay until I'm in my second childhood.

Help me solve a puzzle. In September I received an interesting dried plant in an anonymous envelope. It seems to me today that the handwriting is yours. But that is unlikely: how would you know that I have a keen interest in botany?

What stays with me, in your thanks, is the tone of friendship, and this I know I merit.

1. Now in her sixtieth year and a grandmother, George Sand (born, in 1804, Amandine Lucile Aurore Dupin) was known for the placidity – some called it heaviness or torpor – that masked her habitual and formidable industry. (Her collected works constitute over one hundred volumes.) Her nature was paradoxical: she once said of herself, 'My soul is impatient, sombre, haughty; my temper withdrawn, indolent, calm.' Few writers, and perhaps no woman, can have had more biographers. Chroniclers never tire of recounting her descent on the paternal side, through many misalliances, from Frédéric Auguste de Saxe, seventeenth-century king of Poland, and the eighteenth-century Maréchal de Saxe; her mother was a Parisian bird-seller. The story continues with her marriage to the rustic Baron Casimir Dudevant, the birth of their two children, their separation, her 'liberation' and literary beginnings in Paris, including her adoption of a new name (see p. 413, n. 5); and her affairs with Musset, Chopin and several others. The range of the writings by which she made her living was as wide as that of her friendships; she was a pamphleteer in the Revolution of 1848, during which she was de facto Minister of Propaganda until the June Days. Then came years of laborious rural existence with household, farm tenants and guests, and above all her pen (it was her habit to write twenty pages during the night hours) in the charming old country house inherited from her grandmother at Nohant. The house, about 175 miles south of Paris, is little changed and may be visited today.

To George Sand

[*January 31, 1863*]

Chère Madame,

It's not that I'm grateful to you for having performed what you call a duty. I was touched by your goodness of heart; and your sympathy made me proud, that's all.

Your letter, which I have just received, adds to your article and goes beyond it, and I don't know what to tell you other than, quite frankly, that I love you for it.

M. Aucante has asked me to get you a copy of *L'Opinion Nationale.*[1] You will receive it at the same time as this letter.

No, it wasn't I who sent you a flower in an envelope last September. But what is strange is that at that same time I was sent a leaf, in the same fashion.

As for your very cordial invitation, I answer neither yes nor no, like a true Norman. Perhaps I'll surprise you some day this coming summer. Because I greatly long to see you and talk with you.

All my affection. I kiss both your hands, and am

All yours,
G^ve Flaubert
Boulevard du Temple 42; or Croisset, near Rouen

P.S. I should very much like to have your portrait to hang on the wall of my study in the country, where I often spend long months quite alone. Is the request indiscreet?[2] If not, I send you my thanks in advance. Accept them along with the others, which I reiterate.

1. The issue containing Froehner's article on *Salammbô*. Emile Aucante was Mme Sand's man of business.
2. Mme Sand replied that she would send her portrait later. 'Thank you for wanting to have my face, so insignificant in itself as you well know. What counts for more is the understanding inside the head, and the appreciation in the heart.'

∼

During the next few years their paths sometimes crossed when Mme Sand was in Paris, usually for the opening of a play drawn, either by herself or by a collaborator, from one of her novels. On February

29, 1864, they were together at the triumphant first performance of *Le Marquis de Villemer* in the Théâtre de l'Odéon, where she was the wildly applauded 'Author! Author!' and he a guest with her in Prince Napoleon's box. 'You were so good and so sympathetic to me at the première of *Villemer* that I no longer merely admire your admirable talent,' she wrote him a fortnight later, 'I love you with all my heart.'

Finally, in 1866, they truly discovered each other. It was at one of the Magny dinners – the first to which she (the only woman present) was invited. 'Dinner chez Magny, with my little friends,' she wrote in her diary for February 12. 'They gave me the warmest possible welcome. They are all very brilliant, except the great scholar Berthelot.[1] Gautier, constantly sparkling and paradoxical; Saint-Victor charming and distinguished. Flaubert, impassioned, I find more sympathetic than the others. Why? I don't yet know.' From then on the friendship developed rapidly. In May she asked Flaubert to accept the dedication of the novel she had just finished, *Le Dernier amour*; in August, after a weekend visit to Alexandre Dumas on the Normandy coast, she spent a few days at the Flaubert house in Croisset. 'She is always very natural, not at all a bluestocking,' Flaubert wrote to Princesse Mathilde. 'I'm experienced in that line, you know' – a reference to poor Louise Colet. And for the first time in years he made favourable mention of one of Mme Sand's novels – the one dedicated to him. 'I think you're very severe about *Le Dernier amour*,' he told the princess. 'In my opinion there are some quite remarkable things in this book.'[2]

From then on there was a constant exchange of letters between Croisset, or Paris, and Nohant. In one dated September 12, 1866, George Sand marvelled at the diversity of Flaubert's work – the contrasts between *Madame Bovary* and *Salammbô*, and certain scenes from *The Temptation of Saint Anthony* that he had read to her during the Croisset visit. 'You are a singular being,' she wrote to him, 'very mysterious, and at the same time gentle as a lamb. I greatly wanted to question you, but felt too much respect for you to do so . . . Sainte-Beuve, though he loves you, claims that you are frightfully dissolute. But perhaps Sainte-Beuve sees with eyes that are none too pure?'

1.   Marcelin Berthelot (1827–1907), the chemist.
2.   Perhaps Flaubert was accustoming – or resigning – himself to George Sand's free-flowing style, so different from his own. Stendhal once said, thinking of his own very limited public: 'If the *Chartreuse* were translated into French by Mme Sand, it would be a success, but would require three or four volumes to express what it now does in two.'
  Mme Sand was well aware of her own tendency. 'I wonder why I couldn't have said in twenty lines what has already covered as many pages,' she says of herself in *A Winter in Majorca*. And in her novel *Elle et Lui* (She and He), based on her affair with Alfred de Musset, the painter Laurent says to the heroine, Thérèse: 'I wasn't born like you, with a little steel spring in my brain, so that I'd have only to press the button to set the will to work. *I* am a creator!'

～

To George Sand

[Croisset,] Saturday night [September 22, 1866]

I, 'a mysterious being'! *Chère maître*,[1] come now! On the contrary, I find myself revoltingly banal, and am often thoroughly bored by the bourgeois I have under my skin. Sainte-Beuve, between you and me, doesn't know me at all, whatever he may say.

I even swear to you (by your granddaughter's smile)[2] that I know few men less 'dissolute' than I. What deceives superficial observers is the dissonance between my feelings and my ideas. If you want my confession, I'll make you a full one.

The sense of the grotesque has kept me from slipping into a disorderly life. I maintain that cynicism confines one to chastity. We'll have a great deal to say to one another about this if you're willing, the next time we meet.

Here is the programme I propose. This house will be cluttered and uncomfortable for a month, but towards the end of October or the beginning of November (after the opening of Bouilhet's play), I hope nothing will prevent your coming back here with me, not for a day, as you say, but for a week at least. You will have your room, 'with a table and everything needed for writing'. Is it agreed? There will be just the three of us, counting my mother.

·   ·   ·

I have read, straight through, the ten volumes of your *Histoire de ma vie* (I already knew about two-thirds of it, but only in fragments). What struck me most is the convent life. I have many thoughts about it, which I'll remember to tell you . . . What wish shall I make for you? *My* wish is to see you . . . My mother and I speak of you every day. She'll be happy to see you again.

1. Flaubert's customary salutation to Mme Sand would be this double tribute – the combination of the feminine form of the adjective, *chère* ('dear'), with the masculine *maître* ('master').
2. The infant Aurore, born January 19, 1866, daughter of Maurice Sand and his wife, Carolina ('Lina') Calamatta.

⌒

George Sand to Flaubert

Nohant, La Châtre, Indre, September 28, [18]66

. . . I have packed and sent by express a good proof of the drawing by Couture, signed by the engraver, my poor friend Manceau.[1] It's the best one I have, and it was down here. I have added a photograph of a drawing by Marchal, which was also a good likeness; but one changes from year to year. Age constantly gives another character to the face of people who think and seek; that is why their portraits don't look alike and don't resemble them for very long. I dream so much, and live so little, that sometimes I'm only three years old. But the next day I'm three hundred, if the dreaming was sombre. Isn't it the same with you? Doesn't it seem to you, at times, that you're beginning life, without even knowing what it is, and at other times don't you feel the weight of several thousand centuries, with a vague memory of them, and an impression of pain? . . .

1. Alexandre Manceau, thirteen years George Sand's junior and a friend of her son Maurice, had begun his long role as her secretary, confidant and lover in 1849. His continued presence at Nohant made difficulties between Mme Sand and Maurice, however, especially after the latter's marriage in 1862; and in 1864 Mme Sand had left Nohant to live briefly with the ailing Manceau in Palaiseau, near Versailles. He died there the next year, nursed by her to the end. Soon thereafter she returned to Nohant, using the house at Palaiseau only occasionally. She sold it a few years later.

⌒

To George Sand

Croisset, Saturday night [September 29, 1866]

So now I have that beautiful, beloved and famous face! I'm going to have a wide frame made for it, and hang it on my wall. Like M. de Talleyrand to Louis-Philippe, I can say, 'This is the greatest honour ever paid my house.' But that's a poor phrase, you and I being worth something more than those two fellows.

Of the two portraits, I prefer the drawing by Couture. Marchal saw only the 'good woman' in you; but for me, old Romantic that I am, the other is the 'portrait of the author' that so often set me dreaming in my youth . . .

∽

To George Sand

Croisset, Saturday night [September 29, 1866]
. . .

I do not experience, as you do, that sense of a life that is beginning, the stupefaction of an existence freshly unfurling. It seems to me, on the contrary, that I have always existed! And I am *possessed* by memories that go back to the Pharaohs. I see myself at different moments of history, very clearly, in various guises and occupations. My present self is the result of all my vanished selves. I was boatman on the Nile, *leno* [procurer] in Rome at the time of the Punic wars, then Greek rhetorician in Suburra, where I was devoured by bedbugs. I died, during the Crusades, from eating too many grapes on the beach in Syria. I was pirate and monk, mountebank and coachman – perhaps Emperor of the East, who knows?

Many things would be explained if we could know our *real* genealogy.[1] For since the elements that make a man are limited, mustn't the same combinations reproduce themselves? Thus 'Heredity' is a correct principle that has been incorrectly applied. So it is with that word as with many others. Everybody takes hold of it from a different end, and nobody understands anybody else. The psychological sciences will remain where they are today – that is, at a dim and foolish stage – as long as there is no precise nomenclature, and as long as it is permitted to use the same expression to signify the most diverse ideas. When categories are confounded, farewell Morality!

Don't you find that *basically* we've lost the track since '89? Instead of continuing along the high road, which was broad and splendid, like a triumphal way, we have wandered off along little by-paths and are floundering in quagmires. Perhaps it would be wise to return to d'Holbach for a time? Before admiring Proudhon shouldn't we know Turgot?

But in that case, what would become of CHIC, that modern religion? Chic opinions: being *for* Catholicism (without believing a word of it), being *for* slavery, being *for* the House of Austria, wearing mourning for Queen Amélie, admiring *Orpheus in Hades*, taking part in Agricultural Fairs, talking Sport, cultivating a cold demeanour, being an Idiot even to the point of regretting the treaties of 1815: such are the very latest.

Ah, you think that because I spend my life trying to write harmonious sentences, avoiding assonances, I don't have my own little judgements on things of this world. Alas, I do; and I'll die mad from not having uttered them . . .

1. Flaubert can scarcely have seen Gregor Mendel's *Principles of Heredity*, published in German the previous year. It received little attention until 1900.

~

To Madame Roger des Genettes

[Croisset, November 12, 1866]

I'm so exhausted from having been called out to a fire last night[1] that I can scarcely hold a pen. Actually I don't regret the labour: I was repaid by the spectacle of bourgeois and administrative stupidity in all its splendour. To maintain order, the authorities sent for troops, who proceeded to cross bayonets *against* the firefighters, and also some cavalry, who blocked all the streets of the village. It's inconceivable, the element of confusion that power injects everywhere.

My illustrious friend, Mme Sand, left Saturday afternoon. There was never a better woman, more good-natured and less of a blue-stocking. She worked all day, and at night we chattered like magpies until three in the morning. Though she's a bit too benevolent and benign, she has insights that evince very keen good sense, provided she doesn't get on to her socialist hobbyhorse. Very reserved concerning herself, she talks freely about the men of '48[2] and frankly stresses their goodwill rather than their intelligence. I showed her the sights of Rouen. My mother finds her delightful. Now I must settle down to a steady grind, for every distraction upsets me. What an absurd life mine is, and I want no other! . . .

1. A civic duty – for which there was plenty of water, as the Seine flowed past the village.
2. Mme Sand wrote happily in her diary about her week at Croisset. Her entry for Wednesday, November 7, records in part: 'Flaubert reads me the first part of his novel. It is good, good. He reads from ten to two. We talk till four.' Apart from the sessions with Bouilhet, this is the first mention of any reading aloud from *L'Éducation sentimentale*. Mme Sand would continue to supply Flaubert with memories of 1848 for what are some of the best scenes in the novel.

~

To George Sand

[Croisset,] Monday night [November 12–13, 1866]

You are sad,[1] *pauvre amie et chère maître*. It was you I thought of on learning of Duveyrier's death. Since you loved him, I am sorry for you. This loss adds itself to the rest. How many of the dead we have in our hearts! Each of us carries his necropolis within him.

I've been all at odds since you left: I feel I haven't seen you for ten years. My mother and I speak only of you; everyone here loves you. What constellation were you born under, to be endowed with so many qualities, so diverse and so rare? I don't know what to call the feeling I have for you: it's a very particular kind of affection, such as I have never felt for anyone until now. We got along well together, didn't we? It was nice.

It was so very good, in fact, that I don't want to let others enjoy it. If you make use of Croisset in one of your books, disguise it, so that it won't be recognized. That would oblige me. The memory of your presence here is for the two of us, for me. Such is my selfishness.

I missed you particularly last night at ten o'clock. There was a fire at my woodseller's. The sky was pink and the Seine the colour of red-currant syrup. I worked at the pumps for three hours and came home as tired as the Turk and the giraffe.[2]

. . . A Rouen newspaper (*Le Nouvelliste*) reported your visit to Rouen, with the result that on Saturday, after leaving you, I ran into several bourgeois who were indignant with me because I hadn't exhibited you. The best thing was said to me by an ex-Magistrate: 'Ah! If we'd known she was here . . . We'd have . . .' – pause for five minutes while he hunted for the phrase – ' we'd have . . . *given her a smile!*' That would have been little enough, no?

. . . To love you 'more' is difficult for me. But I do embrace you fondly. Your letter of this morning, so melancholy, went deep. We parted at the moment when many things were rising to our lips. All the doors between us are not yet open. You inspire me with great respect, and I dare not ask you questions.

Adieu. I kiss your good and lovely face, and am

Your

G^{ve} Flaubert[3]

1. George Sand had written: 'On my arrival in Paris I had some sad news. Last night while you and I were talking – and I think that the day before, we had talked about him – my friend Charles Duveyrier died, a man of most tender heart and candid spirit. He will be buried tomorrow. He was a year older than I. My generation is disappearing, one by one . . . I give you the part of my heart that he had: added to what you already have, that makes a very large portion. I wept all night . . . Love me *more* than before, since I'm suffering.' Charles Duveyrier was a Saint-Simonian lawyer, journalist, and dramatist.
2. An allusion to an old vaudeville skit about the first live giraffe brought to France, in 1827. (A.J.)
3. The present editor has followed the example of earlier French editors in not including Flaubert's signature at the end of all his letters. Unlike Mme Sand, who often omitted her 'G. Sand', Flaubert always affixed his 'G^{ve} Flaubert'.

~

To George Sand

[Croisset,] Saturday morning [November 17, 1866]
. . .

Don't torment yourself regarding information about the newspapers [of the 1840s]. They will take up little space in my book and I am in no hurry.

But when you have nothing to do, jot down for me on a scrap of paper what you remember about '48. Then you can fill it out when we talk. I'm not asking you for a treatise, needless to say – just a few of your own recollections.

. . .

If your little engineer has made a vow,[1] and if that vow comes easily
to him, he is right to keep it; otherwise, it's pure folly, between you
and me. Where is liberty to exist, if not in passion? Catholicism,
whose only idea has been to inhibit sexual enjoyment – that is, to
repress Nature – has overaccustomed us to setting a high value on
chastity. We give such things a grotesque importance! One must no
longer be spiritualist or materialist, but *naturalist*. Isis seems to me
superior to the Virgin, as well as to Venus. No! 'In my day' we made
no such vows. We made love! And boldly! But it was all part of a
broad eclecticism. And if we kept away from the 'Ladies', as I did,
absolutely, for two years (from 21 to 23), *it was out of pride*, out of
self-defiance, as a show of strength. After which, we would give
ourselves over to excesses of the opposite kind. We were Romantics,
in short – reds, utterly ridiculous, but in full flower. The little good
left in me comes from those days!

   Adieu, ma chère maître. I love and embrace you tenderly.

                                                     G^ve Flaubert

Do you know, you're spoiling me with all the sweet things you say
to me in your letters.

1. Mme Sand had written to him of a young friend who had promised his
    fiancée to remain chaste during the four years that must elapse before their
    marriage. 'You would tell him he's stupid, but I preach him *my* morality,
    that of an old troubadour.' From now on Flaubert and Mme Sand would
    sometimes refer to themselves as 'two troubadours', perhaps with overtones
    relating to their Romantic pasts and present chaste affection. (See following
    letter, n. 3.)

                              ≈

To George Sand

                    Croisset, Tuesday, 5 o'clock [November 27, 1866]
   You are lonely and sad down there;[1] it's the same with me, here.
Where do they come from, these waves of black depression that
engulf one from time to time? It's like a rising tide. You feel you're
drowning, you have to flee. At such moments I lie flat on my back.
I do nothing – and the flood recedes.

   My novel is going very badly for the moment. Add to that the deaths I have learned of: that of Louis de Cormenin (a friend for twenty-five years), of Gavarni,[2] and then all the rest. But this will pass.

You don't know what it is, to spend an entire day with your head in your hands, taxing your poor brain in search of a word. With you, the flow of ideas is broad, continuous, like a river. With me it's a tiny trickle. I can achieve a cascade only by the most arduous artistic effort. I know them well, the Pangs of Style! In short, I spend my life racking my heart and my brain: such is the true essence of your friend.

You ask him if he sometimes thinks of 'his old troubadour of the clock'.[3] Doesn't he, though! And he misses her. They were very sweet, our night-time chats. There were moments when I had to restrain myself from giving you little kisses, as though you were a big child! Your ears must have burned last night. I dined at my brother's with all his family. We spoke only of you, and everyone sang your praises. Except me, of course: I disparaged you to the limit, beloved *chère maître*.

Apropos of your last letter (and by a natural train of ideas), I re-read old Montaigne's essay called 'Some Lines of Virgil'. What he says about chastity is precisely what I believe.[4] It's the Effort that is virtuous, and not the Abstinence in itself. Otherwise one would have to curse the flesh, like Catholics. God knows where that leads! So, at the risk of always harping on the same string, and of being a Prud'homme, I repeat that your young man is wrong. If he's celibate at twenty, he'll be an ignoble old rake at fifty. Everything has its price! Large natures (and those are the good ones) are above all prodigal, and don't keep such strict account of how they expend themselves. We must laugh and weep, love, work, enjoy and suffer – *vibrate* as much as possible, to the whole extent of our being. Thus it is, I believe, to be truly human.

Try to maintain your serenity. Soon you'll be seeing your granddaughter. That will do you good. And think of this old man, who sends you all his affection.[5]

1. Mme Sand had written from Palaiseau, where, she said, she was 'sharing her solitude with a dead man [Alexandre Manceau], whose life ended here, like a lamp extinguished but still present'.
2. Louis de Cormenin had been one of the editors of *La Revue de Paris* during

its serialization of *Madame Bovary.* Gavarni, the caricaturist, had been one of the founders of the Magny dinners.

3. 'At Croisset do you sometimes think of your old troubadour of the inn clock, who always sings, and always will sing, of perfect love?' Mme Sand had written to Flaubert on November 22. Had they perhaps seen, in some inn, a Romantic-period clock with the figure of a troubadour painted on its case? In *A Winter on Majorca*, Mme Sand had written: 'Like all southern people, the Majorcans are born musicians and poets, or, as their ancestors called them, "troubadours", *trobadors*, which we might translate as "improvisers".'

4. 'I guard myself from temperance as I formerly did from *volupté* – it draws me too far back, even to dullness. I desire to be master of myself in every way. Wisdom has its excesses, and has no less need of moderation than does folly.'

5. Replying on November 30, Mme Sand, after defending her young man and his vow of chastity – since his fiancée is in agreement, why dissuade him? – goes on to speak of sex and the artist:

    'I don't believe in those Don Juans who are Byrons at the same time. Don Juan didn't write poems; and Byron, they say, made love very badly. He must sometimes – one can count such emotions in one's life – have experienced complete ecstasy of heart, mind, and senses; he knew enough about that to be one of the poets of love. No more is required by the instruments of our sensibility. The continual gust of petty appetites would destroy them.'

    And she naively urges Flaubert to try to write more easily, confessing that she does not at all understand the 'anguish' he experiences in his work. She wishes that some day he would 'write a novel in which the artist (the real artist) is the hero . . . The artist is such a fine type to portray . . . You should paint yourself.'

    There exists a somewhat similar letter written by her to Flaubert the previous day and never sent, perhaps because she sensed the ineptitude of her 'advice'. (A.J.)

~

TO GEORGE SAND

[Croisset,] Wednesday night [December 5–6, 1886]
. . .

I'm not a bit surprised that you fail to understand my spells of literary anguish. I don't understand them myself. They exist, however, and are violent. At such times I no longer know how to go about writing, and after infinite fumbling I succeed in expressing a hundredth part of my ideas. Nothing spontaneous about your friend!

Far from it! These last two days, for example, I've been casting and recasting a paragraph, and still haven't solved it. At times I want to weep. I must seem pitiable to you. How much more so to myself!

. . .

As for our subject of discussion (apropos of your young man), what you write to me in your last letter is so much my way of viewing things that I've not only put it into practice, but preached it. Ask Théo! Let's be clear, however. Artists (who are priests) risk nothing by being chaste. On the contrary! But bourgeois – what's to be gained by their being so? *Some* people have to remain within the human race. Happy indeed are those who never stir beyond it!

My view – contrary to your own – is that nothing good can be done with the character of the 'ideal Artist'. Anything of the kind would be monstrous. Art isn't intended to depict exceptional beings.[1] I feel an unconquerable aversion to putting anything of my heart on paper. I even think that a novelist *hasn't the right to express his opinion* on anything whatsoever. Has God ever expressed his opinion? That is why there are so many things that make me gag – things I long to spit out, and which I choke down instead. Indeed, what would be the use of uttering them? Any Tom, Dick, or Harry is more interesting than Monsieur G. Flaubert, because they are more *general* and consequently more typical.

There are days, nevertheless, when I feel I'm at a level lower than cretinism. I now have a bowl of goldfish. And they entertain me, they keep me company while I eat my dinner. Imagine taking an interest in anything so inane!

Adieu – it's late and I have a headache. I kiss you fondly.

1. So says the depictor of Salammbô, St Anthony, St Julian, and Hérodias!

≈

GEORGE SAND TO FLAUBERT

[Paris, December 7, 1866]

Not put anything of your heart into what you write? I don't understand at all, oh, but not at all. To me it seems that you can't put anything else into it. Can you separate your mind from your heart? Is it something different? Can feeling limit itself? Can one's being split itself in two? In short, not to give of yourself entirely in your work seems to me as impossible as to weep with something other than your eyes or to think with something other than your brain. What was it you meant? Answer when you have time.

~

To George Sand

[Croisset,] Saturday night [December 15–16, 1866]

. . .

I expressed myself badly when I told you 'one must not write with one's heart'. What I meant was: don't put your own personality on stage. I believe that great art is scientific and impersonal. What is necessary is, by an intellectual effort, to transport yourself into your Characters – not attract them to yourself. Such at least is the method – which amounts to this: try to have a lot of talent, and even genius, if you can. What vanity, all Poetics, all works of criticism! The complacency of the gentlemen who produce such things flabbergasts me! Oh! nothing daunts those numbskulls!

. . .

~

Flaubert had recently thanked Hippolyte Taine for sending him the second volume of his Italian travels, *Florence et Venise*. Taine replied, mentioning certain unfavourable reviews of the book, and sending Flaubert the following questionnaire in connection with the study he was now preparing, the celebrated *De l'intelligence*:

I need some hypertrophic cases to illustrate what I have to say about imagination and images. I am seeking information from such cases, and you are one of them.

1. When you have reached the point of imagining, in minute detail, a landscape, a character, such as Emma's face and figure, or the horde trapped in the Defile of the Axe, are there moments when you might confuse the intensive imagination with the real object?

2. Having imagined a character or a place with intensity and at length, have you ever become obsessed by it, as by a hallucination, with the character spontaneously changing shape before your eyes?

3. Ordinarily, after looking at a wall, a tree, or a face, when you recall it do you see, with exactitude, its irregularities, the uneven details of its surface – completely, integrally? Or do you perceive merely such and such a gesture, angle, effect of light – in short, three or four fragments, no more?

You are doubtless familiar with the intense but quiet images, and the pleasant hallucinations, which precede sleep. When one is dozing after dinner or beside the fire, one is very aware of them, being still sufficiently conscious. Is there a great difference in intensity between these and the novelist's intuition, or artistic and poetic image, as you know it? Or rather is the difference simply that the images or hallucinations occurring on the verge of sleep are disconnected and involuntary?

You would do me a service, a great service, if, drawing on your own experience, you could reply to some or all of these questions. I am addressing similar ones to Doré, to a chess player who can make his moves without looking at the board, and to a mathematician who can make extended calculations in his head.

Several of Flaubert's replies are incorporated in *De l'intelligence*, where Taine refers to him as 'the most lucid and most accurate of modern novelists'.

∾

To Hippolyte Taine

Croisset, Tuesday night [late November 1866]

Let the blockheads talk away, *cher ami* – your style is neither 'fatiguing' nor 'unintelligible'. The author of the brilliant passages which fill your last book has mastered the art of expressing his thoughts in prose.

Only, travel writing as a genre is per se almost impossible. To eliminate all repetitions you would have had to refrain from telling what you saw. This is not the case in books devoted to descriptions of discoveries, where the author's personality is the focus of interest. But in the present instance the attentive reader may well find that there are too many ideas and insufficient facts, or too many facts and not enough ideas. I'm the first to regret that you don't describe more landscapes, to counterbalance – for the sake of the total effect – your numerous descriptions of pictures. But I have very definite ideas about travel books, having written one myself.[1] We'll talk about that again. Now to answer your questions:

1. Yes, always. For me, the mental image of things is as true as their objective reality, and what has been supplied by reality very soon ceases, for me, to be distinguishable from the embellishments and modifications I have given it.

2. The characters I create drive me insane; they haunt me; or, rather, I haunt them: I live in their skin. When I was writing about Madame Bovary taking poison, I had such a distinct taste of arsenic in my mouth, was poisoned so effectively myself, that I had two attacks of indigestion, one after the other – two very real attacks, for I vomited my entire dinner.

There are many details that I do not write down. Thus, M. Homais as I see him is slightly pitted by smallpox. In the passage I am writing just now I *see* an entire set of furniture (including the stains on certain of the pieces): not a word will be said about all this.

The third question is more difficult to answer. I think that in general (no matter what has been said on the theme) memory idealizes – or, should I say, selects. But perhaps the eye, too, idealizes? Think of our surprise when confronted with a photographic print. *That* is something we have never seen!

In its evanescent character, artistic intuition actually resembles hypnagogic hallucination: it flits before your eyes; and that is when you must grasp it, avidly.

But often, too, the artistic image forms itself slowly, bit by bit, like the various components of a decor that is being assembled.

Incidentally, do not confuse the inner vision of the artist with that of a man suffering from actual hallucinations.[2] I know those two states perfectly: there is a gulf between them. In genuine hallucination there is always terror; you feel that your personality is slipping away from you; you think you're going to die. In poetic vision, on the contrary, there is joy. It is something that permeates you. Nevertheless, here too you lose your bearings.

That is all I can think of to tell you on the spur of the moment.

If you find my answers unsatisfactory, let me know, and I'll try to explain myself better.

1. *Par les champs et les grèves*, of which Flaubert wrote alternate chapters with Maxime DuCamp (see Volume I).
2. Here Flaubert is referring to the hallucinations he experienced in the epileptiform attacks that had played so great a role in his youth (see Volume I), and that seem now to occur very rarely if at all. Responding to a new request by Taine, he describes them in greater detail in the following letter.

~

To Hippolyte Taine

Croisset, December 1 [1866]

Mon cher ami

This is what I experienced whenever I had hallucinations.

1. First, an indeterminate anxiety, a vague malaise, a sensation of expectancy accompanied by distress, *the sort of thing that precedes poetic inspiration,* when one feels that 'something is about to happen'. (A state that can only be compared to the feeling, while fucking, that the sperm is coming and that discharge is about to take place. Do I make myself clear?)

2. Then, suddenly, like a thunderbolt, instantaneous invasion, or rather irruption, *by memory*; for hallucination, properly so-called, is nothing other than that, at least for me. It is a spewing out of memory, an outpouring of what it has stored up. You feel images escaping from you like a haemorrhage. It is as though everything inside your head were exploding all at once, like the thousand fragments of a firework, and you have no time to observe these internal images which follow one another furiously. In other circumstances, the hallucination begins with a single image, which grows, expands, and ends by obscuring objective reality, like, for example, a spark that flits about and then becomes a great flaming fire. In the latter case, one may well be thinking of something else at the same time, and this is almost indistinguishable from the phenomenon called 'black butterflies' – those small shining specks we see floating in the air when the sky is grey and our eyes are tired.

I believe that Will plays a great role in hallucinations. When I have tried to induce them, I have never succeeded; on the other hand, often, in fact usually, I have rid myself of them by force of will.

In my early youth I used to have a peculiar hallucination: when I was in a theatre I always saw skeletons, instead of the spectators; or at least I had that idea so strongly that it resembled a hallucination – where one begins and the other ends can be hard to determine.

I know the story of Nicolai.[1] I have had that experience: *seeing* things that are not there – knowing that they're an illusion, being convinced of it, and yet perceiving them as clearly as though they were real. But in sleep you experience something similar, when you know, while dreaming, that you are dreaming.

So indisputably, for me, does memory play a part in hallucination, that the only way to imitate someone perfectly (to reproduce his voice and portray his gestures) is by great concentration of memory.[2] To be a good mime, your memory must be of hallucinatory clarity – you must actually *see* those you imitate, be permeated by them. It is true that certain bodily organs, too, play their part – the muscles of the face and larynx.

You should ask composers if they actually hear the music they are going to write, the way we novelists see our characters.

In artistic hallucination, the picture is *not definitely circumscribed,* exact though it may be. Thus, I see *perfectly* a piece of furniture, a face, a bit of landscape. But it floats, as though suspended; I don't know where it is. It exists by itself, disembodied from the rest; whereas, in reality, when I look at an armchair or a tree, I see at the same time the rest of the furniture in my room, the other trees in the garden, or at least I perceive vaguely that they exist. Artistic hallucination cannot occupy a large space, cannot move within a very wide frame. If the space enlarges, you [automatically] fall into a reverie, and grow calm again. In fact, artistic hallucination always ends that way.

You ask whether, for me, it adapts itself to the surrounding reality. No. The surrounding reality has disappeared. I no longer know what exists around me. I belong exclusively to that apparition.

By contrast, in hallucination pure and simple you can perfectly well see a false image with one eye and real objects with the other. Indeed, therein lies the anguish.

Adieu. Work well. All yours –

1. An eighteenth-century case history of hallucination, included by Taine in his *De l'intelligence*, I, 105–107.
2. Flaubert was, from childhood, an excellent mime.

❧

To ERNEST FEYDEAU

Croisset, Tuesday [early 1867]

Cher Vieux

I don't know whether you're still in existence, but since I'm writing to ask you a favour I hope you'll give a sign of life. This is the thing – it concerns my book:[1]

My hero Frédéric quite properly wants to have a little more money in his pocket, and he plays the market; he makes a little, then loses everything, fifty or sixty thousand francs. He's a young bourgeois, completely ignorant in such matters – even a three per cent government bond is a mystery for him. This takes place in the summer of 1847.

So: from May to the end of August, what were the securities favoured by speculators?

My story has three phases:

1. Frédéric goes to a broker with his money and follows the broker's advice. Is that how it's done?

2. He makes a profit. How? How much?

3. He loses everything. How? Why?

It would be very good of you to send me this information – the episode shouldn't take up more than six or seven lines in my book. But explain it all to me clearly and exactly.

Keep the date in mind – 1847, the summer of the Praslin and Teste scandals.

And use the occasion to tell me a little about how you are and what you're up to.

1. *L'Éducation sentimentale*, Part II, Chapter 4. Feydeau was well acquainted with the Paris Bourse.

❧

To Edmond and Jules de Goncourt

[Croisset,] Saturday night [January 12–13, 1867]

If it's a consolation for you to know I'm bored, so be it – for I'm none too jolly. I'm working very long hours and feeling fed up. When I say working, it's a figure of speech. I'm giving myself a lot of trouble, and perhaps that's all it amounts to. No matter – I think I've passed the emptiest stretch of my interminable novel. But I'll never again undertake anything of the kind. I'm growing old, and it's time for me to write something worthwhile that I myself enjoy.

I spend entire weeks without seeing a human being or exchanging a word with anyone congenial. Besides, I'm becoming unsociable, like Marat, who is fundamentally 'my man'. I'd even like to put his bust in my study, solely to shock the bourgeois, but he's too ugly. Alas – beautiful morally, but not plastically. With the result (the foregoing being a parenthesis) that at dinner at my niece's in Rouen the day before yesterday I took pleasure in abusing various local people who were present, and made myself thoroughly disagreeable. My balls ache – word of honour! – from my excessive chastity. For I have nothing at hand to empty them into. You'll protest that I do have it (my hand). But I no longer turn myself on . . . Which doesn't prevent Mme Sand from believing that every so often 'some lovely lady comes to see me' – so little do women realize that we can live without them.[1] For company I have a regiment of rats that makes an infernal racket at night, overhead. We gave them poison – which killed my dog. Wind, rain, pitch dark, the river chafing against its banks, and the whistling of the leafless trees – that completes the picture. Here in my study, in the glow of my lamp, I shout out my sentences. I go to bed at four in the morning and get up at noon. Such is the existence of yours truly.

. . . I hope to see you in about a month, when I'll have finished my chapter. Then I'll be at the halfway point in this long book about a poor devil – being one myself, a rather sad one. Come – try to get it up again (your brain, I mean!), and don't be too depressed. *Je vous embrasse.*

1. Flaubert wrote to George Sand by the same post: 'Whatever you may suppose, no *"belle dame"* comes to see me. *"Belles dames"* have greatly

occupied my mind, but they have taken up very little of my time. To speak of me as an anchorite is perhaps a juster image than you think.'

~

GEORGE SAND TO FLAUBERT

Nohant, January 15 [1867]

. . . Why do I love you more than most others, more even than some old and well-tried friends? . . .

The solitude you live in would seem delicious to me in good weather. In winter I think it stoical, and have to remind myself that you don't find regular exercise a necessity for your morale. I had supposed that you employed your strength in a different way during this claustration: as it is, it may be very fine, but you mustn't prolong it indefinitely. If the novel must go on still longer you must inter-rupt it, or vary it with some distractions. Truly, dear friend, think of the life of the body, which grows stiff and resentful if too long neglected. When I was sick in Paris I saw a doctor who was quite crazy but very intelligent. He told me that I was 'spiritualizing' myself to an alarming degree; and when I told him, thinking of you, that it was possible to abstract oneself from everything except work and have one's strength increase rather than the opposite, he replied that there was as great a danger in accumulation as in diminution – and, in this connection, many excellent things that I wish I knew how to tell you.

Of course you know all this, but you take no account of it. So the work you complain of is really your passion, and a grand passion. Then let me tell you what you tell me: for the love of all of us, and especially of your old troubadour, take a little care of yourself.

. . .

~

TO GEORGE SAND

[Croisset,] Wednesday night [January 23–24, 1867]

I have followed your advice, *chère maître*. I have taken some exercise. Am I a splendid fellow, or not? Sunday night at eleven o'clock the moonlight on the river and the snow was such that I was seized by the itch of locomotion. And I walked for two and a half hours – working myself into a state and pretending that I was

travelling in Russia or Norway. When the tide came in and cracked
the ice floes on the Seine and the thin ice covering the farm-courts
– no joking: it was superb. I thought of you and missed you.[1]

I dislike eating alone. I have to associate someone or the idea of
someone with the things that give me pleasure. But that someone is
rare. I, too, ask myself why I love you. Is it because you are a great
man, or a 'charming human being'? I have no idea. What is certain
is that for you I have a *particular* feeling, one I cannot define.

Apropos, do you believe (you who are a Master in psychology)
that one can love two people in the same way? And that one ever
has two identical feelings? I think not, since one's *self* keeps changing
at every moment of its existence.

You write to me beautifully about 'disinterested affection'. That
is true. But so is the opposite, is it not? We always make God in
our own image. At the heart of all our loves and all our admirations
don't we discover – ourselves, or something approaching ourselves?
What matter, if 'ourselves' are good?

My *me* bores me to death at the moment. What a heavy burden
that fellow is, at times! He writes too slowly! And he isn't striking
the slightest pose when he complains about his work. What a chore!
And what an idea, to have picked such a subject! You should give
me a recipe for working faster . . .

You know very well that you have never told me what your
illness is. What is it? Is it serious? Are you going to spend the winter
in the Midi? Don't stay too long, eh? I'd not like it if we weren't to
see each other soon. I'll be in Paris in a month – and you?

I've had a little note from Sainte-Beuve that reassures me about
his health, but is lugubrious nonetheless. He seems disconsolate at
no longer being able to haunt the Cyprian groves! He is right, after
all, or at least right according to his lights, which is the same thing.
Perhaps I'll be like him when I reach his age? I think not, however.
Not having had the same youth, I'll have a different old age. That
reminds me that I once thought of writing a book about Sainte-
Périne.[2] Champfleury treated that subject idiotically. For I see
nothing comic there (either in the subject, or in Champfleury). I
would have made it dreadful, lamentable. I believe the heart does
not grow old. There are even people in whom it expands with age.
I was drier, harsher, twenty years ago than I am today. I've been

feminized and softened by wear and tear – which harden other people. That makes me indignant. I feel I'm becoming too impressionable. I'm emotional over nothing. Everything troubles and agitates me. Everything, to me, is like the north wind to the reed.[3]

Something you said came back to my mind and is making me re-read *La Jolie Fille de Perth* just now. It's charming,[4] whatever they may say about it. That fellow had some imagination, decidedly.

So: *adieu*. Think of me. I send you my best affection.

1.   The river Seine is tidal for forty miles or more above its mouth in the English Channel – that is, beyond Rouen, of which Croisset is a down-river suburb. As for this particular 'locomotion' of Flaubert's, Mme Sand wrote: 'You, my dear, you go walking in the snow, at night. For someone unaccustomed to it, such a promenade is quite mad, and could make you ill, like me. It wasn't the moon, but the sun, I urged you to take advantage of – we're not owls, for heaven's sake.'

2.   That is, a book about old age, set in L'Institution de Sainte-Périne. This was an endowed residence for elderly persons, particularly retired civil servants or their widows, who could afford to pay modest sums for board. Founded in the very early 1800s, under the patronage of the Empress Josephine, it was originally in Chaillot, then transferred in 1862 to buildings in Auteuil. Most of these have now been demolished and are being replaced by modern hospital facilities. Champfleury published his novel *Les Amoureux de Sainte-Périne* in 1859.

3.   An allusion to LaFontaine's fable *The Oak and the Reed*. The oak says to the reed: 'To you everything is north wind, to me all seems zephyr.' (A.J.)

4.   Sir Walter Scott's novel *The Fair Maid of Perth*. Flaubert owned a thirty-two-volume set of Scott's novels in French translation. His adjective for the book is *coquet*: the translation 'charming' could possibly be improved, if one could fathom his meaning here. *La Jolie Fille de Perth* was literally 'in the air' in 1867: Georges Bizet's four-act opera, its libretto taken from the novel, would have its first performance at the Théâtre Lyrique in Paris on December 26.

~

To George Sand

[Croisset,] Wednesday [February 6, 1867]

. . .

First, let's talk about you. Anaemia! I'm not surprised! You *must* take a tonic of iron, and walk and sleep – and go to the Midi, whatever it costs! Yes! Otherwise, made of oak though you may be, you'll crack. As for money, it can be found; as for time, just take it. You'll do nothing that I advise, naturally. Well, you're wrong. And it grieves me.

No, I do not have what are called money worries. My income is very limited, but secure. Only, since it's your friend's habit to anticipate said funds, he's occasionally a little short, and grumbles about it 'within these four walls'. But not elsewhere. Barring the unexpected, I'll always be able to keep myself in food and firewood to the end of my days. My heirs are, or will be, rich. (I'm the poor man of the family.) But enough of that.

As for earning money by my pen, it's something I've never envisaged, recognizing that I'm fundamentally incapable of it. Therefore one leads a modest country life on what one has. Not a supremely amusing existence. But there are so many other people, more deserving than I, who haven't a sou, that it would be wrong to complain. Besides, railing against Providence is such a common way of going on that one should abstain if only for good form.

One more word about lucre, which will be a secret between us. As soon as I'm in Paris, that is from the 20th to the 23rd of this month, I'll be able easily, with no strain whatever, to lend you a thousand francs in case you need it to go to Cannes. I propose this to you bluntly, as I would to Bouilhet or any other intimate. No fuss about it, please. Among conventional folk this would be thought improper, I know, but between troubadours much can be dispensed with.[1]

You are very kind, with your invitation to Nohant. I *will* come. Because I long to see your house. It bothers me not to know it, when I think of you. But I must postpone that pleasure until next summer. Just now I should stay in Paris for a while. Three months is not too long for all I want to do there.

I return herewith the page by the excellent Barbès.[2] Of his *true* biography I know very little. All I know about him is that he is honest and heroic. Give him a handclasp from me as my thanks for his words of appreciation. Is he, between you and me, as intelligent as he is good? I need, now, some men of that camp who will speak frankly with me. Because I'm about to study the revolution of '48.

You promised to look out for me, in your library at Nohant, (1) an article on faïence, (2) a novel by Father X—, a Jesuit, about the Virgin Mary.

But such severity towards old [Sainte-]Beuve, who is neither Jesuit nor Virgin! He bewails, as you say, 'what is least to be regretted, taken in the sense he intends'. Why so? All depends on the *intensity* one puts into the thing. I find you fundamentally tainted (in this matter) with Catholicism, O *chère maître*. Men will always consider sexual pleasure the most important thing in their lives. Woman, for all of us, is the Ogive of the Infinite. This isn't noble, but such is the very core of the Male. There's an immense amount of joking about all this. Thank God there is – for the sake of Literature, and for individual Happiness, as well. No matter! Glory be to Venus!

.   .   .

Ah! I missed you greatly just now. The high tides are superb. The wind is moaning, the river is white and overflowing its banks. It makes one think of the ocean, and one feels the better for it.

Adieu, I embrace you the way I love you – very tenderly.

1. In reply to Flaubert's offer of a loan, Mme Sand wrote (February 8) that *she* had been thinking of offering *him* a thousand francs. 'I kiss you for your kind thought,' she said, 'and do not accept. I would accept, I assure you, if I had no other resource. Let me say that if someone should lend me money, it's Seigneur Buloz [her publisher], who has bought châteaux and many acres with my novels. He has even offered to. So I'll accept from him if it becomes necessary. But I'm in no state to leave.'

2. Armand Barbès (1809–1870), the republican revolutionary, was condemned to death in 1839, charged with murdering a lieutenant of the National Guard. He did not commit the crime, but was the leader of an insurrectionary group one member of which fired the fatal shot. His sentence was commuted to life imprisonment the day before the scheduled execution, when Victor Hugo sent a plea in verse to Louis-Philippe. After four years at Mont-Saint-Michel (at that time used as a prison), he was transferred to the milder climate of Nîmes because of ill health caused in part by maltreatment. Released in 1848 and playing a role in the revolutionary government, he was again imprisoned after the June Days, and in 1854 was once again released, almost against his will, by Napoleon III. At the time of this letter he was living in self-imposed exile in Holland. George Sand, who had been one of Barbès's political comrades, had sent Flaubert a portion of one of his letters to her, in which he praised *Madame Bovary.*

    Writing on February 8, Mme Sand answered Flaubert's question about Barbès: 'Barbès is intelligent, certainly. But single-minded . . . His character can only be compared with Garibaldi's. Incredible in his saintliness and perfection. Of immense value, but a value from which the France of the present moment is incapable of profiting. Born into the wrong milieu – a hero out of another age or another land.' (See also p. 461–4 and 511.)

~

To George Sand

[Paris,] Saturday [April 13?, 1867]

Chère maître

Really, you should seek the sun somewhere. It doesn't make sense to be unwell all the time, so do get away and rest. Resignation is the worst of the virtues.

I need a quantity of them, to put up with the stupidities I keep hearing! You have no idea of the pass things have come to. France, which has had occasional attacks of St Vitus's dance (as under Charles VI), now seems to me to be stricken with paralysis of the brain. Fear is making everybody idiotic: fear of Prussia, fear of strikes, fear concerning the Exposition, which 'isn't going well', fear about everything. You have to go back to 1849 to find such a degree of cretinism. At the last Magny dinner the conversation was on such a servants'-hall level that I swore to myself never to set foot there again. Nothing was talked about except M. de Bismarck and Luxembourg. I'm still fed up to the teeth with it all. All in all, I'm becoming difficult to live with. Instead of getting blunted, my sensibility grows ever more acute; all kinds of trivialities cause me pain. Forgive me this weakness, you who are so Strong and tolerant!

The novel isn't progressing at all. I'm deep in the newspapers of '48. I've had to look into things in various places – Sèvres, Creil, etc. – and have more of that kind of work to do.

Old Sainte-Beuve is preparing a speech on Free Thought which he will read in the Senate, concerning the law on the Press. He has been very stalwart, you know.[1]

1. At the urging of Princesse Mathilde and her brother, the Emperor had appointed Sainte-Beuve a Senator, with a salary of 30,000 francs a year. As will be seen, they were to regret it. His maiden speech, on March 29, 1867, was on the subject of freedom of thought. He was now preparing a second speech, on freedom of the press. (Flaubert's 'Free Thought' is a bit of

absentmindedness.) For Sainte-Beuve's second speech, see Flaubert's letter to Sainte-Beuve of June 27, 1867.

~

To George Sand

[Paris,] Friday morning [May 17, 1867]
. . .

Axiom: hatred of the Bourgeois is the beginning of virtue. As for me, I include in the word 'bourgeois' the bourgeois in overalls as well as the bourgeois in frock coat. It's we, we alone – that is, the educated – who are the People, or, to put it better, the tradition of Humanity.

. . .

~

To George Sand

[Croisset,] Wednesday night, 2 [June 1867]
. . .

Early this week I spent thirty-six hours in Paris in order to attend the ball at the Tuileries.[1] No joking whatever: it was splendid. Indeed the whole trend in Paris now is towards the colossal. Everything is becoming crazy and out of proportion. Perhaps we're returning to the ancient East. I keep expecting idols to come out of the ground. There's the threat of a Babylon. And why not? The *individual* has been so negated by Democracy that he'll be reduced to complete effacement, as under the great theocratic despotisms.

I deeply disliked the Czar of Russia. He seemed a boor. Paralleling the noble Floquet, who with no risk to himself shouts 'Long live Poland!,' we have the chic people who sign the visitors' book at the Elysée.[2] What an era!

As for my novel, it goes *piano*. As I advance, new difficulties arise. It's like dragging a heavy cartload of stones. And you complain of something that takes you six months! I still have two years to go, at least. How the devil do you handle transitions of ideas? That's what's delaying me. Moreover, this book requires tedious research. On Monday, for example, I visited, one after the other, the Jockey Club, the Café Anglais, and a lawyer.

. . .

A week ago I was enraptured by an encampment of gypsies who had stopped in Rouen. This is the third time I've seen them, each time with new pleasure. The wonderful thing is that they were arousing the *Hatred* of the Bourgeois, even though they were harmless as lambs. The crowd looked its great disapproval when I gave them a few sous. I heard some delightful remarks à la Prud'homme.[3] That hatred stems from something very deep and complex. It's to be found in all 'champions of order'. It's the hatred felt for the Bedouin, the Heretic, the philosopher, the hermit, the Poet. And there is fear in this hatred. I'm infuriated by it, being always on the side of minorities. It's true that many things infuriate me. The day I stop being indignant I'll fall flat on my face, like a doll when you take away its prop.

For example, the stake that held me upright last winter was my indignation against our great national historian M. Thiers, who has been elevated to the status of demi-god; and the Trochu pamphlet, and the eternal Changarnier surfacing again.[4] Thank God, the delirium of the Exposition has delivered us momentarily from those buffoons.

. . .

1. Flaubert had written to Caroline a few days earlier: 'Their Majesties wishing to take a look at me, as one of the most splendid curiosities of France, I am invited to spend the evening with them next Monday.' After the ball he wrote to Princesse Mathilde: 'The Tuileries ball stays in my memory as something from a fairy tale, a dream. The only thing lacking was an opportunity to have a closer view of you and speak with you. Don't I sound like Madame Bovary, dazzled by her first ball?'

2. The Palais de l'Elysée was being used during the Exhibition of 1867 to house distinguished official guests, the czar among them. Following the Russian repression of the Polish uprising of 1863, French sympathy for Poland was exploited by those in opposition to the imperial regime at home. During the czar's visit to the Sainte-Chapelle on June 4 someone shouted '*Vive la Pologne*, Monsieur!' Charles Floquet, a leading republican, was generally credited with the 'outrage', but denied it, putting the responsibility on Gambetta. (A.J.)

3. For Prud'homme see p. 370, n. 7. *Le Nouvelliste de Rouen* reported on May 30 that 'Forty-three individuals of the Zingaro type, come from Hindustan, fleeing the invasion of the Mongols', had arrived in the city two days before and set up their tents in the Cours la Reine. On June 8 the same newspaper announced that they had left on the sixth for Le Havre, where they would take ship for America. (A.J.)

4. Adolphe Thiers (for Flaubert as archetypal a bourgeois as Monnier's

Prud'homme) had been officially dubbed 'national historian' by Napoleon III. He was nevertheless in the opposition, and on March 14, 1867, had made a speech, lamenting France's loss of prestige because of misgovernment, which brought him much acclaim.

General Louis-Jules Trochu had recently published a pamphlet attacking the government for its plans to reorganize the French army. An article on the same subject had appeared in *La Revue des Deux Mondes* for April 15, written by the ex-General Nicolas Anne-Théodule Changarnier, who had been arrested during the coup d'état of 1851, expelled from France, and given amnesty in 1859. He had until now been living obscurely in the provinces.

~

To Charles-Augustin Sainte-Beuve

[Croisset,] Thursday [June 27, 1867]

Mon cher maître

All those who aren't sunk in the crassest stupidity, all who love Art, all who think, all who write, owe you infinite gratitude. For you have pleaded their cause[1] and defended their God – our nameless God who is being outraged.

In such a place, it was the only thing to say. The moderation and precision of your language only throw into stronger relief the intemperance and vagueness of their ineptitude. They are decidedly not bright – no, not bright at all.

What a sad thing is mankind! Behold the foremost political assembly of the foremost nation on earth!

No matter: very politely, you have spat the truth at them. It will stick to them. My only regret is that you didn't give them more of it. You can't be very sick, if you're able to speak with such energy!

Ask M. Troubat to give me news of you.[2]

I wish my arms were thirty-four leagues long, that I might embrace you. That is what I count on doing a month from now.

Ever yours, *cher maître.*

1. On June 25, 1867, Sainte-Beuve delivered a second speech in the Senate, this one on freedom of the press. He spoke vigorously against the petition by 'the taxpayers of the city of St Etienne' that Voltaire's *Candide*, Rousseau's *Confessions*, the works of Michelet and Renan, and all novels by Balzac and George Sand be excluded from their public library. The speech was directed

particularly against clerical interference in public matters, and aroused the indignation of Conservative senators.

On the twenty-sixth, immediately after learning of the speech, Flaubert had already sent Sainte-Beuve a short message written on a visiting card: 'Thank you, *Mon cher maître*, for us, for all of us. Damaged though it may be, your bladder can be their lantern!' (Flaubert's words are a somewhat convoluted reference to Sainte-Beuve's diseased bladder and to an ancient proverbial French description of someone who is particularly stupid: *Il prend des vessies pour des lanternes* – 'He takes bladders for lanterns.' A bilingual friend of the present translator suggested, on reading Flaubert's message, the free translation: 'May your liver be their lights.'

2.   Jules Troubat, Sainte-Beuve's secretary.

❧

About Sainte-Beuve's speech, Flaubert wrote to Princesse Mathilde: 'What do you have to say about *le père* Sainte-Beuve? I thought him splendid. He defended the cohort valiantly, and in well-chosen words. His adversaries seem to me of a hopeless mediocrity. Why this hatred of literature? Is it envy, or stupidity? Both, no doubt, with a strong dose of hypocrisy into the bargain.'

The princess's reply was apparently chilly (we shall see later a more pronounced example of her displeasure at a display of independence by her protégé), bringing from Flaubert the following, in a letter also expressing horror at the recent execution of the Emperor Maximilian in Mexico: 'What you say to me about Sainte-Beuve is perhaps true. He perhaps did go too far (from a certain point of view, which I must add is not mine). But his adversaries had set him the example, and then the question of "proper limits" is so difficult. Stay within them and you're a coward; go beyond them, and you're a firebrand. What to do?'

Flaubert wrote more forthrightly to George Sand late in July: 'Speaking of stupidity, it seems that the official world is furious with Sainte-Beuve. Camille Doucet's distress touches on the sublime. From the point of view of future liberty, we must perhaps bless this religious hypocrisy of the worldly, which so revolts us. The later the question is settled, the better the settlement will be. *They* can only weaken, and we grow stronger.'

In September, Flaubert consulted Mme Sand about another matter:

'In my notes I find the following: "*National* of 1841. Maltreatment of Barbès. Kicked in the chest; dragged by beard and hair to be transferred to an *in pace* [oubliette]. Protest by a group of lawyers against these abominations, signed: E. Arago, Favre, Berryer." Find out from him whether that is accurate, will you? I'll be much obliged.' Barbès replied directly to Flaubert:

~

ARMAND BARBÈS TO FLAUBERT

The Hague, October 2, 1867

My dear compatriot,

Our illustrious friend, Mme Sand, has forwarded to me a question you sent her about an incident at Mont-Saint-Michel, and asks me to reply.

The story in the *National* is true.

We were at that time in the 'loge-cells', situated at the very top of the building, where we had been transferred because double or triple grilles were being installed in our ordinary prison quarters.

I don't have to tell you that this transfer was already in violation of all the customary rules of detention, and an act of sheer violence on the part of a jailer, the better to garrotte his captives.

Returning one day to my cell after the usual short, obligatory walk in the former cloister, I saw that they had taken advantage of my absence to close an opening that had always existed in the door of each cell.

I realized that they were beginning with me, but that they intended to do likewise to all my comrades, and I refused to enter until things had been restored to their former state.

My good friend Martin Bernard and others made the same declaration, and all together we asked that the warden be sent for.

Instead of coming, he sent the chief of guards, with his entire squad; and it was then that there occurred that scene, the hideousness and horror of which naturally seem to you scarcely credible.

During the interval in which I had been left as it were master of the cell corridor, the guards having all decamped to organize themselves under their chief's orders on a lower floor, I had opened the door of Martin Bernard's cell and that of another friend, Dessade, which had been merely bolted, not locked.

Seeing the three of us together, the guards (there were at least twenty of them, reinforced in the rear by a company of troops summoned for the occasion) fell on us – no warning being given – the only words uttered being 'Seize them! Hit them!' shouted by their chief.

I was the most severely injured because I was the first they reached. Struck in the face and on all parts of the body, thrown to the floor, throttled with my tie, my beard torn out, dragged from those cells at the uppermost point of Mont-Saint-Michel to the 'black hole' (the lowest level), down flights of stairs with my head striking every step: yes, all that took place.

Martin and Dessade were accorded identical treatment.

In the black hole they made us change into convict's garb – that is, cast-offs that had been worn by non-political prisoners – and they wanted to strip me of my flannel undervest, a kind of garment I have worn all my life, to me like a second skin.

I was able to keep it only by threatening to throw myself on the bayonets and kill myself instantly, since without it I was certain to freeze to death in the glacial place to which they were taking us.

They could see that I was absolutely resolved to do as I said; and when the lieutenant in charge of the soldiers interceded on my behalf I was able to keep my 'second skin'.

Ah! People are trying today to rehabilitate the reign of Louis-Philippe. For my part, I no longer feel hatred for anyone. I even think I can truthfully say that I tend towards leniency precisely because I was harshly treated at that time.

But it was a sad reign and a sad period, I assure you. May Frenchmen not forget! Our beloved France has suffered so much! Violence was done her then; may she fend off the trickery threatening her now: were she to succumb again, the shame and cowardice would be the greater.

This letter is much longer than I intended. Forgive me, in the name of our common cult of George Sand. It was she who asked me to write to you, and you perhaps know that for me she represents, or is, France. I love her as you love her, as we both love our country – humiliated today, but certain to rise again.

George Sand, at least, is always a shining light – ever more so.

In her name, then, forgive my writing at such length, and accept a cordial handshake from one of your admirers ever since *Madame Bovary*, and from one of your friends ever since I learned of the affection in which you are held at Nohant.

A. Barbès.

∼

To Armand Barbès[1]

Croisset, October 8, 1867

I do not know, Monsieur, how to thank you for your letter, so amiable, so cordial, so noble. I have long respected you; now I love you.

The details you send me will be put (quite incidentally) into a book I am writing, in which the action extends from 1840 to 1852. Although my treatment is purely analytical, I sometimes touch on the events of the period. My foregrounds are invented, my backgrounds real.[2]

You know better than anyone many of the things that would be useful to me, and that I ought to hear. But there is no way for us to see each other, since you live where you do and I here. Without Mme Sand, I wouldn't even know how to send you my thanks. I was very touched by what you say of her. She is a religion you and I have in common – and share with others.

Allow me to clasp your hands very firmly, and to declare myself

All yours,
G^{ve} Flaubert

1. Flaubert sent this letter via Mme Sand, Barbès not having given him his address in The Hague. 'Here are a few lines of thanks for Barbès, who wrote me a warm, fascinating letter. Since I have no "patriotic" past whatever, and was bellowing sentences in my study while he was risking his life for liberty in the streets, I didn't think I should write him all the good things I thought about him. I'd have seemed like a kind of fawning courtier.'

    Mme Sand sent Barbès Flaubert's letters to him and to her, with a few words of her own: 'I send you Flaubert's thanks, and also a note he has scribbled to me that contains some open-hearted talk of you. I thank you for giving him exact dates and information. He is a great artist, and one of the few who are *men*.' (A.J.)

2. In *L'Éducation sentimentale* (Part II, Chapter 4), the working-man Dussardier, the novel's most sympathetic character, angrily recalls, in 1847, earlier abuses by the authorities, among them the massacre of the working-class

inhabitants of a house in the rue Transnonain in Paris in 1834 (immortalized in Daumier's lithograph); and the treatment of Barbès in 1841: 'To transfer Barbès to a dungeon, they dragged him by the legs, by his hair! They kicked him in the stomach, and his head bounced against every step on the stairs!' Later (Part III, Chapter 4), Dussardier, uneasy about his own role in the June Days of 1848, is anguished by the reaction that soon followed: 'The workers are no better than the bourgeois! . . . Some wretches are calling Barbès an aristocrat!'

~

To Jules Duplan

Croisset, Sunday [December 1867]

How I'd love to be with you: first because I'd be with you; second because I'd be in Egypt; third because I wouldn't be working; fourth because I'd be seeing the sun, etc.[1] You can't imagine the horrible weather here today. The sky is dirty grey, like a chamber pot long uncleaned, and even more stupid-looking than ugly.

At the moment I'm living alone, my mother being in Rouen.[2] Monseigneur comes to see me almost every Sunday, but today he's at home giving dinner to an upholsterer friend. He is now regaining his serenity and I think is about to begin something, but his change of residence completely unhinged him.[3] The day before yesterday I had a letter from Maxime. He seems to be in very good form, fulminating against M. Thiers, who is now king of France.[4] That's the point we've reached – completely clericalized. Such is the fruit of democratic stupidity. If we had continued on the high road of M. de Voltaire, instead of veering off via Jean-Jacques, neo-Catholicism, the Gothic, and Fraternity, we wouldn't be where we are. France is going to become a kind of Belgium, openly divided into two camps. So much the better! What a culprit is Isidore![5] But since one must always derive some private enjoyment from everything, I *rejoice* in the triumph of M. Thiers. It confirms my disgust with my country and the hatred I feel for that Prud'homme. Can one conceive of more idiotic, irresponsible talk about religion and philosophy! I intend, by the way, to 'fix' him in my novel, when I come to the reaction that followed the June Days. In the second chapter of my Part Three I'll have a dinner where his book on property is praised to the skies.[6] I'm working like thirty thousand niggers, for I want to finish my Part Two by the end of January. In order to complete the whole thing by the spring of '69, so as to publish it two years from now, I don't have a week to spare: you see what I'm facing. There are days, like today, when I feel utterly fagged out. I can scarcely stand on my feet, and I have choking fits when I can scarcely breathe.

Last Thursday I was forty-six – occasion for philosophical reflection! Looking back, I don't see that I have wasted my life, and yet what have I accomplished, God help me? It's time to produce something worthwhile.

Don't forget to observe, for me, the rascally Oriental–Occidental types; store in your memory some anecdotes of the kind I'll need;[7] take notes with me in mind. Don't waste your time in the European cafés. Treat yourself to another visit to the dancing girls, and go to see the Pyramids. Who knows whether you'll ever be in Egypt again? Profit from the occasion: take the advice of an old friend who has had plenty of experience and who loves you. If you think of it, bring me (1) a flask of sandalwood oil; and (2) a trouser belt made of webbing – remember, your friend has a big belly.

. . . By way of reading, I've lately been devoting myself to a study of croup.[8] Never did anyone write in a more long-winded, empty style than physicians! Such windbags! And they despise lawyers! . . .

1. Duplan was in Egypt as secretary to Henri Cernuschi, politician and economist. (Cernuschi's collection of oriental art, which he left to the city of Paris, is housed in his former residence, now the Musée Cernuschi, avenue Velásquez.)
2. Mme Flaubert spent the coldest months in a flat in Rouen.
3. Louis Bouilhet had recently been appointed director of the Municipal Library in Rouen, thanks in part to Flaubert's friendship with Princesse Mathilde.
4. 'Flaubert goes a bit astray here,' Mr Jasper Ridley, author of *Napoleon III and Eugénie* (London: Constable, 1979), writes to the present translator. 'Thiers was certainly not "King of France" in 1867, nor was he a clerical supporter. As the spokesman for big business and the Conservative urban bourgeoisie, he was opposed on many issues to the Catholic Party, which derived its strength from the clergy, the Army, the old nobility, and above all from the great mass of the peasantry; but Thiers, who believed that "the Reds" were the greatest threat to society, always supported the Catholics against the Radicals and the Socialists.'

Thiers' political power was increasing. Following another speech on foreign policy, December 7, 1867 (this one – mistakenly, as it turned out – jeering at the government's warnings about Prussia's military strength), he had become chief of an oppositional 'coalitional majority'.

5. No one seems to know why Flaubert calls Napoleon III 'Isidore'.
6. Actually, in the third chapter. 'They [the Dambreuses' dinner guests] especially praised M. Thiers for his volume against Socialism, in which he showed himself to be as great a thinker as a writer.' The book is Thiers' *De la propriété* (1848).
7. Among Flaubert's never-realized projects was a novel to be called 'Harel-Bey' and laid in the modern 'Orient'.
8. The nearly fatal croup of the Arnoux' young son is one of the determining events of the novel.

∽

To George Sand

[Croisset,] Wednesday night [December 18–19, 1867]
Chère maître, dear friend of Divine Providence,

'*Parlons un peu de Dozenval!*'[1] Let's do some roaring against M. Thiers!

Is it possible to find a more triumphant imbecile, a more abject ass, a more curd-like[2] bourgeois? No! Nothing can give an idea of the vomiting inspired in me by this old diplomatic idiot, rounding out his stupidity like a melon ripening on a manure pile – the manure pile of the bourgeoisie! Is it possible to treat philosophy, religion, peoples, liberty, the past and the future, history, natural history – everything and all the rest – with more naive, inept crudity? To me he seems as eternal as mediocrity itself! I'm flattened by the very thought of him.

But what is really splendid is our glorious National Guard, whom he threw into the clink in 1848, now once again beginning to cheer him! What infinite madness! Which goes to prove that temperament is everything. Prostitutes, like France, have a weakness for old humbugs.

I shall try, in the third part of my novel (when I reach the reaction that followed the June Days) to slip in a panegyric of said gentleman, apropos of his book on Property, and I hope he'll be pleased with me.

What is the best form in which to express one's opinion, occasionally, about affairs of this world without risking being taken later for a fool? It's a difficult problem. It seems to me that the best way is simply to depict the things that exasperate you. Dissection is revenge.

. . .

1. 'Let's talk a bit about Dozenval'. A complimentary copy of the present volume to the first reader convincingly identifying this quotation.
2. *Etroniforme* – term coined by Flaubert.

∼

GEORGE SAND TO FLAUBERT

Nohant, December 21 [1867]

At last, someone who shares my opinion of that political cur! It could only be you, friend of my heart. *Etroniforme* is a sublime word to classify that vegetable species *Merdoïde.*[1] I have friends, perfectly nice fellows, who bow low before *any* symptom of opposition, whatever it may be and wherever it may come from, and for whom that empty-headed mountebank is a god. But they've been keeping their tails between their legs since the last speech with full orchestra. They begin to think he's going a bit far – and perhaps it's all to the good that in order to make himself king of parliament the idiot has shown the world the dead cats and other refuse that make up his entire bag of dirty tricks. That will reach some people. Yes, you'll do well to dissect that cardboard donkey, that cobweb talent. Unfortunately, when your book appears he'll perhaps be gone, and no longer much of a danger, for such men leave nothing behind them; on the other hand, he may be in power – expect anything: in that case, it will be a good lesson.[2]

. . .

1. Term coined by Mme Sand: 'Of the shit family'. A friend suggests a link with *cacafuego*, listed in the Oxford English Dictionary, which cites a 1696 usage: 'A Spanish word signifying Shitefire, and it is used for a bragging, vapouring fellow.'
2. In 1871 the 'turd-like bourgeois' and 'political cur' would of course be elected first president of the Third French Republic.

   When Thiers died, in 1877, and received an immense state funeral, Flaubert wrote rather differently about him, to Mme Roger des Genettes: 'Yes, I too watched old Thiers' funeral, and I assure you it was splendid. That truly *national* manifestation moved me. I didn't love that king of the Prud'hommes – no matter! Compared with those around him he was a giant; and then he had another rare virtue, patriotism. No one exemplified France as he did. Hence the immense effect of his death.'

~

To Alfred Baudry[1]

(1867–1868)

My friend,

I am *not at all* of your opinion, being a born enemy of texts that explain drawings, and drawings that explain texts. My conviction about this is radical, and forms part of my aesthetic.

I *defy* you to cite me one example among the moderns, whose idiosyncrasy this is (the ancients abstained from such sacrilege), which speaks for the contrary. The explanation of one artistic form by another is a monstrosity. You won't find in all the museums of the world a good picture that needs a commentary. Look at exhibition catalogues. The longer the entry, the worse the painting.

. . .

1. Younger brother of the Frédéric Baudry who would play an important role in Flaubert's last years.

~

To Edmond and Jules de Goncourt

[Croisset,] Wednesday [May 20, 1868]

. . .[1]

Returning to my apartment [in Paris] on Sunday night at half past eleven, I go to bed promising myself a deep sleep, and blow out my candle. Three minutes later, a blaring of trombones and beating of drums! It was a wedding at Bonvalet's.[2] Said tavern keeper's windows being wide open (because of the heat of the night), I didn't miss a single quadrille, a single shout. The orchestra (as I have the honour to repeat) was enhanced *by two drums*!

At six a.m., masons again. At seven, I betake myself to the Grand Hôtel.

There, a forty-five-minute prowl before finding a room. Scarcely was I there (in the room), when hammering begins in the room adjoining. Another prowl in the same hotel in search of refuge. At nine, I give up and go to the Hôtel du Helder, where I find a wretched closet, black as a tomb. But the peace of the grave was lacking: shouts of guests, rumbling of carriages in the street, clanking of tin pails in the court.

From one o'clock to three I pack my bags and leave the Boulevard du Temple.

From four to six, tried to sleep at DuCamp's, rue du Rocher. But I had reckoned without yet other masons, who are building a wall alongside his garden.

At six, I transport myself to a bath establishment, rue Saint-Lazare. There, children playing in the yard, plus a piano.

At eight, I return to the rue du Helder, where my man has laid out on my bed everything I required that night for the Tuileries ball. But I hadn't dined, and thinking that hunger was perhaps weakening my nerves, I go to the Café de l'Opéra.

I had scarcely entered, when a gentleman vomits beside me.

At nine, return to the Hôtel du Helder. The idea of dressing exhausts me, like a blood-letting in both arms and both legs. I give up in disgust, and decide to return to the country as fast as I can. My man packs my bag.

That's not all. Final episode: my bag rolls off the top of the cab and crashes on my shoulder. I still have the bruises.

Voilà!

Yours –

1. The first page of the autograph has been lost.
2. A restaurant almost directly opposite Flaubert's flat at 24 boulevard du Temple. The confusion of tenses in this letter is perhaps a consequence of the adventures it describes.

In May 1868 George Sand paid her third visit to Croisset, staying two days. She had a certain interest in phrenology – in her novel *Mauprat* she calls it 'a system which has its good side' – and phrenology lies behind an entry she made in her journal – her only characterization of Caroline's husband: 'Croisset, May 24, 1868. We dine with the others and Monsieur Commanville, whose forehead is *flat*.' In other words, Ernest did not have the pleasantly convex brow that among phrenologists was thought to denote a generous spirit. During Flaubert's later years, which were to be filled with difficulties stemming from the Commanvilles, Mme Sand's references to the niece she knew Flaubert loved would always be of the utmost politeness – 'Your charming niece,' etc. To Commanville she never refers again.

Mme Chevalley-Sabatier, in her book about Flaubert and Caroline (see Appendix I), says of Caroline's unpublished memoirs:

> In the account she gives of [her meetings with George Sand], we find that she did not share the respectful affection displayed by her uncle for the Good Lady of Nohant. Was this a slight touch of jealousy, or resentment that her youth was given insufficient consideration? In any case, Caroline is not indulgent in her description of Mme Sand as 'a little old lady, certainly well past sixty, carelessly dressed, whose only coquetry seemed to be confined to an extraordinary coiffure, which combined black velvet ribbons, white daisies, and barrettes' . . . Mme Sand was very free-spoken, quite bold and crude in her language: that did not please Caroline. When the hour grew late, the latter would retire, and leave the two interlocutors to their seemingly endless dialogue, which sometimes lasted till dawn.

~

TO GEORGE SAND

Croisset, Sunday, July 5 [1868]

. . .

I've been slaving away madly for the past six weeks. The patriots won't forgive me this book, nor the reactionaries either! So much the worse: I write things as I feel them – that is, as I believe they exist. Is this foolish of me? But it seems that our unhappy condition is attributable exclusively to people of our own kind?[1] All the Christianity I find in Socialism appals me! Here, for example, are two little notes now lying on my table:

'This system [Louis Blanc's own] is not a system of disorder. For it has its source in the Gospels. And from this divine source *there cannot flow* hatred, warfare, total conflict of interests. For the doctrine formulated from the Gospels is a doctine of peace, union, and love.' (L. Blanc)

'I even make bold to assert that with the disappearance of respect for Sunday, the last spark of poetic fire has been extinguished in the souls of our rhymesters. As the saying has it: "Without religion, no poetry." ' (Proudhon)

Apropos of the latter, I beg of you, *chère maître*, to read, at the end of his book on the celebration of Sunday, a love story entitled, I think, *Marie et Maxime*. One must know this to have an idea of the Style of our Thinkers. It should be placed with the excursion to Brittany in *Ça et là*, by the great Veuillot.[2] This doesn't prevent some of our friends from admiring these two gentlemen. Whereas they deride Voltaire.

In my old age I intend to write criticism: it will relieve me. For I often choke on suppressed opinions. No one understands better than I Boileau's outbursts against bad taste: 'The stupidities I hear uttered at the Academy are hastening my end.' There was a man for you!

Whenever I hear the steamers passing, one after another, I think of you: I remind myself that you liked the sound, and it irritates me less. What moonlight tonight on the river! . . .

1. By 'patriots' Flaubert means the 'radicals' or 'socialists' defeated during the June Days of 1848; by 'reactionaries' the triumphant, repressive bourgeois (Thiers was their great man); by 'people of our own kind', intellectuals, scholars, Voltairean freethinkers. In *L'Éducation sentimentale*, Dussardier and Sénégal represent the first category; the Dambreuses and their friends the second. (A.J.)

2. Louis Veuillot (1813–1883), Catholic writer. Brittany was, and remains, strongly Catholic.

∾

GEORGE SAND TO FLAUBERT

Nohant, July 31 [1868]

. . .

You disturb me when you say that in your book you'll blame the patriots for all that went wrong [in 1848]. Is that really true? They – the vanquished! Surely it's enough to be defeated through your own fault, without having your nose rubbed in all your stupidities. Have pity! There were so many splendid souls even so. The Christian aspect was a fad. I confess that Christianity has always been seductive. When you see only its gentle side, it wins your heart. But you have to think of all the harm it has done. I'm not surprised that a generous heart like L. Blanc should have dreamed of seeing it purified and restored to its ideal. I too had that illusion, but as soon as you take a step back into the past you see that it cannot be revived, and I am sure that today L. Blanc is smiling at his dream. One must think of that, too. One must tell oneself that all who had some intelligence have come a very long way in the past twenty years, and that it would not be generous to reproach them for what they themselves probably regret. As for Proudhon, I never thought him sincere. He was an orator – of genius, so it is said. I don't understand him. He is a kind of perpetual antithesis, insoluble. I think of him as one of those sophists old Socrates made fun of.

I trust you to be *generous*. With a word more or a word less, with the hand wielding its strength gently, one can flick the whip without causing a wound. You are so good – you cannot be cruel.

. . .

~

To George Sand

Dieppe, Monday [August 10, 1868]

. . .

I expressed myself badly if I told you that my book will 'blame the patriots for all that went wrong', I don't recognize my right to blame anyone. I don't even believe that the novelist should express his opinion on matters of this world. He can communicate it, but I don't like him to state it. (Such is part of my poetics.) Thus I confine myself to describing things as they appear to me, to expressing what seems to me to be true. Hang the consequences. Rich or poor, winners or losers – I take no account of all that. I want to have neither hate, nor pity, nor anger. As for sympathy, that's different. One can never have enough of it. The reactionaries, by the way, will be treated even less gently than the others. For they seem to me more criminal . . .

Now let me say that since I have absolute confidence in the greatness of your spirit, I will read my third part to you when it's done, and if there is something in my work that seems cruel to you I'll remove it. But I'm convinced in advance that you'll make no objection. As for allusions to individuals, there isn't a trace.

. . .

~

To Jules Duplan
                    Croisset, Thursday night [late August or September 1868]
Cher Vieux

Here's the thing.

I tell – or rather, a cocotte in my book tells about her childhood.[1] She was the daughter of workers in Lyons. I need details about the homes of such people.

1. A few lines about the living quarters of Lyons workers.

2. The 'canuts' (as I think the silk weavers are called) work in very low-ceilinged rooms, don't they?

3. In their own homes?

4. Their children work too?

I find the following in my notes: the weaver working at a Jacquard loom is continually struck in the stomach by the shaft of the roller on which the cloth is being wound as it is completed.

5. Is it the roller itself that strikes him? Clarify, please.

In short, I want to write a four-line description of a working-class domestic scene, to contrast it with another interior that comes later – the luxurious establishment in which our heroine is deflowered. Her tambourine is punctured by a Saint-Florent.[2] Unfortunately I have no room to expatiate on these people. If you know one of your compatriots whom you want to 'stigmatize', send me his photograph. But all this is unimportant: what I need is my picture of 'canuts' doing their work amidst their household paraphernalia.

It would be kind of you to send me this information right away. I need it.

. . .

1. Rosanette reminisces with Frédéric in the forest of Fontainebleau. (*L'Éducation sentimentale*, Part Three, Chapter I). Jules Duplan was a Lyonnais.

2. A character in Sade's *Justine* and *La Nouvelle Justine*.

~

To Jules Duplan
                    [Croisset,] Wednesday, 5 o'clock [September 16, 1868]
Dear old chap,

Look what's happened.[1] After making the trip to Fontainebleau and back by train, I was struck by a doubt: and now I'm sure, alas! that in 1848 there was no railroad between Paris and Fontainebleau. This means I have to scrap two passages and begin afresh. I see in *Paris-Guide* (vol. I, p. 1660) that the line to Lyons began only in 1849. You can't imagine what a nuisance this is for me. So – I need to know: 1. how, in June 1848, one went from Paris to Fontainebleau; 2. perhaps *part* of the line was already in use? 3. what coaches did one take? 4. and what was their terminus in Paris? Here is the situation: Frédéric is at Fontainebleau with Rosanette; he hears that Dussardier has been wounded (this is June 25), and he leaves for Paris with Rosanette, who doesn't want to be left behind. But on the way she loses her courage and comes no further. He arrives in Paris alone. Because of the Saint-Antoine barricades he has to make a long detour before reaching Dussardier, who lives at the far end of the *faubourg* Poissonnière.

Can you recall what the ambulances looked like? If you remember any details of the nights in Paris that week, send them to me.

My hero wanders through the streets the last night, June 25–26 (everything ended on the 26th).

Now you see the situation as clearly as I. Be a good chap: try to find me definite information.

My bugger of a novel is draining the very marrow of my bones. I'm dog-tired, and beginning to be depressed.

In 1848 the line between Corbeil and Paris was open. Remains to know how one got from Fontainebleau to Corbeil . . .

1.   Flaubert is verifying details concerning events twenty years past – the end and aftermath of the June Days, 1848, his evocation of which is possibly the most powerful section of *L'Éducation sentimentale*. Over a year later he would still be seeking information, this time from Ernest Feydeau: 'You'd be very kind if you could answer these two questions: (1) In June 1848, where were the posts of the National Guard in the Mouffetard, Saint-Victor, and Latin quarters? (2) The night of 25–26 June (Sunday–Monday), was it the National Guard or the regular infantry that occupied the Left Bank in Paris? I've already asked these questions of several persons, and have had no answer. I'm stuck, with three pages remaining blank.'

About his pages on Fontainebleau, he wrote to George Sand on September 9, 1868: 'I'm working furiously. I've written a description of the forest of Fontainebleau that made me want to hang myself from one of its trees. I had interrupted myself for three weeks, and had great trouble getting back into my stride. I'm like a camel – you can't stop him when he's on the go, nor make him start when he's resting. I still have a year's work ahead. After that, no more bourgeois, definitely. Too difficult, and too ugly. It's time for me to do something good that I'll enjoy.'

~

To George Sand

Saturday night [Croisset, September 29, 1868]

You are surprised, *chère maître*?[1] Not I! I told you, but you wouldn't believe me.

I feel for you. For it's sad to see people you love change. The substitution of one spirit for another, in a body that remains the same as before, is heartbreaking to witness. One feels *betrayed.* I have experienced that, and more than once.

Still, what is your conception of woman, then, O you who are of the Third sex? Are they not, as Proudhon says, 'the desolation of the Just'? Since when have they been able to dispense with chimeras? After love, Piety; that's the way it goes. Sylvanie has no more men; she takes up with God. That's all it amounts to.

Rare are those who have no need of the Supernatural. Philosophy will always be the portion of aristocrats. Fatten the human herd, bed them with straw up to their bellies, even gild their stable – to no avail: they will remain brutish, whatever anyone may say. The only progress to be hoped for is that the brutes may be made a little less vicious. But as for elevating the ideas of the masses, giving them a conception of God that is broader and therefore less Human, I am very dubious, very dubious.

I am just now reading a very respectable little book (by a friend of mine, a judge) about the Revolution in the department of the Eure. It is full of documents written by bourgeois of the period, ordinary small-town citizens. Well, I assure you there are few of that calibre nowadays. They were well-read, admirable people, full of good sense, ideas, and generosity. Neo-Catholicism on the one hand and Socialism on the other have made France less intelligent. Everything is either the Immaculate Conception or workers' lunches.

I told you that I don't flatter the Democrats in my book. But I assure you the Conservatives aren't spared, either. I'm now writing three pages on the abominations committed by the National Guard in June '48, which will make me highly popular with the bourgeois. I'm doing my best to rub their noses in their own turpitude.

You give me no details about *Cadio*.[2] Who are the actors? etc. I'm wary of your novel about the theatre. You are too fond of those people. Have you known many of them who love their art? So many actors are merely bourgeois gone astray![3]

So we'll see each other three weeks from now, at the latest. I'm very happy about that, and meanwhile send you a kiss.

G[ve] Flaubert

What about the Censor? For your sake I hope he'll commit some howlers; indeed it would grieve me were he false to his traditional role . . .[4]

1. George Sand's friend the actress Mme Arnould Plessy ('Sylvanie') had been converted to Catholicism. She had been one of Prince Napoleon's many mistresses.
2. The play adapted by George Sand and her collaborator Paul Meurice from her novel of that name was in rehearsal. She was also in the midst of writing her novel about actors, *Pierre qui roule*.
3. Flaubert is perhaps speaking from intimate knowledge. He and Bouilhet had been having affairs with actresses, Flaubert notably with Béatrix Person.
4. In addition to speaking here as veteran of the *Madame Bovary* prosecution, Flaubert shows himself the former law student in his use of a legalistic phrase: *si elle manquait à ses us*. (*Elle* is *la Censure*, the censorship office.)

~

TO HIS COUSIN LOUIS BONENFANT

Croisset, Thursday [1868?]

Mon cher ami

I haven't thanked you enough. Your account is excellent in every way, and will supply me with some good details. You have done me a real service in sending it. I'm grateful to my little cousin Émilie, too, for her list of Nogent expressions; and I repay her kindness with the blackest ingratitude, because:

I cannot do as she would like, which is to change the name of the hero of my novel. You must remember, *cher ami*, that four years ago I asked you whether there were still in Nogent people named

Moreau? You replied that there were none, and you supplied me with several local names that I could feel free to use. On the strength of your information I went blithely ahead. It's too late to change. A proper name is extremely important in a novel – *crucial.* It is no more possible to change a character's name than his skin; it's like wanting to bleach a Negro.

So much the worse for the Moreaus now living in Nogent!

Not that they'll have any cause for complaint: my M. Moreau is a very elegant young man.

~

Charles Baudelaire had died on August 31, 1867. Now, over a year later, Mme Jacques Aupick, his twice-widowed mother, probably thinking of his friendship with Flaubert and the prosecution they had both suffered – for *Madame Bovary* and *Les Fleurs du mal* – saw to it that Flaubert received a copy of her son's posthumously published *Oeuvres complètes.* Of Flaubert's letter to Mme Aupick, written on December 31, 1868, there is available only the single sentence quoted in an autograph dealer's catalogue of 1968, offering the letter for sale:

'I am very touched by your sending me the works of your son, whom I greatly loved and whose talent I appreciated more than anyone.' In the remaining part of the letter (so says the catalogue), Flaubert recalls his 1851 visit to General and Mme Aupick in Constantinople, where the general, Baudelaire's none too sympathetic stepfather, had been French 'minister plenipotentiary'. The present whereabouts of the letter have not been disclosed by the dealer.

~

TO GEORGE SAND
                [*Croisset, January 1, 1869*] *New Year's Eve, 1 o'clock*
Why shouldn't I begin the year 1869 with the wish that for you and yours it may be 'good, and happy, and followed by many more'? Rather rococo, but I like it.

Now let's chat. I am not 'working myself to death', for I have never been better. In Paris I was told I was 'fresh-faced as a girl', and people ignorant of my biography attributed that healthy look to the country air.[1] Such are ready-made ideas. Each has his own hygiene.

I, when I'm not hungry, can eat only dry bread. And the most indigestible foods, like unripe cider-apples, and bacon, are my cures for stomach ache. And so on. A man who has no common sense mustn't live according to common-sense rules.

As to my mania for work, I'll compare it to a rash. I keep scratching myself and yelling as I scratch. It's pleasure and torture combined. And nothing that I write is what I want to write. For one doesn't choose one's subjects: they impose themselves. Will I ever find mine? Will there ever drop down on me from heaven an idea in perfect harmony with my temperament? Will I be able to write a book into which I put my entire self? It seems to me, in my moments of vanity, that I am beginning to glimpse something that will be what a novel should be. But I still have three or four to write before that one (which is as yet very vague); and at the rate I go it will be all I can do to write those three or four. I am like M. Prud'homme, who thought the most beautiful church of all would have the spire of Strasbourg, the colonnade of St Peter's, the portico of the Parthenon, etc. I have contradictory ideals. Hence, confusion, stoppage, impotence!

As for the cloistered life to which I condemn myself being a 'delicious existence' – no! But what to do! To get drunk on ink is better than to get drunk on brandy. The Muse, crabbed though she may be, is the source of less grief than Woman! I cannot accommodate the two. One has to choose. My choice was made long ago. There remains the question of the senses. Mine have always been my servants. Even in the days of my greenest youth I did with them exactly as I pleased. I am now almost fifty, and their ardour is the least of my worries. This regime is not very merry, I agree. There are moments of emptiness, of hideous boredom. But these grow rarer as one grows older. To be truthful, *living* strikes me as a trade I wasn't cut out for! And yet! . . .

I was in Paris for three days, which I spent doing research and errands for my book. I was so exhausted last Friday that I went to bed at seven o'clock. Such are my wild orgies in the capital.

I found the Goncourts in a state of frantic (sic) admiration for a book called *Histoire de ma vie*, by G. Sand – which goes to show that they are stronger in good taste than in erudition.[2] They even wanted to write to you to express their admiration. On the other hand I found our friend Harrisse[3] stupid. He compares Feydeau to Chateaubriand, greatly admires *Le Lépreux de la Cité d'Aoste*, considers *Don Quixote* tedious, etc.

Are you struck by how rare the literary sense is? A knowledge of languages, archaeology, history, etc. – all that should help. But not at all! So-called enlightened people are becoming more and more inept as regards art. Even what art *is* escapes them. Glosses are more important for them than the text. They value crutches more highly than legs.

. . .

I shan't budge from here before Easter. I count on finishing by the end of May. You'll see me at Nohant this summer, even though bombs should fall.

And your work? What are you doing now, *chère maître*?

When shall we see each other? Will you be coming to Paris in the spring?

Je vous embrasse.

G^{ve} Flaubert

1. A number of phrases in this letter refer to advice that Mme Sand has been giving him, or to comments she has made, about working himself to death, staying holed up in his library and not getting enough fresh air, really finding his cloistered life (about which he constantly complains) a delicious existence, and so on. The tone of her letters is increasingly maternal.
2. Flaubert means that since the last volume of *Histoire de ma vie* had been published in 1855, the Goncourts should have read it before now.
3. Henry Harrisse (1829–1910), born in Paris of American parents, was a lawyer, bibliophile, and historian, author of books on the Abbé Prévost and his *Manon Lescaut*.

~

GEORGE SAND TO FLAUBERT

[Nohant,] January 1, [18]69

It's one in the morning. I have just kissed my children. I'm tired from making a complete costume for a big doll for Aurore, but I don't want to go to bed without kissing you too, my dear friend, my great precious child. May '69 be good to you and see the end of your novel, may you keep well and be always *you*. I can imagine nothing better, and I love you.

G. Sand[1]

1. Flaubert replied, in a letter dated January 14: 'You know, *chère maître*, it's very nice about the two of us – writing to each other simultaneously on New Year's Eve. There is certainly some strong link between us.'

~

To Princesse Mathilde

[Croisset,] Thursday [January 7, 1869]

Your letter of yesterday distressed me, *Princesse*, and I'd have answered it immediately had it not been for the wedding of Mlle Leroy, the Prefect's daughter. A great debauch for me – to Rouen, for an evening party!

Since you are upset,[1] so am I. But let me say it seems to me you're giving a rather inflated importance to the reason. It's never the flag that's to be considered, but what it flies over; *where* one writes is of little importance: the main thing is *what* one writes.

I am not at all defending *Le Temps*, which I profoundly dislike, as for that matter I dislike all newspapers. I hate that paltry way of publishing one's thoughts, and I express my hatred by abstaining completely, despite the money I could earn.

The press is dangerous only because of the exaggerated importance given to it; on this score, friends and enemies are all of one mind, unfortunately! Ah! If only the sceptic might be allowed free rein!

To return to Sainte-Beuve. His greatest offence, to my mind, lies in his doing something that displeases you; and from the moment you asked him not to write for that newspaper he should have complied. Such are my political opinions.

On the other hand, I perfectly understand his fury if they refused an article. One has to be a man of letters to know how wounding such things can be. I brought suit against the *Revue de Paris* when it took upon itself to cut three or four lines of mine.[2] My maxim is that in this regard one must be obdurate.

Therefore I excuse his resentment. But what I would not excuse would be a break with a government that has so greatly honoured him. Surely this is not possible! Despite all you tell me, I still doubt it.

I am re-reading your letter as I write, and it brings tears to my eyes, for I sense that this affair has hurt you to the quick, and that you are suffering from it as from a betrayal.

It would be good of you if you would explain the matter to me more fully; I long to learn that you have been mistaken. Because, in the end, if he writes only purely literary criticism for *Le Temps*, the harm done is slight. But, once again, what I dislike and what I do not forgive him, is that he should distress you. You, you, *Princesse!*, who have been, for him especially, more than good, *devoted.* No: really, from the moment you urged him . . .

Despite my virtuous resolution not to return to Paris before the end of March, I'm promising myself a little visit to you next month.

Ever at your feet, *Princesse*, I kiss your hands, and am

Entirely yours,

G^ve Flaubert

1. Sainte-Beuve had broken with the semi-official *Moniteur Universel* over their insistence that he delete, from one of his weekly articles, an unfavourable reference to Mgr. Le Courtier, bishop of Montpellier. He had gone over to *Le Temps*, the mouthpiece of the liberal opposition, despite Princesse Mathilde's request that he not do so. In her displeasure the princess revealed the spirit of her benefactions to Sainte-Beuve by saying that his acceptance of a senatorship had made him 'a vassal of the Empire'. (André Billy, *Sainte-Beuve: Sa vie et son temps*, 2 vols., Paris: Flammarion, 1952.)
2. Not quite accurate. For Flaubert's quarrel with the *Revue de Paris* over cuts in its serialization of *Madame Bovary,* see Volume I.

To George Sand

Croisset, Tuesday, February 2 [1869]

Ma chère maître:

Your old troubadour is the very picture of exhaustion. I spent a week in Paris verifying boring details (seven to nine hours of cabs a day, a fine way to get rich with Literature! Well . . .). I have just read over my outline. The amount I still have to write overwhelms me, or rather it makes me almost vomit from discouragement. It's always so when I get back to work. It's then that I'm bored, bored, bored! But this time it's worse than ever. That's why I so dread any interruption of the grind. I had no choice, however. I had myself carted to undertakers' establishments, to Père-Lachaise, to the valley of Montmorency, past shops selling religious articles, etc.[1]

In short, I still have four or five months' work ahead of me. What a sigh of relief I'll give when it's done! And what a long day it will be before I tackle the bourgeois again. It's time I enjoyed myself.

I have seen both Sainte-Beuve and the Princess. And I know everything about their break, which seems to me irrevocable. Sainte-Beuve was indignant with Dalloz,[2] and went over to *Le Temps*. The Princess begged him not to. He wouldn't listen to her. That's the whole story. My opinion, if you care to have it, is this: the first offence was committed by the Princess, who was intemperate; but the second and more serious offender is Sainte-Beuve, who acted ungallantly. When you have so accommodating a friend, and when this friend has provided you with an income of thirty thousand francs a year, you owe her some consideration. It seems to me that in Sainte-Beuve's place I'd have said: 'Since it displeases you, let's say no more about it.' He was bad-mannered, inelegant. What disgusted me a little, just between us, was the way he praised the Emperor to me. Yes: to me! Praise of Badinguet! And we were alone.

The Princess took the thing too seriously from the start. I wrote to her, siding with Sainte-Beuve; whereas he, I'm sure, found me cold. It was at that point, to justify himself in my eyes, that he protested his love for Isidore, which humiliated me a little. For it amounted to taking me for an utter imbecile.

I think he's preparing himself for a funeral like Béranger's, and that old Hugo's ability to speak the language of the people makes him jealous. Why write for newspapers when you can write books and aren't starving to death?

He's far from being a sage, that man; he's not like you! Your Strength charms me and amazes me. I mean the Strength of your entire person, not only your brain.

You spoke of criticism in your last letter, saying it will soon disappear. I think the contrary, that it's barely at its dawn. Its trend is the opposite of what it used to be, that's all. (In the days of La Harpe critics were grammarians; in the days of Sainte-Beuve and Taine they're historians.) When will they be *artists*, nothing but artists, *real* artists? Where have you seen a piece of criticism that is concerned, intensely concerned, with the work in itself? The milieu in which it was produced and the circumstances that occasioned it are very closely analysed. But the *unconscious* poetics which brought it into being? Its composition? Its style? The author's point of view? *Never.*

Such criticism as that would require great imagination and great goodwill. I mean an ever-ready faculty of enthusiasm. And then *taste* – a quality rare even among the best, to such a point that it is no longer even mentioned.

What infuriates me every day is to see a masterpiece and a turpitude put on the same level. The insignificant are exalted and the great disparaged. Nothing could be more stupid or more immoral.[3]

. . .

In Père-Lachaise I was overcome by a deep and painful disgust for mankind. You cannot imagine the fetishism of the tombs. The true Parisian is more idolatrous than a black. It made me want to lie down in one of the graves.

1. Flaubert's surviving notebooks testify to his indefatigable investigations in these – and many more – places and establishments.
2. Paul Dalloz, the owner and director of *Le Moniteur Universel.*
3. In a letter written this same February 2, to Turgenev, who had recently visited Croisset and 'charmed everyone', Flaubert repeats his strictures on La Harpe, Sainte-Beuve and Taine as critics, adding: 'I am eager to see your literary criticism, for yours will be that of a practitioner . . . With your kind of feeling, so original and so intense, your criticism will equal your creations, I'm sure.'

~

GEORGE SAND TO FLAUBERT

Nohant, February 11, [18]69

. . .

As for our friend, he is ungrateful, whereas our other friend is too demanding. As you say, both are wrong, and neither is to blame. It's the mechanism of society that makes it so. The kind of gratitude – that is, submission – that she demands, stems from a tradition that the present generation still turns to account (therein lies the trouble), but which it doesn't accept as a duty. The ideas of the person 'under obligation' have changed; those of the one doing the 'obliging' should change also. *She* should tell herself that one doesn't purchase another's moral liberty by performing a good office; and as for him, he should have foreseen that he would be considered as being bound. The simplest would have been not to require 30,000 francs a year. It's so easy to do without it! Let them work it out for themselves. They won't get us mixed up in it – we're not that stupid. You say some very good things about criticism. But to practise it in your sense would require artists, and the artist is too busy with his own work to forget himself in fathoming that of others.

. . .

∼

To George Sand

[Croisset,] Tuesday night [February 23–24, 1869]

What do I have to say about it, *chère maître*? Whether sensitivity in children should be fostered or repressed?[1] It seems to me that in this matter one should not have preconceived ideas. It's according to whether they tend towards having too much or too little. Moreover you can't alter basic character. There are affectionate natures and cold natures – there's no remedy for that. Furthermore, the same sight, the same lesson, can produce contrasting effects. Nothing should have hardened me more than being brought up in a hospital and playing as a small child in a dissecting room. And yet no one is more easily moved than I by the sight of physical suffering. It's true that I'm the son of a man who was extremely humane, sensitive in the good meaning of the word. The sight of a dog in pain brought tears to his eyes. Yet this in no way impaired his efficiency when performing operations. And he invented some terrible ones.

'Show children only the sweet and good side of life, up to the time when reason can help them accept or combat evil' [you say]. Such is not my opinion. For then something terrible is bound to take place in their hearts, an infinite disillusionment; and besides, how can reason develop if it doesn't apply itself (or isn't applied daily) to distinguishing right from wrong? Life is perforce an incessant education. Everything has to be learned, from Talking to Dying.

You say some very true things about the unconscious of children.[2] He who could see clearly into their little brains would discover the roots of human genius, the origin of the Gods, the sap that determines subsequent actions, etc. A black speaking to his idol and a child to its doll seem to me very close.

The child and the barbarian (the primitive) do not distinguish reality from fantasy. I remember very clearly that when I was five or six I wanted to 'send my heart' to a little girl I was in love with. (I meant my *physical* heart.) I pictured it lying on a bed of straw in a basket – an oyster basket!

But no one has gone as far as you in these analyses. Your *Histoire de ma vie* has pages on the subject that are extraordinarily profound. What I say is true, since minds remote from yours have found them amazing – witness the Goncourts.

Have you read their *Madame Gervaisais*? You should.

Your poor daughter-in-law must be very distressed. And Maurice, in consequence? And you too? I'm sorry for all of you. I saw M. Calamatta twice: once at Mme Colet's, and the second time at your house, rue Racine, the first time I called on you. Tell me what news there is of him.

Winter is approaching its end. I have seldom passed a better, despite an abominable grippe that has kept me coughing and streaming for three weeks. In about ten days I hope to begin my next-to-last chapter. When it is well under way (half done), I'll install myself in Paris – towards Easter, not before. I *count* on a reunion with you there. Because, like an animal – or, rather, like a man who prizes things of the mind – I miss you.

Our good Turgenev should be in Paris by the end of March.[3] It would be nice if the three of us could dine together.

I have been thinking more about Sainte-Beuve. To be sure, one can 'do without 30,000 francs a year'. But there is something simpler yet: having such an income, not to spout every week in those bum-wipers called newspapers. Why doesn't he write books, since he's rich and talented?

I am just now re-reading *Don Quixote*. What a giant of a book! Is there anything more splendid?

Soon it will be four o'clock. Time to climb between the sheets.

Adieu. I kiss you on both cheeks – you're like fresh bread – and Mlle Aurore too, with all the affection of your troubadour.

1. George Sand's son, Maurice, and his wife, Lina, had gone to Milan, where Lina's father, the artist Louis Calamatta, was fatally ill. (He was to die on March 9.) Mme Sand, remaining at Nohant with the couple's three-year-old daughter, Aurore, had asked Flaubert for his thoughts about very young children: 'You who have raised a niece who is charming and intelligent.' Mme Sand was not on good terms with her own daughter, Solange, whose marriage to the sculptor Jean-Baptiste Clésinger had failed and whose two daughters by him had died in infancy (as had the first-born, a son, of Lina and Maurice).

2. '*L'inscience des enfants*'.

3. He was, and Flaubert saw him. 'I dined with Turgenev yesterday and the day before,' he wrote to Mme Sand to Nohant (March 31, 1869). 'That man paints such powerful pictures, even in conversation, that he *showed* me G. Sand, leaning on a parapet of Mme Viardot's château at Rosay. Below the turret was a moat; in the moat, a boat. And Turgenev, sitting in that boat, was looking up at you. The setting sun was falling on your black hair.'

    Pauline Viardot-Garcia (1821–1910), 'a great lyric actress and singer' (*Grove's Dictionary of Music and Musicians*, 1935), was a mezzo-soprano, the younger sister of the contralto Marie Malibran – both of them daughters of the Spanish tenor and teacher Manuel Garcia and his wife, Joaquina Sitchez, an actress. In 1841 she married Louis Viardot, writer, critic, and at that time director of the Théâtre Italien in Paris. George Sand, her close friend, depicted her in the novel *Consuelo* and dedicated the book to her. When not in Russia, Turgenev usually lived with the Viardots. Madame Viardot was the love of his life.

∾

As we have seen, Flaubert had thought from the beginning to give his new novel the title he had already used for one of his early, unpublished works; but it was not until it was almost done that he announced to George Sand – on April 3, 1869 – that he had definitely decided to call it *L'Éducation sentimentale*, 'all other ideas having failed'. He now added a subtitle: *Histoire d'un jeune homme* (The Story of a Young Man) – which is printed in all French editions although not in all translations. 'I don't say that the title is good,' he told Mme Sand, 'but so far it's the one that best renders what I had in mind. This difficulty in finding a good title makes me think that the *idea* of the work (or rather its concept) isn't clear. I'd very much like to read you the end.' He did not tell her – at least in any surviving letter – of its being the same title he had long ago given his youthful work. Perhaps Mme Sand, like all but a handful of his old friends, remained ignorant of the existence of that early novel, which would only be published posthumously.

～

To Jules Duplan (?)
> [*Paris,*] *Sunday morning, May 6, 1869, 4 minutes before 5*
Fini! mon vieux! Yes, my book is finished! This calls for your stopping work and coming to embrace me.

I've been at my desk since 8 o'clock yesterday morning. My head is bursting. No matter – there's a tremendous weight off my stomach!

> *A toi –*

～

At this time George Sand was in Paris for a month or more making arrangements concerning her new play, *L'Autre*; Flaubert saw her frequently, and on two occasions read her parts of his novel.[1] '*C'est de la belle peinture,*' she wrote in her diary after the first session; and after the second, 'The end is excellent.' Following that, she read him, in turn, from *L'Autre*, which made him, she wrote to Maurice, 'cry like a calf'.

There were also readings from *L'Éducation sentimentale* in the rue de Courcelles. 'Princesse Mathilde twice asked me to read parts of my novel to her,' he wrote to Caroline. 'At the third request I gave in, and yesterday I read her the first three chapters. Whereupon, enthusiasm from the Areopagus impossible to describe, and I *have* to go on and read her the whole thing – which means (amid my other occupations) four sessions of four hours each.' Two weeks later: 'My last reading to the Princess attained the supreme limits of enthusiasm. (Literally.) A good part of the success must have been due to the way I read. I don't know what got into me that day, but I delivered the last chapter in such a way that I was dazzled myself.'

It is understandable that the reading of the last chapters of *L'Éducation sentimentale*, especially the scene of Frédéric Moreau's reunion with the now white-haired Madame Arnoux, whom he had long romantically loved, should have inspired Flaubert to eloquent delivery. That 'session' must have been charged not only with pride and relief in having completed the work at last, but particularly with thoughts of Elise Schlesinger, the young mother he had met as an adolescent on the beach in Trouville more than thirty years before. He had always romantically cherished the memory of that meeting and of subsequent visits to the Schlesingers' house in Paris during the otherwise dreary winters of his law studies. He had drawn the heroine of his novel in Elise Schlesinger's image; and he knew her now to be ill and unhappy, living with her feckless husband in Baden.

It is also curious to think of his reading to the princess the scenes, near the novel's end, in which he describes the armed repression marking the December 2, 1852, coup d'état of her cousin Louis-Napoleon, the present Emperor. That act of caesarism had led, along with its many other consequences, to her enjoying her present importance – the importance which, in turn, brought her Flaubert's friendship and now the private readings. 'The memory of those five afternoons I spent with you reading my long novel,' Flaubert wrote to her, 'will be with me eternally, as one of the best things in my life.'

The next step, after having the manuscript recopied and before sending it to the printer, would be to go over it – as he had gone over both *Madame Bovary* and *Salammbô* – with Louis Bouilhet, with whom he had been constantly in touch since the novel's inception. But Bouilhet was ill, and had gone to Vichy in hope of relief. 'By the end of next week, Monseigneur will be back in Paris,' Flaubert wrote to Caroline on June 24, 'and we shall set about correcting *L'Éducation sentimentale* sentence by sentence. It will take us at least a fortnight.'

But that was not to be.

1. He had read her three hundred pages of it in May 1868, during one of her visits to Croisset.

~

To Maxime Ducamp

Croisset, July 23, 1869

Dear old Max, I feel the need of writing you a long letter; I don't know whether I'll have the strength, but I'll try.

Since his return to Rouen our poor Bouilhet was convinced he would never leave the place alive. Everybody, I along with the rest, teased him about his pessimism. He was no longer the man you knew; he was *completely* changed – except for his literary intelligence, which remained the same. In short, when I returned from Paris early in June, I found him in a lamentable state. A trip he made to Paris about *Aïssé*,[1] when Chilly asked him to make changes in the second act, so exhausted him that he could barely drag himself from the train to the Odéon. When I went to see him the last Sunday in June, I found Dr Péan from Paris, another brute from Rouen named Leroy, Dr Morel the alienist, and a pharmacist, a good man and a friend, named Dupré. Bouilhet didn't *dare* consult Achille,[2] suspecting himself to be very ill and fearing to be told the truth. Péan sent him to Vichy, whence Willemin quickly dispatched him back to Rouen. On arriving in Rouen, he finally called in Achille. His case was hopeless, as indeed Willemin had written to me.

During that last fortnight my mother was at Verneuil, visiting the Vasse ladies, and letters from Caroline were taking three weeks;[3] you can imagine the anguish I went through. I saw Bouilhet every other day, and *found him improving*. His appetite was excellent, as were his spirits, and the swelling in his legs was subsiding. His sisters came from Cany to make scenes about religion, and were so disgusting that they shocked a decent canon from the cathedral. Our poor friend was *superb*; he sent them packing, telling them in so many words to go fuck themselves. When I left him for the last time, on Saturday, he had a volume of La Mettrie on his bed-table; it reminded me of poor Alfred reading Spinoza.[4] No priest set foot in his house.

His anger against his sisters was still sustaining him on Saturday, and I left for Paris hoping he might still live a long time.

At five o'clock on Sunday he became delirious and began to compose aloud the plot of a medieval drama on the Inquisition. He kept calling for me, to show it to me, and was enthusiastic about it. Then he was seized with trembling, stammered 'Adieu! Adieu!', burying his head in Léonie's breast, and died very peacefully.

On Monday morning at nine my porter woke me with a telegram informing me of the event in telegraphic style. I was alone; I sent the news to you; I went to tell it to Duplan, who was in the midst of business; then I tramped the streets near the station until one o'clock – it was very hot.

From Paris to Rouen, in a crowded car, I had opposite me a cocotte who smoked cigarettes, put her feet up on the seat, and sang. When I saw the cathedral towers of Mantes[5] I thought I'd lose my mind, and am sure I wasn't far from doing so. Seeing me so pale, the cocotte offered me eau de Cologne. That revived me, but what a thirst! Ours in the desert of Kosseïr was nothing to it.

Finally I reached the rue Bihorel: here I spare you details. I have never known anyone better-hearted than young Philippe; he and Léonie, that good, kind woman, gave Bouilhet *admirable* care. They behaved in a manner I consider exemplary: to reassure him, to persuade him that he was not dangerously ill, Léonie refused to marry him; and her son encouraged her in this resistance. Bouilhet had so fully intended to marry her that he had obtained all the necessary documents. On the part of the young man, especially, I find such behaviour *assez gentleman*.

D'Osmoy and I took charge of the funeral. There was a large crowd at the cemetery, at least two thousand people! The Prefect, the Attorney General, etc. – every Tom, Dick, and Harry. Will you believe that as I followed his coffin I relished most keenly the grotesque aspect of the ceremony? I kept hearing remarks he was making to me about it. Inside me, somewhere, he was speaking to me. It seemed to me that he was there, beside me, and that together we were attending the funeral of someone else. The heat was terrible; there was a storm in the offing. I was drenched with sweat, and the climb to the cemetery finished me.

His friend [Gabriel] Caudron (Mayor Verdrel's former clerk) had chosen a plot very close to my father's. I leaned on the railing to catch my breath. The coffin was resting on poles, over the grave. The speeches were about to begin (there were three). At that point I gave up. My brother and someone I didn't know took me away.

The next day I went to fetch my mother at Serquigny. Yesterday I went to Rouen to get *all* his papers. Today I have been reading the letters people have written me . . . Ah, it's a bitter blow!

By his will he leaves thirty thousand francs and something more to Léonie. All his books and papers go to Philippe, whom he directs to consult with four friends as to what should be done with his unpublished works: me, d'Osmoy, you and Caudron; he leaves an excellent volume of poems, four prose plays, and *Aïssé*. Chilly dislikes the second act; I don't know what he will do. This winter you'll have to come here with d'Osmoy and we'll decide together what should be published.

. . . My head is aching too badly for me to go on. Besides, what could I say? . . . Now there is only you, only you! . . . *All* the letters I have received contain the phrase 'Close ranks!' A gentleman *I don't know* sent me his card with these two words: *Sunt Lacrymae!*

1. Bouilhet's drama in verse, *Mademoiselle Aïssé*, which Flaubert would succeed in having produced in 1872. Charles-Marie de Chilly was the manager of the Théâtre de l'Odéon.
2. Flaubert's brother, Dr Achille Flaubert, co-director of the Rouen hospital.
3. Caroline was in Scandinavia with her husband, Ernest Commanville, in connection with his timber business.
4. See Volume I, p. 137.
5. Where Flaubert had spent nights with Louise Colet and where he had often visited Bouilhet when the latter was librarian there.

~

To Frédéric Fovard[1]

[Croisset,] Thursday night [July 22, 1869]

He died of albuminuria, discovered too late to be cured.

His end was hastened by his two sisters, who came to the house and made scenes about religion (and came again yesterday wanting to take away the furniture). He received them like an antique Roman. But the reaction doubtless caused his oedema to mount to his chest and his brain. He became delirious at five o'clock on Sunday and died about ten, unaware of what was happening.

For me it is an irreparable loss. What I buried two days ago was my literary conscience, my judgement, my compass – not to count the rest.

1. Flaubert's notary in Paris.

~

'I have just buried a part of myself,' Flaubert wrote to Princesse

Mathilde; and to Jules Duplan: 'I tell myself, "What's the use of writing, now that he's no longer there?" It's finished – the good talk, our common enthusiasms, our dreaming together about our future work.' Flaubert would never cease to mourn Louis Bouilhet, as he mourned Alfred Le Poittevin.

He accepted Maxime DuCamp's offer to substitute himself as reader and 'corrector' of the manuscript of *L'Éducation sentimentale*, the purpose being – as he had told the Princess of his own final re-reading – to 'eliminate mistakes in French and deprive malevolent critics of as many pretexts as possible. They won't spare me anyway, but as to that I'm quite indifferent.' DuCamp had forfeited much of Flaubert's literary confidence by behaving as he had when serializing *Madame Bovary* in the *Revue de Paris*, and by the superficiality of much of his own subsequent writing; and now Flaubert wrote to Jules Duplan: 'I haven't had the strength to read over my novel, especially since Maxime's comments and suggestions irritate me, justified though they may be. I'm afraid of accepting them all, or of scrapping his entire list.' Eventually, of DuCamp's 251 written objections, most of them on points of grammar, he accepted about two-thirds, rejecting the rest on the authority of Littré's dictionary.[1] The manuscript went off; Lévy paid 16,000 francs for the rights for ten years; and Flaubert, once again putting aside his old *Temptation of Saint Anthony*, devoted himself to negotiating for the production of *Mademoiselle Aïssé* and the printing of a volume of Bouilhet's last poems, for which he would write an introduction.

Then came another loss. 'Sainte-Beuve died today, exactly at half past one,' he wrote to DuCamp on October 13, 1869. 'I arrived at his house by chance at 1.35. Another gone! The little band diminishes! One by one the rare survivors of the raft of the *Méduse*[2] disappear. With whom can one talk of literature now? He loved it, and although he wasn't precisely a friend, his death grieves me profoundly. Everyone in France who wields a pen has suffered an irreparable loss.' And to Caroline: 'I had written *L'Éducation sentimentale* in part for Sainte-Beuve, and he died without knowing a line of it! Bouilhet never heard the last two chapters. So much for our plans! The year 1869 will be marked as a hard one for me – I continue to haunt the cemeteries. Let's talk about something else.'

L'Éducation sentimentale was published on November 17, 1869 –

'the day,' as Flaubert noted in a letter to Caroline, 'of the opening of the Suez Canal.'

1. Maxime DuCamp says, in a passage in his *Souvenirs Littéraires* (which should be read with caution, like all his remarks about Flaubert): 'I had a discussion with Flaubert that lasted three weeks. I would lunch with him, he would dine with me, and we would sometimes battle for fourteen or fifteen hours at a stretch. There were times when I was exhausted. I laugh as I remember those struggles, during which, like Vadius and Trissotin [characters in Molière's *Les Femmes Savantes*], we would hurl blunt truths at each other's heads, without ever causing a wound . . . [Flaubert] claimed, he always claimed, that a writer is free, according to the demands of his style, to accept or reject the grammatical rules which govern the French language, and that the only laws he must observe are the laws of harmony . . . He said that style and grammar are two different things: he would quote the greatest writers, who were almost all incorrect, and point out that no grammarian ever knew how to write. On these points we were on agreement, for his opinions were based on irrefutable examples.'
2. See p. 368, n. 1.

~

George Sand to Flaubert

[Nohant,] Tuesday, November 30, 1869

Dear friend of my heart,

I wanted to re-read your book, and my daughter-in-law has read it too, and several of my young friends, all of them sincere and spontaneous and not at all stupid. We are all of the same opinion, that it is a splendid book, with the strength of the best of Balzac and more real – that is, more faithful to the truth from beginning to end. It takes the great art, the exquisite form, and the austerity of your work to make us willing to forgo the flowers of fantasy. Nevertheless you do fill your painting with poetry, whether or not your characters are aware of it. Rosanette at Fontainebleau doesn't know what plants she's treading on, but she is poetic all the same. It is all the work of a master – so live as calmly as you can in order to last long and produce much.

I have seen two scraps of articles that don't seem to begrudge you your success, but I know little of what goes on except that the papers seem given over to politics. Keep me informed. If they didn't do you justice, I'd be angry and say what I think. That's my right.

. . .

~

To George Sand

[Paris, December 3, 1869]

Chère bon maître,

Your old troubadour is being greatly berated in the press. Read last Monday's *Constitutionnel* and this morning's *Gaulois* – they mince no words. They treat me like a cretin and a scoundrel. Barbey d'Aurevilly's piece in the *Constitutionnel* is a model of this genre, and the one by our friend Sarcey, though less violent, is no less uncomplimentary. These gentlemen protest in the name of morality and the ideal! I have also been flayed in the *Figaro* and in *Paris*, by Cesena and Duranty.

I don't care in the least, but it does surprise me that there should be so much hatred and dishonesty.

The *Tribune*,[1] the *Pays*, and the *Opinion Nationale*, on the other hand, have praised me to the skies.

As for my friends – people who received copies adorned with my signature – they are afraid of compromising themselves, and speak to me about everything except the book. Instances of courage are rare. Nevertheless, the book is selling very well despite the political situation, and Lévy seems satisfied.

I know that the Rouen bourgeois are furious with me because of old Roque and the cellar of the Tuileries.[2] Their opinion is that 'the publication of such books should be forbidden' (I quote verbatim), that I favour the Reds, that I am guilty of fanning revolutionary passions, etc. etc.

In short, I have gathered very few laurels so far, and have been wounded by no folded rose petal.[3]

. . .

All the papers adduce as proof of my baseness the episode of la Turque[4] – which they garble, of course; and Sarcey compares me to the marquis de Sade, whom he admits he hasn't read!

None of this destroys my composure. But I keep asking myself: why publish?

1. The article in the *Tribune* was by the twenty-nine-year-old Émile Zola, of whom more anon.
2. Calling 'Here you are!' the bourgeois Roque, a member of the National Guard on duty at the Tuileries, shoots between the bars of a basement window into a group of prisoners calling for bread.
3. An allusion to one of the 'histories' of the Roman Aelianus (d. AD 140) in which the Sybarite Smindyrides complains of spending a sleepless night because one of the rose petals strewn on his bed was folded in two.
4. The much discussed last scene in the book, when Moreau and Deslauriers recall the fiasco of their adolescent approach to a brothel as having been 'the best moment of their lives'.

∼

To George Sand

4, rue Murillo, parc Monceau,[1]
Tuesday,
4 o'clock [Paris, December 7, 1869]

Chère maître,

The way they're all jumping on your old troubadour is unheard of. People who have received a copy of my novel from me are afraid to talk to me about it,[2] for fear of compromising themselves or out of pity for me. The most indulgent are of the opinion that what I have written is merely a series of scenes, and that composition and pattern are completely lacking. Saint-Victor, who extols the books of Arsène Houssaye, won't write about mine, finding it too bad. *Voilà.* Théo is away,[3] and no one (absolutely no one) is coming to my defence.

Therefore (you can guess what's coming), if you would care to take on that role you'd oblige me. If it embarrasses you, do nothing. No mere indulgence between us two.

. . .

Sarcey has published a second article against me. Barbey d'Aurevilly claims that I pollute a stream by washing myself in it. (Sic.) All that upsets me not the slightest. But God! how stupid people are!

When are you coming to Paris?
Je vous embrasse.

1. Flaubert had recently left his old apartment at 42, boulevard du Temple.
2. Of the hundred and fifty or so people to whom he had sent copies of

L'Éducation sentimentale, Flaubert wrote to Jules Duplan on December 9, thirty at most had replied.

3. Théophile Gautier was in Egypt, sent by the *Journal Officiel* to cover the festivities celebrating the opening of the Suez Canal.

~

George Sand noted in her diary on December 8, 1869: 'Letter from Flaubert. Article immediately . . . I go upstairs early to finish my article.' By the following night at 2 a.m. she could write to Flaubert:

> *Mon camarade*, it's done. The article will go off tomorrow. I send it to – whom? Reply by telegram. I'd like to send it to Girardin.[1] But you may have a better idea. I'm not too familiar with the importance or repute of the various newspapers. Send me a name and an address by telegram. I have Girardin's address.
>
> I'm not entirely satisfied with my prose. I've had fever and a sprain of some kind for the last two days; but we must act quickly.
>
> *Je t'embrasse.*

Flaubert responded immediately, on December 10, by telegram: 'To Girardin.'[2] In his letter of thanks, sent the same day as the telegram, he told her of still more attacks on his novel.

1. Emile Girardin (1806–1881), formerly owner and director of the newspaper *La Presse* and now of *La Liberté*.
2. George Sand's review of *L'Éducation sentimentale* would be printed in *La Liberté* for Wednesday, December 22, 1869, the day before Flaubert's arrival at Nohant.

~

GEORGE SAND TO FLAUBERT

[Nohant, December 10–11, 1869]

. . .

You seem surprised by the ill will. You are too naif. You don't know how original your book is. You don't realize how it *must* vex people by its very strength. You think you write things that will go as smoothly as a letter in the mail. That's what you *think*!

In my article I emphasize the *structure* of your book. That is what people understand the least, and it's the book's strongest feature. I have tried to make simple readers understand how they should read it, for it's the simple readers who make a book a success. Clever, malicious folk don't want others to succeed. I haven't concerned myself with them – it would do them too much honour.

~

GEORGE SAND TO FLAUBERT

[Nohant,] December 14 [1869]

. . .

We're making preparations for our family Christmas celebration beside the fire. We're expecting Plauchut,[1] and I've told him to try to bring you along. If you can't come with him, at least come for Christmas Eve and escape New Year in Paris. It's so dreary! Lina charges me to tell you that you need never wear anything but dressing gown and slippers. There will be no ladies and no outsiders. You'll make us very happy, and you've been promising so long to come . . .

1.   Edmond Plauchut (1814–1909), world traveller and devoted admirer of Mme Sand, was one of the habitués of Nohant. He is buried in the family cemetery there.

~

GEORGE SAND TO FLAUBERT

Sunday, Nohant, December 19, 1869

. . .

Here's the programme for the 24th. We'll dine at six sharp, trim the Christmas tree, and have the marionettes for the children, so that they can get to bed by nine. Afterwards we'll chat, and have supper at midnight . . . You must stay with us a very long time, a very long time; there'll be more merriment for New Year's Eve. This is a crazy, happy house, and it's time for some recreation after our work. Tonight I'm finishing my task for the year.[1] Seeing you, dearly beloved old friend, will be my reward: don't refuse me.

1.   Her novel *Malgrétout*.

~

Flaubert replied on December 20: 'Agreed, *chère maître*! I'll leave for Nohant Thursday by the 9 a.m. train.' George Sand's diary describes Flaubert's stay at the 'crazy, happy house':

Thursday, December 23: . . . Flaubert and Plauchut arrive at 5.30. Much embracing, dinner, talk, playing the python,[1] Arab songs. Flaubert tells stories. To bed at one o'clock.

Friday, December 24: Rain and snow all day. Everyone gay. I come down for lunch with the others at eleven o'clock. Flaubert gives Christmas presents to the little girls, who are enchanted. Lolo [Aurore] carries her doll all day . . . After dinner, marionettes, tombola, fairy-like decorations. Flaubert enjoys himself like a child. Christmas tree on the stage. Presents for all . . . Splendid Christmas Eve. I go upstairs at three o'clock.

Saturday, December 25: Lunch at noon . . . Flaubert reads us his great *féerie*[2] from three to half past six. Delightful, but not destined for success [on the Paris stage]. We greatly enjoy it – much talk about it. Everybody very gay tonight. Flaubert has us dying with laughter at *The Prodigal Son*.[3]

Sunday, December 26: Sunny and cold. We walk in the garden, even Flaubert, who wants to see the farm. We go all over it, show him the ram we've named 'Gustave' . . . At three o'clock Maurice and Edme[4] improvise a marionette show . . . Flaubert splits his sides laughing; he appreciates the marionettes . . . Upstairs at two.

Monday, December 27: Steady snow. Fadet [the dog] refuses to set foot outdoors. Lunch at noon. Lolo dances all her dances. Flaubert puts on woman's clothes and dances the cachucha with Plauchut. It's grotesque – we all behave like lunatics. Visit from M. and Mme Duvernet sobers us . . . Quiet evening of talk. Flaubert makes his farewells.

---

1. So she calls the 'serpent', or 'serpent horn', a now obsolete musical instrument, usually made of wood, consisting of a serpentine tube about eight

feet long – 'the natural bass of the ancient cornet family'. (*Grove's Dictionary of Music and Musicians*, 1935.)

2.   *Le Château des coeurs* (see p. 419–20).
3.   Unidentified. Perhaps one of Flaubert's 'turns' as a mime.

      Thirty years before, in the early 1840s, it had been Chopin who mimed at Nohant, jumping up from the piano to give 'an extraordinary imitation of the Emperor of Austria or an old Polish Jew', and so on. (André Maurois, *Lélia*.) Chopin invented the Nohant theatricals. At first they were pantomimes and more or less improvised short pieces; then Maurice Sand added marionettes, which became the house speciality. Maurice's theatre and his marionettes (many of their costumes made by George Sand) may still be seen at Nohant.

4.   Edme Simonnet, one of Mme Sand's adolescent great-nephews – grandsons of her older (illegitimate) half-brother, Hippolyte Chatiron, who was her father's son by a maidservant. Edme was George Sand's favourite among the many young relatives and friends who were such frequent guests at Nohant as to be members of the household. (There was now a new infant granddaughter, Aurore's younger sister, Gabrielle, born on March 11, 1868.)

                                      ◡

To GEORGE SAND

Monday morning [Paris, January 3, 1870]

Chère maître,

    I wrote last Thursday to tell you that I had a very good trip back. The letter will probably have been delayed, what with New Year and the weather . . .

    I didn't tell you nearly emphatically enough how charming I found the hospitality at Nohant. Those were the best moments of 1869, a year that wasn't kind to me.

    . . . I've begun to read again for *Saint Antoine* . . . Kiss Lolo for me, and don't forget anyone in giving my remembrance and affection, not even Fadet!

    Tout à vous, chère maître.

                                          ◡

GEORGE SAND TO FLAUBERT

Nohant, January 9, [18]70

. . .

    Your book is still being attacked. That doesn't keep it from being a beautiful and good book. Justice will be done later; justice is always done. It hasn't come at the proper time, apparently; or, rather, the time is *too* right. It confirms the present confused state of people's minds all too strongly. It rubs the raw wound. People recognize themselves too clearly in it.

Everyone adores you here, and our consciences are too clear for us to be offended by the truth: we speak of you every day. Yesterday Lina was telling me that she greatly admired everything you do, but that she preferred *Salammbô* to your depictions of modern life. If you had been concealed somewhere nearby, this is what you would have heard coming from her, from me, and from the others:

He is taller, larger, than the average person. His mind is like him, out-size. In this he has at least as much of Victor Hugo as of Balzac, but he has the taste and discernment that Hugo lacks, and he is an artist, which Balzac was not. – Does that mean he is greater than both of them? – *Chi lo sa?* He hasn't yet spoken with his full voice. The immense capacity of his brain confounds him. He doesn't know whether to be a poet or a realist, and since he's both, that troubles him. – He must learn to cope with his own great radiations. He sees everything, and wants to grapple with everything at once. – In that he is unlike the public, which wants to take its nourishment in small mouthfuls, and chokes on anything big. Nevertheless the public will make its way to him, when it understands him. – It will even reach him quite soon if the author will deign to *want* to be understood. – For that, he will perhaps have to make some concessions to the laziness of its intelligence. – But we must think carefully before daring to offer him that advice.

Such is the résumé of what we have all been saying. It isn't without value to know the opinions of good people and young people. The youngest say that *L'Éducation sentimentale* made them sad. They didn't recognize themselves in it, they who haven't yet lived. But they have illusions, and they say: Why does this man, so good, so lovable, so gay, so simple, so sympathetic, want to discourage us from living? It isn't properly thought out, what they say, but since it's instinctive, it should perhaps be taken into account.

. . .

~

Flaubert himself had written a few weeks before to Mlle Leroyer de

Chantepie, the author of one of the few favourable reviews: 'It will be, I hope, with *L'Éducation sentimentale* as it has been with *Bovary*. In the end, people will understand its morality and find it "quite simple".'

XIII

Interlude: Early 1870

Back from Nohant, Flaubert plunged into further reading for the perennial *Saint Anthony*, both at home and in Paris libraries, and began to prepare his preface to Louis Bouilhet's last poems. He was still depressed, and in a low state of energy. And soon he had to mourn another death, that of the faithful Jules Duplan on March 1, 1870. In mid-March came an episode of a kind which almost every writer of fiction encounters in one form or another.

~

To George Sand

[Paris,] Thursday, March 17 [1870]

Chère Maître,

Last evening I received a telegram from Mme Cornu[1] reading as follows: 'Please come. Important.' So I called on her today. And this is the story:

The Empress claims that you have made very unfavourable allusions to her in the last number of the *Revue* [*des Deux Mondes*].[2]

'How could she! With everybody attacking me now! I wouldn't have believed it! And I wanted to have her elected to the Academy! What have I done to her? Etc.' In short, she is very unhappy, and the Emperor as well. He was not indignant, but 'prostrated' (sic).

Mme Cornu vainly insisted that she was mistaken, that you had made no allusion to her whatever, and tried to explain to her how novels are written.

'Well then, have her write to the newspapers that she had no intention of offending me.'

'That she won't do, I'm sure.'

'Then you write to her, and ask her to tell you so.'

'I wouldn't presume to take such a step.'

'But I want to know the truth! Do you know someone who . . .'

At that point Mme Cornu named me.

'Oh, don't say that I spoke to you about this.'

Such is the dialogue that Mme Cornu reported to me. She would like you to write me a letter saying that the Empress was not your model. I am to send your letter to Mme Cornu, who will pass it on to the Empress. That's all.

I find the whole thing idiotic. Those people are certainly sensitive! You and I have to put up with a good deal more than that!

Now, *chère Maître du bon Dieu*, you must do exactly as you please.

The Empress has always been very pleasant with me, and I wouldn't mind doing her a kindness. I have read the passage in question, and find nothing offensive in it. But women's brains are so peculiar!

I am very tired of my own (my brain, I mean), or rather it's at a decidedly low ebb for the moment. Try as I may, I don't get ahead with my work. Things aren't going well at all. Everything irritates and wounds me; and after controlling myself in the presence of others I'm occasionally seized by fits of weeping during which I think my end has come. In short, I'm experiencing something quite new: the onset of old age. The shadows are closing in on me, as old Hugo would say.

Mme Cornu spoke to me enthusiastically about a letter you wrote her concerning a method of teaching. I'm going to see *L'Autre* with my niece next Saturday.

I'm waiting with double impatience for you to return to Paris. Because as soon as you leave it again I'll return to Croisset. Paris is beginning to get a little too much on my nerves.

Did I tell you that I'm taking cod liver oil, like a baby? Pathetic, no?

I embrace you with all my heart.

Your crusty old troubadour.

1. Mme Sébastien Cornu (born Hortense Lacroix) was namesake and god-daughter of the Emperor's mother, Queen Hortense, and was what the French call his *soeur de lait* ('milk-sister'): that is, they had shared the same wet-nurse. She had grown up with him, and was now a confidante of the Empress.

2. The reader will decide for himself whether the beautiful, Spanish-born Eugénie, known for her ambition when she was Mlle de Montijo, had reason to think herself alluded to in the following passage, spoken by a Spanish beauty, Mlle d'Ortosa, in the second instalment of George Sand's novel, *Malgrétout*, in the *Revue des Deux Mondes* for March 15, 1870:

   'I know about all the eminent men, all the powerful women, of the past and the present. I have taken the exact measure of them all, and I fear none of them. The day will come when I will be as useful to a sovereign as I can be today to a woman who asks me for advice on how to dress. I give the impression of attaching great importance to trivialities; no one suspects the serious preoccupations that engross me; this will become known later, when I am queen, czarina, grand duchess . . .'

❧

GEORGE SAND TO FLAUBERT

Nohant, March 19 [1870]

I know, my friend, that you are very devoted to her. I know that *She* is very good to the unfortunate who are brought to her attention: that is all I know about her private life. I have never had either a revelation or a document concerning her, *not a word, not a fact*, that would have enabled me to depict her. Therefore I merely traced a figure of fancy, I swear it: and those who would claim to recognize her in a satirical context would certainly be bad servants and bad friends.

As for me, I never write satire. I do not know what it is. Nor do I paint *portraits*; that is not my profession: I *invent*. The public, ignorant of what invention is, always claims to find models. This is a mistake, and demeans art.

Such is my *sincere* reply. I have just time to put it in the mail.

G. Sand

❧

TO GEORGE SAND

[Paris, March 20, 1870]

I have just sent your letter (for which I thank you), to Mme

Cornu, enclosing it in an epistle by your troubadour in which I permit myself to say *tartly* what I think. The two documents will be submitted to the gaze of the lady, and will give her a little lesson in aesthetics.

⁓

To Madame Hortense Cornu
                              [Paris,] Sunday night [March 20, 1870]

Your devotion caused you to take false alarm, *chère* Madame. I was sure of it. Here is the reply: it reaches me by return mail.

People in society, I tell you again, see allusions where there are none. When I wrote *Madame Bovary* I was often asked 'Was it Mme So-and-so you had in mind?' And I received letters from people completely unknown to me, among them one from a gentleman in Rheims who congratulated me for having 'avenged' him! (His wife had been unfaithful.)

All the pharmacists of the Seine-Inférieure recognized themselves in Homais and wanted to come and give me a whipping; but best of all (I learned of it five years later), in Africa there was an army doctor's wife named Mme Bovaries, who resembled 'Madame Bovary' – a name I had invented by changing the name 'Bouvaret'.[1]

The first thing our friend Maury said in speaking about *L'Éducation sentimentale* was: 'Did you know X—, an Italian, professor of mathematics? Your Sénécal is his living likeness, physically and morally. It has everything, even his haircut!' Others claim that in Arnoux I intended to depict Bernard Latte (the former publisher), whom I never saw, etc.

All this is to tell you, *chère* Madame, that the public is mistaken in attributing to us intentions we do not have.

I was very sure that Mme Sand had no intention of painting a portrait: first because of her high-mindedness, her taste, and her respect for Art, and second because of her character, her sense of decorum and fairness.

I even think, between you and me, that this accusation has hurt her a little. The newspapers bespatter us with filth every day, and we don't answer, even though it's our profession to wield the pen; and people think that in order to make an effect, to win some applause, we set out to lampoon this person or that. No, I assure you! We are not such poor things! Our ambition is higher, and our probity greater. When one respects one's mind, one doesn't go in for the kind of thing required to please the rabble. You understand me, don't you?

But enough. I'll come to see you one of these mornings. Looking forward to that pleasure, *chère* Madame, I kiss your hands and am all yours.

1. Readers may recall that 'Bouvaret' was the name of a hotel-keeper in Cairo, at the time of Flaubert's visit in 1849–1850.

~

TO GEORGE SAND

[Paris,] Monday morning, 11 o'clock [April 4, 1870]
The lovely lady in question has sent me very proper excuses concerning you, assuring me that she had 'never intended any insult to genius'.

~

TO GEORGE SAND

[Croisset,] Saturday night [May 21–22, 1870]
No, *chère maître*, I'm not sick, but I've been busy with my move from Paris and settling in again at Croisset. Furthermore, my mother was not at all well: now she is herself again. And then I've had to sort out the papers left behind by my poor Bouilhet, and have begun my piece about him. This week I've written almost six pages – quite an accomplishment for me; the task is a painful one for all kinds of reasons. The difficulty is to know what not to say. I'll relieve my feelings a little by spouting two or three dogmatic opinions on the art of writing. It's an opportunity to express what I think: an agreeable occupation, which I have always denied myself.

You write to me very beautifully and with great goodness, wanting to restore my courage. I have none, but I proceed as though I had, which perhaps amounts to the same thing.

I no longer feel the *need* to write, because I wrote especially for one sole being who is no more. That is the truth. And yet I will continue to write. But the taste for it is gone, the enthusiasm has vanished. There are so few people who love what I love, who are concerned with the things that are my chief care. Do you know, in all the vastness of Paris, a single house where the talk is about Literature? And when it is alluded to incidentally, it is always in connection with its minor, external aspects – the question of success, morality, utility, timeliness, etc. I feel I'm becoming a fossil, a being unconnected with the life around me.

I should like nothing better than to find comfort in some new attachment. But how? Almost all my old friends are married, set in their ways, thinking all year round of their little concerns, with shooting during their holidays and whist after dinner. I don't know a single one who is capable of spending an afternoon with me reading a poet. They have their worldly involvements: I have none. Note that I am in the same position as regards company as when I was eighteen years old. My niece, whom I love as though she were my daughter, does not live with me, and my poor old mother is growing so old that any conversation with her (except about her health) is impossible. All that scarcely makes for a madcap existence.

As for ladies, there are none available hereabouts, and even if there were! . . . I have never been able to accommodate Venus with Apollo. For me it has always been the one or the other – being, as I am, a creature of excess, given over entirely to whatever I'm engaged in.

I keep repeating to myself Goethe's words: 'Forward! Beyond the tombs!' and I hope to grow accustomed to this new emptiness around me. But no more than that.

The more I know you, the more I admire you. How strong you are!

But you are too good to have written once again to the child of Israel.[1] Let him keep his gold!!! The rascal has no idea of what a fine specimen he is. He thought himself perhaps very generous in proposing to lend me money without interest, but on the condition that I bind myself to him with a new contract. I bear him no grudge whatever, for he hasn't hurt me – he hasn't touched any sensitive spot.

Except for a little Spinoza and Plutarch, I have read nothing since my return, being fully occupied with my present task. This will take me to the end of July. I'm eager to be rid of it, so that I can plunge back into the extravagances of good old St Anthony, though I'm afraid of not being able to wind myself up to the proper pitch . . .

1. Mme Sand had interceded with Flaubert's publisher, Michel Lévy, in an attempt to make him more open-handed. Finding him intractable, she offered Flaubert a loan from her savings. He declined, claiming he had discovered a forgotten nest-egg of his own.

~

The warm welcome at Nohant raised Flaubert's spirits briefly; but continued efforts by George Sand to counter his depression with encouraging letters were defeated by events – and, one must now recognize, by what had become, for Flaubert, habitual melancholy and lamentation.

~

TO HIS NIECE CAROLINE
Croisset, Tuesday, midnight [June 28–29, 1870]
. . .

A week ago I made a sad trip to Paris. What a funeral.[1] I have rarely seen anything so moving. What a state poor Edmond de Goncourt was in! Théo, whom people accuse of being heartless, wept buckets. Nor was I very stoical myself: the ceremony plus the great heat was too much for me, and for several days I was inconceivably tired. Since yesterday I have felt better – thanks, I believe, to bathing in the Seine.

From the seven we were at the beginning of the Magny dinners, we are now only three: I, Théo, and Edmond de Goncourt. In the past eighteen months there have disappeared Gavarni, Bouilhet, Jules de Goncourt, and that's not all. But there's no point in distressing you with my sorrows . . .

1. Jules de Goncourt had died on June 20.

~

TO EDMOND DE GONCOURT
[Croisset,] Sunday night [June 26, 1870]
How I pity you, my poor friend! Your letter, this morning, broke

my heart. Apart from the private detail you confide to me (and which I shall keep to myself, you may be sure),[1] it told me nothing new, or at least I had suspected all you tell me. For I think of you every day and many times every day. The thought of my friends who have died inevitably leads to thoughts of you. A pretty list, during the past year! . . . Your brother, Bouilhet, Sainte-Beuve, Duplan . . . Such are the ideas, like so many tombs, I live with these days.

But with you I dare not complain. For your sorrow must be beyond anything one can feel – or imagine.

You ask me to tell you about myself, my dear Edmond? Well, I am giving myself over to a heart-rending task: I am writing the preface to a volume of Bouilhet's poems. I have scanted the biographical part as much as possible, and will give most of my space to an examination of the work, and still more to his (or *our*) literary doctrines.

I've been re-reading everything he wrote. I've been going over our old letters, stirring up a series of memories, some of them dating back thirty-seven years! Not very gay, as you see! Besides, here at Croisset I'm pursued by his ghost; I find it lurking behind every bush in the garden, on the sofa in my study – even in my clothes, in my dressing gowns that he sometimes wore.

I hope to dwell less on such things when this abominable task is done; that is, in about six weeks. After which I'll try to take up my *Saint Antoine* again. But I have little heart for it. You well know that one always writes with someone in mind. Now, with that someone no longer here, my courage fails me.

So I live alone with my mother, who grows older every day, and more feeble, and complaining. A conversation of any serious kind has become impossible with her, and I have no one to talk to.

I hope to go to Paris in August, and to see you then. But where will you be? Let me have news of you sometime, my poor Edmond! No one pities you more than I.

Je vous embrasse très fortement.

1. Perhaps the fact that Jules de Goncourt had been destroyed by syphilis.

∾

TO GEORGE SAND

Chère bon maître

The death of Barbès[1] has greatly saddened me, for your sake.
We are both of us in mourning. What a procession of deaths during
the past year! It leaves me dazed, as though I'd been hit over the
head. What distresses me (for we always refer everything back to
ourselves) is the terrible solitude I live in. I no longer have anyone
– no one at all – to talk with.

'*Qui s'occupe aujourd'hui de faconde et de style?*'[2] Apart from you
and Turgenev, I don't know a single mortal with whom I can share
the things closest to my heart, and you live far away from me, both
of you.

I continue working, however. I have [now] resolved to take up
my *Saint Antoine* tomorrow or the next day. But to begin[3] a long
and exacting work one must feel a certain liveliness that I lack. Still,
I hope the extravagance of this work will take hold of me. Oh, how
I'd love to be able to stop thinking about my poor *me*, about my
miserable carcass! Actually, the carcass is in very good shape. I sleep
tremendously. 'I'm holding my own', as the bourgeois say.

... Lately I've been reading some deadly theological works,
interspersing them with a little Plutarch and Spinoza ...

Poor Edmond de Goncourt is in Champagne with his relatives.
He has promised to come here at the end of the month. I don't
think that the hope of being reunited with his brother in a better
world is consoling him for having lost him in this. One is the dupe
of empty words in this question of immortality. For the question is
to know whether the *self* persists. The affirmative seems to me a
presumption of our self-pride, a protest by our weakness against the
eternal order! Death has perhaps no more secrets to reveal to us than
life.

What an accursed year! I feel as though I were lost in the desert.
Nonetheless I assure you, *chère maître*, that I'm keeping a stout heart.
And making prodigious efforts to be stoical. But the poor brain is
weak at times. I need only one thing (and that isn't to be had for
the asking): to feel some sort of enthusiasm.

Your letter of two days ago was very sad. You too, you heroic
being: you too feel weary! What's to become of us?

. . .

I have just read the *Conversations of Goethe and Eckermann*. There was a man, that Goethe! But he had everything: everything was in his favour!

1. On June 26. Mme Sand had announced it to Flaubert: 'I am weeping for Barbès, one of my religions, one of those beings who reconcile us to mankind.' Later, writing to Flaubert in 1871 about her own revolutionary past, she would mention Barbès again: 'I have lived through revolutions, and I have seen their leading protagonists at close hand; I have seen the depths of their souls, and I must tell you that their secret is this: *no principles*. Also, no real intelligence, no strength, no consistency: nothing but a personal goal and the means of attaining it. One, only one, had principles – not all of them good, but all sincere, and to him far outweighing personal considerations: Barbès.'
2. 'Who cares these days for eloquence and style?' Unidentified. See p. 468, n. 1.
3. This would be the third 'beginning' of *The Temptation of Saint Anthony*, or rather the beginning of the third, and final, version. Flaubert had first begun the work in 1848, before setting out for Egypt; then again in 1857, during the prosecution of *Madame Bovary* (see Volume I). Both those versions had been put aside. The 'deadly theological works' mentioned in this letter are part of what would be the interminable research for this third version.

   Flaubert had just completed his preface for the volume of Louis Bouilhet's last poems, which was to appear only in 1872.

～

And then it was as though the private troubles had been accumulating only to explode in national disaster.

The burgeoning power of Prussia under the leadership of Bismarck had been alarming France, particularly since the Prussian victory over Austria at Sadowa in 1866. Greatly increased tensions in 1870 brought the two countries to the brink; and in July, in a deceitfully insolent message known to history as 'the Ems telegram', Bismarck tricked France into becoming the 'aggressor'. On Bastille Day, July 14, inflamed Paris mobs chanted 'On to Berlin!' and that night, with special authorization by the Emperor, the singer Marie Sasse, draped in the tricolour, sang *La Marseillaise* at the Opéra, to the cheers of the audience. On July 19, France, though hopelessly unprepared, declared war. (A.J.)

~

To George Sand

Croisset, Friday night, [July 22, 1870]

What has become of you, *chère maître* – you and yours?

As for me, I am nauseated, heartbroken, by the stupidity of my compatriots. The incorrigible barbarism of mankind fills me with blackest gloom. This enthusiasm [for war], unmotivated by any idea, makes me long to die, that I might witness it no longer.

The good Frenchman wants to fight (1) because he is jealous of Prussia; (2) because man's natural condition is savagery; (3) because in war there is an inherent mystical element that enraptures the crowd.

Have we reverted to the wars of the races? I fear so. The frightful butchery now being prepared for lacks even a pretext. It's a craving to fight for the sake of fighting.

I lament the destruction of bridges, the blowing-up of tunnels, the waste of so much human work, such fundamental *negation*.

Peace conferences are anathema for the moment. Civilization seems to me a far-distant thing. Hobbes was right: *Homo homini lupus.*[1]

Here the bourgeois is at the end of his patience. He considers that Prussia was too insolent, and wants to 'avenge himself'. Did you see that a gentleman in the Chamber [of Deputies] has proposed the sacking of the Duchy of Baden?[2] Ah, why can't I go and live with the Bedouins!

I have begun *Saint Antoine*. And it might go well if I could stop thinking about the war . . .

1. 'Man is wolf to man.' Originally what seems to be a proverb, in Plautus, *Asinaria: Lupus est homo homini, non homo, cum qualis sit non novit.*
2. It was the Comte de Kératry, deputy from Finisterre and later prefect of police, who made the proposal. It has been suggested that Flaubert may have been particularly agitated (he will deplore the proposal again in a subsequent letter) because the now elderly Mme Schlesinger, idol of his youth and his inspiration for Mme Arnoux in *L'Éducation sentimentale*, was living in Baden. (A.J.)

XIV

The War and the Commune

1870–1871

WRITING OF THE international tensions of the 1860s in his *Souvenirs littéraires*, Maxime DuCamp describes Flaubert's attitude at that period:

One single man, among my friends, was unaffected by the vague anxiety that preyed on us all: Gustave Flaubert, who was exasperated whenever anyone raised this question on which our very existence might well depend. Flaubert belonged to a group of thinkers, writers, politicians, all of them eminent in their respective fields, who met twice a month, always around the same table, for conversation. These deipnosophists lacked an Athenaeus.[1] One day Flaubert arrived at my house furious and vociferous. He told me he had just walked out of one of those dinners with his friends because they had been talking politics – an indecency among intellectuals. 'What are Prussia and Austria to us?' he said. 'Those men claim to be philosophers, and they spend their time wondering whether the Blues have beaten the Whites; they're nothing but bourgeois, and I find it pitiable to see X and Y discussing annexations, border realignments, dismemberments, reconstitutions, as though they had nothing better to do, as though there were no longer any great poetry to recite, any sonorous prose to be written.' I tried to calm him, without success. 'They're nothing but bourgeois,' he repeated. 'We are neither French nor Algonquins; we are artists; Art is our country: a curse on those who have any other.'

Hot-headed words, which implied no lack of patriotism, for Flaubert would suffer to the point of tears when France surrendered to Germany.

That was in 1866, during the Austro-Prussian War. In 1869, according to DuCamp, Flaubert, paradoxical as always, disapproved the French government's inauguration of a policy of increased liberalism:

The wave of political renovation which seized the country at that time was not at all to his taste. It sometimes exasperated him, and he considered that freedom of the press merely encouraged the diffusion of bad writing. He said that everything that excites public opinion is detrimental to literature, which is made secondary to matters of ephemeral concern. The publication of a poem or a novel, the first performance of a play, was to him more important than any political action. He would have been glad to see legislative discussions replaced by lectures on Goethe, Michelangelo, and Ronsard. Outside literature and art, he saw nothing:[2] that is what sets him apart from his contemporaries and lends him a kind of greatness, limited but powerful. As to his preferred form of government, I have heard him express two opinions, which, though diverse, were directed to the same purpose. He favoured a kind of *mandarinat*: the running of the country would be entrusted to men who, after study, examinations, and competition, were recognized as the most intelligent. In this way, he was sure (he was, of course, wrong), writers and artists would become the masters of the nation's destiny, and this would result in an intellectual flowering beneficial to mankind. When the practical difficulties of such a system were pointed out to him, he would cry: 'Give me a tyrant of genius who will protect arts and letters and lead us out of the mediocrity we're wallowing in!' I don't know whether this was actually his own opinion or whether he had taken it from Théophile Gautier, who all his life called for the reign of a Medici or a François Premier.

Such, according to DuCamp, were Flaubert's expressed political opinions – if political they can be called – at the outbreak of the Franco-Prussian War. Readers of the letters will have noticed that only when he undertook to document the background of *L'Éducation sentimentale* did he begin to discuss political matters to any extent with his correspondents. From then on we have seen him comment on French politics of the '40s, '50s, and '60s, led to do so by his research and by his realization of the fatal continuity of those decades. His hardening opinions were to lead him into conflict – increasing, but always affectionate – with George Sand. Her reply to his letter of (?)July 22, 1870 found them still close to agreement.

1.   'A grammarian of Naucratis, in Egypt, who composed an elegant and miscellaneous work, called *Deipnosophistae*, "Dons at Dinner", replete with very curious and interesting remarks and anecdotes of the ancients.' (Lemprière, *Classical Dictionary.*) The Goncourt brothers, in their *Journal*, parts of which DuCamp probably saw later, are a kind of Athenaeus of the Magny dinners. The 'Blues' and the 'Whites', a few lines below, were rival teams of Roman charioteers.

2.   Here again, as during their youthful trip together to Egypt, there is a notable contrast between DuCamp the journalist, expert in 'current affairs', and Flaubert the novelist, sensitive to the human condition. Throughout his adult life, Flaubert – who truly 'saw nothing' of the ingrown daily world of politicians – was prophetic on the theme of impending world war and the dehumanizing implications of new technology.

~

GEORGE SAND TO FLAUBERT

Nohant, July 26 [1870]

I think this war is infamous; this authorized *Marseillaise* a sacrilege. Men are ferocious and conceited brutes. We are in Pascal's 'half as far'; when will we reach the 'further ahead than ever'?[1]

It is between 40 and 45 degrees *in the shade* here. There are many forest fires – another barbarous stupidity! The wolves come and prowl in our farmyard, and at night we chase them away, Maurice with a revolver and I with a lantern. The trees are losing their leaves and perhaps their lives. Soon there will be no water for drinking. The harvests are almost nothing: but we have war – what luck! Crops are dying, famine threatens, poverty is lurking, waiting to transform itself into a Jacquerie:[2] but we'll fight the Prussians. *Malbrough s'en va-t-en guerre!*

You said rightly that in order to work one needs a degree of cheerfulness. Where is it to be found in these accursed times? Happily, we have no one ill at our house. When I see Maurice and Lina busy, Aurore and Gabrielle playing, I dare not complain, for fear of losing everything.

I love you, my dear old friend, we all love you.

Your troubadour,

G. Sand

1. An allusion to one of Pascal's *Pensées*, which George Sand had copied and kept on her desk. 'Nature progresses *itus et reditus*. It advances and retreats, goes on further, then half as far, and then further than ever. Such are the tides of the sea; the sun too seems to move in this way.' One understands its double appeal to George Sand, given her love of nature and belief in eventual 'progress'.
2. A fourteenth-century revolution of French peasants, which gave its name to subsequent rural uprisings. (Originally from 'Jacques Bonhomme', a name derisively given to peasants by the nobility.)

~

To George Sand

Croisset, Wednesday [August 3, 1870]

What, *chère maître*? You too? demoralized, sad? What's to become of weak souls, then?

As for me, my heart is oppressed in a way that astonishes me. And I wallow in a bottomless melancholy, despite work, despite our friend St Anthony, who ought to distract me. Is it the result of my repeated griefs? Perhaps. But the war has much to do with it. I feel we are entering black darkness.

Behold 'natural man'! Make theories! Extol Progress, enlightenment, the good sense of the Masses, and the sweetness of the French people! I assure you that anyone who ventured to preach Peace here would get himself murdered.

Whatever happens, we're in for a long setback.

Perhaps the wars between the races are to begin again? Within a century, we'll see millions of men kill each other at one go? All the East against all Europe, the old world against the new! Why not? Great international enterprises like the Suez Canal are perhaps, in some other form, outlines and preparations for monstrous conflicts we can only guess at?

And Prussia is perhaps to be given a great drubbing, as part of the schemes of Providence for re-establishing European balance of power? That country was tending to be hypertrophied, like France under Louis XIV and Napoleon. The other organs are unfavourably affected by it. Hence universal disorder. Might tremendous bloodlettings be salutary?

Ah, we intellectuals! Mankind is far from our ideal! And our immense error, our fatal error, is to imagine it is like us, and to want to treat it accordingly.

The reverence, the fetishism, for universal suffrage revolts me more than the infallibility of the Pope (which has just nicely misfired, by the way, poor old chap!).[1] Do you think that if France, instead of being governed, in effect, by the crowd, were ruled by the Mandarins, we'd be where we are now? If instead of wanting to enlighten the lower classes we had busied ourselves educating the upper, we wouldn't have M. de Kératry proposing the sack of the duchy of Baden – a measure the public finds very proper.

Have you been watching Prud'homme[2] these days? He's marvellous! He admires Musset's *Rhin* and asks whether Musset has written anything else. Musset, accepted as the national poet, ousting Béranger! What an immense buffoonery everything is! But a buffoonery far from merry.

Poverty begins to be very evident. Everybody is hard up, starting with me! But perhaps we were too accustomed to comfort and tranquillity. Perhaps we were sinking into materialism. We must return to the great tradition: hold no longer to Life, to Happiness, to money, to anything; but be what our grandfathers were – light, airy beings.

In former times men passed their entire lives in a state of starvation. Now that same prospect looms on the horizon. What you tell me about poor Nohant is terrible. The countryside here has suffered less than yours.

· · ·

1. The doctrine of papal infallibility had been promulgated on July 18. It was followed almost immediately by the loss of the papal states to the kingdom of Italy. Flaubert seems to be making the common mistake of thinking that

the infallibility claimed by the doctrine was total: actually, it is 'restricted' to matters of dogma and morality.

2.   For Prud'homme see p. 370, n. 3.

'*Le Rhin Allemand*' (The German Rhine, 1840), a short patriotic poem by Alfred de Musset, one of George Sand's former lovers, was a rejoinder to a provocative German 'Rhine song', '*Sie sollen ihn nicht haben*' (You shall not have it), of the same year, by Nikolaus Becker (1809–1845). Musset's words had been set to music and were enjoying new popularity at that moment. Lamartine had also answered Becker, in a poem called '*La Marseillaise de la paix*' (1841). (J.B.)

∼

As news from the battlefronts rapidly grew alarming, as military disaster loomed and public panic spread, Flaubert's patriotism flared despite his hatred of 'Isidore'. 'Well, we're in a pretty pickle!' he wrote to Caroline's husband, Ernest Commanville, in Dieppe. 'The Empire is now only a question of days, but we must defend it to the end!' In a letter to Caroline he foretold the siege of Paris, only to change his mind later; and writing to Mme Roger des Genettes he foresaw what total defeat would bring: 'To think we're only in the first act! Because, when peace is made (in one way or another) we'll find ourselves in a revolution.'

∼

GEORGE SAND TO FLAUBERT

[Nohant,] August 15 [1870], evening

. . .

I don't feel very valiant. There is still a woman under the skin of the old troubadour. This human butchery tears my poor heart to shreds. And I tremble for my children and my friends, who may be slaughtered.

And yet in the midst of all this my soul rises up in great bursts of faith. These dreadful lessons we must learn, so as to understand our imbecility, must be of some use to us. Perhaps we are reverting for the last time to the mistakes of the old world. There are sharp, clear principles for all of us today, which must emerge from this torment. Nothing is useless in the material system of the universe. The moral order cannot escape the law. Evil engenders good. I repeat that we are in Pascal's 'two steps back', in order to arrive at the 'further ahead than ever'.

I have finished a novel in the midst of this torment, hurrying lest I break down before the end. I'm as tired as though I were fighting along with our good soldiers.

Je t'embrasse. Tell me where you are and what you are thinking. We all love you.

~

To George Sand

Croisset, Wednesday [August 17, 1870]

I arrived in Paris on Monday and left on Wednesday. Now I know what the Parisian is really like! And in my heart I forgive the most ferocious politicians of 1793. Now I understand them. For I saw such stupidity! Such cowardice! Such ignorance! Such presumption! My compatriots make me want to vomit. They're worthy of being put in the same bag as Isidore! This country *deserves* to be punished, and I fear it will be.

It is impossible for me to read anything whatever: still more, to write. I spend my time like everybody else, waiting for news. Ah! If it weren't for my mother I'd certainly have joined up by now.

Not knowing how to keep busy, I've volunteered as a nurse at the Hôtel-Dieu in Rouen, where my services may be of use, as my brother has no more students.[1] My inaction stifles me to the point of explosion.

If the Germans besiege Paris, I'll go and fight. My rifle is ready. But until then I'll remain at Croisset because I must. I'll tell you why.

The examples of ignominy I saw in the capital are enough to add years to a man's life.

And we're only in the first act, because soon we'll be moving into '*la Sociale*'.[2] Which will be followed by a vigorous and long reaction!

This is what we've been brought to by Universal Suffrage, the new God I consider as stupid as the old. No matter. Do you think it will be abashed, good old Universal Suffrage? Not at all! After Isidore we'll have Pignouf I![3]

What makes me wretched about this war is that the Prussians

are right. Their turn next! Then Russia's. Ah! how I wish I were dead, not to have to think about all this!

At Nohant you must be less tormented than we by the question of money. In a few days all the workers in the Seine-Inférieure are going to ask for relief. My nephew Commanville is very active and keeps his workmen busy despite everything.[4] My brother has abandoned his patients and devotes himself to public affairs.[5] Rouen is arming and maintaining, at its own expense, its entire *garde mobile* – an idea not yet adopted by any other municipality.

Poor literature! Utterly forsaken, *chère maître*. *Saint Antoine* is only at page fourteen. Impossible to keep going . . .

1. They had probably been called up.
2. Current slang for 'Socialist Republic'.
3. That is, 'After Napoleon the Third, Boor the First.' This would be Thiers.
4. Since the end of July the blockade of the Normandy coast had closed factories, causing unemployment and poverty. But Commanville had obtained a government order for his timber mill. (A.J.)
5. On August 10 Dr Achille Flaubert had been elected to the Rouen Municipal Council. (A.J.)

∼

George Sand may have replied directly to Flaubert's tirade against universal suffrage. (Letters from her to him dated, according to her diary, August 22 and September 7, are lost.) In any case, she answered it publicly, with no mention of him, in a few sentences contained in her 'Letter to a Friend' in *Le Temps* for September 5, 1870:

> France, always in the forefront of action, possesses an arm which the Teutons will not snatch from her, and which is the supreme weapon in battles of will: universal suffrage. Recently I have heard it much execrated, even by serious-minded men, this redoubtable missile that has so often been turned against us by our own hands. But so it is with all weapons one doesn't know how to use. This one is the universal safety of the future. This is the machine gun that must resolve, peacefully, all the questions awaiting their answer in days of tumult and terror –

let us not forget it! The day it begins to function properly, errors of Power, whatever they may be, will become impossible.

Thinking to escape a German advance, relatives from Nogent-sur-Seine took refuge at Croisset, crowding the house.

~

To HIS NIECE CAROLINE
Croisset, Wednesday, 5 o'clock [August 31, 1870]
My dear Caro

The Bonenfants seem very happy to be far from 'the theatre of war'. Their girls are no trouble, but poor Bonenfant with his perpetual spitting! Would you believe it, from my bed I hear him spitting in the garden. That's what wakes me in the morning, along with your grandmother arguing with [her maid] Hyacinthe. I swear I can't go on like this, Carolo. If such a life were to continue, I'd go mad or collapse into idiocy. I have stomach cramps and a permanent headache. And no one, you realize, *absolutely no one*, even to talk with! Your grandmother complains endlessly about the weakness of her legs and her deafness. It's all dreadful . . .

~

The next day, September 1, saw the annihilating Prussian victory at Sedan in the Ardennes: 82,000 French troops, and the Emperor himself, surrendered to the enemy and became prisoners of war. French killed and wounded numbered about nine thousand. On September 4 the Third Republic was proclaimed in Paris, its 'Government of National Defence' resolving to continue the fight. On the fifth George Sand wrote in her diary: 'Maurice wakes me, telling me that the republic is proclaimed in Paris without a shot being fired! An immense fact, unique in human history! . . . May God protect France! Once again she has become worthy of His regard.'

~

To GEORGE SAND
[Croisset,] Saturday [September 10, 1870]
Chère maître,

Here we are, 'at the bottom of the abyss'; a shameful peace will perhaps not be accepted.[1] The Prussians want to destroy Paris – such is their dream. Our only rational hope is in *chemistry*. Who knows? Perhaps methods of defence have been found, new ones?[2]

I don't believe that the siege of Paris is imminent. But to force its surrender they will (1) intimidate it by a display of cannon, and (2) ravage the surrounding countryside.

At Rouen, we're expecting the visit of those gentlemen. Since Sunday I've been lieutenant of my company.[3] I drill my men and go to Rouen to take lessons in military art.

The deplorable thing is that opinion is divided; some are for defence to the death and others for peace at any price.

I am dying of grief.

What a house this is! Fourteen people, all groaning, all driving me crazy.

I curse women: they are the cause of all our woes.[4]

I expect Paris to suffer the fate of Warsaw.[5]

And you distress me with your enthusiasm for the Republic. At this moment, when we're being defeated by Positivism at its purest, how can you still believe in Phantoms? Whatever happens, those now in Power will be sacrificed. And the Republic will suffer the same fate. Please note that I defend it, the poor Republic. But I have no faith in it.

Yesterday I saw Dumas at Dieppe, where I went especially to talk with him, to quash an idiotic calumny about the Princess, who has been accused of stealing 51 million *in gold*. In fact she left France with clean hands. But the same cannot be said of her brother, who since the beginning of the war has had the trees at the Château de Meudon cut down and sold for his profit. Splendid, no? Badinguet is (has become?) an imbecile, an idiot. He keeps repeating, like a machine, 'No arms! No supplies!' The Prince Imperial is dying. These last details were given me (indirectly) by Mme Trochu.[6]

That's all I have to tell you now. I have many other things in my head, but can't collect them – I feel I'm drowning in sorrow – in cascades, rivers, oceans, of it. It is impossible to suffer more than this: at times I fear I'm going insane. The sight of my mother's face, when I turn my eyes towards her, drains me of all energy. And I dare not tell you what I sometimes wish for.

This is where our crazy refusal to recognize the truth has led us, our passion for humbug and everything meretricious. We'll become another Poland, then another Spain. Then it will be Prussia's turn – she'll be devoured by Russia.

As for me, I consider myself *finished*. My brain will never recover. One cannot write when one has lost one's self-esteem. I ask but one thing – to die, so as to be at peace.

Adieu, chère maître. And above all, don't try to comfort me!

I embrace you with as much tenderness as is left in me. I feel my heart is withered and dry. I'm becoming stupid and nasty. Once again, all affection.

1. Jules Favre, Minister of Foreign Affairs in the 'Government of National Defence', had published, on September 6, a 'manifesto to the Powers', declaring that France would not surrender 'a single stone of her fortresses, not one inch of her territory'. (A.J.)

2. Flaubert is probably thinking of the 'Scientific Committee for Defence', instituted on September 2. It was presided over by his fellow member of the Magny dinners, the chemist Marcelin Berthelot, and concerned itself chiefly with the manufacture of nitroglycerine and dynamite. (A.J.)

3. The Croisset company of the National Guard.

4. Perhaps a reference to the Empress, who had fled to England on September 7. She was blamed for having encouraged her husband to listen to pro-war advisers; or, more popularly, was hated as the wife of the man who had brought the country to defeat. Crowds were calling for her head when she left Paris. Readers of earlier letters will recall numerous mysogynistic pronouncements by Flaubert; and most of the Nogent refugees were women. But the remark seems particularly offensive in a letter to George Sand.

5. The scene of savage Russian repression following the Polish insurrection of 1863.

6. Princesse Mathilde had left Paris on September 4 and taken shelter with Alexandre Dumas the younger at Puys, near Dieppe. Her baggage had already been put aboard a steamer for England when a rumour arose that it included the crown jewels and pictures from the Louvre. The captain ordered it opened, to convince the crowd of onlookers that it contained only personal effects, and the princess was allowed to depart. The story about Prince Napoleon's trees may also belong to the realm of wartime rumour. Similarly, the Emperor had not lost his mind, nor was the Prince Imperial (the fourteen-year-old son of the Emperor and Empress) dying: after serving in the army he too had gone to England. He would be killed in Zululand in 1879, a volunteer in an English army expedition. Mme

Trochu was the wife of General Louis-Jules Trochu, recently appointed military governor of Paris. (A.J.)

～

To George Sand

[Croisset,] Wednesday [September 28, 1870]

I have stopped being sad. Yesterday I took up my *Saint Anthony* – I had to. We must resign ourselves – accustom ourselves to man's natural condition: that is, to evil.

The Greeks in the time of Pericles devoted themselves to Art without knowing where their next day's bread would come from. Let us be Greek! I confess, however, *chère maître*, that I feel more like a savage. Scholar though I am, the blood of my forefathers, the Natchez or the Hurons,[1] is seething in my veins, and I have a grim, stupid, animal *desire to fight*. Explain that if you can! The idea of signing a peace now infuriates me, and I'd rather see Paris burned, like Moscow, than occupied by the Prussians. But we haven't yet reached that point, and I think the tide is turning.

. . . I have read several letters from soldiers. They are exemplary: a country in which such things are written can't be swallowed up. France is a resourceful jade, and will rise again.

Whatever happens, another world is in the making, and I feel too old to adjust myself to new ways.

My nephew Commanville is making a thousand biscuit-boxes a day for the army, not to mention huts. As you see, we're not asleep in these parts. Paris is overflowing with troops and provisions. In those respects, all is secure.

How I miss you! How I long to see you!

I kiss you all.

Your old troubadour,

G^{ve} Fl.

Here we are resolved to march on Paris should the compatriots of Hegel besiege it. Try to put some guts into your neighbours in Berry.[2] Tell them to help you prevent the enemy from eating and drinking in a country that doesn't belong to them.

The war will (I trust) deal a heavy blow to the 'Authorities'. Will the individual, rejected and trampled on by the modern world, come into his own again? Let's hope so.

1. Flaubert believed, or pretended to believe, the family legend that an ancestor had married a Canadian Indian.
2. In one of her lost letters from Nohant (in the old province of Berry), Mme Sand had apparently written of lethargy or fatalism among her rural neighbours.

∽

Recalling this abrupt resurgence of Flaubert's spirits even as the Germans began to fan out over France, Maxime DuCamp quotes Bossuet: 'The greatest disorder of the mind is wishful thinking.' For a time, euphoria persisted. 'Today I began my night patrols,' Flaubert wrote to Caroline on September 27, 1870. 'I have just made a fatherly speech to my men, informing them that I would run a sword into the belly of the first to falter, and ordering them to shoot me should they see me run away. Your old uncle achieved a truly epic tone. What a weird thing brains are, especially mine! Would you believe it, I now feel almost gay. I began to work again yesterday, and my appetite has returned. Everything wears itself out – anguish included.'

It could not last. The first erosion was caused by the decamping of Caroline herself: she took ship at Dieppe for England (see Appendix I). The visitors from Nogent left Croisset, only to be briefly replaced by French troops. The gate-bell began to be rung by refugees from occupied areas and factory-hands thrown out of work. 'Are you still alive?' Flaubert wrote to George Sand on October 11. 'Where are you, you, Maurice and the others? . . . What wretchedness here! Today I have had 271 poor people at the gate. We gave them all something. What will it be like this winter? The Prussians are now twelve leagues from Rouen, and we have no orders, no one in command, no discipline, nothing, nothing!'

∽

GEORGE SAND TO FLAUBERT

[La Châtre, October 14, 1870]
We are alive, at La Châtre. Nohant is ravaged by smallpox with complications, horrible. We had to take our little ones away . . .

To speak of all the peril and trouble involved in establishing the Republic in the depths of our provinces would be quite useless . . . Don't let's say it's impossible; don't let's think it. Don't let's despair over France. She is expiating her madness, and will be reborn whatever happens. *We*, perhaps, shall no longer be here. To die of pneumonia or of a bullet is – equally – to die. Let's die without cursing our race!

We love you always and we all embrace you.

. . .

~

On her return to Nohant Mme Sand would learn that one of two balloons that the Republican government had sent out from Paris early in October for Tours, carrying delegates to encourage resistance in the provinces, was named the 'George Sand'. The other, which had carried Gambetta, was the 'Armand Barbès'.

The Germans had now encircled Paris, beginning the famous siege; no foodstuffs could enter, and there was an occasional bombardment. To escape that fate, Rouen declared itself an open city. Some sort of postal service continued to function; and alone at Croisset with his mother, Flaubert wrote anguished letters to Caroline in England, to Princesse Mathilde, who was now in Brussels, and to George Sand.

~

To George Sand

[Croisset,] Sunday night [November 27, 1870]

I'm still alive, chère maître, but scarcely the better for being so, such is my sorrow. My reason for not writing earlier is that I was awaiting your news. I didn't know where you were.

For six weeks we have been expecting the arrival of the Prussians from one day to the next. We keep listening, thinking we hear the sound of cannon in the distance. They now surround the Seine-Inférieure, at a radius of fourteen to twenty leagues. They are even closer, since they occupy the Vexin, and have completely devastated it. What horrors! It makes one blush to be a man.

If we have a victory on the Loire, their coming will be delayed. But will we have that victory? When I feel hope I try to suppress it.

And yet, deep within me, despite everything, I can't help hoping a little, just a little.

I think that in all France there is no sadder man than I. (Everything depends on one's sensitivity.) I am dying of grief. That is the truth. And anything said in consolation irritates me. What breaks my heart is (1) human ferocity; (2) the conviction that we are about to enter an era of stupidity. We'll be utilitarian, militaristic, American, and Catholic. Very Catholic! You'll see! This war with Prussia concludes and destroys the French Revolution.

'But what if we're victorious?' you'll ask. That hypothesis goes against all historical precedent. Where have you ever seen the south defeat the north, Catholics prevail over Protestants? The Latin race is in its death throes. France will follow Spain and Italy; the Age of the Boor is upon us.

What a collapse! What a fall! What wretchedness! What abominations! Is it possible to believe in progress and civilization in the face of all that's happening now? What good is science, since that nation, full of scientists, is committing abominations worthy of the Huns! And worse, because they are systematic, cold-blooded, deliberate, without the excuse of passion or hunger.

Why do they execrate us so? Don't you feel yourself crushed by the hatred of 40 million men? The thought of such an immense, hellish abyss makes my senses reel.

There's no lack of ready-made slogans. 'France will rise again!' 'Do not despair!' 'It's a salutary punishment!' 'We were really too immoral!' Etc. Oh, eternal nonsense! No! One does not recover from such a blow.

I feel myself stricken to the core. Were I twenty years younger, I might not think all this; were I twenty years older, I would resign myself to it.

Poor Paris! I find it heroic. But if we see it again it will no longer be our Paris. All the friends I had there are dead or dispersed. I no longer have a centre. Literature seems to me a vain and useless thing. Will I ever be capable of writing again?

I find it impossible to occupy myself with anything. I spend my days in gloomy, devouring idleness. My niece Caroline is in London. My mother grows older by the hour. Every Monday we go to Rouen and stay there till Thursday, to escape from the solitude of the country. Then we return here.

Oh! if I could flee to a country where one doesn't see uniforms and hear the sound of drums! Where there's no talk of massacres, where one doesn't have to be a *citizen*! But the earth is no longer habitable for us poor Mandarins!

Adieu, chère maître. Think of me and write to me. I feel that I would be stronger were you nearby. Kiss all your family for me; and to you, affection a hundred thousand times over from your

old troubadour
G^{ve}

❦

With Paris isolated and close to starvation, the Germans were in no hurry to extend their conquest. Very slowly, one of their armies approached Rouen.

After the war – DuCamp relates in his memoirs – Flaubert described to him 'at least twenty times' his '*émotion poignante*' on the day in December 1870 when he first saw 'the spike of a Prussian helmet glittering in the sun on the towpath at Croisset'. Billeting of the invaders was almost immediate.

❦

To his niece Caroline

Rouen, Sunday, December 18, 1870

My dear Caro,

How you must be worrying about us! Be reassured – we are all alive; we have passed through a time of terrible emotion, and are still plunged in indescribable difficulties. God be thanked that you've been out of it. At times I thought I'd go mad. The night before we left Croisset was horrible. Your grandmother slept at the Hôtel Dieu every night for a week; I spent one night there. At present we are on the quay,[1] with two [Prussian] soldiers quartered on us. At Croisset there are seven, plus three officers and six horses. So far we have had no reason to complain about these gentlemen. But what humiliation, poor Caro! What ruin! What sadness! What wretchedness! Don't expect me to write you an account: it would be too long, and besides I wouldn't be up to it. For a fortnight it has been impossible for us to receive a letter from anywhere, or a newspaper, or to communicate with the outside; from the English papers you must know more about it all than we do. We've been unable to send a letter to your husband, and he has been unable to write to us. Let's hope that when the Prussians are completely entrenched in Normandy they will let us move about. The English consul in Rouen tells me that the Newhaven boat is out of service. As soon as it resumes, as soon as the road from Dieppe to Rouen is clear, come back to us, dear Caro! Your grandmother is growing so old! She longs for you so, needs you so! What months I have spent with her since your departure! My sufferings have been so atrocious that I wish them on no one, not even on those who caused them. When we are not doing errands for the Prussians (yesterday I was on my feet for three hours getting them hay and straw) we are asking each other for news or sit weeping in a corner. I was not born yesterday, and during my life I have suffered many blows; but all was as nothing, compared with what I am enduring now. Nothing, nothing! How can we stand it? I marvel that it is possible.

And we don't know when it will end. Poor Paris is still holding out! But eventually it will give in. And meanwhile France will be completely sacked, ruined. And what will happen then? What a future lies ahead! There will be no lack of sophists to prove that we'll be the better for it, and that 'misfortune purifies'. No! Misfortune makes us selfish and vicious and stupid. This disaster was inevitable; it is in accordance with the laws of history. But what a mockery are the words 'humanity', 'progress', 'civilization'. Oh, poor dear child, if you could know what it means to hear them drag their swords on the footpath, to have their horses whinny in your face! What a disgrace! What a disgrace!

My poor head aches so that I have to make a great effort to write. How will this letter reach you? I have no idea. I was given hope this evening that I could send it to you by a roundabout way. Your uncle Achille Flaubert has had and is still having great difficulty in the municipal council – it held a session while working men were firing rifles outside the windows. I am constantly on the verge of vomiting; your grandmother never leaves the house, and when she walks in her room she has to support herself against the furniture and the wall. When you can safely return, do so. I think it your *duty* to be near her. Your poor husband was very sad because of your long absence, and he must feel worse after the past fortnight. The Prussians are said to have been in Dieppe twice, but not to have stayed. The first time, they were in search of tobacco: people who have it hide it, and it grows steadily scarcer. But we have no definite news at all, for we are cut off as in a besieged city. This uncertainty comes on top of all our other anguish. When I think of the past it seems to me a dream. The Boulevard du Temple – what a paradise! Do you realize that at Croisset they occupy *all* the rooms? There would be no place for us if we wanted to return. It is eleven at night, the wind is blowing, the rain is lashing the windows. I am writing you in your old bedroom, and can hear the snores of the two soldiers sleeping in your dressing room. I toss and plunge in my sorrow like a boat foundering at sea. I never thought my heart could hold so much suffering and remain alive.

I embrace you with all my strength. When shall I see you?

Your old uncle, who can stand no more.

1. In Mme Flaubert's usual winter apartment in Rouen, on the Quai du Havre.

∿

To his niece Caroline

[Rouen,] Monday night, [January] 16 [1871]

. . . Your husband suggested taking us to Dieppe, but (1) your grandmother would have no company (here she has visitors every day); (2) she would worry about your Uncle Achille; (3) the trip would be very uncomfortable. Besides, I don't want to be too far from my manservant, who is alone at Croisset, coping as best he can in the midst of the Prussians. How will I find my study, my books, my manuscripts? All I was able to put in a safe place were my papers relating to *Saint Anthony*. Émile [the servant] has the key to the study, but they keep asking for it, and go in and take books, which they leave lying around their bedrooms . . .

[Rouen,] Monday, [January] 23 [1871])

. . . We are now expecting Mecklenburg's troops, which are to replace Manteuffel's. The men now occupying Croisset will be replaced by others, who may be worse: these have done no damage and have respected my study. But Croisset has lost all its attraction for me, and I wouldn't set foot there now. If you knew what it's like to see Prussian helmets on your bed! What fury! What misery! This frightful war shows no sign of ending! . . .

Rouen, Saturday, [January] 28 [1871]

. . . I went to Croisset this morning – an ordeal . . . Poor Émile is at the end of his tether. In forty-five days they have burned 420 francs worth of wood . . . The cold has intensified again . . . I hear sabres rattling on the paths . . .

⁓

Amid details about the invaders (for a brief time forty Prussians were crowded into the house at Croisset), about the feeble health of his seventy-seven-year-old mother, and about his own desperation, and along with appeals to Caroline to return,[1] Flaubert repeatedly expressed pity for the besieged Parisians. And well he might have. A few words from Maxime DuCamp's account of their plight (his report is one of many describing that terrible time) must suffice here: 'Paris is without meat: Parisians are eating rats, cats, dogs . . . They are cutting down trees, breaking up the wooden benches along the pavements, burning their furniture . . . In January [1871] 19,233 hearses took the road to the cemeteries.' (Four times the normal death rate.) The starving city capitulated on January 28. Ten days before, in the palace at Versailles, the King of Prussia had been proclaimed Emperor of Germany.

1. Flaubert wrote also to Commanville: 'Make Caro come back! . . . Her grandmother absolutely needs her. She is dying of grief and ageing hour by hour.' And: 'What a wretched idea, her fleeing to England! . . . I repeat: her prolonged absence is killing her grandmother. That's all. Simply that.'

⁓

TO HIS NIECE CAROLINE

[Rouen,] February 1 [1871]

Dear Caro,

Your husband wrote to me yesterday that he would urge you to come back as soon as the boat from Newhaven resumes service. Does this mean that the blockade has been lifted? I think not. He adds that he expects to see you within a week. I'm afraid the week will go by without your return. That will be a great disappointment to your grandmother, who is at the end of her strength and her patience. There is always the road from Saint-Valéry, but is it safe?[1]

The capitulation of Paris, even though expected, has plunged me into an indescribable state. One could hang oneself out of fury. I regret that Paris wasn't burned to the last house, leaving only a great black void. France has fallen so low, is so dishonoured, so debased, that I wish she might disappear completely. But I hope that civil war will kill a lot of people for us. Would that I might be included in the number! In preparation for that event, there is to be an election of deputies. What bitter irony! Needless to say, I shall abstain from voting. I no longer wear my Legion of Honour ribbon, for the word 'honour' is French no longer; and so strongly do I feel myself no longer French that I intend to ask Turgenev (as soon as I'm able to write to him) what one has to do to become a Russian.

Your uncle Achille Flaubert threatened to jump off one of the bridges, and Raoul Duval[2] seemed for a time to have gone raving mad. No matter how much you have read in the newspapers, or how vividly you have pictured to yourself what the invasion might be like, *you have no idea of it*, I assure you. Every soul with the slightest claim to pride has been mortally stricken, and like Rachel 'refuses to be comforted'.

Since last Sunday morning, we no longer have any Prussians at Croisset (though many are returning to Rouen). As soon as things have been cleaned up a little, I'll go and take another look at the old house – which I no longer love, and dread to enter, for I can't throw everything those gentlemen handled into the river. If the house belonged to me, I would certainly have it demolished.

Oh! Such hatred! Such hatred! It stifles me. I, who was born oversensitive – I'm choking on gall . . .

1. That is, since the main road from Dieppe (where Caroline would be arriving from England) to Rouen might well be blocked by the Prussians, she should enquire about conditions on the other, secondary road. Caroline returned from England early in February.

2. Lawyer and politician, later deputy from the Seine-Inférieure. He would play an important role in Flaubert's later life.

~

The Germans outside Paris waited a month, giving the National Assembly time to declare the end of the Empire and the Bonapartist succession, and to accept the peace terms proposed. On March 1 they celebrated their victory by entering the city and parading down the Champs-Elysées. On the fourth, from Dieppe, Flaubert wrote to Princesse Mathilde: 'Well, we have swallowed our shame. But not digested it. How I thought of you on Wednesday, and how I suffered! All day I *saw* the bayonets of the Prussians flashing in the sun on the Champs-Elysées, and heard their bands, their hateful bands, playing under the Arc de Triomphe! The man who sleeps in the Invalides must have turned in his tomb with rage.'

After occupying Paris for forty-eight hours, the Germans withdrew: they knew what they were doing – that they could leave the city to its own divided inhabitants. On March 18, 1871, the 'Commune de Paris' was declared, a revolutionary, collectivist state within the regular state, setting off the civil war that Flaubert had hoped would 'kill a lot of people'. His wish was granted. For six weeks, under the eyes of the Germans encamped on surrounding heights, the city was again besieged – this time by the 'Versaillais', the troops of the regular, national government, which was sitting at Versailles. Executions by the Communards, their burning of public buildings, indeed their very existence as Communards, made them the target of savage reprisals by the victorious Versaillais when they entered the city in the last week of May. During that 'Bloody Week' – *La Semaine Sanglante* – thousands of Parisians (some historians say as many as 20,000) were killed by French soldiers. The story of the Commune and its aftermath remains one of the most dramatic and tragic chapters in the history of France, along with that of the macabre years of the later German occupation, Vichy government, and deportations of 1940–1945.

Shortly before the proclamation of the Commune in Paris, the city of Rouen staged a demonstration of a different kind. Prince Frederik Karl of Prussia was to arrive there on Sunday, March 12, to review the occupying troops; on Friday the tenth the Rouennais hung black flags from their houses, shops, and public buildings; and shop windows displayed signs saying 'Closed because of national mourning'. It was on the eleventh that Flaubert, perhaps inspired by unaccustomed pride in his native city, wrote in a letter to George Sand his most celebrated lines about the Prussians – many of whom, billeted on Rouen families, had behaved brutally, in contrast to Flaubert's restrained, though loathed, 'guests' at Croisset.

~

To George Sand

Dieppe, March 11 [1871]

Chère maître,

When shall we see each other again? Paris doesn't sound very gay. Ah! What kind of a world are we going to inhabit? Paganism, Christianism, Boorism: such are the three great evolutions of mankind. It's sad to find oneself at the beginning of the third.

I'll not tell you everything I have suffered since September. How have I stayed alive? That's what surprises me! No one has been more *desperate* than I. Why? I have had bad times in my life, I have suffered great losses, I have often wept, endured much anguish. Well, all those griefs put together are nothing – nothing at all – compared with these. And I don't get used to it. I find no consolation. I have no hope.

I didn't consider myself a believer in progress or a humanitarian. No matter! I did have illusions! What barbarism! What retrogression! I resent my contemporaries for having inspired me with the feelings of a brute of the twelfth century. I am choking on gall. These officers who smash your mirrors with white-gloved hands, who know Sanskrit and fling themselves on your champagne, who steal your watch and then send you their visiting card, this war for money,[1] these savages for all their civilization – they horrify me more than Cannibals.[2] And everybody is going to emulate them, turn military. Russia now has four million troops. All Europe will be in uniform. If we take our revenge, it will be ultra-savage. And you can be sure that we'll be thinking of nothing but that, of avenging ourselves on Germany. The government, whatever it may be, will be able to maintain itself only by harping on that passion. Murder on a grand scale is going to be the goal of all our efforts, France's ideal!

I cherish the dream of going to live in the sun, in some tranquil land.

We must expect new hypocrisies: declamations about virtue, diatribes about corruption, austerity in dress, etc. Officiousness to the last degree.

At this moment I have *forty* Prussians at Croisset. As soon as my poor house (which I now hold in horror) is emptied and cleaned, I'll return to it; then I'll probably go to Paris, despite the unhealthiness of the place. But as to that I don't give a damn . . .

1. The Germans levied taxes on each occupied city, increasing them at the least sign of resistance. In addition, heavy 'reparations' were part of the peace terms. In 1914, at the outbreak of the First World War, France was still paying 'reparations' to Germany for the war of 1870–1871.
2. As future letters will show, Flaubert retained a hatred of Germany for the rest of his life.

～

Of the Paris Commune, Flaubert had no direct experience, but much to say.

On March 17, 1871, the day before the Commune was proclaimed, leaving his mother with Caroline at Neuville, he travelled from Paris by train with Alexandre Dumas the younger to spend four days on a visit of friendship and sympathy to Princesse Mathilde in Brussels. Before returning to France he visited London, writing to Caroline that he had promised Juliet Herbert to do so. Back in Neuville he found a letter from George Sand, written from Nohant the day of his departure. She expressed fears of violence and vengeance among Frenchmen, and added: 'I don't know whether you agree with me, that full and complete liberty [*la liberté pleine et entière*] would save us from such disasters and put us back on the road of possible progress. Abuses of liberty don't frighten me in themselves; but those whom they do frighten always incline towards abuses of power.' Those words, and the disorders that had erupted in Paris, gave Flaubert an opening he did not fail to take.

～

To George Sand

Neuville, near Dieppe, Friday, March 31 [1871]
In reply to yours of March 17.

Chère maître,

Tomorrow, at last, I resign myself to returning to Croisset. It will be hard, but I must do it. I'll try to take up my poor *Saint Anthony* again, and forget France.

My mother will stay here with her granddaughter until it's possible to know where to go without fear of the Prussians or of rioting.

Some days ago I left here with Dumas for Brussels, thinking to return directly to Paris. But 'the new Athens' seems to me to surpass Dahomey in ferocity and imbecility.

Have we reached the end of the swindle? Are we done with the hollow metaphysics and the clichés? All the evil stems from our colossal ignorance. What ought to be pondered, is simply believed, without discussion. Instead of considering, people *tell* you.

The French Revolution must cease to be a dogma, and become an object of scientific enquiry, like everything else that's human. If people had known more, they wouldn't have believed that a mystical formula is capable of creating armies, or that the word 'Republic' suffices to defeat a million well-disciplined men. They would have left Badinguet on the throne *expressly* to make peace, ready to send him to the galleys afterwards. If they had known more, they would have understood what the volunteers of '92 were, and the retreat of [the duke of] Brunswick, bribed by Danton and Westermann.[1] But no! always the same old story! Always nonsense! Now we have the Paris Commune, reviving sheer medievalism. They're frank enough about it! The business about controlling rents is particularly splendid. Now the government interferes in Natural Right, intervening in contracts between individuals. The Commune asserts that we do not owe what we owe, and that one service is not to be paid for by another. It's an enormity of ineptitude and injustice.

Many conservatives who wanted to preserve the Republic out of love of order are going to miss Badinguet and in their hearts call back the Prussians. The people in the Hôtel de Ville[2] have *deflected our hatred.* That's why I resent them. It seems to me that we have never been lower.

We're being tossed back and forth between the Society of Saint Vincent de Paul and the International. But the latter is committing too many idiocies to last long. If it should defeat the Versaillais and overthrow the government, the Prussians will enter Paris and 'order will prevail' – as it did in Warsaw. If, on the contrary, it is beaten, the reaction will be fierce and all liberty strangled.

What can one say of socialists who imitate the methods of Badinguet and Wilhelm: requisitions, suppressions of newspapers, executions without trial, etc.? Ah! What a vile beast the crowd is! And how humiliating to be a man!

Je vous embrasse bien fort.
Your old troubadour
G^{ve}

1. In 1792 the army of the First French Republic repulsed the German invaders in the Battle of Valmy, arousing great popular enthusiasm in France. Considerable surprise was expressed, however, that the German commander, the Duke of Brunswick, should immediately withdraw his troops instead of continuing the campaign, and there were rumours that he had accepted French bribes.

    Flaubert is saying that, just as in 1792 – when victory was won not, as patriotic tradition would have it, by the 'spirit of the Republic,' but by bribery of the enemy – so in 1870 the mystical idea of 'proclaiming the Republic' would not win the war. (J.B.)

2. The government of the Commune, whose headquarters were in the Hôtel de Ville (the Paris City Hall).

~

TO HIS NIECE CAROLINE

[Croisset, Wednesday, 2 o'clock, April 4, 1871]

My dear Caro,

Contrary to my expectations, I find myself *very well off* at Croisset, and I think no more about the Prussians than if they had never come here! It was a very sweet feeling, to be back in my study and see all my little belongings once again. My mattresses have been attended to, and I sleep like a log. On Saturday night I began to work again, and if nothing interrupts me I'll have finished my Heresies by the end of this month. So, my poor darling, the only thing I lack is the presence of those I love; a small group, with you in the front row, my lovely lady.

When we were reunited at the beginning of February, I had lost my bearings completely; but thanks to you, your sweet company and your nice house, I gradually recovered, and now I'm looking forward to the day when you'll come here (for a month, I hope). The garden is going to be very beautiful, the buds are opening, primroses everywhere. Such peace and quiet! I'm quite dazed by it.

On Sunday I spent the day in a delicious stupor. I relived the days when my poor Bouilhet would arrive on Sunday morning with his notebook of poems, when *père* Parain would wander about the house with his newspaper sticking out of his back pocket, and you, poor baby, would be running on the lawn in your white apron. I'm becoming too much of a sheik,[1] burying myself in the past! Let's speak of the present.

Your husband must be relieved: 'our brothers'[2] have just been given a good drubbing. I'd be very surprised if the Commune were to last beyond next week. I was moved by the murder of Pasquier.[3] I knew him very well: he was an intimate friend of Florimont, a chum of your uncle Achille, a pupil of *père* Cloquet, and Mme Lepic's first cousin.

. . .

1. See p. 411, n. 1.
2. The Communards.
3. A military surgeon shot by the Communards.

❧

GEORGE SAND TO FLAUBERT

Nohant, April 28 [1871]

I haven't managed to be alone a single moment since this ugly adventure began without falling into bitter despair. I make great efforts to resist, I don't want to be discouraged, I don't want to forswear the past and dread the future! But my will and my reason struggle against a profound depression that is so far insurmountable. That is why I didn't want to write to you before feeling better; not because I'm ashamed of having these fits of despondency, but because I wouldn't want to increase your already deep sadness by adding the weight of mine.

For me, the ignoble experiment that Paris is attempting or undergoing does nothing to disprove the laws of the eternal progression of men and of things; and if my mind has acquired certain principles, good or bad, they are neither shaken nor changed by it. I have long accepted patience as one accepts the weather, the length of the winter, old age, lack of success in all its forms. But I think that the members of the various parties (those who are sincere) must change their formulas – or perhaps perceive the emptiness of every a priori formula.

That is not what saddens me. When a tree dies you must plant two others. My grief comes from pure weakness of heart, which I don't know how to overcome. I cannot close my eyes to the suffering and even the ignominy of others. I pity those who do the evil; even though I recognize their unworthiness, their moral condition distresses me. We pity a fledgling that falls from the nest: how not pity a vast number of human consciences fallen into the mire? One suffered less during the siege by the Prussians. One loved Paris when it was unhappy through no fault of its own. One pities it all the more today when one can love it no longer. Those who have no love for anything are indulging themselves by hating it mortally. What reply should we make? None, perhaps. Scorn – to be scorned by France – is perhaps the required punishment for the arrant cowardice with which the Parisians submitted to riot and to the desperados who led it. It's a sequel to the acceptance of the desperados of the Empire. Different felons, same cowardice.

But I didn't want to talk to you about this: you roar enough about it as it is! . . .

You haven't told me in what state you found your charming nest at Croisset. The Prussians occupied it: did they soil it, loot it, ruin it? Your books and bibelots – did you find them all? They respected your name, your study? If you *can* resume work there, your mind will be at peace. I must wait for mine to recover, and I know I must assist in my own cure by a certain faith: this is often shaken, but I'm making a duty of it.

Tell me whether the tulip tree escaped freezing last winter, and if the peonies are lovely now. I often travel in my mind: I see your garden and its surroundings. How far away all that is; how much has happened! One is tempted to think oneself a hundred years old . . .

We embrace you and we love you.

∼

Flaubert wrote to Princesse Mathilde on May 3: 'Mme Sand has written me a desperate letter. She sees that her old idol was hollow, and her republican faith seems to me completely extinguished! That's a disaster that won't befall me.'

∼

To George Sand

Croisset, April 30 [1871]

Chère maître,

Let me answer at once your questions insofar as they concern me personally. No, the Prussians did not loot my house. They made off with a few trifles – a dressing case, a box, some pipes; but on the whole they did no damage. My study they respected. I had buried a large box full of letters, and hidden my voluminous notes for *Saint Antoine*. All that, I found intact.

The worst effect of the invasion *for me* is that it has aged my poor mother by ten years. What a change! She can no longer walk alone, and her frailty is heart-rending. How sad it is to watch the slow deterioration of those you love! . . .

To stop thinking about public miseries and my own, I have plunged furiously back into *Saint Antoine*, and if I can continue at this pace without interruption it will be finished next winter. I long to read you the sixty pages that are done. When railway journeys become possible again, come and see me. Your old troubadour has been waiting a long time for you. Your letter that came this morning touched me. What a fine fellow you are, and what a great heart you have!

I am unlike the many people I hear lamenting the [civil] war in Paris. I find it more tolerable than the invasion, because after the invasion any further despair is impossible – another proof of the depths to which we have sunk. 'Ah, thank God the Prussians are there!' is the universal cry of the bourgeois. I put Messieurs the workers into the same bag, and I'd like to throw the whole lot of them into the river. That's where they're headed anyway – and then things will quiet down. We'll become a big, dreary, industrial country – a kind of Belgium. The disappearance of Paris (as the seat of the government)[1] will make France dull and stagnant. She will have no heart, no centre – and, I think, no mind?

As for the Commune, which is in its death throes, it is the latest manifestation of the Middle Ages. Will it be the last? Let's hope so!

I hate democracy (at least as it is understood in France), because it is based on 'the morality of the Gospels', which is immorality itself, whatever anyone may say: that is, the exaltation of Mercy at the expense of Justice, the negation of Right – the very opposite of social order.

The Commune is rehabilitating assassins,[2] just as Jesus forgave thieves; and they are looting the homes of the rich because they have learned to curse Lazarus – who was not a *bad* rich man, but simply a rich man.[3] The slogan 'The republic is above all argument' is on a par with the dogma that 'The pope is infallible'. Always formulas! Always gods!

The God-before-last – universal suffrage – has just played a terrible joke on his faithful by electing 'the assassins of Versailles'.[4] What are we to believe in, then? Nothing! Such is the beginning of Wisdom. It is time to rid ourselves of 'Principles' and to espouse Science, objective enquiry. The only rational thing (I keep coming back to it) is a government of Mandarins, provided the Mandarins know something – in fact, a great many things. The *people* never come of age, and they will always be at the bottom rung of the social scale because they represent number, mass, the limitless. It is of little importance that many peasants should be able to read and no longer listen to their priests; but it is infinitely important that many men like Renan or Littré be able to live *and be listened to*. Our only salvation now lies in a *legitimate aristocracy*, by which I mean a majority composed of something more than mere numbers.

. . .

1. On March 10, 1871, the National Assembly had transferred itself from Paris to Versailles, where it would remain (rebaptized the Chamber of Deputies in 1875) until 1879.
2. Doubtless an allusion to the assassination, more or less approved by the Commune, of generals Lecomte and Thomas. (A.J.)

3. Flaubert misremembered his Luke (16:19–31). Lazarus was the poor man. (A.J.)

4. After the first encounters, on April 2, the Versaillais had shot several prisoners; thenceforth the Commune called the members of the Assembly and the Versailles government 'assassins'. (A.J.)

~

The week that followed the writing of that letter was the Semaine Sanglante. Very shortly thereafter, as soon as entry into the city was possible, Flaubert was given permission to consult books in the Bibliothèque Impériale, still officially closed because of the disorders. (He had known it as the Bibliothèque Royale before 1848, and now it would soon reopen as the Bibliothèque Nationale, as it is called today.) The odour of decaying corpses still hung over the city. Many public buildings were burnt-out shells and would have to be demolished, most prominent among them the Palais des Tuileries, where he had attended Imperial balls, and the Hôtel de Ville (later reconstructed). 'You'll see some mighty ruins,' he wrote to Caroline. 'It's sinister and weird. I haven't seen nearly everything, nor shall I. One should really walk about the city taking notes for a fortnight.'

~

To George Sand

Croisset, Sunday night [June 11, 1871]

Chère maître,

Never did I have a greater desire or greater need to see you than now. I have just come from Paris, and I don't know whom to talk to. I'm choking – crushed, or, rather, disheartened. The odour of the corpses disgusted me less than the miasmas of egotism exhaled from every mouth. The sight of the ruins is as nothing compared with the immense Parisian stupidity. With very rare exceptions it seemed to me that *everybody* ought to be tied up. Half the population wants to strangle the other half, and vice versa. This can be seen plainly in the eyes of the people in the streets. And the Prussians no longer exist! People excuse them, *admire* them!!! 'Reasonable' people want to be naturalized German. I assure you, it's enough to make one despair of the human race.

I was in Versailles on Thursday. The excesses of the Right are frightening. The vote on the Orléans[1] is a concession made to it, to appease it and gain time to prepare against it.

Did you know that Troubat[2] had written articles urging the murder of the hostages? Even so he was not arrested. And he confessed to me that he had been 'imprudent': charming word.

From the general madness I except Renan, who on the contrary seemed to me very philosophical. Our nice Soulié charged me with a thousand affectionate messages for you. Princesse Mathilde several times asked for news of you. She is losing her wits. She wants to return to Saint-Gratien 'despite everything'.[3] I've collected a mass of horrible unpublished details, all of which I spare you.

My short stay in Paris has upset me extremely, and I'm going to have a hard time getting back to work.

What do you think of my friend Maury, who kept the tricolour flying over the Archives throughout the Commune? I think few men capable of such pluck.[4]

. . .

Have you read the outline of a novel by Isidore that was among the documents found in the Tuileries last September? What a scenario![5]

. . .

I wrote you a very long letter about a month ago.

1. The abrogation of the 1848 law exiling members of the French royal houses.
2. Jules Troubat, formerly Sainte-Beuve's secretary, had been secretary to Félix Pyat, publisher of pro-Commune newspapers, but no article by him of the kind mentioned by Flaubert has been found. (A.J.)
3. Part of her property there was occupied by German troops; besides, the local population might be hostile to her as a Bonaparte. She had returned to France a few days earlier. She soon succeeded in obtaining government permission to re-open her chateau and was given German protection there until the end of the occupation. Flaubert found this undignified. 'She returned because she's a spoiled child, unable to school her passions,' he wrote to George Sand. 'That's the entire psychology of the thing. And I made a considerable concession (of which she was quite unaware) in going to see her at Saint-Gratien in the midst of Prussians! There were two sentries at the door. Though I haven't the blood of an emperor in my veins, I blushed to the roots of my hair as I passed them in their boxes. I quite did without my house as long as the Prussians were in it. I think she might have done the same.'
4. Other public buildings in Paris flew the red flag of the Commune. In a

letter to Mme Roger des Genettes, Flaubert added, in a tribute to Maury: 'Which didn't keep him from continuing to write his little articles on the Etruscans. So there are still a few philosophers. I'm not one of them.'

5. The present whereabouts of this outline are not known. It was entitled L'Odyssée de M. Benoît and is said to have been 'probably political, intended to demonstrate the benefits of the imperial regime'! (A.J. and J.B.)

$\sim$

GEORGE SAND TO FLAUBERT

[Nohant, June 14, 1871]

You want and need to see me, and you don't come! That's not nice; for I too, and all of us here, long for you. We parted so gaily eighteen months ago, and so many terrible things have happened in the meantime! To see each other would be the consolation that is our *due*. For my part, I can't stir, I haven't a sou, and have to work like a black. And then, I haven't seen a single Prussian, and want to keep my eyes unsoiled. Ah, my friend, what years we are going through! We cannot revert to what we used to be, for the hope we had then has disappeared, along with the rest.

What sort of reaction may we expect to follow this infamous Commune? Isidore, or Henri V, [1] or the kingdom of the *pétroleuses* [2] restored by anarchy? I, who have had such patience with my species, and have looked so long on the bright side, now see nothing but darkness. I judged others by myself. I had achieved relative mastery over my inborn character, having rid myself of useless and dangerous enthusiasms, I had sown grass and flowers on my volcanos and they were flourishing, and I imagined that all the world could become enlightened, could correct itself, or restrain itself, that the years I had passed with my fellows could not be lost to reason and experience: and now I wake from a dream to find a generation divided between idiocy and delirium tremens! Anything is possible at present.

However, it is wrong to despair. I'll make a great effort, and perhaps I'll become equable and patient once more. But at present it's beyond me. I'm as disturbed as you are, and I don't dare talk, think, or write, I'm so afraid of reopening the gaping wounds in every soul.

I did indeed receive your other letter, and I was summoning the courage to answer it; I'd like to do only good to those I love, especially to you, who feel so keenly. At the present moment I'm up to nothing. Indignation devours me, disgust is killing me.

All I know is that I love you. My children say the same. Embrace your dear mother for me.

G. Sand

1. Henri, comte de Chambord, the Bourbon pretender, who was about to return to France from exile and assert his claim to the throne.
2. 'The name given to women who, during the Commune, are said to have poured parafin on certain buildings to quicken the fires' (*Grand Larousse Encyclopédique*). Their existence is questioned by many historians, but in the hysteria of the reprisals a number of women were executed on the charge.

∼

George Sand has been criticized for basing some of her opinions concerning the Commune, at this time, on false news printed in the Versaillais (anti-Commune) press. Flaubert, wishing to believe that she was abandoning her old attitudes, wrote about her to Princesse Mathilde on September 6: 'Have you read an article by Mme Sand (published [yesterday] in *Le Temps*) on the workers? She is very gradually coming to see the most difficult thing of all: the truth. For the first time in her life she calls the rabble by its name.'

∼

GEORGE SAND TO FLAUBERT

Nohant, September 6 [1871]

Where are you, my dear old troubadour? I don't write to you: I'm perturbed to the depths of my soul. This will pass, I hope, but I am infected with the sickness of my people and my generation. I cannot isolate myself, cannot take refuge in my rationality and my innocence. I feel that great ties have been loosened, almost broken. It seems to me that we're setting out for some unknown destination. Do you have more courage than I? Give me a little of it.

I send you the pretty faces of our little girls. They remember you, and tell me I must send you their portraits . . .

∼

To George Sand

Croisset, September 8 [1871]

Ah! how sweet they are! What darlings! What good little faces, so serious and charming! My mother was greatly touched, and so was I. That is what I call a delicate attention, *chère maître*, and I thank you greatly for it. I envy Maurice! His existence is not arid, like mine.

Our two letters crossed again. That doubtless proves, does it not? that we are affected by the same things, at the same time, and in the same degree.

Why are you so sad? Mankind is displaying nothing new. Its irremediable wretchedness has embittered me ever since my youth. So I am not disillusioned now. I believe that the crowd, the mass, the herd, will always be detestable. Nothing is important save a small group of minds, ever the same, which pass on the torch. As long as no deference is paid to the Mandarins, as long as the Academy of Sciences doesn't take the place of the Pope, all Politics, and Society down to its very roots, will be nothing but an assortment of distressing humbugs. We are floundering in the afterbirth of the Revolution, which was a miscarriage, a failure, a gross blunder, no matter what may be said about it. And the reason is that it had its origin in the spirit of the Middle Ages and Christianity, an antisocial religion. The idea of equality (which is all that modern democracy is) is an essentially Christian idea and opposed to that of justice. Observe how *Mercy* predominates now. Sentiment is everything, the law nothing. There is no longer even any public indignation against murderers. And the people who set fire to Paris are punished less than the slanderer of M. Favre.[1]

If France is to rise again, she must pass from Inspiration to Science, she must abandon all metaphysics in favour of objective enquiry – that is, the examination of reality.

Posterity will consider us very stupid, I'm sure. The words 'Republic' and 'Monarchy' will make them laugh, just as we laugh at 'Realism' and 'Nominalism'. For I defy anyone to show me one essential difference between those two terms. A modern republic and a constitutional monarchy are identical. No matter: there's great squabbling over it anyway – shouting, fighting!

As for the good 'People', 'free and compulsory' education will be the end of them. When everybody is able to read the *Petit Journal* and the *Figaro*, they won't read anything else, since those are the only things read by the bourgeois, the rich gentleman. The press is a school that serves to turn men into brutes, because it relieves them from thinking. Say that! It will be courageous of you, and if you prevail you'll have performed a noble service.

The first remedy would be to abolish universal suffrage, that insult to human intelligence. As it is constituted, one single element prevails, to the detriment of all the rest: *Number* dominates over mind, education, race, and even over money, which is preferable to Number.

But perhaps a Catholic society (which always needs a beneficent God, a Saviour) isn't capable of self-preservation. The conservative party hasn't even the instinct of the Brute (for the brute at least knows how to fight for its lair and its food). It will be absorbed by the Internationals, those Jesuits of the future. But the Jesuits of the past, who had neither Country nor Justice, did not succeed. And the International, too, will founder, because like theirs, its principles are false: no ideas, nothing but greed!

Ah! *chère bon maître*, if you could only hate! That is what you lack: hate. Despite your great sphinx eyes, you have seen the world through a golden haze. That comes from the sun in your heart. But so many shadows have loomed that you no longer discern things. Come, now! Cry out! Thunder! Take your great lyre and touch the brazen string. The Monsters will flee. Sprinkle us with the blood of the wounded Themis.[2]

Why do you feel that 'great ties have been broken'? What is broken? *Your* ties are indissoluble, for your affinity can only be for Eternal things.

Our ignorance of history makes us slander our own times. Mankind has always been like this. A few years of quiet fooled us. That's all. I too used to believe in the progressive 'civilizing' of the human race. We must expunge that mistake and think no better of ourselves than people did in the age of Pericles or Shakespeare, dreadful periods in which great things were accomplished.

Tell me you're in better spirits. And think sometimes of your old troubadour, who loves you.

1. Jules Favre, Minister of Foreign Affairs, had recently been the successful plaintiff in a libel suit. Even though Favre admitted to being guilty of peculation, his accuser was sentenced to a year in prison and a fine of a thousand francs. (A.J.)
2. In Greek mythology, the deity representing divine justice.

~

Mme Sand's response to Flaubert's summons to 'cry out' was immediate, but hardly what he desired.

That her distress over the turn of events was exacerbated by his recent letters – harsh and deliberately insensitive towards her and what he well knew her feelings to be – has been apparent not only in her replies themselves but in their unwonted infrequency. Now she found his call for 'hatred' intolerable. She started to write to him, and her letter took another form, to become one of the most impassioned of all her writings. Her 'Reply to a Friend', which appeared in *Le Temps* on October 3, 1871, is translated as Appendix II in the present volume.

She wrote to Flaubert, advising him of her action.

~

GEORGE SAND TO FLAUBERT

[Nohant, September 16, 1871]

Cher vieux,

I was answering you the day before yesterday, and my letter took on such dimensions that I have sent it as an article to *Le Temps* – I promised to give them two a month.[1] This letter 'to a friend' makes no mention of you even by an initial: I don't want to argue with you in public. In it I give you my reasons for suffering and for continuing to look ahead. I'll send it to you, and it will be like talking with you again. You'll see that my grief is part of me and that I have no right to believe that progress is a dream. Without that hope no one amounts to anything.

. . .

Come, let me suffer! That is better than 'to look on injustice with a serene countenance', as Shakespeare says.[2] When I have drained my cup of bitterness I shall feel better. I am a woman, I feel affection, pity, and anger. I shall never be a sage or a scholar.

. . .

I'm glad you enjoyed the faces of the children. You are so good: I knew you would love them. I embrace you tenderly. Mandarin though you may be, I don't find you Chinese at all, and I love you with all my heart.

1. This was her second in the series. The first had been the 'article on the workers' mentioned by Flaubert to Princesse Mathilde, which had in part inspired his letter of September 8.
2. Mme Sand's words, '*voir l'injustice avec un visage serein*', paraphrase a French translation (by Guizot and A. Pichot, 1821) of a passage from *Julius Caesar*, II, i: 'such suffering souls that welcome wrongs'. The translation reads: *ces âmes patientes de qui l'injustice reçoit un accueil serein*. (A.J.)

~

To George Sand

[Croisset,] Saturday [October 7, 1871]

Chère maître,

I received your article yesterday, and would answer it at length were I not preparing to leave for Paris. I'm going to try to finish up with *Aïssé*.[1]

The middle section of your piece made me 'shed a tear' – without convincing me, of course. I was moved, that was all, but not persuaded.

I comb your article for a certain word and find it nowhere: 'Justice'.[2] All our affliction comes from forgetting utterly that first premise of morality, which to my mind embraces *all* morality. Mercy, humanitarianism, sentiment, the ideal, have played us sufficiently false to make us try Righteousness and Science.

If France does not soon enter a period of self-appraisal, I think she will be irrevocably lost. Free compulsory education will do nothing but swell the number of imbeciles. Renan has said that superbly, in the preface to his *Questions contemporaines*. What we need most of all is a *natural*, that is to say, a legitimate, aristocracy. Nothing can be done without a brain; and universal suffrage as it now exists is more foolish than divine right. You will see some extraordinary things if it is retained! Masses, numbers, are invariably idiotic. I have few convictions, but I have that one, and strongly. Nevertheless the masses must be respected, however inept they may be, because they contain seeds of incalculable fertility. Give them liberty, but not power.

I believe no more than you do in class distinctions. Castes belong to archaeology. But I believe that the Poor hate the Rich, and that the Rich are afraid of the Poor. It will be ever thus. It is as futile to preach love to the one as to the other. The most urgent thing is to educate the Rich, who after all are the stronger. Enlighten the bourgeois first! For he knows nothing, absolutely nothing. The entire dream of democracy is to raise the proletariat to the level of bourgeois stupidity. That dream is partly realized! They read the same newspapers and share the same passions.

The three levels of education have shown within the past year what they can accomplish: (1) higher education caused Prussia to win; (2) secondary education, bourgeois, produced the men of the fourth of September;[3] (3) primary education gave us the Commune. Its Minister of Public Education was the great Vallès,[4] who boasted that he despised Homer.

Suppose that three years from now *all* Frenchmen know how to read. Do you think we'll be the better for it? Imagine, on the other hand, that in each community there was *one* bourgeois, one only, who had read Bastiat,[5] and that that bourgeois was respected: things would change!

I learn today that the mass of Parisians is sorry to have lost Badinguet. A plebiscite would declare for him, I'm sure. So fine a thing is universal suffrage!

However, unlike you I am not discouraged, and I like the present government, because it has no principle, no metaphysics, no humbug.

I'm expressing myself very badly. You deserve a different answer, but I'm very hurried – which doesn't prevent me from kissing you heartily.

Your old troubadour,
G^{ve} Flaubert

Not such a troubadour as all that, however! For the silhouette of the 'friend', as glimpsed by the reader of your article, is that of a not very amiable blockhead and selfish beast.

1. Flaubert was trying to secure a production of Bouilhet's play.
2. It is there – the word itself as well as the implication.
3. Date of the proclamation of the Third Republic, in 1870.
4. Jules Vallès (1832–1885), who took refuge in England after the end of the Commune. Later, following the amnesty, he would revive his radical Paris newspaper, *Le Cri du peuple*.
5. Frederic Bastiat (1801–1850), liberal economist and politician, a strong opponent of socialism in 1848.

~

GEORGE SAND TO FLAUBERT

Nohant, October 10 [1871]

I reply to your *post scriptum*. If [in 'Reply to a Friend'] I had answered *Flaubert*, I wouldn't have – *answered*; for I well know that with you, heart doesn't always agree with mind – a disagreement that all of us, for that matter, are ever compelled to. What I answered was part of a letter from some friend whom nobody knows nor can recognize, since I address myself to a segment of your reasoning that is not the whole *you*.

You are a troubadour all the same, and if I had to write to you *publicly* the character would be all it should be. But our true discussions must remain between ourselves, like caresses between lovers – and sweeter than those, since friendship also has its mysteries, without the storms of personality.

The letter you wrote to me in haste is full of well-expressed truths against which I do not protest. But the link and agreement between your truths of reason and my truths of feeling must be found. France, alas! is neither on your side nor on mine. She is on the side of blindness, ignorance, and folly. Oh! *That* I do not deny – and it is exactly what I deplore.

. . .

~

Mme Sand then changes the subject, and speaks of Bouilhet's *Aïssé* and the present state of the Paris stage. We have seen how she and Flaubert had recognized their fundamental differences from the beginning; and her tact now helped Flaubert to realize that he had perhaps fulminated enough. Not that he could stop abruptly. 'In my opinion the entire Commune should have been sentenced to hard labour. The bloodthirsty fools should have been chained by the neck like common criminals and made to clean up the ruins of Paris.' And, more generally Flaubertian, a sentiment that he might have expressed at any time in his life: 'I'd like to drown my contemporaries in their latrines, or at least rain torrents of abuse, cataracts of invective, on their heads. Why is this? I ask myself.' To those remarks Mme Sand replied obliquely; and, with only a brief faltering, their affection continued as before.

Among Flaubert's expressions of grief and indignation over events related to the war and the Commune, one was directed close to home – to his friend Charles Lapierre, owner-editor of the local newspaper *Le Nouvelliste de Rouen*. Victor Hugo, returning from exile on Guernsey after the fall of the Empire, had (as Enid Starkie puts it)[1] 'turned towards the Left as the revolutionary he liked to think he was', and had written a pamphlet which 'gave the impression that he supported and admired the Commune'. An article in the *Nouvelliste* for May 27, 1871, contained the following paragraph:

> A man whom France for a time believed she could count among her supreme geniuses, and who had the talent to earn an income of many thousand francs by his sonorous phrases and fantastic antitheses, a wretched poet, supporter of the Monarchy, of Bonapartism, and of Republicanism in that order – you will have guessed we refer to Victor Hugo – has just given his opinion on the appalling tragedy we are witnessing. This product of a brain that is utterly softened or deranged is entitled *Paris et la France*.

1. In *Flaubert the Master* (see Works of Related Interest).

~

To CHARLES LAPIERRE

[Croisset,] May 27 [1871]

Confidential

My dear Lapierre,

It is to you alone that I'm writing; therefore, I'm going to unburden my heart to you without constraint.

Your paper seems to me to be 'on a slippery slope', and it is sliding down so swiftly that your issue of this morning scandalized me.

The paragraph on Hugo outdoes everything. 'France believed she could count [him] among her supreme geniuses': that 'believed' is sublime! It means, 'Formerly we had no taste, but revolutions have enlightened us in the matter of art', and it's become abundantly clear that he's only a 'wretched poet', 'who had the talent to earn an income' – are you now attacking money? – 'with sonorous phrases and fantastic antitheses'! Try to imitate him, my good fellow! I find you all very droll, there in the rue Saint-Étienne-des-Tonneliers!

Proudhon[1] has already said 'It takes more genius to be a boatman on the Rhine than to compose *Les Orientales.*' And Augustine Brohan,[2] during the winter of 1853, proved in the *Figaro* that the said Hugo had never possessed the slightest talent. Don't imitate those two – clown and whore. In the interest of public order, and the return to moral standards, the first thing to try to do is to talk about what one knows. Let's choose our arms! Don't let's put our enemies in the right; and, when you want to attack the personality of a great poet, don't attack him as a poet: otherwise those who know something about poetry will shun you.

· · ·

I'm talking too much literature: forgive me. But as an old Romantic I was exasperated by your paper this morning. Old Hugo's foolishness pains me too much as it is, without his being insulted in his genius. When our masters demean themselves, we must do as the sons of Noah did, and cover their shame. Let us at least retain our respect for what was great. Don't let's add to our ruins . . .

1. The socialist writer Pierre Joseph Proudhon (1809–1865), author of the famous definition: *La propriété c'est le vol* ('Property is theft').
2. (1807–1887), an actress at the Comédie Française.

∼

As Enid Starkie points out, Flaubert's letter to Lapierre was written during the Semaine Sanglante, when in Paris Frenchmen were killing Frenchmen by the thousand. After listening at length to Flaubert, the master of self-contradiction, on the subjects of war and politics, it is good to hear him again as artist and champion of art.

Armed with the results of his latest researches – some of them, as we have seen, undertaken in devastated Paris immediately after that bloody week – and writing at last what would prove to be the definitive version of *The Temptation of Saint Anthony,* Flaubert found relief for his spirits in grappling with the mysteries of eastern religions. In response to a letter from his friend Frédéric Baudry couched in the style of those writings, he replied in kind.

~

To Frédéric Baudry[1]

[Croisset,] Saturday night [June 24–25 (?), 1871]

O Bodhisattva! O youth of gentle birth! O perfect Buddha!

Like an old stork, I am sorrowful and dejected in spirit; like an old elephant fallen into the mire, I lack strength.

I need, O youth of gentle birth, the fourth of the medicinal plants that induce well-being in any situation, whatsoever it may be.

I have read the Lalitavistara, O Bodhisattva, I have read *The Lotus of the Wonderful Law,*[2] O youth of gentle birth!

But I would spend innumerable (hundreds) of myriads of Kotis of Kalpas,[3] without understanding, O holy name of God, in what Buddha consists.

I search within myself, to see whether I may not possess the thirty-two qualities of the imbecile.[4]

In short, I'm going to send to you at the end of next week for the Barthélémy-Saint-Hilaire.[5] Thank you for the legend of the deer, but what I especially lack is the theology of Buddhism, the very doctrines of Buddha.

You will probably see me towards the end of July or the beginning of August.

If you see Renan, give him my warm thanks for his book.[6]

It seems to me that politics are calming down. Ah, if people could accustom themselves to living without 'principles', i.e. without dogmas – what progress!

Here are two lines from *The Lotus of the Wonderful Law* that drive me crazy! They concern a house haunted by demons: 'Seizing the dogs by their feet, they overturn them on to their backs; and growling they squeeze them by their throats and take pleasure in choking them to death.' What a picture! How one sees it! Doesn't it make you want to do the same?

Adieu, old Richi.[7] O, the Law! O, the Assembly!

Your disciple,
G[ve] Flaubert

1. A philologist. A Rouennais, he had been a friend of Flaubert's since childhood. He will be heard of again, in subsequent pages.
2. One of the canonical books of Buddhism, in prose and verse, probably dating from the third century AD. There is an English translation (from the Chinese version) by W. E. Soothill (Oxford: Clarendon Press, 1930).
3. Billions of years, a metaphor from *The Lotus*.
4. The allusion is to the thirty-two qualities of goodness that distinguish the sage.
5. Jules Barthélémy-Saint-Hilaire (1805–1895) wrote *Du bouddhisme* (1855) and *Le Bouddha et sa religion* (1862).
6. *La Réforme intellectuelle et morale* (1871).
7. A being of perfect saintliness.

~

'Ouf! I've just finished my section on the Gods!' Flaubert wrote to George Sand on November 14. 'That is, the mythological part of my *Saint Antoine*, which I've been on since the beginning of June. How I long to read it to you, *chère maître du Bon Dieu!*'

The year ended with his receiving a new book by a thirty-one-year-old novelist who had proclaimed himself his disciple, and whose earlier book, Thérèse Raquin, he had praised even while complaining that it was 'not preoccupied above all else with what is for me the goal of art, namely, Beauty.'

~

TO ÉMILE ZOLA

> *[Paris, 4 rue Murillo, Friday night, December 1, 1871]*

I have just finished your dreadful and splendid book [*La Fortune des Rougon*]. I'm still giddy after reading it. It's strong! Very strong!

I find fault only with the preface. In my opinion, it spoils your book, which is so impartial and so lofty. You give away your secret: that is carrying candour too far; and you express your opinion, something which in my poetics a novelist hasn't the right to do.

Those are my *only* reservations.

But you have a noble talent and you are a valuable man.

Send me a line to say when I can come to see you, to talk at length about your book.

I shake your hand most cordially, and am your

G^{ve} Flaubert

XV

The Temptation of Saint Anthony.
The Beginning of Bouvard and Pécuchet.
Le Candidat. Three Tales

1872–1877

'I WANT TO embrace you at the beginning of the new year,' George Sand wrote Flaubert from Nohant on January 4, 1872, 'and to tell you that I love my old troubadour now and always . . . Here we invoked you at the stroke of midnight on Christmas Eve. We shouted your name three times. Did you hear it at all? We are all well. The little girls are growing up. We speak of you often. My children embrace you, too. May our affection bring you happiness!'

But during this year – which was to see the death of his mother – and for some time to come, Flaubert's letters to Nohant would often strain even George Sand's great faith in the power of affection over grief. With Madame Flaubert's disappearance he became the oldest survivor (apart from the servant Julie, who was to inspire one of his *Three Tales*) in his immediate world of Croisset; and, having long since taken to calling himself 'old' – an 'old' Romantic, an 'old' troubadour, a 'fossil' – he now entered, quite wilfully, at fifty, into premature old age.

There were other factors: the approaching death of Théophile Gautier, which symbolized for Flaubert the end of Romanticism; the public's incomprehension of *L'Education sentimentale*; and, not least of all, the terms of his mother's will and the characters and misfortunes of his niece and her husband.

However, his mother's death was the dominating event. Four years later, when his spirits had somewhat revived, he would recognize this, and write to Caroline: 'Shall I tell you my opinion? I think that (without knowing it) I was deeply and secretly sick after the death of our poor old lady. If I'm wrong, how does it happen that for some time now my mind has been functioning more clearly? It's as though a fog were lifting. Physically I feel rejuvenated.'

Flaubert's loyalty to Louis Bouilhet's memory never wavered. He celebrated and defended him in his preface to the posthumously published volume of his verse; he wrote and published a scathing 'Letter to the Municipal Council of Rouen' after that provincial body, by a vote of thirteen to eleven, had declined his committee's offer to pay for the erection of a monument to the poet,[1] and he exhausted himself securing and supervising a production of Bouilhet's play, *Mademoiselle Aïssé*, at the Théâtre de l'Odéon, only to see it be blasted by critics and close after three performances.

There was some consolation in the increasing admiration he received from writers of a younger generation who sent him their works.

1. The monument – a bust of Bouilhet and a fountain – was eventually executed. It stands against the façade of the present Rouen Municipal Library, successor to the building that Bouilhet knew.

~

To Alphonse Daudet

[Paris,] Tuesday morning [March 1872]

It's purely and simply a *masterpiece*! That's the word that springs to my lips, and I'll not take it back.

I began *Tartarin*[1] on Sunday at midnight, and finished it at 2:30! Everything, absolutely everything, kept me entertained, and I burst out laughing several times.

The camel is a marvellous invention, well developed, and providing 'the crowning touch'.

Tartarin on the minaret, fulminating against the Orient, is sublime!

In short, your little book seems to me of the very highest quality. Such is my opinion.

I plan to return to my house in the country in a little under two weeks. Between now and then I'm entirely taken up. But I'd like to see you. How shall we do it? I'll be at home on Sunday afternoon.

And you? When are you free?

Where can I find your brother, whom I haven't yet thanked for his book?

Until soon, I hope, and all greetings.

The hunters, the caps! Barbassou, the negroes eating sticking plaster, the Prince, etc.! Very fine, very fine!

---

1. By 1872, Alphonse Daudet (1840–1897) had already published his *Lettres de mon moulin* and *Le Petit Chose*. Chapters from the immensely popular *Tartarin de Tarascon* would become familiar to generations of secondary-school students of French in England and the United States, but today its coy, racial humour is difficult to swallow. Indeed all of Alphonse Daudet's work is at present in eclipse. The title of one of his plays, *L'Arlésienne*, is known today chiefly as the name of the suite of music composed for it by Georges Bizet.

Ernest Daudet, elder brother of Alphonse, was a respected novelist and historian. The book for which Flaubert had not yet thanked him was perhaps his novel *Thérèse*.

Alphonse Daudet was the father of Léon Daudet, co-founder, with Charles Maurras, of the ultra-nationalist newspaper, *L'Action Française*.

≈

Mme Flaubert died on April 6, 1872. Of the replies to the terse announcements that Flaubert sent to friends, two, written five days apart, are from George Sand, who was ill at Nohant.

I am with you all day, all night, at every instant, my poor dear friend. I keep thinking of all the heartbreaking things that are taking place around you. I long to be near you. Resentment at being pinned down here makes me feel even more ill than I am . . . All I can do is to open a maternal heart to you: it can be no substitute, but it is suffering together with yours . . .

. . . If you should feel like doing some travelling, and lack the wherewithal, I have just earned a few sous, which are at your disposal. Have no more hesitation than I would with you, dear child. *Le Temps* will be paying me for my novel in five or six days . . .

≈

To George Sand

[Croisset,] Tuesday, [April] 16 [1872]

Chère bon maître

I should have answered your first letter at once, it was so sweet. But I was exhausted, I lacked the physical strength. Today I'm at last beginning to hear the birdsong and see the fresh green of the leaves. I've stopped resenting the sunshine! That's a good sign. If only I could feel like working again I'd be saved.

Your second letter (that of yesterday) moved me to tears. How good you are! What a wonderful being! I have no need of money at the moment. Thank you. But if I should feel the need, it is certainly you I would turn to.

My mother has left Croisset to Caroline, with the condition that I retain my quarters here. So until things are finally settled I'll stay on. Before deciding about the future, I must know what I'll have to live on. After that we'll see. Will I have the fortitude to live absolutely alone here, in solitude? I doubt it. Caroline cannot live here now. She already has two places of her own. And the Croisset house is expensive to maintain.

I think I'll give up my apartment in Paris. All my friends are dead. And the last of them, poor Théo, isn't long for this world. Ah! It's hard to grow a new skin at fifty!

I have realized for a fortnight now that my poor dear mother was the being I loved most. I feel as though part of my entrails had been torn out.

I need to see you so badly! So badly! As soon as things are cleared up I'll visit you. If you go to Paris, let me know, and I'll come running to embrace you.

Mme Viardot, Turgenev, and I have a plan – to visit you at Nohant in July. Will this little dream be realized?

I give you a great hug.

Your old troubadour
G^{ve} Flaubert

~

To Caroline he wrote a fortnight later: 'You can't imagine how lovely and how quiet *your* Croisset is. Everything is suffused with an infinite sweetness, and there is a kind of assuagement in the silence. The memory of my poor old lady never leaves me: it hovers around me like a mist – I'm as though enclosed in it.'

And to George Sand: 'Whatever happens, I'll keep my rooms at Croisset. They will be my refuge, and perhaps my only habitation.'

That June he did 'come running' to Paris to see Mme Sand – it was their first meeting in over two years, her first view of the city since the ravages of the war and the Commune. (She found the 'stupor' of the Parisians even sadder than the ruins.) And then, after working obsessively to finish *Saint Anthony* by the end of the month, Flaubert spent several weeks with Caroline at Bagnères-de-Luchon, a watering place in the Pyrenees. (It was during this stay, after her grandmother's death, that she first spoke openly to Flaubert about her unsatisfactory marriage: see Appendix IV.) He did not, after all, accompany Mme Viardot and Turgenev when they visited George Sand at Nohant in September: instead, saying that he had lately been too much of a 'vagabond', and now had to stay at home,[1] he plunged into reading for his next novel.

This would be the book about the two 'troglodytes' whose outline he had put aside in 1864 in favour of *L'Éducation sentimentale*. In a letter of August 1872 to Mme Roger des Genettes, with whom he had apparently discussed the new work, he now speaks of it as 'the farcical story of those two characters who copy a kind of critical encyclopedia. I think I gave you some idea of it. I'm going to have to study many things I'm ignorant of – chemistry, medicine, agriculture. I'm now into medicine. One has to be insane – wildly mad – to undertake such a book!' And to his friend Mme Brainne:[2] 'All this for the sole purpose of spitting out on my contemporaries the disgust they inspire in me. I'm finally going to proclaim my way of thinking, exhale my resentment, vomit my hate, expectorate my bile, ejaculate my anger, purge myself of indignation – and I shall dedicate my book to the shade of St Polycarp.'

He had already decided to call it *Bouvard and Pécuchet*.[3]

Bouvard and Pécuchet, the story of two uneducated, retired copy-clerks and their disillusioning quest for knowledge, will be referred to throughout the remaining pages of the present work. In the form in which it is generally known, the novel is a single volume of ten chapters. Most editions include also Flaubert's outline for an eleventh chapter, unwritten at his death in 1880. Those eleven chapters would have made up the first volume of a planned two-volume work. Flaubert once spoke of a possible subtitle: 'Encyclopedia of Human Stupidity'.

For a summary of *Bouvard and Pécuchet,* never a widely read novel, one cannot do better than quote Jean Bruneau and Jean A. Ducourneau's remarks in their *Album Flaubert* (Gallimard, 1972):

> Flaubert's idea is to show, with the aid of his two characters, the dangers of 'lack of method in the sciences'. After failing in all their experiments, Bouvard and Pécuchet devote themselves to copying a *sottisier* – an encyclopedia of stupid statements and opinions expressed over the years by all mankind, not excepting Flaubert himself. Flaubert imagines a very restricted fictional 'situation', as in *The Temptation of Saint Anthony*: Bouvard and Pécuchet meet by chance on a bench on the boulevard Bourdon in Paris, buy a house in the country, experiment with one science after another, participate in their own way in the events of 1848, undertake a biography of the duc d'Angoulême, dabble in religion, love, the education of boys and girls, and after repeated failure in all these fields they join Flaubert in his judgement of the society of his day. 'Then their minds developed a deplorable capacity – that of perceiving stupidity and finding it insufferable.' They have become Flaubert – just as Flaubert himself, he said, had become them.

What the second volume would have been is not precisely known; but from Flaubert's letters and notes it seems that it would have consisted almost entirely of the *sottisier* – a collection of howlers copied by the baffled and disillusioned clerks from the very books they had hoped would offer them wisdom. Most of that material, as left by Flaubert, is an inchoate mass. It has been tentatively organized and published in French in several versions, but only one section has appeared in English – *The Dictionary of Accepted Ideas,* translated by Jacques Barzun (see Works of Related Interest).

Readers of the first volume of the present work may recall that in the very earliest of the letters the nine-year-old Flaubert already spoke of writing down the 'stupid things' said by 'a lady who comes to see papa'. Apparently he never stopped recording such utterances. He mentioned a projected 'dictionary' of them to Louis Bouilhet in a letter of 1850, and quoted a few items from it to Louise Colet in 1852. His notes also include a 'Catalogue of chic opinions' and an 'Album of the Marquise'. It was apparently a story by Barthélemy Maurice, '*Les Deux Greffiers*' (The Two Clerks), first published in 1841, that suggested the framework which would allow him to present his collected stupidities as the work of a pair of copyists.

Readers of the previous volume may also recall his adolescent infatuation with a young married woman, Elise (Mme Maurice) Schlesinger, on the beach at Trouville. He saw something of the Schlesingers in Paris while he was a law student, he celebrated Mme Schlesinger in his youthful *Mémoires d'un fou* (published only posthumously), and corresponded with her husband after the Schlesingers left France to live in Baden-Baden, where Elise suffered from depression and spent some time in a mental hospital. 'I had only one true passion,' he wrote about her to Louise Colet in 1846. 'I was barely fifteen, and it lasted until I was eighteen.' Then, almost twenty years later, calling on his memories of Elise Schlesinger, he invented the character of Mme Arnoux in the definitive *L'Éducation sentimentale*.

   In 1871, learning of her husband's death, he wrote to her twice, in a tone more openly affectionate than he would have used before her widowhood: 'For me, the sand on Trouville beach still holds your footprints.' Now, in 1872, he wrote to her again.

1.   Actually, 'staying at home' included a secret few days in Paris with Juliet Herbert, Caroline's former governess, who came from England to be with him. The episode is obscure, as is the entire relation with Miss Herbert, with whom he apparently corresponded and whom he apparently saw each year. (See Hermia Oliver, *Flaubert and an English Governess*, in Works of Related Interest.) The multiple presence, during the summer of 1872, of women for whom Flaubert felt affection – Mme Sand, Caroline, Juliet Herbert, and (as we shall see) Mme Schlesinger, not to mention Mme Roger des Genettes and his 'three angels' (see below) – led Hermia Oliver to head her chapter covering these months with a quotation from a letter Flaubert wrote to Caroline on September 24: 'My heart is large enough to contain all kinds of affection: the one doesn't exclude the other, nor the others.'

2.   Mme Charles Brainne (née Rivoire), an attractive widow, who is said to

have 'granted her favours' to Flaubert, and to whom at all events he often wrote quite freely, was a sister of the equally attractive Mme Charles Lapierre, wife of the owner-editor of *Le Nouvelliste de Rouen*. Flaubert sometimes called these ladies, and their friend the actress Madame Pasca (Mme Alice Séon-Pasquier), his 'three angels'. It was the custom of the trio to give him an annual dinner in honour of St Polycarp, one of the Apostolic fathers, whom Flaubert had chosen as his patron out of sympathy with the saint's reputed lament: 'O God, O God, in what a century hast Thou made me live!'

Flaubert was sometimes oppressed by the limitations of these charming bourgeoises. 'My "angels" are pretty silly,' he confided to Caroline after spending an evening at the Lapierres'. 'I think they love the man in me, but as for the mind I'm aware that I often shock them or seem mad.'

3. It may seem strange that for the name of one of his two copy-clerks Flaubert should choose something so similar to 'Bovary'; but variations on the name of his Cairo host (see p. 507, n. 1) apparently fascinated him. There is also the association, in this case, of the French word *buvard* ('blotter' or 'writing pad'). There was an 'actual' Pécuchet – a Rouen banker involved in Commanville's business affairs (see p. 630, n. 2).

~

To Madame Maurice Schlesinger

Croisset, Saturday [October 5, 1872]

Ma vieille Amie, ma vieille Tendresse,

I can never see your handwriting without being shaken. So this morning I eagerly tore open the envelope of your letter.

I thought it would announce your visit. Alas! no. That will be for when? For next year? I should so love to welcome you here, to have you sleep in my mother's bedroom!

It wasn't for my own health that I was at Luchon, but for my niece's, her husband being kept at Dieppe by his business. I returned early in August, and spent all September in Paris, where I'm going again in December to commission a bust of my mother. Then I'll come back here for as long as possible. I'm happiest in solitude. Paris is no longer Paris; all my friends are dead; those who remain count for little, or are so changed that I no longer recognize them. Here, at least, nothing irritates me, nothing distresses me directly.

The spirit of the public so disgusts me that I keep myself detached from it. I continue to write, but no longer want to publish, at least not until better times. I have been given a dog.[1] I take him for walks, watch the effect of the sun on the yellowing leaves, and like an old man dream of the past – for I *am* an old man. For me the future no longer holds dreams, but the days of the past seem as though bathed in a golden mist. Against that background of light, beloved phantoms reach out to me: and the face that stands out most splendidly is – yours. – Yes, yours. Oh, poor dear Trouville!

In the division of my mother's estate, Deauville[2] came to me. But I must sell it and invest the money, to have an income.

How is your son? Is he happy?[3] Do let us write to each other from time to time, if only a word, to show that we are still alive.

Adieu, and ever yours –

1. A greyhound, given to him by his friend Edmond Laporte, of whom more will be heard. A younger man, Laporte was an *avocat-général* (defined in legal dictionaries as 'deputy director of public prosecutions at a court of appeals' – in this case at Rouen), a *conseiller-général* (member of the local council) in the Rouen suburb of Grand-Couronne (across the river from Croisset), and manager of a lace factory there. Flaubert baptized the dog 'Julio' – 'for a number of mystic reasons', he told Laporte: possibly in honour of Juliet Herbert. He quickly developed a particular affection for Julio.
2. A farm there, which we shall see Flaubert selling not 'to have an income', but to pay some of Commanville's debts. One suspects that advice to sell was already being given by Commanville, who was thinking of how he, as Flaubert's 'investment counsel', might profit from what the farm would bring.
3. A few months earlier, Mme Schlesinger had come to Paris for her son's wedding: Flaubert had attended, and, overcome by memories (mixed, no doubt, with thoughts of his novel), he wept – as he wrote to Caroline – 'like an idiot'.

≈

That is the last known letter from Flaubert to his '*vieille Tendresse*': with it, mentions of the Schlesinger family disappear from the correspondence. Mme Schlesinger was to die in 1888, in Baden-Baden, where she had again entered a mental hospital.

Théophile Gautier was not one of Flaubert's frequent correspondents. But for the young Flaubert he had been a star in the constellation, the 'band', of Romantics. To have had the poet become his friend and admirer counted for a great deal with the mature Flaubert. They first met on the eve of Flaubert's departure for Egypt with Maxime DuCamp, in 1849; it was in Gautier's magazine, *L'Artiste*, early in 1857, that the 'second' *Temptation of Saint Anthony* had appeared (the first of the versions to be printed); Flaubert had rejoiced in Gautier's praise of *Salammbô* and been proud to have Gautier's novel, *Le Roman de la momie*, as companion-target in the attack on *Salammbô* by Guillaume Froehner. Gautier died on October 22, 1872.

～

TO HIS NIECE CAROLINE
                    [Croisset,] Friday, 2 o'clock [October 25, 1872]
Loulou,

You are right! The death of my poor old Théo, expected though it was, has laid me low, and yesterday I spent a day that I'll remember. I received the news in a telegram enclosed in a letter, with the result that at the moment I learned of my old friend's death he was being buried.

Having previously made appointments with Caudron and with Mme Lapierre and her sister, I went to Rouen to keep them, so as not to be thought of as a 'sensitive plant'. On the boat from La Bouille, conversation with Emangard. Caudron was on the dock, and we decided certain things concerning Bouilhet.[1] He went with me to the Hôtel-Dieu, where I asked after Pouchet's father. Your brilliant aunt talked about nothing but the hot weather and her own vapours and the quality of the steaks her butcher sent her. After which I crossed the city on foot, meeting three or four Rouennais. The spectacle of their vulgarity, their overcoats, their hats, what they said and the sound of their voices, made me want to vomit and weep at the same time. Never, since I have been in this world, have I been so choked with disgust for my fellow men. I thought continually of the love my old Théo had for art, and felt as though I were being submerged in a tide of filth. For he died, I am sure, of prolonged asphyxiation caused by the stupidity of the modern world.

I was in no mood, as you can imagine, for the jollifications of the Saint-Romain fair.[2] The 'angels' of the rue de la Ferme sensed that, and I went to the cemetery, to see the graves of those I loved. My two friends very kindly went with me; they and Lapierre waited for me at the gate. Such delicacy touched me to the heart. Lapierre was dining out, so I spent the evening alone with the two ladies, and the sight of their kind and lovely faces did me good. I am grateful to them.

When I returned here that night, my poor Julio was all over me with caresses. I don't know why I tell you all this, but you'll gather my state of mind from the details . . .

1. There was regular steamer service on the river, with a stop at Croisset. Gabriel Caudron was treasurer of the committee for the Bouilhet monument. Otherwise unidentified, 'Emangard' is referred to in a later letter as a Rouen bourgeois who on one occasion began a conversation with Flaubert in a way the latter enjoyed: 'Now you're a man who does nothing . . .'
2. The '*foire Saint-Romain*', named for a seventh-century bishop of Rouen whose feast day, October 23, is celebrated in Rouen churches, including the cathedral, on the third Sunday in October. The fair (a tradition of eight centuries) begins on the Saturday closest to October 23 and continues for four weeks. On the Friday immediately preceding its opening there is a one-day horse fair.

    Flaubert frequented the fair from boyhood, and is said to have owed his first acquaintance with the story of St Anthony to a marionette show presented each year in one of the booths. Tormented by devils, who made off with his celebrated pig, the saint cried out in supplication: '*Messieurs les démons, laissez-moi donc! Messieurs les laissez-moi donc!*' Schoolboys and students in the audience were wont to add their voices to the saint's plea. Flaubert inscribed it on the title page of the manuscript of his first version of the work, and it has since been reproduced in printed editions of that version.

～

GEORGE SAND TO FLAUBERT

Nohant, October 26, [18]72

Here is another sorrow for you, this one foreseen but none the less painful for that. Poor Théo, I pity him profoundly – not for dying, but for not having lived for the past twenty years. And if he had consented to live, to exist, to act, to forget his intellectual *personality* a little in order to conserve his actual *person*,[1] he could have lived on for a long time and refreshed his resources, which he had allowed to become too sterile a treasure. They say he suffered great hardship. I understand that he might have done, during the siege, but afterwards? Why, and how?

I'm concerned at having no news of you for a long time. Are you at Croisset? You must have been in Paris for our poor friend's funeral. What cruel, repeated severances! I'm angry with you, though, for becoming such a savage, so at odds with life. It seems to me that you're too inclined to regard happiness as something attainable, and that you're overly angered and astonished by its absence, which is our chronic state. You flee your friends; you plunge into work; and you regard the time you would spend in loving or being loved as time lost. Why didn't you come to us with Mme Viardot and Turgenev? You like them, you admire them, you know you are adored here – and you run off to be alone.

Why shouldn't you marry? Being alone is odious, it's deadly, and it's cruel also for those who love you. All your letters are disconsolate, and they wring my heart. Isn't there some woman you love, and who would find joy in loving you? Take her to live with you. Isn't there a small boy somewhere whom you could think of as your son? Bring him up, make yourself his slave, forget yourself in him.

Living within your *self* is bad. There is no intellectual pleasure like re-entering that self after being outside it for a long time. But to live continually inside that *me* – the most tyrannical, the most demanding, the most capricious of companions: no, that you must not do.

I beg you: listen to me! You are sequestering an exuberant nature in a prison. You are trying to turn a tender and indulgent heart into a deliberate misanthrope, and you will not succeed. I'm worried about you. Perhaps I'm talking nonsense, but we are living in cruel times, and we must not give in to them and excoriate them, but transcend and pity them. There: I love you. Write to me.

1.   Gautier's unhygienic habits were legendary.

∿

To George Sand

[Croisset,] Monday night [October 28–29, 1872]

Chère maître,

You guessed aright that there had been a redoubling of my grief, and your letter is sweet and kind. Thank you. And I embrace you even more warmly than usual.

Even though it was expected, poor Théo's death leaves me heart-broken. With him, the last of my intimate friends is gone. The list is now closed. Whom shall I see now, when I go to Paris? Who is there to talk with about what interests me? I know thinkers (or at least people who call themselves such), but an *artist* – where is there one?

Believe me, he died of disgust with the 'putrefaction of the modern world'. That was his expression, and he repeated it to me several times last winter. 'I'm dying of the Commune', etc. The fourth of September inaugurated an order of things in which people like him had no place. You can't demand apples from orange trees. Deluxe artisans are useless in a society dominated by the plebs. How I miss him! He and Bouilhet have left a great void in my life, and nothing can replace them. Besides, he was so good, and, whatever they say, so *simple*! He will be recognized later (if anyone ever again cares about literature) as a great poet. Meanwhile he is an absolutely unknown writer. But then, so is Pierre Corneille.

He had two hatreds. In his youth, hatred of Philistines. That gave him his talent. In his maturity, hatred of the rabble. That killed him. He died of repressed rage, of fury at being unable to speak his mind. He was *stifled* by Girardin, by Turgan, Fould, Dalloz.[1] And by the present Republic. I tell you this because I have seen some abominable things, and because I was perhaps the only man in whom he confided fully. He lacked the quality that is most important in life – for oneself as well as for others: *character*. His failure to be elected to the Academy was a real source of grief to him. What weakness! What lack of self-esteem! To seek an honour, no matter what, seems to me an act of incomprehensible humility!

That I missed the funeral was due to Catulle Mendès,[2] who sent me a telegram too late. There was a great crowd. A lot of idiots and rascals came to show off, as usual; and today being Monday, the day for theatre news in the papers, there will certainly be articles. He will make 'good copy'.

To sum up, I don't pity him: *I envy him*. For, frankly, life is not much fun.

No, I do not think of happiness as being attainable – but tranquillity, yes. That's why I keep away from what irritates me. I am unsociable; therefore I flee Society, and find myself the better for doing so. A trip to Paris is a great undertaking for me, these days. As soon as I shake the bottle, the dregs rise and spoil everything. The slightest discussion with anyone at all exasperates me, because I find everybody idiotic. My sense of justice is continually outraged. All talk is of politics – and *such* talk! Where is there the least sign of an idea? What is there to hold on to? What cause is there to be passionate about?

Still, I don't consider myself a monster of egoism. My *me* is so dispersed in my books that I spend whole days unaware of it. I have had bad moments, it's true. But I pull myself together by reminding myself that at least nobody is bothering me – and soon I'm back on my feet. All in all, it seems to me that I'm following my natural path. Doesn't that mean I'm doing the right thing?

As for living with a woman, marrying, as you advise, it's a prospect I find fantastic. Why? *I have no idea.* But that's how it is. Perhaps you can explain. The feminine being has never fitted in with my existence. And then I'm not rich enough. And then, and then . . . Besides, I'm too old. And also too decent to inflict my person on another in perpetuity. Deep down, there is something of the priest in me that no one senses. We'll go into all this much better in conversation than in a letter.

I'll see you in Paris in December. But in Paris one is constantly disturbed by 'the Others'. I wish you 300 performances of *Mademoiselle de Quintanie.* But you'll have a lot of trouble with the Odéon. It's an odious place: I suffered horribly there last winter. Every time I've undertaken to lead an active life I've been burned. So – enough is enough! 'Conceal your life,' says Epictetus. My entire ambition now is to avoid trouble. And by doing so I'm certain to avoid causing any to others, which is saying much.

I'm working like a madman, reading about medicine, metaphysics, politics, everything. For I'm undertaking a work of enormous scope, which will require a very long time – a prospect I like.

For the past month I've been expecting Turgenev from one week to the next. But gout constantly prevents him from coming. *Adieu, chère bon maître.* Continue to love me.[3]

1. Girardin, Dalloz and Turgan were editors of newspapers for which Gautier wrote art and theatre criticism. Achille Fould, Finance Minister under

Napoleon III, was responsible for literary pensions. Gautier was granted one (three thousand francs a year) only when decrepit, a year before his death.

2. The poet and dramatist, husband of Gautier's daughter Judith.

3. That same day, or the next, Flaubert wrote to Princesse Mathilde: 'Today I received, from Mme Sand, a letter about Théo that is very kind and contains much advice concerning myself. I'll confess to you, just between us, that her perpetual pious optimism – her peculiar brand of logic, if you will – sometimes sets my teeth on edge. I'm going to answer her with some invectives against democracy: that will relieve me.'

Gautier had been a devoted member of the princess's salon. She had helped him financially by appointing him her 'librarian', at six thousand francs a year.

~

To Ivan Turgenev

Croisset, Wednesday, [November] 13 [1872]

Your last letter touched me deeply, my dear Turgenev. Thank you for your exhortations. But alas! My ailment is incurable, I fear. Besides my personal reasons for grief (the death during the last three years of almost everyone I loved), I am appalled by the state of society. Yes, such is the case. Stupid, perhaps, but there it is. The stupidity of the public overwhelms me. Since 1870 I've become a patriot. Watching my country die, I feel that I loved her. Prussia may lay down her arms: we can destroy ourselves perfectly well without her help.

The bourgeoisie is so bewildered that it has lost all instinct to defend itself; and what will succeed it will be worse. I'm filled with the sadness that afflicted the Roman patricians of the fourth century: I feel irredeemable barbarism rising from the bowels of the earth. I hope to be gone before it carries everything away. But meanwhile it's not very gay. Never have things of the spirit counted for so little. Never has hatred for everything great been so manifest – disdain for Beauty, execration of literature.

I have always tried to live in an ivory tower, but a tide of shit is beating at its walls, threatening to undermine it. It's not a question of politics, but of the *mental state* of France. Have you seen Simon's circular, with its plan for the reform of public education? The paragraph about physical training is longer than the one about French literature. There's a significant little symptom![1]

In short, my dear friend, if *you* weren't living in Paris I'd promptly surrender my flat to my landlord. The hope of seeing you there occasionally is my only reason for keeping it on.

I can no longer talk with anyone at all without becoming furious, and everything I read by my contemporaries makes me quiver with indignation. A fine state to be in! Not that it's preventing me from preparing a book in which I'll try to spew out my bile. I'd like to talk with you about it. So, as you see, I'm not letting myself be disheartened. If I didn't work, my only course would be to jump in the river with a stone around my neck. 1870 drove many people insane, made imbeciles of others, and left others in a permanent state of rage. I'm in that last category. It's the *right* one.

Mme Sand, admirable woman that she is, is probably weary of my bad humour. I hear nothing from her or about her. When is her play to appear? Isn't it for the beginning of December? That is when I hope to pay you a visit.

Meanwhile, take care of your gout, my poor friend, and know full well that I love you.

1. Jules Simon (1814–1896) was Minister of Public Instruction under Thiers. Flaubert's forebodings, in this as in other matters, were amply justified: the ratio of sports 'coverage' to literary matter in any modern newspaper speaks for itself.

∾

Towards the end of this year there arose a situation that was to be chronic during the rest of Flaubert's life: he had to beg Caroline several times to have her husband send him money for household expenses – money of Flaubert's own, which he had unwisely given Commanville to 'manage' for him, and money from Caroline for the upkeep of the house, which was now hers. Here we find Caroline, owner of Croisset for less than a year, already making her fond uncle's heart rebel by reproaching him for careless housekeeping. See Appendix I: one begins now to feel the hand of Caroline's husband and to sense the preaching of 'wifely duty' by her Dominican counsellor. Commanville, who was beginning to have financial difficulties, must have chafed against Mme Flaubert's testamentary provision that Croisset ('expensive to maintain', as Flaubert, probably echoing the

Commanvilles, had written to George Sand) not be sold as long as Flaubert wanted to live there.

~

To his niece Caroline
[Croisset,] Tuesday, 4 o'clock [November 19, 1872]

... As to your financial letter, what was its purpose? You were right in thinking it would depress me. There is no reason to call my attention to my poverty: I think about it quite enough.

Do you expect your remarks to change my temperament? Do you think I can 'keep an eye on what my cook spends'! Suicide is sweet compared with such a prospect – there is nothing to do but sigh and resign oneself.

I still have my flat in Paris, for two and a half years. After that, I'll give it up, perforce – and that will be that. My life is abominably arid, devoid alike of pleasure and of any opportunity to open my heart. But I'm not going to carry my asceticism to the point of worrying about the cooking. Things are dreary enough as it is. *Bonsoir!* Let's say no more about it ...

~

By the following Easter Flaubert was finally willing to take time from planning *Bouvard and Pécuchet* to make his second visit to Nohant. He stayed for a week, Turgenev joining the company for the last few days. Again, George Sand's diary describes the visit.

Saturday, April 12, [1873]: Flaubert arrives during dinner ... We play dominoes. Flaubert plays well, but shows impatience. He prefers to talk, always in an emphatic manner.

Sunday, April 13 (Easter): ... [After dinner,] dancing. Flaubert puts on a skirt and tries the fandango. He is very funny, but after five minutes he is out of breath. Really, he is older than I! Always mentally exacerbated, to the detriment of his body.

Monday, April 14: Flaubert reads us his *Saint Anthony* from three to six and from nine to midnight. It is splendid.

Thursday, April 17: . . . The young people come for dinner. Turkey with truffles . . . Afterwards, dancing, singing, shouting – a headache for Flaubert, who keeps wanting everything to stop so that we can talk literature.

Friday, April 18: Flaubert talks with animation and humour, but all to do with himself. Turgenev, who is much more interesting, can hardly get a word in. They leave tomorrow.

Saturday, April 19: One lives with people's characters more than with their intelligence or greatness. I am tired, *worn out*, by my dear Flaubert. I love him very much, however, and he is admirable; but his personality is too obstreperous. He exhausts us . . . We miss Turgenev, whom we know less well, for whom we have less affection, but who is graced with real simplicity and charming goodness of heart.

Although on his return to Paris Flaubert sent Mme Sand a letter of thanks as warm and affectionate as those he had written in 1869, his behaviour this time amid the young people, the noise, and the gaiety, is eloquent of what had become one of his chief difficulties – adaptation to the habits of others. And he was aware of what was now, following the disappearances of the last few years, the short supply of another quality. He wrote to Mme Regnier: 'Mme Sand is now, with Turgenev, my only literary friend. Those two are worth a crowd of others, it is true, but something nearer the heart would not be unwelcome.'

That companionship he was beginning to find in someone much younger than himself.

Guy de Maupassant, last heard of, in the present volume, in his mother's letter to Flaubert about *Salammbô*, had visited both Flaubert and Bouilhet in 1868–1869, when he had been a boarder in his first year at the Rouen lycée. The men had talked with the boy about literature and read some of his early verse, for Maupassant's dream was to become a poet. Now he was twenty-one and recently demobilized from the quartermaster corps after a period of wartime service in the infantry. He had reluctantly obtained a clerical post in the Naval Ministry in Paris, where his father had friends. He and Flaubert saw something of each other, and Flaubert spoke of him in his answer to a letter from the young man's mother:

~

To Laure de Maupassant

Croisset, October 30, 1872

My dear Laure,

. . .

Your son is right to love me, because I feel a true friendship for him. He is witty, well read, charming – and then he is your son, my poor Alfred's nephew.

The next work I send to the printer will carry your brother's name, for I have always thought of *The Temptation of Saint Anthony* as dedicated 'to Alfred LePoittevin'. I spoke to him about this book six months before his death, and I have at last finished it, after working on it intermittently for twenty-five years. Since he is no longer here, I'd have liked to read it to you in his stead, my dear Laure. I don't know when I'll publish it: the times aren't at all propitious . . .

~

Laure de Maupassant to Flaubert

Etretat [February 1873]

I hear of you so often that I'm impelled to write and thank you with all my heart and soul. Guy is so happy to see you every Sunday, to be allowed to stay for hours, to be treated with such flattering familiarity, that all his letters tell and retell the same thing. The dear boy writes to me about what he does each day, about our friends whom he meets in Paris, about his distractions; and then invariably the chapter ends: 'but the house I like best, the place where I enjoy going more than anywhere else, is Monsieur Flaubert's.' I assure you that I do not find his words monotonous! On the contrary, I cannot describe my joy in knowing that my son is so welcomed by the best of my old friends. For don't I count for something in your graciousness to him? The nephew resembles the uncle, so you told me in Rouen; and I see, not without a mother's pride, that more intimate observation has not entirely destroyed the illusion.

If you want to please me, take a few minutes and tell me,

yourself, some of your news. And talk to me of my son; tell me whether he has read you some of his poems, and if you think they show anything beyond mere facility. You know what confidence I have in you; I will believe what you believe, I will follow your advice. If you say yes, we'll encourage the boy in his chosen path. But if you say no, we'll have him learn wig-making or some such trade. So speak frankly to your old friend.

~

To Laure de Maupassant

Paris, February 23, 1873

You have got ahead of me, my dear Laure, because for the past month I have been meaning to write to you, to send you a declaration of my affection for your son. I can't tell you how charming I find him, how intelligent, good, sensible, and witty – in short (to use a modish term), *sympathique.* Despite the difference in our ages I consider him a friend; and then he reminds me so much of our poor Alfred! Sometimes I'm really startled by the likeness, especially when he lowers his head as he has a way of doing when he recites poetry. What a man Alfred was! He remains in my memory as without peer. Not a day passes that I don't think of him. For that matter, the past, the dead (*my* dead), obsess me. Is this a sign of old age? I think so.

When shall we see each other? When can we talk about '*le Garçon*'? Won't you come with your two sons and spend a few days at Croisset? I have plenty of room for you here now; and I envy the serenity you seem to enjoy, my dear Laure, for I am becoming very sombre. The age we live in, and existence itself, weigh heavy on my shoulders. I am so disgusted with everything, and particularly with polemical literature, that I have renounced publishing. Life is no longer good for people of taste.

Even so, we must encourage your son in his predilection for poetry, because it is a noble passion, because literature can be a consolation in times of misfortune, and because he may have some talent – who knows? So far, he hasn't produced enough to make it possible for me to cast his poetic horoscope; and anyway, where is the man who can determine another's future?

I think our boy is something of an idler, not too fond of work. I should like to see him undertake something long and exacting, execrable though it might turn out to be. What he has shown me is certainly as good as anything published by the 'Parnassians' . . . With time he will acquire an originality, an individual manner of seeing and feeling (which is everything). As to the result, as to his possible 'success', what difference does it make? The principal thing in this world is to keep one's soul aloft, high above the bourgeois and democratic sloughs. The cult of Art gives one pride; no one can have enough of it. Such is my morality . . .

∽

Flaubert's renunciation of publishing was short-lived. As of January 1873, Michel Lévy's rights to *Madame Bovary* and *Salammbô* terminated. Angered by Lévy's neglect of Bouilhet's posthumous volume of verse, Flaubert sold the rights to the two novels to a new, young publisher, Georges Charpentier, who had been recommended to him by Turgenev. In December he sold him *Saint Anthony* as well, to appear in 1874.

Meanwhile he interrupted the planning of *Bouvard and Pécuchet* to prepare the staging of another of Louis Bouilhet's unfinished plays, *Le Sexe faible*. This was never produced. However, stimulated by working in the dramatic form, Flaubert composed a satirical comedy of his own, *Le Candidat*, the story of a wealthy provincial who, bored by everything except the prospect of power, sacrifices all – his wife, his daughter, and his 'honour' – to ensure his election to the Chamber of Deputies. 'Between you and me,' Flaubert wrote to Mme Roger des Genettes, 'I don't attach great importance to this work. I think it's "all right", but no more than that, and I have only two reasons for wishing it success: (1) to earn a few thousand francs, and (2) to irritate a few imbeciles.'

And he added: 'I'm now reading the aesthetics of the noble Lévesque,[1] professor at the Collège de France. What a cretin! A good fellow, and full of the best intentions. But how odd they are, the professors, as soon as they start meddling with Art!'

Léon Carvalho, director of the Théâtre du Vaudeville, was enthusiastic about *Le Candidat*. It went into rehearsal, and after several disquieting postponements finally opened on the night of March 11, 1874. It met the reception all too often reserved for the work of the novelist who has been drawn from his desk by 'the lure of the footlights'.

Mme Sand had been kept away from the première by the illness of her grandchildren at Nohant.

1. Presumably Pierre-Charles Lévesque (1736–1812), a Hellenist and historian.

~

To George Sand

[Paris,] Thursday, 10 o'clock [March 12, 1874]

Chère maître,

If ever there was a flop! People wanting to flatter me insist that the play will catch on with the general public, but I don't believe it for a second.

I know the defects of my play better than anyone. If Carvalho hadn't driven me crazy for a month making one foolish 'correction' after another (I scrubbed them all), I'd have done some retouching and changing myself that might have altered the final result. But as it was, I grew so disgusted with the whole business that I wouldn't have changed a line for a million francs. In a word, I was sunk.

Besides, it has to be said that the audience was detestable, all fops and stockbrokers who had no understanding of what words *mean.* Anything poetic they took as a joke. A poet says: 'I'm a man of the 1830s, you know: I learned to read from *Hernani* and I wanted to be Lara.'[1] That brought a roar of ironic laughter. And more of the same.

And then the public was misled by the title. They were expecting another *Rabagas.*[2] The conservatives were annoyed because I didn't attack the republicans, and the communards would have liked me to throw a few insults at the legitimists.

My actors played superbly, Saint-Germain among the rest. Delannoy, who carries the entire play, is much distressed, and I don't know how to console him. As for Cruchard,[3] he is calm, very calm. He dined very well before the performance, and after it supped even better. Menu: two dozen Ostend oysters, a bottle of iced champagne, three slices of roatsbeaf [sic], truffle salad, coffee, liqueur.

. . . I confess I'd have liked to make some money. But since my fiasco has nothing to do with art or any deep concern, I really don't give a damn. I tell myself, 'At last it's over', and feel much relieved.

The worst of all was the scandal about tickets. Note that I was given twelve orchestra seats and one box (the *Figaro* had eighteen orchestra seats and three boxes). I never even *saw* the *chef de claque*. It's almost as though the management of the Vaudeville set things up for a failure.[4] Their dream came true.

I didn't have a quarter of the seats I'd have liked to dispose of. And I bought a number – for people who then proceeded to knife me during the intervals. The 'bravos' of a few supporters were quickly drowned in a sea of 'Shhhs'. At the mention of my name after the final curtain there was some applause (for the man, not the play), together with two rounds of booing from the top gallery. Such is the truth.

This morning's minor newspapers are polite. I can't ask more of them than that.

Adieu, chère bon maître. Don't pity me. Because I don't feel myself pitiable.

.　.　.

My man said something nice as he handed me your letter this morning. Recognizing your handwriting, he sighed, and said: 'Ah, the best lady wasn't there, last night.'

Which is my sentiment precisely.

1.　The unworldly Flaubert is surprised that a boulevard (corresponding to 'Broadway' or 'West End') theatre audience should laugh at references to Romantic poetry by Hugo and Byron in the midst of a satirical comedy.
2.　A comedy by the popular Victorien Sardou, produced in 1872.
3.　Early in his acquaintance with George Sand, in reply to a burlesque letter from her, Flaubert had composed for her a six-page farcical 'Life and Works of the Reverend Father Cruchard, by the Reverend Father Cerpet of the Society of Jesus, dedicated to the Baronne Dudevant'. Father Cruchard, invented to embody some of Flaubert's characteristics, was a fashionable ecclesiastic who enjoyed hearing the confessions of beautiful society women. (A.J.)
4.　In a note to Alphonse Daudet (March 17), Flaubert says: 'Huegel, one of the administrators of the [Théâtre du] Vaudeville, *booed* me, I am assured by Peragallo [a theatrical agent].' If true, it perhaps means that some of those connected with the Vaudeville were partisans of a play by someone else, which was awaiting its turn to be produced.

~

George Sand to Flaubert

[Nohant,] Saturday [March 14, 1874]

I have passed through that ordeal about twenty-five times, and the worst is the feeling of disgust that you mention. One doesn't see one's play, one doesn't hear it, one doesn't recognize it, one doesn't care about it. Hence the philosophy with which authors who happen also to be artists accept the verdict, whatever it may be.

I already had news of the performance. The audience wasn't a good one. The subject was too close to home to be enjoyable. People don't like to see themselves as they are. There is no longer any middle ground, in the theatre, between the ideal and *dirt*. There is an audience for each of those extremes. Any study of how men and women really live and behave is offensive to people who have no principles; and since there is perhaps no other species nowadays, anything disagreeable is called boring. Well – you're not upset about it, and that's the way one has to be until the moment of requital.

I know nothing of your play, except that it is full of superior talent. (Saint-Germain[1] told me so in a letter, recently, but said he feared it might not appeal to the taste of the day.) You'll send it to me when it's printed, and I'll tell you whether it's Cruchard or the public that's mistaken. Watch the second and third nights, and see whether the different types of audience have differing reactions. That might be helpful to you.

As for tickets being given to everyone except the author, it has always been that way for me. We are too easy-going. And as for friends stabbing you in the back, it has been that way always, with everybody.[2]

I kiss you and I love you. Now be quick and take your revenge. I'm not worried about the future.

1. Gilles de Saint-Germain, the actor who played the role of the opposing candidate, was an old friend of Mme Sand's.
2. Something of this can be found in Edmond de Goncourt's *Journal* for March 12. After recording with obvious satisfaction the failure of *Le Candidat*, the behaviour of the audience, and Flaubert's pitiful attempt,

afterwards, on the deserted stage, to make a show of indifference, Goncourt adds: 'This morning, the newspapers vie with one another in trying to cushion Flaubert's fall. I thought that if it had been I who had written that play, had it been I who had that experience last night, what insults and vilification I would have been treated to in the press. And why? I lead the same exigent life as Flaubert, I have the same devotion to art . . .'

~

To George Sand

[Paris, Sunday, March 15, 1874]

Since there would have had to be a fight, and since Cruchard detests the idea of a struggle, I have withdrawn my play, even though there was five thousand francs' worth of advance sales. Too bad, but I won't have my actors hissed and booed. The second night, when I saw Delannoy come off the stage with tears in his eyes, I felt like a criminal and decided that was enough. (I'm touched by the distress of three people – Delannoy, Turgenev, and my manservant.) So it's over. I'm having the play printed; you'll receive it by the end of the week.

I'm being flayed by all parties – the *Figaro* and the *Rappel*. It's unanimous. People for whom I procured tickets either by plaguing the management or by paying for them myself are treating me like a cretin – for instance Monselet, who *asked* his paper to print an article against me. All of which leaves me untouched. Never have I been less upset. I'm astonished by my own stoicism (or pride). And when I seek the reason for this I wonder whether you, *chère maître*, aren't partly responsible. I remember the first night of *Villemer*, which was a triumph, and the first night of *Don Juan du Village*, which was a defeat. You don't know how much I admired you on those two occasions. The nobility of your character (a thing rarer even than genius) uplifted me! And I said a prayer: 'Oh! May I be like her under such circumstances!' Who knows? Was I perhaps sustained by your example? Forgive the comparison.

Well, I don't give a damn, and that's the truth.

But I regret the several thousand francs I might have earned. My little money-box is broken. I had wanted some new furniture for Croisset. Nothing doing!

My dress rehearsal was deadly. The entire Parisian press! They took everything as a joke. In your copy I'll underline the passages they pounced on.

Yesterday and the day before, those passages no longer bothered anybody. Perhaps Cruchard's pride carried him away.[1]

And they wrote articles about my house, about my slippers, and about my dog![2] They described my apartment, where they saw 'pictures and bronzes on the walls'. In fact there is nothing at all on my walls. I know that one critic was indignant with me for not paying him a call: this morning an intermediary came to tell me that, and asked, 'What answer shall I give him?' – 'Shit.' – 'But Dumas and Sardou and even Victor Hugo aren't like you.' – 'Oh, I'm quite aware of that!' – 'Well, then, don't be surprised if . . .' Etc.

Adieu, chère bon maître. Greetings to all, kisses to the little girls, and to you all my affection.

1. In the opinion of some professionals, *Le Candidat* might have succeeded had Flaubert not impulsively withdrawn it. But, as mentioned above, there were apparently those at the Vaudeville itself who were against the play, and whom Flaubert would have had to 'fight'.
2. One of the reporters wrote of 'the hermitage of Croisset', where Flaubert worked 'shut away for weeks on end, writing at night, sleeping on a rug during the day, with his big dog Salambô [sic] for company.' (A.J.)

~

The letter Mme Sand wrote to Flaubert after reading the printed text of *Le Candidat* was long, detailed, affectionate, and professional. She analysed the difficulties and pitfalls of writing for the stage (as illustrated by what she felt were the defects of his play), she described aspects of the theatrical world of which Flaubert appeared ignorant, and she encouraged him to try another play at once instead of continuing with *Bouvard and Pécuchet.* She was dubious about that novel:

I am afraid, from what you have told me about the subject, that it may be too true, too well observed, too well rendered. You have those qualities in the highest degree; and you have others – faculties of intuition, broad vision, true power, which are superior in other ways . . . You have two publics, one for *Madame Bovary*, and one for *Salammbô*. So bring them together in a theatre and make them both happy.

Flaubert took her words in good part. 'One of the most comical things of our day,' he wrote in reply, 'is the theatrical arcana. It would seem that the art of the theatre exceeds the limits of human intelligence, and that it is a mystery reserved for those who write like cab drivers. Instant success counts for more than anything else. It's a training in demoralization.'

Despite Mme Sand's urging that he persist, *Le Candidat* and his work on Bouilhet's never-produced *Sexe faible* were Flaubert's last writings for the theatre, although to the end of his life he continued to peddle his early effort, *Le Château des coeurs*, the '*féerie*' he had written with Bouilhet and d'Osmoy in 1863, before beginning *L'Éducation sentimentale*. (It too was never produced. In 1879–1880 its text was serialized in a magazine, accompanied by another supposed interview with Flaubert and illustrated with drawings, some of them by Caroline.)

However, although Flaubert never wrote another play, Mme Sand's wish that he might have a theatrical 'revenge' was fulfilled – belatedly and in another country. In 1980, 106 years after its Paris premiere, *Le Candidat*, revived in translation as *Candidato al Parlamento*, was produced in Italy by the late actor-director Tino Buazelli. Flaubert would have tasted recompense in the good notices of his play and the recognition of its timeliness – or timelessness – printed in the newspapers and magazines of Rome, Milan, and Naples. One might wish to have heard comment from him on the easy acceptance by Italian reviewers of his scathing picture of political corruption. Whatever the technical faults of his dramatic satire, Italians of 1980 – less hypocritical perhaps than the French of 1874 – enjoyed its amusing realism.[1]

The Temptation of Saint Anthony was published by Charpentier on March 31, 1874. This third and definitive version (the only one commonly known) is one-third the length of the original composition which Flaubert had read aloud (for thirty-two hours, according to DuCamp) to Louis Bouilhet and Maxime DuCamp before setting out for Egypt in 1849. Most of that version had remained in manuscript following its condemnation by Flaubert's two friends. The definitive version of twenty-five years later incorporates, with some changes, the portions published in Théophile Gautier's magazine *L'Artiste* in 1857.[2]

Sales began well: the first edition of two thousand copies was gone in three weeks – 'Charpentier,' Flaubert wrote, 'is rubbing his hands.' But soon a political crisis involving President MacMahon distracted public attention; the book trade suffered; and meanwhile the journalistic critics were giving *Saint Anthony* their usual kind attention.

1. Two other revivals of *Le Candidat* are mentioned in the *Enciclopedia dello Spettacolo:* by Antoine, for a single night, April 20, 1910, at the Odéon in Paris; and a German 'adaptation' in 1914. The latter was by Karl Sternheim, who, according to the same encyclopedia, after writing a farce called *J. P. Morgan,* produced in 1931 the 'first, pallid satire of Nazism', *Aut Caesar aut nihil,* and soon thereafter was lucky enough to leave his country alive.

2. For the story of the reading of the first *Saint Anthony* to Bouilhet and DuCamp, see Volume I, p. 142, and the present translator's *Flaubert and Madame Bovary.* To say that *Saint Anthony* was of capital importance to Flaubert is an understatement: he called it 'the work of my entire life', and the correspondence contains innumerable references to its prolonged composition. However, the publication and reception of the final version are but briefly referred to in the letters. Readers interested in the peculiar complexity of its content are referred to the recent translation and study by Kitty Mrosovsky listed in Works of Related Interest.

    Literary scholars have always been fascinated by the several versions of *Saint Anthony,* and articles about it abound in international literary journals. One of the early articles on Flaubert to appear in a language other than French was that by George Saintsbury, in *The Fortnightly Review* (London) for 1 April 1878, in which *Saint Anthony* is praised as 'the highest expression of dream literature'. Flaubert was very pleased by the trans-Channel attention. To Mme Roger des Genettes, on September 1, 1878, he wrote: 'In *The Fortnightly Review* for last May 1 [sic] I read an article by a son of Albion which was really marvellous.' And he quoted a line (of verse?): '*C'est du nord aujourd'hui que nous vient la lumière.*' Or, as a contemporary son of Albion put it: 'But westward, look, the land is bright!' (For the French quotation, the offer made on p. 448, n. 1 is repeated here.)

    In his letters Flaubert had always displayed a particular relish for his work on *Saint Anthony,* both in the research and the writing – a double refuge, as *Salammbô* had been, from the modern world, which had grown even grimmer of late. After resurrecting the manuscript from its wartime grave in 1871, he had written about it to Princesse Mathilde: 'In order not to think about [the condition of France], I've gone back to work furiously. I'm happy to be home again, and I continue, as before, to turn sentences. It's just as innocent and useful as turning napkin rings' – a reference to Binet at his lathe in *Madame Bovary.* His total reading in preparation for *Saint Anthony* was probably even more extensive than that for *Salammbô.* The final manuscript was almost indecipherable, so dense was the re-writing. 'The faces of the copyists had to be seen to be believed, such was their bewilderment and exhaustion,' he wrote Caroline. 'They told me the job made them physically sick and that it was "too much for them".' And later, to Mme Sand: 'I won't hide from you that I had a very sad quarter of an hour when the final proofs began to arrive. It's painful to take leave of an old companion!'

~

To Madame Roger des Genettes

Paris, May 1, 1874

... The symphony is complete. Not one of the newspapers fails in its mission ... My God, are they stupid! What asses! Underneath it all I sense personal hatred. Why? And to whom have I done wrong? It can all be explained by one word: I *annoy*; and I annoy even less by my pen than by my character; my isolation (which is both natural and deliberate) being taken as a sign of disdain ...

~

To George Sand

[Paris,] Friday night, May 1, 1874

Chère maître,

'All goes well!' The insults are piling up! It's a concerto, a symphony, with all the instruments playing full blast. I've been torn to pieces by everything from the *Figaro* to the *Revue des Deux Mondes,* including the *Gazette de France* and the *Constitutionnel.* And it's not over yet. Barbey d'Aurevilly insulted me personally, and the generous René Saint-Taillandier, saying I'm 'unreadable', ascribes to me ridiculous expressions I have never used. So much for what's in print. What's being said is more of the same. Saint-Victor tore into me at the Brébant dinner (out of servility to Michel Lévy, perhaps?), as did Charles-Edmond, etc., etc. On the other hand, I'm admired by the professors of the faculty of theology at Strasbourg, by Renan, by *Père* Didon, and by the cashier at my butcher's. Not to mention a few others. Such is the truth.

What comes as a surprise is the hatred underlying much of this criticism – hatred for me, for my person – deliberate denigration; and I keep looking for the reason. I don't feel hurt. But this avalanche of abuse does depress me. One would rather inspire good feelings than bad. However, I no longer think about *Saint Anthony* – it's over and done with.

This summer I'm going to set to work on another book of the same brand, after which I'll go back to novels pure and simple. I have two or three in my head that I'd very much like to write before I die.[1] Just now I'm spending my days in the Bibliothèque [Nationale], making quantities of notes. In a fortnight I'll return to my house in the country. In July I'm going to decongest myself on a Swiss mountaintop, following the advice of Dr Hardy, who calls me 'a hysterical woman' – an observation I find profound.

Turgenev leaves next week for Russia. The trip will interrupt his picture-buying mania: our friend now spends all his time in the auction rooms. He is a man of passions: so much the better for him. I greatly missed you chez Mme Viardot, two weeks ago. She sang arias from *Iphigenia in Aulis*. I can't tell you how beautiful it was – soul-stirring, utterly sublime. What an artist that woman is! What an artist! Such emotions console one for existing . . .

---

1. *Saint Anthony* and *Bouvard and Pécuchet* are books 'of the same brand' in that in each of them Flaubert uses a series of 'situations' as a vehicle for the exposition of ideas – chiefly religious in the one, chiefly scientific in the other, and, in both, social and philosophical as well. In this those two books differ from the 'straight novels', *Madame Bovary* and *L'Éducation sentimentale*.

From Flaubert's correspondence and notebooks we know some of the books he had 'in his head' and never wrote: *Under Napoleon III* (or, *A Parisian Household*, as he later decided to call it), *Harel-Bey* (about the Near East) and *Thermopylae*.

～

Among the 'others' who admired *The Temptation of Saint Anthony* was Victor Hugo, who wrote to Flaubert on April 5:

> A philosopher who is an enchanter: that is what you are. Your book is dense as a forest. I love this darkness and this clarity. Sublime thought and great prose are the two things dear to me; I find them in you. I am reading you and shall re-read you. Until soon: I shall come to see you.
>
> Your friend,
Victor Hugo

Flaubert's letters in these later years mention a number of meetings with Hugo, the hero of his youth whom he still immensely admired 'except when he talks politics to a gallery'. 'The men in my profession are so little of my profession!' Flaubert wrote to George Sand on December 2, 1874. 'There is scarcely anyone except Victor Hugo with whom I can talk about what interests me. Two days ago he quoted to me by heart from Boileau and Tacitus. It was like receiving some gift, the thing is so rare. On the days when there are no politicians with him he is an adorable man.'

There was also a letter from Taine, characteristically if legitimately pedantic (Flaubert had given the gods Roman names rather than Greek, whereas the historic St Anthony, although living in Roman times, spoke only Greek, and so on), but his verdict was in general favourable. He was cautiously impressed by Flaubert's Queen of Sheba: 'Very titillating . . . I am sure that for her moral and physical type, and for her costume, you have authorities, or at least documents, things to go by?'

～

TO IVAN TURGENEV

Kaltbad, Rigi, Switzerland, Thursday, July 2, 1874

I am hot, too,[1] and my condition is superior, or inferior, to yours in that I'm colossally bored. I came here as an act of obedience, having been told that the pure mountain air would un-redden my face and calm my nerves. So be it. But so far, I'm aware only of immense boredom, due to solitude and idleness; besides, I'm no man of Nature – her 'wonders' move me less than those of Art.[2] She overwhelms me, without inspiring me with any 'great thoughts'. I feel like telling her: 'All right, all right, I just left you, I'll be back with you in a few minutes; leave me alone, I need other kinds of amusement.'

Besides, the Alps are out of scale with our little selves. They're too big to be useful to us. This is the third time they have had a disagreeable effect on me; I hope it may be the last. And then my fellow vacationers – the honourable foreigners living in this hotel! All Germans or English, equipped with walking sticks and field glasses. Yesterday I was tempted to kiss three calves that I met in a meadow, out of sheer humanity and a need to be demonstrative. My trip got off to a bad start – at Lucerne I had a tooth extracted by one of the local artists. A week before leaving for Switzerland I made a tour in the Orne and Calvados, where I finally found the place to settle my two characters. I'm impatient to get started on this book, which terrifies me cruelly in advance.

You mention *Saint Antoine*, saying it hasn't found favour with the general public. I knew in advance that this would be so, but I expected to be more widely understood by the elite. Had it not been for Drumont and Pelletan, I shouldn't have had a single favourable review. As yet I've seen none from Germany. But we're in God's hands; what's done is done, and as long as *you* like the book I'm amply rewarded. Popular success has deserted me since *Salammbô*. What I cannot reconcile myself to is the failure of *L'Éducation sentimentale*; the utter lack of understanding that greeted it astonishes me.

Last Thursday I saw Zola, who gave me your news (your letter of the seventeenth arrived the next day). Apart from you and me, no one has spoken to him about *La Conquête de Plassans*, and he hasn't had a single review, either for or against. The times are hard for the Muses . . .

1. Turgenev had written to him from 'Spasskoié, Gov't. d'Orel, ville de Mtensk, June 17 (June 5 Russian calendar)', that the temperature was 16 degrees (Réaumur: about 75 Fahrenheit).
2. 'I'd give all the glaciers for the Vatican Museum,' he wrote to George Sand a day or two later.

❧

On July 12 Turgenev, still in Russia, wrote to him about *Bouvard and Pécuchet*, which they had discussed earlier: 'The more I consider it, the more I think it's a subject to treat *presto*, à la Swift or à la Voltaire. You know that was always my opinion. As you described it to me, your plot seemed charming and funny. But if you overdo it, or fill it with too much learning . . .?'

❧

To Ivan Turgenev
Dieppe, Wednesday, July 25 [really July 29, 1874]
My dear Turgenev
    I shall be back at Croisset on Friday, the day after tomorrow, and on Saturday, August 1, I'll at last begin *Bouvard and Pécuchet*. I have made the vow. There's no more turning back. But such terror as I feel! Such dread! It seems as though I'm embarking on an immensely long journey towards unknown shores, and that I'll not return.
    Despite the enormous respect I have for your critical sense (for in your case the Judge is on the same level as the Creator – which is saying not a little), I am not at all of your opinion as to the way of handling this subject. If it were to be treated briefly, made concise and light, it would be a fantasy – more or less witty, but without weight or plausibility; whereas if I give it detail and development I'll seem to be believing my own story, and it can be made into something serious and even formidable. The great danger is monotony and boredom. That is what frightens me – and yet, there will always be time to compress and cut. Besides, I can never write anything short. I'm unable to expound an idea without pursuing it to the end.

·   ·   ·

Politics is becoming incomprehensible in its stupidity. I don't expect the dissolution of the Chamber. Speaking of politics, in Geneva I saw something very curious: the restaurant run by old Gaillard, the shoemaker and ex-general of the Commune. I'll describe it to you when I see you. It's a world in itself, the world democracy dreams of and that I'll never see, thank God. The things that will hold the centre of the stage during the next two or three hundred years are enough to make a man of taste vomit. It's time to disappear . . .

~

To his niece Caroline

Thursday, 3 o'clock [August 6, 1874]

It was in obedience to your command, dear Loulou, that I sent you the first sentence of *Bouvard and Pécuchet*. But since you refer to it, or rather exalt it, as a 'holy relic', and since one mustn't adore relics that are false, please be informed that the one you possess is no longer authentic. Here is the real one: '*Comme il faisait une chaleur de 33 degrés, le boulevard Bourdon se trouvait absolument désert.*'[1]

So much for that, and you won't know a word more for a long time to come. I'm floundering, scratching out, feeling generally desperate. Last night it all gave me a violent stomach upset.[2] But it will go ahead now: it *must*. Yet this book is fearsome in its difficulties. It may well be the end of me. The important thing is that it will keep me busy for years. As long as one is working, one doesn't think about one's wretched self.

There's nothing more to tell you. I live in solitude, like a quiet little old hermit, with Julio my only company. And speaking of quiet, Fortin[3] is of the opinion that I seem calmer and in better shape. That's possible, but I think Switzerland had the effect of making me a bit stupid: the first step towards becoming a right-thinking member of society.

·   ·   ·

In your last letter you wrote me something sublime: 'I never let anyone touch my beloved volumes of the ancients.' Since you were referring to Seneca, it made me think of Montaigne saying 'An insult to Seneca is an insult to myself.'

1. 'Because the heat had reached 33 degrees, the Boulevard Bourdon was absolutely deserted.' The revised, authentic 'holy relic' remains the opening sentence of the novel. Thirty-three degrees (Celsius) is 91.4 degrees Fahrenheit.

2. Writers, especially those beginning novels, will recognize the symptoms. A month later, Flaubert would again be suffering: 'Since Thursday morning I've been prey to an abominable colic – I can hardly stand on my feet. I do nothing but go upstairs and down again. If I'm not better by Monday I'll employ some energetic methods. This indisposition is so wearing that yesterday I slept for fourteen hours, and last night for twelve.' Anything to stay away from the desk – which remains, nevertheless, the only place one wants to be.

3. According to his obituary in *La Chronique Médicale* (a bi-monthly medical review) for February 1, 1903, [Edouard] Fortin (1831–1902) had served as doctor with the French navy and lived for a time in Peru, before taking up residence at Croisset. Flaubert refers to him (see p. 657) as 'a simple health officer'. (An *officier de santé* was a licensed medical man without an MD degree, who could practise within certain legal limitations. The category was abolished in 1892.) The obituary, in which he is given the title 'Doctor', states: 'Although a simple *médicin de campagne*, Fortin was, we are told, an excellent clinician, of sure judgement and great good sense.'

∾

To Monsieur X—

Croisset, near Rouen, March 17, 1875

I cannot possibly grant your request. On several previous occasions I have already refused to allow *Madame Bovary* to be turned into a play. I think the idea a poor one. *Madame Bovary* is not a subject for the stage.[1]

With all my regrets, believe me
Cordially yours,

1. The various dramatizations that have been made of *Madame Bovary,* for both cinema and stage, are all interesting – in showing how right Flaubert was. It has also been given on television.

~

To Madame Roger des Genettes

Paris, Thursday [April 1875]

. . .

My health is deteriorating. As to what's wrong with me, I have no idea, nor has anybody else – the term 'neurosis' expressing both a number of different phenomena, and ignorance on the part of physicians. They advise me to rest. But why rest? To relax, to avoid solitude, etc., a lot of unattainable goals. I know of only one remedy: time! And besides, I'm bored thinking about myself. If after one month at Croisset I don't feel in better form I'll use Charles XII's remedy and take to my bed for six.

Judging from the way I sleep – ten to twelve hours a night – I have probably done some damage to my brain. Is it beginning to soften, do you suppose? Bouvard and Pécuchet occupy me to such a point that I have become them. Their stupidity is mine, and I'm dying of it. Perhaps that's the explanation.

One has to be under a curse to think up such a book! I've at last finished the first chapter and prepared the second, which will include Chemistry, Medicine, and Geology – all that in no more than thirty pages! and with some secondary characters, for there must be a pretence at action, a kind of continuous story so that the thing doesn't seem like a philosophical dissertation. What makes me desperate is that I no longer believe in my book. The prospect of its difficulties depresses me in advance. It has become a chore for me.

. . .

~

Readers by now familiar with Flaubert's modes of expression in the correspondence will scarcely have to be told that those lines constitute an announcement that the book was progressing.

And then it was harshly interrupted. For that spring there came the crisis in Ernest Commanville's business affairs described in Appendix I. The correspondence for the following months, both before and after Flaubert's imprudent sale of his property at Deauville for the Commanvilles' benefit, contains one agonized letter after another to Caroline. Flaubert finally confided his circumstances to a few friends. Turgenev, back from Russia and staying with his friends the Viardots near Paris, had written, suggesting that he pay a long-deferred visit to Croisset.

~

To Ivan Turgenev

[Croisset, Friday,] July 30 [1875]

My last letter was 'lugubrious', you say, my dear friend. But I have cause to be lugubrious, for I must tell you the truth: my nephew Commanville is *absolutely ruined*! And I myself am going to be very badly affected as a result.

What makes me desperate is the situation of my poor niece. My (paternal) heart suffers for her. Sad days are beginning: lack of money, humiliation, lives upset. *Everything* is bad, and my brain no longer functions. I feel that from now on I'll be capable of nothing whatever. I'll not recover from this, my dear friend. I'm stricken to the core.

Such days as we're passing through! I don't want you to share in them, so we must postpone the visit you suggest in your letter of yesterday. We cannot have you here just now. And yet God knows that an embrace from my old Turgenev would lighten my heart!

I don't yet know whether I'll go to Concarneau.[1] In any case, it won't be for a month or six weeks yet.

For a very long time now I haven't written to Mme Sand. Tell her I think of her more than ever. But I haven't the strength to write to her.

We'll have to gather our wreckage together. It will be a long business. What shall we be left with? Not much. That's what is clearest of all. Nevertheless, I hope to be able to keep Croisset. But the good days are gone, and my only prospect is a lamentable old age. The best thing that could happen to me would be to die.

Such is my selfishness that I haven't said a word about you. I am aware of it. Why don't I have your troubles?[2] I don't wish mine on anyone.

Give me your news, and always love your

Gustave Flaubert

1. Flaubert had planned to go – and in mid-September he would go – to rest at Concarneau in Brittany, where his friend Dr Georges Pouchet (1833–1894) was director of the Laboratory of Marine Biology, a branch of the Museum of Natural History in Paris. In 1879 Pouchet would be named professor of comparative anatomy at the Museum. His father, Dr Felix-Archimède Pouchet, also a naturalist, held theories of spontaneous generation which brought him into celebrated conflict with Pasteur.

2. This is probably a reference to Turgenev's gout, which on several occasions kept him from visiting Croisset.

~

IVAN TURGENEV TO GEORGE SAND

Bougival, near Paris, Friday, August 13, [18]75

Dear Madame Sand

.   .   .

All goes well here, but there is another friend who finds himself just now in a cruel situation – Flaubert, whose letter I enclose. I reproach myself all the more for not having written to you for so long when you see that he never stops thinking of you . . . A letter from you would be a great boon to him. And when I think that I have kept his letter for ten days, ah! truly, I am furious with myself for my indolence and selfishness. I well know that in everything Flaubert says there is the involuntary exaggeration of an impression-able and nervous man, accustomed to an easy, unfettered life; still, I feel that he has indeed been stricken, perhaps even more deeply than he realizes. He has tenacity without energy, just as he has self-esteem without vanity. Misfortune enters into his soul as into so much butter. I have twice asked him to let me visit him at Croisset, and he has refused. In a more recent letter to me he speaks [again] of the mortal wound he has suffered.

.   .   .

~

TO AGÉNOR BARDOUX

Croisset, near Rouen, August 29, [1875]

Mon cher ami,

I cannot tell you how deeply moved I was by what Raoul Duval told me – by what you and he propose.[1] No one could have better friends than the two of you. That you should take the initiative in offering such help makes it doubly precious. But, my dear friend, I ask you to be the judge: were you in my place you would not accept it.

The disaster that has overtaken me is of no concern to the public. It was up to me to manage my affairs better, and I don't think I should be fed from public funds. Remember: such a pension would be published, printed, and perhaps attacked in the press and in the Assembly. What could I – we – reply? Others enjoy this favour, it's true; but what is permitted to others is forbidden to me. Besides, God be thanked, I haven't yet reached *that* point! However, since my life is going to be restricted, if you can find me a post worth three or four thousand francs in a library, along with lodging (such as exists at the Mazarine or the Arsenal), I think that would be good for me. We might think about it and keep our eyes open . . .

For the past four months my poor niece and I have been living in hell. I think that bankruptcy will be avoided. Honour will be safe. But nothing more than that. So, my dear friend: it is understood: do not ask for a pension for me. Because, frankly, *I cannot accept it*. But if you were to find an advantageous sinecure, it would be different. Thank you again for what you have done for me.

1. Flaubert's friends Agénor Bardoux and Raoul Duval were deputies in the National Assembly, the latter from Flaubert's *département*, the Seine-Infér-ieure. Learning of Flaubert's financial difficulties, they had proposed asking the proper ministry that he be granted a government pension. (Duval had already consented, along with Edmond Laporte, to be a guarantor of sums pledged to Commanville's creditors by Caroline. See Appendix IV.) The pension was a form of aid frequently extended to needy men of distinction in various fields: in the case of a man of letters, the grantor would be the Ministry of Education. Flaubert expresses his preference for a government *post*: even a sinecure seems to him more respectable than a dole. The question was to arise again a few years later.

To his niece Caroline

Concarneau, Saturday, 3 o'clock
[September 25, 1875]

Am I going to have a letter from my poor little girl today?

Watch as I may the fish in the aquarium, and stare as I may at the sea, with a walk and a swim every day, I never stop worrying about the future. What a nightmare! Ah! Your poor husband wasn't born to make me happy. But no more of that: what's the use? I assure you I'm being very reasonable. I have even tried to begin something short: I've written (in three days!) half a page of the outline of *The Legend of Saint Julian the Hospitaller.* If you want to know about it, look at Langlois' treatise on stained glass. I'm calmer than I was – on the surface, at least; deeper down everything is quite black.

Here life is pleasantly dull. In bed before ten, up at eight or nine. I do nothing, and my idleness no longer weighs on me. Quite often I manage to think about nothing. Those are the best moments.

My windows look out on a square, with the harbour beyond. In the background are the fortifications of old Concarneau (a crenellated wall with two towers and a drawbridge). I can see the entire length of the quay, with the small boats that go sardine fishing. I have just spent an hour watching them come in, and then had a little nap. Waking up is never cheerful: what a twinge when reality takes over!

Pennetier left us two days ago, and now I'm alone with Pouchet. Such a good fellow, and so self-assured! I envy him that: *I* feel uprooted, like a mass of dead seaweed tossed here and there in the waves.[1]

.   .   .

Here he is, come to get me for our swim – it's our usual time. But the weather seems to be chillier, and the tide is too low. I think I may renege.

6.30

I did renege. It was too chilly. But I enjoyed a splendid sunset. A real Claude Lorrain. Why weren't you here, poor girl, you who love nature so! I was thinking how nice it would be to have you beside me there on the beach, with your easel, hurrying to paint the clouds while they were at their best . . .

1.	When next writing to Caroline, Flaubert would use another image taken from his stay at Concarneau with the naturalist Pouchet: 'Despite your advice, I can't succeed in "hardening myself", dear child. My sensitivities are all aquiver – my nerves and my brain are sick, very sick; I feel them to be so. But there I go, complaining again, and I don't want to distress you. I'll confine myself to your mention of a "rock". Know, then, that very old granite sometimes turns into layers of clay. I have seen some examples of it here, which Pouchet has pointed out to me . . .'

One of the things Caroline had urged him to 'harden himself' to was the sale, for the Commanvilles' benefit, of his last remaining property, a large farm at Deauville called La Cour Bénouville – land forming part of the present racecourse – which he had inherited from his mother. It brought 200,000 francs. 'Yes, the two days at Deauville were hard,' he wrote to Caroline on September 18 from Concarneau, 'but I stood them well: I had the strength not to show what I was feeling.' Of this sacrifice Jacques Suffel has written (*Gustave Flaubert*, Paris Éditions A.-G. Nizet, 1979): 'The gesture was generous, but absurd, because he ruined himself, whereas nothing forced him to do this, and his sacrifice did not put Commanville in the clear. The 200,000 francs brought by the farm covered only a part of the liabilities.' In other words, it would have been more practical had Flaubert let Commanville go into bankruptcy, and helped Caroline with his own income. But it was a question of 'honour'.

∾

The mention of *Saint Julian* to Caroline is the first reference to what would become Flaubert's next book – *Trois Contes* (Three Tales), of which *The Legend of Saint Julian the Hospitaller* would be one. The other two would be *Un Coeur Simple* (A Simple Heart) and *Hérodias*. The trio would refute his remark in a recent letter to Turgenev that he could never write anything short.

E.-H. Langlois, who had been Flaubert's teacher of drawing at the Rouen lycée, wrote his treatise on stained glass in 1832. René Descharmes, in his edition of Flaubert's works, notes: 'The reader will recall the last sentence in *The Legend of Saint Julian the Hospitaler*: "And that is the story of St Julian the Hospitaller, more or less as it is depicted in a stained-glass window in a church in my part of the world." The window is in the Rouen cathedral, on the left of the choir, between the left transept and the apse. Langlois' book describes it in detail, with two illustrations by Mlle Espérance Langlois.'

The Saint Julian window is still in place – or, rather, back in place following its removal before World War II and the subsequent repair of the heavily damaged cathedral. Flaubert had had the story of St Julian in mind for many years. His preparatory reading was, as usual, very wide; and the episodes of the saint's life as he recounts them in his story differ considerably from the iconography of the window[1] – a fact that, as we shall see, was later to give him a peculiar pleasure.

On receiving Turgenev's letter, George Sand had written to Flaubert at once, urging him to take heart; and she wrote also, without telling Flaubert and without immediate result, to a friend highly placed in the government, asking – as Flaubert himself had asked Bardoux – whether some sinecure might be found. Several letters passed between Flaubert and Mme Sand during these months: in one dated October 3 he told her of abandoning *Bouvard and Pécuchet*, of beginning *Saint Julian*, and of his fear of losing Croisset.

1. Benjamin F. Bart and Robert Francis Cook discuss the subject in detail in *The Legendary Sources of Flaubert's 'Saint Julian'* (see Works of Related Interest).

≈

GEORGE SAND TO FLAUBERT

Nohant, October 8, [18]75

Come, come! your health is returning in spite of yourself, since you sleep such long hours. The sea air is forcing you to live, and you have made progress: you have renounced a project that would never have been a success. Write something more down to earth that everybody can enjoy.

Tell me: how much would Croisset bring if your niece were forced to sell it? Is it just the house and garden, or is there a farm, some land? If it's not beyond my means I might buy it, and you could spend the rest of your life there. I have no money, but I'd try to shift a little capital. Do answer me seriously: if I can do it, it will be done.

≈

To George Sand

Monday [Concarneau, October 11, 1875]

Ah, *chère maître*! What a great heart you have! Your letter touched me to tears. You are adorable, simply adorable. How can I thank you? What I long to do is give you a great hug.

Well, this is how things stand. My nephew has devoured half my fortune, and with the remainder I indemnified one of his creditors who wanted to put him into receivership. Once the liquidation is completed, I hope to recover approximately the amount I have risked. From now until then, we can keep going.

Croisset belongs to my niece. We have definitely decided not to sell it except in the last extremity. It is worth a hundred thousand francs (which would bring an annual yield of five thousand), and it brings in no income, as the upkeep is expensive. Any possible income from the stables, gardens, etc. is counterbalanced by the gardener's wages and the maintenance of the buildings.

My niece's marriage contract contained a dowry stipulation, and therefore she cannot sell a piece of land unless she immediately reinvests the proceeds in property or investments. Thus, as things stand, she cannot give Croisset to me.

To help her husband, she has pledged her entire income – the only resource she has.

As you see, the situation is complicated. To live, I need six or seven thousand francs a year (at least), *and* Croisset.

I may perhaps recoup the six or seven thousand francs at the end of the winter.[1] As for Croisset, we'll decide about it later. Such is the present state of affairs. It will be a great grief to me if I have to leave this old house, so full of tender memories. And your goodwill would be powerless, I fear. Since there is no urgency at the moment, I prefer not to think about it. Like a coward, I dismiss, or rather would like to dismiss, from my mind all thoughts of the future and of 'business'. Am I fed up with it! And have been for five months – good God!

I continue to work a little, and take walks. But now it is growing cold and rainy. Still, I won't return to Paris before the eighth or tenth of November.

You approve of my abandoning my bitch of a novel. It was too much for me, I realize. And that discovery is another blow. Despite all I can do to harden myself against fate, I feel very feeble.

Thank you again, *chère bon maître*. I love you: you know that. Your old

Cruchard,

more than ever a stupid old wreck.

1. As usual, Flaubert is vague when writing about finances. He probably means that he may recover some income-producing capital if the liquidation of Commanville's assets, the sawmill and adjoining land, brings enough.

~

It was after his return from Concarneau that Flaubert's Paris Sunday afternoons became the events one reads of in literary chronicles of the period. As we have seen, they had begun in a small way in the boulevard du Temple and continued in the rue Murillo; now his visitors came to the unfashionable end of the rue du Faubourg Saint-Honoré, where his reduced circumstances had brought him. Here, a few Sundays a year, he took concentrated 'revenge' on the long solitudes at Croisset. Despite his lament to George Sand that the death of Gautier had left him with no artist to talk to, and despite his dissatisfaction with 'realists' and 'naturalists' – indeed with almost everybody – Flaubert enjoyed his Paris Sundays: for one thing, they made him forget, for a while, the financial cares the Commanvilles had heaped on him.

'Externally my life [in Paris] has scarcely changed,' he wrote to George Sand on December 16, 1875. 'I see the same people, have the same visitors. My Sunday regulars are, first, the great Turgenev, who is nicer than ever, Zola, Alphonse Daudet, and Goncourt. You have never spoken to me about Zola and Daudet. What do you think of their books? . . . I read nothing at all, except Shakespeare, whom I'm going through again from first to last. How he reinvigorates one, puts air into the lungs as though one were atop a high mountain! Everything seems mediocre beside this prodigy . . .'

There were many other guests at Flaubert's sometimes crowded Sundays, among them Guy de Maupassant, as yet unpublished and still a clerk in the Naval Ministry. Later, Maupassant chronicled Flaubert's 'receptions':

He received his friends on Sunday from one to seven, in a very simple fifth-floor bachelor apartment. The walls were bare and the furniture modest, for he detested artistic fripperies. As soon as a peal of the bell announced the first visitor he covered the papers on his work table with a piece of red silk, thus concealing his tools, sacred for him as objects of worship for a priest. Then, his servant always being free on Sunday, he opened the door himself.

The first to arrive was often Ivan Turgenev, whom he embraced like a brother. Taller even than Flaubert, the Russian novelist loved the French novelist with rare and deep affection. He would sink into an armchair and talk in a slow, pleasant voice, a trifle low and hesitant, but giving great charm and interest to his words. Flaubert listened religiously. Their conversation rarely touched on current affairs, but kept close to matters of literature and literary history. Often Turgenev brought foreign books, and translated aloud poems by Goethe, Pushkin, or Swinburne.

Others gradually arrived. Monsieur Taine, with his timid air, his eyes hidden by spectacles, brought with him historical documents, unknown facts, an aroma of ransacked archives. Here come Frédéric Baudry, Georges Pouchet, Claudius Popelin, Philippe Burty. Then Alphonse Daudet, bringing an air of Paris at its gayest, its most lively and bustling. In a few words he sketches amusing silhouettes and touches everyone and everything with his charming irony, so southern and personal; the delicacy of his wit is enhanced by the charm of his face and gestures, by the polished perfection of his anecdotes. Émile Zola comes in, breathless from the long stairs . . . He flings himself into a chair and looks about him, seeking to gauge from the guests' faces their states of mind and the tone and trend of the conversation. Then still others: the publisher Charpentier, the charming poet Catulle Mendès with his face of a sensual and seductive Christ, Émile Bergerat, his brother-in-law, who married Théophile Gautier's other daughter; José-Maria de Heredia, the marvellous maker of sonnets who will always remain one of the most exquisite poets of the age; Huysmans, Hennique, Céard, Léon Cladel the obscure and refined stylist, Gustave Toudouze. And finally, almost always the last, a tall, slender gentleman with an air of high breeding, Edmond de Goncourt.

Yet another occasional visitor was the young Henry James, climbing to Flaubert's 'small perch' – as he characteristically called it – 'far aloft, at the distant, the then almost suburban, end of the Faubourg Saint-Honoré'. James told his friend William Dean Howells that he didn't 'like the wares' of most of the French writers present; and later he wrote rather primly of their conversation.[1]

> What was discussed in that little smoke-clouded room was chiefly questions of taste, questions of art and form, and the speakers, for the most part, were in aesthetic matter, radicals of the deepest dye. It would have been late in the day to propose among them any discussion of the relation of art to morality, any question as to the degree in which a novel might or might not concern itself with the teaching of a lesson. They had settled these preliminaries long ago, and it would have been primitive and incongruous to recur to them. The conviction that held them together was the conviction that art and morality are two perfectly different things, and that the former has no more to do with the latter than it has with astronomy or embryology. The only duty of a novel was to be well written; that merit included every other of which it was capable.

In his letter to Mme Sand about his Sunday 'regulars' and about reading Shakespeare, Flaubert had said also that he was seeking a new subject for a novel, not being sure that he would ever resume *Bouvard and Pécuchet*.

1. In his introduction to W. Blaydes' translation of *Madame Bovary*, published in London in 1902 by Heineman as volume 9 in the series 'A Century of French Romance'. (A bowdlerized version of this translation of *Madame Bovary* was published in the United States in December of the same year by D. Appleton & Co., as volume 10 in the same series.) James reprinted that introduction as an essay in his volume *Notes on Novelists and Some Other Notes* (New York: Scribner's, 1914); and it was later reprinted by Leon

Edel in the United States in *The Future of the Novel* (New York: Vintage, 1956), and in England in *The House of Fiction* (London: Rupert Hart-Davis, 1957). Another essay by James on Flaubert is included in James's *French Poets and Novelists*, the most recent edition of which, with an introduction by Leon Edel, was published by Grosset and Dunlap (New York) in 1964. Both essays are expected to be reprinted shortly in a new collection edited by Mr Edel.

∼

GEORGE SAND TO FLAUBERT

[Nohant,] December 18 and 19, 1875

At last I find my old troubadour again! He was a source of grief and serious worry to me. Here you are, back on your feet, hoping for natural luck in the realm of external events and rediscovering in yourself the strength to conjure it – whatever it may turn out to be – by work . . .

What shall we do next? You, of course, will go in for *desolation*, and I for *consolation*. What our destinies depend on is unknown to me. You watch them pass, you criticize them, you abstain from any literary appraisal of them. You restrict yourself to depicting them, carefully and systematically concealing your personal feelings. Still, your writings make very clear what these are, and you depress your readers. Whereas I want to make mine less unhappy. I cannot forget that my personal victory over despair was the work of my will, and of a new way of understanding – quite the opposite of that which I had formerly.

I know that you are opposed to the intervention of personal doctrine in literature. Are you right? Isn't this a lack of conviction, rather than a principle of aesthetics? If one has a philosophy in one's soul it is bound to manifest itself. I have no literary advice to give you, I pass no judgement on the writer friends you speak of. I told the Goncourts myself everything I thought. As for the others, I fully believe they are better educated and more talented than I. Only I think that they, and you especially, lack a well-defined and large view of life. Art is not merely painting. Besides, true painting is full of the soul of whoever wields the brush. Art is not only criticism and satire. Criticism and satire paint only one face of the truth. I want to see man as he is. He is not good or bad. He is good *and* bad. But he is something more – nuance: nuance, which is for me the goal of art. Being good and bad, he possesses an internal force that makes him either very bad and slightly good, or very good and slightly bad.

It seems to me that your school is not concerned with fundamentals – that is, it stops too close to the surface. But expending its strength in the search for form, it neglects matter. It addresses itself to the well educated. But we are none of us 'well educated', properly speaking. We are human beings, first and foremost. At the heart of every story, of every fact, we seek the man. That was what was lacking in *L'Éducation sentimentale*, about which I have so often reflected, wondering why there was such dislike of a work so well done and so solid. This lack was the failure of the characters to develop: they submitted to events and never seized control of them. Well, I think the principal interest of a story is what you neglected to put into this one. For the time being you are again feeding on Shakespeare, and you are quite right. He shows men grappling with events: and please note that by his men, whether for better or worse, events are always conquered. They crush them, or crush themselves along with them.

. . .

All the dear ones around me embrace you and rejoice to learn that you are better.

~

To George Sand

[Paris, about December 31, 1875]

Chère maître,

I have given a great deal of thought to your good letter of the eighteenth, so affectionate and motherly. I have read it at least ten times, and confess I'm not sure that I understand it. Just what do you think I should do? Be more specific.

I constantly do all I can to broaden my mind, and I write according to the dictates of my heart. The rest is beyond my control.

I don't 'go in for desolation' wantonly: please believe me! But I cannot change my eyes. As for my 'lack of convictions', alas! I am only too full of convictions. I'm constantly bursting with suppressed anger and indignation. But my ideal of Art demands that the artist reveal none of this, and that he appear in his work no more than

God in nature. The man is nothing, the work everything! This discipline, which may be based on a false premise, is not easy to observe. And for me, at least, it is a kind of perpetual sacrifice that I burn on the altar of good taste. It would be very agreeable for me to say what I think, and relieve M. Gustave Flaubert's feelings by means of such utterances; but of what importance is the aforesaid gentleman?

I think as you do, *mon maître*, that Art is not merely criticism and satire. That is why I have never deliberately tried to write either one or the other. I have always endeavoured to penetrate into the essence of things and to emphasize the most general truths; and I have purposely avoided the fortuitous and the dramatic. No monsters, no heroes![1]

You say: 'I have no literary advice to give you. I pass no judgement on your writer friends, etc.' But why not? I *want* your advice; I long to hear your opinions. Who should give advice and express opinions if not you?

Speaking of my friends, you call them my 'school'. But I wreck my health trying *not* to have a school. A priori, I reject all schools. Those writers whom I often see and whom you mention admire everything that I despise, and worry very little about the things that torment me. Technical detail, factual data, historical truth, and accuracy of portrayal I regard as distinctly secondary. I aim at *beauty* above all else, whereas my companions give themselves little trouble over it. Where I am devastated by admiration or horror, they are unmoved; sentences that make me swoon seem very ordinary to them. Goncourt, for example, is very happy when he has picked up in the street some word that he can stick into a book; I am very satisfied when I have written a page without assonances or repetitions. I would willingly exchange all Gavarni's captions for a few such marvels as Victor Hugo's '*l'ombre était nuptiale, auguste et solennelle*', or Montesquieu's '*Les vices d'Alexandre étaient extrêmes comme ses vertus. Il était terrible dans sa colère. Elle le rendait cruel.*'[2]

In short, I try to think well *in order* to write well. But my aim is to write well – I don't conceal that.

I lack a 'well-defined and large view of life'. You are a thousand times right! But I ask you: how can it be otherwise? You won't illuminate my darkness – mine or anyone else's – with metaphysics.

The words Religion or Catholicism on the one hand, Progress, Fraternity, Democracy on the other, no longer satisfy the spiritual demands of our time. The brand-new dogma of Equality, preached by Radicalism, is given the lie by experimental Psychology and by History. I don't see how it is possible today to establish a new Principle, or to respect the old ones. Hence I keep seeking – without ever finding – that Idea from which all the rest must proceed.

Meanwhile I repeat to myself what Littré once said to me: 'Ah, my friend, man is an unstable compound, and the earth a very inferior planet.'

Nothing comforts me more than the hope of leaving it soon and not moving to another, which might be worse. 'I should prefer not to die,' Marat said. Ah, no! Enough of toil and trouble!

What I am now writing is a little something of no consequence, which mothers can safely recommend to their daughters. The whole thing will run to only thirty pages. It will take me another two months. Such is my verve! I will send it to you as soon as it appears – not the verve, the story . . . May 1876 be good to you all . . .

1. This, from the author of *Salammbô*.
2. 'The darkness was nuptial, august and solemn'; and 'Alexander's vices were extreme as his virtues. His anger was terrible. It made him cruel.'

∽

GEORGE SAND TO FLAUBERT

Nohant, January 12, 1876

Every day, I have wanted to write to you, and there has been absolutely no time. Here at last is a free moment: we're buried under snow. This is weather of a kind I adore: the whiteness is like a general purification, and makes the diversions inside the house all the sweeter and cosier. Can anyone hate winter in the country? The snow is one of the most beautiful sights of the year.

·   ·   ·

L'Éducation sentimentale has been a misunderstood book, as I have told you repeatedly – but you have not listened to me. There should have been a short preface, or, here and there, an expression of judgement, even if only a well-chosen adjective to condemn a wrong, to characterize a defect, to emphasize an aspiration. All the characters in this book are weak and come to nothing except those with evil instincts; that is what you are reproached with, because people didn't understand that you wanted to depict precisely a deplorable society, which encourages those bad instincts and destroys noble aspirations. When people don't understand our work, it is always our fault. What the reader wants, above all, is to penetrate our thought, and that is what you arrogantly deny him. He thinks you scorn him and want to mock him. I understood you, because I knew you. If I'd been given your book without your name on it, I'd have thought it splendid, but strange, and I'd have asked myself whether you were immoral, sceptical, indifferent, or heartbroken. You say that that's how it should be, and that M. Flaubert would violate the rules of good taste if he were to reveal his opinions and the aim of his book. That is false – utterly false. When M. Flaubert writes well and seriously, one sympathizes with him and is ready to sink or swim with him. If he leaves you in doubt, you lose interest in his work, you skim over it, or put it down.

I have already challenged your favourite heresy, which is that one writes for twenty intelligent people and doesn't care a fig for the rest. That is not true, since you yourself are irritated and troubled by lack of success. Moreover, there haven't been even twenty reviews favourable to this book which was so well written and so important. So one mustn't write for twenty persons any more than for three, or for a hundred thousand. One must write for all those who have a thirst to read and can profit from good reading. Then the writer must exhibit his own highest moral principles, and not make a mystery of the moral and beneficent meaning of his book. In *Madame Bovary,* people perceived what that was. If one part of the public cried scandal, the healthier and more numerous part saw in it a severe lesson given to a woman without conscience or faith – a striking lesson to vanity, to ambition, to irrationality. They pitied her: art required that; but the lesson was clear, and it would have been more so, it would have been so for *everybody,* if you had wished it to be, if you had shown more clearly the opinion that you held, and that the public should have held, about the heroine, her husband, and her lovers.

This wish to portray things as they are, the adventures of life as they present themselves to the eye, is not well thought out, in my opinion. It's all the same to me whether one depicts inert things as a realist or as a poet; but when one touches on the emotions of the human heart, it's a different matter. You cannot detach yourself from this consideration; for you are a human being, and your readers are mankind. Your story is inevitably a conversation between you and the reader. If you show him evil coldly, without ever showing him good, he's angry. He wonders whether he is the villain, or you. What you wanted to do, however, was to rouse him and maintain his interest; and you will never succeed if you are not roused yourself, or if you conceal your emotion so effectively that he thinks you indifferent. He's right: supreme impartiality is antihuman, and a novel must above all be human. If it isn't, the public cares nothing for its being well written, well composed and well observed in every detail. The essential quality – interest – is lacking.

The reader also turns away from a book in which all the characters are good, without nuance and without weakness; he sees clearly that this, too, is not human. I believe that art, this special art of narration, is effective only through the opposition of characters; but, in their struggle, I want to see right prevail. Events may overwhelm a good man: I accept that; but let him not be soiled or diminished by them, and let him go to the stake feeling that he is happier than his executioners.

January 15, 1876

I wrote those pages three days ago, and every day I've been on the point of throwing them into the fire; for they are long and diffuse and probably useless. Natures opposed on certain points understand one another only with difficulty, and I fear you won't understand me any better today than last time. However, I send this scrawl so that you can see I'm concerned about you – almost as much as about myself.

You *must* have a success, after the bad luck that has so depressed you. What I tell you will assure that success. Retain your cult for form, but pay more attention to matter. Don't hold true virtue to be a cliché in literature. Give it its representatives; portray the honest man and the strong, along with the maniacs and dolts you so love to ridicule. Show what is substantial, what endures despite these intellectual miscarriages. In short, abandon the conventions of the realists and turn to true reality, which is a mixture of beautiful and ugly, dull and brilliant, but in which the desire for good nevertheless finds its place and its role.

I embrace you for all of us.

~

To George Sand
                              [Paris,] Sunday night [February 6, 1876]
· · ·

And now, *chère maître* – and this is in reply to your last letter – here, I think, is the essential difference between us. You, always, in whatever you do, begin with a great leap towards heaven, and then you return to earth. You start from the a priori, from theory, from the ideal. Hence your forbearing attitude towards life, your serenity, your – to use the only word for it – your greatness. I, poor wretch, remain glued to the earth, as though the soles of my shoes were made of lead: everything moves me, everything lacerates and ravages me, and I make every effort to soar. If I tried to assume your way of looking at the world as a whole, I'd become a mere laughing stock. For no matter what you preach to me, I can have no temperament other than my own. Nor any aesthetic other than the one that proceeds from it. You accuse me of 'not letting myself go' naturally. But what about discipline? What about excellence? What do we do with those? I admire Monsieur de Buffon for putting on lace cuffs before sitting down to write. That bit of elegance is a symbol. And, lastly, I try, naively, to have the widest possible sympathies. What more can be asked of anyone?

As for revealing my private opinion of the people I bring on stage, no, no! a thousand times no! I do not recognize my *right* to do so. If the reader doesn't draw from a book the moral it implies, either the reader is an imbecile or the book is false because it lacks exactitude. For the moment a thing is True, it is good. Even obscene books are immoral only if they lack truth . . .

And please note that I execrate what is commonly called 'realism', even though I'm regarded as one of its high priests.

Make what you can of all that.
· · ·

To try to please readers seems to me absolutely chimerical. I defy anyone to tell me how one 'pleases'. Success is a result; it must not be a goal. I have never sought it (though I desire it), and I seek it less and less.

. . .

I'm touched by the length of your last letter. You do love me . . .

◞

TO GEORGE SAND

[Paris,] Friday night [March 10, 1876]

You make me a little sad, *chère maître*, when you ascribe to me aesthetic opinions that are not mine.[1] I think that rounding out a sentence is nothing. But that *to write well* is everything. Because: 'Good writing implies strong feeling, accurate thinking, and effective expression.' (Buffon.)

The last term is thus dependent on the two others, since it is necessary to feel strongly in order to think, and to think in order to express. Every bourgeois can have heart and delicacy, be full of the best feelings and the greatest virtues, without for that reason becoming an artist. And finally, I believe Form and Matter to be two abstractions, two entities, neither of which ever exists without the other.

The concern for external Beauty you reproach in me is for me a *method*. When I come upon a bad assonance or a repetition in one of my sentences, I'm sure I'm floundering in the False. By dint of searching, I find the proper expression, which was always the *only* one, and which is, at the same time, harmonious. The word is never lacking when one possesses the idea.

. . .

I am writing to Zola to send you his book [*Son Excellence Eugène Rougon*]. I'll also tell Daudet to send you his *Jack*. I'm most curious to have your opinion of these two books, which are quite different in workmanship and temperament, but both very remarkable.[2]

1. 'You no longer look for anything but the well-turned sentence,' Mme Sand had written to him on March 9. 'That is something, but only something – it isn't the whole of art, It isn't even half of it; it's a quarter at most, and

when the three other quarters are fine one does without the one that is not.'
2. '*Testiculos habes, et magnos,*' were among the words of praise Flaubert had sent to Daudet about *Jack*.

≈

'I have a great deal to say about M. Zola's novels,' George Sand wrote on March 25, 'but it will be better for me to say it in an article than in a letter, because it raises a general question that should be explored when one's mind is calm and in repose.'

And she goes on to speak from what seems, under the circumstances, a mind extraordinarily 'calm and in repose':

'How are you? Turgenev tells me that your latest piece of writing is very remarkable.[1] So you're not "done for", as you claim? Your niece continues to improve, does she not? I am better, too, after stomach cramps that were enough to turn one blue, and appallingly persistent. Physical suffering is a good lesson when it leaves your mind free. You learn to endure and conquer it. Of course you have moments of discouragement, when you fling yourself on your bed; but I always think of what my old curé said to me when he had the gout: "Either it will pass away or I shall." And he laughed, enjoying his *bon mot*.'

Mme Sand's 'stomach cramps' were caused by the cancer (yet undiagnosed) that would very soon be fatal. Her letters continued to be spirited, and full of appreciation of others: 'I am enthusiastic about *Jack*, and I beg you to convey my thanks to M. Daudet. Ah, yes! He has talent and heart. How well it is all done and *seen*! I am sending you a volume of old things of mine that have just been put together.'[2]

1. *St. Julian the Hospitaller*, which Flaubert had finished on February 17. On March 15 he wrote the first page of *A Simple Heart*.
2. Alphonse Jacobs thinks that this is probably *La Coupe, Lupo Liverani, Le Toast, Garnier, Le Contrebandier*, which had been published by Calmann-Lévy on March 18. There is an inscribed copy in what remains of Flaubert's library.

≈

To George Sand

[Paris,] Monday night [April 3, 1876]

Chère maître

I received your volume this morning. I have two or three other books here that various people lent me some time ago; I'll make haste to finish them, and will read yours at the end of the week, during a little two-day trip I have to make to Pont l'Evêque and Honfleur for my *Story of a Simple Heart* – a trifle at present 'in the works', as M. Prud'homme would say.

I'm glad you liked *Jack*. It's a charming book, don't you think? If you knew the author, you would like him even more than his work. I have told him to send you *Risler* and *Tartarin*. You'll thank me after reading them, I'm sure of it.

. . . I share neither Turgenev's severity concerning *Jack* nor the 'immensity' of his admiration for *Rougon*. One has charm and the other strength. But neither is concerned *above all* with what is for me the goal of Art, namely Beauty! I remember how my heart throbbed, and what violent pleasure I experienced, when I looked at one of the walls of the Acropolis, a wall that is completely bare (the one to the left as you climb the Propylaea). Well, I wonder whether a book, quite apart from what it says, cannot produce the same effect. In the precise fitting of its parts, the rarity of its elements, the polish of its surface, the harmony of the whole, is there not an intrinsic Virtue, a kind of divine force, something eternal, like a principle? (I speak as a Platonist.) If this were not so, why should there be a relation between the right word and the musical word? Or why should great compression of thought always result in a line of poetry? Does it follow that the law of Numbers governs feelings and images, and that what seems to be outward form is actually essence? If I were to keep going very long on this track I'd find myself in a hopeless predicament. Because on the other hand Art must be humane; or rather, Art is only what we can make it. We are not free. Each of us follows his own path, willy-nilly. In short, your Cruchard no longer has a sound idea in his head.

But how hard it is to understand one another! Here are two men whom I greatly like and whom I consider true artists, Turgenev and Zola. For all that, they have no admiration whatever for the prose of Chateaubriand, and even less for Gautier's. Sentences that enrapture me seem to them hollow. Who is wrong? And how please the public, when those closest to you are so remote? All this greatly saddens me. Don't laugh . . .

∼

In the last letters they exchanged, both friends spoke of literature.

∼

GEORGE SAND TO FLAUBERT

Nohant, April 5, [18]76

. . . I have read *Fromont et Risler.* Please thank M. Daudet. Tell him I spent the night reading him, and I don't know which I prefer, *Jack* or *Risler. Risler* is very winning – I could almost say *riveting.*

I kiss you and I love you. When will you let me read some Flaubert?

∼

TO GEORGE SAND

Monday night [Paris, May 29, 1876]

· · ·

I've been hard at work lately. How I'd love to see you and read you my medieval trifle! I have begun another tale, called *Story of a Simple Heart.* But I have interrupted it to do some research on the period of John the Baptist: I want to write about Herodias' feast.

. . . You will see from my *Story of a Simple Heart* (in which you will recognize your own direct influence) that I am not as stubborn as you believe. I think you will like the moral tendency, or rather the underlying humanity, of this little work.[1]

Adieu, chère bon maître. My greetings to all.

I embrace you most tenderly.

1. 'My *Story of a Simple Heart* advances very slowly,' he had written to Mme Roger des Genettes a few weeks before. 'I've done ten pages – no more. To document it I made a little trip to Pont l'Evêque and Honfleur. This excursion plunged me into melancholy, for inevitably it was a bath of memories. How old I am, *mon Dieu!* How old!'

The touching story, inspired in part by the example of his – and his parents' – servant Julie, who was still alive, was set in parts of Normandy he had known as a child. In writing it, he seems to have taken to heart Mme Sand's urging of the previous October: 'Write something more down to earth that everybody can enjoy.' Millions have enjoyed the tale of the servant Félicité, her life of labour, and her parrot – probably Flaubert's best-known work after *Madame Bovary*.

~

George Sand died at Nohant on June 8, 1876.

~

To Mademoiselle Leroyer de Chantepie

Croisset, June 17, 1876

My dear Correspondent,

No! I had not forgotten you, because I never forget those I love. But I was surprised by your long silence, and wondered about it.

You want to know the truth about Mme Sand's last moments. It is this: she did not have any priest attend her. But as soon as she was dead, her daughter, Mme Clésinger, asked the bishop of Bourges to authorize a Catholic burial, and no one in the house (except perhaps her daughter-in-law, Mme Maurice) stood up for our poor friend's ideas. Maurice was so prostrated that he had no energy left, and then there were outside influences, miserable considerations inspired by certain bourgeois. I know no more than that. The ceremony was immensely moving: everyone was in tears, I along with the rest.

Poor Mme Sand often spoke of you to me, or rather we often spoke of you together; you interested her very much. One had to know her as I did to realize how much femininity there was in that great man, and the vast tenderness in that genius. Her name will live with a unique glory as one of the great figures of France.

· · ·

~

Another unbeliever recently given Catholic burial at family insistence was Louise Colet, Flaubert's mistress of the 1840s and 1850s, who had died on March 8, 1876.

'You understood very well all my feelings on the death of my poor Muse,' Flaubert wrote to Mme Roger des Genettes. 'This revival of her memory made me review the course of my life. But your friend has become more stoical during the past year. I have trampled on so many things, in order to stay alive! In short, after an afternoon given over to days gone by I *willed* myself to think of them no longer, and went back to work. One more thing concluded!

'The family, which is Catholic, took her to Verneuil in order to avoid civil burial, and there was no scandal. The newspapers made little mention of any of it. Do you remember the little apartment in the rue de Sèvres, and all the rest? Ah! God have mercy on us!'

'My heart is becoming a necropolis,' Flaubert wrote to Princesse Mathilde after the deaths of the two women who had played such large parts in his life.

~

To Ivan Turgenev

Croisset, Sunday evening, June 25 [1876]
. . .

The death of our poor Mme Sand grieved me immensely. I wept like a calf at her funeral, twice: the first time, when I kissed her granddaughter Aurore (whose eyes, that day, were so like hers as to be a kind of resurrection); and the second, when I saw her coffin carried past me.

There were some fine goings-on. In order not to offend 'public opinion' – the everlasting and execrable 'they' – her body was taken to the church. I will give you the details of this disgraceful business when I see you. I felt a tightening around my heart, I can tell you, and a positive desire to kill Monsieur Adrien Marx.[1] The very sight of him took away my appetite that evening at Châteauroux. Oh! The tyranny of the *Figuro*! What a public nuisance! I choke with fury when I think of those cocos . . .

You are right to mourn our friend, for she loved you dearly, and never spoke of you without calling you '*le bon* Turgenev'. But why pity her? She had everything life had to offer, and will remain a very great figure.

The good country people wept copiously around the grave. We were up to our ankles in mud in the little village cemetery, and a gentle rain was falling. Her funeral was like a chapter in one of her books.

1. A reporter for *Le Figaro*.

≈

Three Tales now advanced. 'If I have been able to get back to work,' Flaubert wrote to Maurice Sand on October 31, 1876, 'I owe it in part to your mother's good advice. She found the way to re-establish my self-esteem.'

≈

To Edmond de Goncourt

[Croisset, Sunday, December 31, 1876]

Dear old chap,

May 1877 treat you gently! and among other wishes, may *La Fille Elisa* bring you joy! . . .

Turgenev, too, has lost a good deal of money. Fate seems to be giving our little company[1] a drubbing. Poor us!

The thought that you might have to leave your pretty house in Auteuil made me tremble, for at our age habits are tyrannical: to change them is disastrous. How will you get along this year, with your income uncertain? You and I are so incapable of earning our living! It's a sign of a lofty nature, but it's not always gay.

As for my affairs, they show no improvement: they're in the doldrums. I shall be very hard up for another four years,[2] unless my nephew finds some money. But the main thing is that whatever happens I shall not be leaving Croisset, where more and more I love to be. If necessary, I'd rather give up my Paris apartment, but we've not yet reached that point. Besides, during the past year I have learned (not without effort) to stop worrying about the future. Let whatever befalls, befall: each day is sufficient unto itself.

I'm working excessively hard, though my pages fill up slowly. *Hérodias* is now at midpoint. All my efforts go into trying not to make it resemble *Salammbô*. What *will* it be? I have no idea.

I have just read Balzac's *Correspondance*. It shows him to have been a splendid man: one would have loved him. But what a concern for money, and so little love of Art! Have you noticed that he doesn't speak of it a single time? What he sought was Fame, not Beauty. And he was Catholic, legitimist, a landowner, dreaming of the Chamber of Deputies and the Academy; above all, an ignoramus, and provincial to the marrow of his bones: luxury dazzled him. His greatest literary admiration was for Walter Scott. All in all, for me a tremendous figure, but not of the very first rank. His end was lamentable! To die on the very threshold of happiness! Reading his letters was edifying, but I prefer Voltaire's correspondence: the compass spreads a bit wider there.

What more shall I tell you? I'm sturdy as an oak. Yesterday I walked in the woods for three hours. (I never take the air except when I begin to feel stifled.) And last night the moon was so beautiful that I went for a walk again, in my garden, '*à la lueur poétique de l'astre des nuits.*'[3]

Last September I had dizzy spells like yours that alarmed me. They're of no consequence: don't worry about them. Mine came, I think, from wanting to act the young man again during my last stay in Paris. (What's more, I pulled it off.)[4]

Lately I've felt really frustrated at having nobody to talk to about the Germiny case.[5] Poor fellow – I've grown fond of him. And I think France should give him an official compensation: he has kept us all entertained, and every entertainer is a benefactor. That jerking-off of one gentleman by another in a public urinal has entranced the Capital of the Civilized World for a fortnight. Neither the most beautiful works of art nor the greatest scientific discoveries ever generated such excitement when they burst upon the world. The Far Eastern situation is completely overshadowed by this worthy citizen's discharge; and the masturbation with the jeweller (a pearl!) is of greater import than the diplomatic conference at Constantinople. Every Frenchman feels himself haunted by the skin of that man's balls. We feel ourselves entangled in his hair. We're asphyxiated by the effluvia of his urine!

What can we do to rival that fellow? I might apply for a professorship in a Catholic university – but they wouldn't have me. But then I've long been a washout. What an elegy one could make of that [scene in the urinal]! 'By the murmuring stream in a sheltered nook . . .'

Adieu, I embrace you tenderly –

Your Old Reliable

1. The 'little company' probably refers '*les dîners des auteurs sifflés*' – dinners

to which were admitted only a small group of literary men, all of them friends, whose plays had been booed. 'Flaubert was included because of the failure of *Le Candidat*,' Daudet wrote in his memoirs, 'Zola for *Le Bouton de Rose*, Goncourt for *Henriette Maréchal*, and I for my *Arlésienne* . . . As for Turgenev, he swore that he had been booed in Russia, and since that was so far away we didn't bother to go and check.'

2. The reference is to the future liquidation of Commanville's assets, the sawmill and adjoining property, on which Flaubert continued to pin his hopes. This had for some reason been postponed. As we shall see, the sale would take place not in 'four years', but in 1879.

3. 'In the poetic radiance of the star of the night.' (The offer made on p. 468, n. 1 is repeated here.)

4. In the self-congratulations which sometimes appear in the correspondence following Flaubert's meetings with Juliet Herbert, no hint is ever given as to the identity of his partner.

5. 'Eugène Lebègue, comte de Germiny, a prominent Catholic layman, son of the former governor of the Banque de France, born in Paris, July 11, 1841. Appointed in 1875 secretary of the Conseil Général de la Seine. He was surprised in a scandalous attitude with a jeweller's apprentice named Chouard in a *urinoir* in the Champs Elysées [one of those with a "murmuring stream"]. When he was arrested he struck one of the policemen.' (Note in Conard edition of Flaubert's *Correspondance*, VII, 370.)

That winter Flaubert revelled in the grandeur of Renan's 'Prayer on the Acropolis': 'Incomparable,' he wrote to Turgenev, 'in its originality and moral stature.' (His Rouen friends the Lapierres, he noted, hadn't even cut the pages of the December issue of the *Revue des Deux Mondes* in which it was printed; Princesse Mathilde 'didn't understand a word of it', and even Caroline failed to appreciate it and had to be told that it 'summarized intellectual man of the nineteenth century'.)

In a letter to Caroline written the previous June he had revealed, more or less incidentally, his opinion of Stéphane Mallarmé's *L'Après-midi d'un faune*: 'I have received another present, a book from the FAUN, and this book is charming, for it's not by him. It's an oriental tale called *Vathek*, written in French at the end of the last century by an English *milord*. Mallarmé has reprinted it with a preface in which your uncle is praised.'

To *Hérodias*[1] (known especially for its description of Salomé's dance before she asks for the head of John the Baptist) Flaubert devoted historical and archaeological research as painstaking as that for *Salammbô*. It was the last of the three tales to be finished. On February 14, 1877 – 'at three in the morning', as he wrote to Madame Roger des Genettes – it was finally recopied.

During April the three stories were printed separately in newspapers. This was the first time since the incriminating and botched serialization of *Madame Bovary* in the *Revue de Paris* and the unsatisfactory appearance of parts of *Saint Anthony* in Gautier's magazine *L'Artiste* that Flaubert had allowed journals to print any of his fiction. Even now he was reluctant, but he needed the several thousand francs. Charpentier published the volume on 24 April. (Flaubert had the manuscript bound, and gave it to Edmond Laporte, whom he had been seeing more and more frequently and who had accompanied him on his excursion to find suitable backgrounds for *A Simple Heart*.) A few of the reviews were hostile, but in general even the journalistic reception was more favourable than usual: for the first time Flaubert found himself praised in *Le Figaro*, and to his astonishment the book was recommended in the catalogue of a Catholic bookshop.

It has often been remarked that the three tales reproduce the tonalities of three of the earlier books: that *A Simple Heart* is painted in the Norman colours of *Madame Bovary*, that *Saint Julian* joins *Saint Anthony* in Flaubert's hagiology, and that *Hérodias* is no less exotic than *Salammbô*. When Henri Brunetière, in *La Revue des Deux Mondes*, claimed to find in this aspect of the volume an indication that Flaubert's 'invention was flagging', he was quickly taken up by the young Jules Lemaître,[2] writing in *La Revue Bleue*. It was certainly true, Lemaître said, that 'apple trees tend to produce apples, and that from a rose bush more roses can be expected'.

Both Maurice and Lina Sand wrote to thank Flaubert for their copy of *Three Tales* – Lina, a lover of *Salammbô*, said she had been so entranced while reading *Hérodias* that 'she didn't know where she was' – and on August 28, 1877, in reply to another letter from Maurice, Flaubert wrote: 'You speak of your beloved and illustrious mother. After yourself, I think there can be no one who thinks of her more than I. How I miss her! How I need her! I began *A Simple*

Heart exclusively for her, solely to please her. She died when I was in the middle of my work. So it is with all our dreams.'

Three months later he wrote to Mme Roger des Genettes about some of these dreams:

> If I were younger and had the money, I'd return to the Orient – to study the modern Orient, the Orient of the Isthmus of Suez. A big book about that is one of my old dreams. I'd like to show a civilized man who turns barbarian, and a barbarian who becomes a civilized man – to develop that contrast between two worlds that end up by merging. But it's too late. It's the same with my *Battle of Thermopylae*. And *Monsieur le Préfet*! and many others! It's always good to hope, says Martin [in *Candide*]. Desire keeps one alive.

By now he was back at *Bouvard and Pécuchet*.

1. Flavius Josephus and the Gospels were Flaubert's chief sources for *Hérodias*. But again the Rouen cathedral provided inspiration: the sculpture over the left door of the façade, showing Salomé dancing on her hands – as Flaubert, twenty-seven years before, had seen a Nubian girl dancing on her hands at Assuan. At that time, after his Egyptian and Near Eastern travels, in Perugia with his mother, he had made a note of Perugino's fresco of scenes from the life of John the Baptist.

2. Lemaître, who would distinguish himself as a critic, was then a twenty-four-year-old professor in the lycée of Le Havre, making his first appearances in literary magazines. He and Flaubert met, and Flaubert greatly enjoyed his company. 'Jules Lemaître (from Le Havre) is coming to see me on Wednesday,' he wrote to Caroline on February 6, 1880. 'For three days I'll be "talking literature" – supreme joy! That will soothe me.'

XVI

The Last Years. Bouvard and Pécuchet

1877–1880

URING THE short time now left to him, melancholy and labour
would continue to dominate Flaubert's existence. The melancholy, general though it had long since become, would be constantly
exacerbated by events, especially by those pertaining to the Commanvilles; the present labour – the composition of *Bouvard and Pécuchet*
– was in part a product of misanthropy, and also nourished it. Yet,
from letters written in the last weeks of his life, one senses that
Flaubert's spirit was finally eased. The reasons for this, and the
constant interplay, at the time, between principle and circumstance,
give a particular tone to the last scenes of the story.

IN 1864, when he had finished *Salammbô* and was uncertain as to
whether his next novel should be a 'book of passion' or the book
about two copy-clerks, one of Flaubert's reasons for postponing
the latter was the 'frightful difficulties' he foresaw in 'varying the
monotony of the effect'. There is much comedy in *Bouvard and
Pécuchet*, but readers often do find the book intolerably monotonous;
and one suspects that many of them either close it fairly quickly or
skim through it. As a concentration of Flaubert's obsession with
human stupidity, *Bouvard and Pécuchet* has been a mine for savants
and 'explicators'. Many an opinion has been expressed as to whether
his two 'troglodytes' – Flaubert sometimes called them his two
'woodlice' – are buffoons symbolic of mankind, or sympathetic truth-
seekers, or a subtle combination of both. Flaubert himself, who in
1875 had written to Mme Roger des Genettes, 'Their stupidity is

mine, and I'm dying of it,' wrote later to Mme Brainne: 'My (secret) aim is to disconcert the reader to such a point that he goes crazy.' Connoisseurs of the absurd are among the greatest admirers of *Bouvard and Pécuchet.*

The letters that follow were written during Flaubert's struggle, against heavy odds, to complete this formidable book – which Turgenev had urged him to make 'lighter', and which George Sand had congratulated him on abandoning because it 'would never have been a success'.

On April 16, 1877, in the Restaurant Trapp near the Gare St Lazare, a dinner was given by the group of young writers who for publicity's sake had baptized themselves 'Naturalists' – Joris-Karl Huysmans, Henri Céard, Léon Hennique, Guy de Maupassant, Paul Alexis and Octave Mirbeau. The guests of honour were their admired elders – Edmond de Goncourt, Flaubert and Zola; and the menu (at least as reported in the newspapers) included '*Potage purée Bovary,*' '*Truite saumonée à la Fille Élisa,*' '*Poularde truffée à la Saint Antoine,*' '*Artichaut au coeur simple,*' and so on. Flaubert enjoyed himself that evening as he enjoyed having his young admirers attend his Sunday afternoons. But he had no respect for literary 'schools' or for the titles conferred on them. He wrote to Turgenev later that year:

> It's not just a question of seeing. One must order and combine one's perceptions. Reality, according to me, should be only a *springboard.* Our friends are convinced that in itself it constitutes all of Art. Their materialism makes me indignant, and almost every Monday I'm irritated when I read our good Zola's article [in the newspaper *Le Voltaire*]. After the Realists we have the Naturalists and the Impressionists. Such progress! A bunch of jokesters, trying to delude themselves and us into believing that they discovered the Mediterranean.

And to Mme Roger des Genettes:

> My friend Zola is becoming absurd. He wants to 'found a school', being jealous of old Hugo's fame. Success has gone to his head, so much more difficult is it to cope with good fortune

than bad. Zola's self-confidence as a critic is explained by his inconceivable ignorance. I think that there is no longer any love of Art, Art in itself. Where is there anyone who relishes a good sentence? That aristocratic pleasure is in the realm of archaeology.

His favourite among the young writers – and the only one who was an intimate friend – was causing him concern. He wrote to Turgenev in July:

> I have received a pitiful letter from my disciple, Guy de Maupassant. He is worried about his mother's health and feels ill himself. He finds the Naval Ministry, where he works, so tiresome and deadening that he can no longer write, and the 'ladies' are incapable of cheering him up. Besides, since our 'ladies' – even more than our institutions – are the envy of all Europe,[1] they are at present in such demand that it's impossible to come near them. After the Exposition there will be twenty thousand of them dead from overwork.

1. Flaubert refers to the influx of foreign visitors to the Exposition of 1878 and their enjoyment of the pleasures of 'Paree'.

∼

To Guy de Maupassant

Croisset, August 1878

Bouvard and Pécuchet keeps trotting along. Now I'm preparing the chapter on politics. I've made almost all my notes – I've been doing nothing else for the past month – and I hope to begin writing in about a fortnight. What a book! As for expecting that the public will read a work like this – what madness!

· · ·

Now let's talk about you. You complain about fucking being 'monotonous'. There's a very simple remedy: stop doing it. 'The news in the papers is always the same,' you say. That is a Realist's complaint, and besides, what do you know about it? You should scrutinize things more closely. Have you ever believed in the existence of things? Isn't everything an illusion? Only so-called relations – that is, our ways of perceiving objects – are true. 'The vices are trivial,' you say; but everything is trivial! 'There are not enough different ways to compose a sentence.' Seek and ye shall find.

Come now, my dear friend: you seem badly troubled, and that distresses me, for you could spend your time more agreeably. You *must* – do you hear me, young man? – you *must* work more than you do. I've come to suspect you of being something of a loafer. Too many whores! Too much rowing! Too much exercise! Yes, sir: civilized man doesn't need as much locomotion as the doctors pretend. You were born to write poetry: write it![1] *All the rest is futile* – beginning with your fun and your health: get that into your head. Besides, your health will be the better for your following your calling. That remark is philosophically, or, rather, hygienically, profound.

You are living in an inferno of shit, I know, and I pity you from the bottom of my heart. But from five in the evening to ten in the morning all your time can be devoted to the muse, who is still the best bitch of all. Come, my dear fellow, chin up. What's the use of constantly probing your melancholy? You must set yourself up as a strong man in your own eyes: that's the way to become one. A little more pride, damn it! . . . What you lack are 'principles'. Say what you will, one has to have them; it remains to find out which ones. For an artist there is only one: sacrifice everything to Art. Life must be considered by the artist as a means, nothing more, and the first person he shouldn't give a hang about is himself.

. . . Let me sum up, my dear Guy: beware of melancholy. It's a vice. You take pleasure in affliction, and then, when affliction has passed, you find yourself dazed and deadened, for you have used up precious strength. And then you have regrets, but it's too late. Have faith in the experience of a sheik to whom no folly is unknown! *Je vous embrasse tendrement . . .*

1. It is not clear whether, at this time, Flaubert really thought Maupassant's gift was for poetry, or whether he encouraged him to write verse chiefly as a means to improve his prose. Maupassant had already had two stories printed in obscure publications.

    Very soon after writing the present letter to Maupassant (in which he sometimes sounds like George Sand writing to *him*), Flaubert would succeed in having the young man transferred from his office in the Naval Ministry to a more agreeable post under his friend Agénor Bardoux, now Minister of Education. In his letter of recommendation to Bardoux (May 2, 1878), Flaubert had said he thought Maupassant was destined for 'a very great literary future'.

~

To Madame Charles Brainne

Croisset, Thursday, August [1878]

. . .

There are moments when I feel *crushed* by this frightful book. I am now studying Politics. What a mine of imbecility! My scorn for those who devote themselves to it grows stronger every day. It ought to be the science of sciences, and instead it's given over to special interests and passions. Moreover, people were stupider in 1848 than today. There's no difference between the Socialists and the Bourgeois; or rather there are nothing but Bourgeois.

Yesterday I was in Rouen, to return books to the library, and it quite undid me – I have never sweated so much in my life. I collapsed in a café (the Café Dubiez), and ordered a beer – abject! abject! Then – horror of horrors – what did I read, while downing that wretched drink, but the *Figaro*! To such a point of degradation am I reduced by a few hours in my native city.

I have written to young Guy to 'raise his morale'. No answer so far. I think my friend may be slightly lazy. If he worked more, he would be less bored. Life is so abominable that to be swallowed it has to be disguised. If it isn't sweetened with some fabulous drug, one is disheartened. Why so? There are days when happiness seems easy of attainment. And yet, haven't you noticed that without the Concept of Happiness existence would be more bearable? We demand more from it than it can give. There are days like today when I'm sunk in black melancholy. Besides, my penury is getting on my nerves. Money matters are not improving.

Let me end with a pleasant picture. I imagine (since you are taking the waters), I imagine a great room at the baths, vaulted in Moorish style, with a pool in the centre. You appear, wearing a long chemise of yellow silk – and with the tips of your bare toes you test the water. *Crac!* Off with the chemise, and we swim side by side – not for very long, because in the corner there's a lovely divan whereon my dear Beauty reclines – and to the sound of the fountain your

Polycarp and his lady friend spend a delicious quarter of an hour. Oh, why don't those things happen, God damn it? Why? Because there are obstacles to everything . . .

~

To his niece Caroline

[Paris,] Tuesday morning [September 10, 1878]
. . .

I have put aside, to show to you, an abominable (but just) article that appeared in yesterday's *L'Événement* against Maxime DuCamp. It inspired me with 'philosophical reflections', and I felt like having a Thanksgiving Mass said, to thank heaven for having given me the taste for pure Art. By messing about in so-called serious things, one ends in crime. For Maxime DuCamp's history of the Commune has just caused a man to be sentenced to penal servitude. A horrible story. Rather it should be on his conscience than on mine. I felt sick about it all day yesterday. My old friend now has a sad reputation: this is a real stigma. If he had loved *style*, instead of loving publicity, he wouldn't be in the present pass . . .[1]

1. Pierre Ludovic Matillon, chief accountant in the Naval Ministry in Paris, had been arrested in June 1871 and charged with setting fire to houses in the Rue Royale during the Commune. After being held for five months he was discharged for lack of evidence and went to live abroad – some sources say in Antwerp, some in Trieste. His case was reopened in Paris in 1872, and when he failed to appear he was condemned to death in absentia. In 1876 he proposed returning to France to proclaim his innocence and demand trial, but was dissuaded. In 1878, when DuCamp publicized his story in his history of the Commune ('Les Convulsions de Paris', then being serialized in *La Revue des Deux Mondes*), Matillon did return, and on September 4 was sentenced to penal servitude for life. His appeal was rejected, but he was released the next year. (Most survivors among those sentenced for activities during the Commune were amnestied on July 11, 1880.) DuCamp was castigated in *L'Événement* and other radical newspapers for his role in the Matillon affair. In *pièces justicatives* printed in volume III of *Les Convulsions de Paris*, he says that when Matillon wrote to him after reading the instalment in the *Revue des Deux Mondes*, declaring his intention of returning to Paris, he did everything he could to dissuade him.

~

To Madame Charles Brainne

[Croisset,] Tuesday night [December 10–11, 1878]

It was out of affection for you, my dear Beauty, that I didn't write. I didn't want to burden you with the minutiae of my troubles, or rather my penury. You can do nothing about it, and besides it hurts me to talk about it. The news is that we are now at the bottom of the abyss, and things are hopeless. Commanville's sawmill is going to be sold under deplorable conditions – and then what? God knows what will become of us. Perhaps I'm overly apprehensive. Commanville will earn some money in one way or another. No matter: whatever happens, things won't be gay. My heart is heavy, I assure you. And it isn't the lack of money, and the consequent privations, and the complete absence of freedom I'm condemned to, that madden me. No, it's not those things. I feel spiritually *soiled* by all these sordid concerns, by all this commercial talk. I feel I'm being turned into a shopkeeper. Imagine a virtuous woman made to prostitute herself in a brothel, or a fastidious person being dragged about in a garbage cart, and you have my situation. There's great irony in it, and Providence is being hard on me at the moment. No success whatever, no luck. I wanted to earn a few sous with my *féerie* (a work that I consider remarkable, whatever anyone may say). Dalloz didn't even deign to answer, and had his secretary tell me that it 'wasn't suitable for the magazine' but that they would be 'glad to have something else of mine'.

· · · ·

As for a job, a post, my dear friend, never! never! I refused one offered me by my friend Bardoux. Similarly with the officer's cross of the Légion d'Honneur, which he also wanted to give me. If the worst happens, it's possible to live in a country inn on fifteen hundred francs a year. That's what I'll do rather than take one centime of the government's money. Don't you know this maxim (coined by me): 'Honours dishonour; titles degrade; bureaucracy benumbs'? Besides – am I capable of filling any sort of position? After a single day I'd be kicked out for insolence and insubordination. Misfortune doesn't make me more compliant – quite the contrary! More than ever I'm a wild idealist, resolved to die of hunger and fury rather than make the least concession.

I was quite low for several days, but my spirits are improving and I'm working. That's the important thing, after all.

I was touched by your kind thought of me, my poor precious Beauty, but put it out of your mind, I beg you. However, I thank you for the idea, as for a gift . . .

~

Occasionally, in response to Caroline's continued exhortations to economize, he allowed himself a small irony, as in a letter of early January 1879, in which he wrote: 'The weather is mild, and Monsieur is burning less wood . . .'

The Commonvilles gave up their Paris apartment, and crowded their furniture into Flaubert's.[1] 'If I don't come to Paris,' he wrote to Guy de Maupassant,[2] 'it's because I haven't a sou. That's the entire mystery. Besides, I have no place to stay, since I've turned my apartment over to my niece until her husband's affairs are fully settled – and until we know what's to become of us and what he'll be doing.'

Both Commanvilles, it would seem, were now in the habit, in certain situations, of drafting letters for Flaubert to copy, sign, and send – to M. de Fiennes, their Paris landlord; and to Edmond Laporte, who preferred not to be put in closer touch with the Rouen bankers to whom he had given his guarantee.

1. Mme Chevalley-Sabatier, in her book about her aunt mentioned in Appendix I, suggests that this may have been done in part as a precaution against possible seizure of the Commanvilles' 'goods and chattels' by creditors following the sale of the sawmill and other property that was now looming.
2. Maupassant had written: 'I saw Zola last night, and he told me you wouldn't be coming this winter! This news so surprised and saddened me that I beg you to write to me at once whether it's true. To spend the winter without seeing you seems impossible to me. My greatest pleasure of the year was to talk with you every Sunday for three or four hours, and I can't believe the summer can come without my having seen you.'

~

To his niece Caroline

[Croisset, January 18, 1879]

My poor girl

I have just written a letter to de Fiennes following the model you sent me.[1] One more little cup of bitterness! It wouldn't have been difficult to spare me this one. The situation was easily foreseen: a simple visit would have sufficed. But no – your poor husband doesn't seem to me to have a clear sense of justice. De Fiennes is perfectly within his rights, he has been courteous with us, and as thanks we not only don't pay him, but are rude to him.

What I find superb is that Ernest should be indignant with Laporte because he doesn't want to visit Faucon![2] And he accuses him of 'turning against him' – a very clever phrase, which would have put us on bad terms with him but which I removed, fortunately. Here I stop. Because I'd have too much to say. No matter. It's odd to think that others always have obligations towards us, whereas we ourselves have only rights.

1. Flaubert had written to Caroline on December 4: 'I think that de Fiennes resents [Ernest's] not paying the rent the day it was due. This was certainly improper, and you know I was annoyed, and, to tell the truth, humiliated. When one wants to be respected as a Louis XIV, one doesn't behave like a Louis XI. (Between you and me, this little remissness is inexcusable, because I had just handed over to Ernest the 1400 francs from Delehante [the buyer of the Deauville farm] – that is, the very last remains of my capital. He could have used it to pay *my* debts.) Your fine husband does himself harm in people's eyes by many small turns of behaviour he is unaware of.'
2. Faucon, a Rouen banker with an associate named Pécuchet, was Commanville's principal creditor.

∽

Living and working alone at Croisset, under a roof that needed repair, Flaubert added to his January 18 letter to Caroline: 'I satisfy my need for affection by calling in Julie for a talk after dinner and looking at the old black-and-white checked dressMaman used to wear. In the midst of my sadness I continue reading metaphysics for my book – Kant, Hegel, Leibnitz. Not much fun . . .'

The sale of the Commanville assets was postponed, prolonging the uncertainty.

~

To his niece Caroline

[Croisset,] Tuesday, 2 o'clock [January 21, 1879]

My darling

I was expecting this disappointment. So it didn't surprise me. Yet another delay! 'It won't be very long,' you tell me. But on whom does it depend? When will we be finished, *mon Dieu*! When will we have some peace? . . . I long to put it all out of my thoughts, and I am making great efforts of will to do so. But that's impossible. It's becoming an obsession with me.

On Friday and Saturday my mental and nervous state frightened me. I keep mulling over the same recriminations, and constantly wallowing in grief. Then I go back to my books and try to write my chapter. My imagination is aroused; but instead of working on fictitious beings it sets to work on myself, and everything begins all over again.

There's no point in complaining! But there's still less in living! What is my future, now? Who is there to talk to, even? I live alone like an outcast, and the end of my solitude doesn't seem very near; for I'll have to spend two months in Paris this year if I want to finish *Bouvard and Pécuchet*, and during that time you'll be here – so that perhaps I'll not see my poor child till mid-May. As for all three of us living in the little flat in Paris, that is physically impossible – there isn't even a room for the cook. Here at least there's nothing to irritate me; that wouldn't be the case in Paris. Speaking of cooking – what do you do about food?

Today is your birthday, my poor Caro! You were born amid tears – that has brought you bad luck. But I'd better say goodbye now – I'm growing too sentimental. I'm weary of *trying*, though – of straining, of forcing my will: and for what? To what avail? Who is benefiting from all this?

I kiss you tenderly.

Your old uncle

~

Financial strain and mental torment were not all Flaubert had to bear that winter. One night in January, walking along the riverbank in the moonlight, he slipped on a patch of thin ice and fell, breaking a bone in his leg.

◇

EDMOND LAPORTE (AND FLAUBERT) TO ÉMILE ZOLA
Croisset, January 30, 1879

Monsieur,

M. Gustave Flaubert asks me to give you his news.

He is suffering from a very bad sprain, complicated by a crack at the base of the fibula. The inflammation is disappearing, but he has been ordered to rest for three weeks. There is no cause for alarm.

'I'm stuck in bed, smoking a pipe and enjoying three consolations:

'(1) The annoyance the success of *L'Assommoir* is causing your fellow writers;

'(2) the story of the curé of Le Vésinet,[1]

'(3) the fact that our Saviour will probably soon be gone.[2]

'My greetings to your wife.

'Share this bulletin with Maurice Roux and Hennique.'

(Dictated by Flaubert.)

Your faithful servant,
E. Laporte

1. The curé of Le Vésinet remains unidentified, but one can imagine the general nature of the story'. Flaubert rejoiced in the turpitudes of worthies, as in the case of the unfortunate Germiny.
2. The imminent forced resignation of the ultraconservative President MacMahon.

◇

TO CLAUDIUS POPELIN[1]

Croisset, February 11 [1879]

... The accident was more serious than was first thought. The fracture of the fibula was nothing, but articulation was appallingly disrupted – my foot looked like a pumpkin wrapped in red parchment! It was kept in ice packs for ten days. Fortunately the blood was reabsorbed, and the danger is over. Today I'm at last able to get up, thanks to a dextrin boot.[2]

My spirits have remained excellent – I profited from the occasion to give my poor brain a rest. I'll even tell you that this 'misfortune' (as various people have called it) has seemed very slight to me compared with all the others! For during the past three years I have swallowed many a deep and bitter draught. This has even taken my mind off things, and calmed my nerves . . . Don't forget me when speaking with the Princess. Tell her, from me, all the best things you can think of.

1. (1825–1892), painter, enamelist, writer; at this time lover of Princesse Mathilde.
2. 'To answer your question about my "boot", Flaubert wrote to Caroline a day or two later, 'the leg is wrapped in cotton wool and then in several layers of bandage, and on to this is applied a coat of dextrin (which is a resinous substance made from wheat, I believe). As it dries, this delightful preparation turns as hard as iron, and the leg is guaranteed immovable. I couldn't stand this shackle, and thought I'd die of the pain. Fortin slit it from top to bottom and held it together with strips of bandage, so that my foot and leg are now in a kind of cradle. I've had no pain for twenty-four hours, and am back in my study, making notes on spiritualism and religion.'

≈

Flaubert was for a time almost completely immobilized, and for several months his activity would be much curtailed. 'My distraction,' he wrote to Princesse Mathilde, 'consists in watching my dog, who sleeps before my fire, and the boats that pass on the river. I read as much as I can (and not very amusing things – metaphysics and spiritualism); I daydream about my past, like an old man, and then I have much longer thoughts about you, my dear Princess.'

Edmond Laporte made himself errand boy, secretary, and nurse, often spending the night at Croisset, and earning from Flaubert the title of 'Sister of Charity', or 'Little Sister of the Poor'.

≈

TO HIS NIECE CAROLINE

. . . Would you believe the following about the Sister? On Monday he left me by the eleven o'clock boat and was to return by the one at six thirty. As the river road at Couronne was under water, he took off his trousers and waded to the ferry. The Seine was raging. Saint-Martin[1] had been refusing passengers. There's a true friend – who risks drowning, or at least pneumonia, in order not to miss an appointment – which after all could have been dispensed with . . .

1. The ferryman between Croisset and Couronne. In the summer, Flaubert sometimes swam from Saint-Martin's boat.

⌇

To GEORGES CHARPENTIER

Croisset, Sunday [February 16, 1879]

My dear Friend,

I am not 'unjust', for I am not 'angry' at you and have never been so. Only, I thought that you should have told me at once, straight out, that the proposition didn't suit you.[1] In that case I'd have gone elsewhere. Let's not mention it again, and continue good friends.

At the end of *Saint Julian* I wanted to reproduce the stained-glass window from the Rouen cathedral. It was merely a matter of colouring the plate in Langlois' book. And I'd have liked the illustration *precisely because* it is not an illustration, but a historical *document*. Comparing the picture with the text, the reader would have been puzzled, and would have wondered how I derived the one from the other.

I dislike all illustrations, especially where my own works are concerned, and as long as I am alive there shall be none. *Dixi.* I am just as stubborn about my photograph, and almost broke with Lemerre[2] about it. I'm sorry, but I have principles. *Polius mori quam foedari.*[3]

I'm fed up with *Bovary.* The constant mention of that book gets on my nerves. Everything I wrote after it doesn't exist. I assure you that if I weren't in need of money I'd take steps to see that it was never reprinted. But necessity compels me to do otherwise. So – print away! As for the money, there's no need to send it here. Give it to me when I come to Paris. One observation: you mention a thousand francs for two thousand copies, which means ten sous a copy. It seems to me that you used to give me twelve or even thirteen per copy, but I may be mistaken.

Now something else. Next August 10 my contract with Lévy will expire. The rights to *L'Éducation sentimentale* will revert to me. I'd very much like to get something out of it . . .

I am not unaware of everything my friends have been doing for me lately. I send great thanks to Mme Charpentier, and as many again to you, my dear friend . . .[4]

1. Flaubert had suggested that Charpentier print a deluxe edition of *Saint Julian* for the holiday trade, and he had understood that Charpentier agreed. Instead, the special Charpentier book for the 1878–1879 holidays had been Sarah Bernhardt's *Dans les nuages* (In the Clouds), her account of a balloon ascension she had made with the painter Georges Clairin, who illustrated the book.
2. Under an arrangement with Charpentier, the publisher Lemerre issued inexpensive editions of *Madame Bovary* and *Salammbô*.
3. 'Rather death than dishonour.'
4. The reason for Flaubert's thanks will be found in the following letter.

~

To his niece Caroline

Saturday, 2 o'clock [February 22, 1879]

My Loulou

Here's the real truth. I wanted to keep the story from you, to spare you pain, or at least indignation. The upshot is that I was once again wrong in following the advice of others and mistrusting my own judgement. But I'm incorrigible; I always put my trust in outside opinions, and then find myself in trouble. Here goes:

Early in January, Taine wrote to me to say that M. de Sacy was at death's door and that Bardoux wanted to give me his post: 3,000 francs and living quarters.[1] Though I was tempted by the apartment (which is splendid), I replied that the post didn't suit me, because I should be poorer having to live in Paris with a salary of 3,000 francs than I am now at Croisset, and that I should prefer to spend only two or three months in Paris. Moreover, the Princess and Mme Brainne told me that my friends were trying to get me a position 'worthy' of me.

Act Two, Monday. The moment you and Ernest were gone, Turgenev put on a solemn face and said: 'Gambetta[2] asks whether you want M. de Sacy's post: 8,000 francs and living quarters. You must give me your answer at once.' Using eloquence and affection (the latter word is not too strong), and seconded by Laporte, he overcame my distaste for the idea of becoming a civil servant. The thought that I should be less of a burden to the two of you was what really made me decide. After a sleepless night, I told him to go ahead. Everything was to be done quietly, and you were not to be told until all was settled.

Twenty-four hours later I had a letter from Turgenev telling me that he had been mistaken, that the post paid only 6,000, but that he felt he should continue his efforts.

Now Gambetta had promised nothing at all. Goncourt had asked him for a sinecure for me, as had the Charpentiers, who had been quite active about it. They had written to Mme Adam,[3] who was all on my side.

Then came another letter from Turgenev, to say that the post paid not 6,000, but 4,000!

At this point I received a visit from Cordier.[4] He was very helpful and spoke about me to Paul Bert,[5] who said he would do everything for me, and to *Père* Hugo, who then and there wrote a warm letter recommending me to Ferry.[6]

Then came the article in the *Figaro*[7] and Turgenev's departure for Russia. Shortly before that, I had been warned that Maître Senard,[8] one of the mainstays of the cabinet, was demanding the post for his son-in-law Baudry, who he insisted had first claim.

Last Monday came a letter from Baudry, asking (finally!) how I was and announcing his daughter's marriage. This letter is a model: in it the false friend gives himself away completely. He told me that he himself was taking steps to get M. de Sacy's post, and made no mention of those being taken on my behalf. Taine had spoken to him about it, but (said Baudry) the place wouldn't suit me at all. He also shed some tears over my misfortunes and criticized Bardoux for not giving me the post recently bestowed on Troubat: 3,000 francs and obligatory residence at Compiègne! (Charming thought!) Baudry is an *ass*. If he had written to me frankly, and asked me, as a favour to him, to do nothing, my gentlemanly instincts would have obliged me to withdraw from the field. I asked Laporte to answer him that I was too unwell to write, and that I would explain the situation to him when I could once again hold a pen. With a Norman, one has to be a Norman and a half!

That is how things stand now. But I'm sure that Baudry will be appointed,[9] and that I'll look like a fool. I'll be regarded as a blundering schemer: that will be my sole achievement. Furthermore, the article in the *Figaro* will turn Madame Adam against me;[10] and it is already bringing me letters – there was one yesterday from Mme Achille – asking for explanations and requiring answers. A ghastly nuisance. Turgenev has written to me from Berlin to apologize. He has no idea of the authorship of that elucubration, which contains some truths and some untruths.

I confess it has all made me weep tears of blood. To have my penury publicized, and to be pitied by those wretches, who talk about my 'goodness'! It's cruel, cruel! I've done nothing to deserve it! I curse the day when I had the fatal idea of putting my name on a book! Had it not been for my mother and Bouilhet I would never have published. How I regret it now! I only want to be forgotten, left in peace, never spoken of again. I'm becoming odious to myself. Why can't I die, so that I can be left alone? You asked me to tell you the truth, my dear girl: well, now you have it! My heart is bursting with fury; these insults are too much for me.

It's not enough to have to write to de Fiennes and Faucon and ask them for favours: the *Figaro* has to drag me through the mud for its own political reasons. Well, I had it coming to me. I was a coward. I was false to my principles (for I too have principles), and I'm being punished for it. I mustn't complain, but I'm suffering, and cruelly. This is not a pose. The dignity of my entire life is lost. I consider myself disgraced. Oh, Other People! Always Other People! And all this happened because I wanted not to appear stubborn and proud, because I was afraid of seeming to strike a pose.

. . .

N.B. Popelin will probably be coming to see me next week. He'll have lunch or dinner here, and perhaps spend the night. So send me *the key to the cellar*, immediately. Otherwise I'll have only execrable wine to offer him.[11]

1. Silvestre de Sacy (1801–1879), journalist and essayist, had been since 1836 librarian of the Bibliothèque Mazarine, one of the public libraries of Paris,

housing special collections and occupying splendid quarters in the building of the Institut de France. The correct figure for Sacy's salary, as the letter eventually specifies, was 4,000 francs.

2. Léon Gambetta (1838–1882), leader of the then dominant Republican party, had recently been appointed President of the Chamber of Deputies.

3. Mme Juliette Adam, née Lambert (1836–1936), novelist and essayist, had been a friend of George Sand, through whom she came to admire Flaubert. Her salon was frequented by Gambetta and other leading Republicans. She was the founder of *La Nouvelle Revue* (1879–1926) and a strong propagandist for 'La Révanche' (revenge against Germany for the defeat of 1870). This she lived to see in 1918. Later came the German counter-revenge of 1940 and the requital of 1945.

4. Alphonse Cordier (1820–1897), a life senator from Normandy (département de la Seine-Inférieure).

5. Paul Bert (1833–1886), physiologist and deputy, later Minister of Education.

6. Jules Ferry (1832–1893), who had just replaced Flaubert's friend Agénor Bardoux as Minister of Education.

7. The February 17 issue of the anti-Republican *Figaro* had carried, on its front page, a somewhat garbled gossip item, criticizing the government, and especially Gambetta, for not appointing the needy Flaubert to de Sacy's post.

8. Jules Senard (1800–1885), powerful in the legal profession and as a Republican deputy, had been Flaubert's defence lawyer in the *Madame Bovary* trial. We have also met his son-in-law, Frédéric Baudry, the philologist, Flaubert's schoolmate and old friend. Baudry had been a librarian at the Bibliothèque de l'Arsenal from 1859 to 1874, and had then become Sacy's assistant at the Mazarine, at 3,000 francs a year.

9. Flaubert did not yet know that on February 17 Baudry had already been appointed. It is generally considered appropriate that he should have been given the promotion.

10. Not at all. Mme Adam remained cordial, sent Flaubert her books, and begged him to give *Bouvard and Pécuchet* to her magazine for serialization. It did appear there, severely pruned, after Flaubert's death.

11. Presumably the wine that Flaubert habitually drank, while Caroline retained the key to his locked cellar.

～

A few days earlier, Zola had written to Flaubert as spokesman for his disappointed – and apologetic – friends:

～

ÉMILE ZOLA TO FLAUBERT

Paris, February 17, 1879

I wanted to write you, my friend, to tell you that all of us here
have been clumsy in this business concerning you. I beg you: look
on these things with the eye of a philosopher, an observer, an analyst.
Our greatest mistake was to be overhasty – to remind Gambetta of
his promise at a moment when he had been besieged with petitions
all week. Since Mme Charpentier was sick in bed, we had to employ
Turgenev, who was to leave for Russia the next day and had to act
precipitately. The occasion was unfortunate: all kinds of unfavourable
circumstances arose. I'll tell you about it in detail later. In a word, I
think it required a woman to carry off the business promptly and
conclusively. You bear no responsibility for any of it: nothing is lost
as far as you are concerned; and if you are willing, all can be put
right tomorrow.

As for the article in the *Figaro*, I don't know how they learned
about the affair, but I shall find out. The paper acted with its usual
indiscretion and brutality, as it has acted towards all of us since its
inception. I beg you just to look the other way. In what the *Figaro*
said, there is nothing that isn't highly honourable in your regard,
and I assure you it will make no trouble for you with anyone.
Everybody knows the *Figaro*, and is well aware that you have nothing
whatever to do with its editing. We must ignore the press. We must
let it lie about us, slander us, compromise us, without letting it
trouble us, without even wasting a second of our time in reading
what it says. We must pay that price for our peace of mind. I beg
you: treat all this with that noble scorn of yours; don't be upset;
remind yourself of what you so often say – that there is nothing
important in life outside our work.

Reassure us that you remain strong and above it all. None of it
matters. A good page written by you is more important than any of
it. Your friends were not as clever as the occasion demanded; well,
they beg your pardon, and will go no further. If you will allow them
to, they will succeed another time. Light your pipe with the *Figaro*
article, and wait until you are recovered before resuming work. All
the rest is nothing.

I had thought for a moment of coming to see you and telling
you all this in person, but I was terribly busy and moreover was

afraid of tiring you. All of us here love you – you know that – and it would make us happy to prove it to you at this time. The worst thing is the way you are kept confined to Croisset by your wretched fall. I think you would look at things more coolly if you were among us. Let's hope you'll be able to walk soon and come back to us. And if recovery is delayed, please let us visit you for an hour when you're stronger.

I beg you once again: don't be sad. Rather, be proud. You are the best of us all. You are our teacher and our father. We do not want you to grieve in solitude. I swear to you that today you are as great a man as you were yesterday.

As for your life, I know you are somewhat harassed at this moment, but a solution will be found, you can be sure. Get better quickly, and you'll see that everything will be all right. *Je vous embrasse.*

~

To Émile Zola

[Croisset,] Tuesday, 2 o'clock [February 18, 1879]

Mon cher ami

Nobody could be a better chap than you. Thank you for your letter. It put some balm into my blood, as the saying goes.

As soon as I can get down to my dining room, you must come to lunch.

N.B. One word only. What do you mean when you say, ' . . . if you are willing, all can be put right tomorrow'?

Je vous embrasse.

~

On March 4, 1879, Commanville's sawmill was sold disastrously. The 200,000 francs it brought (a third of its estimated value) permitted the payment of some obligations; but neither then, nor even after March 24, when land adjoining the mill was sold for 30,000 francs more than expected, could debts be paid completely, and there would be nothing whatever for Flaubert – a mystery he never fathomed. Amid the murky commercial and legal details, a few seem partially decipherable: not only had Flaubert irrevocably lost all he had advanced in his attempt to save the Commanvilles, but for some of the remaining debts he bore a certain degree of responsibility; and payment had been guaranteed by his friends Raoul Duval and Edmond Laporte. Flaubert's letters to Caroline during the next few weeks showed constant concern for his guarantors:

> As for Raoul Duval and Laporte, *what shall we do*? That's what torments me. Answer me on this.

> . . . I'll be heartbroken if Laporte, next May, is obliged to pay Faucon twelve thousand francs or take out a mortgage on his house.[1] He's putting on a brave front, like the gentleman he is. But I see *perfectly well* that the idea of such a mortgage is infinitely galling to him, less because of the cost of getting it and the interest to be paid, than because of 'what people will say'. He fears it would have an adverse effect on his political position. (That last is conjecture on my part, but I'm convinced of it.) Do you see some way of avoiding this?

> How is it that with these last thirty thousand francs a way can't be found to clear things up completely with Raoul Duval and Laporte? Especially Laporte.

Following the news of this culminating financial disaster, Flaubert learned from Guy de Maupassant, who had been persistent in the Ministry of Education, the answer to the question with which he himself had ended his letter to Zola.

1. It sounds as though Caroline had fallen behind in her annual payments to Faucon, for which Raoul Duval and Laporte stood guarantors, and as though she foresaw incapacity to make them in the future. Raoul Duval was comfortably off, but Laporte was not, and at this moment was in particularly bad financial straits (see Appendix VI).

~

GUY DE MAUPASSANT TO FLAUBERT

[March 7 or 8, 1879]

Mon cher Maître,

I have just been speaking with M. Charmes,[1] and we are in

agreement. Everybody, *everybody*, considers the offer of a pension by the Minister to a man of letters a token of esteem. Princes have always given such things to their great men: why shouldn't our government do the same? And has anything changed, to make what was always considered an honour, painful and humiliating in your eyes?

Besides, the Minister wants to do something that will express his interest in you; and since you don't care about an honorific title, he can give you a pension that nobody will know about. That's the way it's usually done. He will sign an order that will be sent directly to the records office. No announcement will be made; it will be communicated to no newspaper. Only four people will know about it – the Minister, his Chef de Cabinet, Charmes and I: plus the dispatch clerk and the recording officer of the Ministry.

I enquired about the various libraries. Unfortunately there is none, now, of the kind you want. Pensions for men of letters are taking the place of that kind of sinecure; and librarians are now required to be residents of Paris and to be in their offices every other day. You can see that that wouldn't suit you. Regular attendance is required at Sèvres, at the Beaux Arts, etc. – in all the small libraries, which for that reason are better paid than the large ones.

In short, I think you would be better off with a pension than with any kind of post. A pension is a token of esteem, it causes no trouble, it upsets nobody, makes nobody angry; and you can be sure that no newspaper will protest, so natural will it seem to all.

By accepting a post, you . . . enter a hierarchy, you become official. You report to a Director, who in turn reports to the Minister. Nothing of that kind with a pension: it imposes no restriction, it leaves you completely free, and in no way detracts from your dignity. It is a decoration in the form of money rather than a ribbon. You go, or send, to collect it every three months, and that's all there is to it. The day you no longer want it, you write in to say you can do without it, and it will be transferred to somebody else, who probably needs it less than you.

In any case, I have mentioned your scruples and hesitations to Charmes, who will talk about them to the Chef de Cabinet; and I *think* they will offer you a pension, with no attendant publicity. If you absolutely don't want to accept, you will send your 'No, thank you', to Monsieur Rambaud, the Chef de Cabinet. Since you have made no move yourself, it's easy for you. I'm eager to know what happens . . .

1. François Marie Xavier Charmes (1849–1919), '*directeur*' at the Ministry of Education.

~

To Guy de Maupassant
                    [Croisset,] Sunday, 4 o'clock, 9 [March 1879]
Mon cher ami

Since you *assure* me that this pension will remain unknown to everybody, I resign myself, being driven to it by necessity.

But you say: 'It's impossible that any newspaper will protest, the thing will seem so natural to everybody'; and: 'I think no publicity will be given the matter.' So you are not certain? How reconcile those two statements? And on the other hand, you tell me several times it will be a *secret*.

In short, if I can be *sure*, absolutely sure, that the entire thing will remain between the ministry and me – and only on that condition – I accept with gratitude, and on the condition (as I look on it) that it be a loan, a temporary grant.

This is what I intend to do. Once the pension is granted, and as soon as my brother returns from Nice,[1] I shall ask him for the equivalent of the pension. He, his daughter, and his grandson, who will soon be of age, have among the three of them an income of about a hundred thousand francs. They can perfectly well give me five. In that case, I'd go immediately to the minister and give up the pension. Otherwise I'd have to accept it until the time came when I could return it in a lump sum – i.e. all I had received. I would arrange to do this by taking appropriate measures. You cannot imagine how I suffer from being reduced to these expedients.

. . . To sum up: (1) No official title; (2) No publicity. *Absolute secrecy*. In this way I'll only have to say 'Thank you.' I trust you absolutely in this. Don't deceive me out of affection, I beg you. Be the guardian of what I consider (rightly or wrongly) my honour – my only wealth.

When I say 'secret', I mean that even my most intimate friends (including the Commanvilles)[2] should know nothing. I will divulge it as I think proper.

And I don't thank you, my dear boy: that would offend you. But I embrace you affectionately.

Yours –

Thank M. Charmes for me. What have I done that your minister should be so good to me? I am astonished and moved by this.

1. Dr Achille Flaubert, Flaubert's older brother, now sixty-six and retired from his post as chief surgeon at the Rouen Hospital, was convalescing at Nice following a stroke. On his return to Rouen, Flaubert made his financial request, and Achille granted it even before Flaubert finished speaking. But almost immediately the doctor's mental condition greatly worsened; he was never able to carry out his intention; and his wife and daughter showed no inclination to do so. Achille Flaubert died in 1882.

2. In a letter to Caroline written the following week, Flaubert would tell her only that 'I have every reason to believe I'm to be offered a pension' – without revealing the source either of the information or the possible pension itself. Perhaps he was apprehensive – not without reason – that the ill-fated Commanvilles might queer things. (He had learned that Caroline, doubtless 'from the best of motives', had, without consulting him, played an interfering role in the fruitless appeal to Gambetta.) He would tell the Commanvilles of his pension only when it had become a certainty (see p. 649).

~

By the end of May Flaubert felt able to travel to Paris.

~

To Edmond Laporte

[Croisset,] Thursday morning, [May 29, 1879]

Mon Chéri

I leave tomorrow by the afternoon express. (What luck if I were to find my Bab[1] at the station!)

Guy wrote to me yesterday that my nomination is signed, and that in Paris I'll find 750 francs, my first quarter. So the thing is certain.[2]

And you: what's up?

I count on seeing you in Paris very soon, no? We must give ourselves a 'little family celebration': we've certainly earned it.

Quick answer, please, old chap.

Thank you for the magic names.

Your Giant

1. In 1877 Laporte had lost his position as manager of a lace factory in the
    Rouen suburb of Grand Couronne following the death of its owner, and
    he had since been unemployed, with diminished resources – one of his
    reasons for wanting to be relieved of further responsibility in the Comman-
    ville affair. With Flaubert's support he had applied for a government post,
    and was now about to receive official notification of his appointment as
    factory inspector at Nevers. Both before and after ministering to Flaubert
    as nurse and secretary he had been helping him with research for *Bouvard
    and Pécuchet* (most recently for the chapter on magic). 'Bab' would seem
    to be a Flaubertian shortening of the Turkish *baba* ('father').

2. Actually, although Flaubert's 'nomination' for the pension of 3,000 francs
    had probably been decided upon, he would be officially notified only in
    October (see p. 649). This was apparently a normal bureaucratic delay.
    'You know how much time it takes for the slightest thing of this kind to
    be done,' Maupassant had written to him in the spring. If 750 francs, for
    his first quarter, was really already awaiting him in Paris, it was probably a
    special advance somehow made available. The reader will recall that Flaubert
    had other money awaiting him in Paris – a payment he had asked Charp-
    entier to hold for him (see p. 634), perhaps to avoid having to 'share' it
    with the Commanvilles.

    In further reference to Flaubert's pension, there exist portions of a
    correspondence between him and Frédéric Baudry concerning a suggestion
    by Baudry that Flaubert be given the title of *'conservateur honoraire'* at the
    Bibliothèque Mazarine, without duties, in addition to a pension. The aim
    would perhaps have been to make it seem that the pension was a salary –
    a gesture to his pride. Nothing seems to have come of it: Flaubert's name
    does not appear in the records of the Bibliothèque Mazarine.

∾

Flaubert stayed in Paris until June 25. He still limped badly, and
stairs were difficult, but the Commanvilles had gone to Croisset,
and he had his apartment to himself. He paid a courtesy call on 'his'
minister, Jules Ferry, and learned that the support of Victor Hugo
had counted strongly for him in the matter of the pension; he did
more research for *Bouvard and Pécuchet* in the Bibliothèque
Nationale; he was pleased that Charpentier was preparing a new
edition of *L'Éducation sentimentale*; he dined out; and, as before, was
at home to his friends on Sunday afternoons. They poured in.

'Monsieur is overwhelmed by courtesies,' he wrote to Caroline. 'I'm quite surprised. It's evident that many people are glad to see me again, and that of all men I'm not the one least loved by his friends.'

What would follow *Bouvard and Pécuchet*, the story of the two 'wood-lice'? The contrasts of Flaubert's creative temperament were never more apparent: 'Do you know what is *obsessing* me now?' he wrote to Caroline. 'A longing to write the battle of Thermopylae. That idea again has me in thrall.'

After spending the summer at Croisset, Flaubert returned to Paris in late August for a few weeks to correct proofs of the new printing of *L'Éducation*, to arrange for publication of Louis Bouilhet's complete poems, and to talk with the composer Ernest Reyer about music for an opera to be based on *Salammbô*, with libretto by Camille du Locle.[1]

1. The following appears in the English-language edition of *Capri, From the Stone Age to the Tourist Age*, by Arvid Andrén (Göteborg: Paul Aström förlag, 1980), pp. 152–153:

    'About 1880, a middle-aged Frenchman came to the island and settled down in the Villa Certosella by the Via Tragara in Capri. He soon became generally known for his recluse living, his shortness and his sharp tongue: the islanders called him variously "U Francesiello", "the English", or "The Acid Drop". No one knew why he settled on Capri and what he had been doing before he came. He was usually seen strutting about in an impeccable Parisian *complet*, which greatly increased his reputation for being somewhat eccentric. But one day he attracted everyone's attention by appearing in a suit and cape made from the handwoven, rough and uncoloured wool from Amalfi which otherwise was used only by fishermen. No innovation in clothing is so extravagant that it cannot become high fashion. Soon the English and Germans on Capri started appearing in more or less picturesque suits made from the same rustic material. Thus, "the little Frenchman" gave rise to the production of handwoven wool fabrics on Capri which continued right up until a few decades ago, when machine-made products took over.

    'Not until he died in 1903 was it discovered that he, Camille de [sic] Locle, had been the director of the Opéra Comique in Paris, that he had composed libretti for a great number of operas, among others the original text to Verdi's *Aïda*, and had launched several other operas, *Carmen* among them, which, however, received harsh reviews and did not become popular until afterwards. Perhaps it was disappointment which made him leave Paris and his career to hide himself on Capri.'

    Flaubert did not live to hear the Reyer-du Locle *Salammbô*, which had its 'world premiere' only in 1890, in Brussels. It would be first sung at the

Paris Opéra two years later, and at the Metropolitan Opera House in New York on March 20, 1901. And one wishes, too, that Flaubert, who had delighted in the gulf of Naples on his visit of 1851, might have had the pleasure of 'strutting about' with his homespun-clad librettist on Capri – scene of Imperial Roman orgies and other excesses which, as 'reported' by Suetonius, may well have entered into the inspiration for certain scenes of his Carthaginian novel.

Earlier, in 1863–1866, in Russia, the young Modest Mussorgsky (1839–1881) had written a libretto and a voice-and-piano score for six scenes of an opera based on *Salammbô*. After orchestrating three of the scenes he abandoned the project, later using portions of the music in other works, including *Boris Godunov*. Some of Mussorgsky's *Salammbô* music was revised and orchestrated by Rimsky-Korsakov, and can be heard in a recording by the London Symphony Orchestra, conducted by Claudio Abbado (RCA: ARL 1–3988). Mussorgsky's entire score was recently revised, and its orchestration completed, by Zoltán Peskó, and the six scenes, with excellent soloists, were taped live at a concert of the Milan Symphony Orchestra and Chorus of the Radiotelevisione Italiana on November 10, 1980. The two-record album of this performance (CBS Masterworks 79253) includes Mussorgsky's libretto in the original Russian and in English, French, and German translation, and interesting notes by Zoltán Peskó and Rubens Tedeschi. There seems to be no evidence that Flaubert knew of Mussorgsky's *Salammbô*.

Saint Julien would also provide the subject of an opera, *Saint Julien l'Hospitalier, légende dramatique*, music by Camille Erlanger, libretto by Marcel Luguet, first produced at the Paris Conservatory in 1894. A symphonic excerpt from the score, entitled *La Chasse fantastique* (The Fantastic Hunt), became a popular orchestral number after being applauded at one of the Sunday 'Concerts de l'Opéra' in 1895. (*Enciclopedia dello Spettacolo.*)

Additional details concerning scores inspired by Flaubertian texts can be found in the article 'Flaubert' in the fifth edition of *Grove's Dictionary of Music and Musicians.*

~

To Georges Charpentier and Madame Charpentier
Friday evening [Paris, September 1879?]

Monsieur Gustave Flaubert presents his respects to M. and Mme Charpentier. He will be proud and happy to appear next Friday in reponse to their honourable invitation.

He finds the fact that no bourgeois will be present a reassuring prospect. For he has now reached such a point of exasperation when he finds himself in the company of such persons that he is invariably tempted to strangle them, or rather to hurl them into the latrines (if such language be permitted) – an action whose consequences would be embarrassing to the publishing house of Charpentier – which, children and dog included, occupies a large place in his heart.

∼

JULES FERRY TO FLAUBERT
Ministère de l'instruction Publique et des Beaux-Arts
Paris, October 3, 1879

To Monsieur Gustave Flaubert
Croisset, near Rouen (Seine-Inférieure)
Monsieur,

I have the honour to inform you that I have decided you should be awarded an annual grant of three thousand francs, payable quarterly from the funds available in my department for the encouragement of literature, to begin July 1, 1879.

I am happy, Monsieur, to be able to offer you this proof of the interest I take in your work in the field of letters.

Very truly yours,
The Minister
Jules Ferry

∼

But the pleasure that those words from Ferry should have given him was blighted by what was the saddest event of Flaubert's old age – the sudden rupture of his long and close friendship with Edmond Laporte.

For both men this was nothing less than a tragedy. The circumstances (outlined in Appendix VI) are not entirely clear, but they appear sordid. Apparently it was Caroline who insisted on the break, and the episode takes its place in the last act of the drama we have seen slowly unfolding and which could justly be called, in its effect on Flaubert, 'The Curse of the Commanvilles'. In this sad affair his loyalty – or subjection – to Caroline was complete; his suffering, acute. Immediately following the lines of his letter dated October 10, 1879, that are quoted in Appendix VI, he finally told Caroline about his pension: 'This story of Laporte fills me with such bitterness and so utterly spoils my life that I haven't the strength to enjoy a bit of good news that has come my way. Jules Ferry . . . wrote to me yesterday that he was granting me an annual pension of 3,000 francs beginning last July 1. His letter is ultra-amiable.'

His distress overflowed in letters to others. He wrote to Guy de Maupassant from Croisset on October 8, 1879: '*Things aren't going well, my boy.* Something nasty happened recently that has affected my head and my stomach. I'll tell you about it. Suffice it to say that I've seldom been so fed up with existence . . .' And to Mme Roger des Genettes on the same day: 'A man I considered my *intimate* friend has recently displayed the most crass selfishness in my regard. This betrayal is excruciating . . .'

December 12, 1879, was Flaubert's fifty-eighth birthday. It was his last, and one of his unhappiest. The winter at Croisset was long, lonely, laborious, and very cold. 'The house isn't precisely warm,' he wrote to Caroline on December 16. 'Just to walk through the big dining room is enough to numb you.' And on December 21: 'Don't come here now: it's too cold. You'd be too uncomfortable, and for Ernest it might even be dangerous. What a winter!'

The struggle to finish *Bouvard and Pécuchet* seemed endless, as he told Mme Adam in a letter dated December 2, 1879: 'The first volume will be done this coming summer, but when? And the second will need a good six months more – if I'm not finished myself, before the book!'

&

To Mrs Charles Tennant[1]

Croisset, Tuesday night [December 16, 1879]
. . .

What this book is? It's hard to say, in few words. The subtitle might be: 'On lack of method in the sciences.' In brief, I intend to pass in review all modern ideas. Women figure very little, and love not at all . . . I think the public won't have much understanding of it. People who read a book to discover whether the Baroness marries the Viscount will be disappointed, but I am writing for a few special spirits. Perhaps it will be a heavy-handed bit of foolishness? Or, on the contrary, something quite strong? I have no idea. And I am riddled with doubts and utterly exhausted.

1.	Mrs Tennant had been Gertrude Collier, daughter of a British naval officer stationed in Paris in the 1840s. The Flaubert and Collier families had become acquainted at Trouville at that time, and a correspondence had continued.

~

To Madame Roger des Genettes
[Croisset,] Sunday, January 24, 1880

.   .   .

Do you know how many volumes I've had to absorb for my two characters? More than fifteen hundred! My pile of notes is eight inches thick. This superabundance of documents has enabled me to be free of pedantry: of that I'm sure.

I'm finally beginning my *last chapter*. When it's done (at the end of April or May), I'll go to Paris for the second volume, which won't take much more than six months. It's three quarters done, and will consist almost entirely of quotations. After which, I'll rest my poor brain, which is at the end of its tether . . .

I haven't suffered from the cold, but have burned eighteen cords of wood, plus a bag of coke a day. I've spent two and a half months absolutely alone, like a bear in its cave, and have come through perfectly well even though seeing no one: I've heard no stupid remarks. Inability to tolerate human stupidity has become a *sickness* with me, and that word is weak. Almost all human beings are endowed with the gift of exasperating me, and I breathe freely only in the desert.

.   .   .

~

Turgenev, among others, did his best to cheer him.

~

To Ivan Turgenev
[Croisset, December 28, 1879]

Your parcel came last night. The salmon is magnificent – but the caviar makes me groan with voluptuous delight. When shall we eat some of it together? . . . As for Tolstoy's novel,[1] send it in care of my niece. Commanville will bring it to me . . .

1. Turgenev had written to Flaubert on December 27 announcing the dispatch of the 'comestibles' and also of 'a novel in three volumes, by Leo Tolstoy, whom I consider the foremost contemporary writer. You know who, in my opinion, might contest that place.' The novel was *War and Peace*.

~

To Ivan Turgenev

[Croisset, December 30, 1879]

Thanks! triple thanks, O Saint Vincent de Paul of the Comestibles! Upon my word, you treat me like a bardash![1] These dainties are too much! I eat the caviar almost without bread, like jam.

As for the novel, I'm frightened by its three volumes. Three volumes just now, outside my work, is an undertaking. No matter, I'll set to . . .

1. Bardash, a catamite. (OED)

~

To Ivan Turgenev

[Croisset, January 21, 1880]

. . . Thank you for getting me to read Tolstoy's novel. It's first-rate. What a painter, and what a psychologist! The first two volumes are *sublime*; but the third falls off badly. He repeats himself and philosophizes: you see the man, the author, the Russian, whereas hitherto there had been only Nature and Mankind. Sometimes he seems Shakespearean. I cried aloud with admiration as I read – and it's a long novel. Tell me something about the author. Is it his first book? In any case, he has *balls*! Yes! it's very strong! very strong! . . .[1]

1. Turgenev replied: '*Mon bon vieux*, you cannot imagine the pleasure I was given by your letter and by what you say about Tolstoy's novel. Your approval confirms my view of him. Yes, he is very strong, and yet you have put your finger on the spot. He has also conceived a philosophical system at once mystical, childish and arrogant: this has doubly spoiled his second novel (*Anna Karenina*), which he wrote after *War and Peace*, and which also contains some first-class things.'

~

Another, much shorter, masterpiece that was sent to Flaubert gave him a different, more personal pleasure, for he could quite properly feel that he had played a role in its success:

~

To Guy de Maupassant
                            [Croisset,] Sunday, February 1, 1880
                      .   .   .

I'm impatient to tell you that I consider '*Boule de Suif*' a *master-piece*. Yes, young man! Nothing more, nothing less. It is the work of a master. It's quite original in conception, well constructed from beginning to end, and written in excellent style. One can see the countryside and the characters, and the psychology is penetrating. In short, I'm delighted; two or three times I laughed aloud . . .

I have written my schoolmasterly comments on a scrap of paper; consider them. I think they're sound.

This little story will *live*: you can be sure of it. How beautifully done your bourgeois are! You haven't gone wrong with one of them. Cornudet is wonderful and true. The nun scarred with smallpox, perfect! And the count saying '*Ma chère enfant*' – and the end! The poor prostitute weeping while Cornudet sings the 'Marseillaise' – sublime. I feel like giving you little kisses for a quarter of an hour! No, really, I'm pleased. I enjoyed it and I admire it and you.

And now, *precisely* because it is fundamentally strong stuff and will annoy the bourgeois, I would take out two things that are not at all bad but which might bring complaints from idiots because they give the impression of saying 'To hell with you.' (1) . . .;[1] and (2) the word *tétons* [tits]. If you do that, even the most prudish taste can find nothing to reproach you with.

Your prostitute is charming. If you could reduce her stomach a little at the beginning you'd give me pleasure.

Ask Hennique to excuse me. I am really overwhelmed by the reading I have to do, and my poor eyes are giving out. I still have a dozen books to read before beginning my last chapter. I'm now in phrenology and administrative law, to say nothing of Cicero's *De officiis* and the coitus of peacocks. You who are (or rather, were) a rustic, have you ever seen these birds celebrate their love-rites?

Certain parts of my book, I think, will be lacking in chasteness.

I have an urchin with improper habits, and one of my protagonists petitions the authorities to establish a brothel in his village.

I embrace you more warmly than ever.

I have ideas on how to make 'Boule de Suif' known, but I hope to see you soon. I want two copies. Bravo again! *Nom de Dieu!*

1.   Flaubert's first suggestion is incomprehensible in the text.

～

Flaubert's message to Léon Hennique (1851–1935), in the letter to Maupassant, referred to his delay in acknowledging and commenting on *Les hauts faits de Monsieur de Pontbau* (The Great Deeds of Monsieur de Pontbau) (1880), a satire on Romanticism, written in dramatic form, which Hennique, one of the young Naturalists, had sent him. Now he did so, in detail, and he added general observations on Realism and Naturalism.

～

To Léon Hennique

Monday night, [February] 3 [1880]

. . .

This mania for thinking you've just discovered nature, and that you're more true than your predecessors, exasperates me. A storm in Racine isn't a whit less true than one described by Michelet. There is no 'True'. There are only ways of perceiving. Is a photograph a likeness? No more so than an oil painting, or about as much so.

Down with Schools, whatever they may be! Down with words devoid of sense! Down with Academies, Poetics, Principles! I'm astonished that a man of your worth should still let himself fall into such nonsense! . . .

God alone knows to what point I carry scruples regarding documents, books, information, travel, etc. Well, I regard all that as secondary and inferior. Material truth (or what is called such) must be only a springboard, to help one soar the higher. Do you think me fool enough to believe that in *Salammbô* I gave a true reproduction of Carthage, and in *Saint Anthony* an exact depiction of Alexandrianism? Ah, no! But I'm sure that I expressed the essence of each, as we conceive it today . . .

In brief, to finish with this question of reality, let me propose the following: assume that documents were discovered proving that Tacitus lied from beginning to end. What would that do to the glory and the style of Tacitus? Nothing whatever. Instead of one truth we would have two: that of History, and that of Tacitus . . .

~

To Madame Émile Husson[1]

[Croisset,] Monday, February 16, 1880

Kiss old Max for me – and then he should do the same to you. And tell him I'm sorry about his nephritis. I'm not always in top form myself; I've greatly aged in the past two years. But fundamentally I'm in sound shape.

As for the Academy, I fear he may fall foul of some machinations, such as happened to Taine the first time he ran. And if Max doesn't make a lot of visits he'll be defeated and remain a perennial candidate. He who desires the end desires the means. But why let oneself in for such nonsense? A great honour – to be proclaimed the equal of Messieurs Camille Doucet, Camille Rousselet, Mézières, Vieilcastel, etc.! Ah, no! Really too modest, to stoop so low . . . Now if being an Academician paid four thousand francs a year, I'd begin lowering myself at once.

Keep all this to yourself, mon Mouton. For nothing is in worse taste than to joke about the Academy. It's like the Legion of Honour. Money, yes: but 'honour' – thanks!

1. A cultivated Parisian bourgeoise. She, her complaisant husband, and Maxime DuCamp formed a ménage à trois for many years. It was probably her curly white hair that caused her to be called 'le Mouton' (the sheep). Through her, DuCamp had sent word to Flaubert that he was seeking election to the French Academy. It was, and remains, the custom for a candidate to visit Academicians and solicit their votes. DuCamp would win his chair without difficulty – a victory greeted with scorn and indignation by the Left, which never forgave him for his writings about the Commune and particularly for the Matillon incident.

~

To Maxime DuCamp

Croisset, February 27, 1880

First of all, it was good of you to tell me at once about your election, and I thank you for doing so.

Next, why should you think I would be 'irritated'? Since it gives you pleasure, it also pleases me; but I am surprised, astonished, stupefied, and keep asking myself: 'Why? For what purpose?'

Do you remember a skit that you, Bouilhet, and I once acted out at Croisset? We officially welcomed each other into the French Academy! . . . Which 'inspires me with curious reflections', as Joseph[1] would have put it.

Ask the Mouton to give the new academician a kiss from me. *Ton vieux.*

1. Joseph (Giuseppe) Brichetti had been Flaubert and DuCamp's dragoman during their Egyptian journey in 1849–1850.

~

Victor Hugo and others had at various times proposed to Flaubert that he stand for election to the Academy, but he always refused. When Taine and Renan entered the lists in 1878, he wrote to Princesse Mathilde (June 13): 'I find both men exceedingly modest. In what respect can the Academy "honour" them? When you are somebody, why wish to be *something*?' A little later, again to the princess: 'You tell me that everybody, in his heart, wants to belong to the French Academy. Not everybody, I assure you, and if you could read my conscience you would see that I am sincere. Such protestations are in bad taste: no matter, I think I'll not give in. This honour isn't the subject of my dreams. What I dream of, men cannot give me. To tell the truth, I no longer have many dreams. My life has been spent grasping at chimeras. No more.' And to Mme Roger des Genettes, apropos once more of his refusal to stand for election, he quoted from the proud – if possibly apocryphal – motto of the noble Rohan family:

Roi ne puis
Prince ne daigne
Rohan suis

('King I cannot be, Prince I deign not be, Rohan I am.')

About this time, when Flaubert was nearing his death, a change seems to have entered his soul. What it was, one cannot definitely know; but perhaps the very brevity of the sensation of relief engendered by the pension – the almost instant, brutal destruction of that euphoria by the agonizing break with Laporte – made Flaubert resolve to strike out, to seek what pleasure, what comfort, was still possible for him despite the assaults of the Commanvilles.

In March 1880 Commanville had what Caroline reported as good financial news. Flaubert wrote to her warmly about it; but even he must have regarded it, after all that had passed, as probably a will-o'-the-wisp; and in the same letter with his congratulations he made requests in which (as Enid Starkie says)[1] 'one can sense . . . the suppressed irritation of the past years'. Apparently the Commanvilles were planning to move in the autumn to new Parisian quarters of their own; Flaubert, looking forward to more frequent visits to the city, demanded relief from the clutter they had made of his flat.

1. In *Flaubert the Master* (see Works of Related Interest).

∽

To his niece Caroline
                              [Croisset,] Sunday, 4 o'clock [March 14, 1880]
                          · · ·

And now let's talk a little about 'our', or rather *my* apartment. Well, Madame, here are my wishes.

I ask to be liberated from my enemy, *the piano*, and from another enemy, which hits me on the forehead – the *stupid hanging lamp* in the dining room. It is very inconvenient when one has something to do at the table. So, since I'll need the table for my copyist this summer, remove that contraption and put back the simple lamp I had in the boulevard du Temple.

Free me also of *all the rest* – it will be simpler! – the sewing machine, the plaster casts, your *beautiful* glass-front bookcase, your chest. I was so inconvenienced by all that, the last time, that I had to keep my clothes on chairs. Store this superfluous furniture at Bedel's until your next move. But arrange things so I'll feel a bit at home and have some elbow room. Since this apartment is no longer to be of use to you, *empty it.* And please note that I'll need it in May and June, and that I'll probably be back there in September.

. . .

≈

He sent out invitations to a small festival at Croisset, to include Georges Charpentier, a few fellow writers whom Charpentier published, and his own 'disciple':

≈

To Guy de Maupassant

[Croisset,] Wednesday night [March 24, 1880]

My dear fellow,

I don't yet know what day Goncourt, Zola, Alphonse Daudet, and Charpentier are coming here for lunch or dinner and perhaps the night. They are to decide this evening, and I shall know on Friday morning. I think it will be Monday.[1] So if the condition of your eye permits, betake yourself to one of the aforesaid characters, find out when they are leaving, and come with them.

Assuming that all of them spend Monday night at Croisset, since I have only four beds available you will occupy the maid's room – she is absent at the moment.

Note: I have been hearing so many silly and implausible things about your illness that I should like very much, purely for my own satisfaction, to have you gone over by *my* doctor, Fortin. He is a simple health officer, but I consider him excellent.

Further observation: if you haven't the cash for the trip, I have a superb double louis at your service. A refusal on grounds of delicacy would be an insult to me.

Last item: Jules Lemaître, whom I told that you would recommend him to Graziani,[2] will call at your office. He has talent and is a real scholar, *rara avis,* worthy of a better post than the one he has at Le Havre.

He too may come to Croisset on Monday; and since I intend to get you all drunk I have also invited Fortin, to 'heal the sick'.

The festival will be lacking in splendour if I don't have my disciple.

Your old
Gustave Flaubert

1. They arrived on Easter Sunday, March 28.
2. Probably Anton Graziani (1820–1906), 'Chef de Division' in the Ministry of Justice.

～

Edmond de Goncourt wrote about the Easter visit in his *Journal* for March 28:

> Maupassant meets us with a carriage at the Rouen station, and Flaubert welcomes us at the house, wearing a broad-brimmed hat and short jacket, with his big behind in pleated trousers, and his kind, affectionate face.
>
> It is really very beautiful, his place – I hadn't remembered it too well. The enormously wide Seine, with the masts of invisible ships passing by as though against a backdrop in a theatre; the splendid tall trees, their shapes tormented by the sea winds; the garden with its espaliers, the long terrace-walk facing full south: these all make it a fit dwelling for a man of letters – for Flaubert – after having been, in the eighteenth century, the country house of a community of Benedictines.
>
> The dinner is very good: a turbot in cream sauce that is truly a marvel. Many wines of all kinds; and we spend the evening telling broad stories that make Flaubert burst into laughter that is like a child's. He refuses to read from his novel – he can't, he's 'all in'. And we retire to bedrooms that are rather cold and contain a number of family busts.

To the end, the Commanvilles did their best to spoil things.

～

To his niece Caroline
>   *[Croisset,] Tuesday, 10 a.m. [March 30,] 1880*

My Loulou

Do you understand anything about the enclosed letter? More threats! I'm beginning to get used to them, and since I defy anyone to seize my 'property whether real or personal', I remain calm.

I absolutely did not know that I had borrowed fifty thousand francs. Who is M. Legendre? Whom should I consult about this, your lawyer in Rouen, or the one in Paris?

This letter from M. Mesnil has been sent on to me from the rue Murillo. Do what you think proper, as you undoubtedly have instructions.

My reception went off *admirably*!

~

To his niece Caroline
>   *[Croisset,] Thursday [April 1, 1880], April Fool's Day, 6 p.m.*

Darling,

. . . I continue to receive legal documents addressed not only to me, but to others, including the servants! I don't know who has garnisheed the salary of your poor gardener (because of sums he does *not* owe, it seems). In all this I see only one thing: persecution of *me* by fate. Nothing in the world has ever been more intolerable to me. You would have to be in my skin to understand. Whenever anybody mentions money to me, I experience the aesthetic sensation of a person who has been flung into a Latrine!

It was not 400 francs that I advanced, at your husband's request, to Suzanne [the cook-housekeeper at Croisset], but 500. In addition, I gave her, quite apart from the ordinary house expenses, in order not to confuse accounts, 100 francs to pay in full for my reception last Sunday.

Your husband swore by all the gods that by mid-April he would reimburse me those 500 francs! (Note that last winter I paid 300 francs for wood and 300 francs for good wine.) If I advance you 500 more (which I will certainly do), and if it is impossible to reimburse me for that and for the rest, how am I to live in Paris this summer?

On the fifteenth of this month, we must find money to pay the quarter's rent. However, since I am 'a man of order', whatever people may say, I have enough, now, to cover everything. So don't worry, poor kitten; but you *must* learn to be a little more regular about things. Because, regarding these matters my nerves are at the end of their tether. Tuesday was made wretched – spoiled – by that letter from M. Mesnil.

.   .   .

~

To Ivan Turgenev

[Croisset,] Wednesday, April 7 [1880]

Mon bon cher vieux

I rejoice in the thought that in about a month I'll be seeing you . . .[1]

Did your ears burn on Easter Sunday? Here we drank a toast to Turgenev, regretting his absence. The following clinked their champagne glasses to your good health: first your humble servant, then Zola, Charpentier, A. Daudet, Goncourt, my doctor Fortin, and 'that dirty-minded little Maupassant', as Lagier[2] calls him. Apropos of Maupassant, his condition isn't as serious as I thought; he has nothing organically wrong, but the young man is gouty and rheumatic to the nth degree, and totally neurotic.[3] After dining here, the aforesaid gentlemen spent the night, and left the next day after lunch. I was adamant about not reading them anything from *Bouvard and Pécuchet*.

Pradier, when he was working at the Invalides in 1848, used to say: 'The Emperor's tomb will be my own', so exhausting did he find the task.[4] I can say: 'It's time to reach the end of my book – otherwise, I know whose end will come.' Frankly, I'm sick and tired of it. It's turning into a chore, and I still have three months to go, not counting the second volume, which will take me six. All in all, I'm afraid the result may not reward all the effort, and I feel so weary that the denouement may well be anemic and botched. I've got to the point of scarcely knowing what I'm doing; every bone in my body aches, I have stomach cramps, and I scarcely sleep. But enough moaning.

Here are my plans: I hope to be in Paris about May 10, to remain until the end of June; then return to Croisset for two months to make the lists that will comprise most of my second volume; then back to Paris in September for a long stay . . .

My strongest indignation at present is directed against Botanists. Impossible to make any of them understand a question that I find very clear.[5] You'll see this for yourself, and will be amazed by the lack of *judgement* in those brains.

Try to find a few minutes to write to me: that would be good of you. And don't be too long about coming back here to all of us. A great embrace to you . . .

1. Turgenev was still in Russia.
2. The actress Suzanne Lagier (1833–1893), free and easy in life and language; friend of Flaubert and the Goncourts, and the subject of many a scabrous entry in the latters' *journal.*
3. Limited contemporary medical knowledge apparently prevented Fortin, as well as other doctors, from recognizing Maupassant's early syphilitic symptoms.
4. James Pradier (1792–1852) had executed busts of Flaubert's father and sister. Readers may recall that it was in Pradier's studio, where Louise Colet was posing, that she and Flaubert first met, in 1846. The twelve colossal figures of Victories surrounding Napoleon's tomb in the Invalides were in fact Pradier's last works.
5. For a passage in Chapter X of *Bouvard and Pécuchet.* In his indefatigable researches, Flaubert was seeking not only 'exceptions to the rule' in botanical classification, but 'exceptions to exceptions'. He was to write to Caroline on April 28 that Maupassant had found the answer for him by consulting 'the professor of Botany at the Jardin des Plantes'.

∾

TO HIS NIECE CAROLINE

[Croisset,] Sunday night [April 18, 1880]

My Loulou,

. . . This morning I sent your husband yet another summons I have received from a process-server! If this is a bet, to see whether I'll die of pure rage, it's about won. Useless to say more about it, surely? I ask for no explanations, but, in heaven's name, give me some peace! Let me have some peace, and let this persecution stop!

. . . .

Zola, Céard, Huysmans, Hennique, Alexis, and my disciple have sent me *Les Soirées de Médan*,[1] with a very pleasant collective inscription. I suppose Guy will have sent you a copy (unless he doesn't have one). I have re-read '*Boule de Suif*', which I continue to consider a masterpiece.

1. This volume, in which '*Boule de Suif*' was first published, contained a preface by Zola, and one story by each of the writers named by Flaubert. All of them, for purposes of 'publicity', labelled themselves 'realist' or 'naturalist'. Each story recounted an episode of the Franco-Prussian War. The title, 'Evenings at Médan', refers to Zola's house at Médan on the Seine, where the younger writers often gathered. ' "*Boule de Suif*" dwarfs the rest of the volume,' Flaubert wrote to Maupassant. 'The title of the book is stupid.' *Les Soirées* was expertly publicized and sold well.

～

Maupassant's first and only volume of poetry, *Des Vers*, was published a week after *Les Soirées de Médan*. It was dedicated 'To Gustave Flaubert, the illustrious and fatherly friend whom I love with all my heart, the irreproachable master whom I admire above all others.'

～

To Guy de Maupassant

[*Croisset, April 25, 1880*]

Mon Jeune Homme

You are right to love me, for this old man cherishes you. I read your volume at once – of course I was already familiar with three quarters of it. We'll go over it together. What pleases me especially is that it is personal. No chic! No pose! Neither parnassian nor realist (nor impressionist, nor naturalist).

Your dedication stirred up in me a whole world of memories: your uncle Alfred, your grandmother, your mother; and for a while this old man's heart was full, and there were tears in his eyes.

Save me everything that appears about 'Boule de Suif' and about your volume of verse . . .

～

Flaubert's last feast of St Polycarp was celebrated at the Lapierres' in Rouen on April 27, 1880. This year it was embellished with a non-existent orchestra and some farcical messages concocted by Maupassant.

~

To his niece Caroline

[Croisset,] Wednesday [April 28, 1880]

The St Polycarp celebration left me speechless! The Lapierres surpassed themselves! I received more than *thirty* letters, sent from different parts of the world! and three telegrams during dinner. The Archbishop of Rouen, several Italian cardinals, some garbage collectors and members of the floor-waxers' guild, the proprietor of a shop selling religious statuettes, etc. – all sent me their greetings.

As presents, I was given a pair of silk socks, a foulard, three bouquets, a wreath, a portrait (Spanish) of St Polycarp, a tooth (relic of the saint); and a box of flowers is on its way from Nice! An orchestra had been hired, but failed to put in an appearance. Letters from Raoul Duval and his two daughters. A poem by Mme Brainne's son. All the letters (including Mme Regnier's) were adorned with the likeness of my patron saint. I was forgetting a menu composed of dishes all named for my books.

Really, I was touched by the trouble everybody had taken to give me a good time. I suspect my disciple of having had a large hand in the farcical goings-on.

I'm glad you admire '*Boule de Suif*' – a true masterpiece, no more, no less: it stays in one's mind.

. . .

Ten days from now, will I have reached the point I'd like to attain before leaving my dear old Croisset? I doubt it. And when will the book be finished? That's the question. If it is to appear next winter, I haven't a minute to lose between now and then. But there are moments when I feel I'm liquefying like an old Camembert, I'm so tired. But a week spent chatting with '*l'altière Vasthi*'[1] will refresh me.

1. See Appendix IV, p. 684.

~

To Maurice Sand[1]

[Croisset,] Tuesday morning [April 1880]

My dear Maurice

No: *omit* 'Cruchard' and 'Polycarp', and substitute for those names whatever you please. The public mustn't have our all: let's reserve something for ourselves. That seems to me more fitting (*quod decet*).

You don't say whether the edition will be complete? Ah! your dear mother – how I think of her, and how I need her! Not a day when I don't tell myself 'If she were here, I'd ask her advice'.

Until May 8 or 10 I'll be at Croisset. So – whenever you want to come you'll be welcome.

I embrace you all, from the oldest man to the youngest girl.

'Cruchard' to you.

'Polycarp' to the human race.

'Gustave Flaubert' in literature.

1. Maurice was preparing an edition of his mother's letters; Flaubert had sent him all those in his possession.

～

To Guy de Maupassant

[Croisset, May 3, 1880]

. . .

Eight printings of the *Soirées de Médan*? *Three Tales* had four. I'm going to be jealous.

You'll see me at the beginning of next week.

. . .

～

Guy de Maupassant to Ivan Turgenev

Paris, May 25, 1880

Dear Master and Friend,

I am still prostrated by this calamity, and his dear face follows me everywhere. His voice haunts me, phrases keep coming back, the disappearance of his affection seems to have emptied the world around me.

At three-thirty in the afternoon on Saturday, May eighth, I

received a telegram from Mme Commanville: 'Flaubert apoplexy. No hope. Leaving at six.' I joined the Commanvilles at six o'clock at the station; but stopping at my apartment on the way I found two other telegrams from Rouen announcing his death. We made the horrible journey in the dark, sunk in black and cruel grief. At Croisset we found him on his bed, looking almost unchanged, except that his neck was dark and swollen from the apoplexy. We learned details. He had been very well during the preceding days, happy to be nearing the end of his novel; and he was to leave for Paris on Sunday the ninth. He looked forward to enjoying himself – having, he said, 'hidden a nest-egg in a pot'. It wasn't a very large nest-egg, and he had earned it by his writing. He had eaten a very good dinner on Friday, spent the evening reciting Corneille with his doctor and neighbour, M. Fortin; had slept until eight the next morning, taken a long bath, made his toilet, and read his mail. Then, feeling a little unwell, he called his maid; she was slow in coming, and he called to her out of the window to fetch M. Fortin – but he, it turned out, had just left for Rouen by boat. When the maid arrived she found him standing, quite dizzy but not at all alarmed. He said, 'I think I'm going to have a kind of fainting fit; it's lucky it should happen today; it would have been a great nuisance tomorrow, in the train.' He opened a bottle of eau de Cologne and rubbed some on his forehead, and let himself down quietly on to a large divan, murmuring, 'Rouen – we're not far from Rouen – Hellot – I know the Hellots –' And then he fell back, his hands clenched, his face darkened and swollen with blood, stricken by the death he had not for a second suspected.

His last words, which the newspapers interpreted as a reference to Victor Hugo, who lives in the avenue d'Eylau, seem to me unquestionably to have meant: 'Go to Rouen, we're not far from Rouen, and bring Dr Hellot. I know the Hellots.'

I spent three days beside him. With Georges Pouchet and M. Fortin I wrapped him in his shroud. And on Tuesday morning we took him to the cemetery, from which one has a perfect view of Croisset, with the great curve of the river and the house he so loved.

The days when we consider ourselves happy don't atone for days like those.

At the cemetery were many friends from Paris, especially his younger friends, *all* the young people he knew, and even some whom nobody knew; but not Victor Hugo, nor Renan, nor Taine, nor Maxime DuCamp, nor Frédéric Baudry, nor Dumas, nor Augier, nor Vacquerie, etc.

That's all, my dear master and friend. But I shall have many more things to tell you. We shall attend to the novel when the heirs have settled their affairs. You'll be needed for everything.

I wrote the very day of the calamity to Mme Viardot, asking her to tell you, because I didn't know your address in Russia. I preferred you should learn this sad news from friends rather than from a newspaper.

I shake your hands sadly, *mon cher maître*, and hope to see you soon.

Your entirely devoted

GUY DE MAUPASSANT

~

The circumstances of Flaubert's death are known to us through those words by Maupassant.

Maupassant himself was to die insane eleven years later – a victim, at forty-three, of general paresis, one of the forms that can be taken by syphilis in its tertiary stage. Flaubert – who in a number of letters in the first volume of the present work refers to treatments for venereal infection, and to symptoms that are clearly syphilitic – was spared the prolonged wretchedness of such an end. But in modern medical opinion it was probably the same insidious disease, in its tertiary stage, that killed him, at the age of fifty-nine.

Drawing to its close, the nineteenth century thus bore away, as victims of its cruellest realities, one of its most powerful, and one of its most spirited, interpreters.

Volume I

APPENDIX I

A Self-Portrait of Louise Colet[1]

Paris, Saturday, June 14, 1845

WHY BEGIN THIS diary today, instead of ten years ago, when I arrived in Paris – when I was full of enthusiasm, eager to see everything, still with my illusions about great men, about feelings, about fame?

Now I am thirty-four, no more, no less. I have grown stouter, my figure is no longer very slender, but still elegant, well shaped. My bust, neck, shoulders, and arms are extremely beautiful. I am still admired for the smooth curve of my throat and chin: too smooth, perhaps, for the outline of my face is blurred as a result, and lacks length, looks too round. I remedy this defect by the way I wear my hair – very long curls over the temples, which fall to my shoulders, partly covering my cheeks. I am often complimented on my luxuriant hair (very light chestnut: it was quite blonde when I was a child): a coiffeur arranges it skilfully every day. And yet my hair is one of the scourges of my vanity: it is beginning to go white (and when I say 'beginning', I should mention that I found white hairs ten years ago). The short hairs on the temples are almost entirely white. I brush longer hair over them and lacquer it in place. Every Saturday I have any other white hairs plucked out. '*Memento mori*', I always say with a laugh on those occasions, or rather '*Memento vivere*'. I have been doing this for three years, and my hair is so abundant that the thinning leaves no trace. While my hair is being dressed I read or write, so no time is wasted. Thanks to the care I take, I manage to conceal my white hair so well that no one believes me when I speak of it . . . I have a high forehead, very well formed, very expressive; my eyebrows are thick, elegantly arched; my eyes, dark blue, large, very beautiful when they brighten in response to a striking idea or perception, but they are often tired by work or dimmed by tears. My nose is charming – dainty, distinguished, unusual. My mouth is small, fresh-looking, though not remarkable in shape. My smile is particularly pleasant – kindly, naive, I am told: I have never seen myself smile. My teeth are beautiful, in excellent condition, and I have all of them except one rear molar that I had extracted, being unable to stand the pain. My legs are perfect, slender at the ankle; my feet are very small, finely boned, and the contrast between them and my tall, strong figure is greatly admired. My hands, too, are slender, white, fine. Quite a long portrait! I think I am hardly worth the trouble: some day I'll be more concise. As for my moral portrait, it will emerge from the following pages.

1. This self-portrait is the opening section of the fragmentary Memoranda, or 'Mementos', of Louise Colet, reproduced by Jean Bruneau in the Pléiade edition of Flaubert's correspondence from the autographs and typewritten copies in the Musée Calvet at Avignon. All the other 'Mementos' of Louise Colet translated in this book are from the same source.

APPENDIX II

Flaubert and Syphilis

THEODORE ZELDIN, IN *France, 1848–1945*, quoting contemporary sources, writes as follows about syphilis in Flaubert's day:

> It was indeed a major blight on the country. Flaubert, in his *Dictionary of Accepted Opinions*, defined it as being almost as common as the cold: 'More or less everybody is affected by it' . . . Half of syphilitics caught the disease between the ages of fourteen and twenty-one. In the bourgeoisie a tenth caught it at school . . . Visits to prostitutes started at school. On holidays and the Thursday half-day the brothels swarmed with schoolboys.[1]

Flaubert was no exception. One of his letters to Ernest Chevalier, written two months after his seventeenth birthday (see p. 24), tells of visiting a Rouen brothel, and he may have been infected with syphilis even before entering Law School in Paris. Alfred LePoittevin furnished him with the addresses of a number of Parisian 'houses' and the names of some of the girls. The painful chancres mentioned in the letter to Bouilhet from Constantinople (p. 180) resulted from subsequent, recent, probably non-syphilitic venereal infection. There was little medical knowledge of venereal diseases at the time. Mercury, which could produce painful effects of its own, was the standard treatment for syphilis, and Flaubert was one of the many who 'spent one night with Venus and the rest of their lives with

Mercury'. In August 1854, when he was almost thirty-three, approaching the end of *Madame Bovary*, he wrote to Louis Bouilhet:

> Laxatives, purges, derivations,[2] leeches, fever, colic, three sleepless nights – gigantic nuisance – such has been my week, *cher monsieur*. I have eaten nothing since Saturday night, and only now am I beginning to be able to speak. To put it briefly, Saturday night my tongue suddenly began to swell until I thought it was transmuting itself into that of an ox. It protruded from my mouth: I had to hold my jaws open. I suffered, I can tell you. But since yesterday I am better, thanks to leeches and ice.
>
> You should have had a letter from me on Saturday morning – it must have gone astray. For a week I was hideously sick. Terrific mercurial salivation, *mon cher monsieur*; it was impossible for me to talk or eat – atrocious fever, etc. Finally I am rid of it, thanks to purges, leeches, enemas (!!!), and my 'strong constitution'. I wouldn't be surprised if my tumour were to disappear, following this inflammation: it has already diminished by half. Anyway . . . I won't go to consult the great Ricord for another six weeks.[3] Meanwhile I'll keep stuffing myself with iodide.

Flaubert was fortunate that with him the disease did not take the course it did with Jules de Goncourt, Baudelaire, and Guy de Maupassant, all of whom died of paresis in their forties. The extent to which syphilitics infected women with whom they had intercourse during the contagious stage of the disease; the infection transmitted, in turn, by infected women; the effect on children; the personal and social wretchedness – all are part of the history of the disease before the discovery of penicillin.

1. Vol. I, pp. 304, 306.
2. An old medical term. Blistering, cupping, or other means of 'withdrawing inflammation or morbid humour from a diseased part of the body'. (OED)
3. 'Possibly the single most successful doctor of the nineteenth century was Philippe Ricord (1800–89), personal physician to Napoleon III and the national expert on syphilis. Born in Baltimore, the son of a bankrupt French shipowner, he rose to become Paris's busiest and possibly richest doctor.

His house in the rue de Tournon contained five large salons for his patients to wait in . . . His *Treatise on Venereal Diseases* (1838) did rightly distinguish between gonorrhea and syphilis, but he insisted that the latter was not contagious through secondary lesions: he continued to administer his incorrect doctrine to all the rich of Europe, despite the discoveries of the more obscure Joseph Rollet of Lyon (1856).' (Zeldin, I, 24–25, with a footnote mentioning Paul Labarthe, *Nos Médecins contemporains* (1868), 44.)

APPENDIX III

A Letter from Maxime DuCamp

[Paris,] Wednesday, October 29, 1851.

TO ANSWER EVERYTHING in your letter, *mon cher vieux*, would take me six months, and I would have to send you a volume of analyses. So I will only take up a few of your points and the last paragraph. For the rest, I would have to compose a complete treatise on your anatomy (concerning which I think you are often mistaken), and I do not want to do that: the task of dissecting and quartering is deeply repugnant to me,[1] and besides, what purpose would be served?

The matter of publication is very complex, despite its apparent simplicity. Do you merely want to publish? That is easy. Or do you expect to 'arrive' by publishing? That is not easy. You know as well as I that we are no longer living in the days when one became famous overnight by writing *Les Truands* or *L'Écolier de Cluny*.[2] The literary movement, or rather the passion for literature, is a thing of the past; art has fallen on evil days; philosophy and politics have completely usurped its place, and we must resign ourselves to spending many a long day in the dark before seeing the light again. Only in the theatre is it still occasionally possible to become a star overnight, without previous experience. If you want to arrive (I mean secure recognition), you must dig your tunnel quietly, like a miner, and blow up the citadel at a moment when such a thing is least expected. That requires careful preparation of the ground. Will you do it? I doubt it. In this, you are the way you tend to be about everything: you have a violent desire for things when they are impossible or impracticable, and as soon as you have them you are disgusted with them simply because you have them. You used to think a great deal about how you would begin: you wanted to make your mark, you wanted to obtain an instantaneous success and win the support of artists and journalists – that was actually your idea, as I recall. What you expected to do at great expense, I am doing now with nothing – and this is perhaps the real reason why you are offended by my remarks. You think my conduct undignified; you think I should have simply set down my prose and waited quietly with folded arms for admirers to come forward. No! Since I have made a start, since I want to get somewhere, I am not going to falter in my purpose. I am on my way: *bon voyage!* My pistols are in my pockets, I have spent a long time charting my route, and woe to him that stops me! I know I am playing a dangerous game: my life is at stake, and it is up to me to win. You were surprised, on your return from England, to find me so unaccustomedly busy, and you confided your surprise to Gautier. He gave you a very silly answer: had you really known what I am like, you would have understood me without consulting anyone else. Do you remember Rastignac's words in *Le Père Goriot*? What he says so grandly, I say in a smaller way: '*A nous deux, maintenant!*' I have finally got hold of something – a centre of activity where I can do what interests me, let off some of my superabundant steam: I have a very serious campaign to wage; a life-or-death struggle is in the balance. A literary revival is in the offing, and I am determined to be part of it – as a captain, not a private. A month ago I was worried, tormented, actually afraid. Today I am calm and confident: I have won my first battle.[3] I worked, and what is more I put others to work under my orders; and with my very first assault I have breached the walls of the citadel to which I have been slowly and quietly laying siege since 1847. Are you prepared to do all that? You always push things to their wildest extremes, you say, not quite in jest, 'I was not made to be a waltzer.' But *mon Dieu!* Who is suggesting anything of that kind? However, what you need above all is to learn the art of living, of which you are utterly ignorant. That ignorance has already done you greater harm than you can realize, and in your dealings with others it will make you inferior to many a talentless cretin.

You tell me: do what you like with me; make up my mind. That is impossible; I refuse; I cannot take charge of people's souls. Even though you may misunderstand me and take it out on me, I must leave you in your uncertainty; I could show you the two sides of the question, but especially in your case I will never tell you what course to follow. Nevertheless, whatever decision you make, whatever path you choose, I am always here; and believe me, I will spare you the hardest part. Whenever you want to publish, you will find your place ready and reserved – something that few can count on. Never for a moment have I separated you from myself in my thoughts: I have worked for the three of us – Bouilhet, you, and myself. That has long been the case, without your ever suspecting it.

If you publish, what will you publish? Your fragments of *Saint Antoine*, with one or two exceptions, are the kind of thing the public finds boring, and that is to be avoided above everything else; and besides, they are only fragments. What your mother said is right: if you have written something good, publish it. Like her, I can say no more than that. I have made my own success, I am going to make Bouilhet's; send me something good and I will make yours. This is all very serious and important, I know, and I cannot give you a single counsel.

You tell me that because it is to your taste, and after much deliberation, you have *chosen* the life you lead; but in this you are completely deluded. You passively *accepted* that way of life, and it has become your second nature. You accepted it first out of necessity, because of your illness; then out of duty, because of the deaths in your family; and finally, above all, because of the blind hatred of change you carry about with you and because you were afraid of your mother's unspoken reproaches. With her, you have never dared break what early became a habit. The proof of this is the happiness you have experienced whenever you have been able to get away. You enjoy having a good time – don't deceive yourself; and you expressed a profound truth when you wrote to me that you consent to be active only when activity brings you pleasure: that is very true.

Your way of life involves two great drawbacks:

1. It has tied you to your mother, hand and foot. It has given you the terrible habit of depending on others where your everyday life is concerned, and of thinking only of your *subjective* self and never of your *objective* self.

2. It has encased you completely within your own personality. You know how *you* live, but not how others live. Look about you as you may, you see only yourself; and in everything you have written, you have portrayed only yourself.

Those are the two great flaws in your way of life; and the fact is that it is weighing on you, boring you, and making you think that you 'hate life', whereas it is simply *your* life that you hate.

All this is not irremediable: far from it. We live at a time when it is dangerous to isolate ourselves from contemporary intellectual currents. This winter I am going to take courses at the Conservatory, and if I were younger I would study sciences, in order to understand what is going on. Such things are useful, if only to enlarge one's vocabulary. Solitude is beneficial only to the very strong, and to them only when they deliberately seek it for the completion of a task. Are we very strong? I doubt it; and we can never learn too much from others.

If you want to succeed, to arrive, I will say more: if you want to be truly yourself, come out of your hole, where nobody is going to look for you, and move into the daylight. Rub shoulders with the world; contemn it just enough to stand above it; but through this contempt, learn to observe by frequenting it. If you are the stronger, turn it to your advantage. Listen carefully to what it has to say; get to know it; and then talk down to it, and make it listen to you.

Who of all of us had a more favourable start than you? No one. Your life was free of cares, you had money and were known to be in comfortable circumstances, you had the shelter of your mother's house, the certainty that great sacrifices would be made to encourage you, a name made illustrious by your father and already familiar to the public. What have you done with all that? Nothing – and you are thirty years old. If you haven't made a beginning within two years, I don't know what the end will be.

Nowadays we no longer believe in unknown great men. From anyone who claims to have special qualities we pitilessly demand that he show us what he can do; and if he comes up with nothing we have our doubts about him. Be careful not to emulate those pregnant women who tighten their corsets in order to look thin and in so doing give themselves a miscarriage: that is fatal.

As yet, nothing forces you to publish; but if you want to publish eventually, make haste to prepare. As I already said, your place will be kept for you: I have given you my pledge. And the day you come to occupy it you will do as I have done: you will fling yourself so ardently and fiercely at the dish from which others are timidly nibbling, that they will all give way without even so much as trying to stop you.

Now, if you find your way of life adequate, and it leaves you with no regrets, if your work makes you happy, if you are satisfied with what you are writing and feel no need for anything else, if you are so filled with your own personality that you are content to be a great man for yourself alone, I have nothing to say: except that – since happiness comes first – you will do well to continue as you are.

So: as for advice, I give you none and can give you none. This is too serious a matter for me to have the right to do so. I cannot lure you on to a path that is perhaps not the one for you: I do not want to be your tempter. On one occasion[4] I was that, and once is enough. All I can tell you is that if you resolve to publish, I will help you with all my strength, with all my heart, with all my intelligence, with everything I know of life, with all my connections, with all my friends, with all my power, with all my influence: six months from now I will perhaps add 'with all my authority'. In short, count on me for everything – except to make your decision.

Do not doubt yourself – that would be wrong; but at the same time continue to scrutinize yourself with great diffidence. Self-confidence is a splendid thing only when legitimized by success; otherwise it is merely harmful, and makes others laugh while reminding them to be modest about themselves.

In short, when you are alone with your conscience you must know better than anyone else what you have to do. You must know, especially, what you *want* to do, and that is what must guide you.

So there you are, *cher vieux*: make up your mind. At this moment you have two possible options:

On the one hand, complete immersion in your own personality.

On the other: the need to publish something *good* within two years.

That, I think, is a brutal résumé of your position. Make your choice; and as soon as you have a goal, move towards it without looking back and without straying from your path.

One more word and I will have finished with this long letter which has been very painful for me to write and which I would never have undertaken had you not put my back to the wall.

My harsh words hurt you, you say, and you attribute them to your 'normandisms'. You are mistaken. Later, when we are real sheiks,[5] we will talk about all that. All I can tell you now is that I had been loving you for qualities that you do not possess. When I realized that, I had to redirect my friendship to that new nature I discovered in you; and – I tell you this from the bottom of my heart – that was a painful experience which disturbed me for a long time. It was then that I gave vent to those harsh utterances you reproach me for and which I regretted as soon as they were said; it was then that I felt bitter words spring to my lips and – because of my impetuous nature – escape from me despite my constant attempts to suppress them.

Adieu, *cher enfant.* Think carefully about all this; think about it coldly – it is almost like a medical consultation. And whatever happens, never forget that I am

Always yours,
Maxime DuCamp

Thursday night [October 30, 1851]

1. Flaubert had written to Louise Colet in 1846, during one of DuCamp's visits to Croisset:
    'In the mornings he goes to the Hôtel-Dieu to watch the doctors operate and amputate. He enjoys that.' (DuCamp's father, like Flaubert's, had been a well-known surgeon.) Flaubert, in his letter of October 21, 1851, to DuCamp (see pp. 203–6), to which the present letter is the reply, had 'asked for it', though perhaps – as is usually the case – not really wanting it; and in the present letter one does not sense that psychological dissection was in fact any more repugnant to DuCamp than physical surgery. Although the tone and level are in places deplorable, much of what DuCamp says is quite sensible. Even – or perhaps especially – knowing Flaubert as he did, he can be excused for not knowing he was offering *common* sense to a genius.
2. *Les Truands et Enguerrand de Marigny, 1302–1314, Histoire du règne de Philippe-le-Bel,* by Lottin de Laval (Victorien Pierre Lottin), (1832; second edition 1833). *L'Écolier de Cluny, ou le Sophisme, 1315,* by E. Roger de Beauvoir (Edouard Roger de Bully), (1832).
3. The successful launching of *La Revue de Paris.*

4. Perhaps the occasion mentioned on pp. 209–10, n. 1.
5. In a letter to his mother from Egypt, Flaubert had defined the term 'sheik'
as he and Maxime used it between themselves:

'... the sheik is a certain type of elderly [French] gentleman, inept,
living on his income, very respectable, very set in his ways, more or less
senile, always asking us questions about our trip such as the following:

' "And in the towns you've been visiting – is there a little social life?
Are there clubs, where you can read the newspapers?"

' "Are railways making headway? Is there a main line nearby?"

' "I sincerely trust socialist ideas haven't made inroads?"

' "Is the wine good, at least? Are there some special vintages?"

' "The ladies are ... friendly?" ...

'All that in a tremulous voice, with an air of imbecility. Sometimes we
do a double-sheik – i.e. two sheiks in dialogue.'

Flaubert's Niece Caroline

FLAUBERT'S NIECE CAROLINE, one of his most frequent correspondents in the later part of his life, was named for her grandmother and her mother (Flaubert's mother and sister). Two months after Caroline was born, her mother died of puerperal fever. Her death came soon after that of her and Gustave's father, Dr Achille-Cléophas Flaubert. The baby's father, Émile Hamard, had recently lost his own mother and brother, and in the tragic atmosphere of the household he soon showed signs of mental derangement. The child was brought up by her maternal grandmother (Mme Flaubert, Flaubert's mother), by Flaubert himself, and by English governesses – with one of whom, Juliet Herbert, Flaubert would have a long intimacy.

When Caroline superintended the publication of the first edition of Flaubert's general correspondence, in the late 1880s and early 1890s, she prefaced it with an account of her upbringing and her relations with her uncle. These introductory 'Souvenirs intimes' are charming and informative, but leave much unsaid – and, as we know, Caroline suppressed many passages in the letters themselves. Some of the missing facts are supplied in another memoir, *Heures d'autrefois*, written later in her life. This she left unpublished on her death in 1931, and portions of it were printed, with commentary (not all of it reliable) by *her* niece, Mme Lucie Chevalley-Sabatier, only in 1971, in a volume entitled *Gustave Flaubert et sa nièce Caroline*.

From this and other sources we learn of the young girl's loneliness as she grew up almost entirely without companions of her own age;

of the considerable culture she acquired from reading prescribed by Flaubert and from his conversation; and of her love, in late adolescence, for Johanny Maisiat, a young artist who had been engaged to give her drawing lessons. Mme Flaubert and the Flaubert relatives in Rouen quickly took alarm (Maisiat was 'unsuitable', apparently something of a 'bohemian'); and, deciding that an early, safe, bourgeois marriage was essential, they brought forward Ernest Commanville, a successful thirty-year-old timber importer of Rouen and Neuville (near Dieppe). Intellectually there was nothing about Commanville to interest a seventeen-year-old girl who had been educated by Flaubert, and clearly she was not otherwise attracted to him. Nevertheless, the family promoted his candidacy without mercy, and the anguish of the bullied Caroline is pathetically mirrored in Flaubert's letter to her of (?)December 23, 1863. (Her reply, written the next day, is no more mature than one might expect: 'You'd always come to see me, wouldn't you? Even if you found my husband too "bourgeois", you'd come for your Liline's sake? You'd have your own room, with big armchairs, the kind you like', and so on.)

Flaubert seems to have taken no further steps in the matter beyond the affectionate expressions of 'understanding' in his letter: much future grief might have been avoided had he successfully encouraged Caroline in her hesitation. She finally agreed to the marriage on securing from her grandmother a foolish promise that Commanville would be asked to agree that 'there would be no children'. After the wedding, still in her bridal dress, Caroline thanked her husband for his acceptance of that condition, only to learn that Mme Flaubert had simply not delivered the unrealistic message. The Commanvilles' Venetian honeymoon was a torment for both. Flaubert remained ignorant for years of the intensity of Caroline's unhappiness in her marriage.

For a time the Commanvilles seem to have lived rather largely, with a house at Neuville, a flat in Rouen, and a house in Paris. In *Heures d'autrefois* Caroline says that she was never 'unfaithful' to Commanville, but that another infatuation was the reason she left France for England during the early months of the Franco-Prussian War. She does not reveal the name of her suitor. (M. Lucien Andrieu, secretary of the association '*Les Amis de Flaubert*' at Croisset, is at present investigating the possibility that he was Charles Henri Léon

Rivoire, younger brother of two of Flaubert's 'three angels', who was approximately Caroline's age.) He seems to have joined the army, and she could hope to correspond with him more freely from outside France. There is a certain irony here: Commanville seems to have been more or less aware of the situation, and encouraged his wife's departure for England, where she would be farther from her suitor. As the correspondence shows, Flaubert, apparently ignorant of all this, was puzzled both by Caroline's departure and by her husband's acquiescence in it.

After the war, despite painting lessons in Paris and the acceptance of some of her work by the Salon (thanks in part to Princesse Mathilde Bonaparte and other influential friends of her uncle's), despite dinners, the theatre and other distractions, neurotic illness gradually overtook Caroline. Health spas were prescribed; and it was during one of her stays at Bagnères-de-Luchon during the summer of 1872, where Flaubert had accompanied her, that she told her uncle the story of her marriage, infatuation and renunciation. (Rivoire had gone to Algiers, where he died, unmarried, on May 2, 1872.) By this time Caroline had sought consolation and counsel from a fashionable, 'liberal' Dominican priest, *Père* Henri Didon, whose importance in her life Flaubert only now came to understand.

Commanville's timber business suffered badly from the war. By the terms of her marriage contract under the dower system, Caroline could not legally pay debts contracted by her husband, and in 1871 the Commanvilles embarrassed Flaubert by persuading him to ask Princesse Mathilde to lend them 50,000 francs. The princess's lawyers advised her not to do so. In 1872 Caroline's capital came to include the house at Croisset, inherited from her grandmother with the proviso that Flaubert be allowed to spend the rest of his life there. The traditional Church advice to a troubled wife – 'trust your husband' – had doubtless been part of *Père* Didon's counselling.[1] Loyal, therefore, to Commanville, who was 'managing' Flaubert's own modest capital (actually, drawing on it constantly for his own purposes), Caroline displayed a hardness towards her uncle that was perhaps in part reluctant. She urged him to live more economically. The Commanville Paris house and Flaubert's pleasant flat in the rue Murillo were given up, and two small contiguous apartments were taken at the far end of the Faubourg St Honoré.

Things went from bad to worse. In 1875 Commanville's creditors agreed to accept 35 per cent of their claims rather than press for bankruptcy. To pay them in part, Flaubert sacrificed his only property, a farm at Deauville that was his chief source of income. Pending the sale of the sawmill and adjoining property, the bankers Faucon, Pécuchet, et Cie, of Rouen, who either were creditors themselves or represented the creditors, consented to accept 50,000 francs of the remainder in annual instalments, to be paid by Caroline from her personal income. Because this was in fact illegal, they insisted on guarantors and at Flaubert's plea, his friends Raoul Duval and Edmond Laporte agreed to guarantee 25,000 francs each. Flaubert's anguish over this transaction arose from several causes. He feared that he and his beloved niece might be reduced to penury despite his sacrifice of the Deauville land that had come to him from his mother and held many memories; and that a way might be found to sell Croisset itself, despite the terms of his mother's will. It disgusted him that he should be involved in sordid business affairs and be called on to involve his friends as well.

In 1879, after four years of uncertainty, the Commanvilles' last hope, that the sale of the mill and adjoining property might realize more than enough to cover their remaining liabilities, was dashed. They gave up their Paris apartment and moved into Flaubert's adjoining one; Caroline sold silver inherited from an aunt; she gave drawing lessons and painted portraits and fans. Only during the last year of his life (1879–1880) did Flaubert regain a degree of financial comfort, thanks to a modest government pension. This was augmented by a minor commercial success with his volume *Three Tales* and by the reprinting of his earlier books. However, he continued to be persecuted by the creditors with whom Ernest Commanville had involved him. To the Commanvilles he sacrificed also a precious friendship, that of Edmond Laporte (see Appendix VI).

The correspondence reflects Flaubert's constant concern for Caroline: he always remained devoted to her, even though during his last years his affection was sorely tried, and perhaps somewhat impaired,[2] by her steady reinforcement of her husband's financial demands. For her sake he remained on good terms with the rapacious Commanville, and to the end of his life did his incompetent best to suggest persons who might advance still more money to pay pressing creditors. Concerning his complaints about the Commanvilles' harassment, Mme Chevalley-Sabatier says: 'Flaubert perhaps did not remember' – yet perhaps he did – 'that he had, in this case, a certain responsibility. Had he forgotten Caroline's sobs and anger as she sought to refuse a marriage that her grandmother and uncle succeeded in imposing on her?'

Along with the sale of Croisset, one of Caroline's first concerns following Flaubert's death was to see to the publication of *Bouvard and Pécuchet* – that is, of what Flaubert had considered the first volume, left completed except for the final chapter. She and Maurice Sand together prepared portions of the Flaubert–George Sand correspondence for publication in *La Nouvelle Revue* in 1883–1884. In the latter year, a volume containing 122 of Flaubert's letters to George Sand was published by Charpentier, with a foreword by Guy de Maupassant.[3]

From 1886 to 1893 Caroline supervised the first edition of her uncle's general correspondence, omitting most passages reflecting unfavourably on her husband and herself, and – at *Père* Didon's insistence – many which showed Flaubert at his racy and irreverent best.[4] With the aid of Louis Bertrand, Caroline also published several volumes of Flaubert's youthful works that had hitherto remained in manuscript.

Ernest Commanville died in 1890. Enjoying a steady income from the worldwide sale of her uncle's works, Caroline moved to the south of France and built a house at Antibes which she christened Villa Tanit, from the name of the goddess in *Salammbô*.[5] In 1900 she married Dr Franklin Grout, who until his retirement had been director of the celebrated private asylum founded by Dr Esprit Blanche in Passy, where Maupassant had spent his last demented years. In 1907 she published a volume of Flaubert's letters to herself – again, many of them incomplete. She was widowed for the second time in 1921 and died at Antibes in February 1931. She bequeathed Flaubert's most important manuscripts and his correspondence to various French libraries; other manuscripts and some of Flaubert's personal belongings were sold at auction.

Caroline's personality as revealed in Flaubert's letters and in her own memoirs is a blend of the pathetic and the imperious. She had been completely deprived of a mother's affection, and barely knew her deranged father; she was adored by her grandmother and uncle, and though often rebellious against their strict discipline, she knew it to be loving. At seventeen, her heart was broken when this accustomed authority suddenly showed itself ruthless, forcing her into a repellent marriage. From that time, with a momentary faltering when a likely suitor appeared as tempter, duty, 'honour', and materialism ruled her, attended by neurasthenia, the consolations of religion and a demeanour that many found cold. She could certainly be remorseless when she chose – to Flaubert among others. In his later letters her uncle took to calling her *l'altière Vasthi*, after the haughty queen in the book of Esther. (For the impression that Caroline in her old age made on a sensitive, cultivated, talented – 'innocent' – American woman, the reader may consult Willa Cather's charming essay, 'A Chance Acquaintance', in her volume *Not Under Forty*. The two women met by chance at Aix-les-Bains during the last year of Caroline's life.)

Caroline's company and her letters were an incalculable boon to Flaubert, despite the distress that she and Commanville caused him. Her greatest services to us were the preservation of Flaubert's manuscripts, the publication of his youthful writings, and her edition, faulty though it was, of his correspondence. For Caroline's censoring of the latter, Mme Chevalley-Sabatier asks us to forgive her: 'Let us not forget that we are in 1887.'

It is perhaps comprehensible, as well, on grounds other than chronology. A consciousness of her role as reflected in the letters, and of her inability to present her own story in extenuation, no doubt weighed with her. Her role, as it touches Flaubert, is a painful one. And while certain of her actions are indefensible, it is ultimately impossible to judge her. In his preface to Mme Chevalley-Sabatier's memoir, Jean Bruneau adds his voice to hers in urging us to 'understand' Caroline. This note is a brief attempt to do so.

1. The Church apparently retains this position in the present century. A Monsignor who is a professor of nineteenth-century history and literature, when asked by the present editor to comment on these remarks concerning Caroline's situation, replied: 'I do not know what else can be said except a reference to St Paul's injunction to wives that they be obedient to their husbands.'

2. His friend Raoul Duval, who had witnessed much, being close to the scene,

expressed this opinion in a letter to Maxime DuCamp, September 26, 1881. (J.B.)

3. Other editions of the Flaubert–Sand correspondence have since followed, most recently the admirable volume of 422 letters edited by Professor Alphonse Jacobs, published by Flammarion in 1981.

4. This, too, has been followed by many other editions, culminating in that of the Bibliothèque de la Pléiade (Gallimard) being prepared by Jean Bruneau, two volumes of which, out of a projected four, have already appeared at this writing.

5. This might be considered Caroline's second close connection with a Carthaginian name. The first had been a curious verbal coincidence: *Didon*, the name of her spiritual director, is also the French form of *Dido* – name of the legendary queen and founder of the Punic city.

APPENDIX V

'Reply to a Friend' by George Sand

August, 1871 – Nohant[1]

WHAT! YOU WANT me to stop loving? You want me to say that I have been mistaken all my life, that mankind is contemptible, hateful, has always been so and always will be? And you reproach me for my anguish, calling it weakness, childish regret for a lost illusion? You say that the populace has always been savage, the priest always a hypocrite, the bourgeois always craven, the soldier always a brigand, the peasant always stupid? You say you have known all this since youth, and you rejoice in never having doubted it because that has spared you disillusionment in later life. You have never been young, then. Ah! You and I are very different, for I have never stopped being young – if to persist in loving is a sign of youth.

How should I isolate myself from my fellow beings, from my fellow countrymen, from my race, from the great family in whose bosom my private family is merely as one ear of corn in the earthly field? And if only this ear could ripen in a safe place, if only one might, as you say, live for a few privileged beings and withdraw from all the rest! But that is impossible, and your fine intelligence is adapting itself to a supremely unreal Utopia. In what Eden, in what fantastic El Dorado, will you hide your family, your little group of friends, your intimate happiness, so that the lacerations of society and the disasters of the country will not reach them? If you want to be happy through a few, then those few, your heart's elect, must be happy in themselves. Will they be? Can you guarantee them the slightest security?

Will you find me some refuge in my old age, which is drawing to its close? What do I care now about death or life for myself? Supposing that we die entirely, that love does not follow us into the other life, are we not tormented until our last breath by the longing, the imperious need, to assure the greatest possible happiness of those we leave behind? Can we go serenely to our rest when we feel the earth quaking, ready to engulf all those for whom we have lived?

To live along happily in the bosom of one's family despite everything is without doubt a great good, relatively speaking – the sole consolation that one could, or would, enjoy. But even supposing that evil from without does not penetrate into our homes – an impossibility as you well know – I could never agree that we should reconcile ourselves to a source of public misery.

Everything that has come about was foreseen . . . Yes, of course. I had foreseen it as clearly as anyone! I saw the storm brewing; I was aware, as were all thinking people, of the unmistakable signals of the cataclysm. As you watch a sick man writhe in pain, is it any consolation that you are knowledgeable about his disease? When lightning strikes, are we any the calmer for having heard the thunder long before?

No, no, one doesn't isolate oneself, one doesn't sever the ties of blood, one doesn't curse and despise one's kind. Humanity is not an empty word. Our life is made of love, and to stop loving is to stop living.

The populace, you say! The populace is you and I: there is no escaping that. There are not two races; nowadays inequalities due to class distinctions are only relative and usually illusory. I don't know whether you have ancestors who were in the upper reaches of the bourgeoisie; as for me, on the maternal side my roots spring directly from the people, and I feel them ever alive in the very depths of my being. We all have such roots, no matter how much their memory may be obliterated: the first men were hunters and shepherds, then farmers and soldiers. Brigandage triumphant gave birth to the first social distinctions. There is perhaps no single title not acquired by the shedding of human blood. We must certainly endure our ancestors when we have them; but are those remote trophies of hate and violence a glory in which even the least philosophical mind can find a basis for presumption? 'The populace is always savage,' you say. I say, it is the nobility that is always ferocious.

Certainly, together with the peasant, the nobility is the class most obstinately set against progress, and thus the least civilized. Thinkers should congratulate themselves on not belonging to it; but if we are bourgeois, if we are the descendants of serfs and forced labourers, can we love and make reverence before our fathers' oppressors? No! Whoever denies the people degrades himself and displays to the world the shameful spectacle of apostasy. Bourgeoisie! If we want to rise again and recreate ourselves as a class, we have only one possibility: to proclaim ourselves the people, and struggle to the death against those who claim to be our superiors by divine right. For having failed to maintain the dignity of our revolutionary mandate, for having aped the nobility, usurped its insignia, adopted its playthings, for having been shamefully absurd and cowardly, we no longer matter, we are nothing: the people, who should be at one with us, spurn us, and would oppress us.

The populace savage? No: nor is it stupid. But at present it suffers from being ignorant and foolish. It is not the Parisian populace who massacred the prisoners, destroyed the monuments, and tried to set fire to the city. The Parisian populace comprises all who remained in Paris following the siege, since anyone with even the most modest means hastened to breathe the air of the provinces and embrace their absent families after the physical and moral hardships of the blockade. Those who stayed in Paris were the merchant and the workman, those two agents of labour and exchange without whom Paris would cease to exist. They are what directly constitutes the populace of Paris: a single, homogeneous family, whose relations and solidarity cannot be destroyed by political folly. It is now recognized that the oppressors in the turmoil were a minority. Thus the Parisian populace was not inclined to violence, for the majority displayed only weakness and fear. The movement was organized by men already inscribed in the ranks of the bourgeoisie and no longer sharing in the ways of life and the needs of the proletariat. These men were propelled by hatred, by thwarted ambition, deluded patriotism, fanaticism without an ideal, sentimental folly, or natural evil – there was something of all that in them, and even certain tenets of doctrinal pride unwilling to back down in the face of danger. They certainly did not rely on the middle class, which trembled, fled, or hid. They were forced to summon the real proletariat, who had nothing to lose. Well, that proletariat eluded them for the most part, divided as it was into very different shades of opinion, some wanting disorder for their own profit, others dubious of the consequences of involvement, most ceasing to reason because troubles had grown extreme and lack of work forced them to march into battle for thirty sous a day.

Why should you think that this proletariat, confined within Paris, and numbering at most eighty thousand soldiers of hunger and despair, represents the French populace? It doesn't even represent the Parisian populace, unless you want to maintain the distinction I reject, between the producer and the exploiter.

But I want to persist, and ask you on what this distinction rests. On more – or less – education? The dividing line is illusory. If you find men of cultivation and learning at the uppermost level of the bourgeoisie, and savages and brutes at the lowest grade of the proletariat, there nonetheless remains a vast number of people in between – intelligent and wise proletarians on the one hand, and, on the other, bourgeois who are neither wise nor clever. The majority of civilized citizens dates from yesterday, and many who can read and write have mothers and fathers yet living who can barely sign their names.

So it would be simply a greater or lesser amount of acquired wealth that would classify men into two distinct camps? In that case one wonders where the populace begins and where it ends, because affluence shifts every day: one man goes down in ruin, another comes into a fortune; roles change; he who was a bourgeois this morning will rejoin the proletariat this afternoon; and the proletarian of the moment will turn into a bourgeois if he finds a purse or inherits from an uncle.

Surely you see that these labels have become pointless, and that the task of classification, by whatever method, would be insoluble.

Men are above or below each other only in possessing more or less reason and morality. An education that develops only self-indulgence is inferior to the ignorance of a proletarian who may be instinctively and habitually honest. Compulsory education, which we all desire out of respect for human rights, is nevertheless not a panacea. Evil natures will discover in it merely more ingenious and better disguised ways to do wrong. Like all things misused by man, it will be both poison and antidote. The search for an infallible remedy for our ills is illusory. We must all seek, day by day, every means at hand. Today our only thought in practical life must be for improving ways of life and reconciling interests. France is in her agony, that is certain; we are all sick, all corrupt, all ignorant, all disheartened: to say that this was fated, that it must be so, has always been and always will be, is to recite again the fable of the pedagogue and the drowning child. One might as well say, straight out: 'It's all the same to me.' But if you add: 'It doesn't concern me', you are mistaken. The deluge approaches, and death is gaining on us. In vain will you be prudent, and withdraw: your refuge will be invaded in its turn, and as you perish with human civilization you will be no more philosophical for not having loved than those who threw themselves into the flood to save a few shreds of humanity. They are not worth the trouble, those shreds: so be it! They will perish in any case: that is possible; we shall perish with them: that is certain. But we at least shall meet death as warm and living beings. I prefer that to a hibernation in ice, to an anticipated death. Besides, I could not do otherwise. Love does not reason. If I asked you why you have a passion for study, you could explain it no better than those with a passion for idleness could explain their laziness.

So you think me shaken in my convictions, that you preach me detachment? You tell me that in the newspapers you read some fragments by me that reveal a change in my ideas; and those newspapers which quote me benignly do their best to think me newly enlightened; whereas others, who do not quote me, perhaps believe that I am deserting the cause of the future. Let politicians think and say what they will. Let us leave them to their critical assessments. I have no need to object, no need to answer. The public has other matters to discuss than my personality. I have a pen; I have an honourable place for free discussion in a great newspaper; it is rather for me, if I have been incorrectly interpreted, to explain myself more clearly when occasion presents itself. To speak of myself as an isolated individual is something I do as infrequently as possible: but if you think me converted to false notions, I must say this to you and to others who interest themselves in me: Read me as a whole, and do not judge me by detached fragments: a mind independent of party requirements necessarily sees the pros and cons, and the sincere writer tells both, without concern for the blame or approval of partisan readers. However, every rational being maintains some consistency, and I think I have not departed from mine. In me, reason and feelings are always at one in making me repulse whatever seeks our reversion to infancy – in politics, in religion, in philosophy, in art. My feelings and my reason contest more than ever the concept of fictitious distinctions, the inequality of condition that is imposed as a right conferred on some, as a loss deserved by others. More than ever I need to raise what is low and lift what has fallen. Until my heart ceases to beat, it will be open to pity, it will espouse the weak, rehabilitate the despised. If today it is the populace who are under foot, I will hold out my hand to them; if they become the oppressor and the executioner, I will say they are cowardly and odious. What is this or that group of men to me, or these proper names that have become badges, or those personalities that are slogans? I recognize only wise men and fools, the innocent and the guilty. I need not wonder where my friends are, or my enemies. They are where the maelstrom has cast them. Those who have earned my love, yet do not see with my eyes, are no less dear to me for that. The thoughtless abuse of those who have abandoned me does not make me consider them my enemies. Any friendship unjustly withdrawn remains intact in the heart of the innocent. Such a heart is above empty pride; it knows how to await the rebirth of justice and affection.

Such is the rightful and simple role of a conscience not yoked by personal interest to the interests of a party. They who cannot say as much for themselves will surely succeed in their chosen sphere if they have the skill to avoid everything inimical to it; and the greater their talent in that direction, the more readily will they find means to requite their passions. But never summon them before history, to bear witness to absolute truth. From the moment they make a trade of their opinion, their opinion is worthless.

I know some tender, generous, and timorous souls who at this terrible moment of our history reproach themselves for having loved and served the cause of the weak. They see but one point in space, they think that the populace they loved and served no longer exists, because in its place a horde of bandits, followed by a little army of frenzied men, has momentarily taken over the theatre of the struggle. These good souls must make an effort to tell themselves that what was good in the poor, and of concern in the forsaken, still exists; it is only no longer apparent, political turmoil having driven it from the stage. When such dramas are enacted, those who rush in recklessly are the vain or greedy members of the family, and those who let themselves be dragged in are the idiots. That the greedy, the idiotic, and the vain exist by the thousand in France is something that no one can doubt; but there are as many of them, and perhaps more, in other countries. Only let there arise one of those all too frequent occasions that give rein to evil passions, and you will see whether or not other nations are better than we. Wait and see the German nation at work – that nation whose armies have just displayed brutal appetites in all their barbarous crudity, and you will see the nature of its unchained fury! The insurgent populace of Paris will strike you as sober and virtuous by comparison.

This must not be a so-called crumb of comfort: we shall have reason to pity the German nation for its victories, as we pity ourselves for our defeats, because for them this is the first act of their moral dissolution. The drama of their abasement has begun; they are working for it with their own hands, and matters will go very quickly. All those huge materialistic organizations in which right, justice, and respect for humanity go unrecognized are colossi made of clay, as we ourselves have discovered to our cost. Well, the moral abasement of Germany is not the future safety of France; and if we are called on to return evil for the evil she has done us, her defeat will not restore us our life! It is not by bloodshed that races are revitalized and rejuvenated. Some vital breath can still issue from the corpse of France; that of Germany will be a source of pestilence for all Europe. A nation whose ideals have died does not live on. Its death fertilizes nothing, and those who breathe its foetid emanations are struck down by the same pestilence that killed it. Poor Germany! The cup of Eternal wrath is spilt on you as on us; and while you reel in drunken joy, the philosophical spirit grieves for you and prepares your epitaph. This pale, torn, bloody thing called France still grasps a fold of the starry mantle of the future, while you drape yourself in a soiled flag that will be your shroud. Past grandeurs no longer belong in the history of men. It is all over with kings who exploit their peoples, all over with exploited peoples who consent to their own degradation.

That is why we are so ailing, and why my spirit is weary.

But it is quite without scorn that I survey the degree of our wretchedness. I do not wish to believe that this holy country, this cherished race, all of whose harmonious and conflicting chords vibrate within me, whose qualities and faults I love despite every-thing, all of whose responsibilities good and bad I choose to accept rather than disdain – no: I do not wish to believe that my country and my race are stricken unto death. I feel it in my suffering, in my mourning, even in my hours of deepest melancholy; I love; therefore I am alive: let us love and live.

Frenchmen, let us love one another! My God, my God! Let us love one another or we are lost. Let us destroy, deny, annihilate politics, since politics divides us and sets us in arms against each other: let us ask none what he was, or what he wanted, yesterday. Yesterday, everyone was mistaken; we must know what we want today. If it is not liberty for all and fraternity towards all, then let us not seek to solve the problem of equality: we are not worthy to define it, we are incapable of understanding it. Equality does not impose itself; it is a free plant that grows only in fertile soil, in healthy air. It takes no root on the barricades: we know that now! There, it is at once trodden down by the victor, whoever he may be. Let us have the desire to establish it in our way of life, the will to consecrate it in our ideas. Let us give it, for a start, patriotic charity, love! It is insane to think one can issue from a battle with respect for human rights. Each civil war has exacted and will exact its penalty.

O wretched International! Is it true that you believe the lie that force has primacy over right? If you are as multiple, as powerful, as one imagines, is it possible that you profess destruction and hatred as a duty? No: your power is then a phantom, born of fear. A great number of men of all nations could not deliberate and act on a principle of evil. If you are the savage arm of the peoples of Europe, something like the Anabaptists of Münster, like them you will destroy yourself with your own hands. If, on the contrary, you are a great and legitimate fraternal association, your duty is to enlighten your adherents and denounce those who debase and compromise your principles. I yet would like to believe that your body includes many men who are hard-working and humane, and that these men suffer and are ashamed to hear bandits take your name. In that case, your silence is foolish and cowardly. Have you not a single member capable of protesting ignoble crimes, idiotic principles, mad frenzy? Your chosen leaders, your administrators, your inspirers – are they all brigands and cretins? No! It is impossible! There are no groups, no clubs, no crossroads where the voice of truth could not make itself heard. Speak out! Justify yourselves! Proclaim your gospel! Disband and reconstitute, if there is discord among you. Hurl an appeal to the future, if you be something more than the barbarian invasions of antiquity. Tell those who still love the people what they must do on its behalf; and if you have nothing to tell, if you can utter no word of life, if the iniquity of your mysteries is sealed with fear, then renounce all hope of sympathy from noble souls, find your nourishment in the scorn of honest men, and have it out with the jailer and the police.

All France has been waiting for the word: the word of your destiny, which might well have decided her own. She has waited in vain. In my naivety I too waited. Even while censuring the means, I did not want to prejudice the goal. There has always been a goal in revolutions, and the revolutions that fail are not always those least well grounded. Patriotic fanaticism seemed the first sentiment underlying this struggle. Those lost children of the democratic army would perhaps refuse to subscribe to an inevitable peace that they considered shameful: Paris had sworn to be buried in her own ruins. The democratic populace would force the bourgeois populace to keep its word. They seized the cannon; they were going to turn them against the Prussians. It was mad, but it was splendid . . . But no! The Commune's first act is to adhere to the peace; and throughout its entire administration it voices not one protest, makes not the slightest threat, against the enemy. It conceives and commits the dastardly act of destroying, under the enemy's eyes, the column commemorating that enemy's defeats and our victories. What it hates is the power derived from universal suffrage, and yet it invokes that suffrage in Paris, in order to establish itself. It is true that it does not obtain the vote: it dispenses with its desired appearance of legality and functions by brute force, invoking no right except that of hatred and scorn for everything other than itself. It preaches 'positive social science', whose sole repository it claims to be, but not a word of which appears in its deliberations or decrees. It declares it has come to deliver man from his shackles and prejudices, and immediately it exercises unchecked power and threatens death to anyone not convinced of its infallibility. While claiming to revive the tradition of the Jacobins, it assumes the papacy of society and makes itself into a dictatorship. What kind of republic is that? I see nothing life-giving in it, nothing rational, nothing that is or could be constitutional. It is an orgy of self-styled renovators, who possess not an idea, not a principle; not the least solidarity with the nation or outlook to the future. Ignorance, cynicism, and brutality – that is all that emanates from this self-acclaimed social revolution. The unleashing of the lowest instincts, the debility of shameless ambitions, and the scandal of flagrant usurpations – that is the spectacle we have just witnessed. As a result, this Commune inspired the most ardent political men, those most devoted to democracy, with the uttermost disgust. After vain attempts, they realized that no conciliation was possible where principles did not exist; they withdrew from the Commune in distress and sorrow; and the next day the Commune declared them traitors and ordered their arrest. They would have been shot had they remained in its hands.

And you, my friend, you want me to see these things with stoical indifference! You want me to say: 'Man is created thus: crime is his expression, infamy his nature'?

No: a hundred times no. Humanity is indignant with and within me. We must not dissimulate that indignation, which is one of the most passionate forms of love, nor must we attempt to forget it. We must make immense efforts of brotherhood to repair the ravages of hate. We must exorcize the scourge, wipe out infamy with scorn, and inaugurate by faith the resurrection of our country.

George Sand

1. Published in *Le Temps*, October 3, 1871.

APPENDIX VI

The Broken Friendship:
Flaubert and Laporte

FROM THE CORRESPONDENCE, and with some light from other sources, it is possible to piece together an outline of the sad story of Flaubert's break in 1879 with Edmond Laporte, one of his few surviving close friends.

Laporte had repeatedly helped Flaubert with research, accompanied him on a tour of Normandy to find appropriate settings for *Bouvard and Pécuchet*, fetched him home from Switzerland after the 'failure' of *The Temptation of Saint Anthony*, stood co-guarantor for his nephew's debts, and nursed him after his accident. Flaubert called him his 'Sister of Charity', along with many another affectionate nickname, and he was the only friend to whom Flaubert gave one of his manuscripts – the bound pages of *Three Tales*. As late as July 3, 1879, Flaubert wrote to him: 'What's this, my dear fellow? You say that you are "perhaps" my best friend? I'm crossing out "perhaps" and writing "certainly" instead.'

A portion of Flaubert's letter to Caroline of January 18, 1879, makes it evident that he nevertheless allowed his nephew, Ernest Commanville, to use him, up to a point, for the purpose of harassing Laporte concerning renewal of the guarantee the latter had made in 1875. In September 1879 Commanville increased his pressure on Laporte. But Laporte, for at least two good reasons – his own reduced circumstances (he had himself been forced to accept a loan of 500 francs from Flaubert), and increased distrust of Commanville – knew that he must not, and could not, renew. Although he foresaw the possible consequences, he wrote to Commanville expressing his

regrets. Whereupon Commanville, employing his usual method, persuaded Flaubert, who was incapable of refusing any service that
might conceivably benefit Caroline, to beg Laporte to change his
mind. On September 27 and 28, 1879, Flaubert wrote Laporte
pleading letters (not included in the present volume), dense with
commercial language obviously not his own. They make pathetic
reading, especially in contrasting passages where Flaubert attempts
to introduce his own usual tone of jaunty friendship. 'Me no understand what keeps you from signing,' the second letter ends. 'Whatever
you may decide, old fellow, nothing will be changed between the
two of us; but before deciding, I beg you to reflect seriously.'

Laporte wrote Flaubert on September 30, 1879:

> This is just what I feared, my good Giant. You have been made
> to intervene in a discussion from which you should have been
> excluded. I cannot accept you as judge in a matter concerning
> which your friend and your nephew are of different opinions.
> If we tell you all our grievances and justifications, what will
> happen? You will have to decide against one of us, and your
> affectionate relations with that one could be spoiled. So let me
> discuss this business with Commanville alone. If some tem-
> porary unpleasantness should result, at least you won't have to
> take sides. You must know, my dear Giant, that I shall always
> love you with all my heart.

To Commanville Laporte remained firm in his refusal; whereupon Caroline sent Flaubert a letter about which nothing is known
except what can be gathered from Flaubert's replies.[1] He wrote to
Caroline on October 8*:

> I would very much like to know whether Faucon has wound
> things up with Laporte. It is *impossible* for me to work – to
> write, that is – in the intellectual state into which your deplor-
> able story has plunged me. I can't stop thinking about it. I'm
> even more exasperated than tormented. I don't even dare go to
> Rouen (where I should see the oculist and the Prefect and go
> to the library) lest I run into Laporte, not knowing how to act

with him or what to say. So now I have to wait on Faucon's caprices to regulate my personal conduct!

And on October 13:

I have just received a letter from Laporte. He has been at Couronne since Friday night, and counts on seeing me at the Prefect's dinner today. The tone is friendly, as before. Not seeing me there, he'll come here this week, I'm sure. Will he have received Faucon's letter between now and then? What shall I say to him? I'm confused and distressed. When will I ever be calm? When will I be left in peace, once and for all?

What was the 'deplorable story' that Caroline related? And what role had been played by Faucon, the Commanvilles' banker-creditor, whose 'caprices' Flaubert had to take into consideration in determining his 'personal conduct'?

By 'personal conduct' Flaubert can only have meant his conduct towards Laporte; and what that was is quickly told. Flaubert apparently never spoke or wrote to Laporte again – although, as we shall see, in his unhappiness he would have liked to.

A note in the 1954 *Supplément* to the Conard edition of Flaubert's correspondence (probably written by René Dumesnil, one of the editors of the *Supplément* and Laporte's former son-in-law) states that the Commanvilles, furious at Laporte's defection, extracted a promise from Flaubert that he break with his friend. If such was the case, then Flaubert's complaint about having to regulate his personal conduct according to Faucon's caprices makes it appear that the Commanvilles may have acted on orders from that banker, in whose power they now were; and that Flaubert's compliance – reluctant, it would seem – would have had the purpose of sparing them possible trouble with their creditor.

One previous December 31, during the years of their friendship, Laporte had spent the night at Croisset in order to be the first to wish his friend a happy new year. In 1879, probably on December 30, he sent a note:

My old friend,

Whatever feelings you may have been induced to have towards me, I don't want the New Year to begin without sending you all my affection and good wishes. Have no fear of accepting them: they come from someone who is perhaps your best friend. *Je vous embrasse.*

E. Laporte

My best respects to Mme *votre nièce.*

Flaubert wrote Caroline on December 31*: 'By way of New Year's greeting, guess who has sent me a letter, received this morning. Monsieur Laporte! I enclose copy of same. What do you think of it? I'll not answer him, of course.' And on January 4*: 'You don't say anything about the letter from Laporte I sent you a copy of?'

Early in February, a portentous legal document arrived at Croisset. Ever since Flaubert had allowed himself to become involved in the Commanvilles' affairs, his letters to them had abounded in complaints about the flood of official forms that poured in on him: he hated the sight of them, understood none of them, and invariably turned them over to Commanville to deal with. By now his exasperation was close to the boiling point, and seeing on these most recent legal pages the name Laporte (now doubtless spoken only with abhorrence by the Commanvilles), along with the claim that he, Flaubert, was in some way liable for the sum of 13,000 francs, it overflowed in two letters, the second of which sounds almost mad. On February 5 he wrote to Commanville*:

> You must have received, last night, a big envelope containing a legal summons for the thirteenth of this month? I have barely skimmed through it, and what I understand is that it comes from Laporte . . . I'm surprised that he doesn't pay me back my 500 francs before claiming 13,000 more . . .

And the next day, to Caroline:

> The summons from the chivalrous Laporte shocked me, I confess. It's as though someone spat in my face. I haven't read it because of the handwriting and the length, but I saw my

name several times on *stamped legal paper*! And from the last
lines I understood the meaning. (You know the effect legal
documents have on me.) Ah, he's going rather far, that
gentleman . . . It has put me into a torment again. Much as I
try to be 'lofty', as you say you are, in my view of the human
race, this pains me nonetheless . . . What I count on doing
when things are finally cleared up (and it can't be long now) is
to show Monsieur le Conseiller Général that I have Mohican
blood in my veins, and that I can roar as loudly as any bear in
its cave. The letter I shall send him will bring a good price
later, if he keeps it. The rhetoric of that future letter is interfering with my work on *Bouvard and Pécuchet*, so I want to
write it as soon as possible.

The terms of the summons received by Flaubert are unknown,
and there is no certainty that it originated with Laporte. Flaubert,
who 'hadn't read it', but 'understood it from its last lines', was almost
certainly mistaken in taking it to mean that Laporte was suing him
for 13,000 francs. And perhaps the Commanvilles, even if they
allowed him to retain that misapprehension, thought it best to
dissuade him from writing to Laporte about his 'Mohican blood': in
any case, no such letter is known to exist.

On February 22* Flaubert wrote to Caroline that he was
brooding about Laporte and the situation; on March 27* he wrote
to her: 'Received the five hundred francs from Laporte, with a *pitiful*
letter. It forms part of the dossier, and we'll decide together what
my conduct should be.'

Thus it would seem that Flaubert, despite everything, still envisaged the possibility of a reconciliation. But there was none: the
Commanvilles, one may be sure, saw to that.

Laporte made one last appearance, in a scene that is not without its
irony. The other male affection of Flaubert's later years had been
Guy de Maupassant; there is no indication that relations between
Maupassant and Laporte were anything but harmonious; together,
they had supplied Flaubert with what he had said he longed for, in
his letter of January 1873 to Madame Regnier: 'something nearer the
heart'. The day following Flaubert's death Laporte came to Croisset,

wanting to pay his respects. It was Maupassant, delegated by Caroline, who went to the door – we do not know with what degree of willingness – and told Laporte he was not welcome.

1. Of the passages from Flaubert's letters to Caroline and Ernest Commanville included in this appendix, all or parts of those marked with an asterisk were omitted from editions of Flaubert's correspondence published during Caroline's lifetime.

   In certain editions of the correspondence Caroline included a note: 'Business difficulties had arisen between M. Laporte and my husband. This initiated a coldness between M. Laporte and my uncle, which ended in complete rupture.' René Descharmes, an editor of the Conard edition of the correspondence (1926–1933), reprinted that note with a comment: 'The truth is that there were never "difficulties" of any kind between Flaubert and Edmond Laporte, his faithful friend until his death; but only what M. Lucien Descaves, very familiar with the facts, has properly called "the consequences of a petty intrigue". We have seen in earlier letters the services rendered by Laporte to Flaubert, or rather to his nephew Commanville and his niece, at the time of Commanville's financial disaster. The loss of Laporte's friendship was one of the last sorrows of Flaubert's life.'

   It might also be mentioned that among the many letters to Flaubert bequeathed by Caroline to the Institut de France, she included only one from herself.

APPENDIX VII

The Pavilion at Croisset

FLAUBERT DIED IN May 1880. In a letter dated June 11, 1881, to Madame Roger des Genettes, preserved with other Flaubertiana in the Bibliothèque Lovenjoul at Chantilly, Caroline Commanville wrote: 'We have sold Croisset, my husband was never well there,[1] and the property was a heavy charge on us. We were offered a good price for it . . . With only a few days' notice I had to leave all my childhood memories behind me, and – what was even dearer to me – those connected with my beloved uncle, and this seemed to me like a second death.'

The house, with its gardens, terrace, old poplars, and Flaubert's beloved tulip tree, was at once demolished, and in 1882 a distillery (later transformed into a paper factory) opened on the site.

By chance, there survived beside the factory a small pavilion, dating from the seventeenth century, which the Flauberts had called *le petit salon* and used as a summerhouse. Neglected and falling into disrepair, it was rescued by a Rouen committee in the early years of the new century. Its purchase and restoration were paid for by public subscription; and, baptized 'Le Pavilion de Croisset', it was presented to the city of Rouen and inaugurated as a Flaubert museum on June 17, 1907. Caroline did not attend the inauguration ceremonies. 'My health is not good, and I am forbidden any form of agitation,' she wrote to Paul Toutain, president of the committee. She subscribed a thousand francs and presented a copy in watercolour of a view of Croisset she had painted in oil at the age of twelve.[2]

Incongruous in its industrial setting on the riverbank, the pavilion is open to visitors.

1. Edmond de Goncourt, who attended Flaubert's funeral, makes several mentions in his *Journal* of Commanville's behaviour on that occasion: pocketing a twenty-franc piece that Flaubert had left out to pay a locksmith, talking about his and Caroline's future income from Flaubert's works, referring repeatedly to letters from women that he had found in Flaubert's desk and had just been reading. The seeming obsession with this last subject caused Goncourt to wonder whether Commanville might be capable of blackmailing the ladies.

   Considering the role that Commanville had always played at Croisset, one can understand – and even take some satisfaction in the fact – that he 'was never well there'. Such a malaise perhaps implies a slight degree of sensitivity and conscience. Did Commanville – the Commanville we have read of in the letters and now find depicted by Goncourt – really possess even that minimum? One recalls George Sand's brief reference to the gentleman: 'His forehead is *flat*.'

2. In an article in the May 1976 issue of the bulletin *Les Amis de Flaubert*, L. Andrieu says that for the most part it was the '*bourgeoisie lettrée*' who saved the Flaubert Pavilion, though what he calls 'humble folk' also made contributions, including 'Colange, Flaubert's former cook, and Cotelle, the [new] ferryman'. A number of artists – Albert Lebourg, Robert Pinchon, Georges Rochegrosse, Kees Van Dongen, and Jacques Villon among the first – gave paintings, which were auctioned for the Pavilion's benefit.

   Among later items presented to the Pavilion there is a clay urn, excavated at Carthage and said to be Punic. Flaubert would have enjoyed learning that on its importation into France it was classified, after 'research' by customs officials, as an '*objet de toilette*, used by Salammbô for her ablutions', and that as such it was subjected to a 10 per cent luxury tax.

WORKS OF RELATED INTEREST

This brief bibliography is restricted to selected works in English or English translation. A number of other works are cited in the connecting texts and footnotes.

Barnes, Hazel E., *Sartre and Flaubert*, Chicago, University of Chicago Press, 1981.

Bart, Benjamin F. and Cook, Robert Francis, *The Legendary Sources of Flaubert's 'Saint Julien'*, Toronto, University of Toronto Press, 1977.

Brombert, Victor, *The Novels of Flaubert: A Study of Themes and Techniques*, Princeton, Princeton University Press, 1966.

Flaubert, Gustave, *Madame Bovary*, translated with an introduction by Francis Steegmuller, New York, The Modern Library, 1957; revised edition, 1982.
Salammbô, translated with an introduction by A. J. Krailsheimer, London and New York, Penguin Books, 1977.
Sentimental Education, translated with an introduction by Robert Baldick, London and New York, Penguin Books, 1964.
The Temptation of Saint Anthony, translated with an introduction and notes by Kitty Mrosovsky, London, Secker & Warburg, 1980.
Three Tales, translated with an introduction by Robert Baldick, London and New York, Penguin Books, 1961.
Bouvard and Pécuchet, translated with an introduction by A. J. Krailsheimer, London and New York, Penguin Books, 1976.
The Dictionary of Accepted Ideas, translated with an introduction and notes by Jacques Barzun, New York, New Directions, 1954.
The Letters of Gustave Flaubert, 1830–1857, selected, edited, and translated by Francis Steegmuller, Cambridge, The Belknap Press of Harvard University Press, 1980.
November, translated by a Frank Jellinek. New York: The Serendipity Press, 1967; Pocket Books, 1967. London: Michael Joseph, 1966.

Intimate Notebook, 1840–1841, translated by Francis Steegmuller. New York: Doubleday & Co., 1967. London: W. H. Allen, 1967. *The First Sentimental Education*, translated by Douglas Garman. Berkeley, Los Angeles, London: The University of California Press, 1972.

Levin, Harry, *The Gates of Horn: A Study of Five French Realists*, New York, Oxford University Press, 1963.
'A Literary Enormity: Sartre on Flaubert', *In Memories of the Moderns*, New York, New Directions, 1980.

Maurois, André, *Lélia: The Life of George Sand*, translated by Gerard Hopkins, New York, Harper, 1953.

Oliver, Hermia, *Flaubert and an English Governess: The Quest for Juliet Herbert*, Oxford, Clarendon Press, 1980.

Richardson, Joanna, *Théophile Gautier: His Life and Times*, London, Max Reinhardt, 1958.
Princesse Mathilde, New York, Charles Scribner, 1969.

Sartre, Jean-Paul, *The Family Idiot*, translated by Carol Cosman, volume I Chicago, University of Chicago Press, 1981. Only the first volume has appeared. A revised and completed translation is awaited.

Starkie, Enid, *Flaubert: The Making of the Master*, New York, Atheneum, 1967.

Starkie, Enid, *Flaubert the Master: A Critical and Biographical Study (1856–1880)*, New York, Atheneum, 1971.

Steegmuller, Francis, *Flaubert and Madame Bovary*, Chicago, University of Chicago Press, 1977. London, Macmillan, 1968.
Flaubert in Egypt (translated and edited), London, Chicago, The Bodley Head, Ltd., 1972 Academy Chicago Limited, 1979. London, Michael Haag, Ltd, 1983.

Zeldin, Theodore, *France 1848–1945; Volume I: Ambition, Love and Politics; Volume II: Intellect, Taste and Anxiety*, Oxford, Clarendon Press, 1973, 1977.

INDEX